*Psychology
of Exceptional Children
and Youth*

PRENTICE-HALL PSYCHOLOGY SERIES

Arthur T. Jersild, Editor

PRENTICE-HALL INTERNATIONAL, INC., *London*
PRENTICE-HALL OF AUSTRALIA, PTY., LTD., *Sydney*
PRENTICE-HALL FRANCE, S.A.R.L., *Paris*
PRENTICE-HALL OF JAPAN, INC., *Tokyo*
PRENTICE-HALL DE MEXICO, S.A., *Mexico City*
PRENTICE-HALL OF CANADA, LTD., *Toronto*

Edited by

William M. Cruickshank, Ph.D., Sc.D.

School of Education, Syracuse University

Psychology
of Exceptional Children
and Youth

Second Edition

Prentice-Hall, Inc.
Englewood Cliffs, N.J.
1963

© 1955, 1963 by

Prentice-Hall, Inc.

Englewood Cliffs, N.J.

Library of Congress Catalog Card No.

63-10146

Printed in the United States of America

C

Preface

. . . to the Second Edition

SINCE THE publication of the first edition of this book in 1955, a companion volume, the *Education of Exceptional Children and Youth*, has been published by Prentice-Hall, Inc. Together these two volumes provide a remarkable background for the total field of the psychology and education of exceptional children and youth. If the reader will carefully examine the preface to the first edition, he will see the motivation for this book and some of the reasons for its initial publication. These original comments are still true today as the second edition is written or as portions of the original work are revised.

As has been stated elsewhere, the editor of this volume and the contributing authors are of the opinion that the field of the psychology of exceptional children is too complicated and diverse to be treated adequately by a single author. No one individual can be uniformly authoritative on all facets of this broad field so as to be able to treat each with experience, personal investigation, and deep understanding. The strength of this book and of its companion in the field of education lies in part in the fact that each chapter has been prepared by an authority in a given field. In the revision of

v

this work, attempts have been made to strengthen the book even more. Certain chapters have been completely rewritten for this edition by authors who are new to the contributing group. The chapter on mental retardation by Dr. G. Orville Johnson is a unique contribution to the literature. The chapter on the gifted child and youth has been completely rewritten by Dr. Ruth Strang in the light of increased information and understanding. All other chapters have been revised significantly. Oftentimes individual authors have preferred to permit their chapters to stand as in the original edition, but to integrate new research, ideas, and concepts which have developed in the intervening period. The editor and each author have, however, seriously considered each word and sentence to determine whether or not they still provide for the student a continuing base for understanding and appreciation of the essential concepts regarding disability and exceptionality.

Since 1955, much as happened in the United States and elsewhere in the interests of exceptional children, youth, and adults. The Congress of the United States, reflecting movements which were commented upon in the preface to the first edition, has provided grants for research and study which have stimulated the total growth of the field. Leadership personnel have been trained in major universities and colleges through such funds, and these people are beginning to take their places in positions of responsibility throughout the country. The United States Office of Vocational Rehabilitation has brought new life and direction to its program in the several states through direct grants for research, service, and study. The National Institutes of Health have provided leadership for research, training, and the pursuit of knowledge in many related fields, thus bringing new insights to this area of human development. Private foundations have invested their funds generously in major studies and in direct services for all types of children and youth with disabilities. The Panel on Mental Retardation initiated by executive order of President John F. Kennedy and the continuing significant contribution of the President's Committee on the Employment of the Handicapped express a national concern and the concern of many citizens of the United States with these significant problems. Many colleges and universities have responded to this stimulation with stronger programs of teacher and leadership preparation in special education and rehabilitation. Some of these institutions of higher education, utilizing the generous funds of government and private foundations as well as their own resources, have initiated important programs of research, the results of which are turning conjecture and hypothesis into concrete fact and basic knowledge.

While almost every new insight derived from research brings to light two others which need study, the period since the publication of the first edition of this book has been marked essentially by critical investigation. Techniques and research methods, as Drs. Meyerson and Newland so well emphasize in their chapters, need yet to be refined for the investigation of many problems of human life. Suffice to say, however, that there is a current critical attitude toward this professional field which can only result in significant understandings in the future. The contributing authors of this edition commend their chapters to the serious student of psychology and education in the expectancy that many will be motivated to further study, research, and contribution to the understanding of exceptional children and youth.

W. M. C.

. . . to the First Edition

SINCE 1920, the combined effect of several important influences has brought the exceptional child and youth to the attention of professional people in a very dramatic way. World Wars I and II, with their universal military conscription, subjected almost the entire male population of the United States to complete physical, psychological, and psychiatric examinations, and directed public attention to the large percentage of men who, due to physical disability, mental retardation, illiteracy, or psychiatric disorders, were rejected as unfit to assume this major responsibility of citizenship. Similarly, the results of the two wars, together with the conflict in Korea, have created widespread interest in and concern about the general problems of rehabilitation.

Medicine and allied sciences have progressed markedly since the twenties. Psychological inquiries and research have added much to our understanding of the role of handicaps in the lives of children, their parents, and society in general. Medical inquiries have contributed greatly to the control of epilepsy, to an understanding of cardiac disturbances, and to the basic information regarding congenital disorders. True congenital deformities, retrolental fibroplasia, cerebral injuries, and many other problems still pose unanswered questions to the professions. Nevertheless, many advances have been observed in psychological and medical knowledge.

As a result of these factors, most parents of exceptional children now look upon a handicap from a much more mature point of view and consider their children socially acceptable. Parent groups, locally and nationally, have organized to bring these children to the attention of the community.

Long before the pressure of parent groups was felt, many colleges, universities, and social agencies organized professional programs in behalf of exceptional children, youth, and adults. The Council for Exceptional Children, the National Society for Crippled Children and Adults, Inc., together with its many state affiliates, the Office of Education in the United States Department of Health, Education and Welfare, the American Foundation for the Blind, the National Society for the Prevention of Blindness, and many others have been concerned for years with problems relating to the professional preparation of personnel and with the increase of services to handicapped individuals. As a result, thousands of young people throughout the world are devoting themselves to careers that relate to the handicapped.

Although much remains to be investigated concerning the psychological growth and development of exceptional children and youth, psychological understanding has grown sufficiently exact to warrant a single publication dealing with this problem. This symposium, prepared by psychologists, is devoted solely to the psychological considerations of the influence of physical deviation upon the normative growth and development of children and young people. The term "exceptional child" means one who, by reason of a physical or intellectual deviation, is considered unique among children. Thus, chapters that deal with the psychology of the intellectually superior child, as well as with the intellectually inferior child, are included in the book. Chapters that deal with all the major groups of physically disabled children are also included.

In general, the authors approach their respective areas of evaluating psychological theory and research from the point of view of the impact of physical disability or intellectual deviation upon the psychosocial adjustment of behavior. The authors are, in this instance, indebted to Dr. Lee Meyerson for his chapter on the somatopsychology of physical disability, which serves as a backdrop for the later discussions. On the whole, each author has culled from the literature those theoretical statements and psychological research investigations that help in better understanding the implications of deviation for the child. In this connection, chapters dealing with particular deviations have been prepared by Drs. Lee Meyerson, Ruth Strang, G. Orville Johnson, Charles Kram, Jon Eisenson, Joseph Newman, Berthold Lowenfeld, and the editor. The chapter prepared by Dr. T. Ernest Newland is of particular importance in understanding the psychological problems of the exceptional child and youth. His stimulating and provocative comments regarding psychological assessment point to numerous aspects of psychological research for further investigation. Similarly, the excellent statement by Drs. Emory Cowen and Matthew J. Trippe pertaining to psychological counselling and therapeutic treatment of exceptional children, blanketed with knowledge of non-disabled children and youth, reflects the philosophy of all the authors: *The exceptional child must first be considered as a child and in the light of normative growth and development.* At the same time, the chapter brings together the important contributions of psychotherapeutic treatment of these children and their problems.

W. M. C.

The Contributing Authors

EMORY L. COWEN, PH.D., is Professor of Psychology at the University of Rochester. Dr. Cowen is a member of the Division of Clinical and Abnormal Psychology, New York State Psychological Association, and of the Eastern Psychological Association.

WILLIAM M. CRUICKSHANK, PH.D., is Professor of Education and Psychology and Director, Division of Special Education and Rehabilitation, Syracuse University. He is a past president of the International Council of Exceptional Children and a Fellow of the American Psychological Association and of the American Association on Mental Deficiency. He is a member of the American Academy of Cerebral Palsy.

JON EISENSON, PH.D., is Professor and Director of the Speech and Hearing Clinic, Queens College. He is Lecturer in Otolaryngology, College of Physicians and Surgeons, Columbia University. Dr. Eisenson is a Diplomate in Clinical Psychology, Division of Clinical and Abnormal Psychology, American Psychological Association, and a Fellow of the American Speech and Hearing Association.

G. ORVILLE JOHNSON, ED.D., is Professor of Education, Division of Special Education and Rehabilitation, Syracuse University. He is a member of the American Psychological Association, American Education Research Association, National Society for the Study of Education, Council for Exceptional Children, and a Fellow of the American Association on Mental Deficiency. He is also an associate editor of *Exceptional Children*.

DR. CHARLES KRAM, PH.D., is Executive Director of The Epilepsy Foundation, Washington, D.C., and Director of the National Children's Rehabilitation Institute, Leesburg, Virginia. He is a member of the American Psychological Association.

BERTHOLD LOWENFELD, PH.D., is Superintendent, California School for the Blind in Berkeley. Previously he was a Rockefeller Research Fellow, Director of Educational Research for the American Foundation for the Blind, Instructor in Special Education, Teachers College, Columbia University, and visiting professor at various colleges and universities. He is a Fellow of the American Psychological Association, Certified Psychologist of the Board of Medical Examiners of the State of California, and, among other professional assignments, he is a member of the Sensory Study Section, Department of Health, Education and Welfare, Office of Vocational Rehabilitation. Dr. Lowenfeld is the author of many books and publications, among them, *Our Blind Children—Growing and Learning with Them.*

LEE MEYERSON, PH.D., was Visiting Professor of Psychology and Physical Medicine, Stanford University Medical Center, at the time this book was revised, and is now Professor of Psychology at Arizona State University. He is a past president of Division 22, National Council on the Psychological Aspects of Disability, American Psychological Association, and a past recipient of the Research Award of the Division of Rehabilitation Counseling, American Personnel and Guidance Association. He is a Fellow of the Divisions of Clinical, Developmental and School Psychology of the American Psychological Association, the American Public Health Association, and the Society for Research in Child Development.

T. ERNEST NEWLAND, PH.D., is Professor of Education, University of Illinois. He is a Diplomate in Clinical Psychology, Division of Clinical and Abnormal Psychology of the American Psychological Association and a member of the American Educational Research Association, the American Association for the Advancement of Science, the American Association for the Gifted, and the Council for Exceptional Children. Dr. Newland was formerly Chief of the Division of Special Education in the Pennsylvania State Department of Public Instruction and Professor of Psychology and Director of the Psychological Clinic at the University of Tennessee.

JOSEPH NEWMAN, PH.D., is Chief Clinical Psychologist, Veterans Administration Hospital, Pittsburgh, Pennsylvania. Previously, he held a similar position in the Veterans Administration Hospital, Canandaigua, New York and Memphis, Tennessee; was Chief of Advisement and Guidance, Veterans Administration (Tuberculosis) Hospital, Sunmount, New York; and Director of Rehabilitation, Municipal Sanitorium, Otisville, New York. He is a member of the American Psychological Association, Eastern Psychological Association, and Pennsylvania Psychological Association. He is a lecturer in Psychology, University of Pittsburgh. He is also a member of the Society for Projective Techniques.

DR. RUTH STRANG, PH.D., is Professor Emeritus at Teachers College, Columbia University, and Professor of Education, College of Education, University of Arizona. She is a Fellow of the American Association for the Advancement of Science, a member of the Board of Directors of the National Society for the Study of Education, editor of the *Journal* of the National Association of Deans of Women, coauthor of *The Improvement of Reading,* and author of *Helping Your Child Improve His Reading.*

MATTHEW J. TRIPPE, PH.D., is Associate Professor of Special Education and Director of Training for Project Re-ED, George Peabody College for Teachers, Nashville, Tennessee. He is a Fellow of the American Association for the Advancement of Science and a member of the American Psychological Association, the National Education Research Association, and the Council for Exceptional Children. Dr. Trippe was formerly Director of Research in Special Education and Rehabilitation at Syracuse University and Senior Research Scientist (Psychology) with the New York State Department of Mental Hygiene.

Table of Contents

*Psychology
of Exceptional Children
and Youth*

LEE MEYERSON [1]

Director, Somatopsychology Program
Arizona State University

1 *Somatopsychology of Physical Disability*

AT ONE time many people believed that continuing progress in the medical sciences would lead eventually to the prevention or cure of all the disorders we classify as physical disabilities. Today it is clear that we have made great strides in preventing some disabilities and in reducing the severity of others. Blindness as a consequence of untreated syphilis in the mother is practically nonexistent in the United States. Severe crippling following poliomyelitis, which was once common, is now rare. The deformities resulting from osteomyelitis are now prevented by the miracle of antibiotic drugs.

The other side of the picture, however, is not as hopeful. It is becoming increasingly evident that modern medicine is saving lives at the cost of permanent physical disabilities. Premature infants, children, and adults ill with acute infections or the injuries of accidents, and the enfeebled aged, all of whom once would have died, now live; but they live with gross alterations in physique and with severe impairments in physiological functioning.

1

There is presently little hope that illness and disability will disappear. Instead the number, and perhaps the rate, of physically disabled persons is increasing so that today there are more people with physical disabilities in the world than ever before.

Are these millions of people with physical disabilities different kinds of people from others? Are they treated in ways that are unique to those with imperfect bodies? Have they been exposed to life situations that exert a unique effect on behavior? Do we require a special psychology or unique psychological laws to understand them?

Large numbers of professional men all over the world are devoting their lives to the practice of rehabilitation. They make great efforts to assist the disabled person to return to normal society and normal living. Sometimes their efforts result in great success. More often success is limited by variables that are as yet imperfectly understood.

It is clearly important to study the problems that arise from the possession of an atypical physique and to attempt to find answers. A direct attack upon problems that are not well understood, however, is not always the most fruitful. Here we shall begin indirectly by considering the significance that may be assigned to physique generally, without special reference to the physical variations we call physical disability.

Somatopsychology (*soma:* body; *psyche:* mind, soul) is the study of some of the relationships that bind physique and behavior. All of us in everyday life tend to make judgments of people in terms of their physiques and also to evaluate physique in terms of behavior. We may say, "She's a redhead; I'll bet she has a temper," or "He might be a handsome fellow if he didn't scowl all the time." On a more sophisticated level we may say, "She's shy and withdrawn because she's ashamed of being so fat," or "She's fat because she's shy and withdrawn, and eating is her only pleasure."

It is not easy to disentangle the threads of cause-reaction-effect, and moreover, there always seem to be many exceptions. Some fat people are jolly, and some perfectly proportioned people are shy and withdrawn. It is a matter of common observation that the same kinds of behavior may be shown by people who have widely differing physiques, and that among individuals who have the same kind of physique can be found widely differing behavior.

It is the function of somatopsychology as a science to try to make sense out of this confusing array of data. Are there any invariable relationships between physique and behavior so that a science of somatopsychology can be developed, or must we say that each person is a law unto himself?

There are several ways of attacking this problem, and for each way there is some confirming evidence.

1. *There is no relationship between physique and behavior.* It is evi-

dent that normal variations in specific aspects of physique such as the length of fingers, toes, lips, or tongue are not critical factors in behavior. Similarly, it is obvious from impressionistic evaluation of the whole physique that individuals who engage in similar behavior may come in all shapes and sizes. Groups of writers or lawyers or psychologists or realtors are not noted for their physical similarity.

It is equally evident, however, that girls with generous chest measurements seem to behave in ways that are different from girls who are less well endowed. Boys with well-developed muscles engage in activities that are rare for weaker youths. Athletes as a group do not look like bankers or bookkeepers. Men, as identified by physique, behave differently than women.

In addition to common observation, we must also note that there is a large and increasing research literature whose findings lead in a consistent direction. Most of the studies that have been made show a positive correlation between certain aspects of physique and certain kinds of behavior. For example, children who are physically larger in height and weight tend to show leadership, popularity, social success, and good adjustment more frequently than smaller children.[2] The correlations obtained are usually low, but they are positive in relating "good" physique to "good" behavior; and some of the correlations are statistically significant.

How can such data be explained? It must be emphasized that correlation is not explanation. We can be certain only that there are some relationships between physique and some aspects of behavior, but we are still faced with the problem of determining whether these relationships are meaningful. In terms of what concepts can the obtained relationships be explained?

Some of the research findings seem easy to understand. No one in our culture is likely to be surprised that most men tend to marry women who are slightly shorter than they are. This may be a matter of social expectancy. In our culture men are supposed to be taller than their wives. There is no necessary relationship, however. Many men are shorter than their wives. It is also unsurprising that behavioral skill in games is associated with physical strength. To the degree that strength is required for skill, this would appear to be a comprehensible, direct relationship.

It is more difficult, however, to understand Gowin's finding that railroad presidents were significantly taller than railroad station agents, university presidents were taller than small-college presidents, and bishops were taller than small-town preachers.[3] Why do the two characteristics seem to go together with greater than chance expectancy? Similarly, it is not clear why Blair, in a survey of 270,000 men who owned life insurance, found an almost perfect relationship between a person's height and the amount of his insurance policy.[4] The average amount per policy for men who were 6 feet 4 inches tall was $6,180, and the amount consistently decreased with each decrease of 1 inch in height until the average amount per policy for men who were 5 feet tall was only $2,979. Should we say that tall men are more able and therefore earn more money than shorter men; that there are special social reasons why tall men need more insurance than others; or that tallness and the increased ability to buy insurance are both functions of a superior nutritional and social environment?

2. *Physique determines behavior.* One of the oldest ideas in the history of psychology is based on the observation that some individuals are relatively taller than they are wide; some are relatively wider than they are tall; some are relatively well proportioned in both directions; and many cannot be exactly classified.

Since the time of Hippocrates, 2,500 years ago, thoughtful and observant men have believed that there is a systematic and intrinsic connection between physique, or body-type, and personality. The connection has been variously conceived to be genetic or biochemical or physiological so that once the body-type or body was established, predictable behavior necessarily followed.

It is conceivable that the same genes or biochemical conditions that influence the development of body-type also directly influence personality and behavior, but the evidence lends little support to this idea. Correlations, obtained from normal populations, between physical type and psychological type almost invariably have been so low as to be useless for prediction.[5,6,7,8,9,10,11]

Sheldon and associates have developed the most promising modern constitutional typology.[12,13,14,15] They have described three components of structural variation which they claim are independent of nutrition and weight, and three basic components of temperament. In this scheme, a subject is rated on a scale from 1 to 7 for each component of physique and of temperament. Thus, the extreme endomorph (fat and flabby physique) would have a somatotype of 7-1-1; an extreme mesomorph (strong and muscular physique) would have a somatotype of 1-7-1; and an extreme ectomorph (frail and delicate physique) would have a somatotype of 1-1-7. A person who had an average degree of each component would be rated 4-4-4. Similar ratings are made for each of the three primary components of temperament; namely, viscerotonia (general relaxation, love of comfort, food, and people), somatotonia (muscular activity and bodily assertiveness), and cerebrotonia (restraint and inhibition). The creators of this classification reported correlations of the order of +.8 between endomorphic physique and viscerotonic temperament; mesomorphic physique and somatotonic temperament; and ectomorphic physique and cerebrotonic temperament.[16]

These findings, however, have been criticized on the grounds that the criteria for the temperament ratings were often expressed in physical terms. For example, the trait of physical courage for combat was defined as a "confident dependence upon the sturdiness, skill, and muscular strength of the body." The temperamental characteristic of restraint in posture and movement was defined as meaning that the body as a whole is carried stiffly. If temperament ratings are contaminated by body characteristics from the very beginning, it is not surprising that high correlations between physique and temperament were found.

Nevertheless, this theory is a great improvement over earlier typologies, for it recognizes that pure or extreme types of physique or temperament rarely exist and makes provision for the classification of the great mass of men whose physiques and temperaments do not fit exactly into just one of three classifications.

The theory of somatotypes may eventually add to our knowledge of intrinsic relationships between physique and temperament. A somatotyping study of congenitally handicapped persons would be of great interest. At present, however, the theory offers no aid in understanding the behavior of the physically handicapped.

Physique may also directly determine behavior in ways that do not require assumptions about body-type. Men are biological organisms, and as such they are amenable to biological forces, especially deprivations and disease. Lack of necessary endocrine products, for example, may affect both physical and psychological development, although there is little evidence that normal variation in endocrine secretion is related to personality.[17]

Sexual maturity and interest in the opposite sex ordinarily develop together. A person may be sexually mature, however, without being interested in the opposite sex, and a sexually immature child may be highly interested in sexual contact with adults.[18] The presence of the appropriate physique may not necessarily require a particular kind of behavior, and the absence of appropriate physique may not prohibit behavior.

It is predictable that a totally blind child will not respond to visual stimuli nor a totally deaf child to auditory stimuli. It must be remembered, however, that these highly specific limitations on behavior may be resolved in countless ways. Children with the same physical limitation may present markedly diverse personality pictures. It is not possible to predict with accuracy the molar psychological behavior of a child solely from knowledge of the nature and degree of his disability.

Men are also social organisms. In our culture it is predictable that children with male physiques will play with mechanical toys while children with female physiques will play with dolls. Adults with male physiques will be the breadwinners who work outside the home while adults with female physiques will concern themselves with gentler pursuits inside the home. Again, however, it must be noted that exceptions exist. There is no necessary relationship between the physique and the behavior. In some cultures, in fact, women do the sort of work we consider appropriate for men, and men do the work we consider appropriate for women.[19]

3. *Behavior determines physique.* White individuals who uncover their bodies to the sun develop red or brown skins. Individuals who practice the sport of weight lifting develop large biceps. The academic class of a co-ed at Cornell University in Ithaca, New York, where hills are frequent and steep, can be predicted with considerable accuracy from the relative development of the muscles of the calf.

In recent years great emphasis has been placed upon functional or psychosomatic disabilities. It is now well known that how a person thinks and feels may affect his physique. A soldier who runs away from the cries of his wounded buddies may develop "psychogenic" deafness. High-powered executives who function under great pressure for long periods of time are more likely to develop peptic ulcers than individuals who lead calmer lives. Negroes in Africa and Chinese in China rarely develop the heart condition known as essential hypertension, but Negroes and Chinese who live and behave like Americans are as susceptible as other Americans. Similarly, American-born Japanese grow taller and develop a different type of chest structure than their countrymen who grow up in Japan, although there is no reason to believe that the genetic structures of the two groups are different.

A similar process is not unknown among Americans. Theodore Roosevelt was frail and delicate as a youngster. The change in his physique with exercise was not paralleled by similar changes in other frail youngsters who were unable to live in the open and did not develop his interest in "roughing it."

It is evident that all human functions are psychosomatic. Nothing is ever determined simply by heredity or simply by environment.

4. *Behavior and physique may be simultaneously determined by a third variable.* The untreated congenital hypothyroid child simultaneously develops cretin physique and behavioral sluggishness. Both deafness and mental deficiency in a child may be residuals of an attack of meningitis. Development of secondary sexual characteristics and becoming interested in the opposite sex may result from the injection of sex hormones. Some

of these relationships have a *must* characteristic so that direct and accurate prediction from physique to behavior is possible; for example, no cases have been reported of untreated congenital hypothyroid children who did not simultaneously manifest cretin physique and behavioral sluggishness. Other relationships, however, like those in the previous classifications refer to statistical probabilities. Meningitis may or may not cause deafness, mental deficiency, or both.

5. *Behavior is a function of a person interacting with his environment*, $B = f(PE)$.[20] It is now obvious that this is the only formulation that will adequately account for all of the evidence. Behavior is never the result of the person or the environment alone. It is not certain, however, that knowledge of this formula greatly increases our understanding or our ability to predict and control behavior in the individual case. To study all aspects of a person, all aspects of the environment, and all aspects of the interaction between the two is clearly an impossible task. We may limit the field to more manageable dimensions by concentrating not on an understanding of all behavior but rather the more modest aim of understanding what behavior occurs because a person has a particular physique. Even more specifically, we wish to find some way of ordering and understanding the behavior of individuals whose physique is "exceptional" in a negative way—that is, the behavior of individuals whom we call physically disabled.

In the past, one unfortunate effect of formulating a psychological problem in terms of physical characteristics has been to imply that a disability per se is directly responsible for behavior. It is not uncommon to read that the deaf are suspicious, the blind are withdrawn, and the crippled are maladjusted. It is known, however, that some of our deaf, blind, and crippled children are very well-adjusted individuals whose mental health is superior to that achieved by the average physically "normal" child. For such cases the tendency has been to fall back on the bromide that "it all depends upon the person." Since all degrees and kinds of adjustment may be found in the physically disabled, it has been claimed that adjustment depends upon the individual. It is the individual child who with "help" must "accept" or "compensate" or "make up for" so that he may "act as normal as possible" and "be treated as normal," "in spite of" his disability. These formulations place an impossible task and needless strains upon disabled children. As we shall see, except for certain specific behavioral limitations that are directly tied to physique, placing the source of behavior either in the disability itself or in the person is neither helpful nor true.

Understanding the Behavior of the Physically Disabled:
The Cultural Relativity of Disability

THE HISTORY of science shows that progress in understanding phenomena
has often been impeded by the acceptance of "obvious" assumptions
that are not true. It may be of value, therefore, to examine certain assumptions in somatopsychology that appear to be self-evident. For example, what is a physical disability? What is a physical handicap? For
many years, the two terms were frequently used interchangeably, for it
seemed clear that if a person had a disability, he was handicapped for
that ability and the handicap would "spread" to other behavior also.
Undoubtedly there is some truth in this view. A crippled child is limited
not only in physical ability. He *may* also be limited in the kinds of play
experiences that are open to him. His parents, other adults, and children
may treat him differently than if he were not crippled, and he himself *may*
come to feel that he is not only different, but also a less worthy person
than others. It will be observed that different verbs have been used in
this description. The child *is* physically limited, but the effects of the
limitation are restricted to a conditional *may*. Handicaps may or may
not follow from a disability. In recent years it has become common to
make this sort of distinction between the two terms. A disability is seen
as an impairment having an objective or medical aspect,[21] while a handicap is seen as an impairment in a particular kind of social and psychological behavior. Although behavioral data may be equally as "objective"
as physique, this is a useful distinction. It makes explicit the common
observation that children with identical physical impairments may behave in radically different ways and children who behave in essentially
similar ways may have widely differing physiques. It is not certain,
however, that such a distinction is of maximum utility in understanding
the behavior of the people we call disabled. It may be of greater value
to postulate that neither disability nor handicap is objective in the sense
of being simply descriptive. Both are *judgments* which tend to conceal
the implicit values upon which they are based. In strictly objective terms
it can be said only that variations in physique exist. Which variations will
be considered disabilities, impairments, or handicaps is strictly relative
to the expectations of the culture in which the person lives, the tasks
that are required of him, and the meaning the person himself and others
may assign to the variation.

Variations in Physique Leading to Limitation in Ability

Consider a female adolescent whose feet from heel to toe measure just four inches and appear to be "deformed." On observation it is noted that the girl walks mostly on her toes with a shuffling movement, that she cannot walk with the free stride of the typical American girl, and she cannot run. Does this person have a disability? If she were an American girl living in the United States, obviously it would be difficult or impossible for her to engage in many of the activities that we consider appropriate and desirable for teen-age girls. Suppose, however, that this adolescent lived in China a hundred years ago when it was customary to bind the feet of females. In terms of the culture in which she lived, was she disabled? Who should be the judge? There is no question about the variation in physique. The feet of this adolescent and the feet of an American contemporary would differ. An American might say, "She's crippled. Why, she could never play softball like a real American girl." A Chinese might reply, "Barbarians! It is not appropriate for a woman to play softball. This girl has delightfully small feet that her husband will cherish, and she walks with the light and mincing step that is appropriate for a woman. Your American girls with their big gross feet walk like men. We would not allow it in China."

Obviously, it cannot be said that the Chinese girl in the Chinese culture of that time had a disability; on the contrary, the variation in the structure of her foot gave her a positive ability—the ability to walk in the way a woman "ought" to walk. An American girl in China would lack this ability. She would be "different." It would be seen by all that her feet were large and "repulsive." She would be handicapped in behaving like a woman, and if social disapproval were great enough, she might very well develop the maladjusted behavior we commonly refer to as psychological handicap.

Another example from Chinese culture is instructive. It is said that when a powerful man approached the peak of his power, he closed his hands into fists and allowed his fingernails to grow through the palms to the other side. Physically, such a person was in a position similar to that of a bilateral hand amputee, but we cannot say that he was handicapped or disabled. He was in a highly desirable and envied position. He had the ability to live without caring for himself or lowering himself to any kind of labor. In effect such a person was saying to the world, "You see how wealthy and powerful I am? See how fearless I am of the future? See what a wonderful and privileged life I lead? There is nothing I have to do for myself. In all things I have servants at my beck and call."

In our culture, where we value purposeful activity, such a "deformity" would be a horrible disability. Among the elite of China, who value the contemplative life, it was not horrible. It was the height of social distinction. No doubt such behavior sounds very queer and "abnormal" to us but only because we are accustomed to different forms of social honor. The Chinese might very well point to the "deformities" we imposed upon physique when the whalebone-corseted wasp waist and the hourglass figure were considered appropriate for women. The fainting spells and many of the varied "female troubles" common in Queen Victoria's day undoubtedly were traceable to these imposed variations in physique. Similarly, binding of the breasts, required for the boyish figure of the 1920 "flapper," which led to the breakdown of breast tissue and disturbances in lactating ability, probably was not unrelated to the increasing popularity of infant bottle-feeding during the same period. The Chinese might also point to the frequency with which our men, in their unceasing struggle for wealth, success, and power, drive themselves into physical disability and early death from heart disease. Our "jokes" about one-ulcer or two-ulcer executives in the advertising business, as indicators of productivity and merit, would not seem funny to the Chinese.

Other examples of the cultural relativity of disability are easy to find. In our culture, women who have epileptic seizures are considered to have a disability. Among the Shasta Indians of California, however, similar seizures are a rare and valued ability which lead a person to positions of importance, power, and honor. The Ubangi, whom many of us have seen in the circus sideshow, place wooden plugs in their lips to stretch them, so that at adulthood the lips extend five or six inches in front of the face. It is obvious that functions such as nutrition, speech, and the uncommon emotional expression we call kissing must be affected.

Are these people "normal"? Are they "disabled"? One must remember that the Ubangi do not kiss; their lips are not an impediment to their own speech or to their nutrition. They may be considered to have a disability only if kissing were as valued in Africa as it is in the United States, only if they were required to speak English, and only if it were necessary for them to eat American foods. Obviously, however, an American among the Ubangi would have a disability by reason of his shallow lips.

Physical variation among the people of the earth seems to be the rule rather than the exception. There are people who "complete" the body by elongating the neck or molding the skull, by knocking out front teeth, blackening them, or filing them to points. Among some primitive people, it is customary to stretch the labia of the female genitals until they reach the knees. Other groups insert objects into the prepuce of the male genitals. All are examples of variation in physique that, in our culture, would lead us to the judgment of "disability," although they do not do so in the cultures in which they are found.

In addition to imposed variations in physique, it is easy to see that normal variations in height or in musculature may also lead directly to limitations in ability and indirectly to a judgment of "disability." The Pigmy lacks the ability to function efficiently in a society built for tall people. The "normal" white man is relatively lacking in a similar way if he is required to hunt animals by crawling through low grass without being seen. The clothes model of our culture, the highly valued, frail, female with the pipestem shape, would be devalued and handicapped in Okinawa where it is customary for women to be able to row a boat, hoe a plot of ground, and haul in large fishing nets. Where big husky women are required and valued, our beautiful model, by reason of her physique, would lack important physical abilities.

In other words, it cannot be said that a person has a disability without specifying the situation in which he is expected to behave. Disability is not an objective *thing in a person,* but a social value judgment. A society makes a disability by creating a culture in which certain tools are required for behavior. Variations in physique by themselves have little psychological meaning outside of the frame of reference in which they are evaluated.

These examples may seem somewhat "unreal" analogies since there is little communication between primitive cultures and our own and we are convinced of our own superiority. Nevertheless they may help to clarify and make explicit the relativity character of "normal" physique and the judgmental character of the term "disability." Moreover, it can be shown that such analogies are not simply speculations but are similar to culture contacts that have occurred on a large scale. For example, in comparison with the American Indian, who was able to hear the faintest sound of animals in the wilderness and to see the buffalo herds when they were no more than a tiny speck on the plains, the average American pioneer was half deaf and half blind. It is probable that much of the Indians' superiority was a function of training, but it is possible also that they had real physiological superiorities in auditory and visual capacities. It is certain that some early pioneers who did not have or did not differentiate the important abilities of hearing and seeing at a distance sometimes paid for their disabilities with their lives.

The frequency with which intercultural comparisons have been made does not mean that the effects of culture on the judgment of "disability" can be found only by comparing primitive and civilized groups. Intracultural comparisons can be made also. Consider the German male who received a sabre cut on the face in a duel. Such wounds sometimes resulted in muscular and neurological injuries which, like the lips of the Ubangi, affected the person's ability to eat, speak, and kiss. In the United States such an injury might lead to prompt and vigorous application of rehabilitative measures to restore or improve the affected functions. There is no evidence, however, that such "marks of honor" were perceived in pre-World War I Germany as disabilities or as defects that required remedial treatment. They were visible proof of the positive abilities "to be brave" and "to defend one's honor."

Similarly, it is instructive to consider physical abilities (such as acuity for sounds) which have little practical importance in our culture. Some Americans are able to perceive sounds having a frequency of 20,000 cycles per second, but many persons are either lacking or severely impaired in this ability. The perception of such high-frequency sounds is presently of no practical importance in our culture and is hardly differentiated from other hearing abilities except by a few psychophysicists. Impairment in this ability can be precisely measured and rigorously demonstrated. Yet, when it is found, there is no suggestion that it is of any importance, that it has physical, psychological, or social effects upon the person, that he should seek remedial measures, or that he should "compensate" in some way for his lack. The variation in physique leading to limitation in ability is evident; but the judgment of "disability" is withheld. Suppose that sometime in the future the ability to hear frequencies of 20,000 cycles per second should become important. The sequence of social and psychological effects that would follow is clearly predictable.

This type of analysis of the meaning of physique suggests that it may be fruitful to think of physique, and the abilities that are associated with particular variations in physique, simply as tools for behavior. We can then make the following generalization: a disability exists only when a person lacks an adequate physical tool for behavior and when this lack is perceived by the culture in which the person lives as making him less able than his fellows. If a particular tool is not differentiated or required by a culture, its lack or impairment in a person cannot be a disability. If the tool is differentiated and valued by a culture but conflicts with a "higher" physical, social, and psychological ability, the lack or impairment will not be perceived as a disability.

Variations in Physique Leading to Socially Imposed Handicaps

There are some variations in physique that are socially handicapping only. These variations do not directly impose limitations on the abilities that are required by the culture in which the person lives, but they are perceived by the majority as being undesirable.

For example, in some cultures all redheaded infants are considered evil and killed immediately. In our own culture, a black skin, regardless of the brain power that may be under the skin, disqualifies a person from attending some universities. A female physique is a disqualification for many jobs that are well within the capacities of women. Women in the United States do not become barbers to men, although this is a common occupation for women in other countries. Surgeons are rarely female, although the skilled cutting and sewing of small objects that surgery requires is often considered a task at which women excel.

The social discrimination and prejudice against women (and Negroes and members of other minority groups who can be distinguished by their physiques) are commonly known and do not require additional emphasis here. It is evident that some limitations on behavior are not disabilities but socially imposed handicaps. Moreover, it is clear that the handicap is not *in* the body nor *in* the person but is a function of the society in which the person lives. This is true also of handicaps that arise from physical standards. These standards often seem as arbitrary and nonsensical as the killing of redheaded infants. Although they are readily seen to be "funny" rules, and they do not circumscribe behavior as completely as prejudice, they may have as drastic psychological effects in situations where they are imposed. Carious teeth, for example, may prevent a person from securing a teaching credential in the State of California. An airline hostess must be between 5 feet 3 and 5 feet 7 inches tall. Individuals who are "too tall" or "too short" relative to an arbitrary standard may not serve in certain police departments or in the armed forces. The newspapers recently reported the case of twins from Worcester, Massachusetts, who wished to enlist in the Naval Reserve. One was accepted, but his twin who was a quarter-inch shorter did not meet the height requirement and therefore was rejected!

We cannot discuss here the origin of social stereotypes, the reasonableness of arbitrary standards for physique, or the social expectation that certain behavior necessarily follows directly from physique. It may be sufficient to note only that physique is one of the criteria for social classification. It often determines how a person is expected to behave and what he will be permitted to do.

The social criteria are neither universal nor permanent. They may be different for different cultures, and even in the same culture they may change over a period of time.

The criteria for beauty offer an illustrative example. The concept of beauty is a relatively simple one. By the time the average child is four and a half years old, according to the norms of the Revised Stanford Binet Tests, Form L, he is able to perceive and understand that curly hair is more beautiful than straight hair; a Grecian nose is prettier than a broad, flat, or a curved nose; relatively thin lips, and ears that lie close to the skull are nicer than their opposites. Like their elders, children do not see physical characteristics in isolation. Beauty, goodness, prestige, high moral qualities, and social acceptance can rarely be disentangled.[22]

In the light of the evidence cited in the previous section, the cultural relativity of the physical characteristics considered beautiful need not be labored. The cross-cultural evidence makes it clear that, as the philosopher says, beauty is in the eye of the beholder.

There are few, if any, universal standards of attractiveness. In the female, for example, thinness and fatness, powerful muscular physiques and fragile delicate physiques, large, long, pendulous breasts and small upright breasts, flat and narrow buttocks and buttocks protruding to the point of steatopygia are all valued and considered beautiful in some cultures.

Among the Kwoma "the big strapping women, who could carry large loads of produce or firewood up the mountainside . . . were the females that caused Kwoma men to smack their lips and make lewd comments." [23] How would these women behave if they lived in Japan and were required to learn the routine of the delicate, graceful tea ceremony?

Within our own culture, standards for beauty have changed radically in less than two generations. It was not long ago that women who had "skinny" hips emulated Lillian Russell, the glamour girl of the 1890's, by tying pillows over their buttocks and eating without stint to fatten the neck, the shoulders, and the arms. It was only yesterday that the skinny, breastless, hipless "flapper" was the beauty ideal. Today, a casual leafing of any magazine will reveal the social necessity of large breasts on a slender figure.

Assume that three women, each having one of the valued physiques, but entirely unchanged in other respects, were systematically placed in each of the three periods from 1890 to 1955. Would they be likely to change in behavior? Would they become different kinds of people? What would be the critical variable, their physiques or the differing life situations with which they had to cope?

It is evident that social expectations which have the force of standards will influence behavior. A person who has a socially approved physique will be treated differently and will be expected to behave differently than persons whose physiques deviate from the social ideal. Obviously, therefore, the self-image of the person will also be affected. It is difficult to escape becoming the person that others believe one to be. In large measure the self is created by social interaction with others. No person can develop a wholesome personality if he encounters only derogatory attitudes.

It cannot be claimed that the physically disabled are exceptions to these generalizations. It is not correct to state that the physical limitations we have called *disabilities* invariably call forth universal social expectations. The roles assigned to the disabled and the behavior expected from them are not fixed. In Turkey blind men are preferred as readers of the Koran, for their prayers are believed to be more welcome to God than the prayers of others. A blind Catholic, however, cannot become a priest. If the person with a disability has sufficient prestige and status, the desirability of his role may be so great that his disability will be imitated. Princess Alexandra, who became the wife of Edward VII, walked with a limp. At the time she married, a fad spread among thousands of women on the European continent so that they walked with the special, prestigeful, limping gait known as the Princess Alexandra Walk!

Hanks and Hanks have shown that individuals with physical variations that are perceived as disabilities are assigned different roles in different cultures.[24] They may be treated as pariahs or as economic liabilities; they may be tolerantly utilized, granted limited social participation, or just let alone. These variations in assigned role, social treatment, and behavioral expectations are not functions of the disability. Instead, the Hankses hypothesize, the adverse treatment of the disabled is a function of low productivity or unequal distribution of goods in proportion to the size of the population, the maximizing of competitive factors in achievement, and the evaluation of criteria for achievement in absolute ways rather than relative ways.

These are promising hypotheses that appear to agree with the available evidence. Whether or not they are true, or whether other hypotheses are equally tenable, are problems for further investigation. It would be of great help to know why and how variations in physique lead to the imposing of social limitations or handicaps. The origin of social behavior is a problem that cannot be discussed here, however. It is sufficient for our present purpose simply to note that variations in physique, with or without ability limitations, many lead to social emulation, social approval, or social limitation.

It is society, far more than the condition of the body, which determines what a person will be permitted to do and how he will behave. All cultures place values upon certain aspects of physique, although different aspects of physique may be differentiated as important in different cultures, and different values may be assigned to the same variations. Nevertheless, certain generalizations may be made:

1. Physique is a social stimulus.
2. It arouses expectations for behavior.
3. It is one of the criteria for assigning a person to a social role.

4. It influences the person's perception of himself both directly through comparison with others and indirectly through others' expectations of him.

5. Comprehension of the kind, extent, and degree of socially imposed handicaps on persons with atypical physiques is basic to an understanding of the somatopsychology of physical disability.

Variations in Physique Leading to Emotional Handicaps

Some variations in physique do not produce ability limitations, nor do they instigate social handicaps. They may be seized upon, however, and utilized by the person as a defense against facing other problems. For example, a girl may fixate on a small facial mole and moan that it is ruining her life. If only she didn't have the mole—boys would like her better, she'd be less irritable, she'd get along better with her parents, and she'd be able to study better because she wouldn't need to worry about whether other children were looking at her, laughing at her, and criticizing her. There is clearly no ability limitation. In addition, her friends may honestly say that the mole is so small few people even notice it, or if they do, more frequently than not it is considered an attractive "beauty mark." Nonetheless the girl refuses to be comforted. If she seems unfriendly, irritable, and inconsiderate of others, it is "because" the mole on her face makes her so. A similar situation may be encountered in individuals who have normal variations in physique that are socially undifferentiated or not assigned social meaning.

Macgregor and Schaffner have reported that such individuals sometimes seek plastic surgery on the assumption that the change in physique will automatically lead to great social and emotional improvements.[25] They show clearly, however, that the basic problems are psychiatric and not somatopsychologic. If one "blemish" is removed, the individual is either dissatisfied with the result or he readily finds another physical characteristic upon which to project his feelings of insecurity. Physique for such individuals has unique personal meanings that are entirely unrelated to ability limitations or to social handicaps. Moreover, it is questionable whether there is any direct relationship between the variation in physique and the emotional handicap. The body in these cases is simply the excuse for, not the cause of, psychological maladjustment.

These psychiatric cases present separate and complex problems that cannot be considered within the framework of somatopsychology. They are mentioned here primarily because their surface similarity to somatopsychologic problems may confuse the unwary investigator and obscure the essential, underlying relationships between physique and behavior.

It is unquestionable that normal variations in physique and physical disabilities are sources of psychological disturbance for some children. It is equally unquestionable that similar variations and disabilities in other children are not sources of psychological disturbance.[26,27] Workers in somatopsychology may differ as to the reasons why the same physical variation leads to emotional disturbance in one child and not in another, but there is universal agreement that variations in physique need not necessarily lead to emotional handicaps.

Except for the psychiatric cases, the following generalizations seem reasonable:

1. No variation in physique requires psychological maladjustment.

2. If an emotional handicap exists in a person who has a physical disability, it does not stem directly from the disability but has been mediated by social variables.

3. The mediation between physical status and psychological behavior occurs in the following way:

(a) The person lacks a tool that is required for behavior in the culture in which he lives, and he knows that he lacks it.

(b) Other individuals perceive that he lacks an important tool and devaluate him for his lack.

(c) The person accepts the judgment of others that he is less worthy (or, to the degree that he is a product of his own culture, he judges himself as less worthy) and devaluates himself.

The (a) (b) (c) sequence is a unit. If (a) or (b) do not occur, (c) does not occur. If (c) does not occur, there is no emotional handicap.

Variations in Physique Leading to a Combination of Disability and Handicaps

Disability, social handicap, and emotional handicap have been isolated in order to show that they are separate and independent phenomena. Of course, we must now say at once that various combinations are the rule rather than the exception.

The analysis in itself, however, helps to account for the great variation in behavior that may be observed in people who vary in physique. Knowing the components of a combination and their interrelationships, especially in the light of cross-cultural contexts, enables us to begin to understand diverse phenomena that previously were obscure and incomprehensible.

We can begin to understand not only the major question of how it is that two similar individuals with similar disabilities can behave in different ways, but also such apparently diverse phenomena as why the behavior of a child who is blind may change when he understands for the first time that he is blind, and why the task of telling the child is so traumatic for parents.

Moreover, the analysis points to some of the critical variables that affect the behavior of those who have been judged to be disabled. If we are faced with behavior that is undesirable, it is possible to see what has to be changed. We need no longer conceal our ignorance under the guise of respecting individuality. It may be true that "each person is different," but it is neither true nor helpful to "explain" all reactions to disability in terms of characteristic and unchangeable functions of the disability itself or the person.

In actual practice, within a culture that has established standards for physique which seem right and natural, it is difficult for the somato-psychologist to step outside of his own ethnocentrism. An example from within the culture may help to clarify the issue.

> Ever since he was a small boy, Edward G. knew that he wanted to be a policeman. When he was 21 years old, he took the Civil Service Examination for patrolmen, and he passed the mental and physical tests with flying colors—except for one item. He was 5 feet 3½ inches tall, and the regulations said that a policeman had to be 5 feet 4 inches tall.
>
> Edward was desolate. Although he knew that it was not true, he claimed that a mistake had been made in measuring him, and he demanded a remeasurement of his height.
>
> For three days Edward remained in bed and had his friends pull on his legs and his head so that he was stretched out to the fullest possible inch. Then, thirty minutes before he was due to be measured, Edward persuaded a friend to hit him a sharp blow on the top of the head with a piece of wood. The blow raised a lump of considerable size.
>
> Edward immediately raced to the examination and had himself measured. The stretching of the previous few days together with the bump on his head was more than enough to raise his stature to the required 5 feet 4 inches, and he was sworn in as a policeman.
>
> Edward was a good policeman. In three years' service he received several commendations and one award for bravery in capturing an armed robber. One day, however, he was called out to march in a parade and lined up with other policemen who also were supposed to be of minimum height. By comparison, it could be seen immediately that Edward was perceptibly shorter than the others. A "spit and polish" officer measured him on the spot and found that he was now only 5 feet 3 inches tall. Two weeks later, Edward was no longer a policeman.
>
> Dismissal from the police force was a great shock. Some of the people Edward had dealt with in the line of duty now taunted him; others laughed. Edward became more and more convinced that he was no good, not useful for anything. If anyone called him "shorty," he flew into a rage. If he couldn't reach something on a

high shelf, he was morose for days. "If only I were taller," he said again and again.

At last report Edward was in a "nursing home." He was not psychotic, but neither was he mentally well. Severely maladjusted is probably the term that best describes him.

Now how can we explain this case? Did his shortness *cause* his behavior? Obviously, just to ask the question is to realize its absurdity. Did his shortness prevent him from being a good policeman? Well, yes and no. When he was a policeman, he was a good one, but according to the standards, he had a disability for being a policeman and therefore he couldn't be one. Should we say that if Edward had been a different kind of person, if he had courage and social interest, he would not have broken down? Again, all we can answer is yes and no. Every person has his breaking point, and Edward reached his. On the other hand, while he was a policeman, he was a good policeman and a worthy citizen. He did not become maladjusted until he accepted the evaluations of the important "others" and agreed that he was "no good."

Although this case has many important aspects, it is relatively simple in structure and uncluttered with the emotionality that often surrounds the discusion of "real" disabilities. The tool loss leading to social handicap and emotional handicap can readily be seen. It is a good case to remember when platitudes about deafness, blindness, and crippling are offered as explanations for behavior. "*Because* the deaf, blind, or crippled are . . ." or "*because* that's the kind of person he is" are rarely true or useful answers.

In somatopsychology we deal primarily with processes and interrelationships and not with static phenomena. Our further understanding depends upon the development of a human psychological ecology which will permit us to describe in concrete detail the relationships between human beings and their psychological environments in ecological rather than valuative or judgmental terms. A beginning has been made in this section with the description of when and how a variation in physique may become a disability and a handicap.

Understanding the Behavior of the Physically Handicapped: Science and Theory in Somatopsychology

IT IS not enough to have some background knowledge of how disabilities and handicaps are created, in general. Our culture has a well-developed value system relating to variations in physique. To change the negative attitudes of the culture toward those who are judged to be disabled may require hundreds of years of systematic labor. In the meantime we are confronted with the practical problem of helping "the handicapped" to live with some measure of usefulness and happiness.

The evidence on one point is clear. Children who have disabilities, as a group, tend to have more frequent and more severe psychological problems than others. Why does this occur, and what can be done about it?

It is evident from our earlier analysis that it is not sufficient to say, for example, "John is blind; therefore he has severe problems of adjustment." It is necessary to say, "John is blind. In the culture in which he lives people pity those who cannot see. The blind are perceived as dependent individuals who must be taken care of and who cannot compete for many of the most desirable goals in life. John, as a member of his own culture, tends to see himself in this way also. He perceives clearly the low esteem in which he, as a blind person, is held, the prejudice and discrimination that are raised against him, and his lack of status in society. He agrees that he is a less worthy person than those who can see. Therefore, John feels inferior and has severe problems of adjustment."

Expressed in this way, it is clear that not blindness but the social problem is the critical variable. This is true not only of blindness but of other variations in physique also. Some individuals who shrink from the physically deformed are aware that a person is not responsible for how he looks and that avoidance is ethically unjustified. It is contended, therefore, that the repugnance is instinctive, natural, and really can't be helped. There is no reason to believe that this is true. There is every reason to believe that attitudes toward variations in physique are learned. First, the variations that are perceived with horror in one culture are accepted without emotion in another culture. Second, within a culture there are many individuals who do not feel the culturally sanctioned emotions. Not everyone in the United States is emotionally disturbed by the sight of a cerebral palsied child or a congenital amputee. Third, many who do experience emotional distress on first exposure to a particular disability also experience rapid adaptation. The horrified student who sees only disabled bodies at a school for the handicapped changes quickly to the experienced therapist who is only faintly aware of differences in physique but keenly aware of differences in personality.

Disability appears to be as much a problem of the nondisabled majority as it is of the disabled minority. Maladjustment in "normal" individuals with respect to physical disability is widespread. However, we cannot change our society overnight, and social attitudes often present problems that can be dealt with only indirectly.

It appears that a dead end has been reached. If disability is relatively fixed and society is relatively inflexible, that leaves only the person. Inasmuch as the source of behavior is not *in* the person in any psychological meaningful sense, what can be done?

Suppose you are approached by a mother who has a deaf child. "I understand that deaf children tend to become maladjusted," she says. "What can I do to prevent this?"

"Well," you say, "how old is your child? Is it a boy or a girl? How much hearing does he have? Are there any other children in the family? Do they hear well? How old were you when the child was born? Were you ill during pregnancy? Was birth normal? How old is your husband? Is anyone else in your family deaf or hard of hearing? Does the child show signs of maladjustment now?"

The questions, of course, can be endless. A curious thing about them is that there are only common sense reasons, or often no reasons, for believing the answers have any direct relationship to the child's behavior. After the answers are received you may say, "Treat him as if he were normal, but *don't* expect as much of him as if he were normal. Don't spoil him, but on the other hand *do* make allowances for his disability. A special nursery school for deaf children would be a good thing, but then he has to live in a world with normally hearing people, so a regular nursery school would be a good thing too. It all depends on what kind of child he is." In other words, we don't know. We don't know in general, and we don't know what it depends on. The responsibility is passed back to the parent with directions that are contradictory and impossible to fulfill.

Similarly, suppose a parent brings a six-year-old cerebral palsied child and raises the specific question: "Can my child get along in school?" Often we don't know. After asking innumerable questions all that can be said is, "Let's try him out and see." If he gets along, then he gets along, and that's fine. Of course, the waste, frustration, anxiety, and psychological damage to the child if he doesn't get along are unfortunate, but inevitable. Clearly this is an unsatisfactory state of affairs.

It is true that in some instances an individual child can be studied. To some degree it can be determined what "kind" of child he is and how he interacts with his environment. The function of science, however, is to solve problems by means of general laws that can be applied to the individual case. Generalization and certainty of prediction are at the heart of science. Progress in other sciences has occurred only to the degree that the theories were constructed which led to general laws that held without exception. If each case must be studied individually and nothing can be said about the psychological effects of disability in general, there can be no science of somatopsychology.

The problem of individual differences and the search for generalizations that can be applied to every individual case are not unique to psychology. They are common to all science.

Consider the following example from the field of mathematics. What is the area of a circle? In one sense this is a stupid and unanswerable question. It is possible to complain that there are infinite numbers of circles, from a pin point to the circle of the universe, all differing in area. What circle is meant? Where is it? How is it possible to say anything about circles in the abstract? It is indisputably true that the answer to the question depends upon what "kind" of circle it is. If little is known about circles in general, it may be reasonable to ask the following questions: Where is this circle? Is it here on earth, up in the air, or underground? How did it get there? Are there any other circles nearby? Is it hollow or solid? What color is it? Is it made of steel, wood, soap, or is it just a line on paper? How was it formed? When did it get there? Does it surround anything?

Every person who knows the general law, Area $= \pi r^2$, however, knows that these questions are irrelevant and meaningless. The general and invariable relationship between circles and their areas makes only one measurement of importance in determining the area of a particular circle. If this relevant context is known, it is possible to understand and predict the area of any circle by asking just one question: What is the radius? It is then possible to forget the thousand-and-one ways in which circles may differ. These other variables may be important in other relevant contexts, but they are of no value in predicting or controlling area.

If the relevant context is not known, two procedures are possible: (1) An attempt can be made to cover ignorance by asking many irrelevant questions, as is often done in somatopsychology. This procedure will yield meaningless answers that leave us little wiser than before. (2) If, by some fortuitous circumstance, we lived in a world where red circles tended to be larger than black ones, it would be possible to compute a correlation and reach the empirical generalization that red circles tend to be larger in area than black ones. In such a case predictions might be made with better than chance success, but there would still be much uncertainty. Some black circles would have a greater area than some red ones. We could speak only of "tendency" and not of "certainty." Proceeding on the basis of correlational evidence and empirical generalization, as is now often done in somatopsychology, it might be contended that every circle is really different and therefore must be treated individually. The only way to be sure would be to produce a specific circle about which information was desired and measure it. Obviously, this procedure is possible, but it is much more useful to have a general formula that can be applied to any circle. General laws in somatopsychology would be equally useful.

Our goal is to be able to make psychological predictions. The mathematician requires mathematical data in order to make mathematical predictions. Physical characteristics such as color, material, or position in space are not helpful to him. The geneticist requires genetic data in order to make genetic predictions. Physical data such as weight, psychological data such as temperament, or social data such as the number of animals in a cage are useless for genetic prediction.

Is it reasonable to suppose that somatopsychological predictions can be made from the physical data classified as disabilities? Physical characteristics must be the starting point, but they are just as phenotypic or superficial for somatopsychology as they are for genetics. Progress in somatopsychology will come only when a somatopsychological theory is developed which permits the transformation of physical data into psychological data.

A Way of Thinking in Somatopsychology

A COMMONPLACE remark is that we need more research on disabled persons. Undoubtedly that is true, but it is well to understand the kind of research that is required.

There is a myth in our culture about the open-minded scientist who approaches a problem without any preconceptions and reports only the "facts." As we have seen, however, the number of questions that can be asked about any phenomenon is limited only by our ingenuity. Not all questions are equally good questions, and not all "facts" are equally useful in the sense that they lead to further understanding.

For example, we may adopt the role of the open-minded scientist who wishes to study the psychology of the exceptional. What shall be investigated? It is perfectly possible to measure the big toes or the length of the eyelashes of children who are blind and compare the findings with similar data from children who see. No one has done such a study, however, and no one is likely to. Why? Because there is no reason for believing that such measurements will contribute anything to our knowledge of behavior. Even if the two groups were completely different in these characteristics, the result would have no meaning unless there was some way of explaining it. Similarly, it is possible to study the psychology of people who wear size 9 shoes—or even the behavior of people with size 10 feet who wear size 9 shoes—but no one does this. In other words, open-minded is not synonymous with empty-headed. A scientist does not study a problem unless he has some reason for believing it to be important. If he believes that a particular investigation is important, obviously he must have some hunch, reason, or theory for believing so. Before he begins, his preconceptions have already been expressed by the problem he has selected for study and the methods of collecting data that he plans to use. In other words, he has a theory. The random collection of "facts" is not science. Research undirected by a theory of probable relationships is blind and rarely productive. The investigator, before he begins, must have a clear idea of what he is going to look for and how he is going to look. The questions that he asks, in great measure, determine what he will find. If his hunch, hypothesis, or theory is approximately correct to begin with, it is likely that his work will be fruitful.

In somatopsychology it is evident that despite considerable research effort, only limited progress has been made in answering the basic question of how physique may be related to behavior. Examination of the literature shows that considerable progress has been made in other fields, such as medicine, in coping with the problems of disability. In somatopsychology there is still much discussion of the same problems that were seen to be critical one hundred years ago. Answers to these problems are scarce or contradictory, and exceptions to the rule are frequent.

Whenever a question is posed that does not yield generalizations that can be applied without exception to the individual case, it is time to ask whether the questions are meaningful and whether they are answerable.

What Is an Answer or Explanation?

All scientific explanations are essentially descriptions, but there are different levels of adequacy. The least adequate explanation is simply to recognize and affirm that something is and perhaps give it a name. The best explanation describes the greatest amount of data in the fewest terms. A few examples may make these statements more meaningful.

Naming Explanations

It has been observed that salmon are spawned far up in the headwaters of streams. In their second year, they travel downstream to the ocean, which is warmer and saltier and contains less oxygen than do mountain streams. Why do they do this?

In the past it has been customary to label behavior of this kind as instinctive. There is an instinct *in* the fish to behave as it does. This naming of a behavior often yields a satisfying feeling that the behavior has been explained. Actually nothing has been explained. A word has been substituted for an observation of behavior, but we are no wiser than before. The salmon does what it does. First, it is observed that the salmon swims to the ocean. Second, the behavior is labeled an instinct. Third, the behavior is "explained" by saying there is an unknown "something" in the fish that makes it behave this way. It is precisely this unknown that must be investigated. Why do salmon behave this way? Naming the unknown an instinct does not contribute to understanding, and to the extent that it tends to choke off further research, naming is not helpful.

Not long ago it was discovered that the essential factor was the relationship between light and photosensitive receptors in the skin of the salmon. The receptors are covered by pigment which is gradually lost. As the photoreceptors are stimulated by light the fish seeks deeper and deeper streams until eventually it reaches the ocean. This is an explanation. It explains both "instinct" and the lack of it. Prediction and control are possible. If a fish doesn't migrate, the investigator now knows where to look—at the photoreceptors. If it is desirable to prevent fish from migrating, the investigator knows what to control—light.

Young children and primitive people employ many naming explanations. Things are because they are. They act as they do because that is their nature. Heavy objects have the essential nature of heaviness; that's why they fall to earth. A sailboat moves because it *is* a sailboat, and that is its nature.

Of course, older people and civilized people see immediately that an object falls because of its relationship to the earth; a boat moves not because that is its nature but because of the relationship between the area of its sails and the strength of the wind. Expressed in this way, it is clear that prediction is possible because the relevant context is understood. Nothing *is* in itself. Everything occurs in a relevant context.

But how quickly we forget once we move out of the area where the essential relationships are known.

It is observed that a child appears to be wary of adults and clings closely to his mother. He does not mix easily with other children. He is often seen watching other children as if he'd like to join them. Why does the child behave in this way? "Because," we say, "he *is* shy"; that is, the shyness is something *in* the child. It is a "thing" that he carries around with him. This is essentially the same kind of "explanation" that was considered unsatisfactory for the salmon. First the behavior is described, then a name is assigned to the behavior, and finally the behavior is "explained" by the name. The question, "Why does the child behave in this way?" has now been changed to, "Why is the child shy?" but an answer in terms of the relevant relationships has not been given.

The same naming phenomena occur in somatopsychology on a more sophisticated level. It may be observed that a certain person is deaf. He also engages in the behavior that may be classified or described as being suspicious of others. Why does he behave this way?

"Well, this person is deaf. Now it is a finding of psychology that deaf people tend to be suspicious. If this person were blind and suspicious, that would be unusual, but he is deaf and it is not unusual for deaf people to be suspicious. He is deaf. That's why he's suspicious. It is in the nature of deafness or deaf people to be suspicious."

It should be clear at this point that another circular "explanation" has been given that is no more adequate than the concept of instinct. It doesn't help to add that deaf people are suspicious because they believe that other people are talking about them. Not every deaf person is suspicious. Some do not believe others talk about them. Other deaf people may believe it but don't care. Neither the behavior of the suspicious deaf person nor the behavior of the unsuspicious deaf person has been explained.

Naming is not explanation.

Historical and Contemporaneous Explanations

Assume that your class meets in a room without windows. The sun is shining outside, but it is not shining on you. Why isn't the sun shining on you?

Two kinds of explanations are possible. One is based on the history of the objects and might go something like this:

> The sun isn't shining on me because I'm sitting in this room.
> Why are you sitting in this room?
> Well, because I'm going to the university.
> Why are you going to the university?
> There are two reasons. First, because the university is here to go to. Back in 1860 a leading citizen decided to build a university. He made a lot of money in the slave trade and didn't know what else to do with it, so he thought a university would be a good idea. Of course, he made all of this money in the first place because his family had disowned him, and he wanted to prove himself. So, in one sense the sun isn't shining on me or any of the others in the class because the university benefactor wanted to prove himself. The second reason is purely personal and applies only to me. You see, back in 1800 my paternal great-grandfather took his four boys and headed west for Kansas. . . .

It is evident that a complete historical explanation is an infinite regress that leads back to the origins of the universe and to the detailed history of every individual involved. Various shortcuts, of course, can be taken, but the final answer to the question posed must be different for every person in the class. The sun isn't shining on Joe because he is studying to be a doctor. The sun isn't shining on Jim because his parents made him come to college. The sun isn't shining on Mary because she is looking for a husband. Every case is different. These answers sound queer and unbelievable, not because they are false, but because they do not "explain" the relevant context that most of us already know.

In a contemporaneous explanation, no attention would be paid to particular objects. Instead, since this is a physical question, attention would be directed to the physical field forces that are operating: The sun does not penetrate opaque objects. The psychological or social motivations of the individual are irrelevant. A statement may now be made in if-then terms which is always true: If a person is sitting in a room made entirely of opaque substances, then the sun will not shine on him. There are no exceptions. In every case, regardless whether the room is built of brick or stone or building paper, and regardless whether the person is Joe or Jim or Mary, an immediate correct prediction for individual cases can be made. Moreover, since the phenomenon is now understood, it is possible to make the prediction before a room is built and to control the shining-of-the-sun-on-persons-or-objects as we wish. It will be observed that this kind of explanation accounts for both sun-shining-on-objects and sun-not-shining-on-objects. It is independent of any particular objects, and it is independent of the past.

Consider a similar situation in medicine. A child is limping down the street. Why does he limp? Because he had polio when he was five years old. It should be evident immediately that this is a historical explanation which does not explain. The child does not limp because he had polio when he was five years old any more than the sun does not shine on Mary because she is looking for a husband. There are many children who had polio when they were five years old who do not limp. It can be said, of course, that each case is different. Some children who have polio become crippled, and some do not. It all depends on the child. But *what* does it depend on? What should be investigated? If the case histories show that bright children contract crippling polio more frequently than less bright children, as is sometimes claimed, should physicians investigate intelligence?

Fortunately the physician has a contemporaneous explanation that he can apply to individual cases. He may say that if nerves x, y, or z are destroyed the muscles in the legs that are innervated by these nerves will atrophy, and the child will limp. It will be observed that this explanation is independent of any particular child and of any particular disease. It holds without exception in every case. Any injury that destroyed nerves x, y, or z will produce the same behavior. The physician is thereby able to understand why two similar children who had the same disease at the same age may walk differently, while two children who had different diseases may walk in the same way. By testing the nervous function of a particular case he is able to predict before the child takes his first step whether or not limping will occur. The prediction can be made even if the physician has never seen the child before and knows nothing else about him. Control of this behavior is not yet possible, but knowledge of the relevant context between nerves and muscles and limping guides future investigation. It tells the researcher where to look and what to study. The thousand-and-one other ways in which children differ in health and in illness are irrelevant at this point.

Of course, contemporaneous explanation also leads to an infinite regress. How and why are nerves destroyed by disease? The answer to this question will, in turn, permit further questions to be seen. The questions, however, are meaningful, and they are answerable. Historical explanations, except perhaps for certain problems in public health, are dead ends. The implications of this statement deserve to be spelled out.

If a child limps because he had polio, and polio causes crippling, and the polio attack occurred last year, what can be done now? The polio is a past event. The child doesn't have polio now, but only a residual from the polio. It is not possible to influence past events but only the factors that are operating in the present. Historical and contemporaneous explanations lead in two radically different directions, and the influence of direction cannot be overestimated. Historical explanations lead from the present to the past: "It is too bad that the child is crippled because he had polio last year, but that's the way the ball bounces." Contemporaneous explanation leads from the present to the future: "The child is crippled because nerves x, y, or z are destroyed. Is there some way of regenerating these nerves? Is it possible that other intact nerves may be attached to the affected muscles?" Historical explanations lead to excuses. Contemporaneous explanations lead to continuous investigation.

Rehabilitation of the disabled is presently plagued with this problem. Few researchers in somatopsychology are as yet thinking in terms of contemporaneous, field-contextual descriptions. Almost all explanations are in terms of naming, assigning qualities to the individual, or tracing history. For example, a child doesn't talk. Why? Because he lost his hearing when he was two years old, that's why he doesn't talk. An adolescent is very dependent. Why? Because he's been blind since birth. It is too bad, but that is the way deaf children and blind children are.

It is necessary only to see a deaf child who talks and a blind child who is not dependent to realize that historical explanations do not explain. From the standpoint of contemporaneous explanation children who have physical disabilities may tend to show certain kinds of psychological behavior, not because of their histories but because of the psychological forces that are presently acting. If these forces can be understood, behavior will be amenable to change.

Empirical or Correlational Explanations

One way of attempting to solve a problem is to investigate the frequency with which two variables occur together. This is a form of historical explanation projected to the future. It contains certain pitfalls, however, that deserve special mention.

Empirical *method* is basic to science. There are two ways of employing the method, however. One way is to make observations or conduct experiments to test a working hypothesis or a theory. A second way is to try to build up an explanatory theory from the observations. The first way is in general and productive use. The second way has sometimes been characterized as a determined attempt to obtain knowledge from ignorance. The difficulty with the second way is the ease with which human reason may be misled when the relevant context is not known.

For example, there is a statistically significant relationship between sight and intelligence. Blind children, as a group, earn lower I.Q.'s than children who see. There is nothing wrong with such a statement as a description, but it is misleading if it is used as a cause-effect explanation or as a means of prediction for the individual case. It cannot be said that blind children obtain lower I.Q.'s *because* they are blind. There are some blind children who test at the genius level. If the I.Q. of a particular blind child is explained in terms of his blindness, there is no way of explaining the high I.Q.'s of other equally blind children. An example from a field where the true context is known may clarify the matter.

In everyday life there appears to be a close correlation between the lightness of objects and their ability to float in water. Suppose a child shows you a 10-pound iron boat and asks you whether it will float. Depending on your own observations, you reply that it will not because it is "too heavy." Only "light" things will float and not heavy ones. If the boat were made of wood, then it would float, but since it is made of iron it won't. If the child now tells you about a visit to the seashore in which he saw big iron boats floating that weighed ten thousand tons, what can you say? It is apparent that you do not have the correct explanation.

Similarly, consider these empirical observations: An almost perfect correlation has been found between the number of births that occur yearly in the city of Stockholm and the number of storks' nests that are built yearly in Stockholm chimneys. What conclusion can be drawn? Would you draw it even if the correlation over a period of fifty years were perfect?

There is a very close correlation between the number of fire engines that go to a fire and the amount of damage that occurs. Assume that you wish to reduce the amount of damage that occurs at fires, would you suggest that the number of fire engines be reduced?

These are not simply academic examples. They are essentially similar to empirical observations which have misled investigators in the past and continue to mislead in the present. A hundred years ago in the lowlands of Italy it was observed that individuals who left their windows open at night became ill, while those who closed their houses tightly remained well. The disease was malaria, for obviously it came from the bad night air. The man who had a theory that not bad air but the mosquitoes that fly at night were responsible for the disease was obviously a crackpot. In France a hundred years ago it was observed that children who were fed cow's milk sickened and died, while those who were fed wine remained well. In the absence of a correct theory to explain the observation the French were quite right in praising alcohol and condemning milk as food for infants.

It is easy to see the "foolish" errors of others when the true relationships are known. The dangers of empirical explanation are less evident when the relevant contexts are not known.

Suppose a child plays hookey from school. Why is he a truant? An empirical investigation might determine that the school was directly northwest of the child's house. Further, if he left his house and continued in a northwest direction—regardless of whether he walked, rollerskated, or rode his bike—he went to school. On the other hand, if he didn't start out in a northwest direction or didn't continue long enough, he didn't go to school. These are "the facts." What should be done? Clearly, it is necessary to give the child training in walking, rollerskating, and riding his bike in a northwest direction! That will correct his truancy.

No doubt this sounds very funny, but consider these situations. A child says the *w* sound for *r*. It has been found that if a child moves his speech organs in a particular way he will say *r* and not *w*. Therefore, if a child has such a defect, give him training in saying the *r* sound. A child doesn't read. It has been found that in order to read, a child must recognize words. This child doesn't recognize words. Therefore give him special remedial work in recognizing words. These do not sound so funny, but they are based on the same principle as the earlier examples, and they are just as likely to be wrong. Recent research on the successful treatment of reading disabilities by counseling, without remedial work, is highly suggestive.

The world is presently disturbed by the fact that there appears to be a correlation between the number of cigarettes smoked daily and the incidence of lung cancer. On a purely empirical basis, it can also be demonstrated that there is a close relationship between the increased incidence of lung cancer and increase in the following:

(a) consumption of margarine
(b) membership in the Democratic Party
(c) output of comic books
(d) number of aged in the population
(e) social freedom for women

(f) civil liberties for Negroes and other minority groups
(g) number of people who work for a living
(h) cost of living

It is immediately evident that some of these relationships are meaningless or chance relationships that result from the simultaneous operation of independent forces. Some may reflect the influence of a third variable which is not listed here; for example, "tense" individuals may smoke more than others and also be predisposed toward lung cancer. None of the variables will permit precise prediction. Many career women who smoke a lot, eat margarine, belong to the Democratic Party, and read comic books do not get lung cancer.

Correlation is not explanation. An obtained correlation or empirical relationship is meaningless aside from the theory that is used to explain it. The most adequate theory will account for the negative cases in terms of the same concepts that are used to explain the positive cases. The collection of data is not the essence of science. A scientific investigation may be considered successful to the degree that it contributes to the reduction of empirical and quantitative statements and increases the number of qualitative statements that can be made about phenomena.

Inasmuch as many of the conclusions in somatopsychology are based on empirical evidence, these cautions may be worth heeding.

Summary

The task of all science is to order or transform observational data to theoretical constructs in such a way that understanding, prediction, and control of phenomena are possible. The observational data provide a test of the "truth" of a theory, but the theoretical constructs are not directly derived from the data.

If a theory leads to increased understanding, it is considered an explanation. Complete explanation, however, is impossible. Science is truly an "endless frontier" in which a correct answer leads inevitably to further questions.

Adequate explanations appear to have several characteristics in common:

1. They are generalizations which permit application to the individual case.

2. They describe the greatest amount of data in the fewest terms.

3. They reflect a necessary and invariable relationship between certain events that occur in a specified context. The relationship is important rather than the qualities in an object.

4. They lead to understanding of what has to be changed in a relationship in order to bring about change in behavior.

5. They are expressed in dynamic, genotypic, contemporaneous terms and not in empirical, phenotypic, historical terms.

6. They point to further relevant research.

Progress in somatopsychology depends upon discovering adequate theoretical concepts to which data can be ordered. It has been pointed out that revolutionary advances in science have come not from empiricism but from new theories.[28]

Understanding the Behavior of the Physically Handicapped: Some Concepts for Somatopsychology

PHYSICAL DISABILITIES are physical. How it is possible to make psychological sense out of data that are not psychological? It is evident from earlier discussion that physique must be phenotypic for psychology. Psychological investigations based directly upon physique can lead only to naming or to empirical generalizations. Such generalizations can be expressed only in terms of tendency, correlation, or group differences that are significantly different from chance expectancy. If-then-always statements will not be made. There will always be many exceptions, and precise prediction will be impossible.

Examination of the research findings on physical disability indicates that this is an accurate reflection of the current state of affairs.

In this section an attempt will be made to develop a new way of thinking about somatopsychology in dynamic, genotypic, contemporaneous terms. Discussion will be restricted to social psychological adjustment problems. The problems of individual differences, educational method, and physical rehabilitation require extended discussion which cannot be given here.

As psychologists, we are not concerned with physical disability per se, but with the *behavior* that is associated with or appears to result from physical disability. The emphasis is on behavior. Psychological concepts, therefore, are required. Two such psychological concepts which permit the ordering of social-emotional behavior will be described. These are the concepts of *new psychological situations* and *overlapping psychological roles*. These ideas are not original with the present author. They were formulated by the late Kurt Lewin. Their elaboration and application to the physically handicapped were accomplishments of Roger G. Barker and associates. The following discussion draws heavily on their work (See footnote 2).

New Psychological Situations

Figure 1-1 represents a momentary point in time in the life space of a person.[29] It shows a schematic representation of an old or familiar psychological situation and a new psychological situation.

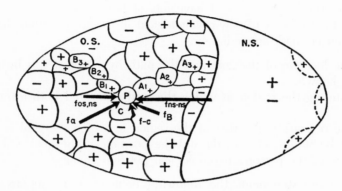

O. S.	Old situation	fa	Force toward subregions A
N. S.	New situation	fB	Force toward subregions B
P	Person	f-c	Force away from subregion C
+	Positive valence	fos, ns	Force in old situation toward new situation
—	Negative valence	fns-ns	Force in new situation away from new situation

FIGURE 1-1. *Old and new psychological situations.*

It will be seen that there are many known subregions in the old psychological situation. Some of the subregions have been labeled "plus" to indicate that they are desired by the person, and some have been labeled "minus" to indicate that they are not desired. Some paths to particular subregions have been indicated. Path A, for example, may represent going to the movies with a friend. The lines between subregions represent barriers that must be overcome. In this case, the barrier in subregion A_1 may represent getting permission from mother to go, A_2 may represent finding a friend to go with, and A_3 may represent having the money to get into the movies. Path B may represent "getting praise from mother"; the subregions to be passed through include making the bed in one's room, picking up toys, and washing one's hands and face before dinner. Path C may represent getting punishment from father, and single subregions may represent "being impudent."

In general, the behavioral possibilities are well structured in an old situation. The person knows where different positive or negative goals are and what paths lead to them. This is true for everyone, handicapped and non-handicapped, adults and children.

In a new psychological situation the entire region is unstructured except for a belief that a positive goal lies out there. In order to reach the goal it is necessary for the person to move out into this unknown region. Since the goal is positive and attractive, but its unfamiliarity is repelling, the region is labeled both plus and minus. An example of a new psychological situation might be leaving home and mother for the first time in order to go to school when all that is known about school is that mother says "you will have lots of fun there."

From the structure of new psychological situations, the following statements can be made immediately:

1. The location of the goal and the path by which it can be reached are not known.

2. Entering the region in which the goal is located both attracts and repels.

3. The person's perception of the region in which the goal is located will not be stable. The region and the position of the goal will appear to change as the person's psychological position changes.

From these statements the following behavioral predictions can be derived:

1. A person in a new psychological situation will engage in wandering, vacillating, unstable trial-and-error behavior. Since the location of the goal and the paths by which it may be reached are unknown, behavior cannot be parsimonious. It must be tentative and cautious. The person will be alert to small cues. He will be easily influenced by peripheral stimuli. Behavior will change as the person's perception of the situation changes. If it appears that he is getting closer to the goal, he will do more of what he has been doing. If it appears that he is moving away from the goal, he will change behavior. Early behavior will be cautious, but if it is unsuccessful, it will be followed by more extreme behavior.

2. The frustration that accompanies repeated trial-and-error behavior will occur. The person will show the emotionality and the disruption of behavior that result from frustration.

3. The person will be in conflict. He will attempt simultaneously to reach the goal in the new situation and to withdraw to the safety of the old situation. The conflict will be intensified if the goal is highly attractive and the old situation relatively unattractive. Conflict will be intensified further if induced forces, external to the person, block the return to the old situation or add strength to the vectors toward the new situation.

It is now possible to make some if-then-always statements: A person will enter a new psychological situation if the psychological forces acting upon him toward the new psychological situation are greater than the forces away from it. (The impelling and restraining forces are amenable to more detailed description, but this will not be attempted here.) If a person enters a new psychological situation, frustration and conflict, and the emotionality and behavior disruption that accompany frustration and conflict, will occur. There are no exceptions. It is true for adults as well as for children. It is true for the physically normal as well as for the physically handicapped.

If this is true, the concept of new psychological situations provides a powerful tool for the understanding, prediction, and control of behavior. The multitudinous, but irrelevant, questions about the past need no longer be asked. The innumerable ways in which individuals differ may be ignored. For this aspect of behavior only one question is relevant: Is the person in a new psychological situation? If the answer is affirmative, the predicted behavior will occur.

We are now in a position to understand why the physically disabled, as a group, tend to have more frequent and more severe problems of adjustment: They are more frequently placed in new psychological situations which place severe, traumatic demands upon them. When a person is placed in a new psychological situation, he *must* behave according to the demands of the situation. People who incur physical disabilities do not become different kinds of people as a direct physical or physiological function of the disability. They remain the same kinds of people, but now, by reason of their disability, they may be placed in different life situations. Especially, they may be placed much more frequently in new psychological situations. Their behavior will change according to the frequency and the degree of "newness" in the situations they encounter.

The behavior of individual, physically disabled persons who are not maladjusted may be understood in the same terms and placed on the same continuum. These individuals, for reasons which remain to be more fully described, are not in new psychological situations.

It may be speculated that some disabled persons successfully avoid new psychological situations. Other disabled persons may be in positions of special status or power. For example, the situation of a blind college instructor who is in a position of power where he can demand the attention of his class is markedly different from the situation of a blind college student. If only because of his greater knowledge of the material that students must learn and his power to give or to withhold grades, the blind instructor is on familiar ground. In high degree he can arrange the class to suit himself, taking full advantage of his skill with words and avoiding his limitations in writing or drawing on the blackboard. In many fields vocal dramatics and the ability to paint compelling verbal pictures are by no means less desired by listeners or inferior to diagrams.

In this instance the blind instructor is not in a new psychological situation and cannot be expected to show the behavior that results from new psychological situations. If he is equally powerful or skillful in other life situations, he will be a blind man who is not maladjusted, and we can readily understand why he is not emotionally disturbed. He would not be an unexplainable exception.

The personal characteristics and the past history of different disabled individuals, of course, may lead to behavior in new situations that is superficially different. Some individuals may be self-conscious, some may withdraw, some may seem to be aggressive. These behaviors, however, are only phenotypically different. Genotypically, they may all be ordered to the "cautiousness" that is required by the new psychological situation. A person can be cautious in different ways. The loud, boisterous person will often agree that he was only putting on a bold front while actually he was quaking in his boots.

One great value of this formulation, like useful concepts in other disciplines, is that it leads immediately to methods of control. If it is undesirable for the physically disabled to be maladjusted, one remedy is clear: *Reduce the "newness" of their life situations.*

It will be observed that a basic requirement for fruitful scientific thinking has been met. Physical data have been transformed to psychological data. The critical variable is no longer the physical disability, with which psychologists can't deal, but the psychological situation of newness. Disabilities have psychological effects not because it is in the nature of disabilities to require certain behavior but because they force the person more frequently into new psychological situations. It is evident that from psychological data, psychological predictions can be made.

Some Dynamics of New Psychological Situations

The situation of a blind student may be taken as an example. In contrast to the well-ordered structure that may be created by a blind professor, the situation of a blind student may become new whenever an instructor writes on the blackboard. The psychological effects of this situation depend upon whether the student is required to enter it.

Figure 1-2a illustrates the critical forces in the situation if the instructor says, "These two words, phenotypic and genotypic, which I have written on the board are important. You must remember them." The situation is not new for the blind student. He can remember the concepts without seeing them written. The goal of remembering is within an old and familiar situation. His blindness will cause no emotionality, no frustration.

Figure 1-2b shows how the situation may change if the instructor draws a diagram but then says, "The diagram shows only what I have just told you. You need not remember it." The situation may be new, but the blind student is not required to enter it. The vectors away from the new situation are greater than the vectors toward it.

Figure 1-2c illustrates the situation if the instructor says, "This diagram is basic. You must be able to reproduce it. I will ask for it on the next examination." If the student does not know how to reach the goal of learning to reproduce the diagram, the situation is new and the student must enter it. The strength of the forces acting on the student in the direction of the new situation is directly proportional to the attractiveness of the goal, that is, the student's aspiration to attain it. The greater the aspiration, either directly for knowledge or indirectly for the ability to give a correct answer on the examination sheet and thereby obtain a

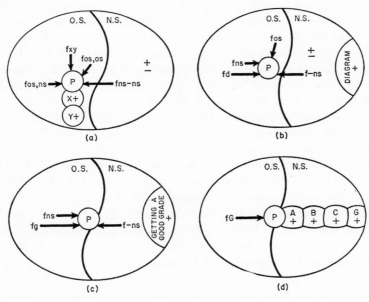

O. S.	Old situation
N. S.	New situation
P	Person
+	Positive valence
—	Negative valence
fos, os	Force in old situation to remain in old situation
fxy	Force toward remembering concepts of phenotypic and genotypic
fos, ns	Force away from remembering the concepts by visual cues
fd	Force toward learning diagram
f-ns	Force away from new situation
fos	Force to remain in old situation and not enter new situation
fg	Force toward goal of getting good grade by reproducing diagram
fns	Force toward new situation
f G	Force toward goal when sequence of steps is known (A+, B+, etc.)
fns-ns	Force in new situation away from new situation

FIGURE 1-2. *Varieties of new psychological situations.*

high grade, the greater the emotionality and behavioral disruption that will occur.

Obviously, the same analysis is possible for other kinds of physical situations and other kinds of physical disabilities.

Individual Differences

In these terms, it is now possible to discuss individual differences in a meaningful way. Not all blind individuals react emotionally when another person draws on the blackboard. Some blind people don't go to college in the first place and thereby avoid the many traumatic, new psychological situations in which blind students may be placed. Among those who do go to college, some, by reason of greater intelligence or better guidance, may prepare themselves in advance so as to reduce the newness of the situations that may be encountered. The blind student who has arranged for a classmate to trace every diagram into his hand, to reproduce it later in three dimensions, and to check the correctness of his practice drawings has made great progress toward his goal. His situation is shown in Figure 1-2d. It will be seen that the situation is not new; it is well structured. The sequence of steps that will lead him toward both momentary and long-range goals is known. The behavior predicted for new psychological situations, therefore, will not appear.

Another "kind" of blind student—perhaps one who is less intelligent, less well guided, or too proud to seek or accept the help he needs, who does not know the sequence of steps that will lead to attainment of the goal—will be in a new psychological situation and will show the predicted behavior. It is evident, however, that this will occur only indirectly because of the "kind" of person he is. The behavior is amenable to change with change in the structuring of the new situation.

New Psychological Situations in Physical Disability

There are three kinds of new psychological situations that may be encountered by the physically disabled person.

1. There are situations that are new because the person has never experienced them. It is common knowledge that the child with a disability is frequently overprotected or rejected by his parents and others. He may be deprived of common cultural experiences that are open to the non-disabled. The cerebral palsied child or the blind child may infrequently or never have been exposed to the learning experiences of "going downtown with mother," "playing outside with the neighbors' children," "going to look at the fire engines with father," or "selecting and buying a toy from his own allowance." Experiential backgrounds in

such cases are obviously limited. The capacity to cope successfully with a wide variety of life situations has not been permitted to develop. In technical terms, the psychological worlds of disabled children may be smaller and less well differentiated than the life spaces of physically normal children.

The practice of institutionalizing disabled children imposes some further restrictions upon the development of their ability to cope with the culture in which they live. Family living experiences, in all their warmth and all their opportunities for learning vicariously, may be drastically reduced. Practice in making decisions, even about such simple things as the time of arising or going to sleep, or when, where, and with whom to play, may be sacrificed to the need for running an institution efficiently. It is not surprising, therefore, that disabled children may reach adulthood without knowledge of the sequence of actions that will lead to the attainment of desired goals. To the degree that they do encounter such new, unstructured situations, they will behave as the situation demands. A schematic representation of the life space of disabled children and the life space of more favored children is shown in Figure 1-3.

It is evident that many situations that are new because they have not been experienced are unrelated to disability. Activities which lead to increasing the scope of behavioral possibilities, and to the structuring

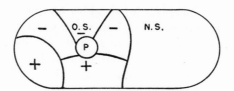

SCHEMATIC DIAGRAM OF LIFE SPACE OF DISABLED
CHILDREN SHOWING LARGE AREA OF NEW SITUATION
AND POORLY DIFFERENTIATED OLD SITUATION

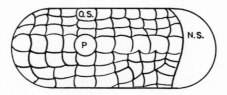

SCHEMATIC DIAGRAM OF LIFE SPACE OF NORMAL
CHILDREN SHOWING SMALLER AREA OF NEW
SITUATION AND HIGHLY DIFFERENTIATED OLD
SITUATION

FIGURE 1-3. *Life space for disabled and physically normal children
(see Figure 1-1 for key).*

of these regions, therefore, will reduce the maladjusted behavior that is a function of newness.

2. Some situations are new because the person lacks a culturally required tool for behavior. He is partially or totally unable to structure the new situations.

It must be emphasized that psychological newness is not equivalent to geographical or physical newness. A motorist may never have driven to Alaska, but if he is able to read maps and follow route markers such a trip would not be psychologically new. The field is well structured. Similarly, if a person is confident of the technique for acknowledging introductions and the etiquette of behavior at a party, he may meet many new people in new surroundings, but since the sequence of steps to "making a good impression on others" is known, the situation is not psychologically new.

On the other hand, a disabled person may enter the same physical situation repeatedly, and it may be new each time. The blind child, for example, may be in a new psychological situation every time he leaves his home to walk around the block. Ditches may have been dug, barriers erected, or there may be obstacles on the sidewalk in places that cannot be anticipated in advance. Each walk, each street to be crossed, may be a new adventure that requires great cautiousness. Similarly, the congenitally deaf child rarely knows in advance if he is going to be able to read the lips of the people who speak to him or if others will understand his laboriously acquired, but imperfect, speech. Each time he tries to speak or to lip-read, the situation is new if it cannot be structured. Knowledge from past experience that communication will be easy, of course, will reduce newness, but knowledge that communication will be difficult leaves the field unstructured.

Behavior in new situations, it will be recalled, is oriented to a goal. The forces toward the goal may arise from the motives of the child, from induced forces from without, or from a combination of both. The deaf child may wish to attend a regular school for normally hearing children or his mother may insist on this. In order to stay it is vital that he "make a good impression" on the teacher. One means to this goal is to have speech that can be understood and to be able to read the lips of others. If, however, the teacher and the other children only sometimes understand the deaf child and only sometimes does the deaf child understand others, each act of communication is psychologically new. The child can't plan consistently. He can never be sure of what to expect. New situations, therefore, are encountered with a frequency that is rarely, if ever, experienced by normally hearing persons. This is true for individuals with other kinds of disabilities, also.

This is inescapable: Every disabled person in our culture is going to be frustrated by those new psychological situations that arise because he lacks an appropriate tool for behavior. The deaf person does not live in an Indian culture, where signs are generally understood and sometimes preferred for communication. The crippled person does not live in an environment where there are no steps to be climbed. He lives in a culture where vocal communication and good locomotor ability are required. To some degree a disabled person is going to be able to function in our culture as well as he would if he were not disabled. But he is going to be exposed more frequently to new psychological situations that are directly related to the disability.

There are no magic solutions here, but the concept of new psychological situations points clearly to the relevant contexts that must be investigated:

(a) Many new situations can be avoided. The deaf person can associate only with individuals who know the language of signs. The blind person can sit at home and listen to the radio or the talking book. What are the positive and negative consequences of such behavior?

(b) Specific skills to reduce newness can be taught. What should a deaf child do if another person cannot understand his speech? What should a crippled child do if he wishes to enter a building but cannot open the door?

(c) It is probable that tolerance for frustration can be learned. Under what conditions is this feasible and desirable?

(d) The potency of some goals can be reduced. For which goals and under what conditions should the disabled person not strive?

3. Some situations are new because of the social stimulus value of the disabled person. Disability has many meanings to others. The disabled person often does not know when he enters a social situation whether he will be an object of curiosity, pitied, sympathized with, "helped," patronized, exhibited, praised for his spunk, avoided, or actively rejected. Only rarely will he be seen as a person who has psychological properties beyond the disability. More frequently he will be identified with the disability and be reacted to in terms of whatever the disability means to the other person. These meanings are often extreme. They are rarely neutral.

Reduction of newness in this situation has two aspects:

(a) The education of the public as to the non-identity of physical characteristics and psychological characteristics.

This requires a change in well-developed stereotypes, and it may be difficult to accomplish. It may be difficult not only because able-bodied persons may have a "need" to perceive the physically disabled as "inferior" persons, but also because disability is not infrequently pheno-typically related to other undesirable characteristics. For example, if large numbers of cerebral palsied persons, through no fault of their own, are poorly educated, or if an appreciable proportion of the cerebral palsied are also cortically brain damaged, a drastic change in customary modes of thinking is required to reserve judgment about a particular, un-known individual who is seen to have cerebral palsy. This is a part of the general problem of prejudice that is experienced by other minority groups also. Enough progress has been made toward the solution of this problem to indicate that reduction of prejudice in the public is possible.[30] Change will not be easy, however, and it will not be accomplished quickly.

  (b) The education of the disabled person in specific social skills which will facilitate his acceptance as a person.

The physically normal person is often well-meaning, but he does not know how to behave toward another whom he perceives to be different. What sorts of behavior will reduce the newness of the situation both for the disabled and for the non-disabled person?

This analysis indicates that the disabled person lives in a world that is frequently ambiguous both for himself and for others. He may fre-quently be placed in a strange and terrifying world in which he is ex-pected to cope with new situations to which he has not previously been exposed; new situations in which his lack of a tool hampers adequate structuring; and new situations in which his social role is not clear.

If new psychological situations have the properties that we have derived, and if disabled persons are more frequently placed in new psy-chological situations, it is not surprising that, on the average, the disabled have been found to be less well adjusted than others. If the theory is true, however, the sequence of steps that will lead to good adjustment is equally clear.

Overlapping Psychological Roles

THE DISABLED person lives in two psychological worlds. Like every-one else, he lives in the world of the non-disabled majority. He also lives in the special psychological world that his disability creates for him. These worlds overlap, as shown in Figure 1-4.

Many activities are common to both worlds, but some activities are engaged in primarily by disabled persons, while other activities are open only to the physically normal. The world of the physically normal is larger in the sense that it contains relatively more behavior possibilities

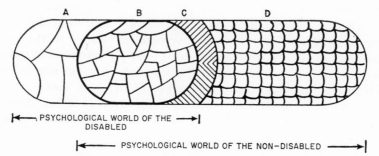

A Small and relatively undifferentiated area open only to the disabled
B Areas open to disabled and non-disabled
C Barrier region preventing locomotion of disabled person to region D
D Larger and well-differentiated region open to the non-disabled

FIGURE 1-4. *Overlapping psychological role situation.*

and is amenable to greater differentiation. This dichotomy is not unique to disability, however. It can also be applied to any of the ways in which individuals differ. There is a psychological world of women and a psychological world of men; a world of Negroes and a world of whites; a world of Catholics and a world of those who have other beliefs; a world of the stupid and a world of those with greater intelligence; a world of the poor and a world of the rich.

Inasmuch as every person holds membership in many different groups, he must play multiple overlapping roles. This in itself is not a source of difficulty. For example, a young man can be simultaneously a son, a brother, a nephew, a fiancé, a college student, a major in English, a fraternity pledge, a Protestant, a football player, and a musician. Each of these roles, in some degree, requires different behavior than the others; but in general they are compatible with each other. The person is able to play the role that is required by the different constellations of psychological and social forces that act upon him.

Interfering Overlapping Roles

At particular times, however, the different roles may be interfering. A man can play football in the afternoon and be a dance band leader in the evening; but he cannot play on the university football team and play in the band simultaneously. The latter situation will create conflict in the degree that the two roles are considered equally desirable and are not seen as different, but equally good avenues of recreation.

The conflict will be resolved as the interplay of psychological forces acting upon the person impels him in the direction of one goal or the other. These psychological forces may arise from the greater, intrinsic desirability of one goal, differences in social prestige attached to the different behaviors, the relative ability of the person to do one or the other well (for example, first trumpet player versus third-string tackle), the amount of time that is required for practice relative to the amount of time needed for study or the wish to have an active social life, the relative scholarships given to football players and trumpet players, plans for the future, and other factors. The important point here is that the person is amenable to the forces that arise from each situation. Both roles are open to him. He can play either or, within limits, change from one to the other.

Antagonistic Overlapping Roles

Conflict will be intensified if the overlapping roles are antagonistic so that responding to one set of role-determiners automatically rules out the other. If a college student brings home his fiancée for a visit, his fiancée-oriented role as a mature person who plans soon to marry, have his own home, and raise a family may interfere with his mother-oriented role as a dutiful son. Suppose one evening his doting mother, who still sees him as a child, says, "Junior, dear. It is raining outside. Be sure to put on your rubbers before you go out." How can the student respond to this childish role to which he has been assigned? If he behaves as a dutiful, docile son he loses status as a mature, capable person in the eyes of his fiancée and of himself. If he rejects his mother's well-meaning meddling in word or action, he loses his role as a dutiful son. He cannot behave both as a mature person and as an immature person; whatever he does, someone will be hurt. The situation will be resolved as before in terms of the relative attractiveness of the two roles and the potency of the psychological forces acting. College students understand why the mother's perception of her son as "my little baby" is unacceptable to him, and why it causes conflict. There are more, and more attractive, behavioral possibilities in the mature role. It is true that college students often are dependent upon their parents in some ways. However, they see no reason why financial dependency, for example, should "spread" to an assumed general immaturity of such degree that they do not know when to come in out of the rain. This sort of role pervasiveness is considered unnecessary and unacceptable. We shall see that this is a serious problem in disability also.

Overlapping Excluding Roles

The greatest conflict occurs when the person rejects the roles that are open to him and strives for a role that he cannot attain or at least that is relatively inaccessible to him. We shall call these "overlapping excluding roles." It does not matter greatly at the momentary point of conflict whether the barrier between the person and a desired role is an ability barrier or a social barrier.

The psychological world of the homely girl, for example, in contrast to the world of the beautiful girl, can be ordered to Figure 1-4. For this variable of beauty, it is evident to any observer that a beautiful girl may behave in ways that are impossible for others. Other things being equal, the beautiful girl will be sought out more frequently. She can be highly selective in whom she will date and where she will go. Even in the classroom, as the author knows from experience, beauty is not unrelated to academic grading. Prestige, status, and privileged behavioral possibilities, not open to homely girls, are open to college "queens." The gains are not only immediate but extend far into the future. Favorable marriages and great social mobility as a function of beauty are not unknown.

These are no trivial or insignificant goals for many college women. It is not surprising that many college girls, when they perceive the great value placed on beauty and the attractive behavioral possibilities it creates, desire this role for themselves. It is possible, within limits, for a homely girl to make the most of what she's got by reducing weight, by adopting culturally approved forms of dress, and by using cosmetics; but only rarely is it possible for a homely girl to become beautiful or to play the role of a beauty.

Many girls who are not endowed with great beauty handle this problem very well. They do not place a high value on the role from which they are excluded. If the beauty behaves as if "beauty is as beauty does," they reply, "Beauty is only skin deep. Other things are more important than how you look."

Some homely girls, however, because of the psychological forces acting upon them, are unable to relinquish the goal of beauty. Perhaps beauty is important to family and friends, and the girl is never permitted to forget that she is not beautiful. She may be referred to as ugly and treated with the rejection and disdain that are reserved for those who lack important attributes. Inasmuch as everyone tends to accept the judgments of important "others," it is extremely difficult to avoid internalizing feelings of inferiority and unworthiness.

For some individuals, beauty is not an end in itself but a means to a goal, so that the psychological forces arise, in part, from within. A girl who wishes to be a movie heroine may perceive that she lacks the necessary pulchritude for this role, but be unable to give it up. She may try all sorts of tricks to attain beauty, but she may also make herself perfectly miserable by sitting in front of a mirror and examining herself: "If only my nose weren't quite so long; if my ears were smaller; if my hair weren't so dry and stringy; if my eyelashes were longer—then the satisfactions that are open to beautiful women would be open to me too. I could be a movie star. I could meet and maybe marry a wealthy and attractive man. I could have fame and other good things."

No doubt, in some degree, this kind of behavior occurs in all psychologically adolescent women in our culture, for there are undoubtedly real advantages in being able to play the role of beauty. If the goal is inaccessible or unattainable, however, it does no good to continue to place a high value on it simply because one feels beautiful inside. Most mature individuals, both male and female, appear to place less value on physical beauty than adolescents do. It is nice to have, but its absence or relative lack does not make a person less worthy nor is it decisive for the judgment of the person.

Similarly, a goal may be unattainable because the path to the goal is blocked by a social barrier. A college girl's highest aspiration may be to pledge Alpha Alpha Alpha sorority. Perhaps, however, she once wore bobby socks on campus or committed the unpardonable faux pas of wearing a slip under an evening gown. Perhaps her family is of the "wrong" race, religion, or economic status. Otherwise she may be beautiful, talented, and a BWOC, but she is blackballed from the sorority. She is now just as effectively prevented from playing the role of "member of Alpha Alpha Alpha" with all its advantages as she would be if she lacked an intrinsic ability. It doesn't matter from the standpoint of behavioral consequences whether the social prejudice is unjust. If the social barrier is strong, only rarely is it possible for the determined person to break through it. Prejudice is usually not amenable to reason nor will it be decreased by "good" behavior on the part of the person. If the person is unable to relinquish a strong emotional attachment to an unattainable goal, the resulting behavior is clearly predictable.

An implicit understanding of this principle is perhaps one reason why it is a normal human tendency to stop comparing oneself with others who are different. The average college student compares his test papers not with Phi Beta Kappas but with others on his own level. The athlete who plays both football and basketball but is able to make only the football team not only plays more football and less basketball, but he comes to consider football a "better" game. The path to mental health is traveled when a person places his highest values on what he has got or can attain and places lower, neutral values or non-comparative values on what he hasn't got or cannot attain.

We are now in a position to make an additional if-then-always statement: If a person, because of his own forces or induced forces, is impelled to strive for a goal that is unattainable because of ability or social barriers, the constellation of behavior commonly referred to as psychological maladjustment will occur. The greater the vectors toward the goal and the stronger the barriers which surround the goal, the greater will be the behavioral disruption.

Application to the Physically Disabled

Individuals who have physical disabilities also have other roles. Like others, they encounter their fair share of overlapping compatible, overlapping interfering, and overlapping antagonistic roles. They are almost unique, however, in being exposed more frequently, sometimes for a lifetime, to overlapping excluding roles. If this is true, it is not surprising that according to available evidence, disabled persons tend to be maladjusted more frequently than others.

The excluding overlap occurs between the role of the disabled person and the role of the physically normal person. The dynamics of the situation are shown in Figure 1-5. It will be seen that the psychological forces acting upon the person in the direction of the world of the physically normal are greater than the vectors toward the world of the physically handicapped. In popular language, it is "better" to be physically normal than to be physically disabled. The reasons are easy to understand. The world of the physically normal is larger and better structured with desirable behavioral possibilities. The world of the physically handicapped is relatively underprivileged.

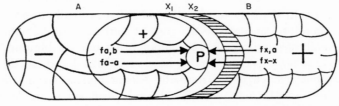

A	Situation of the disabled person	fa,b	Force in A toward B
B	Situation of the non-disabled person	fa-a	Force in A away from A
X_1	Ability barrier	fx,a	Force in X toward A
X_2	Social barrier	fx-x	Force in X away from X

FIGURE 1-5. *Overlapping role situation in disability.*

The slogans prevalent in rehabilitation, that the goal of the handicapped is to "be normal, achieve normality, become as normal as possible, be treated like normal, do the same thing as normal children and in the same way," are not simply figures of speech. They reflect the reality of underlying psychological and social forces. However, the role of the disabled person excludes the role of the non-disabled person in every situation where the disability makes a difference. The disabled person is separated from some desirable normal goals by a strong barrier. This barrier is constructed of ability limitations and social limitations, and both are relatively impermeable. It is dynamically clear, therefore, that disabled persons are often placed in a position where they are impelled to strive for relatively inaccessible or unattainable goals. When the barrier is impermeable and the goal unattainable, the behavior predicted for overlapping excluding roles will occur. Living on the barrier between overlapping excluding roles may be considered a form of psychological suicide.

If it is undesirable for disabled persons to be maladjusted, another solution has become clear: Reduce the frequency of overlapping excluding role situations. A few examples of specific situations may clarify this abstract formulation.

Assume that a person who is blind wishes to be treated like a regular person, just like anyone else. His hostess at a party takes him at his word and asks him to pour the cocktails. How should he behave? Theoretically he has a choice. He can pour like a blind man or he can try to pour like a seeing person. If he pours like a blind man, he will hook a finger over the lip of the glass. When the liquid reaches his fingertip, it is full. Many people, however, are somewhat squeamish about having other people's fingers in their drinks. If he poured in this fashion he would call down upon himself the intense hostility of the assembled group. Perhaps he would hear derogatory comments about blind people being invited to parties. However, he has already rejected the role of the blind person and decided to try to play the role of a normally seeing person. He must, therefore, accept the assignment and attempt to pour drinks like a normally seeing person. He cannot bring out his blindness as an "excuse." He is not a seeing person, however. He is blind. In this situation he cannot behave like a normally seeing person, for he does not have the necessary visual tool. The best he can do is to depend on change in weight or change in sound to estimate when a glass is full. This is both a more difficult and a less effective procedure than visual inspection. Some glasses may be correctly filled, but it would not be surprising if some glasses were filled to overflowing and some were left only partially full. He may go through the motions of behaving like a seeing person, but he cannot actually play the role. He knows, and all who see him will know, that he is blind.

The significance of this example is that similar situations occur with great frequency in the life of every disabled person who rejects the behavioral possibilities that are open to him as a disabled person and strives instead to live a role that is not possible. To the degree that the person's life situation requires "normal" behavior, and to the degree that the person places a high value on entering regions that are partially or totally closed to him, he will be maladjusted. Moreover, the denial of the disabled role will not protect him from the social discrimination of those who perceive that he is disabled. He will be denied acceptance and entrance into privileged situations by those who respond to his disability no less frequently than disabled persons who accept the disabled role when the disabled role is appropriate.

It is easy to contend that the disabled person must "accept" his disability, but this is only a meaningless and contradictory platitude if the underlying situation of disability is not understood. If "acceptance" means that the person must be content with an inferior position that requires him to acknowledge his inferiority as a person and permits him to strive only for intrinsically less satisfying goals, "acceptance" is difficult. If there is no assurance that society will "accept" the disability also and not penalize the person for it, it is unrealistic to endow "acceptance" with the qualities of a panacea.

The Problem of Acceptance

In almost every other overlapping excluding role situation, there are some who will contend sincerely, and not as a sour-grapes mechanism, that the possible role is just as good or better than the excluded role. It is just as good to be a woman as a man; it is just as good to be a Negro as to be white; it is just as good to be Catholic as to hold other faiths; it is just as good to be an independent as it is to be a fraternity man. Many more people believe that it is not good to be too smart, too rich, too beautiful, or too successful. Disability is unique in that almost no one believes it is just as good or better, in any sense, to be disabled than to be non-disabled. No one believes that it is not good to be too healthy. This means that some of the strongest forces in our society act upon disabled people to deny their disabilities and impel them to strive to be non-disabled. We do not wish the disabled to "accept" their disability. On the contrary, we insist that they deny it.

Consider the case of a Negro who feels that many of the most valued goals in our culture are reserved for whites. He aspires, therefore, to the role and position of a white man. How would we evaluate such a person if he exposed himself to X-rays and bought quantities of drugs to lighten his skin, pomades to straighten his hair, and sought plastic surgery to reduce the width of his nose? Every psychologist would say that such a person is seriously maladjusted. His wish to be white in a culture that rewards white skin and penalizes black skin is understandable, but mental health lies only in the direction of accepting himself as a Negro and taking pride in the group to which he belongs.

Consider also the case of a Jew named Goldstein who believes that, like members of numerous other minority groups, he is excluded from highly desirable goals. He suddenly changes his name to Brown and joins the Episcopal Church. Most would agree that he cannot deny himself. Like the blind man pouring drinks, he is only going through the motions. He cannot really be Brown, the Episcopalian. To himself and to his friends he is still Goldstein underneath. To attempt to change in this way is prima facie evidence of emotional disturbance. It would be better to accept himself and take pride in the group to which he belongs.

Consider now the treatment and evaluation of the disabled. A child is deaf. On the one hand we say, verbally, accept the deafness. On the other hand, however, we give him a hearing aid, and compel him to spend most of his waking hours in listening to sounds that he perceives so faintly and distortedly that he cannot interpret them; we urge him to attempt to say sounds that he himself cannot hear or monitor for himself; and we drill him in assigning meaning to the fleeting movements of the lips that are only by-products of the vocal noises of others. In some cases this process is crowned with striking success. Some degree of adaptation occurs in many. For all deaf children, however, we make it clear that the child is not to accept his deafness. On the contrary, he is to exert himself to the utmost to be not deaf. He is not to use the signs which are easier for him. He is to speak, even though his speech will never be as good or as "normal" as the speech of a normally hearing person. He must continue to strive with all his energy for goals that, at best, are only partially attainable. In addition, his adjustment is evaluated, in part, according to the degree to which he associates with normally hearing people and avoids other deaf persons. The inferiority of "the deaf" is made clear to him, for he is encouraged to assert his membership in every other group to which he belongs, but he is not to take pride or seek satisfactions in the psychological world of the deaf.

Deaf children learn quickly that it is "better" to be a hearing person than a deaf person. In the most "progressive" schools where deaf teachers of the deaf are never employed "because they can't teach speech," the children see that the important people, the teachers, the supervisors, and the technicians are hearing people; the janitors, the junior cooks, and the servants are deaf people. Little children who wear individual hearing aids point to them pridefully and indicate, "I hear." Others point to their own empty ears and shrug their dismay.

Similarly, a child has cerebral palsy and doesn't walk. Of course, it is necessary to accept the disability; but, of course, it is equally necessary for the child to struggle with all sorts of therapies to try to overcome at least some aspects of the disability.

This is not an argument for or against particular methods of education, but an attempt to attain clarity. It may be socially desirable that deaf, blind, and crippled children behave, as far as possible, as not-deaf, not-blind, and not-crippled. It may be necessary for them to live on the barrier between overlapping excluding roles. If this is so, however, it is a great advantage to understand clearly the structure of the situation. We cannot justly create situations which lead to maladjustment on one hand and belabor the disabled for their maladjustment on the other.

It is conceivable that there are advantages and values in maladjustment. George Matthew Adams,[31] the newspaper columnist, who often reflects popular feeling recently advised his readers, "Be anxious." Everything worthwhile has been accomplished by people who were anxious to "get ahead."

In a society that worships achievement and "success," perhaps anxiety and insecurity are a small price for progress. It is certain that among the disabled, the highest accolades have gone to those who did not accept, but denied and achieved "in spite of." It is equally certain, however, that they paid for this recognition and praise with anxiety, conflict, and frustration. The former undoubtedly are valuable, but the latter are not the fruits of adjustment. There is nothing to be gained by confusing accomplishment with adjustment. Fortunately, we need not be caught on either horn of the dilemma. If the theory of disability presented in this chapter is true, solutions for some of the critical problems of disability are implicit within it. The application of the theory to a particular disability and to individual cases is described in Chapter 3.[32]

Notes

[1] Close association over a period of years with my colleagues—Roger G. Barker, Tamara Dembo, and Beatrice A. Wright—has undoubtedly led me to assimilate many of their ideas. Their thinking has been so cogent and has become so much a part of me that it is now often difficult to separate the strands of their ideas from my own. The best of what may be of value in this chapter undoubtedly is of their making. The errors, of course, are strictly my own.

[2] R. G. Barker, B. A. Wright, L. Meyerson, and M. R. Gonick, *Adjustment to Physical Handicap and Illness: A survey of the social psychology of physique and disability* (New York: Social Science Research Council, 1953).

[3] E. B. Gowin, *The Executive and His Control of Men* (New York: The Macmillan Company, 1927).

[4] F. B. Blair, "Relations Between the Average Amount of Insurance per Policy and the Height and the Weight of the Insured," *The Record* (American Institute of Actuaries), 29 (1940), 211-223.

[5] D. G. Paterson, *Physique and Intellect* (New York: Appleton-Century-Crofts, 1930).

[6] O. Klineberg, S. E. Asch, and H. Block, "An Experimental Study of Constitutional Types," *Genetic Psychology Monographs*, 16 (1934), 145-221.

[7] P. S. deQ. Cabot, "The Relation Between Characteristics of Personality and Physique in Adolescents," *Genetic Psychology Monographs*, 20 (1938).

[8] R. N. Sanford and others, "Physique, Personality and Scholarship," *Monographs of the Society for Research in Child Development*, VIII, No. 1 (1943).

[9] C. Burt, "The Factorial Study of Physical Types," *Man*, 72 (1944), 82-86.

[10] D. W. Fiske, "A Study of Relationships to Somatotype," *Journal of Applied Psychology*, 28 (1944), 504-519.

[11] H. J. Eysenck, *Dimensions of Personality* (London: Routledge & Kegan Paul Ltd., 1947).

[12] W. H. Sheldon, "Constitutional Factors in Personality," in *Personality and the Behavior Disorders*, ed. J. McV. Hunt (New York: The Ronald Press Company, 1944), chap. xvii.

[13] W. H. Sheldon, S. S. Stevens, and W. B. Tucker, *The Varieties of Human Physique* (New York: Harper & Row, Publishers, 1940).

[14] W. H. Sheldon and S. S. Stevens, *The Varieties of Temperament* (New York: Harper & Row, Publishers, 1942).

[15] W. H. Sheldon, E. M. Hartl, and E. McDermott, *Varieties of Delinquent Youth* (New York: Harper & Row, Publishers, 1949).

[16] Sheldon, *op. cit.*

[17] R. G. Haskins, *Endocrinology* (New York: W. W. Norton & Company, Inc., 1941).

[18] L. Bender and A. Blau, "The Reaction of Children in Sexual Relations with Adults," *American Journal of Orthopsychiatry*, 7 (1937), 500-518.

[19] R. Benedict, *Patterns of Culture* (Boston: Houghton Mifflin Company, 1934).

[20] K. Lewin, *Principles of Topological Psychology* (New York: McGraw-Hill Book Co., Inc., 1936).

[21] K. W. Hamilton, *Counseling the Handicapped in the Rehabilitation Process* (New York: The Ronald Press Company, 1950).

[22] L. A. Spiegel, "The Child's Concept of Beauty," *Journal of Genetic Psychology*, 77 (1950), 11-23.

[23] J. W. M. Whiting, *Becoming a Kwoma* (New Haven: Yale University Press, 1941).

[24] J. R. Hanks and L. M. Hanks, Jr., "The Physically Handicapped in Certain Non-Occidental Societies," *Journal of Social Issues*, 4 (1948), 11-20.

[25] F. C. Macgregor and B. Schaffner, "Screening Patients for Nasal Plastic Operations," *Psychosomatic Medicine*, 12 (1950), 227-291.

[26] H. R. Stolz and L. M. Stolz, "Adolescent Problems Related to Somatic Variations," in *National Society for the Study of Education, Forty-Third Yearbook*, Part I (Chicago: University of Chicago Press, 1944).

[27] Barker, *op. cit.*

[28] J. B. Conant, *Modern Science and Modern Man* (Garden City, New York: Doubleday & Company, 1953).

[29] This figure and the following ones may have practical as well as didactic value. It is suggested that the student attempt to diagram the psychological situations of individuals whose behavior he wishes to study. The diagramming process will help to indicate the information that must be obtained to understand the existing situation and the actions that are necessary to bring about a change in behavior. B. Wright in *Physical Disability—A Psychological Approach* (New York: Harper & Row, Publishers, 1960) provides a rich source of case material on which to practice. N. Cohn in "Understanding the Process of Adjustment to Disability" (*Journal of Rehabilitation*, November-December, 1961) illustrates some simpler diagrams and shows their utility.

[30] G. W. Allport, *The Nature of Prejudice* (Reading, Mass.: Addison-Wesley Publishing Company, 1954).

[31] G. M. Adams, "Be Anxious," *Easton Express* (Easton, Pa.), April 29, 1954, p. 6.

[32] This chapter was prepared while the author was a Public Health Research Fellow of the National Institute of Mental Health.

T. ERNEST NEWLAND

Professor of Education
College of Education, University of Illinois

2 *Psychological Assessment of Exceptional Children and Youth*

THE PURPOSES of this chapter are to review briefly the major assumptions that underlie psychological testing and to indicate major measurement problems regarding these assumptions with respect to exceptional children and youth. Results actually obtained in testing in the different areas of exceptionality will be presented only for the purpose of illustrating assessment problems in this field, since the major psychological findings are incorporated in the chapters on the several kinds of exceptionality. Only a few of the hundreds of devices and techniques will be mentioned—solely to illustrate the problems or attempts at solution of some of the problems which are indicated.

Our discussion of examination procedures and problems will be pointed towards the accomplishment of a maximally meaningful psychological assessment of exceptional children and youth. Yet, to attain this, we would need the contributions of a full and competent staff. Case studies, social studies, the reports of medical diagnostic and treatment specialists, and full educational histories would be required, and we should

need to "staff" such children in the light of all such information before
we could expect to have complete bases for sound and complete psychological assessments of the children. This is beyond the scope of this chapter. We shall limit our concern to problems involved in the obtaining and
integrating of information obtained within the framework of the psychological or psychoeducational clinic. Further, we shall confine ourselves to
a consideration of the nature of the content of psychological reports
rather than the reports themselves.

If this chapter identifies more problems than it settles, it is in part a
result of the status of examination procedures in this field, and in part
a result of the author's desire to have this kind of educational impact
upon the student.

The words "testing" and "assessing" definitely mean different activities.
The term "testing" will be used to denote the exposure of a client to
any given device, whether group or individual, essentially for the purpose
of obtaining a quantitative characterization of one or more traits of that
client. "Assessing," on the other hand, includes both this quantitative
depiction of the client, and the qualitative and integrated characterization of the client as a dynamic, ongoing total organism functioning in a
social setting. Without resorting to an illustrative full-length report of the
assessment of a child, the following excerpted statements may suggest
more clearly the contrast between qualitative and quantitative characterizations:

> (a) He was 5 feet 4 inches tall [quantitative], but he didn't
> really stand up straight while he was being measured [qualitative].
> (b) She earned an I.Q. of 67 on this test [quantitative], but she
> didn't seem to apply herself in the examination situation [quali-
> tative].
> (c) It is interesting to note that he consistently named dif-
> ferences but did not name similarities [qualitative], even though
> he did fail this part of the test [quantitative].
> (d) Her constantly asking the examiner if her responses were
> correct and her frequent biting of her fingernails during the exam-
> ination session suggested feelings of insecurity [qualitative]. This
> behavior, and some others like it, make me wonder if the I.Q. of
> 83 which she got on the Binet [quantitative] gives us a true pic-
> ture of her rate of mental development.

There tends to be relatively less of the qualitative aspect in testing
than there is of the quantitative aspect in assessing. Even though much
of the following discussion will deal with the testing approach, the greater
significance of the use of the assessment approach will, it is hoped,
become apparent.

Even though this book is concerned with exceptional children and
youth up to the chronological age of 21, most of the discussion and the

research cited will pertain to exceptional children from the high-school level downward. The term "exceptional children," as used in this chapter, will signify either this more limited age range or a specific part of it.

It is particularly important in this chapter to bear in mind the fact that the terminology used to denote different kinds of exceptional children is confusing. In the first place, the term "physically handicapped" will be used here to refer to a group of exceptionalities—the orthopedic, the sensorily handicapped, the physically delicate, the brain-injured, the epileptic, and the like. The brain-injured will include both the cerebral palsied and those who have, or are believed to have higher-level neural impairment not reflected in motor dysfunction. The deaf will be regarded as a part of the acoustically handicapped, just as the blind will be regarded as falling in the category of the visually handicapped. The term "mentally retarded" will be used, albeit illogically, to refer to those exceptional children whose intellectual retardation is not so severe as to warrant their falling in the range of mental deficiency nor so slight as to warrant their being regarded as "slow learners." The "mentally retarded," then, will be thought of as having intelligence quotients roughly comparable to 1960 (L-M) Stanford-Binet I.Q.'s falling between approximately 50 and 75 or 80.[1]

In the second place, it certainly is not safe to assume that the different types of exceptionalities are "pure" types. A child with a speech impairment, for instance, also may have a hearing loss, or some higher central nervous system involvement, or he may be socially and emotionally maladjusted. A visually impaired child may be mentally retarded or he may have a speech impairment, or he may also be brain-injured. However, our discussion will be restricted intentionally either to such "simple" types of exceptionality or to types of exceptionality in which the designated conditions are regarded as the *primary*, but not the sole, bases upon which the educational and social needs of such children are being met, or are being studied. The psychological examination and assessment of children of any multiple-exception type involve a compounding of the problems peculiar to each of the involved areas of exceptionality, as in cases such as the mentally superior, severely involved athetoid; the deaf-blind; the blind cerebral palsied; or the speech-impaired emotionally maladjusted.

Assumptions Underlying Psychological Testing

IN CONSIDERING the following assumptions, it is quite likely that the student will think most often in terms of the measurement of the intelligence of a child. The assumptions, however, also underlie the processes of determining such things as the nature of the child's emotionality, his educational achievement, his vocational aptitudes, his motor skills, his height, his weight, or even his temperature.

In this connection, let us use the word "testing" to mean the process of using any device (test, inventory, scale, thermometer) in the examination of an individual. More explicitly, *testing is the controlled observation of the behavior of an individual to whom stimuli of known characteristics are applied in a known manner.* It would follow, then, that if the same stimulus (from the observer's point of view) were applied in the same manner (from the observer's point of view), the differences in the responses of the individuals so stimulated would be a function of differences within the individuals. The following assumptions inhere in this process:

1. It is assumed that *the observer is adequately trained* and skilled in the procedures of getting the subject to respond effectively (rapport), of applying the stimuli (test or test items), of recording the responses of the subject, and of evaluating (scoring) those responses according to the instructions for the standardized use of the device. In the majority of cases, the standardized procedures are adhered to rigidly. Later, we shall consider certain studied departures from these procedures in connection with the examination of certain kinds of exceptional children.

2. It is assumed that *the sampling of behavior* in the test situation *is both adequate in amount and representative in area.* The safest way to judge a basket of strawberries would be to examine each strawberry and then base one's judgment on the total sample. But people don't do that. Some look only at the top, and others tip up the basket and look at a few more. In the area of human behavior, we can't sample all of it, but by acceptable statistical methods we can determine how small a sample we can safely take. Similarly, we can't sample every different area of behavior, but we can and do sample those which, statistically, have been found to yield adequate reliability and validity.

3. It is assumed that *the subjects* being tested *have been exposed to comparable,* but not necessarily identical, *acculturation.* Even if the language problem is ignored, a personality test or inventory or a vocational aptitude test developed for use in the United States could well be of little or no value if used in Thailand or on the Zulus. Certain other tests are nearly as inappropriate when used on certain types of the physically handicapped whose worlds have been seriously circumscribed.[2] Less often, but equally important, certain children may give evidence of having been "hothoused," given rather intensive cultural training consciously or unconsciously, by adults who, quite understandably, want their children to do well.

4. It is assumed that *error will be present* in the measurement of human behavior. Error is present in any measurement, whether it be in the distance to Jupiter, in the weight on the bathroom scales, in the length of a table, or in vocational aptitude, intelligence, or emotional adjustment. Statistical procedures enable us both to ascertain the magnitude of error in any given kind of measurement and to allow for that error in connection with any given measurement. We do not think of a child as having earned an absolute or infallible I.Q. on any given test, but as having an I.Q. on that test falling between a point some 5, 10, or more points above the obtained one and another point some 5, 10, or more points below it.

5. It is assumed that only *present behavior is observed*. Behavior on any given test is as of that particular time on that particular test. It is a sample within a relatively long period of time. It must be remembered that a child is observed as reacting in this way (or these ways) to this stimulation (test) at the time and under the conditions of this test. But this condition does not make futile or meaningless the process of testing or examining because of the next assumption, plus certain kinds of statistical insurance that has been or can be taken out with respect to the validity of the behavior sampled.

6. It is assumed that *future behavior* of the child *is inferred*. The statement "Every diagnosis is a prognosis" illustrates the close association between the process of measuring present behavior and the act of using the results of that measurement in endeavoring to predict how the subject will act, regarding the particular areas of behavior observed, at some later time. The man is significantly overweight now; therefore he will be a less desirable insurance risk. The woman just passed her driver's examination; therefore, the state issues her a permit for future driving. The child does very well on an intelligence test, and someone says he should be good college material. Another child does quite poorly in an examination situation and is therefore regarded as unlikely to respond effectively in future learning situations. Or, even, a child who actually has performed ineffectively in an examination situation is judged (inferred) to be actually capable of profiting from a treatment or training program, because certain conditions are believed to have impaired or distorted his present performance.

This two-step process of measuring and inferring is both reasonable and dangerous. On the one hand, it is the only thing we can do. A child performs normally in the first and second grades. That is to say, he is promoted to the next higher grade in the average amount of time. Therefore we make the guess that he will perform normally in the next higher grade, assuming no intervening distraction. Similarly, he answers correctly the same number of test items as did the average third grader, therefore, we *assume* that he is likely, in other related situations, to behave the way other third graders have behaved. On the other hand, such predictions have three important sources of potential error. Predictions may be faultily based either upon too limited a sample of behavior or upon a sample of behavior that bears no sound relationship to the predicted behavior. A fifteen-minute test involving the manipulation of some blocks can well provide a precarious basis upon which to predict that a child can acquire verbal symbols and use them meaningfully. Even a good sample of behavior which would serve satisfactorily for predicting behavior within the next year or so can lose much of its value for the prediction of behavior five to ten years later. It must be remembered, too, that these predictions are not statements of certainty; they are actually probability statements, made in the sense of "the chances are. . . ."

Measurement in the areas of intelligence and emotionality quite commonly involves an additional inferring process. In the case of intelligence, some kind of achievement often is measured, and then an inference is drawn concerning the capacity which made such achievement possible. In projective testing, for instance, we see inferences drawn with respect to basic personality structures from what often appear to the clinically untrained to be irrelevant behavior samples.

Thus we see that inferences are drawn from a present sample of behavior both with respect to what later behavior will be and with respect to what caused the behavior that was observed in the process of examination or measurement. It is particularly important to recognize that the results obtained in testing or assessing are used as the basis for inferences which have varying degrees of predictive strength. Especially is this realization necessary in dealing with exceptional children since they are, by the varying natures and complexities of their exceptionalities, the ones for whom many of our testing devices and procedures may be at least in part inappropriate.

Variability Among Tests

ONLY VERY slowly are those who deal in the school setting with the results of tests of "intelligence" coming to recognize the necessity of differentiating among those devices. Perhaps even slower is their realization of the extreme importance of clearly denoting the specific measures obtained by means of these devices. Let us examine the importance of such precise communication with respect to "average" children and youth; the major implications of this with respect to the exceptional will become apparent repeatedly.

In order to simplify our consideration, we shall assume that normal, adequate, and otherwise satisfactory conditions existed in all the testings which are discussed. One further clarification is needed as regards the connotation of the term "I.Q." as used in this portion of the chapter. Not infrequently—as in the question, "Is the I.Q. constant?"—one discovers that the person posing the question may use "the I.Q." to denote, in some global fashion, the child's biologically determined potential for learning, a characteristic minimally reflecting the effects of any environmental influence upon it. Others may use "the I.Q." to denote not only this basic capacity of the organism but also the extent to which it may have been modified by the child's rearing and culture, whether in a nurturant manner, in a non-nurturant manner, or in a detrimental way. In this second sense, "the I.Q." is used to denote what may well be regarded as the child's "effective intelligence." However, in addition to this ambiguity—as between just basic, native, biological potential, and potential-as-realized-and-operating—"the I.Q." may denote simply some kind of score by which the child's performance on some test of "intelligence" is characterized. For our purpose in this section, we shall use "I.Q." in this third sense—a score earned on some test of "intelligence." As we shall see, this will improve our communication *somewhat,* but even this has come to contain disconcerting ambiguity.

In the 1920's, the early days of school group intelligence testing, when a group was said to have an average group test "I.Q." of 121, or when any given child was referred to as having "an I.Q. of 85" on some group test, the idea being conveyed was reasonably clear to those communicating. In most communities, a class so characterized would have been a fairly "bright" class; the child was possibly a "slow learner." *As of that time,* when teachers thus described or compared their classes or children, different teachers talked in terms of pretty much the same characteristic. This was due primarily to the fact that the group tests then in use were so similar in content. The behaviors sampled by the group tests of that time tended to be much the same from test to test. (The individual tests of those days, many of them the forerunners of most of our present "performance" tests, sampled considerably more diverse forms of behavior.)

Subsequently, the predominantly verbal group tests came increasingly to be infused with or replaceable by tests which involved less reading and/or less use of verbal response by those taking them. Interspersed among items like "Boy is to girl as man is to (1) house (2) animal (3) woman (4) business," there were items such as " ○ ◁ is to ◁ as □ ○ is to (1) ⊖ (2) ⊡ (3) ▣ (4) ○ ," The child reacting to both of these types of items was called upon to do the same *kind* of thing, but, in the first case, he employed words whose meanings he had learned, whereas, in the second, he did not need to use words to perform successfully. Then there developed complete tests, such as the Cattell Culture-Fair Tests, that employed no verbal content. Later came the kind of group test of "intelligence" which is more common now—that having one section of verbal items and another section of non-verbal, or "non-language" items.

As a result, present group tests of intelligence have become much more heterogeneous: some depending upon sampling only what has been learned by means of fundamental psychological processes; some involving a sampling not only of what has been learned but also of the processes which have been involved in that learning; and some which sample predominantly, or (hopefully) solely, processes which are essential to school learning. The scores (I.Q.'s) earned by means of these different kinds of behavior samplings therefore no longer are as likely to connote the relatively homogeneous sampling of earlier group tests. As a result, it has become even more necessary to qualify the obtained score by the name of the test, such as "Kuhlmann-Anderson I.Q.," "Otis Gamma I.Q.," or "Cattell Culture-Fair I.Q." This kind of specification is additionally necessary by virtue of variations among tests in validity, adequacy of standardization, and other respects. For similar reasons it is necessary to identify clearly the individual test by means of which an I.Q. has been obtained.

If intelligence tests or, better, tests of learning aptitude are to be used to make a sampling of behavior on the basis of which to make some predictions as to likely ease of learning in school, and if the major kind of learning to be predicted is symbol acquisition, the devices used to measure that aptitude should yield reasonably consistent results. Disconcertingly often, educators find this not to be the case, as illustrated by five different average "I.Q.'s" obtained on 284 different twelfth-grade students tested within a single semester: 96.4, 103.7, 105.5, 114.2, and 118.2. One of the tests used was entirely non-verbal; another, a mixture of verbal and non-verbal; and a third, the heavily verbal Primary Mental Abilities Test. Equally extreme variations have been found on first-grade children when they have been given group tests of "intelligence" or "mental maturity."

Chronologically paralleling this confusing state of affairs as regards group tests has been that of individual intelligence testing. Even as the Binet and early adaptations of it were coming into use, "performance" tests were being developed and used. The Seguin Form Board and its adaptations, the Witmer Cylinder, a myriad of form board tests from the Wallin Peg Boards to the more complicated Dearborn and Lincoln Hollow Square tests, picture and figure completion tests, the Kohs Color Cube Test, and maze tests first appeared as separate tests. They then were incorporated, as they were or in modified form, into batteries such as the Pintner-Patterson, the Grace Arthur, the Merrill-Palmer, and the Cattell scales. Since these were individual tests, they were used only clinically. It was out of such a background that the performance part of the Wechsler-Bellevue came into being and thus was included in the Wechsler Intelligence Scale for Children. That children's scores on such non-verbal tests contributed a much less adequate basis for predicting their verbal learning behavior than did their performance on verbal tests was early established, although that fact now appears to be largely overlooked.

The semi-relevance of what has just been said about this group of "performance" tests to what was said earlier about "non-verbal" group-testing attempts must be considered most critically. There is the danger, as shown by uses to which the results of such testing have been put, particularly with respect to certain kinds of handicapped children, of assuming implicitly that, since the item, " O ◁ is to ◁ as . . ." is a non-verbal kind of item and since, say, a figure completion item such as the Feature Profile also is a non-verbal kind of item, they both sample the same kind of psychological process and therefore are likely to have the same or similar predictive value with respect to the child's primary chore in school—that of symbol acquisition. That such an assumption is not warranted is shown by the low correlations, long a matter of record, between the two kinds of performance.

At least some of the confusion regarding results of widely differing tests—all purporting to measure "intelligence"—would seem to be capable of resolution by thinking about such tests in terms of factors which appear to be related to the extent to which scores earned on them increase with age. On the average, scores on the Raven Progressive Matrices, for instance, increase discriminatingly until the age of twelve or thirteen. At the other extreme, increases in scores on the Concept Mastery Test can occur up to the age of fifty. "Maturity" on the Binet is reached from thirteen to fifteen years. Adult performance on the Wechsler increases until twenty to thirty years. Miller Analogies scores may "peak" somewhat after that, but significantly below the CMT.[3] In part, these differences well may be the result of the way in which these tests have been standardized, but, for our purposes here, another psychologically important variable, which well may be thought of as a continuum, seems to parallel the range from the Matrices to the CMT. If we examine the kinds of behavior sampled by the devices mentioned, we note that neither the administration of nor the responding to the Matrices necessitates the use of verbal behavior. Given, for instance a box with three "X's" and a blank space in it occupied by a "?" to be replaced with one of the following: O, △, –, X, ⊂⊃ , the subject quickly and easily can point to the "X" in the series as belonging in the box with the three other "X's." The product of non-verbal learning is needed in comprehending and solving the item. However, if we take an imaginary item to represent those in tests "peaking" later, we find a behavior sampling of this sort: "mortarboard : commencement :: bikini : _____ (1) dancing (2) swimming (3) preaching (4) drawing." Here, the meaning of the pattern —:—::—:— long since has been learned, thus causing the difficulty of the item to inhere in the meaning of the words in order to satisfy the relationship called for in the proportion. It is suggested, then, that the continuum from Matrices-type tests to CMT-type tests can be paralleled by a continuum ranging from sampling learning potential in terms of *psychological processes fundamental to learning* to the sampling of learning potential essentially in terms of the *products of learning.*[4]

The other tests mentioned, as well as still other "intelligence" tests not specifically referred to, can profitably be examined in terms of the extent to which they sample the psychological processes necessary to learning and in terms of the extent to which they sample behavior in terms of what has been learned. Two generalizations integrate the illustrative material which has been presented in this connection:

1. To the extent that the behavior sampled may be regarded as *product* (the result of learning), "maturity" tends to be attained later; whereas, to the extent that the behavior sampled constitutes *process,* "maturity" tends to be attained earlier. Or, "intelligence" test scores which reflect *process* tend to stop increasing at earlier ages than do scores of such tests which reflect *product.* It seems quite possible that at least certain essential psychological processes by which people learn may mature considerably earlier than may have been assumed.

2. To the extent that the behavior sampled may be regarded as *product,* the impact of acculturation upon test performance tends to increase; whereas, to the extent that the behavior sampled constitutes *process,* the impact of acculturation on test performance tends to be reduced.

Such a consideration of the nature of behavior sampled by different kinds of "intelligence" tests should result in much less confusion regarding the varied scores which have been earned. As we shall see, this process-product concept has very definite implications regarding the assessment of the learning potential of exceptional children and youth.

The Meaning of Norms

INDIVIDUAL TEST performances take on meaning when they are thrown into social perspective by means of norms. Measurements which are recorded have to be compared in order to give them meaning. For instance, we say Mary is 51 inches tall—which, in and of itself, is meaningless. It takes on meaning when we are able to say that Mary is taller than her twin brother, or is as tall as the average nine-year-old girl, or is taller than 80 per cent of her fellow seven-year-olds. Knowing how average seven-year-olds, average eight-year-olds, and average nine-year-olds learn, we have a somewhat fuller understanding of Jim's probable ease of learning when we know his mental age to be seven years six months. This was made possible by the fact that the person standardizing the test which was used on Jim had ascertained how a *typical* population at each age level in question had performed on that test. It is of particular importance here to note that a studiously typical population is sought for the standardization of the bulk of the measuring devices used. Mechanically using such devices on certain types of exceptional children, therefore, may be completely without justification. To make modifications of such devices by using only parts of the original standardized device, to modify slightly the material or procedure for even parts of the original standardized device, or to try to combine usable parts of differently standardized devices—each necessitates the carrying out of sound research to show that such tamperings do not invalidate the process of comparing the findings with the original norms.

Obviously, the significance attached to this varies with the kind of exceptional child being examined. If the child is exceptional *only* by virtue of some deviation in intelligence, devices standardized to measure this kind of behavior are applicable as standardized. On the other hand, tests involving speech to any significant extent would yield ambiguous results if used on children with serious motor involvements affecting speech. Certain manipulation tests, used in a standardized, timed manner on certain kinds of motor-handicapped children, would yield completely misleading results. When tests which include a considerable sample of acculturation are used on children who have not had a broadly "normal" exposure to that culture, it is inevitable that questions will be raised as to the validity of the results obtained.

Mainly in areas of exceptionality other than those of the intellectual deviant there is a very real question as to the extent to which the test performances of the severely orthopedically handicapped, or the sensorily handicapped, or of those with marked speech impairments, or even of those who are emotionally maladjusted should be depicted in terms of scores which have been obtained in the "normal" standardizations and uses of the device. If only devices standardized on a random sampling of a "normal" population are used on the exceptional, still excluding from our consideration the intellectual deviant, should the performances of the exceptional be stated in terms of the "normal"? If so, the exceptional stands to suffer by such a comparison since many of the conditions which constitute exceptionality are recognized clinically as conditions which tend to impair rather than to enhance an individual's performance. If, on the other hand, devices are standardized, for instance, on only the specific populations of the physically handicapped, there remains a problem of giving a meaningful social perspective to the performances of such persons on such devices. If, further, normally standardized devices are modified or "adapted" to the conditions of the exceptional, the meaning of the results so obtained, when compared with the norms for the original unmodified or unadapted device, becomes at best ambiguous.

In one sense, the last three sentences in the above paragraph may be regarded as overstatements. Take, for instance, a bead-stringing task for which there are age norms. Assume that an athetotic ten-year-old takes the test and, in the prescribed amount of test time, is able to string only as many beads as the average five-year-old. It still may be socially worthwhile to know the level of the ten-year-old's functioning in this skill even though the test was not standardized on children with a motor involvement such as his. Whether the test was "fair" to this child depends upon the inferences which someone may draw with respect to his performance. In fact, logically, no test is "unfair"; only the user of a test can be "unfair," and his inferences may be unwarranted.

Assuming the appropriateness of norms for the different types of exceptionality, how should the performance of a given exceptional child on a particular device be characterized or interpreted? Should this child be described as being in the bottom one per cent of the general population on a given trait, or should he be regarded as doing very well in view of the conditions operating in his case? On the one hand, his scholastic standing may be far below the grade level at which some persons might expect him to be working. On the other hand, he may be doing as well as he is capable of doing. The mental retardate, for instance, may be succeeding in school as well as can be expected on the basis of his mental capacity, but he still may be doing so poorly that he cannot be expected to succeed as a clerk in a small grocery where he would be required to make out slips, read invoices to check incoming goods, or even read names and addresses when making deliveries. The problem here is not an out-and-out either/or choice; it is, rather, one of deciding which to use when. For purposes of educational planning and motivation, we consider the child's performance in terms of *his* potential. For purposes of vocational planning, and for certain research purposes, however, his status must be conceived of in terms of his skills or lack of them, in comparison with comparable skills in others. The assumption of a constant frame of reference, or a failure to distinguish clearly between different frames of reference, often causes considerable confusion in the assessment of exceptional children and youth.

We have seen, thus far (1) that when any client is tested or assessed he is, in effect, being observed under conditions that are controlled as much as possible; (2) that certain concepts and assumptions are involved in any testing or assessing, whether the client be average or exceptional; (3) that special problems are encountered in testing or assessing the exceptional—whether it be attempted by the mechanical use on the exceptional of a device developed for and standardized upon the non-exceptional, or whether it be attempted by means of a device standardized upon a given kind of exceptional children, or whether one tries to take the short-cut of "adapting" conventional devices for use with the exceptional; and (4) that while these problems vary somewhat from one kind of exceptionality to another, the problems are common to various areas of measurement. Certainly, the more one is sensitive to the problems which have been indicated, the more one is hesitant to accept uncritically I.Q.'s reported on various kinds of the physically handicapped, especially when there lurk in the background implicit assumptions that I.Q.'s (or other quantifications) are comparable in a one-to-one relationship from one device to another, or from one handicapped group to another, or from one handicapped group to a non-handicapped group.

As has been indicated, practically all of the devices which have been used in trying to ascertain the psychological picture of the physically handicapped have been developed on essentially "normal" populations. This is understandable in view of the fact that, in most cases, such devices were the only ones available and because it was desired to depict or describe the handicapped in terms of the non-handicapped population with whom they had to live and compete. Take, for instance, the reporting of mental, or even achievement, test results on the deaf in terms of how they performed on devices which had been standardized on essentially non-deaf subjects. Consider likewise the dangers of this type of characterization of the performances of the severely orthopedically handicapped. However, no research evidence has been presented which demonstrates that the basic assumption regarding exposure to comparable acculturation has been satisfied.

Test Adaptations

THE POINT has been made that any test must be thought of as a controlled pattern of stimuli which is presented to a client in a uniform manner in order that the client's responses to those stimuli can be recorded and measured. Whether or not the original standardized pattern of items can be altered without lowering the validity of the total performance is an important question since, in examining children who are emotionally disturbed or even seriously ill at ease in the examination situation, some psychologists prefer to start their testing with performance or non-verbal items rather than with the verbal items with which the test was started when it was standardized. That such an approach tends more quickly to establish rapport with such subjects is generally accepted among clinicians. Fortunately, some research on the effects of so altering the stimulus pattern of the 1937 Binet indicates that the validity of the total test response is not impaired by this particular type of modification of the test procedure.[5]

It is a not infrequent practice among those making psychological examinations of the motor-handicapped to make other "adaptations" of tests to their clients by omitting certain items on which the examiner feels certain the client cannot perform. Certain vocabulary items are omitted if speech is severely impaired, and manipulation and drawing items are omitted if the client's hands are severely involved. This departure from the standardized stimulus concept of a test both involves a decrease in the sample of the client's behavior and, when "corrections" are made for the whole test on the basis of the parts of the test which were used, usually implies that each item in the test has equivalent measurement value.

Table 2-1 depicts the problem in a considerably oversimplified form. Let us assume that in the test in question ten kinds or "areas" of behavior are sampled, such as vocabulary, comprehension, maze tracing, picture identification, identification of similarities, and so on. Let us assume, also, that four nine-year-olds are examined by means of this device. Child 1 is examined in all ten areas and earns an I.Q. of 150,

Table 2-1

Hypothetical Test Behavior Sampling of Four Children

				"Areas" of behavior sampled in the total test							
Child	I	II	III	IV	V	VI	VII	VIII	IX	X	I.Q.
1.......	x	x	x	x	x	x	x	x	x	x	150
2.......	x	x	x	x	x	x	x	x	x	x	65
3.......	x	x	x		x	x		x	x	x	65
4.......	x	x		x	x		x	x	x	x	65

which becomes part of the basis upon which he may be characterized as mentally superior. Child 2, tested in the same ten areas, performs in a manner that suggests that he may be a candidate for a class for the mentally retarded. Child 3, who has a gross speech impairment, is examined in only eight of the ten areas, and he earns an I.Q. on that test of 65, numerically comparable to the one earned by Child 2. In like manner, Child 4, a manually impaired child, is examined by the "same" test which has been "adapted" to his condition, and he is found to have an I.Q. numerically comparable to those of Child 2 and Child 3. We are justified in assuming psychological comparability among these total test performances only insofar as it has been shown by research that behavior samplings in areas III, IV, VI, and VII are of equal psychological value among themselves and also as related to the other areas of behavior sampled. In spite of the fact that it is yet to be shown by research that these conditions have been met, numerous studies have been published in the field of the exceptional, purporting to show comparisons among exceptionalities, between certain exceptionalities and the non-handicapped, and within certain areas of exceptionality. Such studies have included test adaptations lacking either psychological or statistical justification.

Although this problem is more clearly recognizable in connection with attempts to measure "intelligence," it exists in a slightly modified form with respect to attempts to measure emotional adjustment, vocational aptitudes, and educational achievement. Whereas it is present in such attempts at measurement with the acoustically impaired and the speech-impaired, it is more commonly, and perhaps more dangerously, encountered with the cerebral palsied.

Illustrative of ambiguous, if not misleading, data presented about the cerebral palsied are the following.[6] On the basis of the following I.Q. data, the author of the article stated that 40 per cent of his 300 cases "must be classed as aments":

I.Q.	Per Cent	Age	Per Cent
Below 25	7	1– 5 years	40
25– 50	16	6–10	31
51– 70	15	11–15	20
71– 80	13	Over 15	9
81– 90	17		
91–110	18	*Speech:* Poor	61
111–130	4	Fair	28
131–150	0.3	Good	11
Undetermined	10		

From a psychological point of view, one immediately asks questions such as these about such data: By means of what test or tests were these I.Q.'s obtained? Since the I.Q.'s were all thrown together in the same tabulation, is it not assumed that these I.Q.'s have both numerical and psychological comparability? Were the tests "adapted" to the subjects? If so, do the results from such "adaptations" have numerical and psychological comparability? In view of the fact that 40 per cent of these cerebral palsied clients were less than six years of age, how psychologically meaningful are such I.Q.'s? Since we know that the younger the child the greater the size of error in the psychological measurement of him, how much additional possible distortion resulted due to the crippling condition of these childen? Since 61 per cent were reported as having "poor" (presumably including "no") speech, to what extent are these data further clouded by that factor? What skill did this psychologist possess that enabled him to determine I.Q.'s in all but 10 per cent of his three hundred cerebral palsied clients, 40 per cent of whom were under six years of age, and 61 per cent of whom had poor speech? No small amount of curiosity would be evidenced as to the extent to which these intelligence quotient data would be affected by hearing impairments in these subjects. Questions such as these can well be raised with respect to a number of other reports on the intelligence quotients of the cerebral palsied and certain other orthopedically handicapped children.

When one turns to the severely acoustically handicapped—particularly those born with this handicap or having it from an early age [7]—some of the same questions arise, and new ones occur due to the fact that the psychological conditions attending this latter group differ significantly from those attending, say, those cerebral palsied who have normal hearing acuity. We shall confine our consideration here to problems attending the attempts at the measurement of general mental capacity, but recognize that measurement of emotional adjustment, vocational aptitude, and educational achievement involves certain directly comparable problems. We have difficulty, for instance, in believing that our basic assumption concerning the general comparability of the acculturation of such handicapped subjects has been satisfied, particularly if devices developed for use with the non-handicapped have been used on them and the results stated in terms of a normal population. For a long time, devices standardized on a hearing population were administered to deaf children and youth and their performances characterized in terms of mental ages or I.Q.'s derived from data on children with normal hearing. That the deaf did significantly less well on these devices than the hearing was clearly evident. But did this fact indicate that the basic capacities of the deaf were as low as the test results suggested? Since at least most of the devices which were used sampled heavily in the verbal and conceptual areas, particularly regarding hearing subjects, one very properly can raise the question, "Was the acculturation of the deaf enough like that of the hearing (on whom the devices were standardized) to warrant the use of the same device on the two groups?" Since even most "mental" measuring devices measure achievement (from which capacity to achieve is inferred), had the deaf the same opportunities to achieve (acquire percepts and form concepts) as did the non-deaf standardizing population?

This fact was early recognized and led to two lines of endeavor. Reasoning from the assumption that basic intelligence is likely to be "normally" distributed within a large population (such as the deaf) unless there are factors known to be operating to impair or distort it (as contrasted with affecting the *manifestation* of that intelligence), and that the average of that distribution should not be much, if at all, below the average of a comparable hearing population, ways were sought to obtain a "truer" picture of the basic mental capacities of the deaf. Since the devices used were predominantly verbal, it seemed reasonable to get at the basic learning capacity of the deaf in a non-verbal manner. This seems like a wonderful idea, and it would be if we could be certain that the kinds of non-verbal behavior sampled provided as good a predictive basis (of subsequent school learning) as did the verbal behavior samplings. However, most measures of non-verbal behavior developed on a hearing population do not provide as good a basis for predicting success in school learning as do measures of verbal behavior. In the case of the deaf, the use of hearing-standardized non-verbal tests was found to be more effective in indicating school learning than was the use of hearing-standardized verbal tests. Steps were taken next to improve upon this admittedly makeshift situation by developing non-verbal tests which could be used with the deaf and standardizing these materials on the deaf. A roughly parallel developmental history has existed with respect to the areas of the cerebral palsied and the blind. First, existing devices were employed, with little if any modification from their original form; certain parts of the devices were then omitted and/or substitutes made; then either wholly new devices were made or planned, or administration procedures and norms were developed for the particular exceptionality.[8]

Making adaptations in the individual examination of exceptional children may consist, then, in those adaptations which are made in the testing procedures and in those which involve modifications of the device or devices used. Adapting testing procedures where the content of the device employed remains intact—although possibly presented in a modified order—is essentially a matter of employing psychological tactics in the testing situation. Here, the examiner may read the standardized test items to blind subjects, may allow a child to use a typewriter in giving his responses if he has a major speech or handwriting problem, may observe the eye movements of the subject as he identifies parts of a test item (where other children might write or point with their fingers in responding), might start with motor items rather than with verbal items in the case of a child whose problem involves the communication area, or might even rearrange some Binet items into WISC form if research warranted taking such liberties with the material. Here the primary objective is to obtain as psychologically meaningful responses as possible from the child to the total content of the test employed.

Adaptations which involve modifications of devices, either by the omission of a few of the kinds of behavior samplings or by selecting only certain parts of tests or scales, constitute something quite different. As was indicated earlier, this is done sometimes with no regard for the major psychological and statistical problems involved. Adaptations such as these are made for two reasons. Perhaps more commonly, the examiner employs only those parts of the device for which he can communicate the directions and to which he believes the child is capable of responding. The extreme of this is seen in the case of the use of "performance," non-verbal tests with the acoustically impaired. Attempts have been made to describe adaptations of a number of tests for use with the cerebral palsied.[9] In some instances, only some of the tests which make up a Wechsler or Binet may be utilized, because of insufficient time to administer the entire device or because the examiner believes, for one reason or another, that certain tests, or items, cannot be employed. Usually, arithmetically neat extrapolation procedures (sometimes of questionable psychological validity and limited in statistical justification) are specified for use in estimating what the "whole" behavior sample would have yielded. Generally, however, the communication problem is the major determinant of such adaptations, particularly in the cases of disabled subjects.

On the other hand, the psychologist may decide that he wants to study a child with respect to certain kinds of psychological functionings. He then employs only those parts of tests which he knows, or believes, involve the kind of behavior in which he is interested. He may, for instance, be particularly interested in the child's conceptualization behavior, or in the child's memory spans, or in the child's fund of general information, or how he functions arithmetically, or how he learns in the clinic situation, and the like. Three conditions must be satisfied if the psychologist is going to use test materials in this manner. He must know the parts played by different kinds of behavior in the learning process. He must have evidence that the tests which he uses to obtain such behavior samples throw valid light upon such facets of learning. And he must have a normative background in terms of which he can interpret the results of his sampling. He must understand, for example, the difference in conceptualization behavior between a child who says that a bus and a railroad car are alike because they both have wheels and a child who says that they are alike because they are means of transportation. And he needs to know at what ages children are likely to respond in each of these two manners.

This type of clinical evaluation of children with cerebral defects is well described by Taylor.[10] By means of a variety of tests, for which she provides rationale, directions, and normative data, she samples behavior in terms of perception, reasoning, and learning—paying somewhat more attention to how the child functions than to the rate of development in these areas. Clinically, the procedures she describes have potential value beyond work with the cerebral palsied.

The decisions as to whether and how test adaptations should be made must therefore be based, first, upon the assumptions initially made regarding the distributions of the trait being studied in the particular kind of exceptional subject. Is an essentially normal distribution of learning aptitude assumed as in the case of the visually impaired, the socio-emotionally maladjusted, the orthopedically disabled, or of the total population in terms of which the mentally retarded and the mentally superior are described? Are test adaptations (or selections) made for the usually unstated purpose of causing the deviant to be perceived as less deviant than he really is (for school learning), as in the use of somewhat higher non-verbal performance scores in the place of the predictively more meaningful verbal scores? The psychologist must make his basic assumptions explicit, and is obligated to try to help the educator understand them and interpret test results in terms of them.

Other adaptations are necessary for certain of the exceptional. One kind of such adaptation involves the modification of methods of evoking the desired kinds of responses. These adaptations of the administration of the test are made only for the purpose of improving communication between the examiner and the examined, and every effort must be exerted to do nothing that will alter the psychological nature of the behavior being sampled. Imagine, for instance, a card which has printed on it, in randomly related positions, pictures of a cat, a tree, a bat (mammal), a tricycle, a flower, an elephant, and a house. Suppose that a speech-impaired child is shown a picture of a mouse and is asked to "show me all here (on the large card) like that (the mouse)." The child can, by pointing, give the examiner a psychologically meaningful indication as to whether he functions at a low conceptual level (selecting the cat because of the commonality of the whiskers), or go so far as to include the bat (as one kind of animal), indicating a high level of conceptualization. However, to use a picture of a person as a means of helping the deaf understand that they are to "draw a person" would help him to get the idea of what he is to do, but would limit or invalidate the psychological intent of the test.

Another concept to be kept in mind in making test adaptations is one that was developed earlier to the effect that in certain instances, at least in the cases of the blind and in some of the orthopedically handicapped, learning potential may be more meaningfully sampled only, or primarily, in terms of process rather than in terms of product. The extent to which this kind of adaptation will have merit will necessarily depend upon the age level of the subject whose learning behavior is being predicted. It is quite likely that predicting school learning solely or primarily on the basis of samples of psychological process (classification, eduction of correlates, and the like) may be much more defensible in the case of young children than in the case, say, of high-school level children. This is likely to be true due to the fact that learning at the higher level, or even at the later elementary school level, depends not only upon the pupil's being adequate as regards the psychological processes essential to his learning but also to his having benefited from those processes by learning some things (products) which are needed in order to learn higher order things. At the kindergarten or pre-school level, psychological processes are the primary means by which the child comes to learn that many different objects can be called "dog"; this concept must be acquired (product) before he later can differentiate between the labels "canine" and "feline"—it can be a contributive step to his learning what "animal life," or "transportation," or "shepherding" means.

The matter of adapting tests for use with the exceptional must be evaluated in terms of the whole range of points developed in this section. Particular areas of exceptionality present their unique demands, and the nature of the adaptations justifiably will need to vary also among the areas of psychological measurement—whether learning aptitude, academic achievement, socio-emotional adjustment, or vocational aptitude.

Measurement Approaches and Problems

WE HAVE considered at some length certain assumptions basic to and difficulties inherent in attempts to examine the exceptional. On the basis of these, the student should be able to determine for himself certain possible uses of specific devices and procedures.

The number of devices which have been well developed for the purpose of sampling different kinds of human behavior runs frustratingly into the hundreds. Other less well-standardized and validated devices which have been used, many of which might add significantly to our understanding of human behavior if they were provided with scientifically acceptable bases, increase the total amazingly. To consider each of the best and most promising of these, with respect to particular types of exceptionality, would lead us into a mass of detail that would be interesting but, in large part, highly transitory. It will better serve our purpose here to consider only illustrative attempts at measurement of certain types of behavior in certain of the areas of exceptionality. Some of these attempts have been made, others are being initiated, and some need to be undertaken.

Psychologically, we strive continuously to think in terms of the "whole individual" reacting in varying situations. However, measurement in this molar sense has not been accomplished. What we have to do is, consciously, artificially, to deal, one at a time, with certain facets of the individual, and then to reconstitute the individual into a dynamically meaningful whole. For our purpose, we shall concern ourselves with selected measurement approaches and problems in specific areas: limited aspects of physical condition, intellectual potential, socio-emotional adjustment, educational achievement, and vocational aptitude.

As we consider these facets of different kinds of exceptional children and youth, we recognize that some evidences of some of these areas overlap to varying extents with certain evidences of others. A child needs a certain amount of intellectual capital and educational achievement in order to comprehend and react meaningfully to an inventory on social adjustment or to certain tests of vocational interest. Even if the items in such devices were read to him, he must be able to understand and remember what is read if his responses are to have even elementary validity. In spite of this, the areas can be regarded as partially and, if competent research has been done on the devices used, identifiably discrete. Bear in mind, too, that we shall refer to the exceptionalities as though they were single rather than multiple exceptionalities.

The Physical Area

During the early years of an individual's life, inferences concerning intellectual growth are based essentially upon evidences of physical growth and development. This is understandable because the nervous system must grow in order that muscles will function. When certain muscles are seen to function, this is taken as evidence that certain neural growth has occurred. When normal stimulation does not evoke a given motor response, it is inferred that neural growth has not occurred, due either to lack of time for such growth or to the presence of some pathological condition. If the nature of a variety of motor responses of an 18-month-old infant is comparable to the nature of those of only a nine-month-old, then one is usually highly suspicious of "mental" retardation or of some contributing pathology, or of both. (One does not generalize wisely on a single sample of behavior!) As a result, the physical developmental picture serves as a major basis on which inferences are drawn concerning "mental" development. Particularly useful in ascertaining and interpreting this physical developmental picture of infants and young children is Gesell and Amatruda's *Developmental Diagnosis*, although, in using the information in this book, one must constantly bear in mind the fact that the normative statements are in terms of averages and that perfectly normal individuals can fall somewhat above and below the averages which are presented.[11]

Using the normative data of the Gesell Developmental Schedules, Blum and Fieldsteel have prepared development charts on which child growth may be plotted.[12] The charts provide for the systematic recording of 28 samples of motor behavior and of 32 samples of functional behavior. The systematic description of the motor performances (and functions) of children of whatever type of exceptionality has value, even when their behavior is compared with that of non-exceptional children, since in doing so, the *range* of any child's behaviors may be more suggestive than the fact of his having deviated from the "normal" in any of them. Assets thus tend more quickly to be capitalized upon and liabilities often may suggest remedial or corrective steps to be taken.

In interpreting behavior samples of this sort, one must remember that the manifestations of some mild neuropathological conditions may not appear until later. Illustrative of this is the case of a child who, at the age of 18 months, was very thoroughly and apparently competently examined, both neurologically and psychologically, in a clinic of high repute. The official report of that clinic, undoubtedly justified at that time, contained not even a suspicion of any neurological involvement. When the writer saw the child, at the age of five, there were motor and sensory responses that suggested some neural involvement. Subsequent examination of the child by a competent medical authority, confirmed the suspicion of mild athetoid involvement with an accompanying moderate hearing loss.

The problem of characterizing the motor levels of children handicapped by neuromuscular disorders has been attacked by Johnson, Zuck, and Wingate.[13] Drawing upon Gesell's developmental data and preparing situations and devices which call for more complex behaviors, they have constructed an individual test by which they endeavor to ascribe motor ages to such handicapped children. Standardized originally on "normal" children, for which the original data unfortunately are not available, norms are established for functioning both with upper extremities and with lower extremities. The children can be examined both with and without braces, thus making possible a determination of the benefits of bracing and the effects of other corrective work.

Illustrative of a different basis for the study of the motor competencies of children, youth, and adults with neuromuscular involvements are the check lists prepared by Brown and others.[14] Her Daily Activity Record provides a means for checking 100 routine behaviors—including speech, dressing, undressing, eating, locomotion, rising, and sitting down—and for recording progress in learning such physical activities. The Brown-

Bogert Pre-Vocational Motor Skill Inventory [15] is intended for use with "any person of any age who has one or more extremities free for motor skills." One hundred activities are listed in this device, also, but they differ from the essentially self-care activities of the Daily Activity Record by including behaviors such as fixing a plug on an electric cord, extracting a nail, packing groceries in a carton, and putting a key in a padlock. While the time allowances for both these devices and the age placements of the items in the latter inventory still may require more rigid statistical validation, the instruments and their underlying rationale have much to commend them. Some evaluations of over-all motor coordination have been made, especially with the mentally retarded, by means of the Oseretsky test.[16]

If we disregard the psychogenic aspects of speech impairment and instead deal with it essentially as a motor function, then the problem of identifying the behaviors that constitute speech impairment is facilitated by the many check lists, sets of pictures, and other stimuli for evoking speech behavior which are described in the chapter on speech-handicapped children.[17]

While it is not within the proper domain of the psychologist to make diagnoses regarding the presence or absence of brain damage, he often can detect behavioral cues on the basis of which to invite consideration by the neurologist. Sometimes his suspicions are aroused by electro-encephalographic tracings, by digit, letter, or figure reversals, or rotations on intelligence and on some projective tests, or by certain bizarre or stereotyped perceptual behavior.[18] (Such hunches tend to be dangerous when they are expressed by the neophyte; they are not 100 per cent certain with experts!) Illustrative of psychologists' validated attempts to ascertain the presence of brain injury are the Graham-Kendall Memory-for-Designs Test, the Iowa Visual Retention Test, and the work of Reitan.[19] No research has yet been done to ascertain whether these approaches can validly be used with the deaf or the blind.

The measurement of auditory and visual efficiency will not be discussed here, since those procedures and problems are discussed in the chapters on the acoustically and the visually handicapped. Suffice it to point out here that certain problems in these areas parallel those in the area of measuring intelligence. In all three areas, for instance, there is first the problem of gross and reasonably effective screening, as a result of which children so screened out undergo more intensive and extensive individual examination by more highly trained persons. Audiometrics and vision screening procedures vary in validity just as group intelligence tests do. Further, just as a child of normal or above-average mental capacity may not do well on a group intelligence test because of emo-

tionality or a number of other factors, just so, for instance, may a child
"fail" in a group testing situation because of wax in his ears, a cold, or
other causes.

Helpful to some extent in the total psychological assessment of exceptional children and youth are the evaluated measurements of their
different gross structural features. Clinicians vary in the amount of attention they give to such aspects as body type, head girth, cephalic index,
changes in chest size with inspiration and expiration, and stage of development of the wrist bones. Height and weight norms, interpreted in
the light of the nature of the child's parental stock and health history,
can be helpful in understanding and characterizing these aspects of the
child. Widely used norms continue to be those of Baldwin and Wood.[20]
Much more recent and carefully obtained data on the heights and
weights of children and youth, ages 5 through 20, are now available, however.[21] Developmental age-normative data, compiled by Olson, include
additional information on permanent dentition and strength of grip, and
extend the height-weight norms by sex down to the 30-month level.[22]
Recording and studying the physical developmental history of children,
by teachers and parents in checking gross growth and by pediatricians
in working correctively on growth problems, are facilitated by the Wetzel
Grid technique.[23] Based upon the fact that children tend to have their
own physical growth rates, successive plottings of height-weight status
can reveal departures from the children's channels which, in turn, are
taken to be indicative of some disturbance of growth patterns due to
physical or emotional factors.

The physical behavior pattern of a child may be distorted not only
by neuromuscular and structural anomalies and physiological dysfunctions but, also with at least equal prevalence, by excessively solicitous
and inhibiting parental care. Unless one is clinically highly perceptive
of traces of cues in such cases, the degree of physical involvement is
likely to be regarded as considerably greater than it actually is. In such
instances, the orthopedist, the neurologist, or the pediatrician can give
the psychologist some valuable cues and, often, the psychologist can
find behavior potentialities of much value to the medical specialists.

The Area of Intelligence

The earlier discussion of assumptions and problems of measurement
in general and the illustrations presented to show how easily the results
of attempts at measurement of intelligence in particular can be contaminated are both of particular import with respect to the problem of
ascertaining the learning capacity of all types of exceptional children.

General problems. As this discussion has progressed, the reader has probably become concerned about the seeming confusion of the measurement of "intelligence" as a total, all-inclusive something with the measurement of aptitude for school learning. It is hoped, also, that he has become concerned with allusions to "basic" learning capacity and illustrations of measured learning capacity. An understanding of these terms will contribute much to a comprehension of the significant measurement problems of the exceptional, to a sound basis for critical evaluation of the studies reported in this field, and to an adequate background in light of which to perceive the strengths and weaknesses of current and future attempts at measurement in this area.

Granted that it would be psychologically significant to be able to measure an over-all, all-inclusive intelligence either within a given area of exceptionality or among all areas, the bulk of the efforts have been, and probably will continue to be, directed toward the measurement of those aspects of intelligence which are most directly related to the learning of a certain kind of behavior that seems to play a major part both in just living with people and, more specifically, in learning in school situations. Since the provision of school learning situations constitutes the bulk of society's organized efforts in the interests of children, the measurement of the "intelligence," or "mental capacity," of these children becomes largely, if not essentially, the measurement of learning aptitude geared primarily to school situations but also to many non-school situations. In the discussion here, it is assumed that the major, if not the sole, learning activity is the acquisition of symbols.

Within this structure, then, the following definition of "intelligence" is employed: *Intelligence is the potential of the organism to acquire symbols, to retain those symbols, and to communicate meaningfully by means of those symbols.* This "educator's definition" includes much more than vocabulary acquisition. Symbols may be spoken or written. They may be verbalized or non-verbalized. Symbols represent both objects and relationships between objects. The child, for instance, may rub his stomach as a non-verbalized symbol to communicate the idea that he is hungry, that he likes something, or that he has a stomach ache. He may say, "John is taller than Sue," using the symbol "taller" for the relationship between two persons. He may cringe, in a completely unverbalized manner, at a frown because this facial "symbol" in another portends a threatening relationship between another and himself. Having acquired these symbols he uses them in "intelligence" tests, in personality inventories, in vocational aptitude tests (either verbal or non-verbal), in educational achievement tests, or in projective devices. In the light of this, then, the measurement of this aspect of intelligence becomes the measurement of the child's susceptibility to acquire symbols.

The second terminological problem here arises with respect to our belief, or evidence, as to how close we come to the measurement of this susceptibility to symbol acquisition. When test performance is minimally contaminated by such conditions as emotional overlay, sensory impairment, motor involvement, or abnormal acculturation ("hothousing" or gross deprivation), we regard such test behavior as very closely indicative of basic capacity. To the extent that test performance is clouded by any of these conditions, we get results that do not accurately reflect that *basic* capacity. The term "basic capacity," or "basic intelligence," is used here to denote more nearly the biologically inherent learning potential of an organism. We continually hope that the behavior which reflects it is as little culturally contaminated as possible but have the constantly lingering suspicion that it is at least a little so distorted.

The likelihood of test performances validly reflecting the basic capacities of children varies with the population of which those children are a part. If they were a group randomly selected out of a large heterogeneous public school population, basic capacities would be likely to be pretty accurately reflected in significantly more than half of those in such a group. If the children were among a random selection of those brought into a psychological clinic for examination, the basic capacities would be reasonably clearly reflected in only a small minority of them. Again, (and this is most important for us here) if the children were all exceptional, it would be highly unlikely that basic capacities would be reasonably clearly reflected in more than a very small percentage of the group. For reasons that have been suggested in this chapter and that have been presented in the other chapters of this book, the test performances of a very large percentage of exceptional children tend to be clouded by these conditions of emotional overlay, sensory impairment, motor involvement, and abnormal acculturation. Whereas such likely contaminations are recognized in the area of tested educational achievement and are suspected in the areas of emotionality and vocational aptitudes, they are particularly significant psychologically in the area of mental capacity measurement, both because of the higher frequency of attempts at measurement in this area and because of the cruciality of attempts at such measurement.

It appears desirable, then, to distinguish clearly between *basic* capacity and *manifest* capacity. We shall use the term "manifest capacity" to denote that performance level which is immediately and most easily apparent in the test situation, the interpretation of which is unaffected by any qualitative explanations. It is the test indication of what the client did—how he scored according to standardized procedure of test administration. It involves no guessing by the examiner as to how much better or worse the client "really" is. It is the unmitigated performance at the time of testing. It is reasonably safe to assume that by far the major percentage of published reports of the "intelligence" of various types of exceptional children are reports of this manifest capacity. To the extent that readers of such reports assume that these manifest capacities are synonymous with the basic capacities of these children—to that extent may harm be done these children by means of distorted educational and social planning for them.

Since it is the manifest capacity which is indicated by the gross performance on the test, it should be noted that the basic capacity is inferred by the clinician. To the uninitiated, this inferring process may seem quite nebulous and the result of such inferring only a wild guess. To the person who has worked clinically, rather than mechanically psychometrically, with children, this process is psychologically sound and real, and the results of it are supportable estimates. In some instances, basic capacity is taken to be indicated more by certain parts of certain tests (vocabulary versus memory span, for instance); in other instances, the clinician's inference as to basic capacity stems from the quality of performance rather than from the quantity of performance in the examining situation. This is admittedly a subjective process, but the subjectivity occurs within a trained clinician's frame of reference rather than within the frame of reference of a psychologically untrained person. The chances for and magnitude of error in such "measurement" of this basic capacity are clearly greater in such estimations by properly trained persons than is the case in the standardized use of psychological devices in ascertaining evidence of manifest capacity, but the clinician believes that a more meaningful psychological indication of the child's real potential is thereby obtained.

An illustration or two may help clarify the matter. An emotionally disturbed ten-year-old boy earned a Revised Binet Form L mental age of eight years and six months under competent examination (his manifest capacity). However, it was apparent to the examiner that the boy's basic capacity was greater than the one reflected in the examination situation. In fact, it was estimated that the boy's real potential would be nearer that of an average ten- or ten-and-a-half-year-old if the boy could be helped in his emotional adjustment. After the boy was put for a year in a therapeutic situation which, in the judgment of the clinical staff, had been partially successful, he earned a Revised Binet I.Q. of 105.[24] This was still believed to be somewhat below his "true" rate of intellectual development. A seven-year-old cerebral palsied girl was examined by a psychometrist by means of parts of the Revised Binet and parts of several performance scales. The results were reported in terms of intelligence quotients and the girl was recommended for exclusion from the public schools because her performance (manifest capacity) appeared to indicate that she was considerably lower than a Binet I.Q. of 50 would suggest. Yet, on re-examination by a psychologist, there were qualitative indications that she was functioning then, with allowances made for the motor handicap, at a five- or six-year level (her basic capacity). The results of a year's trial in a treatment center and special class for the cerebral palsied supported the findings of the psychologist rather than those of the psychometrist.

It should not be assumed from the foregoing that only the basic capacity is psychologically and socially significant. Knowing the manifest capacity of a child, one is helped to know at what level one can expect the child to function *at that time*. Having some idea of the basic capacity of that same child, if the two be different, one can know what to expect of that child, if and when the extenuating conditions or factors have been changed or if the child is helped to learn methods of compensating, in whole or in part, for them.[25]

It should be emphasized that such disparities between manifest and basic capacities do not always exist. In a few cases, they are large; in some, little, if any, disparity exists. The likelihood of such disparities in the case of the exceptional is greater than in the case of the non-exceptional. As a rule, basic capacity tends to be greater than manifest capacity, although clinics are not without instances of children "testing beyond themselves." The frequency and size of error tend to be greater in the case of group devices than in the case of devices competently individually administered. Certain group devices have greater chances for error than others, even when they are competently administered and scored. The age of the child tested is also a factor to be considered. A comparable situation exists with respect to the various individual tests and scales. For reasons of this kind alone it will be seen why no small number of published studies presenting the I.Q.'s of handicapped children, or even of studies on reportedly non-handicapped children, have been confusing and actually misleading to the uninformed. As has been suggested, the very fact that some children are exceptional should make us at once highly critical of the results obtained on such children by merely conventional approaches to the measurement of their mental capacities. This in no way vitiates devices used in conventional ways to ascertain the intelligence of not less than three-fourths of our school age children, under the assumptions that have been stated; it suggests only that an intelligent caution be exercised with respect to the undertaking of this task in the cases of at least those 15 to 20 per cent of our pre-school and school-age children and youth who constitute the exceptional group. Healthy skepticism is rightly maintained at all times with respect to all test results; it is only more so with respect to the exceptional.

It is essential to emphasize, then, especially regarding group tests, that low test scores always are much more suspect than are high scores. The chances of errors being present in an obtained low score are much greater than in high scores. A low score that is "untrue," or is not accurately indicative of the basic capacity of a child, still has psychological significance because it is of value to know that the child scored "artificially" low and to know that there are, or can be, times when he can or will stumble.

Good group intelligence tests have their major value (still short of perfection), as screening devices, for the initial identification of the mentally superior; have decreased screening value (but still practical) with respect to the mentally retarded; and are of still less screening value in reflecting verbal learning capacity as we go from the socially and emotionally maladjusted to the speech-impaired, the sensorily handicapped, and the seriously involved orthopedically handicapped. In the case of the orthopedically handicapped, the tests have high practical screening value provided the children on whom they are used have no interfering motor impairments and no major cultural impoverishment. With respect to children with cerebral palsied conditions, the possible effect of conceptual dysfunctions needs also to be considered.

The need for more definitive depiction of the learning capacities of exceptional children and for reduction in the error of such measurement necessitates individual examination of them. In such an individual examination approach, greater adaptation of the procedure is possible in terms of the characteristics of the child. Rapport is established in the face-to-face situation, whereas indifference or fright may exist under group testing. The child who, for purely physical reasons, is enabled under individual examination procedures to take his time or to react only to situations that have been selected so as not to prejudice the sampling of his behavior, is not cut short by time limits or forced to enter into, or to avoid completely (fail), a variety of test situations that were found to have meaning with respect to the non-handicapped. Less culturally contaminated behavior samplings can be made by means of certain individual procedures in the case of the child who presents a history of marked cultural deprivation as a result of sustained physical confinement, whereas most conventional group devices may involve a heavy sampling of behaviors that are completely irrelevant to such a child's psychological history.

The way in which an exceptional child's performances in test situations may be represented varies with the social and clinical factors attending those examinations. Most frequent characterizations of these performances have tended to be in terms of intelligence quotients. Less frequently, mental ages, test ages, centile, and standard score designations have been used. Still less frequently in the past, though increasingly now in most clinics, these performances have been characterized in broader, less definitive, terms. Intelligence quotients indicate only *rates* of mental development. The "deviation quotients" of the Wechsler scales and of the 1960 (L-M) Stanford-Binet can be taken roughly to indicate relative rates of development, but differ in certain respects from their forerunner, the computed intelligence quotient, which was obtained by dividing an obtained mental age by the chronological age, and multiplying the result by 100. All such quotients, however, have primarily administrative value. Educationally, they have somewhat more value at the time a child normally enters school, have very limited value between that point and the high-school level, and acquire more value from the high-school age on up. Mental ages, however, have primarily educational value, since they indicate *levels* of mental development and thereby can be suggestive of the levels at which the child might be expected to work in school. Test ages, in the sense employed with respect to the WISC, may have somewhat less educational value, depending upon the relationship known to exist between the behavior sampled by any particular test and the educational performances under consideration. Centile and standard score characterizations have less educational value below the high-school level. Some rightly regard all such specific designations as unwarranted with respect to certain of the more physically handicapped and use such characterizations as "roughly the potential level of an average nine-year-old," or "educable," "trainable," and "sub-trainable." The majority of our considerations in this chapter are in terms of *level* characterizations.

We shall consider, mainly, representative examples of individual examination approaches that have been tried, adapted, and developed for certain of the exceptionalities. Some of these devices and approaches will be seen to be employable with more than one kind of exceptional child; some will be usable with only one kind.

The cerebral palsied.[26] Children who have neuromuscular involvements present difficult assessment problems. The picture is considerably more complicated with respect to those handicapped by cerebral palsy. While this section deals with problems pertaining only to the latter group, it will be apparent that many of these apply to children with orthopedic involvements.

The greatest liberties in endeavoring to "adapt" individual examinations have been taken with respect to the cerebral palsied. The greater the physical involvement of such children, the greater has been the need either to make such "adaptations" or to develop examination procedures appropriate to the demands of this type of exceptionality. In fact, in the absence of individual devices suitable for use with the cerebral palsied, a "cafeteria" approach generally has been used. Depending upon the condition of the particular child, certain items from one scale are used in connection with other items lifted from other scales on the assumption that all such items, taken together, psychologically rather than additively, would give at least a general idea of the mental level at which the child was functioning, or could function. In the hands of the psychologically less well-trained, this procedure can be dangerous, particularly if the assumption is implied that such items from different devices, and often sampling quite different kinds of behavior, are comparable on a one-to-one basis. However, when such items are selected with a view to the sampling of consciously presumed or known types of psychological functioning, and when the examiner has an adequate background of training and experience with normal children, reasonably meaningful qualitative and quantitative approximations of the intellectual potential of such a child can be obtained. Obviously, a definitive I.Q. characterization of the cerebral palsied child by the former procedure is based upon assumptions that still need to be supported by research and hence may be misleading. Some rough ideas of the rates of mental development of these children by these procedures can be inferred, but pinpointing by I.Q.'s is a psychometrist's and statistician's dream rather than a psychological reality.

The measurement of the learning capacities of the cerebral palsied [27] presents problems that are considerably more challenging than is the case with respect to the other types of exceptionality. Test results obtained in the process of identifying the mentally superior and the mentally retarded are comparatively easy to verify in terms of social and educational criteria, even though the extent to which such test results are a function of non-hereditary organic pathology in the mentally handicapped is not yet clear. In the cases of children with other handicapping conditions, excepting *perhaps* those with aphasia and epilepsy, there is reason to assume that organic pathology per se plays little or no part in the actual lowering of the basic learning capacities of such groups. When we come to the cerebral palsied, however, our realization that the condition results from brain-centered central nervous system pathology and our still relatively great ignorance of the extent to which basic learning capacity is thus impaired combine to provide us with extremely ambiguous criteria on which to evaluate results obtained from existing measuring devices or on which to standardize new devices suited to the unique perceptual and communication needs of this handicapped group. Some psychological research reveals a limited picture of their perceptualization processes, and these can contribute to, or even be a part of, faulty conceptualization. With our definition of basic learning capacity, such conceptualization impairment would appear to be grounds on which reasonably to suspect some basic retardation. The question is, "How much?"

The need, therefore, for the development of devices and procedures which can be used with the cerebral palsied is at once apparent. The problem here is not so much with those who are only mildly involved, since, with moderate caution, available approaches can be used. The major difficulties exist with respect to the examination of those of moderate and severe neuromuscular involvement. In such cases, communication is a problem, both regarding the use of verbal responses by the subjects and, in some cases, regarding the sensory impairment of such cerebral palsied children. In some instances, where these handicapped children are physically unable to speak, they also are unable to point. In such cases the examiner may have to rely upon the child's eye movements, and, if nystagmus renders this avenue of communication doubtful, even upon the facial expression of the child.[28] In addition to the problem of communication, there are those of the meaninglessness of rigid time limits, the highly varying and often grossly distorted cultural backgrounds, the possibility of the confusion of figure and ground in at least the visual field, the wide age range, the possible relatively higher fatigability as compared with the non-handicapped, the possible interference of more and greater emotional factors such as excessive dependency on the parents, and conditioning against clinical settings. Add to all these problems the fact that the term "cerebral palsy" has come to include a variety of conditions that might materially complicate the psychological picture, and it will be seen how difficult the intellectual evaluation of these handicapped children actually is. The fact that this handicapped group is numerically smaller, for instance, than the blind group, even after correcting for Phelps' underestimation of prevalence, and regarding as blind those with a Snellen rating of 20/200 and worse in the better eye after maximal correction, also adds to the difficulty of soundly standardizing a test or a test battery on this population.

Since some of the difficulties attending the intellectual evaluation of the cerebral palsied are in common with those encountered with other types of exceptional children, it is understandable that attempts would be made to develop devices that could be used with other kinds of children as well. Illustrative of one attempt of this sort is the Columbia Mental Maturity Scale, which was developed for individual use with children in the mental age range from three to at least ten years. Somewhat sensitive to acculturation, especially in items at the upper end of the scale, this device may be administered either orally or by pantomime, although no data indicate whether the latter procedure affects the results.[29]

From the time of the early Binets, young subjects have been asked to point out parts of a pictured doll, to give the verbal symbols for pictured objects, and to use words in describing pictures. That there would appear complete tests based upon vocabulary (symbol acquisition, in the terminology of this chapter) should be quite understandable, since measures of this kind of achievement would be highly predictive of further, similar achievement. Some of the group intelligence tests of the 1920's were entirely vocabulary tests, and vocabulary per se constituted a significant portion of the total behavior sampling of many others. Among individual intelligence tests, the 1929 Van Alstyne Picture Vocabulary Test, revised in 1960, antedated the Ammons Full-Range Picture Vocabulary Test and the Peabody Picture Vocabulary Test.[30] The Van Alstyne Test is limited to the mental age range of two through seven years, the Ammons Test has norms ranging from kindergarten through the twelfth grade, and the Peabody Test has normative data for levels from one year nine months to eighteen years. Each of these devices involves confronting the subject with cards, each bearing pictures about which the subject is asked questions and to which the subject can point in giving his responses. For exceptional children and youth who have gross difficulty in speaking, these tests help meet the communication problem. On any of them, differences among scores for pre-school and for in-school children have quite different connotations, since they so fully sample *product*.

Less culturally contaminated are the Raven Progressive Matrices,[31] which consist of geometrical designs among which relationships must be ascertained in order that the subject can select, from a multiple choice situation, that design which will complete correctly the whole pattern, or matrix. Tracht [32] and Taibl [33] have used the 1938 matrices with cerebral palsied. The psychometric results obtained by means of this device (some suggesting less mental retardation among the cerebral palsied than has been generally reported) do not concern us particularly here, since they, too, need to be evaluated in terms of the concepts developed thus far in the chapter. The theory underlying the construction of the items in this test gives it psychological appeal. Its adaptability, especially with respect to means of communication by the one using it and by the one taking it, makes it clinically desirable. However, some of its users, on both the handicapped and non-handicapped, have felt some dissatisfaction with the adequacy of its standardization, even on British subjects.[34] With well-established American norms, and with research showing that the figure-ground idiosyncrasies of the cerebral palsied are not clouding the picture, this device could well be found to have much value in psychometric work with this kind of exceptional child. Regardless of the extent to which Taibl's psychometric data may be found to be valid, the pains to which he went in ascertaining and establishing a pyschologically sound means of communication with the cerebral palsied children can well serve as a goal for those who would examine such children.

Not completely unrewarding and unpromising, but as yet non-definitive, exploratory attempts have been made to adapt other devices for use with the cerebral palsied. These have consisted of taking extant test items and setting them up in a multiple choice form in which the child can point to his answer to the question; of "blowing up" items, such as the Porteus Mazes, which the child may normally attempt or in which the child may direct the examiner how to proceed; or of the examiner's offering test item responses with respect to which the child indicates the correctness or incorrectness of the examiner's statements.

It is well to keep in mind the fact that the learning behavior of cerebral palsied children, and other children with at least major orthopedic involvements, is, perhaps much more so than in the cases of other exceptional children, only partly a function of their basic capacities. Of at least equal importance are the nature and strength of his motivation. The cerebral palsied child who communicated by hitting his chest or leg to indicate "yes" or "no," and the one who used a typewriter as a means of communication, and the one who turned pages by means of a rubber-tipped stick, and countless ingenious others, all give evidence of learning and, therefore, can be presumed to have capacities to learn. But of at least equal importance is the fact that they have a *drive* to do that learning.[35] The different combinations of drive and intelligence in such children present different kinds of challenges to the clinician. Consider, for example, the following kinds of children:

(a) The child who has a strong drive and high intelligence presents the simplest clinical challenge because he is so highly responsive.
(b) The child who has a strong drive and low intelligence presents less of a challenge to the clinician because there is a good basis for communication, although the parents of such a child often mistake effort or perseveration for achievement.
(c) The child who has a weak drive and low intelligence usually is reasonably quickly and clearly identified as such, but the clinician needs, nevertheless, to make additional efforts to check the intellectual aspects pretty carefully lest he be misled by the behavior sampled.
(d) The child who has a weak drive and high intelligence is most likely to be faultily diagnosed, since communication has pretty badly broken down.

Teachers and therapists who work with such physically handicapped children benefit little from evaluations that throw light upon only learning capacity.

The brain-injured. This group of the exceptional is included here more to acknowledge its existence than for the purpose of considering the problems of psychological assessment in any extensive manner. Logically, this group includes the cerebral palsied. Often, however, the term "brain-injured" is used to denote only those individuals without relatively easily identifiable motor involvement. Even thus used, the category includes a frustratingly wide range of degrees of neural damage which must be considered in terms of the part or parts of the brain involved. Care must be taken to make certain whether, in any given subject, the term denotes damage per se or improper development (agenesis or dysgenesis). Mentioned at the end of this chapter are only a few illustrative studies bearing on this group.[36] Two quite diverse testing approaches, by McCarthy and Kirk and by Frostig, may have possibilities for use in diagnosis— the former in the area of linguistics and the latter in the area of visual perception.[37]

One of the continuing questions that bothers the person who tries to make a psychological assessment of the brain-injured concerns the extent to which the aberrations which he finds in his behavior samplings can validly be attributed to the neural damage per se and to what extent they may be as plausibly attributed to some other condition. Nudd,[38] for instance, compared the free responses of brain-injured children and those of non-brain-injured children to pictures depicting social interaction and found that the non-brain-injured children gave more of the kind of response usually expected of the brain-injured. Some of her evidence suggested that emotional rather than neurological factors might be playing the larger determining role.

The deaf. The psychological problems associated with attempts at the measurement of the intelligence of the deaf are of particular significance. Here, the problems of cultural deprivation and emotional overlay continue to demand recognition. But more important and fundamental factors enter the picture. Whereas in the case of the cerebral palsied a major problem is the means and clarity of communication by the child to the examiner, in the case of the deaf a major problem is the communication of the examiner to the child. Of at least equal psychological significance is the fact that the conceptualizations, if not actually the conceptualization process, of the deaf may well be grossly impaired. The deaf child not only receives fewer stimuli on which to conceptualize, but also runs a greater risk of perceiving those stimuli in manners other than those intended by the examiner. Whether or not this impairs the conceptualization process is not the concern of the chapter; the fact that conceptualizations are impaired is relevant, since normal or average acculturation consists of the acquisition of enough conceptualizations for ordinary communication. The significance of this is at once apparent with respect to the possibility of measuring the learning potential of the deaf. Such measurement aims at getting evidence of either the capacity of the individual to conceptualize on presumably novel stimuli, or the extent to which conceptualization has occurred (achievement), from which the capacity to do so is inferred. As the ease and adequacy of communication increase, both conceptually and auditorially, the unique measurement difficulties tend to disappear, and we approach only the "normal" problems of measuring basic learning capacity.

As is apparent in the chapter on the acoustically impaired, the "deaf" do not constitute a homogeneous group, whether defined in terms of hearing acuity or in terms of adequacy of communication, or some combination of both. Our line of reasoning concerning these is at once seen as more plausible with respect to those born with the hearing losses indicated in our definition, or acquiring them early as a result of conditions other than, say, scarlet fever, meningitis, and athetosis. In such cases, the part played by neural pathology raises still further complicating questions.[39]

Intentionally omitted from specific mention here are the numerous studies of the performances of the acoustically impaired on tests originally developed for use with the non-handicapped, attempts at standardization on this group of such devices, and studies of the correlations between tests highly varied in purpose. These can be investigated more fruitfully by the interested student in the summaries in the Pintner, Eisenson, and Stanton book (*op. cit.*, pp. 110-130), and in original form in the *Volta Review*, in the *American Annals of the Deaf*, and in *Exceptional Children*.

The Pintner Non-Language Mental Tests constituted the first and most extensive approach made to the group intelligence testing of the deaf by one who comprehended the complexities of the problem. The difficulties of communicating, even in the necessarily small group situations, and the highly varied structurings of the different psychological and physical characteristics of deaf children helped materially to shift interest to individual examination of the deaf. Illustrative of attempts to develop devices specifically for the individual examination of deaf children are the Ontario School Ability Examination which appeared in 1936 and the Nebraska Test of Learning Aptitude which became available in 1941.[40] Both of these devices were standardized on and for deaf subjects. The Ontario was standardized on an age range of five through twenty-two, whereas the norms for the Nebraska are for children between the ages of four and ten inclusive, although one-year extrapolations are provided at both extremes.

Without attempting to delineate the strong points and weaknesses of these tests, it is interesting to observe how they both illustrate a common step in adapting and developing measuring devices for the handicapped. On page 89 are listed the names of the items that constitute each test. No significance as to item placement in the test is indicated in the listing, although mental level increase is vaguely reflected in the Ontario from Examination I through Examination VI.

Here, again, we see the evidences of the "cafeteria" approach which was mentioned with respect to examination procedures employed on the cerebral palsied with, however, the manner of communication altered in view of the impaired hearing acuity. Here, though, the items selected in the "cafeteria" have been assembled and abetted by others statistically, into what the authors believe to be effective devices for the indication of the learning potential. This is one step slightly in advance

Ontario

Examination I—Manipulation
   Series A. Locomotion (standing and stepping alone)
   Series B. Paper folding (similar to Gesell and Binet)
   Series C. Block building (adapted from Gesell)
   Series D. Form identification and construction (adapted from Stanford Revision IV, 2 and V, 5)
   Series E. Knot tying (adapted from Stanford Revision VII, 4)
   Series F. Healy-Fernald Puzzle (Stanford Revision, X, alt. 3)
   Series G. Weight discrimination (adapted from Drever and Collins)
Examination II—Color patterns (adapted from Drever and Collins, Kohs)
Examination III—Knox blocks
Examination IV—Dominoes (adapted from Drever and Collins Visual number memory)
Examination V—Drawings
   Series A. Imitative (adapted from Gesell)
   Series B. Copying (adapted from Gesell and the Stanford Revision)
   Series C. Design Pair (adapted from Stanford Revision X, 3)
   Series D. Ring design
Examination VI—Tapping

Nebraska

Memory for colored sticks
Bead stringing (copying and memory)
Pictorial association
Block building (from pictures)
Memory for digits (subject reproduces one to five digits, presented visually and then hidden)
Completion of drawings
Pictorial identification
Paper folding
Visual attention span (one to six pictures briefly exposed to be selected from 15 possibilities)
Puzzle blocks (cubes, variously cut up to be reassembled)
Pictorial analogies (pictorial equivalents of the type: Man: House:: Bird: ————)

of the present status of testing the cerebral palsied. This step, it will be noted, is predicated upon the assumption that the types of behavior sampled by the Binet and others from which the items were adapted or upon which they were modeled are psychologically crucial in the measurement, either directly or indirectly, of basic learning capacity.

The non-verbal parts of the Wechsler Adult Intelligence Scale and the Wechsler Intelligence Scale for Children are being tried on deaf children and youth.[41] Opinions, yet to be supported systematically by meaningful data, are generally favorable to such partial uses of the Wechslers, just as they were with respect to the desirability of the earlier performance tests over verbal tests. The Leiter International Performance Scale, although not specifically developed for use with the deaf, has been used on them. Leiter results on deaf children have been reported, with interesting and ambiguous disparities found between them and those obtained on the Arthur Performance Scale and on the Nebraska. A few are trying the Progressive Matrices on the deaf and are entertaining the suspicion that this device will be found to be still more rewarding. On the basis of the responses of 1,400 hearing and 1,054 deaf subjects, all between the ages of three and sixteen, a revision of the Snjiders-Oomen Non-Verbal Intelligence Scale has been made. It involves a variety of behavior sampling—block design, picture completion, picture arrangement, visual memory, drawing and copying of designs, and sorting of objects and cards. The scale is structured in terms of "psychological viewpoints": form, combination, abstraction, and memory.[42]

Considerable work in the area of individual intelligence testing of the deaf still is needed before the situation can be reasonably stabilized. Particularly germane with respect to testing in this area of exceptionality is the general question of what kind of behavior sample can provide the best basis for predicting the school learning of those so tested. The tendency has been for workers in this area to take those parts of tests which most easily can be communicated to the deaf and then to seek to identify that pattern of such tests which either discriminated between successive year levels or which yielded positive correlations with the amounts learned, or both. The size of such correlations leaves much to be desired. This approach has tended to result in almost exclusive use of performance-type tests—long known to yield results which correlate poorly with the results of schooling, at least in the case of the hearing. The convenience in the use of such performance tests plus the chance of evoking higher scoring responses on such tests (this latter being a boon at times to many working with the mentally retarded as well) have tended to impede the development of a pattern of behavior sampling that might be significantly more predictive of the deaf's acquisition and use of symbols. Many of these tests appear to sample *process* more heavily than *product*. Here, the problem would appear to lie, however, in the possibility that secondary psychological processes are being sampled rather than those processes more fundamental to the symbolic learning of the deaf. On the basis of the process-product concept developed earlier, one would assume that the kinds of behavior sampling involved in the Leiter and the Raven Matrices should be more fruitful, particularly with the young deaf.

It must be remembered that learning capacity tests are given for the purpose of getting indications of how well children will learn in school. The learning product of the public schools, with non-handicapped children, is still a great deal more clearcut and generally agreed upon than is the learning product of the deaf. Here, the picture is tremendously clouded by a confusion of goals such as "learning speech-reading, language, speech, and school subjects," "learning in a sign-dominated world," "learning in a speech-reading-dominated world," "learning to adjust," and the like. The ambiguity of any one of these and the use of different ones in different studies make for an elusive predictive target against which to validate any test of the learning aptitude of the deaf.

The blind. With the blind, as with the other kinds of physically handicapped, the a priori assumption has been made that their learning potential, whether basic or manifest, is made up of the same component parts which are present and operative to the same extent in the case of the non-handicapped. This is probably a much more convenient point at which to start than if we were to assume the psychological naïveté of, say, Binet when he first undertook the task of identifying those kinds of behavior which served as indicators of learning capacity, or if we were to start back at the point where many performance tests were made in the hope that some of them would have predictive value for at least something. Our success in discovering those kinds of behavior which in combination are reasonably predictive of the learning behavior of children who are predominantly non-handicapped, while helpfully suggestive in attacking this problem for the handicapped, must be regarded as potentially restrictive of our perception of all the psychological factors operating in the case of the handicapped. Because of perceptual or conceptual impairment or distortion and because of the unique communication problems of the various handicapped groups, certain behavior samples which are important with respect to the non-handicapped may be of much less or of no significance with respect to the handicapped, and vice versa. For a thoroughly adequate approach to this area of measurement we need a factor analysis, within each handicap area, of a wide variety of both old and new test approaches in order to ascertain for the different kinds of handicapped what the primary mental abilities are and the relative part each such ability plays. Until we know that the primary mental-ability pictures for all the kinds of handicapped are the same as those for the non-handicapped, we must accept only provisionally the majority of our current testing approaches in this area.

This is not to imply that what has been done in the area of the total and severely visually impaired is without value. Research evidence that has been accumulated by Samuel P. Hayes, his early co-workers, and his students on the improvement of mental test scores with chronological age, on the relative stability of the intelligence quotients of blind children, and on the correlations between intelligence test performance and educational achievement indicates quite the contrary. The question remains whether or not the adaptations of the Binets and the Wechslers, significant as they have been, represent a psychologically adequate sampling of the behavior of the blind and severely visually impaired.[43]

Viewing this area, as we did the cerebral palsied and the deaf, we again see that unique problems arise with respect to communication, perception, and conceptualization. Communication is much more nearly normal than in the former areas; when it is impaired, it is essentially as a result of perceptual and conceptual distortions. "White as the driven snow," "blood red," and "sneeringly" mean something quite different to the blind than they mean to other physically handicapped who can see, since to the blind they may well mean "cold-wet-slippery," "warm-wet," and a particular voice quality or word sequence. Perceptual restrictions of this sort, with the attending conceptual impoverishment, have a direct bearing upon our assumptions of comparable acculturation. Test items which are known to involve this kind of contamination are, fortunately, identifiable and replaceable. Whereas no small part of the blind child's communication with his world is through the senses of touch and kinesthesis, we have yet to ascertain statistically, the part these as well as other senses play in his learning behavior. These avenues are only slightly tapped and little explored in present intelligence test procedures.[44]

In the physical exploration of their total environment, the blind are markedly less mobile than the deaf. In the psychologically crucial years of infancy and early childhood, their physical dependency has tended to approach that of the severely orthopedically handicapped. This often contributes to the impairment of the communication process in the examination situation. The sampling of the behavior of any dependent child is always a real problem for the clinician; it is considerably more so in the case of the blind. It must constantly be kept in mind that, first, it is difficult to get certain behavior samples from such children, and, second, there is the ever-present question of the extent to which the sample which is obtained has been psychologically contaminated by a long, impoverishing, constricting relationship with adults. A further problem, perhaps a psychological corollate of the above, that often affects communication between the psychological examiner and the blind, is the occasional presence of "blindisms," those socially irrelevant, and often bizarre, motor behavior patterns (twisting, squirming, gesticulating, posturing) that are often misleading to the lay person and distracting to the clinician, especially if he has had limited experience with the blind.

With respect to this area, too, we need to raise questions on the validity and implications of this generalization: To the extent that blindness is independent of an inheritable defective syndrome, and to the extent that blindness is independent of neural pathology directly involving the higher mental processes—to such an extent we should expect a distribution of basic learning capacity similar to that of the total (normal) population. Note that this has been suggested with respect to only *basic* capacity and not to manifest capacity, since we already have considered some of the major factors that can contribute to considerable disparity between the two.

As has been indicated with respect to the deaf, the accuracy of the measurement of learning capacity is reflected in the degree to which such measurements agree with the amounts learned. The learnings of the blind are quite different from those of the non-handicapped, though probably less so than those of the deaf, and the presence of emotional problems often impairs the efficiency of the learning process, particularly in the cases of the adventitiously blind.

As we consider the whole area of intellectual measurement of the exceptional, we see that the problems related to it, particularly with respect to those who are seriously handicapped, are numerous and complicated. The professional and scientific literature on exceptional children teems with reports of results obtained by administering intelligence tests to these children. To the psychologically untrained, the reported results may well seem hopelessly confusing. Some data are taken to indicate improvement of basic intelligence; some, to indicate the uselessness of the tests by which the results were obtained; some, to indicate the relative brightness of different types of exceptional children. The differences between I.Q.'s obtained at successive times on the same populations, or between children with different kinds of problems, or between different kinds of tests on the same groups of children have caused some to jump almost blindly to conclusions on the nature of the social promise of some groups of children, or of some specific children; to enthuse hastily concerning the merits of given methods of treatment, education, or medication; or, even, to solve dilemmas by arbitrarily, and with no small amount of psychological blindness, taking the highest of a number of scores or performances as valid. It is no wonder that so many psychologically less well-oriented educators have decided to avoid these apparent contradictions and confusions by avoiding the use of even well-standardized intelligence tests, or that they have protected their teachers and children by "salting away" in their files such seemingly errant data.

If, hypothetically, only one person were to have used only one measuring device, variations or differences still would have existed for the reasons we have considered thus far. But different people used different devices intended to measure different aspects of the potential of different children at different times and under differing conditions. Even had the proper persons used the proper devices on the proper subjects, normal errors of measurement would have been disconcerting to the uninitiated. The presence of the highly varied and major psychological problems in the examination of different types of exceptional children, especially the physically handicapped, serves to complicate the picture to such an extent that one actually tends to be surprised at the relative consistency of such

results rather than to be dismayed at seeming discrepancies.[45] Two understanding and protective attitudes will help:

1. We need to feel a persistent and healthy concern and to employ
every legitimate checking procedure we know in the cases of all children
who make test scores that suggest mental retardation.

2. So long as we recognize that our examination procedures, with their
inherent assumptions, shed immediate, quantitative light on what the
operating levels of the children are at the times of those procedures
—their manifest capacities—and so long as we, or some others, draw
inferences from those examination results as to what the basic capacities
are, we shall be safeguarding the interests of those children, their parents,
their teachers, their therapists, and society.

The Socio-Emotional Area

The designation of this area is intentionally broad because it is the
bias here that, whatever the emotional picture of the individual may be,
it is the impact of that emotionality upon interpersonal relationships that
is of major importance. This is not to deny the value of studying the
social development or status, or the emotional development or status, per
se in order to obtain a psychologically sound picture of an individual;
it is, rather, to emphasize the interrelatedness of these aspects of behavior in that individual. Whenever we consider these subareas separately,
it will be with the constant realization that they have been only artificially
isolated for the sake of descriptive convenience.

In fact, it is difficult, if not impossible, to consider the social behavior
of a child without introducing factors or conditions that, in themselves,
are not social, but are really physical, intellectual, or emotional. Regarding the child socially, we can think of a child's ability to get around in
his environment. (Does he play in different parts of the house, at times
away from his adults? Does he play with children in the block? Does
he go to the store for his mother? Does he participate in social group
activity such as clubs, games, etc.? Does he date?) Or we can think
in terms of his physical growth and development (Can he crawl, walk
or run?), or we can think in terms of his being able to communicate
with those in his environment (speech, sensory adequacy, conceptual
development). We can think in terms of his having sufficient mental
maturity to enable him to go about the neighborhood with reasonable
caution, or to enable him to remember what he went to the store for or
how to go to and from the store, or to enable him to understand or
count when he plays games, or we can think in terms of whether he is
sufficiently emotionally independent of his parents to explore his house

or his neighborhood, or of whether he is sufficiently outgoing to enjoy being with and to be accepted by his peers.

Take, for instance, the item, "Cares for self at table," which appears at the IX-X level of the Vineland Social Maturity Scale. The extent to which a child can do this adequately can be determined by a number of factors, singly or in combination, as in the case of any of the following nine-year-olds: a child, of average intelligence, having a highly over-protective or exacting mother, or a blind child, or a manually involved cerebral palsied child. The scale is a highly useful device with which to quantify social competence, but its author and wary users of it are well aware that it reflects also "limitations imposed by intelligence level, emotional attitudes, social conditioning, disposition, and the like," and fully recognize that scores earned on it must "be interpreted with due regard for special limiting circumstances" [46] which include physical handicapping conditions.[47] The difficulty of conceiving of social development and/or maturation as a completely discrete behavioral entity has resulted in the development of very few devices purporting to measure it, and helps account for the larger number forthrightly purporting to measure socio-emotional development or adjustment.

The social frame of reference. The determination of over-all social status, in terms of social distance from the group, or from members of the group, by means of a sociometric approach [48] has been attempted with a number of the types of exceptional children. This seemingly innocuous and plausible method of asking children to name those of their classmates whom they like as leaders, playmates, friends, neighbors, and the like (to mention only the positive nominations), recording frequency of nomination, and plotting the interrelationships indicated by the nominations has raised disturbing questions as to the validity (Is actual social status thus identified?), the permanence (How evanescent is the status identified?), and the generality (Is over-all social status truly represented by high frequency of nomination as a seat-neighbor, for instance?) of the data so obtained. The fact that this and other sociometric approaches, such as the "guess who" technique, which was first used by Hartshorne and May,[49] must be used only on those children who either can read or can comprehend the statements which are presented to them tends to limit their valid use insofar as young children or mentally handicapped children are concerned.

The majority of attempts to ascertain "social adjustment," "socio-emotional adjustment," or "emotional adjustment," whether so named or only implied, by means of rating scales, check lists, and inventories have been for the purpose of finding out whether or not the kind of exceptionality under study differs from "the normal" group, or whether or not a specific exceptional child is "normal." Reports of the extent to which the sensorily handicapped, the orthopedically handicapped, and the intellectual deviants have problems, or are "maladjusted," have appeared with considerable frequency in the literature of this field. With respect to these the student may feel obliged to raise questions such as the following concerning the meaning of such findings. Generally, are the norms, on the basis of which any such comparative observations are made, psychologically meaningful with respect to the kind of exceptional children on whom the device was used? Certain personality inventories and check lists may be used quite appropriately with mentally superior children of given ages, but how appropriate are they when used on mentally retarded children who cannot read effectively enough to respond meaningfully, or on some physically handicapped children whose backgrounds and experiences have been distorted in the sense of their not having had certain opportunities to respond in situations sampled by means of the devices? The reading of the items to children of either of these handicapped groups not only does not avoid these difficulties but also introduces at least two others—auditory memory span and auditory comprehension. Often overlooked in the uses of generally standardized devices involving the child's responding, either directly or indirectly, concerning himself are the nature and extent of conceptualization present in the child so responding. In one kind of examination setting it is definitely psychologically meaningful for a child to respond to the word "spells" either as a verb or as a noun, but to assume, as is the case in the normative uses of these devices, that all children will respond solely in terms of only one meaning can lead to at least ambiguous results. Consider the difference in the underlying meaning attached to the same answer "yes" to the question "Do you prefer a play to a dance?" when that reply is given by a youth with no orthopedic or other physical involvements and by a paraplegic. Both would receive the same score, but each would have different psychological meaning.

The use of rating scales, the results of which are evaluated in terms of norms, involves some of these same problems. In these, the behaviors tend to be more objectively described in order to facilitate the use of such devices. However, the term "withdrawing" can have one meaning, when checked for a physically handicapped child in a non-handicapped group, and quite another for a non-handicapped child in the same group. Further, unless the behavior is quite specifically described, such a term can be interpreted variously by different raters. In fact, a very real question remains concerning the extent to which the one doing the rating of a child projects himself into the ratings, thus producing a picture that is a mixture of what some of the child's behavior may be and of how the rater feels about, or perceives, that behavior. The distortion of "true" pictures, obtained by such inventories, check lists, and rating scales, or by the subject's so describing himself, or by having another describe him is a factor that always has to be taken into consideration but, with judicious use and cautious interpretation, such evaluations can be of some value.

A recent attempt to get around the verbal aspects of self-reporting on social adjustment is Jay's *A Book About Me* [50] intended for use by kindergarten and first-grade children. With this device, the child is confronted with a variety of pictured situations under headings such as "My Mother," "My Daddy," "My House," "Things We Have at Our House," "Things I Do at Home," "Things I Can Do All by Myself," "People I Know, See, and Like," and "Which I'd Rather Do"—all social situations in which he is to identify himself. Pictured under "Things I Am Afraid Of," for instance, are a fire, a child being spanked, a storm, a snake, a policeman, a doctor, a father scolding a child, a larger boy shaking his fist at a smaller one, an oncoming car at a street intersection, a child going into a dark room, a bulldog, and bugs, flies, and a spider. While this has been intended primarily for the average early school child, it itself, and other possible approaches patterned after it, should be of much value if used individually with a variety of exceptional children.

The individual frame of reference. The approaches illustrated thus far are intended primarily to throw light on the adjustment of individuals to groups or how individuals representing the groups react to other members in that group. The emphasis was on the social frame of reference within which the individual is operating. In addition to this necessary and useful conception of the problem of adjustment, it is very helpful to find out, if possible, the dynamic emotional structure with which the individual reacts to the members of his group and in terms of which his social peers react to him. The emphasis here is upon such aspects of the individual as his perceptions of himself, his needs, drives, and emotional tensions.

The responses of any person to any stimulus at any time are psychologically colored, often unconsciously, by the way he feels at the time and by his background of emotional and intellectual experiences. No small amount of research has been done to tease out and identify emotional manifestations involved in, or constituting parts of, performances on intellectual, achievement, and aptitude measuring instruments. Enthusiasms having varying amounts of validity have been expressed, for instance, with respect to intelligence test responses wherein a child consistently goes the longer way in the Binet child-to-school mazes, or wherein a child completely ignores (rejects) his immediate environment in the word-naming item, or wherein digit memory span is at variance with other test behavior. Starting at least with the early work of Binet and the users of free association tests, many psychologists have endeavored to devise test stimuli which, without appearing to the subject to do so, would evoke responses that would throw greater light on the emotionality of subjects.[51] The assumption here is that the nature of his responses to such stimuli will be more a function of the subject's emotionality than of the stimuli themselves. In current terminology, the subject "projects" himself into the stimuli in terms of his own needs, tensions, and emotional outlook on life, and the devices are called projective tests.[52]

The apparent plausibility and the seeming lack of threat to the subject being so examined have contributed heavily to the development of some two hundred of these devices on the basis of varying kinds and qualities of research. A child may model an innocuous chunk of clay into a person, a chair, a cube, a ball, a snake, or some other object or animal. He may complete the sentence, "What I want is . . ." by adding "to go home," "to be an aviator," "to get even with Harry," or a number of other possibilities. He may draw lines more away from himself than toward himself. He may fill in solidly a geometric figure, or only a part of it, or he may attach drawings to it. He may draw a house with smoke coming out of the chimney, or with many or few openings, using a whole page for his drawing or using only a very small portion of it. In all these and other projective test stimuli situations, there is at least reduced likelihood of his feeling personally threatened by his being asked, or allowed, to do these things, and he is not likely to be aware that he is throwing some light on his emotional adjustment—a thing about which he may not feel able to talk and for which he may not have the verbalizations or concepts with which to talk.

The potential values of using such tests with the exceptional appear to be great. The importance of the emotional adjustment of the various kinds of exceptional children and youth, especially the handicapped, with respect to their education, their social adjustment, and their vocational placement and adjustment is only beginning to be recognized.[53] That each area of exceptionality would be explored, at least in part, by this time by means of at least one kind of projective approach is understandable. Thus far, children who were mentally retarded, blind, and non-sensorily physically handicapped have been studied the most by projective approaches.

Our concern here is with the problems attending the use of projective approaches as a part of the total examination or psychological assessment process, rather than with the enumeration of the types used or with the study of the results reported. It is interesting to observe that, in general, the initial use of projective methods of getting at the nature of the emotionality, or of the emotional adjustment, of individuals has followed much the same basic pattern as characterized the initial use of tests of mental capacity. In both, a very few were well standardized before they were generally used, but a large number of devices have sprung up mushroom-like. Just as certain responses to intelligence tests were regarded as throwing some light upon the emotionality of those taking them, just so have some responses to projective devices been interpreted as throwing light upon the mental capacity of the subjects. In both cases, many inadequately trained persons made use of the devices, gaining a false sense of competency and dealing with their response data with an unwarranted sense of the definitiveness and implications of the behavior so elicited.

Attending the use of projective approaches are essentially the same assumptions and the same problems as in the use of mental capacity measures. Behavior is sampled. A general comparability of background, both experiential and developmental, is assumed. Responses are taken as *indicative* of emotional conditions rather than being taken as the condition they indicate, and thus these behavior samples are taken as the bases for inferences. There is "error" in such measurement, due to sizes and natures of samplings and to the possible variability within the individual from time to time. The validation problem is, perhaps, greater in the projective area due to the difficulty in setting up acceptable criteria and to the greater possible impact of subjectivity on the scoring and analysis of the subject's responses.

To these disturbing but not necessarily invalidating difficulties or problems, which are present in the use of such approaches on the non-exceptional, we must add also those which are involved in working with the exceptional. Here, too, are the problems of communication and conceptualization. We can't present the ambiguous sound stimuli of one device to the deaf, but we can use it with certain other types of exceptionality. If for projective purposes we present bas-relief outlines of a horse to blind subjects, to what extent and in what ways can we safely compare their responses with those of sighted subjects? Deviant experiential backgrounds, perhaps even further impaired by mental retardation, may render useless pictorial or incomplete-sentence projective materials. The verbal responses to certain projective stimuli may be impaired or distorted due to limited conceptualization; such responses may well have a significance that renders them non-comparable with those of non-handicapped subjects.

In spite of all these problems that figure importantly in the use of projective devices and procedures on the exceptional, important additional information can be obtained by this type of approach. This is true, however, only under these conditions, which are not unique to this area:

1. The devices must be used by persons who are competently trained in their uses and well oriented in the personality dynamics in the light of which inferences are drawn concerning emotionality, and in the assumptions underlying psychological measurement.

2. The devices must have validity which has been established with respect to the type or types of exceptionality on which they are used. Implied or expressed assumptions of such validity, however plausible they may seem, must be based on sound research.

3. The devices must be such as to permit clear communication *to* the exceptional child or youth, to permit unambiguous and adequate communication *from* the subject, and must not presume the use of concepts, verbalized or otherwise, which, for any physical, social, or intellectual reason are not reasonably likely to be in the repertoire of the subject.

Commonality of acculturation. We have emphasized with respect to both the intelligence and socio-emotional areas the effect of the impact of grossly deviant backgrounds upon the responses of exceptional children and youth to devices in these areas. To understand the significance of this acculturation problem, two questions need to be answered: (1) How much can a child's background differ from those of other children and still be within the "normal" range? (2) When does a child's response become bizarre—completely at odds with the "normality" of the responses upon which the test is statistically or clinically standardized—and therefore have some special significance? To some, these questions are regarded as so unanswerable that they view the use of standardized examination procedures with thorough apprehension. This extremist position of throwing the baby out with the bath does not seem warranted even though specific categorical answers may not be given to the questions. Rough limits, within which the answers can be sought, can, however, be indicated.

Environmental backgrounds can be thought of as ranging from psychologically impossible, absolutely identical environments of two or more persons through some that are quite similar, through some others that are roughly similar, to highly dissimilar, and on out on the continuum to the completely unique background for a single person. No test is standardized for general use on an unattainable identity of backgrounds. Nor are any tests standardized on the logical impossibility of unique personal backgrounds. The use of "unselected" populations for standardization purposes, even on the basis of prior selections such as deaf children, blind children, cerebral palsied children, or even mentally retarded or gifted children, carries with it the recognition of the presence of an admittedly wide variety of normally different yet roughly common backgrounds. Here, also, normality is a range and not a point on our continuum, but the range does not include the extremes of gross cultural deprivation we have mentioned. Put more specifically, our cerebral palsied, for instance, come from homes that vary considerably in emotional atmosphere, cultural level and opportunity, presence and kind of siblings, amount and kind of orthopedic attention, educational facilities, and the like. But a few children, and these occur also in other areas of exceptionality, come from backgrounds that are even more different and will have had even more limited opportunity to come into contact with magazines, television, radios, interpersonal and interobject contacts. Hence they will have lacked in both the stimulation value and in the experiential value which normally, though still in widely varied manners, would have been present in the lives of their more fortunate peers. In the cases of exceptional children, then, it is not the response alone of the child who has been so deprived, but rather the response-as-having-come-out-of-his-background. Again, once a device is selected by the clinician as appropriate to a child of a given type of exceptionality, it can be used rather forthrightly on a major percentage of his group (hence, such testing tends to have an over-all value), but great care must constantly be exercised with certain other children of this type of exceptionality regarding the nature of their responses in the light of their backgrounds.

The Area of Educational Achievement

In considering the problems of measurement in this area, we concern ourselves more with the *what* of the individual than with the *why* and *how*. Here, the primary concern in examining the individual is to find out what he has learned, what he can do educationally. Regardless of his handicaps or his superiority, he reads at some part of a particular grade level, and that is the place at which the educator must work with him in reading. Such educational levels are the points from which the educators try to bring him up to those indicated by capacity tests and in the light of the facilitating or hampering effects of his emotionality and exceptionality. Measurements in the areas of learning capacity and socio-emotional adjustment contribute to the total picture of the individual by helping us understand how he was able to achieve as much as he did or why he wasn't able to achieve any more than he did.

This contrast between the purpose and the nature of the results of measurement in this area and those of the areas considered earlier is of value primarily in showing the reasons why some of the assumptions made with respect to measurement of learning capacity and emotional adjustment do not apply here. We try to measure educational achievements in order to find out what they are; we do not draw inferences on the basis of them as to how well adjusted a child is socially or emotionally (although we may well want to find out if his emotional condition is or has been such as to impair the effectiveness of his learning). Regarding the results of measured educational achievement themselves, we do not have the manifest performance-basic capacity gap problem which we have with respect to measured learning capacity. Nor do we have in this area, quite as much as in the measured emotional adjustment, the tendency to generalize with respect to more global behavior. As in other measurement areas we accept, understand, and allow for, both statistically and clinically, the presence of our errors of measurement, both because we are working with a normally varying individual and because we have to use a sampling approach in our measurement. Similarly, we use the depictions of educational performance, whether they be in terms of educational grade status or centile points, as having meaning only in terms of the population on which the achievement tests were standardized.

Insofar as most of the types of exceptionality are concerned, we recognize the appropriateness of the use of such norms in understanding the particular child, but in some cases we purposely depart from certain standardized test administration procedures and, at times, certain of the content. In the case of an emotionally disturbed child, or of a motor-involved child, we may give the test under normal, timed conditions, but have him mark how far he got at the designated time limits. We may then let him proceed with the tests as far as he can in the hope of getting fuller understanding of his total educational output. Spelling tests, usually administered orally, have to be adapted into multiple choice, synonym, or some other method of presentation. Special consideration must be given to test items involving either sound words—the crowing of a rooster, the screeching of a car's brakes, and the like, or color and certain object depiction words in the cases of deaf or blind children who may encounter them in standardized tests or word lists. These alterations have to be kept in mind in trying to interpret the test performances of such children in the light of the norms which are provided. Some have endeavored to regard any such limited performances as percentages of what the total might have been and then have characterized the child's "true" educational performance in terms of this "corrected" total. So long as the results so obtained are regarded as even coarser approximations than are obtained in the normal use of such devices, this method can have some value.

The conceptualization-communication problem exists in this area, too, but with impacts that differ somewhat from the situation in the two previous areas of measurement. Achievement test approaches have been modified by the use of large-type achievement tests for children who are partially sighted, by the development of achievement tests in braille for those who are blind, by the motor handicappeds' use of the typewriter, by use of objective test items in the place of handwritten responses for children with certain motor handicaps, and by the reading of test items to children with other kinds of handicaps, thus facilitating communication both to and from these kinds of children. Regarding the conceptualization aspect of our examination problem, it takes on a different significance in this area of measurement since our interest here is in ascertaining whether or not the conceptualizations being tested have been acquired by the children as a means both of communication and of acquiring other concepts. Here, the conceptualizations are the products being measured rather than the means by which one tries to get a picture of learning capacity or emotional adjustment.

Thus far no mention has been made of group averages. At times there may be merit in endeavoring to find out the average educational test performances of epileptic, cerebral palsied, blind, or deaf children of different ages (ignoring the false implications as to any homogeneity of such age groups). From the standpoint of stimulating research on the learning processes of, especially, the sensorily handicapped, there may well be some value in knowing, for instance, that the educational achievements of the deaf tend with frustrating consistency to run below those of their chronological peers. This type of information by itself is of limited value; when it is thrown into relationship with their learning potentials, it takes on added and truly provocative meaning. But with exceptional children and youth in particular we are obligated to deal with and think in terms of *individual* performances. In the area of educational measurement, the key problem is the consideration of the amount of achievement in the light of the individual's capacity to achieve. In terms of their ages or grades, the mentally superior tend to do exceptionally well, in one sense, on such achievement tests, and the mentally retarded tend to do poorly. But these performances take on entirely different meanings when we view them in light of the learning potentials out of which they come. It is then that we see clearly that the mentally retarded tend to work up to their capacities and that the mentally superior are the more educationally retarded. Allowing for all of the errors which we know exist in our measurements of the exceptional, it is still beneficial and desirable to evaluate each individual's educational achievements in terms of his capacity to achieve.

The Area of Aptitude Measurement

In the preceding paragraphs we considered the outcomes of such educational measurement primarily as direct evidence on status. The child was found to read at third-grade level, could perform simple arithmetic operations at a fifth-grade level, or had language-usage competence similar to that of an average fourth grader. This contrasted with the purposes of measurement in the two preceding areas which, to varying degrees, were to ascertain *the basis for* further work with the exceptional child or youth—his susceptibility to learning in school, and perhaps, certain aspects of his promise under therapy. In a manner largely similar to the orientation in physical and educational status measurement, measurement of aptitudes is largely the ascertainment of the amounts of particular skills and interests which can function as they are, and partly measurement of susceptibilities to further training toward given job competencies.

The term "aptitude" is taken here to refer to certain of those habits (including attitudes) and muscular coordinations of an individual which are known to predispose him to acceptably efficient performance in a given type of activity. Unless specifically indicated, this activity is regarded as either vocational or pre-vocational in nature. This predisposition may be "embryonic" and relatively simple, as in the case of certain speed of movement tests, or it may be heavily structured and involved, as in the case of the use of pliers or other tools in an object assembly test of considerable complexity. "Intelligence" has been dealt with in this chapter as learning aptitude or susceptibility to learning. Reading readiness tests are intended to measure a certain kind of aptitude for, or susceptibility to, learning to read. Emotional adjustment can affect general aptitude as in the case of an "unstable" person, or it can be a factor in determining whether an individual would do well in a given kind of work, as in the case of an "outgoing" person, or as in the case of a person who would feel more secure in the laboratory or among bookshelves. A "motor age" of an individual who is crippled may well have an important bearing on whether he can be expected to work at a drill press, or on a watch repair job, or as a keeper of a tool cage in a large plant. In like manner, whether a person can read or compute (educational achievement) can have particular significance with respect to a wide variety of occupations. All of these areas of potentiality and skills have a bearing upon, and can well be a large part of, the basis for vocational placement, as can sensory acuity, yet there remain certain other behavior samplings that research has shown to be relevant to success in certain occupations. It is in the sense of these areas of behavior that we shall consider the measurement of aptitude.

Behavior sampling in this area has been essentially of two kinds: attempts to ascertain the nature of the interests of the individual, insofar as they are known to be relevant to certain occupations, and attempts to ascertain the nature of muscular coordinations which are known to be or are regarded as playing important parts in the performance of given tasks. The inference gap, to which we have referred in other areas of measurement, is greater with respect to the measurement of interests than in the case of measurement of motor skills. But the reasoning is straightforward and the limitations are reasonably apparent. If the interests and preferences of, say, successful architects can be found to be significantly different from those, say, of successful computing machine operators, or real estate salesmen, then, depending to some extent on the age of the individual, if a person's interests and preferences most closely resemble those of architects, such a person has at least that much in his favor if he desires to become an architect. If a person just doesn't have fine motor coordinations and, perhaps, good visual memory, he might well have difficulty in succeeding at watch repairing.[54]

In each of the other areas, measurement in only one of them has little, if any, value. Just so does aptitude measurement alone have limited value. Interests have value in suggesting aptitudes, but must be supported by certain amounts of intelligence, certain kinds of emotionality, mobility and other motor competencies, and educational skills. Similarly, errors are present in our behavior samplings, and we need research assurance that the behavior sampled has adequate predictive value with respect to given occupations or occupational areas. Rapport and good motivation are needed in the examination, just as in any other area.

Since our primary concern here is with direct evidence of the compatibility of present interests and preferences with given established occupational areas and also with the present susceptibility of the individual to training to a competency level in a given occupation, or family of occupations, it is understandable that few tests need to be developed specially for the exceptional. As a result, only a few aptitude measuring devices have been developed specifically for the exceptional, and the major effort has been in improving the means of communication with respect to existing devices. This has resulted in more work with the blind than with other exceptionalities. The relative instability of interests in the younger age groups and the attending delay in specific vocational guidance have understandably narrowed to the upper end of the age scale of our group the approaches to the measurement of their aptitudes. However, in the case of the mentally retarded, it is apparent that at least certain of the measurement approaches present unique problems in the area of concept adequacy on their part and the resulting communication efficacy of the devices which might be used. The most promising area of exploration with respect to this problem might well be the development and use of pictorial approaches involving the use of pictures to be checked (after Jay's *Book About Me*) in addition to the pictures of tools, machines, gear movements, and belt or rope routings over pulleys.[55]

It is well to keep in mind that in this area, too, we are dealing in terms of probabilities. We are still in the realm of "the chances are . . . ." Further, we are safer in our guesses or estimates when we recognize the fact that we use the results of some of our measures of vocational interest more to suggest the undesirability of a given occupation or group of occupations than to indicate clearly the desirability of a given occupation or group of occupations. Given the results of one or more vocational interest inventories on a youth, our statement to him might well run in this fashion: "More than your responses or scores on these devices is needed to help you make a decision about what you might consider as a kind of life work. However, as far as the results of these devices alone are concerned, the chances are about seven out of ten that _____ might be a good type of work for you to consider favorably, but the chances are eight or so out of ten that _____ would be a good area to avoid."

The Assessment Process

Analysis

Regardless of the kind of exceptionality the individual possesses and regardless of the age of the exceptional individual, the sampling of various areas of behavior must be carried out for the purpose of throwing light upon specifiable and psychologically significant aspects of the individual. In contrast to a testing approach which results from giving *a* test to get *a* score, there is the more important need to study the individual in terms of certain psychological constructs, or from certain psychological frames of reference which bear clearly upon the situation with respect to which the individual is being studied. A very significant approach of this sort is the one described by Taylor, as mentioned on page 70. A somewhat different structuring of the clinician's task is presented in the next few paragraphs. The assessment process will be considered in terms of obtaining behavior samples which will enlighten the clinician regarding the subject's conceptualization behavior, his interpersonal relationships, his communication, his energy level, and the validity of information obtained about the subject from others. This will be done by stating only a few questions which illustrate what the clinician must be asking himself about the client as he works with him.

Conceptualization. What is his present level and quality of conceptualization? In view of the subject's history, what reasonable implications can be drawn regarding the client's subsequent conceptualization—his rate and ultimate level of growth in this area? What has been the nature of the subject's acculturation? Has he had a "normal" exposure? Or has he been reared in an impoverished or culturally "sterile" environment?

Or has he been "hothoused?" If the child shows the effects of such "hot-housing," what are the implications of the results of such activity with respect to the child's capacity to benefit from it? How does he learn in the clinic situation?

Interpersonal relationships. How does the subject relate to the clinician? How has he related to others in his environment? Is he "outgoing"? If so, is this behavior of good quality? Does it have a compensatory basis? Is it soundly compensatory, or is it over-compensatory? Is he "withdraw-ing"? Is this behavior really a manifestation of good quality self-suffi-ciency? Or is it the result of his having learned to retire to situations which must be, for him, less threatening? Is he quite distractible? Is this a function of his basic insecurity or other emotional tension? Or is it better attributable to low mentality? Or to hearing loss? How does he respond to motivation in the clinic situation? Does he become interested in the test situation, or is he concerned primarily with pleasing you? Is he excessively concerned with meeting time limits, or does he excessively seek approbation? Is he aggressive in the clinic situation? If so, is he justified in being so? Have the significant adults in his world taken him so often to clinics for examination and treatment that he resents being with you in another one? Or has he become resigned to it? How much residual psychological integrity has he?

Communication. How well is he "receiving"? Does he, possibly due to a hearing loss, give evidence of misinterpretation of words he hears? Is his asking for repetition of directions due to hearing loss, emotional need, or "short attention span"? Are any of his posturings or the closeness with which he watches you suggestive of any possible hearing loss? Is "inattentiveness" due to hearing loss, legitimate fatigue, or some other condition? Does he see well what is shown him? Are there any posturings or other physical adjustments which may be compensatory for poor vision? Are there any cutaneous-kinesthetic anomalies affecting his re-ception of stimuli? Are there any anomalies in the motor area? May they be due to inadequate maturation? To neural impairment? To emotional tension? Is motor anomaly limited to eye movement, speech, locomotion, manipulation, breathing, or common to two or more? (Questions regard-ing the mediation aspect of the communication process—what happens after the stimulus is "received" and before the response is made—will not be raised here specifically, since much that has been said [and asked] in regard to conceptualization and in regard to Taylor's procedures applies here.)

Energy level. Is the vigor of his response appropriate to the demands of the situation? Does he "over-react"? If so, is this a healthy, "animal" energy? Does it have a plausible emotional basis, as in certain over-compensatory behavior? If below the demands of the situation, may it

have resulted from repressive treatment? From a debilitated physical condition? From understandable fatigue? From medication? From his rejection of the clinical situation?

Nature of information. To what extent is your clinical evaluation of
the subject based primarily upon what you have actually observed? To
what extent are you dealing with your own inferences as though they
were observed behavior? To what extent is the developmental and social
background information which you obtained from someone else a careful
report of specific behavior, or to what extent does it consist of ambiguous,
inferred generalities, such as "nervous," "stubborn," "withdrawn," and
the like? Has your information about the subject come from a hyper-
critical, or excitable, or basically insecure person? To what extent has
your background information on the child come from an adult who is
excessively ambitious for (or rejecting of) the child? Or has it come from
a person of low psychological perceptive acuity?

These are only some of the many questions the psychologist always
asks himself as he seeks to acquire an understanding of any individual—
exceptional or otherwise—in order to try to make a psychologically sound
assessment of him. It is apparent that, to do so, he cannot be "test-
bound." But, in doing so, he needs four things:

1. To have a normative background in terms of which he can decide
that a given child's conceptualization is that of an average ten-year-old,
or decide that the child is insecure, or that he has good psychological
integrity. To be able to do this, he needs to have acquired much experience in terms of which he has valid expectancies for average nine-
month-old infants, seven-year-olds, ten- and fifteen-year-olds. He needs
to know the various ways in which children handle their feelings of insecurity. He must be able to differentiate between psychological integrity,
or ego strength, and psychological façade.

2. To have a knowledge of what behaviors may *not* suggest as well as
of what they may suggest. The child hastily diagnosed as a "mirror
writer" may after all be only a youngster, like one with whom the writer
worked, who "saw her sister write this way and get a lot of attention"
and similarly wanted attention. Or perhaps the child reported as "shifty
eyed" and untrustworthy is actually nystagmic. Or, the child reported as
"clumsy" may be a developmental problem; or he may be fearful of
running and going up and down stairs because his crossed eyes render
him deficient in depth perception; or he may be "clumsy" because he is
muscularly tense as an integral part of an emotional problem; or, least
likely, he may have some central nervous system impairment. Or, the
situation may be something like the case of the child who had shown
"uncontrollable behavior" at various times over a period of three years

and who was found to have an infection of the ear that became severe and "drove the child wild."

3. To have a sound understanding of and a deep feeling for the legitimacy of differentness. While the clinician must have an understanding of the "normal," in terms of which he can understand deviants, he, perhaps more fully than most parents and teachers, is constantly aware that in the psychological sense a norm is only a statistical statement, an average, for some defined group. To him, such a norm need not be something to be attained by a given youngster, because it may be unreasonably high for one child or restrictingly low for another. The exceptional child has a "right to be different," and to expect the school and society both to understand his difference and to capitalize upon it.

4. To be sensitive constantly to the importance of the interaction of the many facets of behavior which he necessarily explores in isolation.

Synthesis

Let us imagine a piece of cloth that has been woven out of a variety of colored threads. An intricate design is woven into this piece of cloth. Due to the nature of some of the dyes, parts of some of the exposed threads have faded and other parts have been soiled, so that the color you see in them is quite different from that you would find if you turned the cloth over or if you pulled those threads out of their sheltered positions within that pattern. Some of the cloth is well worn, meaning that some of these threads are thinner, even a bit shaggy, in spots. Perhaps, by some fluke in the patterning and weaving process, some particularly strong or well-dyed thread figures only to a very minor extent in what one sees on looking at the whole piece of cloth. One could look at the whole piece of cloth and make certain meaningful observations to the effect that it is soiled, faded, thin, worn, in need of replacing, usable for certain things, and so on. These are socially appropriate evaluations of this piece of cloth, given the implied frames of reference for them.

Certain persons, because of their particular functions in society—such as the weaver, the dyer, and the patternmaker—may well decide to describe (an elementary kind of evaluation) the pattern in terms of the number of threads per inch, the percentage of color to a square inch, the use of straight-line or curved-line elements in the pattern, the tensile strength of the threads used, the chemical analysis of the dyes used, or any one of a number of other facets of this piece of cloth. Each of these will have a social value within its frame of reference. Given enough samples of each of these separate elements, socially meaningful (but not meaningful insofar as this one piece of cloth is concerned) generalizations could be made concerning such thread strengths, stability of such patterns, permanency of such dyes, and so on. But none of these studies of single aspects of this piece of cloth can be taken to represent the cloth; clothwise, such single evaluations or descriptions are meaningless.

The analogy with the examination of the individual—particularly if he is exceptional—need not be labored. The layman or novice tends to make gross evaluations, all of them psychologically valuable and some of them valid regarding the person so evaluated. But the psychologist, aspiring to the objectivity of the scientist, is faced with the two problems of science. He must analyze the whole individual into parts or functions in order that he can get clearer and more objective pictures of those functions. Then, if society is to benefit from his intensive studies of these elements, he must try to reassemble those functions into the whole individual, emphasizing certain of those functions for some purposes, and emphasizing others for other purposes, but at all times concerning himself with the whole individual. This synthesizing process gives psychological meaning to the studies of the artificially isolated functions, enhancing some, limiting others. The psychological tester tends to stop with, or to describe the individual primarily in terms of, his work at the analysis stage. If the psychologist would *assess* the individual, he goes through the analysis stage, making as many controlled observations as he deems necessary in order to synthesize his findings into a psychologically meaningful picture of the total functioning dynamic individual. This is not simply an additive process. A person's health may be somewhat below average and his intelligence may seem less than average, yet the strength and nature of his motivation may well be such that he performs on a job considerably better than either of the first two characteristics would lead one to expect.[56]

This need for synthesis holds where any sound psychological evaluation of an individual is undertaken. It is often difficult to achieve when working with the non-exceptional. It is doubly necessary and much more difficult in connection with the exceptional, since misleading or obscuring conditions so often enter their behavioral pictures. This difficulty often is compounded by the fact that, because of a dearth of appropriately well-trained persons, less well-qualified individuals endeavor to make assumptions and use procedures that have much more validity in a non-exceptional frame of reference.

While it was necessary for convenience of discussion and description to concern ourselves with aspects or functions of the exceptional as though they were pure, isolated identities, the interrelatedness of these five areas of measurement repeatedly became apparent. The paradox of the psychological absurdity of dealing with functions one at a time and the scientific impossibility of meaningfully concerning ourselves with an undifferentiated total called an individual constitutes a continuum within which the psychologist must always operate.

The point was made, in the discussion of intelligence measurement of the severely physically handicapped, that the psychologist had to use an almost intuitive approach, but that in doing so he had a fairly meaningful set of reference points as a result of having been well grounded in his training and experience with less handicapped children. As a result of the important part played by such basic training, we encounter the point of view that effective measurement in markedly atypical cases is much more a matter of the person making the examination than it is of the particular device used. Even though reasonably adequate psychological pictures thus can be obtained of the handicapped, the kind of data so obtained often is recognizably inadequate for rigid statistical analysis. In other words, the determination of the mental level or rate of mental development in such cases tends more to be an art than a science. This being the case within a given area of measurement, the synthesizing of these areas of measurement tends even more to be a matter of art. Calling either of these processes something less than scientific need not cause us to reject them as useless and completely meaningless. The need for rigorous research on the validity of these important and necessary processes is unmistakably apparent.[57]

Summary

THE CONCEPTS and assumptions fundamental to all measurement underlie the examination and assessment of the exceptional. We sample behavior and assume, with varying degrees of confidence, that our samples give us adequate cues as to the totality of learning-proneness, emotionality, achievement, or aptitudes. For a number of reasons, but especially since the organism we are observing under controlled conditions is a growing and adapting one, and since we have to resort to samples of its behavior, we are bound to have errors in our measurements. At times the behavior we observe has to serve as a basis for inferring a capacity for further similar behavior, as in the case of the measurement of mental capacity. Both the performance under observation and the inferred basic capacity to perform are of psychological importance. In the case of the exceptional the gap between the two tends to be greatest. At other times there is less, if any, need for such inference since it is the degree of skill in evidence at the time of observation (testing) that is of primary social value, as in the case of educational achievement or certain vocational aptitudes.

Certain of our assumptions and problems are common to all the areas of the psychological evaluation of the exceptional. Even though measurement error is known or knowable, it is at times not recognized. But it can be reduced. Pervading the processes of psychologically evaluating the exceptional are problems pertaining to the nature and status of their conceptualization processes, and problems involved in communication. The first of these necessitates the careful consideration both of the verbalized content employed in the behavior sampling process and of the evaluations made of the responses given in the examination situations. This latter bears also upon the means of communicating, by the exceptional child or youth, with the examiner, and also makes special demands regarding the sensory avenues employed in "getting through" to him. The communication problem appears to have received more attention than the conceptualization problem.

The examination of exceptional children and youth is, by the very nature of their being exceptional, an exacting and difficult task requiring the services of highly skilled and qualified persons. The presence of motor and sensory handicaps and of major emotional involvements, singly or in combination, materially complicates the process. The psychological assessment of these children and youth, the necessary synthesizing of the results of physical, intellectual, socio-emotional, achievement, and aptitude measurements, is even more difficult. While sound research is badly needed to show us how to make these processes more scientific and less a matter of art, their results can still play a significant part in educational and social planning for, and in our understanding of, the exceptional.

Notes

[1] Hereafter, any unqualified reference to intelligence quotients or mental ages will be in terms of the 1960 Binet. If either has been ascertained by any other test, the name of that test will be used—as Otis IQ, or PMA mental age, or WISC test age.

[2] M. J. Berko, "Some Factors in the Mental Evaluation of Cerebral Palsied Children," *Cerebral Palsy Review,* XIV (1953), 6, 11, 15.

[3] See: Nancy Bayley and Melita H. Oden, "The Maintenance of Intellectual Ability in Gifted Adults," *J. Gerontology,* 10 (1955), 91-107; Nancy Bayley, "On the Growth of Intelligence," *American Psychologist,* 10 (1955), 805-818; and W. H. Guertin, A. I. Rabin, G. H. Frank, and C. E. Ladd, "Research with the Wechsler Intelligence Scales for Adults," *Psychological Bulletin,* 59 (1962), 1-26.

[4] Interestingly related to this conceptualization, which was arrived at clinically, is Cattell's positing, on the basis of results obtained by factor analysis, a fluid general ability, perhaps somewhat similar to the author's "process," and a crystallized general ability, quite similar to the author's "product." See: R. B. Cattell, *Personality and Motivation Structure and Measurement* (New York: Harcourt, Brace & World, Inc., 1957), Appendix 11, "Intelligence in Personality: Culture-fluid and Culture-crystallized General Ability Tests," pp. 871-880. Using data collected since his 1957 statement, Cattell recently has submitted for publication material for an article entitled "The Theory of Fluid and Crystallized Ability: A Check on the First Hypothesis."

[5] See, for example, A. N. Fransen, B. R. McCullough, and D. R. Stone, "Serial versus Consecutive Order Administration of the Stanford-Binet Intelligence Scales," *Journal of Consulting Psychology,* XIV (1950), 316-320.

[6] N. B. Bond, "Cerebral Palsy Profile in Mississippi," *Exceptional Children,* XX (1953), 98-99.

[7] For convenience, hereafter called the "deaf."

[8] Regarding the initial basic assumption (concerning the normality of learning potential distribution) as equally plausible with respect to the deaf and the blind may seem, at first blush, defensible. However, the author questions its validity with respect to at least those who have been born deaf. He suspects that in the born deaf the major psychological process underlying all learning—the innate predisposition of the organism to generalize—does not receive as much reinforcement, both intentional and incidental, as is true in the case of individuals without such acoustic disability. As a result, it is believed, this process which originally may have had a potential of "normal" operation, well may come to function at something lower than its original potential due to lack of stimulation. This concept of reduced effective stimulation logically is part of a picture of deprived acculturation, a special case of faulty acculturation as that term is used in this chapter. The possible fruitfulness of this concept with respect to other kinds of exceptional children also should be explored. See, for instance, T. E. Newland, "Language Development of the Mentally Retarded Child," in *Language Development and Language Disorders: A Compendium of Lectures.* (Nancy E. Wood, Editor), Monographs of the Society for Research in Child Development, Serial No. 77, Vol. 25, No. 3 (1960), pp. 71-87.

[9] R. M. Allen and M. G. Collins, "Suggestions for the Adaptive Administration of Intelligence Tests for those with Cerebral Palsy," *Cerebral Palsy Review,* Part I, 16 (1955), 11-14, 25 and Part II, 19 (1958), 6-7; E. Katz, "The 'Pointing Modification' of the Revised Stanford-Binet Intelligence Scales, Forms L and M, Years II through VI: A Report of Research in Progress," *American Journal of Mental Deficiency,* 62 (1958), 698-707 and E. Katz, "A Method of Selecting Stanford-Binet Intelligence Scale Test Items for Evaluating the Mental Abilities of Children Severely Handicapped by Cerebral Palsy," *Cerebral Palsy Review,* 1 (1956), 13-17; D. J. Sievers and R. D. Norman, "Some Suggestive Results in Psychometric Testing of the Cerebral Palsied with Gesell, Binet, and Wechsler Scales," *Journal of Genetic Psychology,* 82 (1953), 69-90.

[10] Edith M. Taylor, *Psychological Appraisal of Children with Cerebral Defects* (Cambridge: Harvard University Press, 1959).

[11] A. Gesell and C. S. Amatruda, *Developmental Diagnosis,* 2nd ed. (New York: Paul B. Hoeber, Inc., 1947).

[12] L. H. Blum and N. D. Fieldsteel, *Blum-Fieldsteel Development Charts* (New York: Harcourt, Brace & World, Inc., 1953). See also: A. Gesell and staff, *Gesell Developmental Schedules* (New York: The Psychological Corporation, 1949).

[13] M. K. Johnson, F. N. Zuck, and K. Wingate, "The Motor-Age Test: Measurement of Motor Handicaps in Children with Neuromuscular Disorders Such as Cerebral Palsy," *Journal of Bone and Joint Surgery,* XXXIII-A (1951), 698-707.

[14] M. E. Brown, "Daily Activity Inventories of Cerebral Palsied Children in Experimental Classes," *Physical Therapy Review,* 30 (1950), 415-421; and M. E. Brown, "Daily Activity Inventory and Progress Record for Those with Atypical Movement," *American Journal of Occupational Therapy,* IV (1950), 195-204, 261-272 and V (1951), 23-29, 38.

[15] M. E. Brown, "Pre-vocational Motor Skill Inventory: Preliminary Report," *American Journal of Occupational Therapy,* VII (1953), 153-163, 188.

[16] *Oseretsky Tests of Motor Proficiency* (Manual), ed. E. A. Doll (Minneapolis, Minn: Educational Test Bureau, 1946). See also: M. K. Distefano, Jr., N. R. Ellis, and W. Sloan, "Motor Proficiency in Mental Defectives," *Perceptual and Motor Skills,* 8 (1958), 231-234.

[17] Illustrative of such aids to the teacher and the speech correctionist in sampling speech behavior is material in the book *Diagnostic Manual in Speech Correction* by W. Johnson, F. L. Darley, and D. C. Spriestersbach (New York: Harper & Row, Publishers, 1952).

[18] Z. Piotrowski, "Positive and Negative Rorschach Organic Reactions," *Rorschach*

Research Exchange, IV (1940), 147-151. Included here as illustrative. Bear in mind that organic signs are believed to be found also in other projective test responses. See also, for example, J. R. Wittenborn and S. B. Sarason, "Exceptions to Certain Rorschach Criteria of Pathology," *Journal of Consulting Psychology,* XIII (1949), 21-27. E. A. Doll, "Psychometric Pitfalls in Clinical Practice," *Journal of Consulting Psychology,* XI (1947), 12-20.

19 F. K. Graham and B. S. Kendall, "Performance of Brain-Damaged Cases on a Memory-for-Designs Test," *Journal of Abnormal and Social Psychology,* XLI (1946), 303-314; and "Further Standardization of the Memory-for-Designs Test on Children and Adults," *Journal of Consulting Psychology,* XII (1948), 349-354. See also: A. L. Benton, "A Multiple Choice Type of the Visual Retention Test," *American Medical Association Archives of Neurology and Psychiatry,* 64 (1950), 699-707; R. M. Reitan, *The Effects of Brain Lesions on Adaptive Abilities in Human Beings* (Indianapolis: Indiana University Medical Center, 1959); and M. Korman, "Some Problems in the Psychological Diagnosis of Brain Damage: An Overview," *Texas Reports on Biology and Medicine,* 18 (1960), 214-221.

20 B. T. Baldwin and T. D. Wood, *Weight-Height-Age Tables for Boys and Girls* (New York: American Child Health Association, 1932).

21 W. E. Martin, *Children's Body Measurements,* U. S. Office of Education Special Publication 4 (Washington, D.C.: Government Printing Office, 1955).

22 See also W. C. Olson, and B. O. Hughes, *Manual for the Description of Growth in Age Units* (Ann Arbor, Mich.: The Edwards Letter Co., 1950).

23 N. C. Wetzel, *The Treatment of Growth Failure in Children* (Cleveland: National Education Association Service, 1948).

24 See also E. Z. Johnson, "Individual Patterns of Emotional Functioning in Children of Comparable I.Q.'s—Implications for Education," *American Journal of Mental Deficiency,* LVII (1953), 681-686. This involves relationships between Revised Binet and Progressive Matrices data on mentally retarded children.

25 The term "effective intelligence," as used by many, denotes much the same as "manifest capacity."

26 The term "cerebral palsy" is used in the sense of the definition "Any abnormal alteration of movement or motor function arising from defect, injury, or disease of the nervous tissue within the cranial cavity."

27 See also E. Haussermann, "Evaluating the Developmental Level of Cerebral Palsied Pre-School Children," *Journal of Genetic Psychology,* LXXX (First Half, 1952), 3-23. A discussion of problems and possible procedures rather than of completed techniques. And H. V. Bice, "Psychological Examination of the Cerebral Palsied," *Journal of Exceptional Children,* XIV (1948), 163-168.

28 The author worked with one cerebral palsied child who indicated "yes" by thumping his fist against his chest, and "no" by hitting his leg.

29 L. H. Blum, B. B. Burgemeister, and I. Lorge, "The Mental Maturity Scale for the Motor Handicapped," *School and Society,* LXXIII (1951), 232-233; *Columbia Mental Maturity Scale* (New York: Harcourt, Brace & World, Inc., 1954). The only information supplied in the manual for the 1959 revision is a normative data sheet which provides norms for a mental age range from 3 years 5 months to 13 years 11 months, but the norms above 10 years suggest the use of extrapolative procedures. The sigmas of the I.Q.'s for the separate age levels have been reported as distractingly large.

30 Dorothy Van Alstyne, *Van Alstyne Picture Vocabulary Test* (New York: Harcourt, Brace & World, Inc., 1960); R. B. Ammons and H. S. Ammons, *Full Range Picture Vocabulary Test* (Missoula, Mont.: Psychological Test Specialists, 1948); L. M. Dunn, *Peabody Picture Vocabulary Test* (Nashville, Tenn.: American Guidance Service, Inc., 1958).

31 There are two series of these matrices. The 1938 series consists of five sets of twelve items each, the items arranged in a presumed order of difficulty and the sets increasing, overlappingly, in difficulty. The 1947 series, intended for children from five through eleven years of age, consists of the first two sets of the 1938 items plus

an interposed set, with colors used in all three sets. The normative data are British. Available in this country through The Psychological Corporation, New York, N.Y., and Western Psychological Service, Box 775, Beverly Hills, California.

[32] V. S. Tracht, "Preliminary Findings on Testing the Cerebral Palsied with Raven's Progressive Matrices," *Journal of Exceptional Children*, XV (1948), 77-79, 89.

[33] R. M. Taibl, "An Investigation of Raven's Progressive Matrices as a Test for the Psychological Evaluation of Cerebral Palsied Children" (Doctoral dissertation, University of Nebraska, 1951).

[34] This has been shared abroad, as witness the article, "An Item Analysis of the Progressive Matrices Test," by Charlotte Banks and Unra Sinha in the *British Journal of Psychology*, Statistical Section, IV, Part II (1951), 91-94.

[35] For our purpose here, a child is regarded as having a "strong drive" to the extent that he appears to be outgoing in his relationships with his environment (people, objects, and conditions), if he is inquisitive and curious, if he "bores in," if he is active. Aggressive behavior is regarded psychologically as more of an asset than a liability. The significance of a "strong drive" is tempered but not lost if it is compensatory in nature.

[36] H. Werner and A. Strauss, "Types of Visuo-Motor Activity in Their Relation to Low and High Performance Ages," *Proceedings of the American Association on Mental Deficiency*, 44 (1939), 163-168; V. N. Rowley, "Analysis of the WISC Performances of Brain Damaged and Emotionally Disturbed Children," *Journal of Consulting Psychology*, 25 (1961), 553; B. M. Hunt, "Differential Responses of Mentally Retarded Children on the Leiter Scale," *Exceptional Children*, 28 (1961), 99-102; W. Quast, "The Bender Gestalt: A Clinical Study of Children's Records," *Journal of Consulting Psychology*, 25 (1961), 405-408; E. E. Lessing, "A Note on the Significance of Discrepancies between Goodenough and Binet I.Q. Scores," *Journal of Consulting Psychology*, 25 (1961), 456-457; and I. W. Scherer, "The Prediction of Academic Achievement in Brain Injured Children," *Exceptional Children*, 28 (1961), 103-106.

[37] J. J. McCarthy, "Qualitative and Quantitative Differences in Language Abilities of Young Cerebral Palsied Children" (Doctoral dissertation, University of Illinois, 1957); S. A. Kirk and J. J. McCarthy, "The Illinois Test of Psycholinguistic Abilities—An Approach to Differential Diagnosis," *American Journal of Mental Deficiency*, 66 (1961), 399-412; Frostig-LeFevre-Whittlesey, *Developmental Test of Visual Perception* (Los Angeles, Calif.: Marian Frostig, 7257 Melrose Avenue, 1961). The former is based upon Osgood's conception of psycholinguistics; the latter purports to measure behavior of young children in the areas of eye-motor coordination, figure-ground discrimination, shape constancy, positional perception in space, and spatial relationships.

[38] Ellen M. Nudd, "Perception of Pictured Social Interaction by Brain-Injured and Non-Brain-Injured Children of Normal Intelligence" (Doctoral dissertation, University of Illinois, 1957).

[39] See, for instance, R. Pintner, J. Eisenson, and M. Stanton, *The Psychology of the Physically Handicapped* (New York: Appleton-Century-Crofts, 1941).

[40] See also S. A. Kirk and J. Perry, "A Comparative Study of the Ontario and Nebraska Tests for the Deaf," *American Annals of the Deaf*, XCIII (1948), 315-323; and J. R. Birch and J. W. Birch, "The Leiter International Performance Scale as an Aid in the Psychological Study of the Deaf," *American Annals of the Deaf*, XCVI (1951), 502-511. Includes some comparative data on the Arthur Scale and the Nebraska Test.

[41] E. E. Graham and E. Shapiro, "Use of the Performance Scale of the Wechsler Intelligence Scale for Children with the Deaf Child," *Journal of Consulting Psychology*, XVII (1953), 396-398.

[42] J. Th. Snijders and N. Snijders-Oomen, *Non-Verbal Intelligence Tests for Deaf and Hearing Subjects* (Groningen, Holland: J. B. Wolters, 1959).

[43] See also M. K. Bauman, "Diagnostic Procedures in Rehabilitation of the Blind," *Journal of Rehabilitation*, XVIII (1952), 7-11. Specifically illustrative of some of the problems discussed in this chapter. And R. E. Simmons, "Psychological Testing of the

Blind," *Outlook for the Blind,* XLIV (1950), 131-135. A discussion of problems with respect to vocational counseling.

[44] In process of standardization by the author is a non-verbal, bas-relief learning aptitude test for the blind involving only cutaneous-kinesthetic exploration of the items. No braille reading ability is involved. It is believed that primarily *process* is sampled. For a description of the proposed device and the results obtained on 937 born-blind residential- and day-school children, see T. E. Newland, "The Blind Learning Aptitude Test," pp. 40-51 in *Report of Proceedings of Conference on Research Needs in Braille,* American Foundation for the Blind, Inc., 15 West 16th St., New York, N.Y.

[45] See, for instance, R. F. Street, "I.Q. Changes of Exceptional Children," *Journal of Consulting Psychology,* 6 (1942), 243-246.

[46] E. A. Doll, *Vineland Social Maturity Scale* (Manual) (Minneapolis: Educational Test Bureau, 1946).

[47] This type of device has been used for goal-setting purposes by following this line of reasoning: Granting that the various behaviors which are to be checked on such a scale represent competency expectancies for the different age levels, to what extent can children not yet having the competencies normally expected at or near their age levels be helped or trained to do such things for themselves? The possibilities of this use of the Vineland, not unrecognized by workers with the handicapped, are, for instance, at once apparent with respect to the mentally handicapped, the blind, and the deaf.

[48] H. H. Jennings, *Sociometry in Group Relations* (Washington, D.C.: American Council on Education, 1948).

[49] H. Hartshorne and M. A. May, *Studies in Service and Self-Control* (New York: The Macmillan Company, 1929).

[50] E. S. Jay, *A Book About Me* (Chicago: Science Research Associates, Inc., 1952).

[51] F. L. Goodenough, "The Appraisal of Child Personality," *Psychological Review,* LVI (1949), 123-131.

[52] J. E. Bell, *Projective Techniques* (New York: Longmans, Green & Co., Inc., 1948). A descriptive compilation of the major types of approaches used. L. K. Frank, *Projective Methods* (Springfield, Illinois: C. C. Thomas, 1948). A good statement of the rationale of projective testing. P. B. Symonds, "New Directions for Projective Techniques," *Journal of Consulting Psychology,* XIII (1949), 387-389; L. E. Abt and L. Bellak, eds., *Projective Psychology: Clinical Approaches to the Total Personality* (New York: Grove Press, 1959).

[53] L. B. Ames, J. Learned, R. W. Metraux, and R. N. Walker, *Child Rorschach Responses* (New York: Paul B. Hoeber, Inc., 1952). Exceptional children reported on include emotionally maladjusted delinquents, mentally superior, endogenous and exogenous defectives, enuretic children, children with extremes in reading skills, and those with tics. See also: N. H. Ledwith, *Rorschach Responses of Elementary School Children* (Pittsburgh, Pa.: University of Pittsburgh Press, 1959); A. I. Rabin and M. H. Haworth, eds., *Projective Techniques with Children* (New York: Grune & Stratton, Inc., 1960); and L. B. Ames *et al., Adolescent Rorschach Responses* (New York: Harper & Row, Publishers, 1959).

[54] Intentionally omitted here is the consideration of the usual gamut of aptitude tests. Devices such as the Detroit Mechanical Aptitude Test are heavily loaded with samplings of knowledge about things mechanical—whether, for instance, the subject knows a pipe wrench from a claw hammer. In a sense, one who is better informed regarding an area of activity has a better "aptitude" for it. In the case of tests of musical aptitude, behavior is sampled in terms of aspects such as tonal discrimination, tempo discrimination, memory for each, and the like. Graphic artistic aptitude tends to be tested in terms of appreciation. Certain recently publicized tests of "creative writing ability" depend so heavily upon verbal factors already identified in most intelligence testing that their unique contributions as tests of creative writing aptitude is by no means clearly established.

[55] Some work has been done along this line. See K. P. Weingarten, "The Measure-

ment of Interests in Non-Professional Vocations by Means of a Pictorial Inventory," *California Journal of Educational Research*, V (1954), 7-10. The Geist Picture Interest Inventory (Missoula, Mont.: Psychological Test Specialists, 1959), thus far developed only for male adults, also is illustrative of possibilities which could be explored, particularly for use with the vocabulary-limited mentally retarded. Approaches such as these should be helpful with others whose language is seriously impaired.

56 T. E. Newland, "Are Exceptional Children Tested or Assessed?" *Exceptional Children*, XIX (1952), 51-55; P. B. Symonds, "Case-Study and Testing Methods," in *Handbook of Child Guidance*, ed. Ernest Harms (New York: Child Care Publications, 1947), 266-314; G. H. Kent, *Mental Tests in Clinics for Children* (Princeton: D. Van Nostrand Co., Inc., 1950). While not specifically pertaining to exceptional children, quite relevant in spots. C. M. Louttit, *Clinical Psychology of Exceptional Children*, 3rd ed. (New York: Harper & Row, Publishers, 1957). Chap. iii, "Clinical Psychological Testing" is particularly relevant.

57 W. A. Hunt, "Clinical Psychology—Science or Superstition," *American Psychologist*, VI (1951), 683-687.

LEE MEYERSON[1]

Director, Somatopsychology Program
Arizona State University

3 A Psychology of Impaired Hearing

EVERYONE KNOWS what impaired hearing means. A person who does not hear sounds as well as other people has impaired hearing. This seems extremely simple; but as scientists readily learn, everything is more complex than it seems in the beginning. In this case we need ask only a few questions: What is meant by "hear"? What sounds? What other people? Under what conditions?

None of the answers is unequivocal. Hearing is a subjective phenomenon. If two listeners say they hear the same sound, we have no way of knowing that they are experiencing the same sensations. If one listener says he doesn't hear, there is no way of getting inside of him to verify his statement. It is possible to define hearing only in terms of the specific kind of stimulus, the specific way in which it was presented to the listener, and the specific kind of response that was obtained from a specific person or group.

There are many kinds of sound stimuli. There are many ways in which these stimuli can be presented. There are many ways in which a response can be observed. The hearing of a person varies with the way in which it is tested. Moreover, the results of different methods of measurement do not necessarily bear a simple or a close relationship to each other. In comparison with "other people" one may have good hearing under some conditions and poor hearing under other conditions.

Additional variation is introduced for some kinds of hearing by variables related to the person, such as pathology of the peripheral or the central auditory system, age, intelligence, education, motivation, and training. A child may have extensive ear disease without having impaired hearing, or he may have impaired hearing without having observable disease. He may have impaired hearing for pure tones but not for speech, or impaired hearing for speech but not for pure tones. He may have impaired hearing in quiet but not in noise, or impaired hearing in noise but not in quiet.

It is evident that impaired hearing presents complex problems for medicine, physiology, neurology, psychophysics, and education as well as for psychology. These disciplines, however, are not concerned with the same kinds of problems. They share the cultural heritage of the common-sense meanings of hearing, impaired hearing, and deafness, but in scientific work they either do not use these terms or they assign to them special and precise meanings. The psychologist, too, must develop concepts that have special and precise meanings.

The Problem of Relevant Variables

HEARING ACUITY is most frequently measured with a pure tone audiometer. This is an instrument calibrated to produce, at the will of the examiner, sounds of different frequency and intensity. Under ordinary conditions the subject listens for a sound transmitted to his ear by an earphone, and indicates, perhaps by raising or lowering a finger, when he hears and when he no longer hears the sound. The point at which the subject consistently responds correctly is usually considered the threshold for that frequency. Each frequency is tested separately, and each ear is tested individually for each frequency. The results are recorded on an audiogram.

These data yield one kind of basic information that is operationally related to the concept of impaired hearing. Other kinds of auditory sensitivity and discriminative abilities, in addition to the threshold of hearing for pure tones, are equally important.

For the psychologist, the ability to perceive and comprehend speech at conversational levels of intensity is one of the most crucial kinds of hearing. Much progress has been made in developing precise measures of hearing for speech,[2] and the routine use of such tests may be expected in the future. However, these measures were not used with the acoustically handicapped children who were the subjects of past psychological investigations. Even today, among children who have impaired hearing, the threshold audiogram for pure tones is often the only information available.

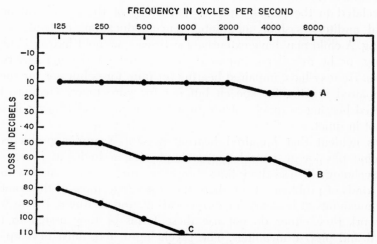

FIGURE 3-1. *Audiograms of the better ear in three individuals.*

Figure 3-1 shows a sample audiogram. It will be observed that the frequencies, in cycles per second, are plotted on a logarithmic scale. Hearing loss is plotted in decibels on a linear scale.[3] The sounds used in taking an audiogram do not represent the limits of human audition. The standard audiometric frequency scale is limited to only part of the sounds human beings can perceive. The frequencies from 100 to 8,000 cycles per second, however, are the most important for human communication.[4] Similarly, the zero line of the decibel scale does not represent the absolute threshold of normal human audition for pure tones. It is a statistical average of the best responses given by young adults as measured by a particular empirical investigation.[5]

With this brief background, consider the schematic curves, A, B, and C, which have been drawn on the audiogram blank. Let each curve represent the better ear of three separate individuals. The data show that each person has a measurable impairment of threshold hearing for pure tones, and that the three can be ranked in degree of impairment from A to C.

These curves contain some important information. While they do not tell us what the individuals can hear, they do indicate at what level pure tones are not heard. For some kinds of physiological problems, no further information is needed. Clinical, educational, and social psychologists, however, are rarely interested in threshold acuity for pure tones as such. Rather, they are concerned with the effects that a sensory impairment may have upon behavior. Psychophysical measurements are important in somatopsychology primarily as a means of simple classification. Like other quasi-psychological variables, such as skin color, religion, age, or sex, they serve as reference points for gross attributes of a particular person or group.

It must be emphasized that these attributes remain biological, physiological, or sociological. They cannot take on psychological meaning until some way is found to transform them into psychological data. In technical terms, it is necessary to discover the variables that intervene or mediate other attributes and behavior.

How can this be done for auditory sensitivity? What reference points should be used? Neither classification of the psychophysical data nor transformation into psychological data is an easy task. First, all sounds are not equally important. If a child had a total loss of hearing for all frequencies above 8,000 cycles per second, but no other impairment, he might be a medical or physiological curiosity. No one, however, would consider him a "deaf" or a "hard of hearing" person. Hearing for such high frequencies is not required in our culture except perhaps for piccolo players. The impairment would be physiologically real but, so far as we now know, psychologically meaningless. Second, for sounds that are known to be important in our culture, it is not possible to jump directly from physiological classification to psychological meaning. Cases A, B, and C have in common some degree of impairment of threshold hearing for pure tones. What can be said about them psychologically? One might venture the hypotheses that Case A can enjoy music, Case B will receive less satisfaction from music, and Case C will not enjoy music. This is not necessarily true. Case A may be "tone deaf" and not enjoy music at all. Neither hearing for music nor enjoyment is measured by the pure tone test. Case C might represent a person like Beethoven who created some of his finest symphonies after he became "deaf."

It is obvious that gross physiological hearing impairment is phenotypic for psychology. Nevertheless, we must consider two quasi-physiological classifications of acoustically handicapped children that are in common use.

The White House Conference on Child Health and Welfare proposed the following definitions: [6]

> The *deaf* are those who were born either totally deaf or sufficiently deaf to prevent the establishment of speech and natural language; those who became deaf in childhood before language and speech were established; or those who became deaf in child-

hood so soon after the natural establishment of speech and language that the ability to speak and understand speech and language has been practically lost to them.

The *hard of hearing* are those who established speech and ability to understand speech and language, and subsequently developed impairment of hearing. These children are sound-conscious and have a normal, or almost normal, attitude towards the world of sound in which they live.

The Conference of Executives of American Schools for the Deaf was strongly opposed to this classification.[7] They said the problem was simply one of auditory capacity and the only appropriate definitions were as follows:

The *deaf:* those in whom the sense of hearing is non-functional for the ordinary purposes of life. This general group is made up of two distinct classes based entirely on the time of the loss of hearing: (a) the congenitally deaf—those who were born deaf; (b) the adventitiously deaf—those who were born with normal hearing but in whom the sense of hearing became non-functional later through illness or accident.

The *hard of hearing:* those in whom the sense of hearing, although defective, is functional with or without a hearing aid.

The White House Conference definitions represent a conscious effort to apply educational and psychological meaning to the phenomena of impaired hearing. The general idea is that speech and language—activities unique to man—are basic for the subsequent development of the person. The deaf are those who can learn speech and language only by special instruction. The hard of hearing are those who have learned speech and language in the ordinary developmental way. The intent is to recognize that the educational techniques and psychological guidance of a child who has a foundation of speech and language can and should proceed along lines markedly different from the techniques used in the education of a child who must first learn speech and language in an artificial way.

According to the White House Conference definitions, the audiogram is largely irrelevant. The critical question concerns the time and the method of establishing speech and language. Application of this view leads to some paradoxical results. If Case B had his 60-decibel loss of hearing since birth, he would be called deaf; while if Case C lost his hearing at the age of twelve years, he would be called hard of hearing.

More serious is the emphasis placed upon a past event. The definitions say nothing about the child's present behavior. Some children who are born with the degree of hearing loss shown in Case C eventually acquire intelligible speech and excellent language and move into social and vocational positions in the normally hearing world. Others with the same degree of physiological hearing loss from birth never learn speech or adequate language. The two groups present striking, unmistakably different, behavioral pictures.

Similarly, a child who loses part of his hearing after speech and language are well established may be educated in such a way that both deteriorate into unintelligibility. He may identify himself and associate only with those who neither hear nor speak. He may be more "deaf" behaviorally than a child born without hearing who has artificially acquired the tools for functioning in a normally hearing world. The use of an historical scheme for classifying cases of impaired hearing can lead only to psychological confusion.

The definitions proposed by the Conference of Executives of American Schools for the Deaf have the merit of being based, in part, upon present functional auditory status. However, "functional" hearing and "ordinary purposes of life" are vague concepts that require precise description. Hearing cannot be dichotomized into discrete categories of functional and non-functional. Rather, it shades gradually along a continuous distribution. It is unlikely that hearing ever becomes non-functional short of total loss, and total loss of hearing is extremely rare. In an extensive clinical practice the author has never encountered such a case. Moreover, all of the available evidence is consistent in showing that relatively small amounts of residual hearing may serve useful functions even in children who appeared to be "deaf" from birth.[8]

The recent achievement of Wedenberg emphasizes how little we know about the variables that influence function.[9] He reported that two young children who had 99 per cent bilateral loss of hearing learned to speak spontaneously and to interpret speech through their ears after several years of intensive auditory training!

Most important, however, is the psychological confusion that results when the definitions of the Conference of Executives of American Schools for the Deaf are applied. The functioning of a child's ears is not the only or even the most important fact about him. A child with a great amount of residual hearing, like Case B, may grow up to be a finger-spelling, signing, deaf adult who lives almost entirely in the world of the deaf. Another child with relatively little residual hearing, like Case C, may grow up to be a speaking, lip-reading person who lives primarily in the psychological world of the hearing. Their behavior will be markedly different. A psychological investigation which classifies both of them as deaf because neither has functional hearing cannot fail to be misleading. Impaired hearing is the phenomenon with which the investigator may begin, but he cannot make accurate behavioral predictions from it.

If these considerations have merit, they mean that future investigators will be remiss if they "label" rather than describe their samples. In a situation where the relevant variables cannot be pinpointed with precision, there is no substitute for the fullest operational description of the subjects. *The terms "deaf" and "hard of hearing" are outgrown for scientific use. Information on multiple parameters and much finer distinctions among the attributes of individuals are necessary.*

Although all of the component factors that mediate impaired hearing and behavior are not known, the minimum acceptable description of subjects must include detailed information of the following areas: auditory status, educational status, psychological status, and sociological status. It is probable that the variables which are of critical relevance will be different for different investigations. The clinical psychologist, for example, may be concerned with what constellations of hearing abilities, in what amount, and in association with what other factors, and under what conditions are required for the learning of spontaneous speech. The social psychologist may consider impaired hearing not directly in terms of degree but rather in terms of the sorts of psychological situations it creates for individuals whose other characteristics are known and described. For all, however, the day is long since past when the pure tone, threshold audiogram could be considered sufficient in itself.

The Problem of Empirical Evidence

THERE HAVE been a great many psychological investigations of the deaf and the hard of hearing. The meaning of the findings, however, is uncertain. Much of the difficulty arises from the fact that investigators have rarely given an adequate description of the populations they studied. They have used labels such as *deaf, hard of hearing, children with auditory defects, acoustically handicapped children,* and the like without specifying the operational definitions that would make the labels meaningful. For example, it is likely that some investigators used the term "hard of hearing" when they meant children with measurable, but not necessarily handicapping, threshold losses of hearing in one ear. Others probably used the same term to indicate children whose hearing for speech was defective, but functional. A third group undoubtedly was guided by the recommendations of the White House Conference. They used "hard of hearing" to mean any child who, regardless of the degree of auditory impairment, had developed speech and language without special instruction. In other words, comparisons of results from different investigations which purported to study the same group are hazardous. Samples from different psychological universes are jumbled together.

In addition, psychologists, for the most part, are not specialists in disability. It is understandable, therefore, that when an investigator wished to study disabled children he went to a place where subjects were readily available—special classes and special schools. This means that in a very real sense we do not have good data for a psychology of exceptional children and youth. We have primarily a *sociology* of children who attended special schools and classes.

What are the characteristics of children who attend special schools for the deaf? Tabulation of pupils by degree of "functional" hearing is no longer made, but in 1954 about 20 per cent of the children were classified as hard of hearing.[10] In residential schools for the deaf with which the author is familiar, there have been children who play the piano for their own amusement and children who regularly use the telephone! This is not unusual, although the population of residential schools has been changing in recent years and it is no longer common. Beginning with the very first solid experimental study of deaf children, there has been considerable doubt about the psychological universe that was being sampled. Pintner and Paterson [11] noted that at least one of the "deaf" children they tested had "a considerable amount of hearing." He could hear "without any difficulty" when spoken to slowly and distinctly in a quiet room. The authors do not mention speaking loudly. Undoubtedly there are similar children in every school for the deaf.

In addition to subjects who have mild, moderate, or even questionable losses of hearing, the author has examined children in schools for the deaf who were feeble-minded or mentally retarded; mongoloid children; children who had congenital canities, thyroid and pituitary disorders, brain damage, aphasia, epilepsy, various kinds of cerebral palsy, impaired vision verging on blindness, and emotional disorders ranging from psychic deafness to pre-psychosis. Some of these children had physiological impairments of hearing so mild that they probably would not be handicapping if it were not for their other disabilities. Other children had severe losses of hearing, but the hearing impairment was not their greatest problem nor the major contributing source of their behavior.

In classes for the hard of hearing with which the author is familiar, there are children who have better hearing for pure tones and for speech than some other children who are progressing well in regular classes. There are also many children with less psychophysical hearing than the majority of cases in schools for the deaf.

The author knows of no psychological study of deaf subjects in which it can be said with assurance, "These children had impaired hearing and no other disability." However, progress in clarifying the issues has been made. Licklider [12] and Hirsh [13] offer able expositions of the different kinds of hearing abilities and some ways of measuring them. Myklebust [14] gives a detailed clinical procedure for distinguishing among auditory disorders due to peripheral deafness, aphasia, psychic deafness, and mental deficiency.

It is reasonable to believe that future investigators will pay more attention to these presently uncontrolled variables. We may hope for un-contaminated data upon which a psychology of impaired hearing may be built. Understanding of the presently available empirical evidence, however, requires a clear comprehension of the problem of relevant variables and of the following points:

1. Investigations that have been based upon populations attending special schools have been weighted for non-normality in respects other than hearing. Special schools do not contain unbiased samples of the universe of children with impaired hearing. Some children with impaired hearing never attend special classes. Others attend only for relatively short periods of time. These children who do not go to special schools are often children who have exceptional intelligence, academic aptitude, and social flexibility, or children who live in other kinds of highly favorable social psychological environments. They are able to attend regular public or private schools for non-disabled children, or in some cases they receive private tutoring. These able children are under-represented in institutional populations. Children who are less able, children who live in less favorable social psychological environments, and children who have multiple disabilities in addition to impaired hearing are over-represented. In other words, children who adjust readily to school work tend to go to regular schools and to remain there. "Problem children," regardless of the degree of physical disability, are easy candidates for special education.

2. Deaf children are most frequently educated in residential schools. Of the 21,545 pupils enrolled in schools and classes for the deaf in the United States in 1953, approximately 75 per cent were in institutions. In 1961, 58 per cent of 28,529 children with hearing impairments resided in institutions.[15] It is common knowledge that institutions do not offer an optimal environment for rearing children.[16] Orphanage children, for example, develop less well both mentally and physically than children living in their own homes. The full effects of institutionalization have not been completely explored, but enough is known to demonstrate that there are detrimental influences. This is not a criticism of residential schools for the deaf. Much can be done to improve such institutions in the direction of providing more favorable psychological environments. Investigation of the relative merits of special day schools, special classes, special teachers in regular schools, and other administrative arrangements for educating the deaf should also be fostered. For many children, however, the restrictions and limitations of institutionalization are but a small price to pay for the boon of education. It is far preferable to the false

freedom of growing up in ignorance, isolation, and idleness, if that is the only alternative.

When institutional children with impaired hearing are found to be different from a control group of physically normal children living in their own homes, it is impossible to determine how much of the difference is a function of impaired hearing and how much is a function of institutionalization. Studies in which institutionalized handicapped children are compared with institutionalized physically normal children are rare.

In this situation the explanatory value of comparisons between standard test norms and the scores of institutionalized deaf children is slight. Test norms almost invariably assume that subjects to whom the norms will be applied live in life situations comparable to the life situations of the group upon whom the test was standardized. Where this is not true, the meaning of the norms is uncertain. No one, for example, would assume that children of a savage tribe were feeble-minded because they achieved low scores on the Stanford-Binet Scale. The life situations of these children are different from the standardization population.

Despite these limitations on the available empirical evidence, the data offer the only starting point. The earlier investigations were not wrong or useless. They exemplify the state of psychological knowledge at the time they were made. The data and the findings must be employed not as the final words but as stepping stones to better investigations that will further increase our knowledge. Science rarely discovers a complete answer once and for all. It is a series of successive approximations in which an idea leads to some knowledge, knowledge leads to improved methodology and theory, and these in turn lead to further knowledge.

It is appropriate therefore to consider the present state of our knowledge concerning children with impaired hearing. We shall do so under three major headings: Intelligence, Educational Achievement, and Personality. The deaf and the hard of hearing will be considered separately, following the terminology used by the original investigators. The obscure meanings of these classifications should be kept in mind.

Intelligence

The deaf. Pintner and Paterson, using the Goddard Revision of the Binet-Simon Scale, found that the mean I.Q. of 18 deaf children was 63.[17] If the obviously feeble-minded cases were eliminated, the average I.Q. was raised to 73. The method of typing out the questions and having the child reply in writing was found to be ineffective because many subjects did not understand the questions. When signs and finger-spelling were used, comprehension of the questions occurred and answers could be obtained.

The investigators, however, placed little faith in their findings. They stated that the language of the questions was too difficult and that deaf children did not have the same opportunities for the life experiences that the test items assumed were common for all children. For example, some of the questions concerned stamps and money, but these deaf children rarely handled either. Inasmuch as the authors were interested in measuring intelligence and not either language ability or environmental deprivation, they concluded that verbal tests of the Binet type were unsuitable as measures of intelligence of the deaf.

Levine disagreed with this conclusion.[18] She believed that some verbal tests of intelligence can readily be used with deaf subjects and that the results provide important information about certain aspects of intellectual functioning that cannot be tapped by other kinds of tests. She administered the Wechsler Bellevue Intelligence Scale for Adolescents and Adults to thirty-one selected "normal deaf" adolescent girls. On the *verbal* portion of the scale her subjects obtained a mean I.Q. of 89.6. This is significantly lower than the mean I.Q. of the normally hearing group upon whom the test was standardized. The investigator believed that the results accurately reflected the low average "abstract" intelligence of the deaf.

Almost all other investigators have restricted their experimentation to tests that require little or no knowledge of language. These tests may be classified as follows:

(a) Individual Performance Tests. These measures require the subject to perform some action. Instructions may be given in pantomime. No language is required either from the examiner or from the subject.

(b) Group Non-Verbal and Non-Language Tests. These are paper and pencil tests that can be administered to large numbers of children at the same time. The non-verbal tests assume that the subject has enough language to comprehend the examiner's instructions. The non-language tests do not. Neither kind of test requires language or the understanding of language for successful response.

The findings of the major investigations may be summarized briefly. Compared with normally hearing "control" groups or the normally hearing children on whom the particular test was standardized, the following relative results have been reported for deaf children.

1. *Individual Performance Tests:*

(a) Lower I.Q.'s (Lyon and others,[19] MacKane,[20] Amoss,[21] Peterson,[22] Roth,[23] Zeckel and van der Kolk,[24] Morrison,[25] Capwell,[26] Johnson,[27] Oleron [28]). The median I.Q. of the means reported by these investigators was 91.

(b) I.Q.'s that were not different (Drever and Collins,[29] Schick and Meyer,[30] Schick,[31] Bishop,[32] Kirk,[33] Streng and Kirk,[34] Lane and Schneider,[35] Burchard and Myklebust,[36] Amin,[37] Lane,[38] Hood,[39] Borelli[40]). The median I.Q. of the means reported by these investigators was 100.

(c) Higher I.Q.'s (MacPherson,[41] MacPherson and Lane,[42] Levine[43]). The mean of the mean I.Q.'s reported by these investigators was 110.

2. *Group Non-Verbal and Non-Language Tests* (including the Goodenough Drawing-of-a-Man Test):

(a) Lower I.Q.'s (Reamer,[44] Day, Fusfeld and Pintner,[45] Peterson and Williams,[46] Shirley and Goodenough,[47] Lyon and others,[48] MacKane,[49] Streng and Kirk,[50] Springer,[51] Johnson[52]). The median I.Q. of the reported means was about 85.

(b) I.Q.'s that were not different (Shirley and Goodenough,[53] Louttit,[54] Kellogg,[55] Johnson[56]). The reported I.Q.'s were close to 100.

The hard of hearing. Investigations of the intelligence of hard of hearing children are in agreement that on *verbal* tests these children obtained slightly, but statistically significant, lower I.Q.'s than their normally hearing controls (Waldman, Wade and Aretz,[57] Madden,[58] Pintner and Lev[59]). The median difference reported was 5.4 I.Q. points. One investigation in which a *non-language* test was used found hard of hearing children were slightly, but not significantly, lower in intelligence (Pintner and Lev).

Educational Achievement

The deaf. Early studies of educational achievement by means of standard tests revealed that children in schools for the deaf were retarded from three to five years (Reamer,[60] Day, Fusfeld and Pintner,[61] Hall[62]). The amount of retardation increased with age, so that older deaf children were more retarded than younger children. Day, Fusfeld and Pintner reported that the educational quotient (educational age divided by chronological age) was 71 for twelve-year-olds and 67 for fifteen-year-olds. Others have reported E.Q.'s of 79 and 89.[63]

More recent investigations have supported the conclusions of the earlier work.[64] There is general agreement that greatest retardation occurs in understanding the meaning of paragraphs and words. Least retardation is found for arithmetic computation and spelling.

An excellent study by Fusfeld offers the most enlightening contemporary evidence.[65] He administered the Stanford Achievement Test, Advanced Battery, Form J, to 134 candidates for admission to the Preparatory Class (twelfth grade) associated with Gallaudet College. These students

130 LEE MEYERSON

may be considered to represent the intellectual and academic *élite* of students graduating from residential schools for the deaf. Their performance relative to the *average* child in the different grades of the test standardization population is shown in Table 3-1.

Table 3-1

School Grade Achievement of Applicants to Gallaudet College on the Stanford Achievement Test

Part	Q_1	Median	Q_3
Language	9.6	11.6	12.8
Arithmetic Computation	9.4	10.5	11.5
Spelling	9.2	10.5	11.5
Social Studies	8.3	9.9	10.7
Arithmetic Reasoning	8.1	9.4	10.8
Study Skills	6.9	8.4	10.3
Paragraph Meaning	6.8	8.2	10.0
Science	6.4	7.7	9.4
Word Meaning	5.3	6.7	9.1
Grade Equivalent for Entire Test	8.2	9.2	10.2
Range of Grade Equivalents	4.5+	to	12+

It will be seen that the median student of the 1953 Gallaudet élite attained a median grade achievement of 9.2 years. A similar finding was reported in 1929 by Hall. How much retardation this represents depends upon the interpretive criteria that are used. Fusfeld's subjects were tested in the spring before they were to enter twelfth grade. Their median grade achievement, therefore, should have been at least 11.8 years. On the other hand, less than 15 per cent of residential schools for the deaf offer instruction beyond the tenth grade. In terms of actual subject matter covered, perhaps it would be fairer to expect 10.8 years as the median grade achievement. Finally, the mean age of this group was 18.9 years (range: 14 to 26.5 years) and they had spent on the average 12.8 years (range: 8 to 17 years) in school. In other words it had taken 19-year-old students almost 13 years to reach a median grade achievement of 9.2 years. This level is reached by the average 15-year-old child. The retardation of the students applying for admission to Gallaudet College Preparatory may be variously considered to range from 1.7 to 4.8 years depending on the criterion used. The retardation of the *average* student at public residential schools for the deaf undoubtedy is much greater.

Inspection of Table 3-1 shows that retardation is not uniform in different subjects. There is a range of five years between achievement in Language and achievement in Word Meaning. Ordinarily, as Fusfeld points out, one might expect achievement in Language, Word Meaning, and Paragraph Meaning to go together. In this test, however, Language dealt with exercises in correct forms of capitalization, punctuation, and grammar, whereas Word Meaning and Paragraph Meaning required understanding of language in use. The differential achievement may reflect the essence of the present educational difficulties of the deaf. They have been taught and have learned the forms of language, but they do not grasp the meanings.

The evidence relating educational achievement to variables such as intelligence, degree of deafness, age of onset of deafness, and number of years spent in a school for the deaf is conflicting. Restudy of this problem by research adequate in methodology is urgently needed. Two findings, however, are worthy of notice. Upshall reported that children who attended day schools for the deaf made significantly greater educational gains than children who attended residential schools.[66] The difference could not be accounted for in terms of the higher intelligence, greater amount of hearing, or the later age of becoming deaf of the day school children. Johnson's data indicated that residential school children who were taught by the acoustic method had higher E. Q.'s than children of equal intelligence, amount of hearing, and age of onset who were taught by other methods.[67]

The hard of hearing. Several investigations have shown that children with defective hearing are retarded in school progress frequently, or more frequently than normally hearing children.[68]

When hard of hearing children were matched for verbal intelligence with normally hearing controls and achievement was *measured* by the Stanford Achievement Test, however, the difference between the groups was not statistically significant.[69] Sprunt and Finger argued that these findings were misleading because the matching should be done on the basis of non-verbal intelligence.[70] They found that the achievement scores of a group of hard of hearing children were significantly lower, at the four-per-cent confidence level, than the scores of normally hearing controls. This finding is in agreement with similar results obtained by Prince.[71]

Personality

The deaf. Most experimental investigations of the personality characteristics of the deaf have employed paper-and-pencil tests, questionnaires, and inventories. The results are in general agreement that, according to the test norms and interpretations derived from normally hearing children, deaf children were less well adjusted. They obtained lower scores on scales labeled "general adjustment," "school adjustment," "social adjustment and school adjustment." They obtained higher scores on scales purporting to measure characteristics such as emotional instability and neuroticism.[72]

The results of four studies using the Rorschach Test are in agreement that institutionalized deaf children gave responses that were similar to the responses of rigid, neurotic, normally hearing, non-institutionalized persons of similar chronological age.[73] The data may mean that deaf children are neurotic; that their reactions to the Rorschach Test are similar to younger, normally hearing subjects; that they are making an adequate response to their institutionalized life situation; or that different reactions to the Rorschach Test are appropriate for normal deaf children. It is not possible from the present data to determine which interpretation or combination of interpretations is most reasonable.

On the Haggerty-Olson-Wickman Behavior Rating Schedules, teachers of the deaf described their pupils as having more frequent behavior problems and less desirable character traits.[74] When deaf subjects were equated with a normally hearing control group for age, intelligence, and socioeconomic status, however, the differences disappeared.[75]

Two studies of social maturity have found that institutionalized deaf children obtained lower scores on the Vineland Social Maturity Scale than normally hearing children living in their own homes.[76] Children attending a day school for the deaf, and pre-school deaf children, however, appeared to earn normal social maturity quotients.[77]

Among the most interesting and promising of recent investigations using deaf subjects are several studies of psychological rigidity and level of aspiration behavior. *Rigidity* refers to the tendency to persist in an action that is no longer appropriate and to be unable to perceive new ways of responding to the same stimuli. For example, a child may be given nine blocks that can be classified according to color, shape, or size. A flexible child is able to classify the blocks in all three ways. A rigid child, however, classifies the blocks in just one way. He is unable to restructure his perceptions so as to see that there may be more than one right answer to the problem. Despite great pressure on the child to "do it *another* way," the child rigidly sticks to his first classification.

McAndrew and Oleron reported that institutionalized deaf children were more rigid than normally hearing children.[78] Wall found there were no differences between the two groups.[79] Johnson concluded that rigidity has many dimensions.[80] Deaf children were more rigid than hearing children on some tasks and less rigid on others. It depends upon the specific situation.

Level of aspiration refers to the situation in which a child is told his score on a task such as crossing out every letter *e* in a paragraph. He is then asked to predict what his score will be on the next trial. Maladjusted children have been found to have unrealistic levels of aspiration. They aspire too high or too low and are unable to change their aspirations in the light of their performance. Well-adjusted children tend to aspire just slightly above what they have achieved in the past and readily raise or lower their aspirations in accordance with performance.[81]

McAndrew reported that institutionalized deaf children were more rigid than normally hearing children.[82] Johnson and Rutledge, however, are in agreement that level of aspiration behavior varies with the nature of the task.[83] Sears reached the same conclusion for normally hearing children.[84] Where the task does not penalize the deaf child, his level of aspiration is not different from the hearing child.

The hard of hearing. According to all of the available evidence, hard of hearing children obtain scores on personality inventories, questionnaires, and rating scales that are markedly similar to the scores obtained by normally hearing children.[85] However, hard of hearing children may more frequently have speech defects [86] and may be named more frequently by teachers as presenting classroom problems.[87]

The Meaning of the Empirical Evidence

IT IS evident that empirical investigations result in no magical solutions. The evidence is usually contradictory. Even where the results are consistent, they must still be interpreted and evaluated. It is possible to be consistently wrong by ascribing *cause* to irrelevant or misleading variables. Evidence is relevant when it facilitates the answering of questions. The kinds of answers that are obtained, however, are functions of the kinds of questions that are asked. Investigators tend to find what they look for. One of the hardest tasks in any science is learning to ask the right questions.

Let us be clear at the outset about the kinds of questions that can be asked about children with impaired hearing. Basically there are three questions.

1. What are the characteristics of children who attend schools and classes for the acoustically handicapped?
2. What are the other characteristics of children who have impaired hearing?
3. How does impaired hearing affect behavior?

The first question is the one that past investigations have most frequently asked. It may be an important clinical and educational question. By measuring repeatedly, the school administrator is kept informed on how well his school is doing its job. If pupil achievement suddenly drops, for example, he may find an explanation for it in terms of poorer intellectual qualifications or underprivileged home environments of recently admitted students. Or perhaps he may find that there has been a sudden influx of multiple-handicapped students. If he discovers that his pupils, on the average, are socially immature, he can institute a remedial program or change some of the regulations in his school.

Repeated measurement may be considered an educational public health task. Before a problem can be solved, there must be some way of discovering that it exists. Like medical public health service reports, which supply a continuous stream of information about who is ill, of what, and where, educational public health data yield important information about the current state of affairs. Sometimes comparative information leads immediately to gains in knowledge. For example, an Australian public health physician found that an unusually large number of deaf children were born about the same time. In attempting to find an explanation for this phenomenon, he discovered that the children were conceived during an epidemic of rubella. We now know that maternal rubella during the first trimester of pregnancy is associated with deafness in the off-spring.[88] By exposing females to rubella before they reach maturity, one kind of deafness can now be prevented. Similarly, it may be found that remarkable school achievement in one class is associated with a new audio-visual aids program. By exposing all children to a similar program, the general level of achievement may be raised.

Without underestimating the importance of this kind of research, we may still raise the question of how much it contributes to our knowledge of the psychology of deafness.

What universe does the population of a special school represent? We have observed that different "kinds" of children are found in a school for the deaf and that they seem to be enrolled for different reasons. A school which admits children with I.Q.'s at the idiot [89] or imbecile levels,[90] or serves as a dumping ground for children who cannot be placed elsewhere, is a special kind of school. It is strikingly different from a school that employs a psychologist and rigorously bars mentally defective children. Obviously the group characteristics of the pupils in these schools will differ. Similarly, Pintner's finding that the more able students tend to leave special classes for the visually handicapped and the less able remain is probably true of the acoustically handicapped also.[91]

This is the rock upon which many, if not most, investigations have floundered. In itself it may account for a large portion of the discrepancies among the different investigations. The available findings do not represent the universe of children with impaired hearing. In many cases no generalizations are permissible beyond the specific group that was tested. Moreover, it seems certain that the evidence will change with changes in school procedures. The trend is already evident. Later studies present a more favorable picture of the deaf than earlier reports. It is likely that the available data reflect to a far greater degree our ignorance of how to rear children with impaired hearing than they reflect any inherent characteristics of the deaf. As more schools add psychologists to their staffs and the atypical but not deaf children are gradually assigned to other institutions, as parent training programs increase, as pre-school education becomes more widespread, as improved hearing aids and methods of auditory training enable deaf children to attend classes for the hard of hearing and hard of hearing children to attend regular schools; as all these occur, it would be suprising if changes in the measured characteristics of acoustically handicapped children did not also occur.

The question concerning the other characteristics of children with impaired hearing is also one that is worthy of investigation. The considerations noted above apply to this question as well if the cases are selected by reason of their membership in special schools or classes. However, there have been some investigations of acoustically handicapped children in which school classification was not a variable.

It will be agreed that the physical characteristics of hearing-handicapped children are not of direct concern to the psychologist who is attempting to establish a psychology of impaired hearing as distinct from a sociology of impaired hearers. If it were established that deaf children have visual impairments [92] or some other physical disorder more frequently than other children, that would be interesting and helpful to the clinical psychologist. There is no reason to believe, however, that visual impairment is a function of auditory impairment. The two impairments may be independent, or they may be related only via a third variable. Such findings, therefore, contribute little to a psychology of impaired hearing. Children with multiple defects present separate and special problems. Only by isolating the relevant variables can it be determined what behavior is a function of auditory impairment, what behavior is a function of visual impairment, and what behavior is a function of both occurring together.

The "other" characteristics with which the psychologist must be concerned are psychological characteristics. Here also, however, great care must be exercised in identifying the *sources* of psychological behavior. If a child becomes both deaf and mentally defective as a result of meningitis, we cannot ascribe his impaired mental functioning to deafness. The behavior of mentally retarded deaf children is of interest, but if a particular experimental sample is loaded with such children, the significance of deafness as an independent variable may be obscured.

Similarly, sociological controls are needed. If (a) 29.6 per cent of the deaf are children of farmers,[93] and (b) farmers make up only 18.7 per cent of the general population, and (c) children of farmers, as a group, have lower I.Q.'s than others, and (d) deaf children, as a group, have lower I.Q.'s than others, then (e) the lower I.Q.'s of deaf children cannot be ascribed to the influence of deafness unless a correction is made for the excess number of farmers' children among the deaf.

The student will readily think of comparable examples that apply to the hard of hearing. For instance, the frequency of moderately impaired hearing as a result of disease is said to be greater among children of lower-class parents than among others. Perhaps lower-class parents are less able to purchase adequate medical care for minor physical disorders, or perhaps they do not understand the importance of preventive medicine. In any event, some studies have found that hard of hearing children show significantly greater school retardation than others, and it is well established that children of lower-class parents, on the average, show less progress in school than children of middle-class parents. If it is true that hard of hearing children are significantly retarded in school progress, what other data are needed in order to evaluate this information?

This extended discussion of the association of impaired hearing with other characteristics has been made to emphasize the dangers of drawing direct conclusions from empirical relationships. Where the relevant variables are not known, it is always a great temptation to draw conclusions from the obvious.

Among the Greeks, it was obvious that the deaf *were* ignorant and unlearned. It was concluded, therefore, that they *could not* learn. It is reported that in some Greek cities deaf infants were systematically exposed to die.[94] Within the time of living men, it was equally obvious that the deaf did not speak. The *did not* was interpreted to mean *could not*.

We know better today, but the same point of view arises repeatedly in ever-new form. It has been established empirically that as of today the deaf appear to be stronger in motor and mechanical ability than in verbal intelligence and academic achievement. An eminent scientist concluded, therefore, that "for most deaf children the emphasis should be on the motor, the mechanical, the concrete. . . . Shopwork, home economics, trade training of all kinds, dramatics, gardening . . . would be the main subjects." [95]

As a matter of present educational policy such a course may have much to recommend it. Its ultimate result, however, would be to establish a group of second-class citizens. It must be emphasized that all of the data are not in, and much of the evidence available we do not fully understand. As in the past, it is probable that the deaf have the ability to learn but the culture in which they live lacks the ability to provide conditions under which learning may occur. Investigations of "other" present characteristics of the deaf can contribute little to the solution of this problem.

One kind of question remains: What effects does impaired hearing have upon behavior? It seems to the author that this is the only relevant question upon which a psychology of impaired hearing can be based. It is a dynamic question in which only the forces that are operating in the present need be considered.

An advantage of this kind of formulation is that it makes no assumptions concerning inherent characteristics *in* a person. Rather, the emphasis is upon the constellation of variables in particular situations that coerce certain kinds of behavior. Knowledge is power. When the dynamic relationships become known, it is reasonable to believe that understanding and control of behavior will be possible. The task of the future is to determine what psychological variables are dynamically related to what behavior. Changes in behavior in desired directions will then become possible and controllable by the introduction of changes in the psychological situation.

Psychologists, of course, will have to assign more precise meanings to the concept of impaired hearing as a means of identifying the group to be studied. Some descriptive ways of doing this have already been suggested. More fundamentally, it seems to the author that a minor revolution will occur in the next decade in the somatopsychology of impaired hearing. It is becoming clearly evident that the medical problems of diseased ears and the psychological problems of impaired ability to communicate are separate and distinct. In the future psychologists will pay less attention to gross physiological auditory sensitivity and more attention to the psychological situation as it exists for the person. Physical disabilities will be perceived as part of a physical situation which *may* frequently create extremely difficult psychological situations for the person. The emphasis will not be upon the disability but upon behavior. This means, for example, that for psychological investigations deaf subjects will be not classified initially according to the type of medical pathology, degree of physical impairment, time of onset, or other non-psychological variables. They will be classified according to the properties of the psychological situations in which they live and behave.

Auding. Hearing for speech undoubtedly will become a central concept. Great efforts will be made to measure this function precisely and to uncover the variables upon which it depends. Appreciable progress toward this end has already been made.[96] It seems clear that the psychological function of hearing for speech, which the author has termed *auding*, is one way of transforming the physical data into psychological data. The psychologist will study all children who have impairments in auding. It does not matter initially whether the impairment is associated with diseased ears or not. Impaired auding ability presumably has similar psychological effects regardless of its origin. It is these behavioral effects, which he can deal with effectively, that the psychologist must study.

Different kinds of remedial work, of course, may be necessary for different children. The relatively small number of children with treatable medical pathology, for example, should be examined by physicians. The remainder may be helped by psychological and educational methods.

The situation is similar to the problem of impaired reading ability. No one now seeks to discover poor readers by measuring their visual acuity. Impaired reading ability may be related to many variables. The psychologist studies them all after first classifying his subjects as poor readers. Some children need visual corrections; the great majority have impaired reading ability because of other than physiological reasons.

It is only a matter of time before a similar transformation will occur with respect to auding. It seems probable that the future will see as many school hours devoted to auding and to remedial auding as are now devoted to reading and remedial reading. Two great discoveries of our time are that hearing for speech is learned and that it can be taught.

If this view of the psychological significance of impaired hearing has merit, a vast new and fruitful field for research will be opened. The problem of 20,000 American deaf children who may have no auding ability is relatively insignificant by comparison with the larger number whose auding is impaired but remediable.

For the deaf and those who cannot learn to aud well, additional quasi-psychological subclassifications may continue to be necessary. Classifications based on speech and lip-reading ability, place of residence, level of aspiration, values, and other variables will be required. For example, if two children cannot aud, speak, lip read, or communicate by language, they must be classified psychologically according to their present abilities and the kinds of psychological situations to which they are exposed. It does not matter if they have different degrees of hearing loss for pure tones or if the time of onset was different. For a psychology of impaired hearing, their situations are similar. It does matter if one is taught from infancy in an "oral" environment and the other is not. Their situations, then, are different.

Similarly, if two children have equivalent degrees of hearing loss for pure tones, but one can aud, speak, and communicate by language, and one cannot, psychological clarity requires that they be classified differently.

There are other behavioral variables also, but these are basic. By classifying according to the behavior and the situation, it may then be possible for future investigations to determine what constellations of variables are necessary for what kinds of outcomes. The present evidence indicates that a child may be well adjusted regardless of the method by which he is taught, the way in which he communicates, or his place of residence. If that is true, the persistent problem of what kind of teaching method—acoustic, oral, manual, combined, or simultaneous—or what kind of school—regular, special or residential—is *best,* can be seen to be meaningless. The psychological classification that has been proposed will facilitate a systematic attack on the more meaningful problem of what kind of education, for whom, at what time, leads to what results. Comparative studies of children with known and fully described characteristics who live in different environments will be seen in the light of their true importance. Testable theories of minimal determinants which are required for different kinds of educational and clinical treatments and for different ultimate growths would greatly assist the investigative process.

Against the background of this reasoning, it may be helpful to consider what meanings should be assigned to the experimental findings. Other things being equal, it would be reasonable to place more faith and more emphasis on those studies in which the number of subjects was larger, in which some effort had been made to attain representativeness, and in which some control of irrelevant variables was obtained. As we have seen, however, other things have not been equal or even relevant.

The following conclusions appear to be reasonable:

1. Most samples of deaf children obtained markedly lower scores on measures of intelligence, educational achievement, and personality than the groups with which they were compared. There is marked disagreement, however, concerning non-verbal intelligence and some aspects of personality.

2. The particular samples of hard of hearing children obtained slightly lower scores, often not statistically significant, on measures of intelligence, educational achievement, and personality than the groups with which they were compared.

3. There is no convincing evidence that hearing impairment is directly or necessarily related to intelligence, educational achievement, or personality.

The major reasons for the apparent paradox of the last conclusion have already been outlined. Some further considerations, however, may be of interest.

The Deaf

The measurement of intelligence is based upon the following assumptions:

(a) the children to be tested have lived in similar past environments;
(b) they have had similar interests; and
(c) they have had equal opportunities to explore these interests.

These assumptions are not true for deaf children in general or for institutionalized deaf children in particular. When a verbal test of intelligence is administered to deaf children, the results show that the deaf have not progressed well in one kind of subject matter—language. Predictions from these tests to performance on other kinds of learning and problem-solving tasks are rarely supported. Moreover, when deaf adolescents have an understanding of language equivalent to that of the average eighth-grade child, at least one study shows that they did not do less well on a collegiate-level verbal test of intelligence than others.[97] In view of their other experiential limitations, this is remarkable.

With respect to performance and non-language tests of intelligence, part of the confusion can be readily resolved. Two of the studies which showed that the deaf have higher performance I.Q.'s than others, used speech-defective children as controls.[98] These controls had delayed speech, spastic speech, motor aphasia, and other symptoms that are not typical of intellectually normal children. In the remaining study, the investigator pointed out that the test items were similar to materials which had been used in the education of deaf children.[99] In other words, the superior performance of the deaf might easily have been a function of practice.

The discrepancy among the other studies may be ascribed to the following variables:

1. Low correlations between different tests of intelligence. This has been reported by many investigators for both deaf subjects and for hearing subjects. The only operational definition for intelligence is that it is whatever the intelligence tests measure. Different intelligence tests have been constructed and standardized in different ways, and they may measure somewhat different functions. Birch and Birch reported that five tests commonly used with the deaf gave different results.[100] Children classified as mentally retarded on some tests earned superior and gifted scores on others. Theoretically, it seems quite feasible to devise a test of "intelligence" upon which deaf children might consistently attain superior scores.

2. Differences in the samples of deaf children tested with respect to institutionalization, environmental conditions, frequency of multiple handicaps, and socioeconomic groups from which drawn.

3. Differences in the control groups with which the deaf subjects were compared.

From a positive standpoint, if impaired hearing makes a difference in measured intelligence, one might expect that congenitally deaf children would test lower than the adventitiously deaf, that children who became deaf early in life would test lower than children who became deaf later in life, and that children with greater impairments in hearing would test lower than children who had lesser impairments. The available evidence is almost unanimous that this does not occur. It is not possible to give a precise estimate of a person's intelligence from knowledge of his hearing loss or the age at which it was incurred. Moreover, it is known that some deaf children are highly superior intellectually. This, in itself, leads toward the conclusion that deafness alone does not prohibit normal or superior intellectual growth. Many investigators have identified the normal, non-language I.Q.'s obtained by the deaf as "concrete" intelligence as contrasted to a higher form of "abstract" intelligence that presumably is measured by verbal tests.[101] However, if deaf subjects who have adequate language are not inferior on verbal tests of intelligence, this is just another way of saying that in our culture language may be associated with the ability to abstract, and the deaf are inferior in language.

Whether language is invariably associated with abstract thinking is doubtful. Eberhart [102] and Borelli [103] showed that the world of the deaf child is organized beyond the concrete level. In the beginning, at least, language is not necessary for abstraction. The young deaf child learns words for ideas that he already has. The ability of deaf adults, who have limited language, to perform adequately on complex tasks like automobile repairing, points in the same direction. Visual abstraction may occur without being mediated by language.

Variables other than deafness may bear upon this problem also. Institutionalized, normally hearing boys [104] and other kinds of isolated children [105] obtain better non-verbal than verbal I.Q.'s. Further research to determine the contributing effects of institutionalization and social isolation upon the abstract intelligence of the deaf would be desirable.

The evidence on the educational achievement of the deaf is clear cut. Deaf children are hindered in learning the language in which they are instructed. It is not surprising, therefore, that deaf groups, normal in other respects, may learn less. Again, however, we must note that the relationship between deafness and language is not necessarily simple or invariable. Some congenitally deaf individuals have a superior command of language. Some have earned college degrees with a major in English. Others are employed as editors, press agents, and salesmen. Deaf persons who are able to speak and read fluently in several languages are not unknown.

Assigning meaning to the educational data is complicated by at least three other variables: (a) experiential and social deprivations; (b) institutionalization; and (c) methods of instruction.

Consider some deprivations of the early years of the deaf. They miss the constant flow of auditory language in which the normally hearing child is immersed. They may also be deprived of verbal play and other kinds of warm social contact with the adults in their environments. As they grow older, they learn relatively little until they begin school. Then they must first learn a socially approved means of communication before they can learn other things. The language deprivation is obviously great, and some have felt that heroic steps must be taken to overcome it. In some pre-school classes attempts are made, with some success, to teach four-year-olds to read. Formal schooling at such a tender age, however, hampers normal play experiences and may be considered an additional deprivation imposed on top of the deprivations associated with deafness.

It is not known what results might be achieved if all deaf children were taught finger spelling from infancy and encouraged rather than restrained from using the natural gestures of childhood. Proponents of the oral method contend that a visual medium of communication would be so easy and attractive to deaf children that they would resist learning speech and language. The able description by Hofsteater of his own education does not support this view.[106] In the present climate of opinion, however, it is unlikely that the effects of enlarging the child's experiential world by this means will be tested. Fortunately, it may not be necessary. The tremendous growth of the pre-school movement and the emphasis upon auditory training in infancy for deaf children may change appreciably the future picture of the educational achievement of the deaf. Stone and Fine, and others have shown that pre-school training for the deaf can be conducted along lines that are similar to any well-run nursery school.[107] The results, in terms of skills acquired, depth of learning, and freedom from rigid, drilled, submissive behavior, are not poorer and may be better than the results obtained by early formal instruction.

For the present and past generations of the deaf upon whom the test results were obtained, language and communication skills have lagged far behind intelligence, chronological age, and interests. This situation has presented difficult problems in finding appropriate teaching materials which are not too difficult in language to be understood. Anyone who has observed the boredom of deaf adolescents as they struggled through reading materials intended for much younger children will not find it difficult to understand one reason why the educational retardation of the deaf has seemed to increase with age.

The pernicious effects associated with institutionalization must again be mentioned. It is well established that children who live in institutional environments are among the most seriously retarded in language development.[108] This is not to say that institutionalization *accounts* for the language difficulties of the deaf. Obviously, that is not true. Day-school deaf children also have language problems, but they appear to be less serious.[109]

Consider, finally, methods of teaching the deaf. At one time it seemed obvious that since speech could be broken down into component sounds, the individual sounds were basic. The atomistic sounds were taught hand in hand with the alphabet. It was ultimately discovered that it was quite possible for a child to be able to say individual sounds perfectly, in isolation, and yet be unable to put them together to make speech.

There is general agreement today that better progress is made when larger "whole" units are taught. The whole, psychologically meaningful act has properties that are different from the sum of the individual parts. The advantages of "whole" or gestalt methods of instruction, however, and the techniques for implementation, have yet to be discovered in many areas of the education of the deaf.

These are but several of the relatively unexplored variables that must be investigated before it can be concluded that deafness in itself prevents adequate educational progress. At present it seems reasonable to believe that the deaf have greater potentialities than their group achievement scores indicate.

The problem for the future is to determine in what degree lesser educational achievement is necessarily related to deafness and to what degree it may be overcome by improved educational methods.

The evidence on the personality of the deaf, like the evidence on intelligence and educational achievement, must be treated with great caution. As in the other areas, the assumptions implicit in personality tests are not met when the subjects are deaf children. In addition, inasmuch as almost all of the studies were methodologically inadequate with respect to sampling, administrative technique, and use of controls, their conclusions cannot be accepted as demonstrated.[110]

The most reasonable conclusion seems to be that deafness is not directly related to personality in the sense that it requires a particular kind of adjustment. Different kinds of specific behavior may be necessary to cope with the special situations that are imposed by impaired hearing. These are not necessarily poorer or less desirable kinds of behavior. They may be of equal value with respect to orientation to reality, stability, and maturity. It is noteworthy that the experimental evidence is invariably more favorable to the deaf when institutionalization was controlled. The best controlled studies show the fewest differences between the deaf and others. It is a reasonable expectation that as other variables are controlled it will be possible to understand how physically impaired hearing may exert psychological effects. When the process by which impaired hearing is mediated into behavior is better understood, measures of control may become feasible.

The Hard of Hearing

Little meaning can be assigned to the experimental findings on hard-of-hearing children because of great uncertainty about the nature of the populations that were sampled. It can be said only that the results apply to whatever populations the samples represented.

Early investigators often used the 4A audiometer in combination with the 2A audiometer to identify cases of impaired hearing. However, Meyerson has shown that the 4A audiometer test was an unreliable measure of whatever it was that was tested.[111] The 2A audiometer, like present-day tests of threshold, pure tone hearing, screened out children with physiological impairments that may or may not have had psychological significance. Sometimes the impairment was in one ear only. Sometimes the impairment was measurable, but the subjects were unaware that they had it. Sometimes the impairment was found in two or three frequencies beyond the speech range and apparently did not affect hearing for speech. It is not reasonable to consider such subjects hard of hearing in any psychologically meaningful sense.

Additional investigations are urgently needed in which the characteristics of the subjects and their situations are better described. Identification of subjects by tests of auding ability may be more meaningful for psychological and educational investigations than other measures. It seems essential that the strait jacket of physiological measurements for psychological variables be broken.

In addition, to the extent that intelligence, educational achievement and personality are related to parental social class, economic status, and occupational status—either directly via heredity or indirectly via the opportunities that different "kinds" of parents are able to provide for children—judgments of the former cannot be made without consideration of the latter. As the author has noted elsewhere, "Where a difference is found between disabled and non-disabled samples, the difference may not be interpreted as due to the disability if differences on other significant variables were not controlled." [112]

The Problem of Adjustment

DESPITE OUR relative lack of knowledge concerning the ways in which impaired hearing may directly influence behavior, the psychologist is not powerless in dealing with some practical problems of adjustment. Impaired hearing in this section refers to the impairment ("hard of hearing") or loss ("deaf") of a tool for behavior. It may be considered operationally as the limited or absent ability to speak and understand the speech of others. In our culture, individuals who have such impairments may be placed more frequently in special kinds of psychological situations. It is with these situations that the psychologist must be concerned rather than with the degree of physiological impairment directly. If the relevant variables have been correctly identified, this is one line along which future psychological progress will develop.

One effect of the loss of a tool for behavior is that it more frequently places a person in new psychological situations. The maladjusting consequences of new psychological situations which were described in Chapter 1 will occur in cases of impaired hearing also. The same solution for the reduction of maladjustment is indicated: reduce newness.

The easiest way to reduce newness is to remove, limit, or replace with a substitute tool, the impairment that acts as a barrier to the structuring of new regions. Sometimes auditory training combined with a hearing aid and instruction in lip reading will serve these functions. Often, however, they will not.

We must face realistically the fact that in the light of our present knowledge, and for a long time to come, the communication barrier for deaf children is not going to be removed. Many will not be able to learn speech and lip reading. Some who do will find they are not able to function satisfactorily in a normally hearing world, or that the effort required to meet normal communication standards is greater than the value of the benefits obtained.

If this is true, other ways of reducing newness should be studied. It may be beneficial for those with impaired hearing not to enter some new situations where the possibility of successful structuring is slight. In other situations it may be desirable for the counsellor to give specific help in structuring. Educators and psychologists in special schools and classes can do much more than has been done in the past in preparing acoustically handicapped children for the life situations they will later face.

Another effect of the loss of a tool for behavior is that it may more frequently place a person in antagonistic, overlapping role situations. Several of the possible kinds of overlapping role situations are shown in Figure 3-2.

Adjustment Pattern 1

Figure 3-2*a* shows a type of adjustment pattern that is selected by many. These individuals withdraw to the relatively small, restricted, but safe, life spaces provided by clubs of the deaf and societies for the hard of hearing. They reject and are rejected by the world of the normally hearing. Their major goals and aspirations are confined to situations in which they can function at equal advantage with the hearing.

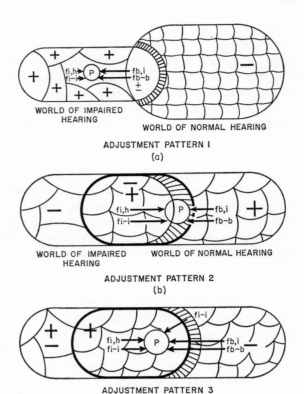

fi,h   Force in world of impaired hearing toward world of hearing
fi-i   Force in world of impaired hearing away from world of impaired hearing
fb,i   Force in barrier toward world of impaired hearing
fb-b   Force in barrier region away from barrier region

FIGURE 3-2. *Varieties of adjustment patterns.*

The amount of overlap or commonality with the life space of the normally hearing is slight. The valence of the overlap is simultaneously positive and negative. It is positive because some areas, like earning a living, cannot often be restricted to the psychological world of impaired hearing. It is negative because a situation open equally to hearers and impaired hearers often requires the impaired hearers to function at a disadvantage. For example, the deaf individual in applying for a job is not certain whether he will be evaluated negatively as a deaf person or positively as a person who has the necessary skills for the position. Because of the communication barrier he is often less able to present his qualifications in a favorable light.

Similarly, a person with impaired hearing may enjoy driving his car—a region that is open to both groups—but if he has an accident, his case may be prejudged because of unwarranted assumptions about the influence of hearing on driving skills. It is not surprising that many deaf individuals perceive safety in a small and restricted but well-organized world.

Adjustment Pattern 2

Figure 3-2b shows the life space of a person who rejects the world of impaired hearing and aspires to the world of the normally hearing. He desires to do exactly the same things as the normally hearing and in exactly the same way. As in 3-2a, however, the ability and social barriers to participation in the world of the normally hearing are strong. Individuals who select this adjustment pattern live on the barrier between two ways of life—a world whose goals are relatively inaccessible to them and a world whose goals they reject. Sometimes the efforts of an extremely able person are strikingly successful. He is admitted to some limited areas of the normal world where others who have similar disabilities are not accepted. It is not always certain that the gains achieved are in proportion to the amount of effort that has been required to attain them. For others who are less able or in less favorable social situations the barriers are never breached, even after a lifetime of intensive effort and years of insecurity and anxiety.

Adjustment Pattern 3

Figure 3-2c is a schematic representation of the life space of a person who eagerly enters and values the large area of commonality that exists between those who have impaired hearing and those who have normal hearing. Such a person perceives himself as one who shares many behavioral areas with others. Impaired hearing is correctly perceived to be only one of his characteristics: he has many others. For example, he may be a bowler, an amateur photographer, a professional printer, a parent, and a worker for the Community Chest. Hearing does not necessarily have a central position in these activities. The person may feel as able to participate in them as normally hearing individuals.

Other activities which require hearing can be entered by different methods. A lecture can be listened to, translated into signs, or written down. The same goal can be reached by a variety of methods.

The special activities in the psychological world of impaired hearing are accepted also as additional regions for rich and fruitful living. For example, a hard of hearing man may attend a special class in lip reading —an activity not usually entered by those with normal hearing, but of interest and value to him. A deaf person may attend an alumni meeting of his state school and communicate with some of his friends by means of signs and finger spelling.

These special activities may have negative as well as positive valence for some. The negative valence may arise because the person perceives the negative values that are attached to impaired hearing in our culture. If deaf people are considered inferior, and if it is true that a person is judged by the company he keeps, participation in the special activities of the deaf may have clear negative components.

There is no uncertainty, however, about the special areas that require hearing for participation. The person whose life space is represented in Figure 3-2c rejects them. He does not attend musical concerts simply to show that he behaves like "normal" people. He has no desire to play the piano like a typewriter. He does not aspire to jobs such as telephone operator, radio announcer, or opera singer. He perceives clearly that specific ways of behaving may be different without being "better" or "worse."

There are numerous other arrangements of commonality, barriers, and valences. The three that have been outlined, however, may be considered examples of the major types.

Which adjustment pattern is best? This is a question that cannot be answered by a scientific psychology. The solution must be approached through a philosophy of counselling.

The Problem of Counselling

It is not usually the function of the counsellor to advise that one pattern of adjustment is "better" than another. This is a problem that every person should be free to decide for himself. It is the function of the counsellor, like the scientific advisor in any field, to understand the field forces that affect behavior and to help apply them to the individual case.

The patterns of adjustment that have been outlined are all useful, but for different purposes. Their suitability depends in large part upon the cognitive, perceptual, and motor capacities of the behaving person; upon his needs, tensions, strengths, and skills; and upon the host of variables that may be specific to his situation.

Undoubtedly there are some individuals who are exceptionally able in using cues other than hearing to structure new psychological situations quickly. Others may have greater tolerance for the ambiguity of overlapping psychological roles. The good counsellor helps the client to discover his own needs and abilities and to match them to the best fitting adjustment pattern. The type of adjustment that may be satisfying and self-actualizing for a congenitally deaf child of average ability may be highly inappropriate and unrewarding for a recently deafened war veteran. There is no one best pattern.

Adjustment Pattern 1

Adjustment Pattern 1 is often called "withdrawal" and condemned as undesirable by practically all except those who practice it. It is a threat to many normally hearing people because it amounts to challenging the values of the normally hearing world as the only values or the best values. It is a claim that one can live a full and happy life without speech, without lip reading, and with limited language that is communicated by finger spelling, signs, and writing.

Is it "better" to be a big frog in a small and quiet puddle or a small frog in a big and dangerous pond? The answer depends more on the values and philosophy of the person who judges than upon the objective situation. Psychology can only point out the consequences of each role.

It is evident that the psychological world of impaired hearing is smaller and less well differentiated than the world of hearing. There is safety in it, however. The demands upon the person are fewer, more readily anticipated and more easily met.

Withdrawal is not necessarily an undesirable or maladjusted reaction. In many cases it is appropriate and realistic. In some degree it decreases the opportunities for varied satisfactions and gratifications. However, it also solves the problem of antagonistic overlapping role situations.

Advantages and Consequences of Adjustment Pattern 1

The deaf individual who chooses *Adjustment Pattern 1* knows clearly the group to which he belongs and the role that he will play. In great measure he is protected from conflict, insecurity, frustration, and the anxiety and humiliations that are a consequence of trying to compete on equal terms with unequal tools. He does not devaluate himself as an inferior person because he cannot meet normal standards for speech and hearing, nor does he pursue the ghost of a different, but not necessarily better, ideal—the life of a normally hearing person. Within his world he may find understanding, friendship, love, status, success, and other gratifications that might never fall to his lot as a marginal person.

He does not carry the burden of trying to behave "as if" he had normal hearing. The boundaries of his world are clear. He is able to accept help when it is needed without feeling inferior. He refuses to judge himself as a person, or to allow himself to be judged, only on tasks where he is inferior because he lacks the appropriate tools. He insists that other qualities and abilities, for which he has adequate tools, are equally important. From a psychological standpoint such an adjustment is based upon reality. It may not be optimal but it is not unhealthy unless the scope for behavior is unduly restricted.

It is significant that many of the adult deaf, including some who have been educated in oral schools, seem eventually to fall into this pattern. They maintain stoutly that as persons they are "just as good" as hearing people, that signs and finger spelling are "just as good" as speech, and that pad and pencil are "just as good," or better, for effective communication as lip reading. They appear to have a strong group "we-feeling," and are active in defending what they consider their inalienable rights.

The relative narrowness of the deaf world, and the tendency toward egocentricity and provinciality that it induces in its inhabitants, should not be overlooked. Neither, however, should it be unduly exaggerated. The deaf are often pictured as miserable, maladjusted, isolated individuals who are burdens to themselves, their parents, and their community. Nothing could be farther from fact. Within the psychological world of the deaf, once it and its values are accepted, there are numerous opportunities for self-fulfillment. Because they are not widely publicized, normally hearing people are often unaware that these opportunities exist.

The deaf hold numerous social events and have many clubs and organizations for varied interests. For example, in New York City the Union League of the Deaf is so large that it occupies a building which rents for $6,000 a year. The deaf publish their own magazines and newspapers. They own their own insurance company. They sponsor a periodic World Conference of the Deaf and a World Deaf Olympics in addition to regular nation-wide and regional conventions in the United States. They have their own churches and spiritual advisors. They love, work, and play in ways which do not appear dynamically different from the way others do these things. Their family life does not appear to be less stable. Their children—both deaf and hearing—are often outstandingly successful by any standards. As a group they are employed, law-abiding, home-owning, respectable members of their communities.

Unlike some other disabled groups they have always taken care of their own social service work. It is not a grammatical error that leads them to call their organizations Clubs *of* the Deaf. It is their way of emphasizing that they are not the recipients of other people's charity. They have organized and supported these clubs themselves, with relatively little help from the normally hearing. Their disability is deafness, not incompetence. They are vigilant in combatting the small group of deaf peddlers or beggars who try to trade upon their deafness and thereby infringe upon the good name and self-respect of other deaf people.

Their independence is shown in other ways also. In recent years when

Senator Langer of North Dakota proposed that the deaf be permitted an additional $600 income tax exemption, similar to what is now allowed the blind, the organizations for the deaf were unanimous in opposition. They successfully killed the bill with their statement that they wished no favors. There are practically no legal benefits for the deaf, in contrast to many special privileges for the blind, for example.

This description, of course, has meaning largely for deaf children who grow up to identify themselves with the deaf. It is not an easy process. An analogy is sometimes made between the disabled and other types of social and cultural minority groups. This is only an analogy, however, and must not be pushed too far. Most deaf children are born to normally hearing parents, and not infrequently they have normally hearing siblings. The deaf child, especially outside of the larger cities, may not be a member of a minority group. He may be simply an isolated and rejected individual without group support. For years he may not know that there are others like him in the world. He may be the recipient of ambivalent and hostile attitudes. His parents may feel guilty over having brought a defective child into the world. Their oversolicitude or rejection may fail to meet his needs for social and emotional approval until the child stigmatizes himself as inferior, unworthy, or evil. Unlike members of religious or racial minority groups, which have a high degree of continuity and tend to encourage group pride and group belongingness,[113] he actually has no group with which he can identify. He has no group support to sustain his courage and reinforce his claim of equal worthiness. He is a maverick, subject to all the psychological forces that act upon mavericks and ugly ducklings. His parents and sibs are likely to be normally hearing and to maintain the standards of the normally hearing.

Even schooling may not change this situation. In many schools for the deaf he and his classmates are evaluated in terms of the degree to which they meet hearing standards. There may be no deaf teachers to serve as models for an ego-ideal. If there is a conflict between adjusting to self and adjusting to a normally hearing society, the former must yield.

For many children it is not until after they leave school that they have an opportunity to choose their own adjustment pattern. Then, however, they encounter additional problems. Unlike the Negro, who is often discriminated against from childhood and may learn to cope with it, the disabled child frequently lives in an outwardly protective and sentimental environment. Many of us have different attitudes toward sweet and "helpless" handicapped children than toward the grosser disabled adult. Benedict has ably described, in another context, the devastating psychological effects of such cultural discontinuities.[114] It is not until post-school experience that the deaf child encounters the full force of the hostility and discrimination that is directed against his group. From the standpoint of mental hygiene, fewer problems might arise if deaf and other kinds of physically disabled children were actually members of a psychological minority group from birth.

A second problem the child faces is that the world of the deaf does overlap with the world of the hearing. The deaf person must live and work in a world that is composed largely of non-deaf individuals. If he does not wish to cut himself off from family and from sources of livelihood, he must make an effort to meet some of the standards of others. Apparently this can usually be done. The individuals who employ *Adjustment Pattern 1*, like normally hearing people in similar psychological situations, can comply with foreign standards without placing a high value on them or considering them better than their own.

Although the *deaf* child has been used in this discussion as a basic frame of reference, it must not be thought that *Adjustment Pattern 1* is limited to the deaf. There is in much lesser degree a psychological world of the hard of hearing also. There are some individuals whose entire lives seem to revolve about the activities of the local Society for the Hard of Hearing.

It must be noted, also, that the suitability of *Adjustment Pattern 1* is not necessarily dependent upon the degree of hearing loss. A child may have a great amount of residual hearing, passable speech, and fair lip-reading ability, but he may lack other qualifications for living in a normally hearing world. If he has lived a marginal and frustrating life of failure and humiliation during his school years, he may wish to enter the world of the deaf where greater satisfactions may be open to him. He may live thereafter as a deaf person who has some hearing rather than as a psychologically hearing person whose auding is impaired. In some cases that the author has counselled, this kind of adjustment has seemed to be the most realistic and appropriate.

Adjustment Pattern 2

In *Adjustment Pattern 2*, there are also positive and negative aspects. On the one hand, the psychological world may be larger and better differentiated. On the other hand, the person may be uncertain about the boundaries of his world, about the group to which he belongs, and about his status in the world of the normally hearing. This pattern is often considered "best" by the normally hearing. It is an affirmation that the role of the normally hearing person is preferable. It does not challenge the values of the dominant majority. The person who employs this pattern is frequently perceived to have "spunk" and courage. He does not withdraw from the activities of the dominant world. He fights and compensates. Because of his impaired hearing, or to make up for it, he tries to be better than others. By identifying himself with values of the majority and rejecting the values of the deaf minority, he hopes to escape the imputation of inferiority and the underprivileged status that is the fate of other individuals with impaired hearing.

The counsellor must remember that the social and ability barriers are not completely impermeable. They can be breached. Sometimes because of exceptional skills, exceptional wealth, or exceptional social connections, the barriers are successfully penetrated. For example, one would not ordinarily expect a deaf man to be a psychiatrist,[115] a dentist, a heart specialist, a professor, or a world famous advertising executive.[116] Yet there are adventitiously deafened men who are successfully functioning in these roles. Congenitally deaf men, known to the author, are successfully functioning among the normally hearing as insurance salesmen, engineers, medical illustrators, editors, bacteriologists, librarians, cartographers, and chemists.

Among the hard of hearing, other things being equal, one would hardly expect to find a popular singer like Johnnie Ray. Other things equal, a position that requires frequent and effective oral communication on delicate problems is not entirely suitable for a hard of hearing person. Since other things are not equal, however, we have had as an able Assistant Secretary of State, a long-time hearing-aid wearer, Herbert Hoover, Jr.; and an able advisor to presidents in deafened Bernard Baruch. The occupations of these men, however, tell us little about their psychological adjustment pattern. It is necessary to know their values.

For some, impaired hearing may be simply one of their acknowledged characteristics. It is neither more nor less important than any other characteristic. It would be "a good thing" to have better hearing just as it would be a good thing to be more intelligent, own a better home, look handsomer, or earn more money. The possession of good things is an asset, but lack of them does not make the *person* inferior or less valuable. Individuals who have a value system of this kind are not in an antagonistic overlapping role situation, and they will not behave as that situation requires. They see themselves as people who are entirely worthy of full acceptance by society. They do not devalue themselves or feel inferior to people who have good hearing. Other "possessions" of the person are of equal or greater importance.

For others, impaired hearing may become the center of existence with great effort being devoted to reduce it, disguise it, or compensate for it. Some acoustically handicapped individuals, for example, avoid like the plague all others who have a similar impairment. They live among the normally hearing and share their values. They devalue the non-speaking, non-lip-reading deaf, or those who are members of a society for the hard of hearing more strongly than their hearing counterparts do. They are sure that it is better to associate with hearing people than with acoustically handicapped people. Hearing people as *people* are better, more valuable, more likable, than those who have impaired hearing. These individuals suffer from the fact that fate has short-changed them and dealt them a bitter blow. Nevertheless, if they themselves are the objects of impatience, discrimination, and hostility, it is only right and natural because people with impaired hearing *are* inferior and less worthy. The most one can do about it is to double and redouble one's efforts to make up for it. Such persons are in an antagonistic overlapping role situation and they will behave with the guilt and conflict that the situation requires. They share the stigmatizing attitudes of the majority, and they do devalue themselves. They refuse to be comforted by the assurances of friends with more insight that "your deafness is not you." [117] Regardless of their ability, if they are ashamed of their disability, if they try to deny it, or to behave "as if" it did not exist, they divorce themselves from reality without gaining the general social acceptance they crave. There is no assurance that penetrating a particular ability barrier will automatically lead to a relaxation of social barriers. The ability barrier may be breached in the occupational region while the social barriers remain as strong as before. This is shown in Figure 3-3. The deaf psychiatrist, for example, is more likely to be perceived as a deaf person than as a psychiatrist, and he may have great difficulty in building a practice.

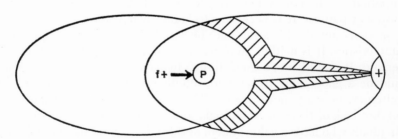

FIGURE 3-3. *Schematic life space of hearing impaired individual showing penetration of occupational barrier and achievement of occupational goal while social and other barriers remain strong toward goal (f+ = force toward goal).*

It is probable that both the person who is ashamed of his impaired hearing and the person who is not will be pitied and devalued by others who place a high value on hearing. They will both be discriminated against, avoided, and denied entrance to desirable behavioral regions.

There is an important difference between the two attitudes, however. As Dembo and others have pointed out, the person who is ashamed will feel that his nonacceptance is logical, reasonable, and justifiable.[118]

The person who is not ashamed will see clearly that it is the maladjustment of the normally hearing individuals which leads them to devaluate and reject him. He will see that the difficulty is not in the disabled person who has adjusted and coped adequately with his loss of a tool. It is the non-disabled persons who show maladjustment and lack of respect for reality by their inability to understand that hearing is only a tool.

> A considerable part of the suffering due to nonacceptance by others is thereby removed; because the negative evaluations of others are seen as unwarranted, because the injured person does not blame himself, they hurt less. Instead, the person who holds them may in turn be devaluated and seen as ignorant and prejudiced.
> Whereas the maladjusted injured person wishes to be accepted by the non-injured though he feels he ought not to be accepted, the adjusted person will care less to associate with those whose values he does not share or respect. The adjusted injured person gains a considerable degree of emotional independence and freedom from the non-injured.[119]

The kinds of suffering that result from attempting to meet artificial and inappropriate standards can be easily perceived in several autobiographies.[120]

To apply this reasoning to children, it is necessary to begin with parents. Although a child often shows a healthy respect for what he can do and a noncommittal or neutral attitude toward what he can't do, he sees parents as all-powerful beings. From them he tends to derive standards, values, and self-image. A harsh, uncertain, or overprotective parent with extreme ideas about "normality" may easily lead to the child's perception of himself as one who is inferior and unable to deal with his environment. He will then behave as if he were inadequate, even though he has the necessary capacities. If parents are able to understand that hearing is only a tool, one characteristic, one value, and that a child has many others, they will not feel ashamed. They will not consider their child inferior or less valuable than other children, and the child will not blame himself.

This is rarely a problem for deaf parents. Normally hearing parents not unreasonably wish to build the child in their own image. For some it is unquestionable that every person, to be a complete human being, *ought* to be able to hear well. They are unable to adjust themselves to the fact that an individual can be a very fine person and yet not hear or not see or not walk. For others, the *ought,* as an imperative, applies to speaking, understanding the speech of others, appreciation of music, or whatever the particular function that the physical impairment interferes with. They may say, "I want my deaf child to learn to speak and to become as normal as possible." They advise each other that the best way to evaluate a school is to talk with some of the older pupils and see how good their speech is—"and beware of schools that permit signing or finger spelling or have deaf teachers. Deaf teachers can't teach speech and they have queer ideas" (that is, different values). Why this harping on the very areas in which the child is handicapped?

Everyone will agree that speech and lip reading are useful tools for the deaf child. In their finest development they enlarge the life space of the child tremendously, permit increasingly finer differentiations or growth, and reduce the communication barriers between the child, his family, and the world. For reasons that are presently unknown, however, not every deaf child learns to speak and lip read. For reasons we can only conjecture, many who do learn, after twelve to fifteen years of continuous drill, later do not use their hard-won skills. Perhaps they discover the deceit of the implicit promises held out to them that "if only you learn these skills and behave like other people, society will accept you." Perhaps many discover that their speech and lip reading are good only in a limited circle of family and friends. Outside of it they may experience great difficulty in understanding or being understood. They may discover that others are amused or annoyed at their voices.

Is a child necessarily a less valuable child if he uses other modalities and communicates by finger spelling or pad and pencil? Is nothing else so important as speech and lip reading? It is true that in some schools there is a tendency to establish a status hierarchy of "good" oral pupils and "poorer" manual pupils, but there is no psychological justification for this. Perhaps parents should evaluate a school by determining whether its students have anything worthwhile to communicate beyond being able to say "a top, a ball, a fish." Perhaps they should ask if the children have learned to solve problems by themselves, whether they have learned to take turns and respect the rights of others, and whether they have "good" adult power figures with whom they can easily identify.

This discussion should not be misconstrued. Speech and lip reading or any communication skill, are valuable and worthy of great effort to acquire. When they are effective, they may produce near-miraculous changes and open vast behavioral possibilities. Parents perceive this. They would be less than human if they did not desire these fruits for their own. Speech and lip reading may be a way of salvation after what seems to be catastrophic misfortune. It is not surprising that they apply great pressure on the child to learn these difficult things. Deaf children, however, like other children, respond to parental and educational pressure with tension, frustration, anxiety, guilt, and shame. How can they help but feel inferior when they cannot satisfy the expectations of those upon whom they are most dependent? [121]

Most parents undoubtedly wish their children to be happy. They are not to blame if they follow their own values and the best advice they can find. They may not anticipate the pathological reactions that may occur when a person is faced with a task that is impossible to cope with and yet must be coped with. They may not know the hazards of creating emotional attachments to unattainable goals. If they do know, they may still hope that their child may be one of those who has exceptional aptitude for language. Language aptitude is sufficiently well distributed, therefore the hope is perhaps not unrealistic.

It is fortunate that deaf children who are not talented in this respect are sufficiently flexible to resolve as well as they do the great tensions that beset them. It is puzzling that the sensory, educational, and social deprivations presently associated with impaired hearing can be resolved with so relatively little psychological disturbance. By any standards the post-school adjustment of the deaf must be considered a tribute to the deaf themselves, their parents, their teachers, and others who have had a part in their rearing. Nevertheless, there is much to be said, from the standpoint of mental hygiene, for educational practices based on normal growth motivation rather than on deficiency motivation.

The Adequacy of Pattern 2

In considering the suitability of *Adjustment Pattern 2* for the deaf child, or the adult he will become, it is necessary to remember two things:

1. There is no evidence and no reason to believe that deafness carries with it any kind of superiority. Exceptionally able children will be found among the deaf no more frequently than in other groups. The number of deaf individuals who will be able to penetrate even the ability barrier will be small.

2. The deaf person to survive in this antagonistic overlapping role situation must have not only exceptional ability but also highly developed tolerance for frustration. Entrance to the privileged situations of the normally hearing requires the very tools that the deaf person lacks. His voice and speech may not meet the standards of the normally hearing in pleasantness, modulation, rhythm, speed, accent, or pronunciation. Lip reading is more fatiguing, less easy, less flexible, and less certain than communication by hearing. There will be times when neither his speech nor his lip reading will be adequate to the demands of the situation. He will frequently be placed in new psychological situations in which his tool loss will hinder him from structuring the unknown regions. He will frequently have to deny his own perceptions in favor of the perceptions of others who have better tools. No matter whether he behaves then "as if" he were normally hearing or with behavior appropriate

for the deaf, he will be seen as inferior and devalued. He will meet with ambiguous and hostile attitudes, and he will not have the emotional support of others whose perceptions are like his own. Frustration, tension, and conflict in high degree are inevitable. In brief, while he may make a more or less effective adjustment to normally hearing society, he will be more or less disorganized and maladjusted as a person.

The second point should not be misinterpreted. Maladjustment is a description whose meanings have been specified. The values of maladjustment to self must be weighed against the values of maladjustment to society with the person himself as the judge.

Although little attention has been devoted to the hard of hearing in the discussion of *Adjustment Pattern 2*, the dynamics are the same as for the deaf. The tool loss in moderately impaired hearing is smaller and creates a less rigid ability barrier than deafness. It is easier for the hard of hearing to pass through. At the same time, however, to the degree that the lacking tool is necessary for achievement, and uncertainty exists about meeting normal communication standards, the hard of hearing person will be subject to the same forces and show the same psychological reactions as the deaf person.

Adjustment Pattern 3

In the light of these considerations, *Adjustment Pattern 3*, or some variation of it, would appear to encompass great advantages. On the one hand it avoids the provinciality and egocentrism inherent in small, restricted, and poorly differentiated psychological worlds. On the other hand it also avoids the heart-searing conflicts, the disorganization, and the growth-inhibiting threats that inevitably arise from strong emotional attachments to unattainable, or only partially attainable, goals. Simultaneously, it offers a sufficiently large scope for a full and rich life. The increase in commonality between the world of those with impaired hearing and the world of the normally hearing can be increased gradually as the ability of the person increases and the resistance of social barriers decreases. Moreover, the enlargement of the life space can be accomplished without emotional disturbance because the person sees each increase as a positive gain. He may perceive that some have skills and privileges that he does not have and others do not have some of the skills and privileges that he has. However, he does not feel the necessity for making value comparisons and does not overvalue the former or devalue the latter. He places his highest values on what he can do and on what he has reasonable expectations of achieving. Other abilities may be "a good thing" but they do not make the person who has them "better" nor the person who does not have them "worse." They are neutral.

To many the face value of this type of adjustment appears compelling. Why don't individuals with impaired hearing just accept it when it is so reasonable to do so? It is not a simple task, but difficult and complex. Some reasons for the difficulty have been discussed in Chapter 1 (see "The Problem of Acceptance").

It should not be necessary to point out that the problem is not unique to the acoustically handicapped. Ordinary psychotherapy for the physically normal is basically a process of leading a client to explore his limitations and disabilities and accept them as *part* of himself without devaluing himself as a person. The dynamics of adjustment that have been outlined have great generality. They are equally applicable to everyone. An example from everyday life may illuminate the issue.

> Jim Smith is the son, grandson, and great-grandson of physicians. He, too, aspires to be a physician. Unfortunately, however, he lacks a tool for adequate behavior as a physician: he is not bright. His I. Q. is of the order of 100, and his academic record is poor. Despite rigorous application to his studies, he just isn't smart enough to gain the necessary knowledge that will enable him to be a good physician. What are the alternatives in this situation? He can say, "I'm stupid," or "I do not have the aptitudes for medicine." He can say, "It's a good thing to be a physician, but many occupations are just as good. Medicine is not for me. I'm pretty good at athletics, though. Maybe I'll become a football coach."
>
> Jim, however, cannot say this. In part he is under great pressure from his family to carry on the tradition, and he has accepted their values. In part, he has seen for himself the desirable and privileged life that physicians lead. In addition to their rewards of "serving humanity" and receiving the gratitude of patients who have been helped, there are better pay, high social status, and many other desirable goals in the life space of a physician. For these reasons also, Jim is unable to accept the suggestion that he become a medical technician. This would bring him closer to the desirable areas, but he would still be outside of the highly privileged regions.
>
> Jim, therefore, continued to strive persistently. Because of this persistence, family influence, and other factors, Jim managed to squeak through college and medical school, although it took him ten years instead of eight. His family and others applauded his spunk. He now had an M.D. Is he really a physician, however? Is he really in the privileged area of medicine if he practices?
>
> The life situation of a capable physician is markedly different from the life space of one who is not confident of his skills. The able M.D. feels secure in his ability to meet new situations as they arise. His training has already partially structured them. He knows in a general way the sequence of steps that will lead to help for the patient. This was not the situation for Jim. Jim, despite his degree, was simultaneously in the situation of a person lacking

medical ability and important knowledge, and in the situation of a person who was expected and required to behave as a competent physician. He was attempting to play an antagonistic overlapping role. Like the blind person pouring cocktails, he could go through the motions but he could not simultaneously play both roles.

From this information alone it is predictable that Jim will have attacks of acute anxiety whenever he is called to a case. He couldn't know in advance whether he would be able to handle it. He will not behave adequately in emergencies, but will try to cover up as best he can. He will be afraid and ashamed to talk with other physicians and will have few friends among them. Since he is behaving only "as if" he were a physician, he can't have close friends for fear that someone will find him out. It is like living a lie—one can neither advance nor withdraw. He must continue to strive to be something he is not. As a consequence of striving for goals that he can never reach, Jim will be a frustrated, anxious, and unhappy person despite the prerogatives of his degree. The unhappiness will not be localized to medicine but will spread to other regions and relationships also. This, in fact, is what happened.

Most people, upon reading the case history, seem to agree that Jim would have been "better off" if he had been able to accept his limitations and to value the other good behavioral possibilities that were open to him.

The situation is not different for the disabled person who tries to behave "as if" he were not disabled. The anticipated advantages of the large life space, in reality, may be greatly circumscribed. It is not a larger life space if one is unable to move about freely within it. It is not greater freedom to live a fuller life if one must constantly compare himself unfavorably with others on abilities that the objective situation demands. There may be more real freedom in a life space that has fewer "objective" advantages but also fewer barriers. Freedom exists when one can cope adequately with the environment and feel successful. Adjustment exists when a person's values are consistent with his needs and abilities.

The development of values and the process of value change are not well understood. That is one reason why psychotherapy is such a long, expensive, and painful process. It seems certain, however, that children, as more helpless and dependent persons, have less freedom in selecting values than adults. The responsibility of their parents and teachers, therefore, is great.

In fulfilling this responsibility some other advantages of *Adjustment Pattern 3* may be considered.

Advantages of Pattern 3

1. It allows and encourages the child to believe in his own percep-

tions. We have noted that some of the skills and much of the behavior that children with impaired hearing may be socially required to learn are based on the needs and the perceptions of others. In speech and lip reading, for example, the child may be unable to monitor his own productions. He must constantly look to a "helper" to tell him when he is right and when he is wrong, for he frequently cannot perceive the stimuli that would enable him to know for himself. It is something like learning to shoot a rifle at a target that cannot be seen, with a helper to punish poor shots and reward good ones; or learning to drive a car when blindfolded. It is possible, and some may develop great skill, but it is nervewracking. One soon learns to respond to the promptings of others rather than to the goal.

This situation, in itself, may account for a large part of the rigid, drilled, anxious, submissive, and insecure behavior of the deaf that has been reported by many observers. Could it also be one reason it is so difficult to make speech and lip reading training stick? Have deaf children learned to please their teachers rather than to structure paths to goals?

There have been no investigations of this problem among the deaf. Asch, however, in a brilliant investigation, has described some of the psychological effects of social pressures upon a person to deny his own perceptions.[122] He presented a group of subjects the task of selecting one of three lines that mostly nearly matched the length of a standard line. Two of the comparison lines were always perceptibly different from the standard line, as in Figure 3-4. When the subject did the task alone he was able to make the correct matches.

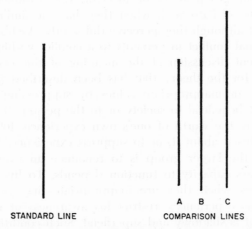

A B C

STANDARD LINE   COMPARISON LINES

FIGURE 3-4. *Lines used in Asch's (1952) experiments [from Solomon E. Asch, Social Psychology (Englewood Cliffs, N.J.: Prentice-Hall, Inc., 1952), reproduced with permission].*

Asch then formed groups of seven subjects in which each person was required to announce publicly his decisions about the correct matching lines. However, six of the seven subjects in the group were collaborators of the experimenter. They had been instructed to give a certain number of false reports. In Figure 3-4, for example, they would respond that Line C best matched the standard line. The seventh subject—a minority of one—was the critical person. The task was exquisitely simple. The evidence was right in front of him. From a purely perceptual standpoint the experimental subject could always answer correctly and be sure that he was right.

What actually happened when the experimental subjects found that their perceptions were different from the majority? As a group, they yielded! No subject disregarded the judgments of the group. Most of them saw the difficulty as being not in the false reports of the majority but in themselves. They assumed the blame for lack of agreement and disruption of the experiment. They doubted and condemned themselves. They felt shame, guilt, and inferiority. They assumed from the outset that they were wrong and the majority was right. By doing so they became less free to look at the evidence in front of their eyes. Being "correct" and not exposing oneself as different was of greater concern than mastering the task. Because they had a great need not to be excluded from the group, they tried hard to see the lines in the same way as the majority. Sometimes they succeeded in inducing this confusion in themselves. If they could not succeed, they knowingly falsified their reports. Few were able to remain independent and report their own true perceptions without anxiety, tension, and conflict. Most would not say or imply that the group might be in error. Like disabled persons who employ *Adjustment Pattern 2,* when they have a similar need not to appear different although they perceive differently, Asch's subjects transferred an external conflict in percepts to a conflict within themselves.

Asch's eloquent discussion of the meaning of this experiment offers strong support for the theory that has been described in this chapter. Sharing foreign or inappropriate values by suppressing one's own experiences is not beneficial to society or to the person. It is a malignant process. To deny the worth of one's own experience, to permit oneself to become confused about it, or to suppress experiences that cannot be assimilated by the larger group is to renounce an essential condition upon which one's capacity to function depends. To live up to the demands of others when they are inappropriate may require that the person blunt his experiences, restrict his awareness of reality and develop a self that is shadowy and superficial. Such conditions chronically overtax the capacity for orientation, for reality appears always to be shifting. There is no common ground with others, but only yielding to others. These conditions put a stop to the testing of reality so that the person tries not to observe, not to understand, and not to feel. Contact with reality is impossible when one must behave in a contradictory and threatening world as if it were a consistent and understandable world.

Human beings faced with demands beyond their capacities for orientation and lacking the perceptions for independent action do more than distort and exclude the content of unmanageable situations. In the effort to achieve a new but now artificial stability they are forced to modify their mode of orientation in the direction of *not* responding adequately to objective requirements, including their own needs. The consequences are that ultimately they become estranged from both their culture and themselves.

It is not a contrary argument that some with impaired hearing or other disabilities embrace the injustice from which they suffer. This is a common effect of extreme social pressures. Men cannot endure being only losers and victims; they cannot face indefinitely the consequences of resignation and defeat.

Asch continued his experiments by introducing *two* naive subjects into a group of five collaborators. The results now were strikingly different. The two naive subjects might not show any evidence of being aware of each other, but their emotional disturbance was much less. "The presence of a single voice pointing to the true state of affairs had an unmistakable liberating effect. With one person at their side most subjects were able to face the majority with independence and the weakest were spared the extremes of yielding." [123]

These experiments suggest a basic function of the counsellor: He must supply at least one single voice that encourages the disabled child to believe in the worth and validity of his own perceptions. The perceptions of children with impaired hearing may be different, but they are just as true as the perceptions of the hearing. It is vital to the mental health and adjustment of the acoustically handicapped that the counsellor does not try to force them into a psychological "iron maiden." He must be able to say that the majority—society—is wrong. You do not have to submit by denying yourself.

There is no direct evidence on this problem for the acoustically handicapped, although it is one of the most potentially rewarding areas for future investigation. Cutsforth offers some evidence concerning the blind which is in general agreement with Asch's later work.[124] He asked blind children what they would say about certain stimulus words. These words had been selected because they could be responded to in terms of several modalities. For example a rose may be red, sweet-smelling, soft, velvety, and bitter-tasting. Cutsforth found that the great majority of responses were of visual qualities, especially color. When there was a double response, the children tended to feel that the visual attribute was the more valid. In responding to blood, a child said, "Sticky-red. It's sticky, but it's *really* red." What is the experiential significance of color for the blind?

Cutsforth raised the important question of whether we are justified in leading the blind child into the realm of visual unreality and away from his own world of valid experience. Why should the blind child employ visual concepts when other sensory concepts are equally available and much more meaningful in experience. Why should they overvalue the experiences of others and undervalue their own. We may well raise similar questions for the deaf. Do we wish them to live by words rather than in reality, and what are the implications of the former behavior on personality and social adjustment?

Adjustment Pattern 3 does not require the child to deny his own perceptions or encourage him to place a high value on the perceptions of others.

2. A related characteristic of *Adjustment Pattern* 3 is that it facilitates cognitive clarity. The boundaries of the situation are clear so that at a given point in time the child is not uncertain about what behavior is possible and what is not. Of course, as the child grows, the life space may be greatly enlarged and the boundaries pushed back. His behavior, however, is cognitively guided. He is not at the mercy of the perceptions and values of others nor is he impelled to react automatically to stimuli that are inappropriate for him. With respect to his hearing characteristics, he is able to answer the questions: Who am I? In what psychological world do I live?

Everyone, it will be recalled, lives in multiple overlapping role situations. The hearing impaired: hearing dichotomy has been singled out for analysis here, but it should not be forgotten that there are many additional multiple overlaps—all of which sometimes operate simultaneously. For example, the person with impaired hearing may also play the roles of the white, middle-class, Jewish adolescent. All of these, in some degree, require different behavior than is appropriate for a Negro, upper-class, Christian child. Cognitive clarity for these other group membership roles is also desirable. A large and well-balanced variety of group memberships does not cause disturbance. It is uncertainty about one's "belongingness" that creates psychological conflict. Where "fate" has made a child a member of one minority group it is essential that he should recognize and accept it and take pride in his membership. This is a necessary basis for developing strong and secure loyalties to other groups.[125] Shame and attempts to escape identification with an undervalued minority make the child uncertain about where he belongs. Pride in group membership, identification with group goals, and achievements and concern for favorable changes in the social status of the group are adjustive behaviors.

No part of the devaluation and discrimination against the deaf is directed to them as persons. Rather, it is prejudice against the group to which they belong.

The counsellor who insists on the following is not helpful: (a) The person with impaired hearing is only an individual and not a member of a group; (b) he is not different from others who hear; and (c) behavior which appears "normal" or most closely approaches "normality" is the most highly desirable goal. All of these values impose great and unnecessary burdens upon the person. They demand behavior which may be considered undesirable for mental health if it is achieved. In effect they demand that the person with impaired hearing place himself on the barrier between the life spaces of hearing roles and impaired hearing roles and submit to the buffeting forces that inevitably act upon persons in antagonistic role situations.

The person with impaired hearing who has no pride in the group to which fate has assigned him and tries to escape does not thereby free himself from the treatment that is directed toward other members of the group. He simply loses the valuable support of others who are attempting to cope with a similar situation. The independence, respectability, and courage of the deaf provide an excellent base for the feeling of group belongingness.

Consequences of Pattern 3

Some consequences of *Adjustment Pattern 3*, therefore, are the following:

The person is easily able to say, "I have impaired hearing." He does not devalue himself or his group. Differences can be neutral. He sees the value of "hearing behavior" as an asset, but "impaired hearing behavior" does not affect the worth of the person. If he is placed at a disadvantage in a normally hearing world it is because of the difficulty of the task and not the incompetence of the person. He, therefore, does not blame himself or feel guilt and shame. Because he is cognitively clear about this, his behavior is flexible and not bound by anxiety. He can cognitively guide his behavior in a conscious, goal-directed, and voluntary way and describe what he is doing to others. At one stroke he frees himself from ambiguous group memberships and their conflicting group demands.

Counselling Adventitiously Impaired Persons

THE SAME principles that apply to individuals with congenital impairments apply also to those who have incurred impairments. The latter are more likely to be attracted to *Adjustment Pattern 2* and to reject *Adjustment Pattern 1*, but this does not invariably occur.

A major difference between the two groups is that the life space of the congenitally impaired is gradually built up and differentiated. The adventitiously impaired, however, may already have a well-organized life space which must now be restructured. The counsellor must not be too cheerful, too soon. Hearing is a valuable asset. It is necessary and desirable for the person to mourn his loss before he is able to assimilate his present situation and reassess his goals. Unlike the congenitally impaired, who can easily see new enlargement and differentiation of the life space as a gain, the adventitiously impaired person must set up a new base line from which to evaluate himself. If he previously shared the stigmatizing attitudes of the majority toward the group to which he now belongs, he will apply these judgments to himself. He will devalue himself as an imperfect normal person and be unable to see himself as a whole and good person whose impaired hearing is just one attribute. In this situation no matter how often he does as well or better than normally hearing persons, he will still feel inferior. If it were not for his defective hearing, he might have done even better.

The function of the counsellor is to help set up a new base line which is rooted in the present and does not require any comparisons with the previous state of the person. From this new base line the adventitiously impaired, also, will be able to perceive each positive gain as a gain. If an individual was not able to lip read and can now lip read a little, that is an objective gain. There is no need to devalue it because hearing was easier.

The basic principles have already been stated. Figures 3-5, 3-6, and 3-7 show some additional ways in which the counsellor can assist in the restructuring process.

The client often comes with the feeling that he is imprisoned by impaired hearing. The barrier, however, "in reality" need not surround the person, but only certain areas of the life space. Many activities do not require hearing. It is possible to show also, as in Figure 3-6, that desirable activities which appear to require hearing do not do so. Effective communication, for example, may be mediated by vision, as in lip reading or finger spelling; by motor activities, as in writing, and by emotions, as in scowling or kissing. In addition, the counselor can show, as in Figure 3-7, the relatively small portion of human capacities that are

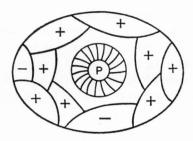
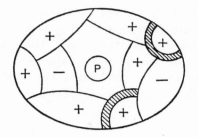

LIFE SITUATION AS THE CLIENT   LIFE SITUATION AS IT IS
          MAY SEE IT

FIGURE 3-5. *Perception of life situation.*

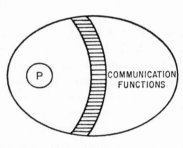
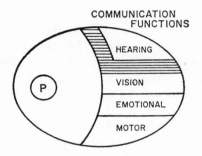

LIFE SITUATION AS THE CLIENT   LIFE SITUATION AS IT IS
          MAY SEE IT

FIGURE 3-6. *Perception of life situation.*

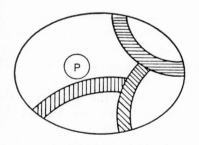
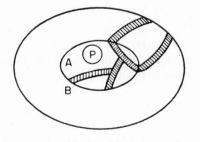

LIFE SITUATION AS THE CLIENT   LIFE SITUATION AS IT IS
          MAY SEE IT

P—PERSON   A—PRESENT FUNCTIONING   B—CAPACITY & POTENTIAL FOR
                                                        FUTURE DEVELOPMENT

FIGURE 3-7. *Perception of life situation.*

effectively utilized by the average person. There are persons with excellent hearing who engage in conversation no more stimulating than "He said, and then I said." They may never attend a lecture or a concert or use their auditory capacities for enriching their lives. The same is true of other modalities. The child with impaired hearing has a greater potential for psychological growth than he will ever develop to the full.

Recent Advances

THIS CHAPTER has been devoted primarily to the presentation of a point of view intended to contribute to the clarity with which students of the psychology of impaired hearing will perceive *some* of the critical problems in this field. Hopefully, it will prevent perpetuation of some of the misunderstandings of the evidence, and repetition of some of the mistakes that have been made in the past.

The reader should be cautioned, however, that it is largely a *social-psychology* that has been presented; the emphasis has been placed on some ways of evaluating and thinking about children with impaired hearing rather than on an extensive review of the literature. In addition, many other fields of psychology have made important contributions to our knowledge of hearing impairment. There are many more problems, much evidence, and many other points of view that have not been mentioned here. The study of impaired hearing is a large, complex, and active field of investigation, and the literature is extensive. The serious student will wish to consult the book-length treatments [126] and the technical periodical literature that have been appearing in steadily increasing quantity in the last ten years.

Fortunately, the identification of relevant material is now a relatively easy task. Since 1960, *DSH Abstracts* has provided world-wide coverage of the literature on deafness, speech, and hearing by regularly examining the contents of more than two hundred fifty scientific journals and exchanging information with eleven other abstracting services which search thousands of other journals.[127]

The abstracts are sufficiently detailed to facilitate the decision of the specialist in one aspect of impaired hearing as to whether a particular article should be read, while simultaneously keeping him informed of advances in other aspects. The latter is important because the psychology of impaired hearing cannot be understood in isolation from other knowledge in hearing and deafness. For the beginning student, browsing in the *DSH Abstracts* will convey the flavor of the similarities and differences in the approaches, results, and interpretations not only of investigators who write in English but also of foreign investigators who publish in languages that most American students cannot read. It can be a fascinating and instructive experience to observe how some data reported from different countries can be convergent or congruent, while other data, opinions, attitudes, treatment, and evaluation of those with impaired hearing remain quite divergent. It becomes clearer that there are social and cultural determinants of much behavior that we may unthinkingly ascribe directly to auditory deficit. The student will observe, too, the great gains that are occurring in our understanding of the hearing process, in hearing evaluation and audiological diagnostic methods, in medical treatment of impaired hearing, in hearing-aid technology, in educational applications, and in solving problems that a decade ago were hardly perceived.

It cannot be said that experimentally-based knowledge of the psychology of impaired hearing has increased at the same rate as knowledge of some other aspects of hearing and deafness. Studies of improved technical quality concerned with counting, measuring, correlating, and comparing such variables as intelligence, achievement, personality, and adjustment have continued to appear. The data reported do not require the revision of present generalizations, however, and the studies do not contribute appreciably to the solution of the problems outlined in the first part of this chapter. Except for a report by Myklebust, they will not be discussed here.

A small but increasing number of studies are new in that they do more than report simply the measured characteristics of a group of hearing-impaired children, affirm that some of those characteristics are related in some more or less statistically significant way, or show that those with impaired hearing are similar or different from the normally hearing on some global function. There are attempts to identify relevant variables that are operating, to describe process as well as outcome, and sometimes to induce desirable change in some behavior. A few of these studies will be reviewed briefly.

Perception and Concept Formation

Myklebust has summarized the evidence of group differences between deaf and hearing children in visual perception and concept formation.[128] He interprets his findings as indicating that the deaf demonstrate inferiority in these functions as a necessary consequence of deafness itself. In his view, impaired hearing is one kind of sensory deprivation that reduces the input of total experience and thereby creates an imbalance in all psychological processes.

It is possible to place other interpretations on the same evidence and to advance the thesis that physical deafness directly creates nothing except an inability to respond to auditory stimuli. It is more fruitful, however, to identify and isolate possibly relevant variables and manipulate them experimentally in such a way as to reduce the number of different interpretations that can be placed on the results. Several investigators have recently done this.

Furth examined the responses of young deaf and hearing subjects to a variety of concept learning tasks.[129] The solution of some of the tasks could be facilitated by the language experience of the normally hearing subjects while the solution of other tasks could not. For example, for the concept "opposite," which was not in the language experience of the deaf: if the experimenter selected the largest of one set of objects, the subject's task was to select the smallest—and vice versa. For the concept "the same," which was in the language experience of the deaf, the task was to select the pair of identical objects from a set of two pairs. In the latter tasks, that is, the deaf and hearing subjects were on an equal level with respect to language, and concept formation was left free to vary independently of language variables. The hypothesis was that where language experience does not favor the hearing child, there are no differences in abstract thinking or concept formation between the deaf and the hearing. The results supported the hypothesis.

Similarly, Rosenstein, using a different set of tasks, found no significant differences between deaf and hearing children in the ability to perceive, abstract, or generalize.[130] He concluded that where the language involved in the tasks is within the repertoire of deaf children, their performance on the task does not differ from hearing children. Oléron's data can be interpreted in the same way.[131]

Carrier threw an oblique but penetrating light on the relationship between language and thinking by showing that language experience sometimes facilitates the formation of *incorrect* concepts.[132] He was concerned with science education and the formation of science concepts by very young children. One of the persistent problems in this field arises from children's limited language and lack of precision in language use, relative to the adult, which sometimes inhibits problem-solving or concept formation. The task for the science educator, which parallels that of the teacher of the deaf, is either to improve language function or find nonlanguage ways of teaching scientific concepts. It is instructive that science educators devote little effort to attempt to demonstrate that children's concept formation is "impaired" or that because of their "immaturity" little can be done to teach science until they grow up. It is an example that might well be emulated in some other fields.

In his experiment, Carrier was concerned with the influence of color on judgments of weight. Children incorrectly judge objects of darker color to be heavier than the same objects displayed in lighter colors.

Carrier demonstrated that linguistic influences were responsible for the formation of this incorrect concept by showing that, to a statistically significant degree, all of his hearing subjects and his older deaf subjects performed incorrectly but his younger deaf subjects, who had the least language experience, did not.

The importance of this experiment is that it lends support from another direction to the conclusions derivable from the experiments of Furth, Rosenstein, and Oléron. In these experiments it was clear that where the linguistic abilities of deaf children were sufficient, there was no conceptual deficit. Carrier's experiment indicates that where misleading linguistic influences hinder correct concept formation, deaf children who had the least language experience performed better than hearing children, while older deaf children whose language experience was larger were misled in the same way as were the hearing. Pointing in the same direction as other recent evidence on visual perception, visual memory, and cognition,[133] the experiments lend strong support to the belief that the poorer or retarded performance of the deaf as a group in tasks that require abstract thinking is mediated by language and does not reflect incapacity in perception or concept formation.

This conclusion will come as no surprise to many educators of the deaf who have emphasized repeatedly that the developmental problems of the deaf arise not from factors inherent in deafness itself, nor even from lack of speech, but from inadequately developed language. From a remedial standpoint, however, attention might well be directed toward the numerous, unexploited, non-verbal ways of teaching concepts such as are common in science education.

In general, the trend of the *evidence* in recent years, but not necessarily an investigator's conclusions, has been to show small or no differences between the capacities of deaf and hearing children. Differences in reported performance on non-auditory tasks are more frequently interpreted as functions of the deaf person's educational treatment and social experience, and these are perceived as being amenable to change. The sensory impairment and the language retardation are not denied, but the tendency is to suggest that their contaminating effects can be minimized or eliminated by more stringent experimental controls. When this is done the deaf child who is not otherwise neurologically damaged seems remarkably similar in capacity to his hearing fellows. The educational and psychological tasks are to find paths around the impaired ears so as to liberate the undamaged capacities which remain.[134]

Lip Reading and Sign Language

The interpretation of English speech from only the visible movements associated with phonation appears to be theoretically impossible. The work of Woodward and Barber on the simple discrimination of pairs of consonants with a common vowel as "alike" or "different," indicated that the movements associated with the phonation of English consonants are distributed among only four categories that are visually contrastable to each other.[135] These movements may be described as bilabial, rounded labial, labiodental and non-labial. Almost all phonetic dimensions and all variables of articulation except the labial were virtually undiscriminable by visual perception. If the lip reader can decode the varying patterns of the twenty-four vocal signaling units which occur in English speech, it seems apparent that he must be responding to more variables than the four signal reception units that are consistently available to him by vision. The identity and the operation of these variables are not known. Woodward and Barber speculate that the determinants of visual speech perception will be found in the nature of language itself as a meaningful functioning system. Their research, based on the theory and method of structural linguistics, is a promising first step in this direction.

Other kinds of research toward understanding the relationships between oral-aural stimuli and oral-visual communication have yielded largely negative or conflicting results. Because of the numerous and complex variables in the speaker, the stimuli, the receiver, the environment—and the interrelationships among them—it is not easy to isolate the relevant determinants. Present evidence indicates that lip-reading skill is not significantly or consistently related to age, sex, intelligence, academic achievement, personality or to more discrete variables such as pure tone hearing loss, age of loss, visual skills, visual-motor co-ordination, memory span, concept formation, reading ability, amount of instruction in lip reading or years of experience in communication by lip reading.

This does not mean, of course, that such relationships may not exist but only that present evidence is negative or equivocal. It may be doubted, however, that the usual counting and measuring approach used in these studies is likely to prove rewarding. It may be more fruitful to concentrate on specifying the nature of the lip-reading stimuli and the conditions under which lip reading occurs. In this way the environmental variables that facilitate lip reading and those that inhibit it may be revealed. Such knowledge, which would contribute to the improvement in lip-reading ability by all who must use it, would seem to be more valuable than attempts to "explain" impairment in lip-reading skills in terms of some unmanipulable "trait" in the lip reader.

Simmons [136] and O'Neill and Oyer [137] offer bibliographical and evaluative guides to the studies of lip reading that have appeared in recent years.

Two investigations reflect a re-growth of interest in a neglected aspect of the psychology of impaired hearing—the language of signs. Tervoort made a genetic and psycholinguistic analysis of the visual symbols used for communication by Dutch and American deaf children.[138] He traced the growth of language from the natural gesture level to formal signing and formal symbolization. Stokoe, using the methods of structural linguistics, analyzed the sign language of intelligent adults who use it skillfully, and he also devised a method of reducing the language to writing.[139]

The evidence from both studies indicates that the visual communication system of the deaf is a language, or it is at least "language-like" in nature and function. Although psychological implications are presently limited, the possibilities for further development of this field of study are impressive.

There appear to be greater interest and scholarly activity relating to the study of manual communication and its effects upon behavior than have been observed in the recent past.[140] Additional developments undoubtedly are in the making.

"Change" Experiments

The accepted ways of treating deaf children, particularly young children, have changed greatly in recent years. The acceptance and spread of new methods have not been a function, in any great degree, of systematic research showing that the new procedures were superior to the old. Rather, change occurred by way of consensual validation and the informal, unsystematic observations of many parents, teachers, and clinicians that, in practice, an addition or elimination of some kind did yield better behavioral results. There are at least two small but important studies, however, in which change was deliberately engineered and the effect of the change was measured.

Stone, Fiedler, and Fine changed the pre-school program of a public day school for deaf children by introducing nursery school procedures in place of formal teaching methods and imposing the early use of individual hearing aids at a time when neither practice was as common as it is today.[141] It was predicted on theoretical grounds that certain desirable gains in speech production and perception, academic progress, and personality growth would occur and would be measurable several years after the experimental treatment had ceased. The results showed clearly that, even under the less than optimal experimental conditions that can be obtained for research in a public school setting, a freer educational environment and the wearing of individual hearing aids had beneficial effects on the behavior of deaf pre-school children. It also showed the degree to which the changed educational environment, the hearing aid, and the interaction between the two contributed to the improvement that was obtained. The full investigation is too complex to be summarized briefly, but will be valuable to those who study it. It is a different and more rewarding research approach than investigating the kinds of characteristics *in* deaf children that are "naturally" associated with differences in speech, academic progress, and personality.

Falconer approached the problem of language impairment in deaf children as a problem in establishing the environmental conditions under which learning can occur.[142] Using a "teaching machine" and a procedure based on the learning theories of B. F. Skinner,[143] he taught eight young deaf children more than thirteen nouns in about fifty minutes. Retention, when measured after two weeks, was nearly perfect. Such performance is far better than deaf children usually achieve. This first step toward the improvement of one kind of learning in the deaf by means of behavior methods can surely lead to further gains—if it is suitably exploited.

Some Observations on Research

IN PSYCHOLOGY, since the first printing of this book, there has been little abatement of the measurement and correlational studies reporting the group characteristics of various samples of individuals with impaired hearing or their comparability to a "matched" group of normally hearing children. The limited conclusions that legitimately may be drawn from such investigations have already been discussed. Essentially, well-designed measurement studies may provide good evidence of the current status and performance of the population with which we are concerned but no evidence that the current status is inevitable or unchangeable. Similarly, good comparison studies, even with matched groups, focus on current status rather than on the possibilities for change or the conditions under which change may occur. In both kinds of studies the temptation seems almost irresistible to conclude that an *obtained* psychological or educational outcome is a *necessary* outcome, and to "explain" it as a direct consequence of the physical disability. This process tends not only to lead to probably erroneous conclusions but also to choke off more fruitful, dynamic investigations.

For example, in the usual comparison of personality or adjustment in "matched" normally hearing and impaired hearing subjects, it may be found that the responses of the two groups were similar or different. In general, if the responses of the subjects with impaired hearing are different from the normally hearing group's responses, it is concluded that those with impaired hearing are retarded, maladjusted, or defective. If the responses of the two groups are similar, the implication is that those with impaired hearing are the same as others. Neither conclusion appears to be reasonable or helpful. First, as several generations of investigators have discovered, matching of subjects or groups can be done on only a few of the possible variables which may affect the results, and there is little assurance that the relevant rather than the easiest variables are controlled. Second, individuals who are handicapped by impaired hearing lack an important tool for behavior in our culture, and they may live under conditions that are markedly different in some respects from the normally hearing. Under the traditional testing-correlating-comparing strategies, however, the results tell us little about the conditions under which the person with impaired hearing develops, learns, and adjusts, to what variables he adjusts, or how he does it. Results that are expressed as static, judgmental "facts," while they may be useful to the clinical psychologist and the educator in making the day-to-day decisions and predictions which cannot be postponed until more adequate knowledge is available, may also choke off the further study of *how* the handicapped child develops, learns, achieves, and adjusts.

Description is the fundamental level of scientific investigation, but it is not the acme. The most fruitful kind of research is concerned with change and the specification of the conditions under which change occurs. Hence, one of the most important questions that can be raised in evaluating the adequacy and helpfulness of a research study at the next higher investigative level to which somatopsychology is now prepared to move, is the following: Does the study contribute to the specification of the manipulable, environmental *conditions under which* the behavior investigated occurs, varies in strength or fails to occur? Only this kind of study can resolve and perhaps systematize in a meaningful way the divergent and contradictory results which continue to clutter the literature. Only this kind of study will move us forward from simple description and classification to the more precise prediction, control, and improvement of the behavior of children with impaired hearing.

A major limitation hindering the further development of empirical documentation for a psychology of impaired hearing is the continued utilization in research of non-manipulable variables. A science develops, after an initial stage of description and classification of the phenomena, by manipulating an independent variable in some way so as to produce some change in a dependent variable and, by so doing, obtain knowledge about the functional relationships that exist between one variable and another. In much current somatopsychological research, however, variables are not manipulated, but relatively unmanipulable conditions such as age, sex, intelligence, degree of hearing loss, personality, and other global characteristics are counted, measured, correlated, or compared. This kind of work results in the continued piling up of static descriptions (no longer needed except perhaps for record-keeping purposes) of the characteristics of children with impaired hearing.

Few of the generalizations that can be stated about the psychological functioning of "the average deaf child" are different or more profound today than they were ten years ago. Where counting and measuring studies have indicated the occurrence of some change, plausible, common-sense speculations may suggest some of the relevant independent variables which must have been operating to have produced the change; but speculation is not a good substitute for systematic investigation, nor can it yield the control over phenomena which will facilitate desirable changes and inhibit undesirable ones. Studies which correlate the relationships among the characteristics of those with impaired hearing or make comparisons with the normally hearing have continued to appear without adding appreciably to our knowledge. Enough is already known of the many detrimental behavioral effects that are associated with impaired hearing in our culture to make reasonably good behavioral predictions for the different subgroups of the population of impaired hearers, but prediction for the individual is still uncertain, and techniques for control of undesired behavior are generally lacking. Additional statistical studies probably will show changes in the performance of the population, but unless an independent variable is "naturally" or experimentally manipulated, the findings are unlikely to result in understanding.

For example, recent studies of the intelligence of the deaf show that the gap between the deaf and the hearing has narrowed.[144] That is interesting and hopeful, but, if the change is real and not an artifact of measurement, what accounts for the improvement in the intellectual level of the deaf? The physical characteristics of the subjects do not appear to have changed with respect to degree of hearing loss or age of onset, and some of the measuring instruments were the same as those used in earlier studies. It seems reasonable to believe that some unspecified non-experimental change in the environment of the deaf is facilitating their development. Perhaps it reflects the influences that are related to earlier diagnosis, the increasing sophistication of parents and professional people, the use of hearing aids, pre-school training, some unidentified improvement in educational treatment or personnel, or some combination of these. Since the nature of the independent variable is not known, it is not clear what should be done for all deaf children in order to improve their performance.

This example, of course, illustrates that research and experimentation are not the only paths to knowledge. Improvement does often occur by trial and error procedures that have common-sense criteria. These procedures, however, are slower, less certain in yielding new knowledge, and less precise in application. In a scientifically oriented world, they tend to become the main channels for change only when scientists bog down in unprofitable kinds of investigation and fail to provide the knowledge and the leadership for orderly, systematic solution of important problems. The field of somatopsychology of impaired hearing may be in this position.

It is noteworthy that the two disciplines that have made the most spectacular gains in the field of impaired hearing during the last quarter century are medicine and audiology. One major reason for their growth and progress is that each discipline has an improved way of manipulating a heretofore relatively unmanipulable variable. The physicians, with a host of medical and surgical techniques, have learned to change some pathological conditions in the person's auditory apparatus so that communication with the environment is improved. The audiologists, with the aid of psychophysicists and engineers, have learned to apply an instrument for changing the auditory environment so as to bring it within the range of impaired sensory capacities. The two ways together illustrate the task for a fruitful somatopsychology. Some change must be induced in the person or in the environment in such a way that the interaction between the two produces a change in behavior.

The time is ripe for psychologists to cease counting, measuring, and correlating relationships among static variables and to begin systematically manipulating variables. It is not so important to give additional documentation of what behavior is manifested "naturally" in persons with impaired hearing in our culture as it is to discover or invent procedures for changing detrimental or undesirable developmental, social, and psychological behavior. Some developments in behavior theory have led to a plausible framework and some sophisticated techniques which hold promise for the solution of these problems.[145]

Perspectives to the Future

Two MAIN lines of development in the future can be anticipated. One is concerned with the improvement of "hearing," and the other with the amelioration of some undesirable effects of "deafness." The former has by far the greater momentum, but the latter could develop rapidly. Present evidence is largely anecdotal and clinical, although systematic investigation probably is not far away.

Hearing

As a function of advances in medicine, audiology, and hearing-aid technology, a minor revolution has occurred in the psychological situation of individuals who manifest impaired responsiveness to sound. Many impairments of the peripheral auditory system are now improvable, correctable, or reversible either by direct medical or surgical intervention in the person or by changing the perceived environment via amplifying

its sounds. This has led, on the one hand, to a blurring of the traditional
distinctions based on measured, unaided hearing acuity; and, on the
other hand, to the perception of sources of impaired responsiveness to
sounds that were previously undifferentiated.

For example, many public school children with normal pure-tone thresholds now receive systematic instruction in the discriminative function
that we have called "auding" (to distinguish it from the purely atten-
tional variable) but which is more commonly known as "listening training." An increasing number of children who previously would have been
"hard of hearing" have been restored medically and gained or regained
normal functioning. Many children whose unaided hearing remains impaired to a degree that previously would have classified them as "hard
of hearing" have little functional, communicative deficit when sound
reaches them through a hearing aid. Finally, amplified sound applied
early and consistently now permits many children who previously would
have been classified as "deaf" to function as "hard of hearing." The
tremendous effects of improved communicative functioning on the psychological situations and the behavior of these children have not been
studied systematically. Most, if not all, of earlier descriptive studies of
behavior, which used unaided hearing thresholds as the main condition
against which outcomes were plotted, are now obsolete. Hopefully, such
studies will not be repeated without major improvement in experimental
design.

Fortunately, attention has now shifted from exclusive concentration
on "how much" impaired responsiveness to sound exists to increased concern for differentiating auditory impairment, deficiency, deprivation, confusion, inhibition, and other conditions whose sources may not arise in
the peripheral auditory apparatus. Not responding to sound, especially
speech sounds, may result from lack of sufficient exposure to it (which
may occur for many reasons) or from central nervous system disorders
which have neurophysiological and neuropsychological effects that go
far beyond the ears. Not responding, which is the only information that
most audiometric tests yield, may mean not attending, not sensing, not
perceiving, not discriminating, not remembering, or actively inhibiting a
response to an auditory signal as a function of any one of a number of
causes.

With so many parameters available, it is now easier to focus on the
questions: Under what conditions do these phenomena occur, and under
what conditions will change occur? It has also become easier to see that
a relatively large impairment is not necessarily behaviorally catastrophic
nor is a relatively small deficit unimportant. Sensitivity to the problems
of differential diagnosis and the awareness of the existence of multiple
disabilities that are sometimes found in association with reduced respon-

siveness to sound have made it more difficult to "explain away" all undesirable or retarded behavior of those with impaired hearing as inevitable consequences of reduced acuity.

One of the most exciting developments in the improvement of hearing is the indication, crude and uncontrolled as yet, that responsiveness to sound may develop in relatively unresponsive infants and children if they are exposed to auditory stimulation.

As the age of discovery of hearing impairment in children has dropped steadily downward, an increasing number of audiologists have diagnosed severe or profound deafness in an infant and then found several months later that normal responsiveness could be demonstrated. Sometimes it appears that the mother of such an infant was unwilling to "accept" the fact of deafness and talked directly into the infant's ear for hours at a time, but often no such evidence is available. Similarly, a child may show increasingly lower pure-tone thresholds on repeated testing over a period of years. It is common to explain the former situation as a "mistake" in diagnosis, and undoubtedly mistakes sometimes do occur. The latter situation is often attributed not to an increased capacity to hear but to improved discrimination or performance, and improvement in discrimination surely does often occur. One may speculate, however, as to whether these answers are the full answers. Not all infants are born with the same degree of maturation nor do they develop at identical rates. Perhaps some infants were "deaf" at the time they were tested. Perhaps some improvement in sound thresholds in older children reflects a real gain in sensitivity as well as in discrimination.

Griffiths placed binaural, wearable hearing aids on more than thirty infants who had been diagnosed as deaf by the parents' otologist and who showed limited or no responsiveness to sound in her own testing.[146] All of the infants were under eight months of age, and they wore the aids during all of their waking hours. She found that after several months of experience with amplification, almost all of them showed normal responsiveness to sound without the aid. Similar results appear to have been obtained on fewer cases by several other therapists, although none of it has been formally presented in a form that will allow inspection and independent evaluation.

Some professional individuals become highly emotional at such reports and condemn them in terms that range from "impossible" to "charlatanism." It is of interest, however, that some of these individuals are those who not too many years ago counselled parents against the use of a hearing aid until a child was seven or eight years old and "able to take care of it himself," that is, prevent it from being damaged. They were also indignant later about the very idea of imposing hearing aids on two- or three-year-old babies and bringing amplified sound to children in other ways that are quite common today. There is no reason to suspect deception in the descriptive reports, although mistakes in interpretation are possible.

The evidence, such as it is, is impossible to interpret and will remain impossible to interpret until controlled experimentation is carried out. Initially, all that may be required is to place hearing aids randomly on half of a group of infants, of similar developmental level and home environments, who appear unresponsive to sound. Meanwhile, amplified sound will be withheld from the other half of the group. Observation of the developmental process and progress will show if the two groups differ.[147]

It must be remembered that present procedures for evaluating responsiveness to sound in infants are crude and unprecise. Differential developmental rates in infants constitute another variable. It seems probable that many infants who appear, or are, unresponsive to sound during the early months of life may later mature naturally without induced stimulation and develop normally, although it is not known how frequently this occurs. For other infants who are impaired rather than retarded, it seems unlikely that stimulation with sound could be a remedy for all of the numerous conditions that are associated with reduced responsiveness to sound. A very real obstacle impeding experimentation by many investigators is that the results claimed for early auditory stimulation appear too good to be true.

Nevertheless, it is the author's speculation that within the next decade it will be established that the administration of amplified sound can induce a reversal of some kinds of unresponsiveness to sound that otherwise would be permanent. It may be speculated that auditory stimulation, in some cases, may trigger an impeded biochemical, neural, psychological, or experiential process that is necessary for the development of hearing. Such speculations are consistent with what is presently known about the impaired or aberrant sensory responsiveness of maternally deprived children, of animals reared in darkness, and of humans who have had infantile cataracts of the eye removed in adulthood. Hearing is a learned function, and perhaps it cannot be learned effectively if consistent exposure to above-threshold sounds is delayed beyond infancy. Amplifying the sounds of the environment appears to be a reasonable procedure for bringing this experience within the sensing range of infants who have a *quantitative* auditory impairment only. It may be fully effective only in underdeveloped organisms and not in the maldeveloped infants that obstetricians can now deliver and pediatricians can keep alive. Even for maldeveloped infants and older children, however, the plasticity of the human organism is such that probably some degree of successful adjustment and responsiveness often can be made to incomplete or distorted sound stimuli if the optimal learning conditions can be specified. Further, to the extent that increased knowledge of the encoding, transmission, and decoding processes of hearing leads to induced environmental changes which can augment the incomplete and unscramble the distorted, much more progress in the improvement of hearing can be anticipated.

Psychologists have not contributed so importantly to the solution of these problems on the applied experimental level as they have on the psychophysical level, but there are obviously many intriguing problems, in the transitional, hypothesis-generating stage subsequent to clinical observation, that are ripe for investigation.

Deafness

At a meeting of the World Health Organization in Switzerland several years ago, an audiologist said to a teacher of the deaf:

"The trouble with you residential-school people is that you know nothing about hearing."

"That may be so," was the reply, "and the trouble with you speech and hearing therapists is that you know nothing about deafness."

There is a measure of truth in that wry exchange. Although there have been signs of rapprochement and increasing cooperation between the two groups, the gulf of divergent values, experiences, and expectations which separate them is wide and deep. The two groups are alike in viewing language and communication as central problems of those with impaired hearing and in perceiving hearing, speech, and lip reading as highly desirable tools for behavior if the person has or can obtain efficient functioning with them.

The groups disagree, however, in the degree to which they see such skills as simple tools for communication or as personal characteristics that every human being "ought" to have and use. They disagree about whether obtaining a limited degree of aural-oral functioning is worth the cost that presently is imposed on every American deaf child. They disagree in their willingness to accept other means of communication, such as finger spelling and signs, and they disagree in their evaluation of the degree of personal life satisfaction that is open to those who communicate by visual means. Finally, they differ in the experiences they have had in successfully teaching auditory discrimination, speech, and lip reading to those with impaired responsiveness to sound, and they differ in their expectations of frequency and degree of success in these activities that can be expected in the future.

Perhaps the heart of the dispute is based on the observation that children with severely impaired hearing tend to be, or to become, visually coupled to the environment to the near exclusion of aural-oral couplings. One kind of question is: Is this atypical development desirable and inevitable or is it unduly restrictive and can it be changed? One kind of reply is: A visual orientation presently is fact for large numbers of individuals who will not or cannot benefit in the foreseeable future from experimental advances in the improvement of hearing. Another kind of question is: Should effort be expended exclusively on strengthening the functioning of a child's weakest sensory channel and his responding to stimuli that are weakly perceived, or should some effort be devoted to developing his natural sensory strengths and his responding to stimuli that are strongly perceived? These questions have many social and cultural ramifications, and in the absence of data about the effects of alternative procedures, they are not easy to answer.

The normally hearing student is often quick to judge that aural-oral communication is better than visual-manual communication, and that the deaf person should seek the former whatever the cost, resulting proficiency, or probability of failure. This is not surprising. There are many good, or at least plausible, reasons for such a judgment, although not everyone will agree. It is not possible to reach a sound conclusion in this matter unless one is acquainted with the issues and the arguments that are advanced on both sides. Unfortunately, the student is more likely to be exposed to personal documents written by orally-trained individuals such as Molly Sifton, author of "Fulfilment," [148] and less likely to see her sequel, written eleven years later, which she titled, "I Changed My Mind." [149] He is more likely to see such articles about the deaf as appear in the Volta Review [150] than equally eloquent but opposing articles by deaf persons such as are published in the Silent Worker [151] and the Silent World.[152]

It is a measure of the power of the oralist movement in the United States that every child in a school for the deaf is exposed to instruction in speech and lip reading, and no such child receives formal instruction in the language of signs. For many psychologists, however, the issue is by no means foreclosed. Just as it seems a wise procedure to bring amplified sound to the ears of infants who appear unresponsive to ordinary auditory stimuli, so it also appears reasonable to encourage the use of other modalities which may serve as a means of communication and facilitate a child's knowledge of the external environment. The latter issue seems likely to assume increased importance as workers in differential diagnosis begin to identify, with greater regularity and precision, those children whose unresponsiveness to sound is associated with other central nervous system disorders. Among these children are those who do not benefit appreciably from training in auditory discrimination, speech, and lip reading, and the investigation of the conditions under which they might benefit has barely begun. For these children, and perhaps for others, development and learning might be facilitated by expert instruction in the language of signs and in finger spelling.

Several arguments have been used to oppose the use of a visual-manual language by the young deaf child. The social argument contends that the use of signs and finger spelling sets the child apart from the larger society and limits his intercourse to the small number of individuals who know his special language. That may be so. It has not been demonstrated, however, that the social position or functioning of the orally taught child is better during early childhood; it may be poorer.

The psychological argument is based on the assumption that once the use of a more easily perceived visual language is begun, the child's speech and language will not develop as readily or as well. From an empirical standpoint, there is no convincing evidence that this argument is true, and there is some evidence that it is not true.[153] Investigators in Russia [154] have reported that the early use of finger spelling facilitates the growth of oral communication, and these data are congruent with what might be expected on the basis of many theoretical considerations. For example, what principles of psychology would suggest that learning should begin with the most difficult and complex discriminations, in which self-monitoring feedback is largely lacking, rather than with easier tasks?

The linguistic arguments state that the language of signs is an impoverished, esoteric language in the sense that is has no symbols, unprecise symbols, or private symbols for many common English words. It also has a different structure than English. Both arguments appear to be true but not inevitable. When one considers that the language has not been formally taught for almost a hundred years, that its development was the responsibility of no grammarians, no lexicographers, no linguists, and that it has been passed on, literally, from hand to hand of a relatively uneducated group, its viability is astounding. It is a language that can be enriched, and its structure can be formalized either as a separate language or as the gestural equivalent of English. The recent upsurge of interest in this field and in the additional possibilities inherent in finger spelling gives good indications of further developments to come.

In other aspects of deafness, the psychophysicists and the learning psychologists are active in new and promising investigations, but the social, developmental, and clinical psychologists are not. A recent conference on the researchable problems of deafness resulted in an impressive list of problems in search of answers.[155] Hopefully, the next decade will be a fruitful one.

Notes

[1] This chapter was originally prepared while the author was a Public Health Service Research Fellow of the National Institute of Mental Health. Its revision was accomplished while he was Visiting Professor of Psychology and Physical Medicine at the Stanford University Medical School.

[2] I. J. Hirsh, *The Measurement of Hearing* (New York: McGraw-Hill Book Co., Inc., 1952). Also, L. Meyerson, "Hearing for Speech in Children," *Acta Oto-Laryngologica*, Supplementum CXXVIII, Stockholm: 1956.

[3] Decibel is a unit used in expressing the relative power of the sounds produced by the audiometer. Plotting decibels on a linear scale is conventional, but it is important to remember that the scale is actually logarithmic. Thus 20 decibels is not 20 times as great as 1 decibel but 100 times as great:
$1 \text{ db} = 1$; $10 \text{ db} = 10^1 = 10$; $20 \text{ db} = 10^2 = 100$; $30 \text{ db} = 10^3 = 1000$; etc.

[4] S. S. Stevens and H. Davis, *Hearing: Its Psychology and Physiology* (New York: John Wiley & Sons, Inc., 1938).

[5] W. C. Beasley, *The National Health Survey: 1935-1936. Normal Hearing by Air and Bone Conduction*, Public Health Reports, Hearing Study Series (Washington, D.C.: Government Printing Office, 1938). Also, J. C. Steinberg and M. B. Gardner, "On the Auditory Significance of the Term Hearing Loss," *Journal of the Acoustical Society*, 11 (1940), 270-277.

[6] White House Conference on Child Health and Protection, *Special Education, The Handicapped and the Gifted: Report of the Committee on Special Classes* (Section III, Education and Training), Volume III-F (New York: Appleton-Century-Crofts, 1931).

[7] Conference of Executives for the Deaf, "Report of the Conference Committee on Nomenclature," *American Annals of the Deaf*, 83 (1938), 1-3.

[8] W. A. Hughson, A. Ciocco, E. G. Witting, and P. S. Lawrence, "Studies of Pupils of the Pennsylvania School for the Deaf, III. An Analysis of Speech Characteristics in Deafened Children with Observations on Training Methods," *Child Development*, 13 (1942), 131-158.
H. R. Myklebust, "The Use of Individual Hearing Aids in a Residential School for the Deaf with Implications for Acoustic Training," *American Annals of the Deaf*, 91 (1946), 255-261.
A. W. G. Ewing and I. R. Ewing, "Educational Treatment of Deafness," *Lancet*, 253 (1947), 628-630.
E. H. Johnson, "The Ability of Pupils in a School for the Deaf to Understand Various Methods of Communication," *American Annals of the Deaf*, 93 (1948), 194-213; and "The Ability of Pupils in a School for the Deaf to Understand Various Methods of Communication—II," *ibid.*, 93 (1948), 258-314.
C. V. Hudgins, "The Response of Profoundly Deaf Children to Auditory Training," *Journal of Speech and Hearing Disorders*, 18 (1953), 273-288.

[9] E. Wedenberg, "Auditory Training of Deaf and Hard of Hearing Children," *Acta Oto-Laryngologica*, Supplementum XCIV, Stockholm: 1951.

[10] "Tabular Statements of American Schools for the Deaf, October 31, 1951," *American Annals of the Deaf*, 99 (1954), 1-236.

[11] R. Pintner and D. G. Paterson, "The Binet Scale and the Deaf Child," *Journal of Educational Psychology*, 6 (1915), 201-210.

[12] J. C. R. Licklider, "The Perception of Speech," in *Handbook of Experimental Psychology*, ed. S. S. Stevens (New York: John Wiley & Sons, Inc., 1951).

[13] I. J. Hirsh, *op. cit.*

[14] H. R. Myklebust, *Auditory Disorders in Children* (New York: Grune & Stratton, Inc., 1954).

[15] "Tabular Statements of American Schools for the Deaf, October 31, 1951," *op.*

cit. and also those for October 31, 1961, *American Annals of the Deaf*, 107 (1962), 158.

[16] R. Ripin, "A Comparative Study of the Development of Infants in an Institution with Those in Homes of Low Socio-Economic Status," *Psychological Bulletin*, 30 (1933), 680-681.

W. Goldfarb, "The Effects of Early Institutional Care on Adolescent Personality," *Journal of Experimental Education*, 12 (1943), 106-129.

A. Freud and D. Burlingham, *Infants Without Families* (New York: International Universities Press, Inc., 1944).

R. A. Spitz, "Hospitalism: An Inquiry into the Genesis of Psychiatric Conditions in Early Childhood," *Psychoanalytic Study of the Child*, 1 (1945), 53-74.

J. Bowlby, *Maternal Care and Mental Health* (Geneva: World Health Organization, 1951).

L. J. Stone, "A Critique of Studies of Infant Isolation," *Child Development*, 25 (1954), 9-20.

[17] R. Pintner and D. G. Paterson, *op. cit.*

[18] E. S. Levine, "An Investigation into the Personality of Normal Deaf Adolescent Girls" (Doctoral Dissertation, New York University, 1948, University Microfilms No. 1156).

[19] V. Lyon, *et al.*, "Survey of the Illinois Schools for the Deaf," *American Annals of the Deaf*, 78 (1933), 157-175.

[20] K. MacKane, *A Comparison of the Intelligence of Deaf and Hearing Children*, Teachers College Contributions to Education, No. 585 (New York: Columbia University Press, 1933).

[21] H. Amoss, *Ontario School Ability Examination* (Toronto: Ryerson Press, 1936).

[22] E. Peterson, "Testing Deaf Children with Kohs Block Designs," *American Annals of the Deaf*, 81 (1936), 242-254.

[23] S. Roth, "Survey of the Psychological Examination Given by Dr. Stella Bowers, May, 1937," *West Virginia Tablet*, 61 (1938).

[24] A. Zeckel and J. van der Kolk, "A Comparative Intelligence Test of Groups of Children Born Deaf and of Good Hearing by Means of the Porteus Test," *American Annals of the Deaf*, (1939), 114-123.

[25] W. J. Morrison, "Ontario School Ability Examination," *American Annals of the Deaf*, 85 (1940), 184-189.

[26] D. F. Capwell, "Performance of Deaf Children on the Arthur Point Scale," *Journal of Consulting Psychology*, 9 (1945), 91-94.

[27] E. H. Johnson, "The Effect of Academic Level on Scores from the Chicago Non-Verbal Examination for Primary Pupils," *American Annals of the Deaf*, 92 (1947), 227-233.

[28] P. Oleron, "Conceptual Thinking of the Deaf," *American Annals of the Deaf*, 98 (1953), 304-310.

[29] J. Drever and M. Collins, *Performance Tests of Intelligence* (Edinburgh: Oliver & Boyd, Ltd., 1928).

[30] H. Schick and M. Meyer, "The Use of the Lectometer in the Testing of the Hearing and the Deaf," *American Annals of the Deaf*, 77 (1932), 292-303.

[31] H. Schick, "The Use of a Standardized Performance Test for Pre-School Age Children with a Language Handicap," *Proceedings of the International Congress on the Education of the Deaf* (Trenton, 1933), pp. 526-533.

[32] H. Bishop, "Performance Scale Tests Applied to Deaf and Hard of Hearing Children," *Volta Review*, 38 (1936), 484-485.

[33] S. A. Kirk, "Behavior Problem Tendencies in Deaf and Hard of Hearing Children," *American Annals of the Deaf*, 83 (1938), 131-137.

[34] A. Streng and S. A. Kirk, "The Social Competence of Deaf and Hard of Hearing Children in a Public Day School," *American Annals of the Deaf*, 83 (1938), 244-254.

[35] H. S. Lane and J. Schneider, "A Performance Test for School Age Deaf Children," *American Annals of the Deaf*, 86 (1941), 441-447.

[36] E. M. L. Burchard and H. R. Myklebust, "A Comparison of Congenital and Ad-

ventitious Deafness with Respect to Its Effect on Intelligence, Personality and Social Maturity. Part I: Intelligence," *American Annals of the Deaf*, 87 (1942), 140-154.

37 D. L. Amin, "Differences Among Deaf and Hearing Children," *Indian Journal of Psychology*, 21 (1946), 91-92.

38 H. S. Lane, "The Relation between Mental Test Scores and Future Achievement," *Proceedings of the National Forum on Deafness and Speech Pathology* (St. Louis, 1947).

39 H. B. Hood, "A Preliminary Survey of Some Mental Abilities of Deaf Children," *British Journal of Educational Psychology*, 19 (1949), 210-219.

40 M. Borelli, "La Naissance des Operations Logiques Chez Le Sourd-muet," *Enfance*, 4 (1951), 222-228.

41 J. MacPherson, "A Comparison of Scores of Deaf and Hearing Children on the Hiskey Test of Learning Ability and on Performance Scales" (Master's thesis, University of Washington, 1945).

42 J. MacPherson and H. S. Lane, "A Comparison of Deaf and Hearing on the Hiskey Test and Performance Scales," *American Annals of the Deaf*, 93 (1948), 178-184.

43 E. S. Levine, *op. cit.*

44 J. C. Reamer, "Mental and Educational Measurements of the Deaf," *Psychological Monographs*, XXIX, No. 132 (1921).

45 H. E. Day, I. S. Fusfeld, and R. Pintner, *A Survey of American Schools for the Deaf* (Washington, D.C.: National Research Council, 1928).

46 E. Peterson and J. Williams, "Intelligence of Deaf Children as Measured by Drawings," *American Annals of the Deaf*, 75 (1930), 242-254.

47 M. Shirley and F. L. Goodenough, "A Survey of Intelligence of Deaf Children in Minnesota Schools," *American Annals of the Deaf*, 77 (1932), 238-247.

48 W. Lyon, et al., *op. cit.*

49 K. MacKane, *op. cit.*

50 A. Streng and S. A. Kirk, *op. cit.*

51 N. N. Springer, "A Comparative Study of the Intelligence of a Group of Deaf and Hearing Children," *American Annals of the Deaf*, 83 (1938), 138-152.

N. N. Springer, "A Comparative Study of Behavior Traits of Deaf and Hearing Children of New York City," *American Annals of the Deaf*, 83 (1938), 255-273.

N. N. Springer, "A Comparative Study of Psychoneurotic Responses of Deaf and Hearing Children," *Journal of Educational Psychology*, 29 (1938), 459-466.

52 E. H. Johnson, "The Effect of Academic Level on Scores from the Chicago Non-Verbal Examination for Primary Pupils," *op. cit.*

53 M. Shirley and F. L. Goodenough, *op. cit.*

54 C. M. Louttit, *Clinical Psychology* (New York: Harper & Row, Publishers, 1936).

55 R. E. Kellogg, "The Relative Value of Verbal, Non-Verbal and Performance Tests of Intelligence in Predicting School Achievement of Deaf Children" (Master's thesis, University of Chicago, 1940).

56 E. H. Johnson, "The Ability of Pupils in a School for the Deaf to Understand Various Methods of Communication," *op. cit.*

57 J. L. Waldman, F. A. Wade, and C. W. Aretz, *Hearing and the School Child* (Washington, D.C.: Volta Bureau, 1930).

58 R. Madden, *The School Status of the Hard of Hearing Child* (New York: Columbia University Press, 1931).

59 R. Pintner and J. Lev, "The Intelligence of the Hard of Hearing School Child," *Journal of Genetic Psychology*, 55 (1939), 31-48.

60 J. C. Reamer, *op. cit.*

61 H. E. Day, I. S. Fusfeld, and R. Pintner, *op. cit.*

62 P. Hall, "Results of Recent Tests at Gallaudet College," *American Annals of the Deaf*, 74 (1929), 389-395.

63 N. N. Springer, *op. cit.;* also E. H. Johnson, "The Ability of Pupils in a School for the Deaf to Understand Various Methods of Communication," *op. cit.*

[64] E. H. Johnson, *ibid.;* E. S. Levine, *op. cit.;* V. Lyon *et al., op. cit.;* also the following:

F. Heider and G. M. Heider, "Studies in the Psychology of the Deaf: No. 2," *Psychological Monographs,* 53 (1941).

H. S. Lane, "The Rate of Educational Progress of the Deaf Child," *Oralism and Auralism* (Columbus, Ohio, 1949).

I. S. Fusfeld, "A Cross-Section Evaluation of the Academic Program of Schools for the Deaf," *Gallaudet College Bulletin,* 3 (1954).

[65] I. S. Fusfeld, *ibid.*

[66] C. C. Upshall, *Day School vs. Institutions for the Deaf* (New York: Teachers College, Columbia University, 1929).

[67] E. H. Johnson, *op. cit.*

[68] J. L. Waldman, F. A. Wade, and C. W. Aretz, *op. cit.;* also the following:

F. W. Bock, *Deafness Prevention* (Rochester, N. Y.: Rochester League for the Hard of Hearing, *circa* 1928).

J. H. Humphrey, "Hard of Hearing Children in the St. Louis Public Schools," *Volta Review,* 30 (1929), 644-646, 666.

F. A. Laurer, "Hearing Survey Among a Group of Pupils of Syracuse Schools," *American Journal of Public Health,* 18 (1928), 1353-1360.

H. L. Warwick, "Hearing Tests in the Public Schools of Fort Worth," *Volta Review,* 30 (1929), 641-643.

E. B. Sterling and E. Bell, "Hearing of School Children," *Public Health Reports,* Washington, 145 (1930), 1117-1130.

D. A. Caplin, "A Special Report on Retardation of Children with Impaired Hearing," *American Annals of the Deaf,* 82 (1937), 234-243.

J. W. Sprunt and F. W. Finger, "Auditory Deficiency and Academic Achievement," *Journal of Speech and Hearing Disorders,* 14 (1949), 26-32.

[69] J. L. Waldman, F. A. Wade, and C. W. Aretz, *op. cit.;* R. Madden, *op. cit.;* J. N. Boone, "A Study of the Effect of Hearing Loss on Freshmen at the University of Florida on Selected Measures of Their Achievement" (Master's thesis, University of Florida, 1951).

[70] J. W. Sprunt and F. W. Finger, *op. cit.*

[71] J. W. Prince, "The Effect of Impaired Hearing at Various Frequencies on Grades and Citizenship," *Journal of Educational Research,* 42 (1948), 234-237.

[72] V. Lyon *et al., op. cit.;* E. H. Johnson, *op. cit.;* M. Shirley and F. L. Goodenough, *op. cit.;* C. M. Louttit, *op. cit;* also the following:

L. Brunschwig, *A Study of Some Personality Aspects of Deaf Children* (New York: Teachers College, Columbia University, 1936).

I. Gregory, "A Comparison of Certain Personality Traits and Interests in Deaf and in Hearing Children," *Child Development,* 9 (1938), 277-280.

N. N. Springer and S. Roslow, "A Further Study of the Psychoneurotic Responses of Deaf and Hearing Children," *Journal of Educational Psychology,* 29 (1938), 590-596.

H. W. McCormick, *Acoustically Handicapped Children* (New York: New York City Board of Education, 1941).

M. Albright, "Mental Health of Children with Hearing Impairments," *Exceptional Children,* 19 (1952), 107, 110-113, 124.

[73] E. S. Levine, *op. cit.;* also the following:

J. P. Altable, "The Rorschach Psychodiagnostic as Applied to Deaf-Mutes," *Rorschach Research Exchange and Journal of Projective Techniques,* 11 (1947), 74-79.

H. McAndrew, "Rigidity and Isolation: A Study of the Deaf and the Blind," *Journal of Abnormal and Social Psychology,* 43 (1948), 476-494.

C. Berzmann, "Some Considerations Concerning the Rorschach of Deaf Mutes," *Enfance,* 3 (1950), 33-48.

[74] S. A. Kirk, *op. cit.;* E. M. L. Burchard and H. R. Myklebust, *op cit.*

188   LEE MEYERSON

75 N. N. Springer, *op. cit.*
76 K. P. Bradway, "The Social Competence of Deaf Children," *American Annals of the Deaf,* 82 (1937), 122-140; E. L. M. Burchard and H. R. Myklebust, *op. cit.*
77 A. Streng and S. A. Kirk, *op. cit.;* C. Avery, "Social Competence of Acoustically Handicapped Children," *Journal of Exceptional Children,* 15 (1948), 71-73.
78 H. McAndrew, *op. cit.;* P. Oleron, *op. cit.*
79 K. B. Wall, "A Study of Rigidity in the Personality of the Deaf" (Master's thesis, Emory University, 1952).
80 D. Johnson, "A Study of Rigidity in the Personality of Deaf Children" (Master's thesis, University of Kansas, 1954).
81 K. Lewin, T. Dembo, L. Festinger, and P. Sears, "Level of Aspiration" in *Personality and the Behavior Disorders,* ed. J. McV. Hunt (New York: The Ronald Press Company, 1944).
P. S. Sears, "Levels of Aspiration in Academically Successful and Unsuccessful Children," *Journal of Abnormal and Social Psychology,* 35 (1940), 498-536.
E. W. Gruen, "Level of Aspiration in Relation to Personality Factors in Adolescents," *Child Development,* 9 (1938), 277-280.
82 H. McAndrew, *op. cit.*
83 D. Johnson, *op. cit.;* L. Rutledge, "Aspiration Levels of Deaf Children as Compared with Those of Hearing Children," *Journal of Speech and Hearing Disorders,* 19 (1954), 375-380.
84 P. S. Sears, *op. cit.*
85 R. Madden, *op. cit.;* H. W. McCormick, *op. cit.;* also the following:
S. Habbe, *Personality Adjustments of Adolescent Boys with Impaired Hearing* (New York: Teachers College, Columbia University, 1936).
R. Pintner, "An Adjustment Test of Normal and Hard of Hearing Children," *Journal of Genetic Psychology,* 56 (1940), 367-381.
R. Pintner, "Intelligence Testing of Partially Sighted Children," *Journal of Educational Psychology,* 33 (1942), 265-272.
86 S. Habbe, *op. cit.*
87 M. F. Fiedler, "Teachers' Problems with Hard of Hearing Children," *Journal of Educational Research,* 42 (1949), 618-622.
88 N. E. Murray, "Deafness Following Maternal Rubella," *Medical Journal of Australia,* 1 (1949), 126-130.
89 O. Bridgman, "The Estimation of Mental Ability in Deaf Children," *American Annals of the Deaf,* 84 (1939), 337-349.
90 D. F. Capwell, *op. cit.;* E. M. L. Burchard and H. R. Mycklebust, *op. cit.*
91 R. Pintner, *op. cit.*
92 E. Stockwell, "Visual Defects in the Deaf Child," *Archives of Ophthalmology,* 48 (1952), 428-432.
93 H. E. Day, I. S. Fusfeld, and R. Pintner, *op. cit.*
94 H. Best, *Deafness and the Deaf in the United States* (New York: The Macmillan Company, 1943).
95 R. Pintner, J. Eisenson, and M. B. Stanton, *The Psychology of the Physically Handicapped* (New York: Appleton-Century-Crofts, 1941).
96 L. Meyerson, *op. cit.;* J. C. R. Licklider, *op. cit.;* J. C. R. Licklider, D. Bindra, and I. Pollack, "The Intelligibility of Rectangular Speech Waves," *American Journal of Psychology,* 61 (1948), 1-20; J. C. R. Licklider, and I. Pollack, "Effects of Differentiation, Integration and Infinite Peak Clipping upon the Intelligibility of Speech," *Journal of the Acoustical Society,* 20 (1948), 42-51; E. Wedenberg, *op. cit.*
97 I. S. Fusfeld, "Research and Testing at Gallaudet College," *American Annals of the Deaf,* 85 (1940), 170-183.
98 J. MacPherson, *op. cit.;* J. MacPherson and H. S. Lane, *op. cit.*
99 E. S. Levine, *op. cit.*
100 J. R. Birch and J. W. Birch, "The Leiter International Performance Scale as an Aid in the Psychological Study of Deaf Children," *American Annals of the Deaf,* 96 (1951), 502-511.

[101] R. Pintner, J. Eisenson, and M. B. Stanton, *op. cit.;* G. J. Alves, "Recherches sur le Langage, la Mimique et la Psycho-Motilité des Sourds-muets," *Journal de Psychologie Normale et Pathologique,* 45 (1952), 464-483; P. Oleron, *op. cit.*

[102] M. Eberhardt, "A Summary of Some Preliminary Investigations of the Deaf," *Psychological Monographs,* 52 (1940), 1-5.

[103] M. Borelli, *op. cit.*

[104] C. Rogers, *Clinical Treatment of the Problem Child* (Boston: Houghton Mifflin Company, 1939).

[105] M. Sherman and C. B. Key, "The Intelligence of Isolated Mountain Children," *Child Development,* 3 (1932), 279-290.

M. Sherman and T. Henry, *The Hollow Folk* (New York: Thomas Y. Crowell Company, 1933).

E. J. Asher, "The Inadequacy of Current Intelligence Tests for Testing Kentucky Mountain Children," *Journal of Genetic Psychology,* 46 (1935), 480-486.

[106] H. Hofsteater, "An Experiment in Pre-School Education," *Gallaudet College Bulletin,* 8 (1959), 1-17.

[107] L. J. Stone and C. G. Fine, "The Effects of a Revised Pre-School Program on the Personality Development and the Communication Efficiency of Young Deaf Children," *Progress Report, Public Health Service,* Research Grant B-331, July, 1953.

[108] D. McCarthy, "Language Development in Children," in *Manual of Child Psychology,* ed. L. Carmichael (New York: John Wiley & Sons, Inc., 1946).

[109] C. C. Upshall, *op. cit.*

[110] R. G. Barker, B. A. Wright, L. Meyerson, and M. R. Gonick, *Adjustment to Physical Handicap and Illness* (New York: Social Science Research Council, 1953).

[111] L. Meyerson, *op. cit.*

[112] L. Meyerson, "The Visually Handicapped," *Review of Educational Research,* 23 (1953), 476-492.

[113] R. B. Goodwin, *It's Good to Be Black* (Garden City, N. Y.: Doubleday & Company, Inc., 1953).

[114] R. Benedict, "Continuities and Discontinuities in Cultural Conditioning," *Psychiatry,* 1 (1938), 161-167.

[115] D. J. Farber, "Written Communication in Psychotherapy," *Psychiatry,* 16 (1953), 365-374.

[116] E. E. Calkins, *and hearing not*—(New York: Charles Scribner's Sons, 1946).

[117] G. E. Murphy, *Your Deafness Is Not You* (New York: Harper & Row, Publishers, 1954).

[118] T. Dembo, G. Ladieu, and B. A. Wright, *Adjustment to Misfortune, A Study of the Social-Emotional Relationships Between Injured and Non-injured People* (Army Medical Research and Development Board, Office of the Surgeon General, War Department, April, 1948).

[119] T. Dembo, G. Ladieu, and B. A. Wright, "Acceptance of Loss-Amputations," in *Psychological Aspects of Physical Disability* (Washington: Rehabilitation Service Series No. 210. Superintendent of Documents, *n.d.*).

[120] G. E. Murphy, *op. cit.*

[121] We cannot consider here the extensive literature on the growth-inhibiting effects of threat and frustration. Barker, Dembo, and Lewin (1941) will provide a start for students interested in investigating this problem. The literature on animal neurosis also offers suggestive leads for hypotheses about education of the deaf.

[122] S. A. Asch, *Social Psychology* (Englewood Cliffs, N.J.: Prentice-Hall, Inc., 1952).

[123] *Ibid.* See also, L. Meyerson, "Some Observations of the Psychological Roles of the Occupational Therapist," *American Journal of Occupational Therapy,* 11 (1957), 1-4.

[124] T. D. Cutsforth, "The Unreality of Words to the Blind," *Teachers Forum,* 4 (1932), 86-89.

[125] K. Lewin, *Resolving Social Conflicts* (New York: Harper & Row, Publishers, 1948).

[126] G. von Békésy, *Experiments in Hearing* (New York: McGraw-Hill Book Co., Inc., 1960); R. Bender, *The Conquest of Deafness* (Cleveland: Western Reserve University Press, 1960); H. Davis and S. R. Silverman, *Hearing and Deafness*, rev. ed. (New York: Holt, Rinehart & Winston, Inc., 1960); F. L. Darley, ed., *Identification Audiometry* (American Speech and Hearing Association, 1961); A. Ewing, ed., *The Modern Educational Treatment of Deafness* (Washington, D.C.: The Volta Bureau, 1960); K. W. Hodgson, *The Deaf and Their Problems* (New York: Philosophical Library, 1954); E. A. Levine, *The Psychology of Deafness* (New York: Columbia University Press, 1960); H. R. Myklebust, *The Psychology of Deafness* (New York: Grune & Stratton, Inc., 1960); H. A. Newby, *Audiology* (New York: Appleton-Centurn-Crofts, 1958).

[127] *DSH Abstracts*, National Index on Deafness, Speech, and Hearing, Gallaudet College, Washington 2, D.C.

[128] Myklebust, 1960, *op. cit.*

[129] H. G. Furth, "The Influence of Language on the Development of Concept Formation in Deaf Children," *Journal of Abnormal and Social Psychology*, 63 (1961), 386-389.

[130] J. Rosenstein, "Cognitive Abilities of Deaf Children," *Journal of Speech and Hearing Research*, 3 (1960), 108-119.

[131] P. Oléron, *Recherches sur le Developpement Mental des Sourds-Muets* (Paris: Centre National de la Recherche Scientifique, 1957).

[132] E. O. Carrier, *The Influence of Language in the Color-Weight Associations of Hearing and Deaf Children*. Science Education Research Report. (Cambridge: Harvard Graduate School of Education, 1962).

[133] F. X. Blair, "A Study of the Visual Memory of Deaf and Hearing Children," *American Annals of the Deaf*, 102 (1957), 254-263; D. G. Doehring, "Color-Form Attitudes of Deaf Children," *Journal of Speech and Hearing Research*, 3 (1960), 242-247; D. G. Doehring, "Visual Spatial Memory in Aphasic Children," *Journal of Speech and Hearing Research*, 3 (1960), 138-149; D. G. Doehring and J. Rosenstein, "Visual Word Recognition by Deaf and Hearing Children," *Journal of Speech and Hearing Research*, 3 (1960), 320-326; H. G. Furth, "Visual Paired-Associates Task with Deaf and Hearing Children," *Journal of Speech and Hearing Research*, 4 (1961), 172-177; H. G. Furth, "Scholastic Ability of Deaf Children and their Performance on Non-verbal Learning Tasks," *Journal of Clinical Psychology*, 17 (1961), 370-373; R. B. Hughes, "Verbal Conceptualization in Deaf and Hearing Children," *Exceptional Children*, 27 (1961), 517-522; S. L. Kates, W. W. Kates, J. Michael, and T. M. Walsh, "Categorization and Related Verbalizations in Deaf and Hearing Adolescents," *Journal of Educational Psychology*, 52 (1961), 188-194; A. L. Larr, "Perceptual and Conceptual Abilities of Residential School Deaf Children," *Exceptional Children*, 23 (1956), 53-66, 88; P. Naffin, "Die Psychologischen Voraussetzungen der Erziehung des Taubstummen Kindes" in *Padagogische Psychologie*, ed. H. Hetzer (Gottingen: Hogrefe, 1959); J. Rosenstein, "Perception, Cognition and Language in Deaf Children," *Exceptional Children*, 27 (1961), 276-284; K. Stafford, "Problem Solving Ability of Deaf and Hearing Children," *Journal of Speech and Hearing Research*, 5 (1962), 169-172; M. C. Templin, *Development of Reasoning in Children with Normal and Defective Hearing* (Minneapolis: University of Minnesota Press, 1950).

[134] An investigator found that more deaf children than hearing children *responded* according to color in a situation where the responses could be based upon differences in either color or shape. He concluded that deaf children do not *perceive* visual stimuli in the same manner as do hearing children. In view of the training procedures commonly employed with deaf children, was that a reasonable conclusion?

[135] M. F. Woodward and C. G. Barber, "Phoneme Perception in Lipreading," *Journal of Speech and Hearing Research*, 3 (1960), 212-222.

[136] A. A. Simmons, "Factors Related to Lipreading," *Journal of Speech and Hearing Research*, 2 (1959), 340-352.

[137] J. J. O'Neill and H. J. Oyer, *Visual Communication for the Hard of Hearing:*

History, Research and Methods (Englewood Cliffs, N.J.: Prentice-Hall, Inc., 1961).

138 B. T. Tervoort, "Esoteric Symbolism in the Communication Behavior of Young Deaf Children," *American Annals of the Deaf*, 106 (1961), 436-480.

139 W. C. Stokoe, Jr., *Sign Language Structure: An Outline of the Visual Communication Systems of the American Deaf*, Studies in Linguistics, Occasional Papers, No. 8 (Buffalo: University of Buffalo, 1960).

140 H. M. Moser, J. J. O'Neill, H. J. Oyer, S. M. Wolfe, E. A. Abernathy, and B. M. Schowe, Jr., "Historical Aspects of Manual Communication," *Journal of Speech and Hearing Disorders*, 25 (1960), 145-151; H. M. Moser and others, "Distance and Finger Spelling," *Journal of Speech and Hearing Research*, 4 (1961), 61-72; R. Paget, "Education of the Totally Deaf," Advancement of Science, 9 (1953), 437-441; E. L. Scouten, "Helping Your Deaf Child to Master English Through Finger Spelling," *American Annals of the Deaf*, 105 (1960), 226-229.

141 L. J. Stone, M. F. Fiedler, and C. G. Fine, "Preschool Education of Deaf Children," *Journal of Speech and Hearing Disorders*, 26 (1961), 45-60.

142 G. A. Falconer, "A Mechanical Device for Teaching Sight Vocabulary to Young Deaf Children," *American Annals of the Deaf*, 106 (1961), 251-257.

143 B. F. Skinner, *Science and Human Behavior* (New York: The Macmillan Company, 1953) and *Cumulative Record*, Part III (New York: Appleton-Century-Crofts, 1961).

144 C. P. Goetzinger and C. L. Rousey, "A Study of the Wechsler Performance Scale, Form II, and the Knox Cube Test with Deaf Adolescents," *American Annals of the Deaf*, 102 (1957), 388-398; M. S. Hiskey, "A Study of the Intelligence of Deaf and Hearing Children Through a Comparison of Performances on the Separate Standardizations of the Nebraska Test of Learning Aptitude," *American Annals of the Deaf*, 101 (1956), 320-339.

145 L. Meyerson, J. L. Michael, O. H. Mowrer, C. E. Osgood, and A. W. Staats, "Learning, Behavior and Rehabilitation," in *Research in the Psychological Aspects of Rehabilitation* (Washington, D.C.: American Psychological Association, 1963.

146 C. Griffiths, HEAR Foundation, Los Angeles, California, Personal Communication, and V. Victoria, "Hearing Aid Babies," *Audecibel*, X, No. 1 (1961), 4, 13.

147 Experimentation of this kind has not as yet been done and perhaps won't be until the screening of infants for hearing impairment is done routinely in hospitals by individuals who are not ethically obligated to initiate remedial measures. The moral problem for the therapist who believes in the effectiveness of her treatment is graphically described, in connection with a similar situation, in Sinclair Lewis' novel, *Arrowsmith* (New York: Harcourt, Brace & World, Inc., 1925).

148 M. Sifton, "Fulfilment," in I. R. Ewing and A. W. G. Ewing, *Opportunity and the Deaf Child* (London: University of London Press, 1947).

149 M. Sifton, "I Changed My Mind," *The Silent World*, July 1958 (reprint).

150 *The Volta Review*, Volta Bureau, Washington, D.C.

151 *The Silent Worker*, 2495 Shattuck Avenue, Berkeley 4, California.

152 *The Silent World*, 105 Gower Street, London, WC1, England. See especially, P. Abrahams, "Tell the Truth," 16 (1961), 173-175; "Without Speech," 17 (1962), 8-10; and "Education and Welfare," 17 (1962), 40-41.

153 A. Shaw and L. Meyerson, "Signs, Finger Spelling and Speech," (unpublished manuscript).

154 B. V. Morkovin, "Experiment in Teaching Deaf Preschool Children in the Soviet Union," *The Volta Review*, 62 (1960), 260-268, and M. F. Titova, "Peculiarities in Mastering Pronunciation Amongst Deaf Children Who Are Beginning to Learn Speech Through Dactylic Language," Abstract 1197 in *DSH Abstracts*, 1 (1961), 343.

155 M. Rogers and S. P. Quigley, eds., "Research Needs in the Vocational Rehabilitation of the Deaf," *American Annals of the Deaf*, 106 (1960), 335-370.

JON EISENSON

Director, The Speech and Hearing Clinic
Queens College

4 The Nature of Defective Speech

What Is Defective Speech?

From the point of view of the listener, any child who speaks so that attention is distracted from what is being said to the manner of its production may be considered to have defective speech. The amount of distraction and therefore the degree and significance of the defect may vary. Objectively, a child's speech is significantly defective when the amount of distraction is sufficient to make it difficult for him to communicate readily with a normal listener. A normal listener is one whose hearing, visual perceptive abilities, intelligence, expectations, and motivations make it possible for him to wish to and be able to understand what the speaker is attempting to communicate.

Defective speech has another aspect, a subjective one. From this viewpoint, speech may be considered defective if the speaker is unduly self-conscious or apprehensive about objectively small deviations. Any speech deviation is a defect when it looms large enough in the speaker's mind so that it becomes a factor which contributes to his maladjustment.

Specifically, speech may be considered defective if it is characterized by any one or more of the following:

1. It is not readily audible.
2. It is not readily intelligible.
3. It is vocally unpleasant.
4. It is visibly unpleasant.
5. It is labored in production or lacking in conventional rhythm and stress.
6. It is linguistically deficient.
7. It is inappropriate to the individual in terms of his age, sex, and physical development.
8. The speaker responds to his own speech as if one or more of the above were present.

Speech as a Developmental Process

It must constantly be appreciated that children do not learn, all at once or at any given time, how to speak with adult proficiency. Children arrive at proficiency for each of the components of speech—gesture, voice, articulated sound, and language—at different developmental periods. A fair amount of proficiency in the use of gesture is attained before words begin to be used meaningfully. Some degree of voice control for the expression of feelings precedes word usage and the control of voice for the communication of thought. Language growth is a continuous attainment which does not end with childhood. Articulatory control, though it begins before single words are evoked, may not be a proficient accomplishment for many children until they are in the second or third grade of school. Templin found that vowels and diphthongs were correctly produced by most children in 90 per cent of their verbal utterances by age three.[1] Comparable proficiency for some consonants, however, was not reached by most girls until age seven and by most boys until age eight.

Types of Speech Defects

SPEECH DEFECTS are frequently divided into four major types:

1. Defects of articulation (sound production).
2. Defects of phonation (voice production).
3. Defects of rhythm (stuttering and cluttering).
4. Language dysfunctions (delayed speech and aphasia).

For practical purposes, a second type of classification may be considered. This classification is based on categories of speech-defective individuals rather than on speech defects. For example, a cerebral palsied child may show defects of language delay, voice, and articulation. Most children with cleft palates have defects of articulation as well as of voice. With this in mind, the following classification should be found useful:

1. Defects of articulation, including omissions, distortions, or substitutions of speech sounds.
2. Defects of voice, including those of quality, loudness, pitch, variety, or adequate duration.
3. Stuttering (stammering) and cluttering.
4. Delayed language development.
5. Cleft-palate speech.
6. Cerebral palsy speech.
7. Impairment of previously developed language function (aphasias).
8. Speech defects associated with defective hearing.

Incidence of Speech Defects

A 1959 SURVEY conducted by a Committee on Legislation of the American Speech and Hearing Association found that 5 per cent of school age children (ages five to twenty-one) and 1.3 per cent of children under five years of age had defective speech.[2] The Committee on Legislation estimated that in the year 1960 at least 3,000,000 children in the United States would require remedial attention for their defects of speech or of hearing because of the implications of these defects for educational, social, and emotional adjustments. Table 4-1 summarizes the findings of the report.

It will be noted that the largest category, exceeding all the others

Table 4-1

Estimated Number of School-age Children per 10,000 with Each Type of Speech or Hearing Problem

Type of Problem	Per Cent of Children with Serious Problem	Number of Children with Serious Problem
Articulation	3.0	300
Stuttering	1.0	100
Voice	.1	10
Cleft-palate speech	.1	10
Cerebral palsy speech	.1	10
Retarded speech development	.2	20
Speech problem due to impaired hearing	.5	50
Total	5.0	500

combined, is that for functional articulatory defects. It is likely that among the children with less severe speech defects an even greater proportionate number fall into this category.

Sex Distribution

The consensus of evidence indicates that the number of boys exceeds that of girls among school-age children with defective speech. Among typical studies which bear out these findings are those of Mills and Streit [3] and Roe and Milisen [4] in relation to articulatory defects. Probably the greatest sex differences are to be found in regard to stuttering. Schuell made an extensive study of sex ratio among stutterers as found in the current literature. Schuell concluded that:

> A sex difference of from two to ten males to one female is found among stutterers, the magnitude of the ratio varying according to the age and educational status of the population studied, and according to the methods used in obtaining samples and making surveys.[5]

It has long been recognized that girls begin to speak earlier, arrive at articulatory efficiency earlier, and have somewhat better language development in the early years than do boys. Now it may be added that, even when allowances are made for the later initial age of speaking for boys, the quality of the speech for many years is on a lower level for boys as a group than it is for girls. It apparently continues to be so even on the university level. Morley, for example, found that at the University of Michigan, the proportion of speech-defective students was consistently higher among the male than it was among the female student population. The ratios ranged from 1.6 to 1, to as high as 3.4 to 1, during World War II.[6]

Causes of Defective Speech

ONE MUST never lose sight of the fact that a speech defect is the defect of *a person*. What may constitute a primary cause of a defect for one individual may have little or no etiological significance for another. Some children with minor organic anomalies of the articulatory mechanism, such as malocclusions, may have unmistakable articulatory defects. Others, with measurably greater anomalies, may have entirely adequate articulation. Some children regress in speech proficiency when new siblings are brought into the family. Other children take the arrival of new brothers and sisters in apparently easy stride. Even stutterers, who as a group are fairly predictable as to what factors will increase or decrease the severity of their stuttering, vary extensively when considered as individuals. The causes of speech defects which we shall consider refer to the various groups of speech defectives when they are studied as groups. In the final analysis, the only certain way of knowing why a given child has a speech defect, and what this defect may mean to him, is to study him as a whole child.[7]

Organic Causes

Some speech defects are clearly organic in origin. The articulatory and vocal difficulties of the child with a cleft palate can, at least initially, be attributed directly to the type and severity of the cleft. Hearing impairment, if it begins early and is relatively severe, may directly account for defects of both articulation and voice. Malocclusions and dental irregularities, if severe, may be responsible for some degree and some types of defective articulation, though such physical abnormalities, as indicated earlier, do not make it inevitable that a given child will have faulty articulation. Cerebral palsy conditions which involve the speech mechanism are directly responsible for defective speech. Aphasic involvements, by definition, are impairments of established language ability on the basis of brain pathology.

Functional Causes

Many children with apparently normal speech mechanism nevertheless have defects of articulation and/or of voice. In some instances, imitation of an older sibling, a playmate, or an adult may account for the defect. Children learn to articulate, vocalize, and use language "by ear." If what they hear is faulty, and if they have no cause to be negatively inclined to what they hear, they will learn to speak in a faulty manner. In an important sense, speech faults which are based on imitative patterns may indicate normal adaptive behavior. If the influential and respected members of a child's environment speak in a given way, the child, having no basis to determine that such speech is not appropriate, should be expected to imitate what he hears, *unless he is negatively inclined either to the individuals or to the general environment.*

Psychogenic Causes

Numerous studies have supplied data which support the clinical impression that many defects of speech are basically psychogenic. When the defects are found in children, their origin, when not organic or imitative, may often be associated with the children's reactions to their environment, particularly to their parents. It is not at all surprising that some investigators have interpreted their findings to indicate that the primary maladjustments exist in the parents of the speech-defective children. Wood, for example, found that, on the whole, a group of fifty speech-defective children showed better adjustment than the parents. Despite this, about half of the children to whom the Thematic Apperception Test was administered revealed dynamisms which suggested frustration, withdrawing tendencies, and a sense of lack of affection. Only three of the twenty-five children to whom the TAT was administered manifested no preponderance of unfavorable dynamisms. Maladjustments of the parents were determined on the basis of the findings of the Bernreuter Personality Inventory and the California Test of Personality. Both mothers and fathers tended to have poor adjustment scores. Eighty-six per cent of the children had one or both parents who were below the 35th percentile in self-adjustment; 64 per cent had one or both parents who were below the 35th percentile in social adjustment. The mothers, as a group, were significantly totally less well adjusted than the fathers. A specific significant finding was that the social standards of the mothers were very high in comparison with other adjustment scores.

> When this is viewed in relation to the emotional instability of the maternal group, it appears probable that the speech-defective children had imposed upon them a set of very high standards in an atmosphere of habitual emotional outbursts on the part of the parents.

In general, Wood concludes

> . . . on the basis of this study that functional articulatory defects of children are definitely and significantly associated with maladjustment and undesirable traits on the part of the parents, and that such factors are usually maternally centered.[8]

Moncur compared the responses of the mothers of stutterers and non-stutterers on questionnaires designed to reveal tendencies toward parental dominance and the holding of children to excessively high standards. Moncur found the mothers to be much like those studied by Wood. As a group, the mothers of stutterers tended by their responses to reveal a variety of dominating actions which included ". . . domination by disciplinary action, domination by oversupervising and overprotecting the child, domination by holding the child to excessively high standards, and domination by adverse parental criticism." [9]

The findings of Wood and Moncur in regard to these special populations can probably safely be generalized to include other types of speech-defective children. Investigations at the Queens College Speech and Hearing Clinic suggest that the parents of delayed-speech children tend to be unrealistic, rigid, and overprotective. Mothers tend to be so to a greater degree than fathers. This observation is consistent with the findings of Peckarsky who studied and compared a population of twenty-six mothers of children with psychogenic delayed speech and a control group of mothers whose children had normal speech.[10] As a group, the mothers of the delayed-speech children were found to be "overprotective, rigid individuals, who are restrictive in their demands upon the children." The home environment is reported to be characterized by "confusion, tension, and a lack of organization in the performing of routine tasks." In fairness to the mothers of the delayed-speech children, it should be noted of the control group mothers that their attitudes were not necessarily different, but were more moderate.

Intelligence and Speech Defects

THE STUDIES which we will consider will be divided into three categories:

1. The relationship of speech defects to intelligence in children of school age as a whole.
2. Intelligence of speech-defective children with physical handicaps.
3. The incidence of speech defects among children known to be of below average intelligence.

Carrell analyzed a school population of 1,174 children.[11] He found that the speech-defective children, taken as a group, were lower in average intelligence than the general population. Craig surveyed and analyzed a population of 692 first-, second-, third-, and fourth-grade children enrolled in four Negro schools in Augusta, Georgia, for the incidence of speech defects and factors of intelligence, reading abilities, grade placement, and socioeconomic background.[12] He found that in regard to intelligence, at the fourth-grade level the children with severe speech problems tended to fall below the non-defective group.

Among physically handicapped children with speech defects, the cerebral palsied and the deaf show a higher proportion of those mentally below average than does the total population. Stanton, after surveying the literature on the intelligence of crippled children, noted that the cerebral palsied group showed the lowest mean scores.[13] Most objective findings, even when allowances are made for the nature of the motor disabilities, indicate that a disproportionately large number of cerebral palsied children are also mentally retarded. Wolfe, for example, found that 26 per cent of the subjects of his study were so limited in intelligence that they had to be considered uneducable.[14]

Deaf children as a group fall below the mean intelligence level of hearing children. This general observation holds when either individual or group tests are used.[15] Hard of hearing children were found to fall slightly but significantly below the normal hearing on tests of verbal intelligence. A slight but not significant difference was also found in a non-language test.[16] Oleron, using the Raven's Matrices Test, concluded that the deaf were equal to the hearing in concrete mental functioning but inferior to them in abstract intelligence.[17]

The Mentally Deficient

The consistent finding of studies of speech defects among mentally deficient children is that the incidence of defects is considerably higher than it is among the population as a whole. In a pioneer study Kennedy found that 42.57 per cent of children in the moron group (I.Q.'s ranging from 50 to 69) had speech defects; 31 of 32 imbeciles (I.Q.'s from 21 to 47) had speech defects; and all of the children in the idiot range (I.Q.'s from 20 to below test level) had defects of speech.[18] Lewald found that 56 per cent of speaking feeble-minded children had speech defects.[19]

More recent studies present data which support the earlier findings. Sachs, for example, studied the incidence and nature of speech defects in a group of 210 mentally deficient children between the ages of ten and twenty.[20] He found that speech defects were present in 57 per cent of the children. Gens reports an even higher percentage.[21] According to Gens, 70 to 75 per cent of institutionalized mentally deficient children have disorders of speech.

Smith, after surveying the recent literature on the relationship between mental retardation and defective speech, concluded "The incidence of speech problems was found to range from 8 per cent up to 79 per cent, depending on the intellectual range being studied. With retarded, specifically, language development was delayed, articulation problems were more prevalent, and voice problems occurred commonly." [22]

Educational Achievement

The consensus of evidence shows that children with defective speech (including students on a college level) are somewhat retarded in school progress as compared with children with normal speech.[23] The amount of retardation would, of course, be much greater if we were to include those speech-defective children who are also mentally deficient and who must therefore either attend special schools or be institutionalized as uneducable. Surveys, such as those of Carrell, upon which the general conclusion of slight educational retardation is drawn, are concerned with children in regular schools and so exclude the severely mentally deficient and other special groups who are more greatly retarded.[24]

The ASHA Committee on the Midcentury White House Conference

includes the following among the well-established effects of speech disorders.

> Speech defectives appear to be retarded scholastically and to fail to take advantage of opportunities for college training, out of proportion to expectations based on intelligence test data.[25]

Reading Ability and Speech

Although research findings are not unanimous, most of the evidence indicates that difficulties in speech and in reading are somehow related. A recent study suggests that these lack of proficiencies are correlated even at the stage of reading readiness. Weaver, Furbee, and Everhart [26] found that in a population of 638 first-grade children there was a steady decrease in reading readiness as the number of articulatory faults increased. The relationship, as might be expected, is greater when oral reading disability is correlated with speech disability, especially for articulation and for stuttering. Hildreth, for example, considers a number of language and speech defects that retard reading.[27] These include: indistinct, inaccurate articulation; poor auditory discrimination of speech sounds; stuttering; bilingual background; and emotional conflicts due to speech defects which interfere with articulation in oral reading, as well as with the comprehension and interpretation of the written page. Jackson found that, in comparison with 10 per cent of the accelerated readers, 23 per cent of the retarded readers had speech defects.[28] Artley, after reviewing the literature, concluded that a majority of studies ". . . lead one to the generalization that speech and reading defects are to a substantial degree associated. Particularly is this true when oral reading is involved.[29]

The possibilities to explain the relationship between speech and reading disabilities may be put into three categories: (1) The two disabilities have a common cause; (2) speech disability may cause reading disability, especially when children are taught reading by the oral method; and (3) reading disability may cause speech deficiency.

Eames believes that both reading and speech disabilities are likely to have a common cause on the basis of a neurological lesion of the language centers.[30] Emotional reactions may increase the degree of difficulty in either reading or speech or both. Although it is difficult to demonstrate this relationship in young children who do not show obvious neurological involvement, the relationship is frequently demonstrated in cases of acquired aphasia in children and in adults. Limited intelligence, probably more than specific neurological deficit, is likely to be a common cause for speech disability and general linguistic deficiency.

The possibility that speech defects may be the cause of reading disability can be explained along the following lines. Defects of articulation may cause errors of pronunciation and so cause errors in the interpretation of the written word. It is also possible, especially in insecure children, that the child's awareness and concern over his defective speech may reduce his ability to concentrate on and so to comprehend what he is reading. A third factor is that faulty speech, especially faulty articulation and stuttering, may disturb the rate and rhythm of reading, interfere with proper phrasing, and therefore with the comprehension of the written symbol. A fourth possibility is that a child, aware of his speech deficiency, may become negatively inclined to all forms of oral expression. The attitude may be generalized to silent reading, and so may indirectly influence an area of achievement which the child might otherwise enjoy and in which normal proficiency might otherwise be expected.

The likelihood that reading disability might be the cause of defective speech, except possibly for stuttering, is remote and small. For most children, articulatory proficiency is attained for a large majority of speech sounds before formal training in reading ordinarily begins. This is especially true in schools which have a flexible program in the teaching of reading and do not begin formal teaching until reading readiness is clearly demonstrated. In regard to stuttering, the possibility exists that small children who have difficulty with oral reading may generalize this difficulty to include oral recitations, and possibly to conversational speech. Several stutterers who have been treated by the author date the onset of their stuttering to unhappy incidents associated with oral reading. Artley, after noting the absence of research to support the possibility that reading defects may cause speech defects, concludes that "where reading defects exist as a cause of speech defects, an explanation may lie in the fact that reading defects may result in fears, tensions, and various types of nervous behavior that may impair normal speech." [31]

Relationship of Speech Defects to Other Defects

Physical Defects

Most speech-defective children are physically normal. At least, their defects of speech cannot be directly attributed to the existence of a specific physical disability. Among children with serious defects of speech, approximately 320,000, or 16 per cent, have physical disabilities etiologically associated with their defects of speech. Chief among these are cleft palate, cerebral palsy, and hearing impairments. Deformities and growths of the larynx or pharynx, and neurological impairments affecting the control of the vocal bands, soft palate, or muscles of the throat, may be the cause of vocal defects. These conditions, however, occur relatively infrequently in children. Enlarged adenoids is a much more common cause of voice disturbance. In addition, there are minor organic anomalies such as dental malocclusions and high palatal arch which are found to occur more frequently among speech-defective children than in the population at large.

Of late, considerable interest has been shown by orthodontists and speech pathologists in oral irregularities and articulatory defects associated with "tongue-thrust" swallow. Many children who habitually protrude their tongues between their teeth in the act of swallowing, also demonstrate extreme tension in the mouth-enclosing musculature. The forward thrust of the tongue tends to produce oral malocclusion characterized by anteriorly displaced incisors. In a study of a population of children between six to eighteen years of age which included 668 with tongue-thrust swallow, 230 of the group were found to have sibilant distortion.[32] This incidence is considerably larger than would be expected by chance and significantly larger than the incidence of sibilant distortion among the children in the study whose normal swallowing habits were free of tongue-thrust.

It is likely that residuals of infant neuropathologies have continued influence in the form of retarded speech development or in defective articulation. Although it is not always possible to demonstrate this relationship, the impression of many speech pathologists, including the present writer, is that it exists among many young children with retarded or distorted speech.

A supporting study along this line was made by Eustis.[33] He reports that 48 per cent of individuals over six years of age of a family tree covering four generations, in addition to specific speech and reading disabilities, showed one or more of the following conditions: left-handedness, ambidexterity, body clumsiness. Eustis believes that these conditions suggest a syndrome, hereditary in origin, which is characterized by a slow rate of neuromuscular maturation and probably implies retarded myelination of the motor and association nerve tracts. "It is suggested that this inherited tendency to delayed neuromuscular maturation is the single factor from which all the various aspects of the syndrome may develop."

Basically the same point of view is expressed by Eames, who holds that many defects of speech and reading are etiologically associated, both essentially being "neurophysiological with psychological overtones."[34]

Motor Development and Motor Abilities

Although it is frequently not possible to find evidence of specific neurological deficit, or of motor involvement, as an etiological associate of defective speech, there is a fair amount of evidence to indicate that the general picture of the development of motor abilities is less favorable for the defective in speech than for the population at large.

Bilto administered a series of tests measuring large-muscle abilities to a group of 90 speech-defective children (stutterers and articulatory defectives) who ranged in age from nine to eighteen years and who had no observable organic defects basic to their speech disturbances.[35] The tests were also administered to a control group of children with normal speech. The test performances called for the use of appropriate rhythm, coordination, and the application of strength. Bilto found that approximately two-thirds of the speech-defective children were inferior to the normally speaking children in the tested abilities. It is important to note, however, that no single specific type of physical disability characterized the speech-defective children.

Patton found that articulatory defectives tended to show less kinesthetic sensibility than a matched control group of normal elementary school children.[36] Karlin, Youtz, and Kennedy found that children with distorted speech were inferior to a matched group in their ability to perform tasks requiring motor speed.[37]

Albright [38] compared 31 college students with good articulation and 36 with poor articulation, in tests of motor and articulatory skills.[38] The students with poor articulation were inferior to the control group in motor skill and in three of four tests specifically related to articulatory skills.

The results of some studies are not as conclusive as those just considered. Fairbanks and Bebout compared a group of 30 young adults with functional articulatory defects with 30 free from articulatory defects.[39] Their study was confined to four measurements of the tongue: (1) Maximum length of protrusion; (2) length of the tip; (3) maximum amount of tongue force; (4) percentage of error in duplicating a tongue position. They reported small, inconsistent, and not significant differences between the groups. In another aspect of the study with the same group, Fairbanks and Spriestersbach compared the rate of repetitive movements of the organs of articulation.[40] They found a significant difference for the males only in regard to lip movement.

Reid made a study of functional articulatory defects in elementary school children.[41] She concluded that degree of neuromuscular control and degree of kinesthetic sensitivity are not related to articulatory ability. She observed, however, that ". . . there are minimum levels of maturity . . . that are requisite for articulatory ability." Reid did find a significant correlation between articulation ability and the ability to discriminate between speech sounds.

Contrary to the findings reported in most of the studies we have considered are those of Mase.[42] He studied matched groups of 53 fifth- and sixth-grade boys with respect to six factors commonly believed to be associated etiologically with functional articulatory defects. These factors included rate of movement of the articulators and general muscular coordination. Mase found no significant differences between his experimental and control groups on any of the factors studied.

It may be that the differences in findings cited may be based on differences in populations studied, instruments, and measurements employed, or sizes of groups studied. The present author in reviewing the literature noted that, as a general finding, the higher the incidence of males in the experimental population, the greater the likelihood that significant differences were found. Males, as noted earlier, exceed the number of females in the speech-defective population. There is apparently also a greater incidence of both delayed maturation and retarded motor development among males than among females. In any event, it is reasonably safe to conclude that the evidence suggests that some degree of motor involvement is etiologically associated with defective speech development. (We are excepting, for the moment, the obvious relationship between the cerebral palsied and others with definite motor impairment.)

Sensory Disabilities

If we approach this matter from the point of view of the handicapped child with specific sensory disabilities, such as the hard of hearing, the deaf, and the blind, we will find a larger incidence of speech defects than we would in the population at large. If we exclude these special populations with significant hearing and visual losses, we will find a lack of unanimity in the results of studies related to sensory disabilities among speech-handicapped children. Most of the studies are of children with articulatory defects. Most, also, are concerned with some aspect of auditory ability.

Hall found that articulatory defectives at either the university freshman or elementary school level were not inferior to normal speakers on measures of auditory acuity, auditory discrimination of either simple or complex speech patterns, or in regard to auditory memory for speech sounds.[43]

Hansen employed three tests of sound discrimination and compared the results with small groups of adult, untrained articulatory defectives, trained defectives, and normal speakers.[44] He found no significant differences in discrimination ability between the groups on either the Seashore Measure of Timbre, the Travis Glaspey Speech Sound Discrimination Test, or a specially devised vowel discrimination test.

Reid found no significant relationship between auditory memory span and articulatory ability.[45] She did, however, find that the ability to discriminate between speech sounds "stands out as being positively related not only to severity of speech disorder but also the response made to special speech training."

Van Riper, working on the assumption that articulatory defectives are weak in auditory discrimination, prescribes detailed exercises for improving sound discrimination as a basic technique in the treatment of articulatory disorders.[46]

The assumption that difficulty in sound discrimination is etiologically associated with defective articulation is made by Curtis. He says many persons with articulatory defects ". . . do not have a clear auditory impression of what the correct sounds should be or how they differ from their errors." He also emphasizes that "This means that with a large number of cases . . . teaching the child to produce the correct sound must be preceded by some systematic ear training." [47] It would appear, however, that Curtis, on the basis of further study, does not believe that persons with articulatory defects have a generalized difficulty in sound discrimination.

Spriestersbach and Curtis question the assumption that a generalized disability in sound discrimination characterizes the speaker with functional articulatory defects.[48] They found that children tend to be fairly consistent in making omission errors of articulation and sound discrimination errors in the same phonetic contexts (correlation of .75). Interestingly, however, they found that children were much less consistent in committing substitution errors and sound discrimination errors in the same phonetic context (correlations of .25).

Van Riper and Irwin emphasize that the techniques for testing sound discrimination may explain the inconsistent results in the literature pertaining to persons with articulatory defects.[49] They suggest "(1) that our existing tests of speech sound discrimination are not testing speech sound discrimination ability except in a crude and oblique fashion, and/or (2) that poor discrimination may be only one of many factors important in the case's ability to recognize error-signals in his own speech." Van Riper and Irwin look upon speech sound (phonetic) discrimination as a complex of several factors that includes auditory memory span and phonetic analysis as well as the ability to monitor one's own sound production. A test of the ability to discriminate speech sounds should seek to single out the factors involved in the total complex.

Hearing Acuity

It is not surprising, of course, to find defects of voice and articulation among children who have significant degrees of hearing loss. The American Speech and Hearing Association's Committee on Legislation lists impaired hearing as the third largest category of causes of defective speech. (See Table 4-1) Estimates of the incidence of impaired hearing in the school population vary from about 3 to as much as 10 per cent. Glorig reported that 3 per cent of a male population between the ages of ten through nineteen were found to have a hearing loss of 15 decibels or more.[50] This figure is based on a sample of approximately 400,000. Davis and Silverman are aware that there is considerable variability in estimates of hearing loss.[51] They say "Our best estimate is that 5 per cent of school-age children have hearing levels outside the range of normal . . . and that from one to two of every ten in this group require special educational attention." These estimates refer to hearing impairments of such degree that the individual is likely to be aware and think of himself as an acoustically handicapped person. In the speech-defective population as a whole, smaller amounts of hearing loss may have an influence on the quality of speech, even though the speaker may have no awareness of his reduced hearing acuity.

A study by Sullivan revealed that in the Minneapolis elementary school population of 25,708, 22.2 per cent of the speech-defective children had a loss of 10 decibels or more in one or both ears, compared with 18.8 per cent of the normally speaking children.[52] Fiedler found that among public school children in grades 1 to 3, the incidence of speech defects was higher among children with hearing loss (19.28 per cent) than among their normally hearing classmates (6.73 per cent).[53] A diagnosis of hearing loss was made on the basis of a 20-decibel loss on two or more frequencies in either ear as measured by individual pure-tone testing on the ADC audiometer. Few of the children found to have hearing loss were identified as such by their teachers.

The specific form of defective speech varies considerably with the type, degree, and age of onset of hearing loss. Children with congenital hearing loss severe in degree are almost always delayed in beginning to speak and continue to be slow in language development. Beyond this, the oral speech they are able to develop is likely to be characterized by articulatory distortion, faulty rhythm, and general vocal inadequacy. Even if the hearing loss is acquired after the normal onset of speech, speech defects are likely to become part of the over-all habilitation problem. We may accept the observation of Davis and Silverman as a truism that "If the ear can no longer serve as a monitor when one talks, slow degeneration of speech results. The sharpness and precision of enunciation disintegrate. The melodies of speech become monotonous. Intonations lose their life. The quality of the voice becomes rigid. Finally, control over the loudness of the voice suffers."[54] For a more detailed consideration of the relationship between hearing loss and speech, the reader may consult Berry and Eisenson, *Speech Disorders,* chapter 19.[55]

Auditory Memory and Sequencing

AUDITORY MEMORY span has been a subject of psychological study for many years, going back to the initial investigations of Ebbinghaus.[56] Most recent studies of auditory memory span have used series of digits or of non-sense syllables as basic measures. The assumption that auditory memory is a factor in intelligence is expressed in the frequent inclusion of memory span tests employing digits forward, digit series to be recalled in reverse order of presentation (digits backward), and recall of meaningful material as in reproduction of sentences and of units of meaning after the oral presentation of contextual material. There is ample evidence that memory span as measured by recall is positively related to intelligence and to mental development. Many speech pathologists believe that poor auditory memory is related to defective speech, though the results of research are by no means consistent. An excellent brief review of the subject may be found in Van Riper and Irwin.[57]

Despite the inconsistent results of controlled investigations, many speech pathologists, including the present author, maintain their clinical impression that speech-defective children with retarded language development and articulatory defects are indeed defective in auditory memory. Perhaps the reason for the difference lies in the nature of the experimental design. Immediate recall when a child is not concerned with meaning calls for a different integration than recall with meaning. Even more crucial, we believe, is the need to distinguish between recall of material to be imitated (immediately reproduced) and a more complex ability to sequence a series of sounds into a *phonetic and meaningful unit.* Young children who are just beginning to develop verbal habits often transpose sounds and syllables and may say *pests* for *pets* or *ephelant* for *elephant.* Such transpositions also feature the paraphasic output of adults who have cerebral damage and become aphasic. Van Riper and Irwin indicate that children with defective articulation are frequently lacking in their ability to combine and analyze speech sound sequences. Because of this lack, "The articulation case can understand the word spoken by another, can recognize it as correct, yet cannot say it correctly himself. . . . When we find cases with marked deficiencies in phonetic ability of either the analytic or synthesizing type, we can expect difficulty in articulation therapy." [58] Children who are retarded in language development may, we suspect, be lacking in a fundamental ability to analyze any but the shortest auditory sequence, to identify and recall the first item of an aurally received event, or to hold this and succeeding items in mind until a series is recognized as having been completed. Beyond this, the child must be able to synthesize the series of auditory items into an event appropriate to the demands of a speaking situation.

Auditory events, unlike visual ones, do not "stay put." Impressions received aurally can be reproduced only by adequate feedback. Such feedback is a function not only of the total number of items that can be recalled, but of the sequence or order in which they need to be recalled for acceptable verbal behavior. When recalled, the items must be organized into recognizable verbal events (linguistic units) and be reproduced so that they are intelligible to another listener. For this, the ability for auditory discrimination and production, as we have already noted, must also be adequate. For many young children, and especially those with brain damage, the demands for this complex ability seem to be excessive. As a result, they are slow to talk and often defective and retarded after they begin to talk. The need to help brain-injured children to *hear and distinguish* sounds was an integral part of an experimental program conducted by Cruickshank and his associates.[59]

Personality Aspects and Adjustment Problems

THE APPROACH in this section will be first to consider studies and points of view on the speech-defective population as a whole and then to consider the specialized studies of particular types of speech defectives. Some of the studies and points of view have already been considered in our discussion of the psychogenic basis of defective speech.

Speech Defectives as a Group

Van Riper is especially impressed with the speech defective's tendency to employ either aggressive or withdrawal behavior reaction to the penalty behavior of his associates. Hostility and anxiety seem to be the key behavioral traits of speech defectives.

> When an individual is constantly frustrated and at the same time deprived of any chance to express his hostility, to find a substitute reward, or to escape from the situation, a good deal of anxiety is aroused. This is painful, and the person tries in many ways to reduce the discomfort. He may begin to worry about his health, about his job, about school marks, and actually to create difficulties in each of these areas so that they, instead of the speech problem, can be considered the true difficulty.[60]

Van Riper, in common with many speech pathologists, believes that speech defects are in themselves frustrating and serve both to produce and impair the need for "blowing off steam." Observations such as Van Riper's are made on the basis of clinical experience. The behavioral traits are certainly not unique for speech-defective persons but are found among many persons with minor as well as major adjustment problems. Yet the relationship between speech deficiency and maladjustment is likely to be causal rather than merely coincidental.

Glauber, approaching the problem from a Freudian, psychoanalytic point of view, observed that speech disturbances are common in psychoneurotic patients. In relationship to psychoneurotic personalities, Glauber says:

> Speech may be overvalued in all categories. It is most voluminous and indistinct in the oral-clinging, is rapid and distinct in the compulsive, mostly highly developed in the exhibitionistic and competitive types, and most disturbed in the orally-aggressive and the masochistic which creates the greatest amount of conflict, with resultant tendencies towards repression and other defenses. . . . The speech disorder or idiosyncrasy is a reflection of a disturbance or idiosyncrasy of the total personality. . . .[61]

With a different orientation, Johnson summarizes the effects of speech disorders on personality to highlight their circular influence.

> The psychology of the handicapped is basically the psychology of frustration. The handicap of impaired speech is no exception to this general rule. In fact, there is hardly anything more frustrating, in ways that matter deeply, than something that constantly interferes with our relationship to other people.
>
> . . . .
>
> The relationship between speech and personality is . . . a two-way affair. They affect each other. And the effect is not only circular, but also cumulative . . . speech characteristics, once created, tend to affect the personality in ways that insure their further development.[62]

Up to this point, we have presented the opinions of writers in the field of speech correction and psychiatry and their observations, based largely on personal experience, of the relationship between defective speech and personality maladjustments. No attempt has been made to indicate causal relationships. It is fairly apparent, however, that Glauber has in mind that speech defects of the kinds he describes are manifestations of maladjusted personalities. Van Riper, and the authors of the Midcentury White House Conference report, on the other hand, are thinking primarily in terms of the effect on the personality of a speech defect, whatever the origin of the defect may be. Berry and Eisenson, after reviewing some of the research literature on the relationship between personality traits and defective speech, conclude:

> There seems to be a tendency for speech-defective individuals to present a personality picture which includes traits considered to

be socially undesirable. Tendencies towards maladjustments seem
to increase as the speech defectives grow older. . . . The tendency
for speech defectives to have other limitations such as poor motor
control, lesser intellectual capacity, and somewhat lower educational achievement makes it difficult to determine the direct relationship between the personality maladjustment and the defective
speech. It may be that together, the speech defect *and* the other
limitations constitute a constellation which is conducive to maladjustment. . . .[63]

Without at this time trying to answer whether the chicken came before,
after, or with the egg, we will turn our attention to more specialized
studies of particular groups of speech defectives. The implications of
some of the studies may provide partial answers to the question, "Which
may be the cause and which may be the effect?"

Retarded Language Development

Definition

The child with delayed or retarded language development is one
whose language development is significantly below what we would have
a right to expect on the basis of his age and an estimate of his intelligence.
In a broader sense, the synonymous term "delayed speech" may be used
to characterize any significant retardation in language development or
articulatory proficiency based on age expectancy alone. In that broader
sense, a mentally deficient child or a deaf child, or a child with severe
motor involvement, may be said to be delayed in speech if he does not
have a normal vocabulary and articulatory proficiency by the age of
three. The immediately following discussion *excludes* those children who
have any known specific organic or intellectual deficiency to which the
delay in language development may be directly attributed. We might,
however, emphasize that mental deficiency is the most frequent cause of
delayed or retarded language development.

Parental influences

In our earlier discussion of the psychogenic causes of defective
speech, reference was made to several studies concerned with the parents
of speech-defective children. These studies tended to indicate that parents, and especially the mothers, of young speech-defective children
were more maladjusted than control group parents. Among the undesirable traits and attitudes found to exist to a greater degree among the
test group parents were increased neurotic tendency, lower self- and
social-adjustment, greater over-all emotional instability, rigidity, perfec-

tionism, overprotectiveness, and restrictiveness. In addition, many of the mothers were found to have unrealistically high expectations of what constitutes appropriate language performance for their children. Peckarsky, for example, found that mothers of children with delayed speech were overprotective, rigid, highly critical, and restrictive in their demands upon their children.[64] Frequently, when a child physically and intellectually normal fails to develop speech, the basis of the retardation may be found in the child's reaction to his parents' maladjustments. The speech delay may often be both a reaction to the psychological environment and a manifestation of the child's own maladjustment.

Rejection

Much of the attitude of the parents considered in the studies previously cited probably constitutes an unconscious rejection of the children. A child who senses such rejection and who cannot identify himself with his parent, and especially with his mother, is likely to be delayed in speech development. Mowrer points out that a child must first identify himself with his parent with respect to speaking behavior before he can begin to wish to speak. He must, of course, be physically and intellectually mature and ready before the identification will motivate true speech. The rejected child either makes no such initial identification or may lose the identification once rejection is sensed.

Parental rejection which takes the form of continuous disapproval and criticism, of speech as well as of other forms of behavior, may cause the child to stop talking, or to reduce his amount of talking. Where the rejection takes the form of indifference, the ordinary rewards which strengthen speech behavior and which stimulate renewed efforts at speaking are absent. Speech, then, may continue on an infantile level.

Goldfarb, discussing the schizophrenic child, observes:

> . . . the speech model presented by a pathologically perplexed parent may be diminished in phonatory and rhythmic range. Further, in the face of unstructured emotional communication by this kind of parent, the child responds with confusion and unawareness of what is expected of him, so that he never achieves the complicated techniques required for connotative expression.[66]

Ruesch in his discussion of autistic, withdrawn, or outright schizophrenic children and their disturbances in communication, or their failure to develop conventional communicative skills, also considers the parents' own behavior to be the fundamental cause. "The parents' unresponsiveness in non-verbal terms prevents the child in the early years of life from learning how to relate through *movement and action*. The absence of early appropriate and gratifying communication through action, gesture, and object leaves traces." [67] Some of the traces are in inadequate speech both for the expression of affect and for developing normal relationships through conventional communicative behavior.

Negativism

When the rejection takes the form of excessive criticism, the child may demonstrate that rejection is a mechanism he too can use. He may begin by rejecting his own parents. If he does so, he may also negate speech, through which he became aware of the parental criticism and disapproval. Such a child may occasionally become overtly unresponsive to human sounds and manifest a conscious awareness only of mechanical or animal noises. He may either fail to develop speech or, if he had begun to use speech, regress to a preverbal stage of speech development.

The intelligent child who is severely retarded in speech has a deficient tool for making adjustments to his environment. As he grows older, without adequate means for expression and communication, he must frequently deny his own developing needs and so entertain frustration. If he does not engage in self-denial, he invites frustration by having no proficient means to communicate his wishes or to elicit responses for their satisfaction.

Behavioral Traits Accompanying Delayed Speech

It is, of course, not possible to make any direct inquiry or study through adjustment inventories of what is disturbing the child with delayed speech. Conclusions must be drawn from observations of the child's environment, from personality studies of the child's parents, and from direct observation of the child's behavior. Conclusions and implications have been drawn relative to the influence of parental maladjustment on the child. Observations will now be made of the behavior of the child, of what he does in the company of other children. For the most part, these will be limited to direct observations of the child with delayed speech in a play situation in a speech clinic. The author has been in charge of such a clinic since 1946 and has had delayed-speech groups under the immediate supervision of a psychologist and one or more speech clinicians since that time. The groups have varied in size from four to nine children.

Most idiopathic delayed-speech children resort to direct means to make their wants known or to impress their feelings upon others. These direct means may include literally forcing another child, or an adult, to enter into a situation and striking out at an undirected object or person. Frequently, the object or person struck at may be one very recently brought into the situation created by the child. The striking out may probably be considered the child's way of responding to something or somebody that does not readily understand why it was wanted and what role it was expected to assume.

Some children with delayed speech isolate themselves, as far as the physical situation permits, from others in the room. They will spend periods of up to an hour or more "playing" with a single toy object, or just sitting off to one side apparently doing nothing. One boy of five spent his first four months in the clinic sitting high up, silent and alone, on the top of a 4-foot jungle gym.

Some delayed-speech children appear to enjoy close physical contact with older persons and with inanimate objects. They may be seen to rub their bodies along the walls as they move from place to place. They rub their faces against their toys. Occasionally and very impulsively, they will grab hold of another child, or a clinician, and cling with great force for a moment before releasing the person. Apparently, there is a need for sensuous contact which the child obtains from accepting individuals or unsuspecting objects.

Emotional lability characterizes the behavior of many delayed-speech children. They act with impulsiveness and excessiveness, at least when compared with most normally speaking children. They yell and cry quickly and more loudly, break toys, knock down block houses, fling objects around, tear papers, throw pencils, chalk, and crayons, and in general keep things flying about them.

All the characteristics just considered do not set the child with delayed speech off from other children. As a group, delayed-speech children differ in degree from normally speaking children. Their mechanisms of adjustment or maladjustment are like those of other children, except that they are less expertly used. Some delayed-speech children are even well behaved and appear to have made an adjustment to not speaking. Some reveal no factors in their case histories which can explain why they do not speak. Most, fortunately, learn to speak after a while and improve in their adjustment patterns as speech is developed.

Congenital Aphasia and Language Retardation

THE TERM *congenital aphasia* is almost an "Alice in Blunderland" term that may mean just about what the individual clinician wishes it to mean. So, indeed, some authorities do not accept the term at all but direct attention to the development and behavior of the so-called congenitally aphasic children, which are remarkably like those of schizophrenic children. They feel that the omnibus term *schizophrenic* carries sufficient variations of meaning as well as divergent personalities to include the congenitally aphasic. This, we believe, is the position of Lauretta Bender.[68]

Our own position is that congenital aphasia is a separate syndrome that must be considered among the organic causes of language retardation. An individual who makes the diagnosis of congenital aphasia must first make certain that the child so designated is not mentally retarded, is not suffering from significant hearing impairment, and is not one who is primarily autistic or schizophrenic. On the positive side, a diagnosis of congenital aphasia implies a need for the diagnostician to establish that the individual had a cerebral neuropathology before language could be normally established, or else to establish that the individual had atypical cerebral development on a congenital basis.

Differential Diagnostic Features

An aphasic child is one who, as a result of cerebral damage or cerebral dysfunction, presents a syndrome of linguistic and non-verbal behavioral manifestations that distinguish him from other children, both normal and deviant. The following are critical features:

1. Developmentally, the child shows generalized perceptual differences —if not dysfunction, auditory inefficiency beyond any audiometrically determined hearing loss, and intellectual inefficiency over and above any "measurable" intellectual deficit.

2. Specific behavioral manifestations include morbidity of attention, perseveration, inconsistency of response, emotional lability, and frequently general hyperactivity.

3. Linguistically, the child shows a marked amount of retardation in the comprehension, evaluation, and production of language, and a *disproportion and unevenness in the anticipated comprehension-production linguistic ratio.* Developmentally, the child does not show expected increments or the "ordered" pattern by which most children increase their linguistic abilities for communicative language.

4. The aphasic child is distinguished from other non-verbal children by the likelihood that his behavioral manifestations, such as perseveration and over-all lability of performance, as well as sensory, perceptual, and intellectual inefficiency, increase as he confronts a verbal-symbol situation and he realizes that a verbal-symbol response is required of him.

Clinical Picture of the Congenitally Aphasic Child *

The designation or characterization of the congenitally aphasic child embraces the following in the clinical background: established brain

---

* For a detailed consideration of the hyperactive brain-damaged child, including approaches to diagnosis and treatment, see Cruickshank, *et al., A Teaching Method for Brain-Injured and Hyperactive Children.* (Footnote 59)

damage, atypical cerebral development or developmental history, behavioral manifestations, and general intellectual functioning comparable to the child with cerebral pathology. These would include:

1. Perceptual dysfunction in one or more (not necessarily all) avenues; figure-background confusion.
2. Laterality confusion, often with associated difficulty in spatial orientation.
3. Inconsistency of responses to sounds, and especially to verbal situations.
4. Specific defects in linguistic symbol behavior. Developmental unevenness and disparity in the comprehension of auditory, visual, and motor experiences. Marked disparity between intake and output of language. Productive language not on the level of expectancy in the light of receptive ability.
5. Morbidity of attention.
6. Morbidity of response (difficulty verging sometimes to inability to change a response) once one has been made. This is frequently associated with difficulty or inability to change an initial frame of reference.
7. Auditory inefficiency; the child's functional hearing (proficiency of hearing) is below what would be expected from audiometric results.
8. Lability of non-verbal expressive behavior, with lability increasing as verbal behavior is normally expected.

*Developmental Background: Phasic Development
and the Dys-phasic Child*

Children who fail to develop language or are significantly retarded in some aspect of language development because of congenital cerebral pathology or pathology with onset before true speech is normally achieved (by the end of the second year) are frequently found to be *out-of-phase* in their general sensory, motor, and perceptual development. In regard to these functions they are literally dys-phasic, in that they do not follow anticipated patterns in the development of their sensory-motor skills and the behavior that is associated with such skills. Their sequential development is more highly individualized than our norms lead us to expect. Developmental manifestations which normally go together—which correlate and are in phase for normal children—show a lack of such correlation or phasing in children with known brain damage.

Clinicians are often confronted with assessing non-verbal children for whom brain damage or atypical cerebral maturation cannot be clearly demonstrated by either clinical history or neurological diagnosis. We consider the diagnosis of congenital aphasia to be in order if the developmental history and psychological evaluation show the predominant features of the child with established brain damage.

The clinician would need to be certain that mental retardation and/or hearing deficiency is not singly, or in combination, basic to the language delay. Beyond this, he would need to be mindful that some clinicians consider such children to be schizophrenic. It might be of some comfort to appreciate that the term *childhood schizophrenia* is really an omnibus designation that in some important respects overlaps our criteria for congenital aphasia. Goldfarb acknowledges this in describing the setting of his research on childhood schizophrenia. Says Goldfarb "The Staff was impressed with the great variation among the children in the single diagnostic category 'childhood schizophrenia'." The children differed markedly with respect to symptoms, defenses, and general level of ego development. They also differed in responsiveness to treatment." [69] With all due concern that diagnosis may determine treatment, we may conclude that in the final analysis the proof of the diagnosis is in the individual's responsiveness to a program of treatment.

Stutterers

IT IS probably fortunate that the limitations of this text do not permit an evaluation of the theories of causation of stuttering, or of the vast literature concerned with providing information about how stutterers are or are not different from other persons. The literature on stutterers and stuttering (or stammering) is ancient, vast, contradictory, and inconclusive. Any person with a bias can find there what appears to be considerable evidence to support his bias or substantiate his point of view.

In *Stuttering: A Symposium,* six authorities present their viewpoints as to the essential cause or causes and therapeutic approaches for stutterers.[70] The present author, who is also the editor of and a contributor to the *Symposium,* believes that the viewpoints on stuttering in this monograph and in general can be classified into three major but not altogether discrete groups along the following lines:

1. The stutterer has difficulty in speaking—he blocks, hesitates, repeats, grimaces, and so forth—because of an unconscious (repressed) need to do so. The stutterer is essentially a neurotic individual who expresses his neuroticism in part through his deviant speech.

2. Stuttering constitutes a breakdown or failure in functioning of the complex of neuromuscular and intellectual activity required for communicative speaking. This breakdown may occur temporarily for any speaker, but it is likely to be relatively chronic for those who are either emotionally or constitutionally predisposed to such impairment.

3. Stuttering is a learned act characterized by "anticipatory struggle" behavior. It thus becomes an avoidance reaction that is associated with a fear of hesitation in speech, or otherwise of speaking in a manner the individual has learned to regard as stuttering.

We shall not, in our discussion, seek to support or to refute any of these theoretic positions. Instead we shall evaluate some of the recent literature as it touches upon psychological implications of being a stutterer. We shall be especially concerned with studies that seek to discover: (1) how the psychological environment of stutterers is different from that of normally speaking children, and (2) how the adolescent and young adult stutterers differ psychologically from adolescents and young adults who do not stutter.

Environmental Influences of the Young Stutterer

Johnson, an eminent student of stuttering and stutterers, argues:

> So-called stuttering children are not different from children not so diagnosed, with respect to birth injuries, other injuries, diseases, and general development. . . . They are not different with regard to intelligence. In general they are normal children.[71]

Despite this, Johnson believes that an essential difference between the child who begins to stutter and the child who does not may be found in the reaction of his parents to the way he speaks. The parents of the young child who becomes a stutterer are anxious about the child's speech. They tend also to generalize their anxieties so that they become worried not only about his speech but about his conduct in general. The young child is looked upon as being nervous, unstable, or "defective in some way." The implication made by Johnson is that the only significant difference between the young child who becomes a stutterer and the child who does not is in the way his parents respond to him. This is characterized by a specific anxiety in regard to the child's speech, a generalized anxiety in regard to the child's total behavior, and an unrealistic expectation as to what normal speech and normal behavior in general should be.

> In all my years of counselling parents who have been concerned about their children's speech, the one thing about them that has impressed me most has been their degree of perfectionism. They differ among themselves, of course; . . . but in general they have appeared, as a group, to be inclined to demand a little more of their children in the way of growth and development than would seem to be realistic.[72]

Unreasonable expectation of speech performance was also found by Bloodstein, Jaeger, and Tureen.[73] They asked 24 parents of young stutterers and 24 parents of young non-stutterers to diagnose as "stuttering" or "normal" the recorded spontaneous speech of 6 stuttering and 6 non-stuttering children. They found that the parents of the stuttering children significantly exceeded parents of the non-stutterers in the extent to which they diagnosed both the stuttering and the non-stuttering children as stutterers.

Moncur designed an interview form comprised of 330 items by which he distinguished the attitudes of mothers of stuttering and non-stuttering children in regard to domination. Domination was revealed by the types of disciplinary actions and the standards of performance the mothers had in regard to their children. Moncur concludes that there is a syndrome of environmental factors which seems to precipitate or aggravate stuttering with significant regularity. The syndrome includes a variety of parental actions which include "domination by disciplinary action, domination by oversupervising and overprotecting the child, domination by holding the child to excessively high standards, and domination by adverse parental criticism." [74]

Glasner made a study of 70 stuttering children under the age of five.[75] Although he believes that young children who stutter are frequently and initially different in personality type from children who do not stutter, he found that on the whole the stuttering children had a background significant for overprotection and pampering, and overanxious, excessively perfectionist parents.

Emphasis on the early familial influences also comes from studies of older stutterers. Some of these will now be considered.

Adolescent and Young Adult Stutterers

Home Influences

Glauber reported on a clinical study of mothers of stutterers. According to his report, the stutterer is an inadequate male who identifies himself almost completely, but defectively, with the mother. The basic fault, and the cause of the stuttering, is to be found in the personality of the mother, in her ambivalent attitudes to the stuttering child in particular as well as to other members of her family, including her own mother. Glauber holds that the nuclear etiological factors in the stuttering syndrome lie in specific elements in the personality structure of the mother.[76] In a later writing Glauber characterized the mother as suffering from maternal anxieties. ". . . birth, nursing, weaning, and onset of speech were felt by the mother as anxious experiences, with a special quality compounded of both separation and clutching. Also the child's taking control of his own locomotion, elimination, the development of his will in its negative and positive aspects, and of his intellect—all these landmarks of his ego development—were felt by the mother as the child's provocative acts of moving away." [77] Glauber came to his conclusions in regard to stutterers and their mothers on the basis of ". . . an extensive study of the family constellation of stutterers and material from psychoanalyses of stutterers and of their mothers." Some of the observations differ in at least a few important respects from those previously considered.

Douglass and Quarrington differentiate between stutterers according to their motivation and degree of success in controlling the outward, secondary manifestation of stuttering.[78] The interiorized stutterers—those who generally succeed in controlling visible and audible aspects of stuttering, but who feel and think of themselves as stutterers—are characterized by their sensitivity to their social world. This sensitivity, apparently, originates with their families. On the basis of their case histories and clinical studies, Douglass and Quarrington observe:

> The interiorized stutterer appears to come from a family that is upwardly oriented and employs child-rearing practices and methods of discipline particularly suited to the development of a child who will strive to maintain and enhance the social status of the family. Moral training in such a family is by means of anxiety-producing threats to withhold affection or actual withholding of affection until the child conforms with the expectations of the parent.
>
> Parental expectations in such upwardly-oriented families are characteristically high in respect to most aspects of the child's life.

Another approach to the probable influence of the parents on the personality and speech of the stutterer was undertaken by Moore, Soderberg, and Powell.[79] They employed questions from the Sacks Sentence Completion Test to evoke spontaneous speech from a group of 16 adolescent male stutterers ranging in age from thirteen to twenty-one. The questions were on the topics of parents, future hopes, misdeeds, fears, associates, and good times. Moore and his associates found that the severity (duration) of stuttering was significantly greater when the stutterers talked about *parents* than on any of the other topics.

Duncan investigated and compared the home adjustment of 62 stutterers and a control group of 62 non-stuttering college students. On the basis of answers to questions on the Bell Adjustment Inventory, Duncan found significant differences in regard to 5 items. As a group, the stutterers more often than the non-stutterers felt that they were not understood by their parents, that there was a lack of real affection in their homes, that their maturity was underestimated, that they entertained strong desires to run away from their homes, and that their parents were disappointed in them.[80]

Sheehan reviewed studies on personality aspects of stutterers that employed projective techniques as the instruments of investigation. Sheehan evaluated the results and concluded: (1) Findings based upon projective studies are inconsistent; (2) Stutterers as a population do not show a definite personality pattern; and, (3) There is very meager evidence "to show that stutterers are different from anyone else." Sheehan did find, *in keeping with some of his own studies*, that lower levels of aspiration existed among stutterers.[81]

Social Adjustments

Except for the subjective opinions in the psychoanalytic literature, in which stutterers tend to be characterized as severely neurotic individuals, there is considerably less unanimity on the over-all social adjustment of stutterers. It may very well be that psychoanalysts are correct in their judgments in regard to the limited number of stutterers they treat who may be severely neurotic. Objective studies, for the most part, do not support the generalized judgments of the psychoanalysts. On the other hand, it should be appreciated that most studies of adolescent and young adult stutterers are made with college students as subjects. These students may be a selected group of comparatively well-adjusted stutterers who attend college and accept therapy because they have succeeded in adjusting socially despite their speech impediment. With these reservations in mind, some of the objective studies will now be reviewed.

Fiedler and Wepman investigated the self-concept of stutterers by comparing a group of ten adult male stutterers and a control group of six non-stutterers in their responses to 76 statements descriptive of personality traits taken from Murray.[82] They concluded that the stutterer's self-concept showed no characteristic difference from that of the non-stutterer.

Duncan, in the study cited earlier, found significant differences for stutterers as compared with non-stutterers in only 5 of 35 items related to "home adjustment" on the Bell Adjustment Inventory.

Schultz compared adult stutterers (20 college students) with psychoneurotics in a non-directive counselling situation and investigated the responses of the stutterers on the Adult Form A, California Test of Personality. Schultz concluded: "These stutterers had many symptoms common to psychoneurotics. The stutterers . . . had many serious social and self-adjustment problems." [83]

Spriestersbach compared the evaluation reaction of a group of 50 male stutterers enrolled at the State University of Iowa, 183 normally speaking male students, and 20 male psychotic patients at an Iowa State hospital. The evaluations were of a series of pictures which were to be rated upon the degree to which they fitted such words as *fun, undesirable,* and *worthwhile.* Spriestersbach concluded that the stutterers displayed evaluated reactions differing somewhat from the non-stutterers in a way which suggested relatively mild degrees of social maladjustment. The stutterers differed markedly from the psychotic patients in their evaluated reactions.[84]

In an earlier study, Richardson compared the responses of a mixed group of thirty adult stutterers and a matched control group of thirty non-stutterers.[85] The examination inventory consisted of the Rorschach, Thematic Apperception, and the Guilford Inventory of Factors STDCR. Richardson found few differences between the two groups based on their Rorschach and TAT responses. Significant Rorschach differences based on the stutterers' failure to see movement and color were interpreted to mean that they tended not to recognize their inner promptings and that they failed to respond impulsively to outside environment. The Guilford Inventory, however, yielded results which indicated several significant differences. The stutterers were found to be more socially introvertive, more depressed, and less happy-go-lucky than the non-stutterers.

Murphy and Fitzsimons, based on their own studies and a broad review of the literature, consider that the stutterer's self-concept is dominated by feelings of inadequacy and insecurity, both born of parent-related anxiety.[86] The stutterer's speech as well as his over-all adjustment problems are characterized by underlying lower self-concept—lower in comparison with that of ideal-self—than we are likely to find among peer non-stutterers.

Other Groups

The personality and adjustment problems of the hard of hearing, the deaf, and the cerebral palsied will not be considered in this section. Some aspects of the problems of the groups of speech defectives with special sensory or motor disabilities were taken up in the general review of types of speech defectives.

These groups are being considered in more detail by other writers of this text under the categories of the exceptional consistent with their primary disabilities.

Summary

THE DEFECTIVE in speech differ in degree but not in kind from the normally speaking population. Taken as a group, the differences are not great. On an individual basis, the difference may be great, small, not discernible, or non-existent. Taken as a group, speech defectives, stutterers excepted, are somewhat retarded intellectually and educationally.

They all, stutterers included, have somewhat more difficulty in their ad-justment efforts than do the normally speaking. In individual instances it is not clear whether these adjustment problems are caused by the defect in speech, or whether the speech defect is but one additional manifestation of the somewhat maladjusted personality.

Objective studies relating to the personality pictures and adjustment problems have, for the most part, been undertaken with adolescents and adults. Some attempts to do as much for children have been reported. On the whole, the differences appear to be greater as the children grow older. The adolescent and adult speech defectives appear to have con-siderably more problems in adjustment than do the children. This observa-tion, however, may really mean that our measuring devices for adjust-ment differences are better when applied to older speech defectives than they are when applied to children.

Notes

1 M. C. Templin, "Norms on a Screening Test for Articulation for Ages Three Through Eight," *Journal of Speech and Hearing Disorders*, XVIII, No. 4 (1953), 323-331.

2 American Speech and Hearing Association Committee in Legislation, "Need For Speech Pathologists," *ASHA*, I (1959), 138-139.

3 A. W. Mills and H. Streit, "Report of a Speech Survey, Holyoke, Massachusetts," *Journal of Speech Disorders*, VII (1942), 161-167.

4 V. Roe and R. L. Milisen, "Effect of Maturation upon Defective Articulation in Elementary Grades," *Journal of Speech Disorders*, VIII (1942), 37-50.

5 H. Schuell, "Sex Differences in Relation to Stuttering: Part I," *Journal of Speech Disorders*, XI (1946), 277-298.

6 D. E. Morley, "A Ten-Year Survey of Speech Disorders Among University Stu-dents," *Journal of Speech and Hearing Disorders*, XVII (1952), 25-31.

7 See N. W. Freestone, "The Wish for Defective Speech," *Journal of Speech and Hearing Disorders*, XIII (1948), 119-130, for a detailed consideration of this point of view.

8 K. S. Wood, "Parental Maladjustment and Functional Articulatory Defects in Children," *Journal of Speech Disorders*, XI (1946), 255-275.

9 J. P. Moncur, "Parental Domination in Stuttering," *Journal of Speech and Hearing Disorders*, XVII (1952), 155-164.

10 A. Peckarsky, "Maternal Attitudes Towards Children with Psychogenically De-layed Speech" (Doctoral Dissertation, New York University, School of Education, 1952).

11 J. A. Carrell, "A Comparative Study of Speech-Defective Children," *Archives of Speech*, 1 (1936), 179-203.

12 R. S. Craig, "The Nature and Frequency of Speech Defects Among First, Sec-ond, Third and Fourth Grade Children in Four Negro Schools of Augusta, Georgia" (Doctoral Dissertation, Northwestern University, 1951).

13 R. Pintner, J. Eisenson, and M. Stanton, *Psychology of the Physically Handi-capped* (New York: Appleton-Century-Crofts, 1941), chap. 9.

14 W. G. Wolfe, "A Comprehensive Evaluation of Fifty Cases of Cerebral Palsy," *Journal of Speech and Hearing Disorders*, XV (1950), 234-251.

15 See R. Pintner, J. Eisenson, and M. Stanton, *op. cit.*, pp. 110-130.

16 R. Pintner and J. Lev, "The Intelligence of the Hard of Hearing School Child," *Journal of Genetic Psychology,* LV (1939), 31-48.

17 P. Oleron, "A Study of the Intelligence of the Deaf," *American Annals of the Deaf,* XCV (1950), 179-195.

18 L. Kennedy, "Studies in the Speech of the Feeble-Minded" (Doctoral Dissertation, University of Wisconsin, 1930).

19 J. Lewald, "Speech Defects as Found in a Group of 500 Mental Defectives," *Proceedings and Addresses of the American Association for the Study of the Feeble-minded,* XXXVII (1932), 291-301.

20 M. H. Sachs, "A Survey and Evaluation of the Existing Interrelationships Between Speech and Mental Deficiencies" (Master's thesis, University of Virginia, 1951).

21 G. W. Gens, "Speech Retardation in the Normal and Subnormal Child," *The Training School Bulletin,* XLVIII (1950), 32-36.

22 J. O. Smith, "Speech and Language of the Retarded," *The Training School Bulletin,* LVIII, No. 4 (1962), 111-124.

23 M. F. Berry and J. Eisenson, *Speech Disorders* (New York: Appleton-Century-Crofts, 1956), chap. 9.

24 J. A. Carrell, *op. cit.*

25 ASHA Committee on the Midcentury White House Conference, "Speech Disorders and Speech Correction," *Journal of Speech and Hearing Disorders,* XVII (1952), 129-137.

26 C. H. Weaver, C. Furbee, and R. W. Everhart, "Articulatory Competency and Reading Readiness," *Journal of Speech and Hearing Research,* III (1960), 174-180.

27 G. Hildreth, "Speech Defects and Reading Disability," *Elementary School Journal,* XLVI (1946), 326-332.

28 J. Jackson, "A Survey of Psychological, Social and Environmental Differences between Advanced and Retarded Readers," *Journal of Genetic Psychology,* LXV (1944), 113-131.

29 A. S. Artley, "A Study of Certain Factors Presumed to be Associated with Reading and Speech Difficulties," *Journal of Speech and Hearing Disorders,* XIII (1948), 351-360.

30 T. H. Eames, "The Relationship of Reading and Speech Difficulties," *Journal of Educational Psychology,* XLI (1950), 51-55.

31 A. S. Artley, *op. cit.,* 359-360.

32 S. G. Fletcher, R. L. Casteel, and D. P. Bradley, "Tongue-Thrust Swallow, Speech Articulation and Age," *Journal of Speech and Hearing Disorders,* XXVI (1961), 201-208.

33 R. S. Eustis, "The Primary Origin of the Specific Language Disabilities," *Journal of Pediatrics,* XXXI, 448-455.

34 T. H. Eames, *op. cit.,* 51-55.

35 E. W. Bilto, "A Comparative Study of Certain Physical Abilities of Children with Speech Defects and Children with Normal Speech," *Journal of Speech Disorders,* VI (1941), 187-203.

36 F. E. Patton, "A Comparison of the Kinesthetic Sensibility of Speech Defective and Normal Speaking Children," *Journal of Speech Disorders,* VII (1942), 305-310.

37 I. W. Karlin, A. C. Youtz, and L. Kennedy, "Distorted Speech in Young Children," *American Journal of Diseases of Children* (1940), 1203-1218.

38 R. W. Albright, "The Motor Abilities of Speakers with Good and Poor Articulation," *Speech Monographs,* XV (1948), 164-172.

39 G. Fairbanks and B. Bebout, "A Study of Minor Organic Deviations in Functional Disorders of Articulation: 3. The Tongue," *Journal of Speech and Hearing Disorders,* XV (1950), 348-352.

40 G. Fairbanks and D. C. Spriestersbach, "A Study of Minor Organic Deviations in Functional Disorders of Articulation: I. Rate of Movement of Oral Structures," *Journal of Speech and Hearing Disorders,* XV (1950), 60-69.

41 G. Reid, "The Etiology and Nature of Functional Articulatory Defects in Elementary School Children," *Journal of Speech Disorders,* XII (1947), 143-150.

[42] D. J. Mase, *Etiology of Articulatory Speech Defects,* Teachers College Contributions to Education, No. 921 (New York: Columbia University Press, 1946).

[43] M. Hall, "Auditory Factors in Functional Articulatory Speech Defects," *Journal of Experimental Education,* VII (1938), 110-132.

[44] B. F. Hansen, "The Application of Sound Discrimination Tests to Functional Articulatory Defectives with Normal Hearing," *Journal of Speech Disorders,* IX (1944), 347-355.

[45] G. Reid, *op. cit.*

[46] C. Van Riper, *Speech Correction,* 3rd ed. (Englewood Cliffs, N.J.: Prentice-Hall, Inc., 1954, pp. 221-234.

[47] J. F. Curtis, "Disorders of Articulation," in *Speech Handicapped School Children,* ed. W. Johnson (New York: Harper & Row, Publishers, 1956), p. 113.

[48] D. S. Spriestersbach and J. F. Curtis, "Misarticulation and Discrimination of Speech Sounds," *Quarterly Journal of Speech,* XXXVII (1951), 483-491.

[49] C. Van Riper and J. V. Irwin, *Voice and Articulation* (Englewood Cliffs, N.J.: Prentice-Hall, Inc., 1958), pp. 22-26.

[50] A. Glorig, "Hearing Conservation Past and Future," *Proceedings of the Working Conference on Health Aspects of Hearing Conservation,* Supplement to the Transactions of the American Academy of Ophthalomology and Otolaryngology (November-December, 1959), 24-33.

[51] H. Davis and S. R. Silverman, *Hearing and Deafness,* rev. ed. (New York: Holt, Rinehart & Winston, Inc., 1960), p. 416.

[52] E. M. Sullivan, "Auditory Acuity and Its Relation to Defective Speech," *Journal of Speech Disorders,* XI (1944), 127-130.

[53] M. F. Fiedler, "Teacher's Problems with Hard of Hearing Children," *Journal of Educational Research,* XLII (1949), 618-622.

[54] H. Davis and S. R. Silverman, *op. cit.,* p. 389.

[55] M. F. Berry and J. Eisenson, *op. cit.,* chap. 19.

[56] H. Ebbinghaus, *Memory: A Contribution to Experimental Psychology,* trans. H. A. Ruger and C. E. Bussenius (New York: Columbia University Press, 1913).

[57] Van Riper and Irwin, *op. cit.,* pp. 26-29.

[58] Van Riper and Irwin, *op. cit.,* p. 29.

[59] W. M. Cruickshank, F. A. Bentzen, F. H. Ratzeburg, and M. T. Tannhauser, *A Teaching Method for Brain Injured and Hyperactive Children* (Syracuse, N. Y.: Syracuse University Press, 1961), pp. 182-183.

[60] C. Van Riper, *op. cit.,* p. 81.

[61] I. P. Glauber, "Speech Characteristics of Psychoneurotic Patients," *Journal of Speech Disorders,* IX (1944), 30.

[62] W. Johnson, J. Curtis, C. W. Edney, and J. Keaster, *Speech Handicapped School Children* (New York: Harper & Row, Publishers, 1956), pp. 59-60.

[63] Berry and Eisenson, *op. cit.,* p. 17.

[64] A. Peckarsky, *op. cit.*

[65] O. H. Mowrer, "Speech Development of the Young Child: The Autism Theory of Speech Development and Some Clinical Applications," *Journal of Speech and Hearing Disorders,* XVII (1952), 263-268. See also Mowrer's *Learning Theory and the Symbolic Process* (New York: John Wiley & Sons, Inc., 1960), pp. 79-86.

[66] W. Goldfarb, *Childhood Schizophrenia* (Cambridge: Harvard University Press, 1961), p. 200.

[67] J. Ruesch, *Disturbed Communication* (New York: W. W. Norton & Company, Inc., 1957), p. 133.

[68] L. Bender, "Psychiatric Aspects," *The Concept of Congenital Aphasia from the Standpoint of Dynamic Differential Diagnosis,* ed. S. P. Brown, American Speech and Hearing Association Symposium, 1958.

[69] W. Goldfarb, *op. cit.,* p. 7.

[70] J. Eisenson, ed., *Stuttering: A Symposium* (New York: Harper & Row, Publishers, 1958).

[71] W. Johnson, *Speech Handicapped School Children, op. cit.,* p. 197.

72 W. Johnson, *Stuttering and What You Can Do About It* (Minneapolis: University of Minnesota Press, 1961), p. 95.

73 O. Bloodstein, W. Jaeger, and J. Tureen, "A Study of the Diagnosis of Stuttering by Parents of Stutterers and Non-Stutterers," *Journal of Speech and Hearing Disorders,* XVII (1952), 308-315.

74 J. Moncur, "Parental Domination in Stuttering," *Journal of Speech and Hearing Disorders,* XVII (1952), 155-164.

75 P. J. Glasner, "Personality Characteristics and Emotional Problems in Stutterers under the Age of Five," *Journal of Speech and Hearing Disorders,* XIV (1949), 135-138.

76 I. P. Glauber, "The Mother in the Etiology of Stuttering," abstract of an address in *The Psychoanalytic Quarterly,* XX (1951), 160-161.

77 I. P. Glauber, "The Psychoanalysis of Stuttering," in Eisenson's *Stuttering: A Symposium, op. cit.,* p. 99.

78 E. Douglass and B. Quarrington, "The Differentiation of Interiorized and Exteriorized Secondary Stuttering," *Journal of Speech and Hearing Disorders,* XVII (1952), 377-385.

79 W. E. Moore, G. Soderberg, and D. Powell, Relations of Stuttering in Spontaneous Speech to Speech Content and Verbal Output," *Journal of Speech and Hearing Disorders,* XVII (1952), 371-376.

80 M. H. Duncan, "Home Adjustments of Stutters and Non-Stutterers," *Journal of Speech and Hearing Disorders,* XIV (1949), 255-259.

81 J. Sheehan, "Projective Studies of Stutterers," *Journal of Speech and Hearing Disorders,* XXIII (1958), 18-25.

82 F. E. Fiedler and J. Wepman, "An Exploratory Investigation of the Self-Concept of Stutterers," *Journal of Speech and Hearing Disorders,* XVI (1951), 110-114.

83 D. A. Schultz, "A Study of Non-Directive Counseling as Applied to Adult Stutterers," *Journal of Speech and Hearing Disorders,* XII (1947), 421-427.

84 D. C. Spriestersbach, "An Objective Approach to the Investigation of Social Adjustments of Male Stutterers," *Journal of Speech and Hearing Disorders,* XVI (1951), 250-257.

85 L. H. Richardson, "A Personality Study of Stutterers and Non-Stutterers," *Journal of Speech and Hearing Disorders,* IX (1944), 152-160.

86 A. T. Murphy and R. M. Fitzsimons, *Stuttering and Personality Dynamics* (New York: The Ronald Press Company, 1960), chap. 6.

BERTHOLD LOWENFELD

Superintendent, California School for the Blind

5 *Psychological Problems of Children with Impaired Vision*

THE BLIND

Introduction

Impairment of vision causes many practical as well as theoretical problems. The psychological aspects of these problems will be treated here under three headings: Cognitive Functions, Mobility, and Personality and Social Factors. In general it can be said that blindness creates problems *sui generis* only in the area of cognitive functions and mobility. The congenitally and totally blind child experiences the world around him by sensory functions which the seeing child does not employ for this purpose, and he builds up his knowledge of the object world in ways that are essentially different from those of seeing children. As a result, it appears to be as impossible for the seeing to imagine the world of the blind as it is for the blind to really understand the experience of seeing. In achieving mobility the blind also make use of sensory means rarely if ever employed by the seeing. The personality and social effects of blindness, however, are similar to those caused by other conditions which either handicap the individual or set him apart in one way or another from the normal, the majority, the customary, or the better-organized. A blind child may develop feelings of insecurity because of negative parental attitudes due to his blindness just as other children may develop them for the same or for different reasons. Thus social and emotional effects of blindness are non-specific, although they may be characteristic as reactions to blindness or environmental influences caused by it.

For reasons of presentation the three factors are treated separately. In reality such separation does not exist. Cognitive functions and mobility have their strong emotional and social implications, while emotional and social factors may intensely influence cognitive functions and mobility.

Some problems caused by blindness have received a good deal of attention and investigation, but others have fared less well. The comparatively small number of blind children with the resulting wide scatter in age, intelligence, socioeconomic background, and geographic location has retarded research. It makes research based on large groups or on matched groups rather difficult and often impractical. If we consider this obstacle in addition to the others which obstruct research in general, we cannot be surprised that the literature on the psychological effects of blindness in children is limited, and that in many areas experiences, observations, and theoretical presentations are the only contributions available.

Psychological problems of blindness received early attention in the eighteenth century with the question of how a successfully operated congenitally blind person would react to his first optical impressions. The philosophers Locke, Berkeley, and, later, Diderot theorized considerably about sensory problems of the blind. During the early period of scientific psychology, William James, as well as Wilhelm Wundt and others, discussed in their standard works problems of the blind, particularly their spatial perception. The first systematic study dealing with psychological problems of blindness as such also dates back to the experimental laboratory of Wundt where Theodor Heller conducted investigations which he reported in his *Studien zur Blinden-Psychologie* (1895). Psychological research in the field of the blind has dealt mainly with problems of sensory experiences of the blind as compared with those of the seeing, with the ability to perceive obstacles, and with the measurement of intelligence, a field in which Samuel P. Hayes made the outstanding contribution. In 1933 Thomas D. Cutsforth's *The Blind in School and Society* was published as the first major work dealing with personality problems of the blind. Since then the emotional and social implications of blindness have received increasing attention.

A unique contribution was made by Helga Lende when in 1940 the American Foundation for the Blind published her *Books about the Blind: A Bibliographical Guide to Literature Relating to the Blind,* of which a new revised edition appeared in 1953. More recently, in 1960, Graham published a survey, *Social Research on Blindness*, which reports the literature as well as the then on-going research.[1]

Definition of Visual Impairment

There are mainly three ways in which pathological conditions in the eye may result in impaired vision. The visual acuity may be reduced, the field of vision may be limited or defective, and color vision may be imperfect.

Visual acuity is measured by the use of the Snellen Chart and expressed in the form of a fraction. A visual acuity of 20/200 means that the eye can see at the distance of 20 feet what a normal eye can see at 200 feet, or in other words, an object that a normal eye can see 200 feet away must be brought to within 20 feet in order to be discerned by the eye with a visual acuity of 20/200. In this pseudo-fraction the "numerator" and the "denominator" may be changed. In visual acuities better than 20/200, the denominator is usually changed, as for instance in 20/70; in visual acuities below 20/200, the numerator is usually changed, as for instance in 5/200. This is proper enough since such low acuities are actually measured at distances less than 20 feet.

The *field of vision* may be affected in two ways: an eye may have central vision with the peripheral field restricted to a certain angle, or the eye may have a scotoma, a spot without vision, which, if in the center of the field of vision, may cause loss of central vision. Restrictions in the field of vision are mapped out with the perimeter, an instrument which indicates the field limitations in the various directions on a chart.

Color vision is determined by the discrimination of the three qualities of color: hue, saturation, and brightness. In the rare case of total color blindness, all colors are seen as shades of black, gray, and white. Most color blindness is partial, the person having difficulty in distinguishing between certain colors, usually reds and greens. Color blindness by itself, though a visual impairment, is generally not regarded as coming within the scope of visual handicaps. However, some eye conditions which reduce vision also result either in total or partial color blindness.

According to the most widely accepted definition of blindness, a person is considered as blind if he has "central visual acuity of 20/200 or less in the better eye, with correcting glasses; or central visual acuity of more than 20/200 if there is a field defect in which the peripheral field has contracted to such an extent that the widest diameter of visual field subtends an angular distance no greater than 20 degrees."[2] Under this definition, individuals who are totally blind, who have light perception (ability to distinguish darkness and light), or light projection (ability to indicate the source of light), who can distinguish hand movements in front of their eyes, who have form- or object-perception, who have "travelling vision," and whose vision can be measured with the Snellen Chart up to and including 20/200, are all considered as "blind." This definition does not take into consideration the important factor of near- or reading-vision, or any defects within the peripheral field which do not result in a contraction of the field itself but block out certain areas.

During an era in which ophthalmologists were cautious about the use of the eyes, particularly for reading, the definition of blindness given above was a fairly adequate tool in determining educational placement of children. While a few decades ago the use of the eyes was considered as harmful for many types of visual handicaps, ophthalmologists recommend now that visually handicapped children use their sight without any special restrictions. The eyes are visual receptors and just as a camera does not suffer from use, neither do the eyes. This change of approach made the previously defined demarcations of visual acuity far less meaningful. Many children with visual acuities considerably below 20/200 are able to read print, large type or even regular size, if they can bring it close to their eyes or use magnifying glasses, as they are now encouraged to do. A "functional" definition of blindness is sought which will realistically determine for educational purposes which children should be considered as blind or as partially seeing.

Jones [3] reported statistics on the degree of vision of 14,125 legally blind students enrolled in residential schools and local public schools, as registered with the American Printing House for the Blind in January, 1960. This constituted possibly more than 90 per cent of all blind children receiving education in the United States. Of these children, 6,407 (45.4 per cent) attended residential schools and 7,718 (54.6 per cent), local public schools. Their degree of vision is distributed as follows: 24 per cent are totally blind, 16 per cent have light perception only, 28 per cent have vision ranging from perception of hand movements up to but not including 20/200, and 31 per cent have 20/200 visual acuity. This registration does not include any children, attending residential schools or local public schools, whose vision is better than 20/200, though there are many enrolled in some of these schools. Of the children enrolled in residential schools, 52 per cent are totally blind or have light perception only, while the corresponding figure of such children with no useful vision in local public schools is only 29 per cent. On the other end of the visual acuity range, 17 per cent of the children in residential schools have 20/200 visual acuity, while in local public schools 43 per cent have that much vision. A full description of educational facilities for blind children is given by Abel.[4]

Causes of Blindness

The cause of blindness often has psychological implications for the individual. Whether blindness is inherited or acquired through accident or disease may, for instance, be an important factor in explaining an individual's reaction toward his parents. The most recent national data on causes of blindness among school age children are those published by Kerby [5] pertaining to the school year 1954-55 which included 4,426 of 7,000 blind students, then estimated as attending schools in the United States. The following percentage distribution of causes of blindness was reported:

Infectious Diseases		7.4
Ophthalmia neonatorum	1.6	
Syphilis	1.4	
Toxoplasmosis	.7	
Rubella	.6	
Meningitis	.6	
Tuberculosis	.4	
Other and not specified	2.1	
Injuries		4.9
Sharp or pointed objects	1.2	
Blows or falls	1.0	
Firearms, airguns, fireworks, other explosives	.9	
Burns	.3	
Other and not specified	1.5	
Poisonings		19.3
Excessive oxygen	19.3	
Tumors		5.1
General Diseases		.7
Prenatal Influence		56.1
Genetic origin (established or presumed)	14.3	
Cause not specified	41.8	
Etiology Undetermined or Not Specified		6.5

These statistics show that by far the largest known cause of blindness in children of school age was retrolental fibroplasia (19.3 per cent). Retrolental fibroplasia (referred to as RLF) is an eye disease which since 1942, but mainly between 1949 and 1954, caused blindness almost exclusively in prematurely born babies. After intensive and painstaking medical research, it was found in 1954 that the major cause of this condition was the administration of high concentrations of oxygen over prolonged periods of time to prematurely born infants. Since 1954 the application of oxygen in incubators has been carefully controlled, and RLF is virtually eliminated. In the peak years of this disease, 1949-54, some states reported that almost 80 per cent of their blind pre-school children were blind as a result of it. It has been estimated that RLF caused blindness in approximately 10,000 babies who are now growing through childhood and adolescence into adulthood.

The statistical data for 1954-55 do not reflect the full impact of RLF as a cause of blindness in the school-age population, since the children born during its peak years reached school age between 1955 and 1960 and will remain in school for many years.

The large percentage of blindness due to Prenatal Influence (56.1 per cent) for which no specified cause can be given, shows that our medical knowledge of causes of blindness is still far from satisfactory.

Age at Onset of Blindness

Visually handicapped individuals may have been born with a visual impairment or may have lost their sight completely or partially at any time during their lives. The extreme case of blindness is one in which the person is totally blind from birth. According to observations made by Zoltan Toth and others, individuals who have lost their sight before about five years of age do not retain any useful visual imagery.[6] In a more recent study Schlaegel confirmed this, stating that visual imagery tends to disappear if vision was lost before the age between five and seven years.[7] He also found that subjects with the poorest vision had the least number of visual responses. Various studies on dreams of the blind, reported by Blank,[8] confirm that the critical period for retaining visual imagery in dreams is if sight was lost at the age between five and seven years. This "is also the period of cerebral structural maturation, the completion of early childhood ego development, and the beginning of latency." Therefore, children who lost their sight completely during the early years of their lives must also be regarded as extreme cases. If children have some sight, they observe visually and also visualize in their memory. Those who lose their sight completely or partially after five years of age may retain a more or less active visual frame of reference. They may, for instance, observe an object by touch and form a visual idea of it based on their past visual experiences. Of course their visual observation is limited according to the degree of sight retained.

On the basis of this discussion, we must distinguish the following gradations of visual impairment so far as influence on sensory and memory activities is concerned:

1. Total blindness, congenital or acquired before the age of five years.
2. Total blindness, acquired after five years of age.
3. Partial blindness, congenital.
4. Partial blindness, acquired.
5. Partial sight, congenital.
6. Partial sight, acquired.

Of these six categories, the first four come within the definition of blind-ness, and children who belong to these four groups are considered as blind for educational purposes. Those who belong to the fifth and sixth groups are partially seeing children who will be discussed elsewhere.

Kerby's report shows that 51.5 per cent of her group of students were born blind, and that 35.4 per cent became blind during birth or up to but not including five years. This gives a total of 86.9 per cent who were born blind or became blind before five years of age.

It is estimated that there are about 35,000 blind individuals (by legal definition) below 21 years of age in the United States. Since the total number of individuals below 21 years of age in the United States is about 71.5 millions, a ratio of one blind individual to 2,000 seeing individuals in this age group can be estimated. This ratio is an inflated one due to RLF. Jones states: "If present trends continue, there is reason to believe that, after the children blinded by retrolental fibroplasia have been graduated and many children who would formerly have been taught by braille methods are taught to read print, the incidence of blindness will drop to about one child to every 7,000 or 8,000 of the school population. Today, however, more blind children are reaching school age than at any time in our history." [9]

It has been pointed out that a visual acuity test is in most cases used as the indication of a person's degree of sight. Such a test, however, does not always give a true indication of the individual person's "visual ef-ficiency." Many experienced observers have noted that some children with very low vision make much better use of it than others who have a higher visual acuity. Such factors as general intelligence and environ-mental influences are assumed to be influential. Viktor Lowenfeld con-siders inclination toward the visual type or the haptic type as the most important factor determining whether the remaining sight is an asset or an irritation for the individual.[10] Barker and others also call attention to this fact and state: "It is the adequacy of each individual's vision for the particular tasks of his life that is crucial for a somatopsychological defini-tion of blindness rather than optically measured visual acuity." [11]

In the following discussions it must be kept in mind that the effects of blindness are fully operative only in those children who have no sight and no workable visual imagery. For all others, adaptations and modifica-tions in kind as well as in degree will have to be made according to the extent of their visual handicap.

Cognitive Functions

Experiencing the Object World

Children who are blind or have lost their sight early in life must rely upon their remaining senses for gaining knowledge of the world around them. In attempting to determine the importance of the remaining senses for the blind child's development, it is necessary to understand the basic functions of hearing and touch as cognitive means. Hearing gives certain clues in regard to distance and direction of the object, provided the object makes any sound. It does not convey any concrete ideas of objects as such. A blind person may, for instance, walk under a tree and hear the wind blow through the leaves. His past associations and experiences may enable him to interpret what he hears so that he can say whether the tree has leaves, needles, or is barren, whether the leaves are dry or fresh, how far away from the ground they are and how thick the foliage is. His olfactory impressions may permit him to say whether the tree is in bloom or even what kind of a tree it is. But all these clues will not give the blind person any idea of the shape and size of the leaves, the formation of the branches and of the trunk of the tree, and of its general appearance. Knowledge of the spatial qualities of objects can only be gained by touch observations in which kinesthetic sensations take part. The importance of hearing is in the area of verbal communication, in locomotion, and in general as an indicator of audible clues.

Lacking sight, actual knowledge of the object world can be gained only by touch experiences. Berthold Lowenfeld points out that tactual space perception of the blind is different from the visual space perception of the seeing.[12] The main reason for the difference is to be found in the fact that tactual perception requires direct contact with the object to be observed. As a consequence, blind people can observe only those things which are accessible to them. The sun, the moon, clouds, the horizon, and the sky are inaccessible and can be explained to blind people only by the use of analogies from other sensory fields. This method must also be used in explaining to blind people such visual phenomena as shadows, perspective, and reflection of light. Many objects are too large to be observed by touch, for instance, a mountain or a large building. Other objects are too small and cannot be observed by touch with any degree of accuracy, for instance, flies or ants. Of course, microscopic observations can only be made visually and are entirely impossible for the sense of touch. Fragile or delicate objects like butterflies, certain flowers or parts of flowers, snowflakes, or a spider's web also cannot be observed tactually. Objects in motion, live objects, and objects in certain conditions such as burning, boiling, or cooking cannot be observed by touch because they either change their shapes or positions or because direct contact with them would be dangerous. Liquids do not have shapes of their own and are often difficult to observe by touch when kept in containers. This is also the case with mercury in narrow glass tubes as used in thermometers and various gages.

Many of these restrictions in observation hold true not only for the blind person who has never seen but also for the person who becomes blind later in life. Although he may have a very clear idea of the visual appearance of these objects, he cannot actually observe the object itself. He may, for instance, know what a thermometer looks like but cannot read the temperature it indicates. If it is understood that visual observation permits perception of a situation as a whole and of the objects within the situation according to size, shape, distance, position, and color, it must also be recognized that tactual observations have their own characteristics and advantages. Touch perceptions relate, with the restrictions already discussed, the size, shape, and position of objects. In addition, they also give such experiences as surface quality (roughness, smoothness, evenness), temperature, and weight. These qualities cannot be gained by visual observations, although seeing people may secure them if they bring their touch organs into play. The average person is inclined to neglect tactual observations almost completely because of the dominance of sight over all other senses. For instance, most seeing people are completely satisfied by looking at a sculpture without giving themselves the stimulating experience of observing it by touch. Another most important advantage of touch, as compared with vision, is that it does not depend upon light. Also, it is often easier to explore with the fingers rather than to get into a position where sight could be applied. Often tactual observation is the only observation that can be made, as in some medical examinations.

There is a further important difference between sight and touch so far as activity of these senses is concerned. When a person is awake, his eyes are almost continuously open to stimulation coming from the outside world. This is different for touch activities. The hands as touch organs must be actively applied for the purpose of observation. Also, when they are applied, the horizon of touch extends only to the limited area of the outstretched hands. Observations beyond that limit can only be made if the person moves toward or follows the object to be observed. It is true that the exposed areas of the skin are open to stimulation by air currents and temperature, but this in no way compares with the perceptual activity of sight.

Hearing enables a blind person to gain information through verbal communication and to keep in contact with his social and physical environment. However, in respect to the latter, his efficiency is curtailed. People may stop talking or may not talk at all so that he is unaware of their presence; persons may move away or enter a room without being heard; it may not always be obvious to the blind person to whom the comment of somebody else is directed; many things do not give any sound while others which do sound may not always do it, or they may sound only under certain conditions, such as leaves when the wind is blowing; continuous sound such as that of rain may drown out all other audible clues; and snow deadens sounds which may indicate changes in the environment. All these factors contribute to more chances for being less adequate in meeting the demands of the situation. Therefore, it can be assumed that they increase a blind person's nervous tension and insecurity.

With the exception of taste, which permits touch observations since the tongue and the mouth envelop or at least touch the object, the other senses relate only sensory clues indicating the presence, location, or nature of certain objects. In passing by a garden one can, for instance, smell if there are certain trees or plants around, provided the wind does not blow in the opposite direction. As one walks on the street, such places as a drug store, a shoe store, or a food market can be ascertained by their specific odors. Also, the exposed skin surface reacts to changes in air current and in temperature, which may give a blind person clues concerning the spatial characteristics of his surroundings. Walking along the walls of buildings feels entirely different from walking along a garden fence, along shrubs, or in open space.

Space and Form Perception

The process by which space perception by touch is attained has been the subject of considerable research. Heller [13] and Steinberg [14] agree that the touch sense is the only original spatial sense of those who were born blind. Heller distinguishes two types of tactual perception by the hands: enveloping touch in which small objects are enfolded by letting either one or both hands observe the object. This type of tactual perception he called "synthetic touch" because the form of the object is perceived as a whole, more or less simultaneously. In observing an apple, for instance, children will gain an idea of the shape of the fruit by enfolding it in their hands. This enveloping touch is applied not only to smaller objects but also to larger ones when only parts of them are subjected to closer observation. The other type of tactual perception is applied to large objects which extend beyond the limited scope of one or both hands, as in the observation of a chair. Here the moving hands follow the shape of the object and, if it is a very large one, the whole body may actively participate in the process. This method has been called "analytic touch" because it consists of successive impressions gained by observing parts of the object. These successive impressions, however, cannot remain isolated, but must result in a unified "touch idea" of the object. Without such unification, blind people would not have any workable concept of larger objects nor of their environment.

German psychologists considered this phenomenon of unification the central problem of blindness, and various explanations have been given for it. Steinberg assumes, as a result of experimentation in which Gestalt psychological principles were applied, that there is a mental process of "expansion of tactual space." [15] Heller believes that there is a contraction of tactual space in which large objects are reduced by a special mental act until a simultaneous idea of the total object is achieved.[16] Another theory postulates the perseveration of the earlier perceptions until they combine with the later ones into a spatial and temporary continuum, a spatial Gestalt. Senden (published in German, 1932, and translated into English, 1960) reviews the reports and studies of others concerned with the problem of the perception of space and shape in congenitally blind persons who recovered their sight after eye surgery.[17] He comes to the conclusion that tactual perceptions do not result in awareness of space. The congenitally blind person creates temporal schemata and verbal concepts which are "a surrogate for the spatial awareness he lacks." Others disagree with this point of view, and so do even those who discuss in an Appendix to the book the significance of Senden's work for related disciplines.

Whatever the explanation may be, the fact that blind individuals are able to reproduce all kinds of objects, small and large ones, in modeling and handwork, and that they can recognize objects on the basis of previous observations, is evidence that they must be able to unify separate perceptions into one total concept of the object. This central problem of space perception, however, needs further investigation.

All tactual observations of the fingers, hands, arms, or other parts of the body have a kinesthetic component because muscle sensations are involved in these movements. For example, in observing a chair with both hands, the touch movements of the two hands and arms may proceed in different directions and with changing distances between them. Therefore, the actual spatial experience is made up not only by the touch contacts with the object, but also by the variety of muscular sensations accompanying the touch movements.

Tactual perception results not only in spatial experiences but in a number of other touch sensations. The surface of the skin has specialized nerve endings which are the receptors for pressure, pain, warmth, and cold. Sensitive spots for these sensations are dispersed over various areas of the body in varying density. Experiments reported by Hayes have shown that blind individuals have no better discrimination in regard to cutaneous sensitivities than the seeing.[18]

Color Ideas

Space and form can be perceived through sight as well as touch. Color perception, however, is a function of the retina, and no other organ can take it over. When the retina is destroyed, when it cannot be affected by light stimulation, when the stimuli received by the retina are not carried back to the interbrain and the cortex, or when the visual areas of the brain are destroyed, total blindness occurs and color vision is absent.

Therefore, persons who have been born blind or lost their sight so early that they do not have any visual memory do not have any real ideas of color. Since they live in a world which makes constant use of color observations and color references, they build up substitutive ideas for color on the basis of verbal, sensory, and emotional associations. They hear people talk, for example, about the blue sky and, as a result, all or some of the different sensations and emotions caused by fine weather may build up as a substitutive idea for the color blue, in this case a pleasant one. On the other hand, the commonly unpleasant connotation that this color carries in the proverbial "blue Monday" may give the word *blue* a different emotional character. Because such color associations vary from individual to individual, and also from time to time, the substitutive color ideas are not constant. Blind children learn the common color associations such as blue sky, red blood, white snow, and green grass because they are a part of their socially needed vocabulary. However, since they cannot experience color, their attention should be directed toward aspects of situations and objects which can be experienced by them in order to avoid purely verbal preoccupation. Excessive and unrealistic use of color words by blind individuals is not rare and can, in many cases, be regarded as a compensatory mechanism.

Colored audition, which is a form of synesthesia, plays an important role in the ideational life of many persons who have lost their sight either during childhood or later on. In this phenomenon color sensations are closely attached to auditory sensations and may appear regularly in response to certain auditory stimulations. These secondary sensations of color are called photisms. Photisms may be attached to a variety of experiences and ideas. Wheeler and Cutsforth have jointly and separately published research on this problem and examined the function of synesthesia in learning,[19] in the development of meaning,[20] and of concepts,[21] and in other thought processes. Voss, in his extensive study of color hearing of the blind, enumerates photisms attached to: timbre of tones and sounds, especially of various musical instruments; varying pitch of tones of an instrument; single tones within a scale; major and minor scales; voices of persons; vowels and consonants; various emotions; numbers; days; months; geographical names, particularly those of cities and countries; names of the notes of the scale, and so on.[22] These photisms, once present in an individual, are quite inflexible, although they vary from person to person. Of course only persons who have seen colors can experience colored audition, since imagination cannot create anything which was not experienced previously by the senses.

Sensory Acuteness

The assumption that the loss of one sense is compensated for by a more or less automatic improvement in the acuity of the other senses is one of long standing and perseverance. Three explanations might be considered for this fact. The wish to have nature act according to justice and thereby relieve one of feelings of guilt or the responsibility to help, ascribes to other minorities similar facilities. The fact that blind individuals may learn to use their senses better than those who can rely upon sight gives some actual support to this assumption. Finally, there is a widespread tendency to consider anything the blind can do as admirable and superior, which only disguises a tendency to consider them inferior.

It is not surprising that experiments to determine the differences in sensory acuteness of the blind and the seeing were performed to a considerable extent around the turn of the century, when experimental psychology began to be practiced in many laboratories, particularly under Wilhelm Wundt in Germany and William James in the United States. Hayes reviews in detail the various studies which tested the comparative abilities of the blind and the seeing to distinguish the direction of sound, to determine the distance of sounds, and to discriminate the intensity of sounds; also studies of acuteness of smell, taste, and touch, discrimination of lifted weights, of passive and active pressure, and of tactual space, sensitiveness to changes in temperature, and acuteness of the vibratory sense, particularly in the deaf-blind.[23] All these studies gave evidence that the blind are not superior to the seeing in their sensory acuteness; some of them even indicated that they are somewhat inferior. There is no experimental research available on pain sensitivity, on the sense of balance, and on the organic sense. Hayes investigated the memory of blind children—rote memory, recall, and logical memory—and found no superiority in this field either.[24] He concludes, "In memory, as in sensation, compensation is not a gift but the reward of persistent effort." Therefore, any higher efficiency of the blind in interpreting the sensory data perceived, must be the result of attention, practice, adaptation, and increased use of the remaining faculties.

Almost twenty years later Axelrod [25] examined the effects of blindness on two levels of sensory functioning: A basic tactile level where light-touch sensitivity and two-point acuity of three finger tips were tested; and a "higher level" where sense data received through the haptic and auditory modalities were utilized. He did not find any generalized rise of sensory acuity in the early-blind group; on the contrary, they did significantly less well than sighted subjects on the "higher level" complex-task performance. These results stress the importance of early visual learning for later problem-solving. Axelrod adds that "brain damage associated with, or consequent to, blindness of early onset cannot be ruled out as a factor" but continues: "The difference between early-blind and sighted groups on the complex tasks were, though statistically significant, nonetheless small; they should not be regarded as evidence of gross impairment of intellective processes." [26] A great deal of hypothesizing was required to bring some coherence to the interpretation of the data of this study. This indicates that the last word on the problem of "sensory compensation" may not yet have been spoken. There may be processes in operation which so far have eluded experimentation.

With the exception of an early study by Ralph V. Merry, no research can be reported on the widely assumed superior abilities of the blind in music.[27] Merry used the Seashore Musical Talent Tests with a selected group of 44 blind students. The majority of them made superior ranks in the six tests, but since they represented a selected group, their superiority does not permit any general conclusions. Even in this group, Merry points out, there was a significant percentage of inferior performances. Although further research would be needed to clarify the question of superior musical ability of the blind, various factors stand in the way of such an undertaking. Blind children are usually encouraged to listen to music, to practice music, and to take part in musical activities far beyond opportunities offered to seeing children. This does not only support the general impression that the blind are more musical, but also promotes their efforts and interests to an extent which gives them unquestionable advantage over an otherwise equal group of seeing children.

The belief that blind people have a superior ability to interpret human voices also belongs in this category. It is unquestionably true—and we know it from various autobiographical and other reports—that some blind persons can remember and recognize many voices even after a long lapse of time. They also develop through continuous practice the ability to discern in voices moods, emotions, attitudes, and such traits as sincerity, tact, friendliness, and their opposites. On the other hand, it often happens that blind individuals rely too much upon the voice as an indicator of a person's character and either accept or reject the person on that ground alone. In this respect they are not different from seeing persons who form impressions on the basis of pleasant or unpleasant appearances. Cantril and Allport conducted some experiments in which blind and seeing subjects were asked to judge from voice the vocation, age, interests, and such features of personality as introversion and extroversion.[28] They found, contrary to the popular belief, that the blind are less accurate in their judgments than the seeing. They explained this by the fact that the blind have fewer opportunities to observe and to study personality and also have no visual assistance in correcting their errors in judgment. These experiments have been made with a small number of persons and can only be considered as preliminary. The problem of interpretation of voices and its influence on the blind is one that should receive further attention. Regardless of the objective validity of the judgment which blind people form in listening to voices, it is a fact that they are strongly influenced by them and find in the variety of timbres and modulations a source of enriching social experiences.

Intelligence Test Results

Samuel P. Hayes has, since 1918, reported on his studies in connection with the standardization of intelligence tests for blind children. In his *Contributions to a Psychology of Blindness*,[29] he reports results of the use of the 1930 Hayes-Binet Intelligence Tests in seventeen residential schools for the blind. This report covers the largest number of children tested and includes 2,372 pupils. The mean I.Q. obtained for them was 98.8. The mean I.Q.'s in the seventeen schools ranged from 108.1 down to 92 with standard deviations from 15.24 to 22.62. Of the total, 10.3 per cent had I.Q.'s of 120 and above, while 9.2 per cent had I.Q.'s of 70 and below. Subsequent reports give the same general picture as a result of more recent adaptations of the Binet scale and of the Wechsler scale.[30, 31] According to these reports, the percentage of blind pupils falling into the "average group" is somewhat smaller than the 50 per cent for the seeing. A slightly larger percentage of superior pupils is found among the blind and a considerably larger percentage of below-average pupils. Since there is a good deal of variation in the actual percentage figures, it seems reasonable to indicate only the general pattern of the distribution. Hayes has also published at various times reports on the distribution of intelligence at a single school, Perkins Institution, which confirm the above facts.

Hayes followed the distribution of I.Q.'s of pupils entering two residential schools for the blind from 1915 to 1940, and found in practically all years a mean intelligence of slightly above 93.[32] There were considerable variations in the percentages falling into the various intelligence groups with no trend apparent in the changes over the years. The percentage in the inferior group was consistently higher than that in the superior group. These data not only demonstrate that in the years surveyed the schools did not receive poorer material, but also confirm the previously mentioned characteristics of the distribution of I.Q.'s among blind children.

The question whether congenitally and adventitiously blind children show any difference in their intelligence was also examined by Hayes.[33] He found no correlation of general intelligence with the age at which sight is lost, and achievement in different school subjects also did not show any differentiation. He concludes, "The *mental constitution* of those born blind may well be essentially different from that of the other group, but the *functioning* of their minds as measured by our tests shows no such difference." [34]

To compile a distribution of I.Q.'s of pupils in schools for the blind and draw from this general conclusions upon the intelligence of blind children as compared with seeing children is a somewhat uncertain procedure. Schools for the blind must admit and retain for shorter or longer periods of diagnostic observation children who are of questionable educability. In the case of the seeing school population, such children would not be included in regular classes. Thus the borderline and dull brackets of the intelligence distribution may be overweighted according to the tolerance of a school for low intelligence children. Hayes ascribes the retardation frequently found in pupils entering school to "the inferior environment in which many blind children grow up, and the restrictions placed upon them in their homes," and notes that under the favorable conditions of a good residential school, many of these children "blossom out" although this may not occur for several years.[35] Komisar and MacDonnell confirmed this in a study of retests of 89 children in a residential school.[36] They found significant gains in I.Q. (mean gains of 6.3 I.Q. points) which increased with the years spent at the school. Children with lower I.Q.'s gained more than those at average or above average levels.

Another factor to be considered in this connection is Hayes' own recognition that the Hayes-Binet Scale is not entirely satisfactory if used with younger and older children.

> Although we have fairly convincing evidence of the general validity and reliability of the Hayes-Binet Scale, the author has long realized that both ends of the scale were far from satisfactory— the tests for very young children have never been properly standardized because so few cases come to the attention of schools and their testers, and the tests above the fourteen year level are too few and too restricted in range to give an adequate measurement of bright adolescents.[37]

Since Hayes made this statement, the verbal parts of the Wechsler scales which avoid some of these shortcomings have become widely used in testing the visually handicapped. Hayes recommended their use and reported consistent high correlations between the Interim Hayes-Binet Intelligence Tests for the Blind 1942 and the Wechsler Bellevue Scale.[38] In an item analysis of the latter, he showed its value in use with blind students. Lewis confirmed the correlations mentioned before and also showed that there is a positive relationship between measured mental ability and academic achievement and survival of blind students in a residential school.[39]

The verbal parts of the Wechsler scales, however, need to be supplemented with performance test items so that a measure of an individual's global intelligence can be secured. Wattron reports a successful attempt to use adapted Kohs-type blocks which have smooth and rough sides instead of the white and red colors.[40] Other researchers are at present working on the development and standardization of performance test scales for the visually handicapped.

In the past years many things have happened which suggest a re-evaluation of the whole problem of intelligence testing of blind children: the increase in blindness in children due to RLF which did not follow any socioeconomic stratification; the increase in the number of blind children attending local public school facilities (in 1961 about 8,250 as compared with approximately 7500 in residential schools); [41] the better understanding of parents in bringing up their blind child because of growing emphasis on parent education; and the recognition that tests devised for seeing children may not adequately measure the intelligence of visually handicapped children, particularly if they rely only on verbal items. These are some of the factors which advocate a revision of our testing procedures and of the conclusions drawn from them in the past.

Achievement Test Results

The first report on the use of an achievement test with the blind was published in 1918 by Hayes, who used a reading test with blind pupils. In 1927, Maxfield published her *Adaptation of Educational Tests for Use with Blind Pupils*,[42] in which she gave directions for the administration of parts of the Stanford Achievement Tests and the Gray Oral Reading Check Tests. Since then many achievement tests have been used and adapted for use with the blind, such as the Metropolitan Achievement Tests, the Sones-Harry High School Achievement Test, and the Myers-Ruch High School Progress Test. The Stanford Achievement Tests in their various forms have been used most widely in schools for the blind. The College Entrance Examination Board also offers its tests in braille for those blind students who plan to enter college. Hayes found two basic changes necessary in adapting achievement tests for use with blind pupils: (1) Greater detail in preliminary instructions and (2) an increase of three times the time allowance given for seeing pupils.[43] This ratio was indicated as desirable in a study by Caldwell.[44]

In general the results of studies on the achievement of blind pupils revealed that, grade-by-grade, children acquire about as much school information as seeing children do, with the exception of arithmetic in which their scores are generally lower. Lowenfeld noted a drop in the achievement in literature and in history in the curves showing results of the *New Stanford Achievement Test* in seven schools for the blind.[45] He explains this drop in subjects which per se should not present particular difficulties to the blind, by the slowness of braille reading which confines the blind pupil to a much smaller amount of reading than his seeing peers. He stresses in this connection the importance of using Talking Books which enable blind students to read about three times as fast as their average braille reading rate.

Although blind pupils show grade-by-grade about the same achievement as seeing pupils, Hayes points out that "blind children average at least two years older than seeing children in the same grades, so comparisons by age, either chronological or mental, demonstrate their retardation." [46] Lowenfeld reports on the age-grade relationship for 481 pupils in four grades of twelve schools for the blind.[47] In the third and fourth grades, the blind showed an over-age of 2.5 years, in the sixth grade of 2.9, and in the seventh grade of 2.8 years. Various factors are responsible for this age-grade retardation, such as environmental influences resulting in lack of opportunity for observations, slower acquisition of knowledge due to lack of sight, and slower braille reading. No recent data have been published on age-grade relationships, but it may be possible that such findings would show a change due to the increased use of aural sources of information, such as the Talking Book and the radio, and to the greater integration of blind children with seeing children.

It must of course be recognized that whatever is said about blind pupils as a group does not permit any conclusion concerning the achievement of individual blind students. Many of them finish high school in competition with seeing students in public schools at an equal age and excel even in such subjects as arithmetic, geometry, and physics.

The most valuable source of information on tests and testing techniques for use with blind pupils and adults is *A Manual for the Psychological Examination of the Adult Blind*,[48] which also includes information concerning special considerations of a blind client's history and sources for securing testing material.

The Use of Touch in Cognition

If blind children are to gain experiences comparable in reality value to those of seeing children, they must acquire them through touch observations. Such experiences are particularly essential during the elementary grades when children form the basic concepts of their environment. Objects or situations can either be observed in reality or as models. If an object is too large, the model will represent it in a contracted form; if an object is too small, the model will show it enlarged and most likely also reinforced. A model is only a substitute for the real experience and is always in some way incomplete or distorted. For example, if animals are represented in stuffed form, they may be true to size, shape, and surface quality, but do not give the feeling of warmth, life, and motion which one gets when observing the animal alive. If only a model of the animal is used, size and texture are given up, the motion is "frozen," and the only quality preserved for observation is shape. These shortcomings are, in one or the other combination, true for all teaching models. It is, therefore, necessary for teachers to take great care that their pupils will not form misconceptions about certain qualities of the object presented, particularly in regard to its actual size.

Although almost no research is available concerning the psychological and educational problems of touch observation, a few comments based on experience are offered here. The ability to observe by touch and to manipulate develops with the child. The cutaneous senses, prehensory and grasping abilities, kinesthetic sensations, time experiences, and last but not least, coordination and intelligent interpretation, are brought into action according to the child's developmental level. The younger the child is, the simpler must be the experiences from which he can gain. At first he will be limited in observing as well as in verbalizing his experiences, but by practice he will acquire the ability to observe better, to differentiate objects according to size, weight, shape, material, surface, temperature, and to give verbal reports of his observations. Simultaneousness is characteristic of visual observation, while successiveness is characteristic of touch observation. Every part of the object must be covered by or brought under the touching hand, often not only once, but frequently, so that the large forms as well as the finer details can be observed. In addition to this individual need for more time, there is a group factor which must be considered. Many children can, at the same time, look at an object while only one child can observe it by touch. If touch observation is limited to the hours of instruction only, it will either consume too much time or the individual child will be confined to only a cursory inspection of the object. For this reason, material for observation should be left in the classroom so that the pupils can continue their observation during their free time. The teacher may call the attention of the pupils to certain characteristic features and let them proceed on their own with the actual observation—either in preparation or in follow-up of the instruction period. In this directed but unsupervised observation, totally blind children and those with partial sight gain mutually from their experiences.

The fact that blind children must rely in their acquisition of actual object knowledge on the touch sense puts them at a serious disadvantage in experiencing objects and situations in their totality. In seeing children, sight is the unifying agent which enables the individual in a short time to observe situations in toto and to combine part experiences into wholes. Sight also serves as an organizer of discrete experiences and facilitates the reduction of form varieties to simpler patterns or schemata. The blind child gains many impressions by the use of his senses: he may hear or smell something, he may feel air currents or temperature changes, and he may have actual touch contact with the object or situation or with parts of them. But all these experiences are discrete and unorganized and remain so, unless guided observation or teaching lends organization and structure to them. Teaching by the unit method has, therefore, a special purpose in the blind child's education. It gives him those unifying experiences which he often cannot gain because of his lack of sight.

The young blind child forms his own concepts of his environment as he grows into it. These concepts, incomplete and distorted as they may be, suffice for his purposes and satisfy the child's restricted curiosity. A desire to know more about things and to know them in reality and fully must often be awakened and encouraged in blind children. The pre-school years should encourage such inquisitiveness in the young blind child, but often it is suppressed by an ill-conceived "touch taboo." Then the more difficult task of reestablishing this desire for exploration is left to the teacher.

In the process of his observations, the child does not react with one sense but with his total sensory equipment; he hears, smells, and, if given opportunity, tastes. Hearing and smelling have, in common with sight, the characteristic that they need not be applied but are continuously open to stimulation; the sense of taste, like touch, functions only when its organ comes into direct contact with the object to be tasted. Thus, children will hear and smell while they are awake, although their observations need to become conscious ones in order to be of real value. Children, and also adults, may listen to the twitter of birds again and again without noticing the great variety of bird sounds—it is just twitter to them. Once their attention is called to the specific song of, say, the robin, and this recognition is sufficiently implanted, they will not fail to recognize it and to know when one of these singers is around. Or, in walking through a wood, one may smell a peculiar odor which can be traced to rotting wood. Once this connection between the odor and its source is firmly established, the child will know how to make use of it as a clue to the presence of rotting wood or other material in the same condition. Thus, besides recognition, "implanting" and "establishing" are necessary processes before an experience can become of value for future use. The concept of "passive" and "active" knowledge as elaborated in the field of creative growth by Viktor Lowenfeld is a most useful one in this connection.[49] The methods by which education succeeds in transforming passive into active knowledge are the same for seeing and blind children and include motivation, insight, exercise, activity, repetition, and various forms of reinforcement. Which of these will be used in a given situation with the individual child or with a group of children is a decision which must be left to the teacher.

Confirmation of the need of blind children for practical knowledge of objects comes from the area of vocational testing. Bauman states that studies of test results

> . . . point very strongly to the desirability of including in the education of blind children far more contact with practical materials of possible vocational value, such as tools. The inability of some blind individuals to deal with this type of material suggests lack of previous contact with it rather than lack of fundamental ability to comprehend it.[50]

Normally a child acquires his knowledge of tools by observing when anyone in the family does some work in which tools are used, or when he can watch a workman performing his job. Where the seeing child can watch from a distance, the blind child must have direct contact with the object to be observed, and this is his greatest obstacle to the casual acquisition of knowledge and experience. It implies that blind children must be given special opportunities for observation in order to make their environment real to them. This will help them avoid falling into a pattern of unreality which so often interferes with their later adjustment to the requirements of life.

Deutsch investigated the effect of lack of sight on the sense of reality in the person born blind.[51] He gave 28 blind pupils a box containing seven wooden blocks of various shapes which the subjects were asked to name and arrange in the order of preference. They were asked to enumerate the forms of the blocks from memory, and it was also observed how they reacted to removal of one or more of the blocks while they were playing with them. Deutsch noticed that the curiosity of the person born blind was more quickly satisfied than that of the seeing, that some subjects were inhibited about feeling the figures, and that observation of loss of some blocks resulted in a striking readiness to give up reality and to escape into fantasy.

The ability of blind children to recognize by touch simple embossed pictures has been studied and reported on by R. V. Merry and F. K. Merry. On the basis of a series of experiments, they reached the following conclusions:

> It seems unwise to expand any considerable amount of time teaching blind children how to recognize tactually pictures of three-dimensional objects. If, however, the needs of the child demand instruction upon the identification of simple figures in two dimensions, time for such work seems justified. . . . It may be of value to make use of embossed designs of a bi-dimensional type in the education of blind children, but it is very doubtful if embossed pictures of tri-dimensional objects, wherein perspective is involved, possess any real meaning for children without sight even after systematic instruction.[52]

The idea of using embossed pictures in the education of blind children is an old and often tried one. In addition to the experiments just discussed, the accumulated experiences of teachers of the blind also prove that embossed pictures of three-dimensional objects are of no practical value. Usually they are made by using three-dimensional dots or lines or raised surfaces for the purpose of making tangible two-dimensional outlines of objects as perceived by vision. Thus, perceptual qualities of vision, such as perspective, base line, light and shadow, and distinctness are presented to the sense of touch which does not function according to them. To be concrete, the embossed outline of a dog gives the shape of this animal as it is seen. The hands, observing a real dog, or a part of it, by touch, move in three dimensions and embrace the object or parts of it in an act of three-dimensional perception. They do not follow the visually perceived outline of the object. In an embossed drawing, the dog's four legs are represented in one plane, while to the sense of touch they are actually at the "four corners" of the dog's body, as a blind child expressed it. The embossed outline, therefore, constitutes not a representation but a symbol of the object which becomes meaningful only by added verbal interpretation and explanation. Of course, the situation becomes far more involved if different objects of varying size and positions requiring perspective drawings are presented.

The Merrys' conclusions indicate that the use of embossed material in the teaching of geometry, geography, and other subjects should be successful and, also, that embossed pictures of essentially two-dimensional objects, such as a wheel, a hand, or a pair of scissors, can be recognized.

Creative Activities

Viktor Lowenfeld has studied extensively the creative activities of blind and partially seeing children and the psychological factors involved.[53, 54] He distinguishes two different modes of perception, the haptic and the visual perception. The haptic mode is based on immediate bodily experiences and is primarily concerned with the tactual space around the individual. The visual mode is concerned with his environment and with the visual integration of it. Lowenfeld found that the amount of sight is not a determining factor in the person's inclination toward one or the other type. A haptically minded individual might be disturbed by his remaining sight, while a visually minded individual will be greatly aided by it. Creative activity, which permits the individual child to express himself according to his mode of functioning is an important means of adjustment. By releasing emotional tension and rigidity, it can help to overcome feelings of inferiority and isolation from the environment. The author exemplifies his findings with numerous illustrations which show the importance of his distinction as derived from visually handicapped children for the general field of art education. His observations, concerning the tactual-kinesthetic perception of space, show that the blind are capable of achieving simultaneous spatial images through an act of integration of successively perceived tactual impressions. He also concludes that, in the modeling of the blind, objects receive their proportion by the value they have for the individual in a given situation. Thus the perspective of the blind in modeling is a perspective of value. So far as creative activities of blind children are concerned, he warns of the danger of imposition of visual characteristics by the teacher, and stresses "that the most primitive creative work born in the mind of a blind person and produced with his own hands is of greater value than the most effective imitation." [55]

Speech

The congenitally and totally blind child cannot be aided in his learning of speech by imitation, which plays a great role in the development of seeing children. He can only learn from what he hears and from occasional touch observation. Therefore, his progress in speech development may be slower than that of seeing children. But it is not only the speech development but also the acquisition of word concepts which is affected by blindness. Cutsforth refers to this as "verbal unreality" since the blind child may learn to name many things without having any real experience or idea of them.[56] He investigated this tendency toward verbal-mindedness in two groups. He used 39 totally blind pupils of whom 13, at one time, possessed good sight and were visually-minded, and 26 were congenitally blind. The subjects had to respond to the names of forty selected objects with some quality of the object. Fifty-four per cent of all responses were visual qualities, the congenitally blind giving 48.2 per cent and the adventitious group giving 65 per cent. Tactual responses followed next, with the congenital group giving 35.7 per cent and the adventitious group giving 24.2 per cent. This showed a strong tendency of the blind children participating in this study to employ visual concepts, when other sensory concepts were just as available and would have been much more meaningful and familiar in experience. Naturally, a large number of wrong visual responses was found. Cutsforth believes this indicates that the pupils preferred risking a doubtful visual response rather than giving their own experiences.

In a recent study Nolan [57] repeated Cutsforth's experiment and found that significantly fewer visual responses were made by his group of blind children. He concludes "that 'verbal unreality' is not a significant problem for the group studied." He also reports that responses to four of the stimulus words were available for 1,000 sighted children. In a comparison of these with the ones obtained in his study, the responses of the blind children closely resembled those of normally seeing children. Though Nolan's data do not give any reasons for this change, one can assume that modern methods used in the education of present-day blind children may have something to do with it and that Cutsforth's findings by themselves, reinforced by the observations of others, are in part responsible for the change.

Maxfield published a preliminary study of the spoken language of eight pre-school blind children based on the verbatim report of observations.[58] Although she regarded her work more as a methodological study, it contains some interesting results. Among the older children, 40 to 50 per cent of the responses (about twice the percentage found in seeing children) were concerned with things. Blind children asked more questions and gave fewer commands than seeing children. Their responses also were more frequently incomplete and emotionally toned. Blind children used proper names of persons more frequently than seeing children, and they also asked more questions than seeing children. Maxfield considers some of these differences as indications of the blind child's need for gaining security.

Stinchfield [59] discusses speech disorders among blind children and found, in a survey, that about half of the children showed some speech defects, ranging from mild oral inaccuracies and letter substitution to lateral lisping, sigmatism (a form of stammering with imperfect pronunciation of the "s" sounds), and severe oral inaccuracies. She recognizes that in blind children such speech defects are usually remedial, and that the prognosis is much better than in the case of deaf children. The development of speech disorders in blind children is due to the fact that the congenitally blind child must learn speech without being able to learn the formation of speech sounds and the accompanying bodily movements and gestures by visual imitation. He depends solely on the acoustic imitation and production of speech. Stinchfield found more dyslalia (speech defects of organic or functional origin, dependent upon malformation or imperfect innervation of the tongue, soft palate, or other organs of articulation) than any other type of speech defect. In a speech survey of 220 children in a residential school, she found letter substitution, lisping, and stuttering the most frequently occurring speech defects besides unspecified mild oral inaccuracies. Various authors have suggested psychological causes for speech defects among the blind such as infantilism, egocentricity, emotional gratification, feelings of inferiority, and overcompensation, but no study has actually demonstrated for blind children the connection between speech defects and any particular psychological reaction pattern.

Brieland summarizes observations of various authors on differences of speech in blind and seeing children as follows:

> (1) The blind show less vocal variety. (2) Lack of modulation is more critical among the blind. (3) The blind tend to talk louder than the sighted. (4) The blind speak at a slower rate. (5) Less effective use of gesture and bodily action is typical of the blind. (6) The blind use less lip movement in articulation of sounds.[60]

Berry and Eisenson consider monotony and lack of appropriate modulation to be characteristic voice defects of the blind.[61] Cutsforth discusses voice and speech and their relationship with personality development.[62] He mentions particularly lack of stimulation, faulty sound analysis, synesthetic imagery, and faulty projection as causes of speech defects. The last-mentioned he considers the most common one and calls the use of a loud voice without specific directional projection the "broadcasting voice of the blind."

Brieland, in his own study, compares the ratings on speech performances of 84 matched pairs of blind and sighted pupils twelve to eighteen years old.[63] The ratings indicate that there were no significant differences in general vocal effectiveness or in vocal variety; the blind were judged significantly superior in pitch modulation, while the sighted were favored in ratings of bodily action and in degree of lip movement. He concludes that his findings "failed to show the inferiority in the use of the voice which the literature on speech of the blind would lead one to expect." [64] The superiority in pitch modulation may result from a greater reliance of the blind upon verbal means of expression, while the superiority in bodily action of the seeing is due to the influence of the visible components of social communication. He suspects that observers become unduly sensitive to small defects in the blind and thus tend to judge them more unfavorably than they would seeing persons.

A survey by Rowe [65] arrives at conclusions which even favor the blind. She screened 148 school-age blind children for speech defects and took tape recordings which were independently judged by two speech therapists. Her findings indicate that the percentage of speech defects found was low when compared with general estimates and percentages for the normal school population. She ascribes these favorable results to good pre-school counseling services, to the fact that in the surveyed group no cases with major secondary handicaps were included, and to the good schooling which these children received. The methodology of this study, however, is open to serious questioning.

Touch Reading

The psychological processes involved in reading are complex and not less so if the reading organs are the fingers rather than the eyes. Blind children learn to read and write braille, which is a system of embossed dots to be read by the fingers. The full braille sign consists of six embossed dots, two vertical rows of three, of a size which can be covered simultaneously by the pulp of a finger. Braille Grade One is written in full spelling, and Braille Grade Two makes use of contractions representing letter combinations, syllables, or words.

While a great amount of research on reading in general has been done, the research on touch reading has largely centered on the mechanics of the reading process. Bürklen published his important experimental study on touch reading in German in 1917 (translated into English in 1932).[66] He agrees with Heller that the vertical arrangement of six dots is the best possible one for touch reading.[67] The readability of the various letters of the alphabet is not determined by the number of dots, but by their characteristic formation. He found that all fingers could be used in touch reading, but that the first and second fingers of both hands are the preferred ones. The index fingers of both hands are predominantly used as reading fingers. There are different touch motions employed in reading: the up-and-down motion and the horizontal motion. Good readers move their fingers horizontally with a minimum of up-and-down motions, while less skilled readers interrupt their horizontal movement by frequent up-and-down motions which may also form loops. Bürklen also recognizes that the touch motions are connected with different pressure of the fingers. Good readers exert slight and uniform pressure, while poor readers employ strong and variable pressure. There is little decrease of touch sensitivity even after hours of touch reading, which is also not particularly fatiguing. Touch reading is three to four times as slow as visual reading. Reading of words and sentences is done by a unifying perception of word pictures similar to visual reading. Only with difficult or unknown words is a dissection of the word picture necessary. Reading with both hands is fastest, but the left hand alone reads somewhat better than the right hand.

Maxfield wrote the first book dealing with methods of teaching braille reading and agrees largely with Bürklen, except that American experiences have demonstrated that one-handed readers who use the right hand are more efficient than those who use the left.[68] She under-lines the importance of relaxation and correct posture in reading and recommends that children should be trained to read silently without lip movement or inner speech. She observes that many of the best readers read ahead on a lower line with the left hand before the right has finished the preceding line and recommends that this be encouraged if children show any inclination toward it. She also recommends the word method of teaching braille reading and the early teaching of contracted braille.

Holland and Eatman made moving-picture records of the finger move-ments which revealed, among other facts, the importance of the amount of time spent in making return sweeps—between 6 and 7 per cent of the total reading time—with good readers spending less time than poor readers.[69] Also good readers make fewer regressive movements than poor readers, whose performance is in general less uniform. Holland also studied the speed and pressure factors in reading braille and confirms Bürklen's findings.[70] He observed that pressure varies within a given line, with less variation in the case of fast readers. Poor readers tend to increase pressure toward the end of a paragraph. Fertsch also used a moving picture camera in studying hand dominance.[71] She explains the discrepancies in past findings by the differences in performance of good and poor readers. Readers whose hands are equally effective in perceiv-ing braille read faster, and among them are fewer poor readers than among those who use either the right hand or the left hand dominantly. Those with the right hand dominant perform better than those with the left hand dominant. Good readers read a substantial amount of material with the hands functioning independently, of which the right hand reads about twice as much as the left hand. Poor readers read very little ma-terial with the hands independently, since they keep right and left fingers close together.

In another study, Fertsch found silent braille reading considerably faster than oral braille reading.[72] Independence in the functioning of the hands is characteristic of good readers in making return sweeps as well as in regressive movements. She also found that reading habits be-come established by about the time a pupil has reached the third grade and do not change noticeably with increase in reading experience.

Horbach published a study in which he reports observations and experiments on touch reading.[73] He concludes that these experiments give full confirmation to his initial assumption that the processes of tactile and visual reading are the same not only in their final results, but also in the progress of the reading act. Differences found, particularly in the rate of reading, are only of a gradual nature. Thus he confirms many of the assumptions of Bürklen's early study.

Although a beginning has been made, the whole area of touch reading poses many problems as yet unsolved, and even uninvestigated. Readability of letters and contractions, the mental processes involved in touch reading, methods of teaching touch reading to children and to adults, reading readiness and its indications, are all problems which need investigation.

Touch reading is slow, and this slowness has been made responsible for retarding blind children in their educational progress. The fact that only a limited amount of reading matter is available in braille also exerts its influence, because much of it must be read aloud to the students. Lowenfeld compared rates and comprehension of braille and Talking Book reading, the latter with and without sound illustrations.[74] Talking Books are long-playing phonograph records on which texts are recorded by professional readers, and which can make use of sound effects as "illustrations." Talking Book reading was found to be about three times as fast as braille reading. For younger children (third and fourth grades), comprehension by Talking Book reading is superior to that of braille reading, particularly for pupils in the lower I.Q. range. Older pupils (sixth and seventh grades) comprehend story-telling material equally well by braille and by Talking Book reading, but comprehension of textbook material is better by braille than by Talking Book reading. Children indicated a preference for Talking Book stories which were illustrated with sound effects. Therefore the use of Talking Books, for supplementary reading, is recommended on all grade levels, particularly with slow learners, while textbooks should be studied in braille.

A further speeding up of Talking Book reading was suggested by Enc and Stolurow [75] who conducted experiments to determine whether "time compression" as developed by Fairbanks, Gutman, and Miron [76] would result in more efficient reading. It was found that over the range of 160 to 233 words per minute, faster rates were more efficient than slower ones. Iverson found in a trial that a 35 per cent compression was considered most desirable for general fiction material.[77] There is need for further research on the optimum conditions for reading and learning by listening.

The American Printing House for the Blind in Louisville, Kentucky, has embarked on a research program which, according to Nolan, includes applied research in the field of reading, writing and printing, and also basic behavioral research.[78]

Mobility

FOR THOSE who are totally blind or who have only light perception, the task of getting about is one of the most difficult to perform. Chevigny and Braverman stress that the most complex expression of skill for the blind is the ability to travel independently.[79] No comprehensive research on the psychological factors involved in mobility is available. Work on the perception of obstacles, which occupied European scientists around the turn of the century, received particular attention in Cornell University studies published from 1944 on. Obstacle perception, however, is only one factor of importance in the ability to get about. It received more intensive scientific attention only because the blind seemed to possess an ability which the seeing appeared not to have, namely, to avoid obstacles without having bodily contact with them. This fact was recognized already by Diderot in 1749 when his "Letter on the Blind for the Use of Those Who See" was published.

Obstacle Perception

Bürklen [80] and Hayes [81] report extensively on the anecdotal and autobiographical material as well as on the first scientific attempts to investigate the hypothetical obstacle sense. Hayes provides a summary of theories to explain the obstacle sense covering the research up to 1935. He distinguishes four different types of theories explaining the obstacle sense: (1) A heightened response of some sense organ, known or unknown; into this category belong the pressure theories, the auditory theories, and the temperature theories. (2) Perceptual interpretation of cues from one or more sense organs, such as a combination of pressure, sound, and temperature changes. (3) An indirect and complicated response to sensory cues; Dolanski assumes, for instance, that cues from any sense organ may suggest danger, arouse fear, and produce contraction of muscles under the skin, causing sensation of obstacles.[82] (4) Occult explanations which assume magnetic or electrical phenomena, vibrations of the ether or of some other hypothetical substance, vestigial organs in the skin (paroptic vision), and give other subconscious or miraculous explanations.

Around the turn of the century, German scientists engaged in a heated and often acrimonious controversy in which each of them defended a theory stipulating a heightened response in one or the other sense organ.

Truschel claimed that his experiments proved that stimulation of the organs of hearing by reflected sound waves is responsible for obstacle perception.[83] Kunz opposed him and claimed that the blind have a "distance sense" (Ferngefühl) based on abnormal sensibility of the skin for pressure and perhaps temperature differences.[84] Krogius opposed both and considered temperature sensations as the factor responsible for distance perception of obstacles.[85] The experiments of Truschel were perhaps more scientifically conducted than those of his two opponents, but experimental psychology at that time was not ready to attack the problem with any hope of general agreement. James discussed "How the Blind Perceive Space" and considered "tympanic pressure" sensations as the responsible factor.[86] Villey was critical of Kunz and Krogius and thought that audition is mainly responsible for obstacle sensations.[87] He stated that they may not be recognized as auditive impressions, although they belong to the auditive order, and that the pressure sensations reported by many blind persons may be auditory illusions for which there is at present no physiological explanation. Dolanski conducted extensive experiments with 42 subjects in which he moved, without noise and without production of air currents, small disks toward the subject seated in a chair.[88] The disks were moved either in "frontal approach" or in "lateral approach" toward the subject's face or one of his ears. The distance at which disks of a given size were detected was always greater with the lateral approach than with the frontal approach. He used a variety of materials for the disks, but the material of the disks did not affect the results. Dolanski experimented with his subjects in four conditions: with the face uncovered; with thick paper flaps affixed to the sides of the head in perpendicular direction and in front of the ears; with a cardboard mask covering the face; and with ears plugged with cotton. His results indicated that audition is responsible for obstacle perception. In the second series, no obstacles were detected on the frontal approach which made audition impossible, while the lateral approach permitting audition showed the same positive results as in the first series where the face was left uncovered. No obstacles were detected in the fourth series in which audition was eliminated. In the third series, when a cardboard mask covered the face, the disks were discovered as well with as without the mask which indicated that pressure and temperature cannot be responsible factors. Jerome and Proshansky regret that Dolanski did not present any data on the frequency of mistakes when subjects claimed to detect an object that was not present, and also criticize that he did not include any catch-tests in his test procedures.[89]

The most extensive research on the perception of obstacles by the blind was undertaken by a team of psychologists at Cornell University and continued elsewhere. In the first of these studies, Supa, Cotzin, and

Dallenbach used blind and blindfolded subjects who were placed at various distances in front of either a wall or a portable masonite board approximately four feet square with its lower edge two feet above the floor.[90] In walking toward the obstacle, they were asked to indicate their "first perception" of it and then to approach it as closely as possible without touching it—the "final appraisal." Experiments in which hearing was not eliminated were conducted, once with the subjects walking on hardwood floor with shoes on, and once walking in stockinged feet on a soft carpet runner. The "first perceptions" of the two blind subjects were better than those of the two sighted subjects, while in the "final appraisals" the sighted subjects did approximately as well as the blind. In the four main experiments, various controls, similar in effect to those used by Dolanski, were introduced in order to reduce or eliminate certain sensory cues. Two different receptors of sensation were considered: (1) the exposed areas of the skin, and (2) the ears. The stimuli acting on each of those receptors could be either (a) air currents and air waves which are outside the auditory range arousing only cutaneous sensation, or (b) sound waves which could be heard and which also might arouse cutaneous sensation in the ear or on the exposed areas of the skin. In the first main experiment the exposed areas of the skin were covered, and in the second the ears were plugged and shielded from all stimulation. In the third experiment, the exposed areas of the skin were left open to air and sound waves as in the second, but all stimuli which might have reached the ears were drowned by means of a sound screen—a constant, continuously sounding tone of moderate intensity, conducted by wires to a set of headphones worn over the ears of the subject. In the fourth experiment, the stimuli were reduced to sound waves, and their action was limited to the ears. This was achieved by placing the subject in a soundproof room with high-fidelity headphones over his ears through which he could listen to the sounds of the experimenter who, carrying a microphone, walked in another room toward the obstacle. The latter arrangement was criticized by Jerome and Proshansky because "electrical transmission systems usually respond to sounds in a manner that differs from the ear's response in a number of important ways. Those differences that are probably most relevant to the present problem are amplitude and directional response." [91] The results of the experiments of this study led to the following conclusions:

> 1. Stimulation of the face and other exposed areas of the skin by "air-" and sound waves is neither a *necessary* nor a *sufficient* condition of the perception of obstacles by our Subjects.
> 2. Stimulation of the skin by reflected breath is neither a *necessary* condition nor, as far as "facial pressure" is concerned, a *sufficient* condition for the "final appraisals" by our Subjects.

3. The pressure theory of the "obstacle sense," insofar as it applies to the face and other exposed areas of the skin, is untenable.
4. Aural stimulation is both a *necessary* and a *sufficient* condition for the perception of obstacles by our Subjects.[92]

In 1947, Worchel and Dallenbach followed up the first study with an investigation on the perception of obstacles by the deaf-blind.[93] In it they wanted to determine whether the aural mechanisms found to be responsible for obstacle perception are auditory or cutaneous, or whether both were involved. They found that their deaf-blind subjects did not possess the obstacle sense and were incapable of learning it; and that stimulation of the cutaneous surfaces of the external ears (meatuses and tympanums) is not sufficient to the perception of obstacles. They concluded that the pressure theory is untenable and that audition was confirmed as the aural mechanism responsible for the perception of obstacles by the blind. This study still left open the question whether intensity (loudness) or frequency (pitch) is the auditory dimension involved. This question was the subject of experiments reported in 1950 by Cotzin and Dallenbach.[94] In preliminary experiments it was established that continuous sounds are as adequate as intermittent sounds to the perception of obstacles under like conditions. The main experiments indicated conclusively that changes in loudness are neither a necessary nor a sufficient condition for the perception of obstacles. Changes in pitch were established both as a necessary and a sufficient condition for the perception of obstacles and considered a result of the Doppler effect (the phenomenon in which the pitch of a sound rises when the source of the sound approaches the listener). It was also established that at normal walking speed high frequencies of approximately 10,000 cycles and above are necessary, while frequencies of about 8,000 cycles and below are insufficient for obstacle perception. The authors recognize that there still remains an unsolved problem: the relation of wave length and velocity of movement to distance at which obstacles are perceived.

McCarthy and Worchel [95] experimented with an unusually capable blind boy who rode his bicycle over a course on which two movable obstacles had been placed. When riding as swiftly as he could, he was able to avoid obstacles almost as well as in the slow trial runs. This demonstrates that higher speeds do not impair object perception, a finding which lends support to the Doppler shift theory.

The Cornell experiments were repeated outdoors by Ammons, Worchel and Dallenbach under conditions more nearly approximating everyday situations where cues other than auditory ones could be utilized.[96] Though no single condition was found necessary for obstacle perception, the results confirmed auditory cues as the most reliable, accurate, and universal ones. Other sensory cues such as cutaneous, olfactory, and temperature were utilized when auditory cues were not available.

Worchel, Mauney, and Andrew examined the distribution of the ability to perceive an obstacle under usual outdoor conditions among 34 totally blind students.[97] The study indicated large individual differences in the "first perceptions" and consistency in the "final appraisals" in those who had the obstacle sense. It was found that seven of the 34 subjects did not possess the obstacle sense. Worchel and Mauney used these seven failures in another study to determine the effect of practice on the perception of obstacles.[98] These seven subjects were given 210 training trials under conditions favorable for learning. The tests after the practice showed that these subjects had developed the ability to perceive obstacles to an extent equal to that possessed by experienced subjects. The authors conclude that "a systematic course in perceptual recognition and detection of objects for the blind may be of considerable aid and shorten the period of trial-and-error procedure usually adopted by the blind." [99]

There is one further study dealing with a problem in this area. The tendency to veer in one direction, when attempting to walk straight, has been ascertained for blindfolded seeing subjects. Rouse and Worchel confirmed this also for the blind.[100] This tendency is consistent in direction for the same subject, with most subjects veering to the right. Removal of auditory cues and elimination of facial tactile cues does not increase veering tendency.

Training normal hearing to greater usefulness was the aim of experiments carried out by Norton [101] at the Cleveland Society for the Blind. Binaural tape-recordings were made with two microphones located at the normal two-ear distance, picking up the sounds which were played back through earphones, one to each ear. In one part of the training situation, recordings of various sounds were offered for the purpose of locating and identifying these sounds. In another part, "passive listening" was employed in which the trainee responded verbally to situations recorded under active travel conditions. This arrangement permitted him to concentrate fully on various aspects of his changing environment. The studies are continuing, and a manual has been published describing the project and the training procedures.

In search for a guidance device the Haskins' Laboratories examined the problem of the obstacle sense. Jerome and Proshansky found certain deficiencies in the experiments conducted in the past, particularly the failure to include catch-tests in the regular procedures of some of the earlier studies.[102] They used four blind subjects in their own experiments. In a "differentiation test," the blind person's ability to differentiate between the presence and absence of objects in his immediate environment was examined. It showed that they all possessed an obstacle sense operating with various degrees of accuracy at different distances. With the increase of distance between the subject and the test object, a regular decrease in obstacle perception occurred, but marked individual differences were noted. The subsequent "avoidance test" was designed to test the more complicated task of avoiding obstacles while attempting to circulate among them either with or without aural obstruction. Real obstacles and symbolic obstacles were used and rotated on an obstacle course through which the subject had to make his way without contacting any of the objects. Contacting a real object and passing so close to a symbolic object that it would have been touched were the criteria used. If a subject had no obstacle sense, he should have made as many errors on real obstacles as on symbolic ones; if aural cues were not necessary, he should have made as many errors on real obstacles with ears unobstructed as with ears obstructed. There was a reliable difference between scores on real and symbolic obstacles when no sensory obstruction was used. Also, on real objects, the difference between aural obstruction and no obstruction was reliable. However, the differences between errors on real and symbolic objects were negligible with aural obstruction. These data indicate that the avoidance of obstacles depends upon aural sensations, and the authors conclude:

> . . . because these studies were carried out in a sheltered area from which air currents and abrupt temperature changes were almost completely eliminated, the results must be interpreted as indicating that, when other sources of information have been excluded, the blind person is capable of avoiding obstacles on the basis of aural cues alone.[103]

The study reports further on testing procedures for the evaluation of obstacle avoidance devices.

Griffin,[104] in his chapter "Echolocation by the Blind," reviews the literature on orientation and makes challenging suggestions for future research in this field. He asks the question whether we can learn from the bats and recommends that we first study "the language of audible echoes" and also explore "what kinds of sound field will produce the most information and the most readily recognized echoes." He recommends research to determine the type of sounds which are most effective in echolocation, as for instance, the frequency-modulated pulses used by certain types of bats. "Any human adaptation of echolocation would necessarily require that the blind man generate clearly audible sounds, probably a series of clicks." [105] Blind people, he believes, will not want to make themselves conspicuous unless they can secure real independence in mobility by it. He warns of continuing hasty attempts to construct portable guidance devices and recommends instead a more patient program of basic research.

Although it is recognized that obstacle perception as such is only one factor influencing a person's mobility, the other factors have received little attention and almost no scientific investigation. There is, for instance, no study available which would show the effects of the restriction in mobility on the personality formation of the blind, or on his relations to others on whom he must frequently depend in order to get about. It is obvious that blind individuals are from infancy restricted in their ability to expose themselves to experiences as compared with non-handicapped individuals. Since blindness imposes limitations in the perceptual area, this added restriction due to limited mobility calls for special instructional methods if it is to be compensated for at least partially. Lowenfeld discusses the effects of this restriction and notes that differences in mobility show themselves already among young blind children.[106] Some hardly dare to step out into unfamiliar grounds and hesitate even in familiar surroundings, while others show a surprising facility in getting about. While the blind child is very young, he leaves his environment only when accompanied by others. When he gets older and must adjust to living in the world at large, his restriction in mobility becomes a factor of major importance. If he has not been encouraged to develop his ability to move about and has not achieved a reasonable degree of independence in it, his whole success may be jeopardized. He may, in the extreme case, not only take help for granted, but may develop a generalized expectancy of help characteristic of regression. He may also develop a resentment against his dependency and project this resentment toward the seeing society as a whole. Educators of the blind are familiar with these reactions although they have not been the subject of systematic studies.

Many have recognized that the task of getting about results in increased nervous strain for the blind person. Cutsforth also stresses the unavoidable injury to the ego of the blind person as result of his position of dependency in locomotion:

> Since the blind live in a world of the seeing, it is necessary to procure visual aid and information. Whether this be volunteered or solicited, it represents a curtailment of self-expression and is registered emotionally as such. Thus, the act of asking a stranger the name of an approaching street car is an admission of inferiority for which there must be compensation. And the thoughtful, kind-hearted guide through a traffic jam must be pleasantly thanked for his assistance—society demands it—while the emotions demand that he be cursed or struck down with the cane.[107]

Orientation and Locomotion

Lowenfeld points out that mobility has two components: mental orientation and physical locomotion.[108] Mental orientation has been defined as the "ability of an individual to recognize his surroundings and their temporal or spatial relations to himself," [109] and locomotion as "the movement of an organism from place to place by means of its organic mechanism." [110] Both functions are necessary for mobility but are of a different nature. In the task of orientation, the blind person must keep in his mind a "mental map" and relate himself to it while he is moving toward his intended destination. If he is experienced, he will rely upon various clues coming to him from his environment, as for instance, the audible traffic signal at a certain corner, the change in ground level at a certain point, the air current indicating open space, and of course all kinds of odor sensations. He also will make use of his "muscular memory," which Villey discusses and describes as follows:

> It is by it that, without counting the steps and without looking at them, we know that we have reached the top of our staircase. Our legs have registered, in a way, the number of contractions they had to make. Not only can this muscular memory retain very well the height of a staircase, but also the dimensions of a room and the distance between two walls. It instigates the blind man to repeat, with perfect regularity, the movements that have become habitual to him.[111]

He also employs his time sense in tracing his position on the mental map. The more familiar he becomes with his route, the more mechanically he recognizes his surroundings and his own relation to them. But in order to move about safely and in a goal-directed way, the blind person must also be able to follow a safe path and to avoid harmful obstacles. In doing this he makes use of all his senses. His sense of hearing is constantly active in observing all kinds of sounds, including echoes; he interprets odors in relation to their various sources; he notices changes of temperature and air currents and what they indicate; his feet follow the surface of the ground and notice changes in it; he observes distances, not by counting steps but in terms of time, movement, and sound. Thus any observation he can make and any clue he can obtain is interpreted for the purpose of locomotion as well as orientation. Obstacle perception as such also has its important place in it although it cannot be employed effectively in many situations; for example, in moving in crowded or noisy places, or under unfavorable weather conditions when rain and winds drown out and snow deadens the necessary perceptions.

In the task of getting about, blind persons have always relied upon human assistance. They also have made use of the cane and, lately, of guide dogs. Human assistance can take over both factors of mobility, locomotion as well as orientation. The cane which functions as a lengthening touch organ or feeler indicates to the blind person, if skillfully used, an obstacle-free spot on which he may put his foot. The guide dog indicates an obstacle-free space into which the blind person may safely move. Both cane and guide dog leave the task of orientation to their user.

Educators and rehabilitation personnel are giving increased attention to mobility training as an essential part of a blind individual's adjustment. Training in mobility under all kinds of conditions and in the use of the cane are included in many school and rehabilitation programs. Although no experimental evidence of the superiority of any method of cane travel is available, practical usage has confirmed the superiority of the Hoover technique of cane travel, which was developed in the rehabilitation program for war-blinded servicemen. According to this technique, the cane is used in a pendulum-like scanning motion to make certain that the place where the foot will be moving is free of obstacles. A white cane which is longer than the usual cane—it should reach to the breastbone of the user —is required. Techniques to meet various situational demands have been worked out, and training in the use of the cane proceeds according to a set course of study.

Finestone, Lukoff, and Whiteman completed an extensive study dealing with the demand for dog guides and included in it a chapter dealing with "Aspects of the Travel Adjustment of Blind Persons." [112] Their findings indicate that "human guide users represent minimal travel performance, cane travelers achieve a midway position well above human guide users, while dog guide users are in turn markedly above both groups."

Worchel investigated space perception and orientation in the blind by three experiments for which he used 33 totally blind students and a matched group of sighted students.[113] In the first experiment, he wanted to determine the role of visualization in tactual form perception. He used simple geometrical blocks and found that in reproductions by drawing and in verbal descriptions sighted subjects were significantly better than the blind and accidentally blinded subjects significantly better than the congenitally blind. He interprets this as indicating that touch alone is not as efficient in the perception of tactual forms as touch aided by visual images. However, in the test on form recognition, in which the subjects had to select among four blocks one that was similar in shape to the stimulus block, the blind and sighted did equally well. In this test visualization was not required. The author indicates that the tests were done with simple forms and that more complicated ones may show different results. The second experiment required the imaginal construction of a total form after parts of the form had been perceived by touch. The results indicated again that "the use of visual imagery is of definite aid to the sighted and to the accidentally blinded in imaginally manipulating tactual perceptions." It is interesting to note that the ellipse and circle were easiest recognized after tactual perception of parts of them, while the semicircle was most difficult. The third experiment is the one dealing directly with the problem of spatial orientation and with the role of visualization in it. The subjects were led along two sides of eight different-sized, right isosceles triangles and asked to return without guidance via the hypotenuse to the starting point, or they were led along the hypotenuse path and asked to return without guidance along the two legs of the triangle. The experiments were made in an open area where auditory cues gave no undue advantage to the blind. The sighted subjects were significantly superior to the blind, and there was no difference between the accidentally and the congenitally blinded. The results indicated that the blind missed the initial position because of angular deviations rather than by errors in estimating the distance. Introspective reports given by some of the subjects indicated that the blind and the sighted used time in estimating distances. The sighted used visual imagery in determining direction. The study demonstrates the importance of visual imagery in orientation and confirms that besides auditory cues time assists the blind in distance orientation.

Worchel's findings, that in the performances which he tested, the sighted were superior to the accidentally blind and to the congenitally blind, were confirmed by Drever in experiments using spatial tests.[114] His findings also suggest the existence of certain basic skills built up through the early years, and that later learning has little effect.

Geographic orientation in the blind was the topic of another study in which Worchel cooperated with McReynolds.[115] In their geographic orientation tests the congenitally blind did as well as the accidentally blind, and degree of blindness, etiology, age at blindness, age, I.Q., and sex were not significant factors in geographic orientation. They conclude that "visual imagery does not seem necessary to geographic orientation."

Garry and Ascarelly [116] conducted training experiments in orientation and spatial organization with a group of congenitally blind "good" and "poor" performers. They reported positive effects of training in these skills, though the trained "poor" performers did not achieve the level of the untrained "good" performers.

Maze tests have been used to determine learning ability and evaluate intelligence. Studies by Koch and Ufkess,[117] Knotts and Miles,[118] and R. V. and F. K. Merry [119] showed that the stylus maze is more difficult for the blind than for the seeing, while the high-relief finger maze is less difficult for both groups; that the ability to learn the maze correlated higher with mental age than with chronological age; and that the finger maze is a valuable supplement in testing the intelligence of blind children. There is no agreement concerning the superior or inferior maze-learning ability of the blind as compared with the seeing. Duncan found that past visual experience influenced success in maze learning more than the actual degree of sight present, and also that those who had perfect vision for at least a year seemed to be the most successful ones in learning the maze.[120] She also observed that 15 of the blind group of 59 failed to draw square corners in reproducing the maze, and that the greatest degree of vision among these 15 was "finger perception." Only two of the thirty sighted subjects failed to draw square corners. This observation tends to support the Worchel findings concerning the difficulty of directional orientation without visualization. MacFarland was interested in observing in a maze-learning situation the methods used by blind subjects, by seeing subjects who were tactually oriented, and by seeing subjects who were visually oriented.[121] He found that tactual methods had more lasting effect than visual orientation, that motivation affected the degree of learning, and that blind persons seemed more motivated than the others. The method of solution used by blind persons was different from that of the other groups.

> They worked slowly and carefully in the first trials, exploring every part of the maze; then they began to eliminate errors systematically. It was apparent that this group employed an attack based at least in part on "visualization" (ultimate construction of a mental image of the entire board) plus kinesthetic memory.

This ability to construct a mental image of an object or situation as a result of successive observations of parts of it seems to be a decisive factor. Its importance is also stressed by Viktor Lowenfeld in his research on the drawings of partially blind children and on the modeling of the blind and the deaf-blind.[122]

Two important distinctions were added by a study on maze learning by Berg and Worchel.[123] They added to the visual and tactual-kinesthetic factors, verbalization as an aid in maze learning and also concluded that different mazes call for the use of different sensory processes. They used a multiple U maze which was held to be a motor and visual maze, and a unidirectional X maze which was held to require verbalization for its mastery. Their subjects were 28 totally blind, 28 deaf, and 28 normal children, matched on the basis of age, sex, I.Q., and age at the onset of the sensory loss. On the U maze they found the normals and blind equal, and each surpassing the deaf, suggesting that verbalization plays a significant role in the mastery of this kind of maze. On the X maze, normals performed better than the blind and they in turn better than the deaf. This is interpreted as indicating that while verbalization is important, visualization is also an aid in the learning of this kind of maze.

Personality and Social Factors

PERSONALITY IS the psychophysical organization of the individual as modified by his life experiences and thus includes hereditary as well as environmental factors. The child who is congenitally blind experiences the world in his own way, which is different from that of most other children, and must also cope with special difficulties in getting about. His personality is affected by these differences, and it can be assumed that, by reason of his handicap, he is more likely to be under nervous strain and to harbor feelings of insecurity and frustration. But before discussing the findings concerning the effects of blindness on the individual, another source of possible conflicts must be considered, that is, the attitudes toward blindness and the blind.

The Influence of Environmental Attitudes

The attitudes of the public toward the blind have been discussed in many articles, and practically all authors of books dealing with the blind felt called upon to make some statements about this topic. Barker *et al.* have reviewed publications on attitudes toward the blind and found that "there is almost universal agreement among the blind and those who work with them that blind persons are commonly perceived to be helpless and dependent and are frequently placed in underprivileged social situations." [124]

Rusalem [125] supplied, in 1950, one of the first experimental studies on this problem. One hundred and thirty graduate students in a social psychology class were given a questionnaire listing 20 physical, 14 sociological, and 26 psychological traits allegedly characteristic of the blind. The answers indicate the following primary clusters of identifying characteristics: Physical—carry canes, use guide dogs, wear dark glasses, have lack of facial expression; Sociological—attend separate schools, rarely work in industry, are economically dependent; Psychological—have very great sense of touch, have keen hearing, have better than average memory. These on the whole favorable responses do not support the negative attitudes generally assumed to be operative toward the blind. The 59 subjects who had had contact with visually handicapped individuals did not significantly differ in their responses from those without previous contact with the blind. Rusalem recognizes a number of factors which limit his findings, such as a biased and exceptional group of subjects, the possibility that a list of items does not give opportunity for free expression of attitudes, and that the consciously selected items may not be significant for the unconscious tendencies. He calls attention to "the urgent need for highly organized social psychological research into the dynamics of attitudes towards the blind" and suggests that "these attitudes are highly complex and may never be explained in terms of a single simple hypothesis." [126]

Chevigny and Braverman discuss at length the attitudes of the public toward the blind and of those in work with the blind.[127] They call attention to the fact that the blind are a minority group, and that while the content of the set of ideas about the blind may be different from that entertained about other minorities, the manner of operation is the same. They examine the underlying reasons for the particular attitudes toward blindness and the blind in psychoanalytic terms and attempt to give an explanation of the adjustment and reorganization process required in meeting those ideas about blindness which form the constant in the social environment.

Attitudes Toward Blindness contains three papers representing various fields of learning. The first deals with the problem from the point of view of the psychiatrist,[128] the second considers the cultural-sociological aspects,[129] and the third presents the approach of the clinical psychologist.[130]

The minority status of the blind and other attitudinal problems toward blindness were explored in two important recent studies. Gowman [131] examined the sociological position of the war blind in American social structure, and Lukoff and Whiteman [132] published a preliminary report of their experimental research on attitudes toward blindness. The latter research, as many others, was supported by a grant from the Federal Office of Vocational Rehabilitation. Since both studies, though dealing with problems of the adult blind, have in some parts implications for the status of blind youth, their pertinent results will be reviewed here.

Gowman's book has a chapter, "Attitudes Toward Blindness," [133] in which he reports on a questionnaire study exploring attitudes of high-school seniors toward blindness. When asked to rank five potential injuries as to their impact upon themselves and their prospective mate, four fifths of them placed blindness for themselves in the first position. There is greater variability concerning the mate, but blindness is still considered the most difficult disability to accept. Middle-class males were the only ones who assigned blindness to the second position as far as its impact on their mate is concerned. The questionnaire also included thirteen interpersonal situations to which alternative responses had to be selected and a series of agree-disagree questions concerning the blind. Lower-class subjects showed a tendency to react to blindness by focusing on assumed limitations and by stereotypical conceptions. Middle-class subjects related more to the visually disabled because of an apparent sophistication and their middle-class humanitarian values.

Lukoff and Whiteman [134] investigated the attitudes of sighted persons toward blindness by questioning three major groups: graduate social work students, undergraduate college students, and a group of middle- and low-income housing inhabitants. Their findings confirm the importance of environmental attitudes for the kind of adaptation the blind person makes to his handicap. Family members and sighted friends of the blind person are most likely to influence his attitudes of independence. Their findings suggest four relatively independent components of sighted people's perception of the blind: (1) The degree to which sighted persons perceive blindness as personally frustrating; (2) The conception of blindness as distinct from attitudes toward blind people; (3) Readiness to interact with blind people; and (4) Differences in the degree of feelings among the sighted in thinking about or interacting with blind people. The question of how blind people perceive the sighted was examined by an analysis of data derived from a sample of 500 blind individuals in New York State. A majority of them believes that sighted people have little understanding of the blind, that they are surprised if a blind person can do something, that they consider blind people braver than the average sighted, and that most sighted people pity the blind. Members of the blind sample also tended to agree that they expect favored treatment in regard to pensions and job opportunities. Their interaction with sighted people is characterized by a pattern of submissiveness.

The authors summarize the reciprocal perceptions of the blind and sighted groups as follows: Blind people's perception of the sighted is realistic in considering them as naive, lacking understanding of blind people, and as overly pitying—all of which they are. They are unrealistic in ascribing to the sighted both negative and positive stereotyping attitudes which they do not have, since almost half of them contended that blind people are capable of doing just about everything without help. Lukoff and Whiteman intend to focus in their future research on various aspects of how attitudes and their psychological and social correlates affect interaction and how changes can be produced.

Parents are the most important persons in the social environment of the child and their attitudes profoundly affect his life. They also reflect in some way those of the general public of which the parents are a part. Sommers [135] has made a thorough study of "some of the factors conditioning the behavior and the personality of the adolescent blind, and to find out whether there exists a relationship between parental attitudes and actions and the blind child's behavior pattern and attitude toward his handicap." [136] She obtained her results by three different methods: (1) The California Test of Personality was administered to 143 adolescent blind. (2) A questionnaire especially designed for blind children was answered by 120 of the adolescent blind subjects and another questionnaire by 72 of the parents of these subjects. (3) Controlled interviews were conducted with 50 blind subjects and their parents.

The scores of the California Test of Personality indicated that the personal and social adjustment of blind adolescents as a group was below that of the seeing, and that blind girls were slightly better adjusted than blind boys. Sommers concluded, however, that this test, like other personality tests designed for the seeing, does not adequately measure the personal and social adjustment of this group. A test should be designed, especially for use with the blind, which would evaluate the effects of blindness in relation to the total growth pattern and total social environment of the blind individual.

The questionnaires revealed a wide variety of attitudes and feelings among the visually handicapped. They indicated that emotional disturbances and maladjustments result more frequently from the conditions and social attitudes of the blind person's environment than from the sensory handicap itself. The lack of uniformity in the reactions also disproves any assumption that blindness by itself can be the dominant cause of behavior deviations. The blind children were most aware of their handicap in such social situations as when people refer to their handicap or feel sorry for them or try to help too much; at sports and games requiring sight; when going to or eating at a strange place; when crossing streets, travelling, or window-shopping. The question, "What do you feel one misses most by being unable to see?" brought replies clustering around the following activities: sports, games, car-driving, travelling; enjoyment of sights of nature; facial expressions; movies, exhibitions, reading material; independence; normal home life, social life in general. More blind than seeing children indicated that they worried. Three times as many blind as seeing children worried about their own future and the future of the world (finding a job, financial insecurity, and the like). But schoolwork, tests, and teachers were the main worries of both blind and seeing children.

The interviews with the parents disclosed that:

> Persistent feelings of frustration on the part of the parent seemed to arise from a sense of unfulfillment resulting from the fact that the birth of a child with a handicap as apparent as blindness failed to meet the concept of the kind of child which the mother had expected; while the contradiction between maternal devotion and an irrepressible sense of repulsion caused by the blindness seemed to create feelings of irreconcilable conflict.[137]

The case studies indicated four different reasons why parents manifest conflicts in their relationship with their handicapped child: (1) Blindness is considered as a symbol of punishment and parents look upon their blind child as a visitation of divine disapproval. (2) Fear of being suspected of having a social disease. (3) Feelings of guilt due to transgression of the moral or social code or to negligence; resentment of the state of pregnancy, attempted abortion, marital discord, and the like may be reasons for these feelings. (4) Blindness in a child is considered a personal disgrace to the parents.

The ways in which the parents reacted to the handicap of their children fell into five fairly distinct categories:

Acceptance of the child and his handicap. The parent has accepted the handicap in an objective way and shows genuine devotion and high evaluation of the child. No apparent guilt feelings or rebellion against the handicap are expressed. The attitude is "we must make the best of it." In most cases religion gives mental and spiritual support.

Denial reaction. It is denied that the handicap has an emotional effect on the parent and that the child is actually handicapped. Educational and vocational plans for the child indicate that the parent does not accept or recognize any limitations for the child. Overambitious ideas are imposed on the child, and the parent insists on high achievement.

Overprotectiveness. Parents are overwhelmed by a feeling of pity which expresses itself in oversolicitous and overprotective handling of the child. The mother's own need for a love object may induce her to keep her child on an infantile level. The child's care indicates loving affection and excess of attention.

Disguised rejection. The handicap is considered a disgrace. The negative attitude and resentment toward the child is concealed by oversolicitous and anxious concern about his welfare and by an exaggeration of the duty of being a good mother.

Overt rejection. The child is openly resented, and the parent is aware of hostile feelings but builds up defenses to justify them. Society, the doctor, or teachers are blamed for their prejudice toward blindness. By the process of projection, the parent achieves a feeling of self-justification for her own hostility and a relief from her intense feelings of guilt.

Sommers stressed that sharp lines of demarcation cannot be drawn and that some overlapping of attitudes is to be expected. Acceptance of the child and denial reaction are considered positive attitudes since they permit the child to grow, to develop, and to participate. Overprotection and disguised and overt rejection are negative attitudes which interfere with or stunt the child's growth. Although the number of parents reported in Sommers' study is too small to permit any generalization in regard to the distribution of parental attitudes, it is of some interest to know that out of the 50 parents, nine showed acceptance, four denial reactions,

270   BERTHOLD LOWENFELD

13 overprotectiveness, 16 disguised rejection, and eight overt rejection.

Important for the general formation of attitudes toward a blind child is the following statement which Sommers made in connection with parents:

> The meaning the child's handicap held for his parents, especially his mother, the intensity of her emotional reactions, and the kind of adjustment she was able to make seemed to depend largely on the psychological makeup of the individual parent, her marital relationships, and her own personal and social adjustment to life.[138]

It is interesting to note that Sommers' five types of parental attitudes resemble very closely those which Leo Kanner [139] distinguishes as operative for children in general: acceptance, perfectionism, non-rejecting overprotection, rejection, overt hostility and neglect. The category of perfectionism closely resembles Sommers' denial reaction.

The adjustive behavior of the blind adolescents studied by Sommers was closely related to the parental reactions and showed the following six patterns:

Wholesome compensatory reactions. The limitations resulting from the handicap are recognized and accepted, and the subject tries to minimize them by substituting for his limitations. A sound competitive spirit with respect to accesible goals is demonstrated, and in discussing problems regarding his handicap, no evasiveness is shown (seven out of 50 subjects).

Hypercompensatory reactions. Extreme aggressiveness, strong competitive drives, and resentment of criticism are evidence of antisocial character traits. The crusader for the cause of the handicapped belongs in this group (seven subjects).

Denial reactions. Actual limitations resulting from blindness are not admitted as evidenced in the subject's educational and vocational planning, activities, and interests. Denies that blindness is any handicap and evades discussing problems regarding the handicap (six subjects).

Defensive reactions. Rationalization or projection is used to give socially acceptable reasons for the subject's behavior, who thus protects himself from the necessity of acknowledging the real reasons for his failures. Blames society for prejudice against blind people and feels unfairly treated (14 subjects).

Withdrawal reactions. Thoughts and activities center around the handicap. The individual retreats emotionally or on a rational basis. Avoidance of social contact and of competition except with those similarly handicapped and feelings of inferiority are characteristic for withdrawal. Also concentration on solitary activities and daydreaming (nine subjects).

Nonadjustive behavior reactions. The subject remains unadjusted, being unable to deal with the problems of life. Maladjustment is shown in a variety of symptoms such as strong self-centeredness, emotional instability, intensive worrying, and anxiety (seven subjects).

Sommers considers only the last-mentioned behavior as strictly non-adjustive. So far as the individual is concerned, the other reactions reduce emotional tension and assist him to adjust to his environment although they may not always be approved socially. Even withdrawal assists the individual in making some kind of adjustment to his disability. While in general one particular adjustment mechanism is predominant, in some instances, several modes of adjustment were used.

Sommers also studies the relationship between the child's adjustment and parental attitudes as rated by a series of twelve evaluation scales covering the physical, cultural, and emotional environment of the home, the parental attitudes toward the child, and the child's attitude and reactions. The statistical data presented by Sommers only complement her qualitative findings and insightful analysis.

Sommers warns against attacking directly a specific personality maladjustment in a handicapped child, because this means merely to battle against the symptoms and not to attack the underlying trouble. According to the findings of her study,

> The answer to the problem of how to effect a more satisfactory development in the personality of handicapped children would seem to lie in building up in the parents of these children wholesome attitudes toward the handicap, as well as in the education and guidance of the child himself.[140]

In this she finds herself in agreement with others who have studied the emotional problems of physically handicapped children.

Meyerson,[141] in his 1953 review of educational research, points out that the Sommers study, though most valuable, has certain weaknesses, particularly in its lack of statistical support. He points to the urgent need for additional research along similar lines. The volume, *Adjustment to Visual Disability in Adolescence,* by Cowen, Underberg, Verrillo, and Benham carries forward our research efforts in this area. It will be discussed later because its main emphasis is on personality adjustment, though it deals in some parts with parental attitudes.

The motor performance of visually handicapped children was studied by Buell, who compared scores of the blind, of the visually handicapped, and of the seeing in such activities as track and field, the Iowa Brace Test, in running, jumping, throwing, and so on.[142] Of the 865 pupils in this study, 309 had no useful vision, and 556 were partially seeing; their age ranged from 10 to 20 years. Buell asked teachers and staff members of the schools to indicate those children whose parents appeared to overprotect them and found that 27 per cent of the blind boys and 30 per cent of the blind girls were considered overprotected, while only 13 per cent of the partially seeing boys and 9 per cent of the partially seeing girls were thus classified. Buell found that overprotective attitudes of parents influenced performance in track and field events and in a stunt type test in a significant way. Neglected children were found to perform normally in motor acts. He concludes that "as far as motor performance is concerned, parental neglect is to be preferred to overprotection." Therefore, "one cannot overemphasize the harm done to visually handicapped children by overprotective parents." [143]

While considerable research has been done on the attitudes of parents toward their visually handicapped children, the important problem of attitudes of professional workers toward the blind has received only scant attention. Blank [144] discussed from a psychoanalytic point of view the unconscious conflicts about blindness which may interfere with the professional worker's efforts in helping blind individuals. Among these conflicts are overidentification, subjective "blind spots" about blindness, unconscious sadistic trends, and erotic countertransference reactions. He recommends making psychoanalytic consultation available to case workers, teachers, and supervisory personnel, but warns against considering psychoanalysis a panacea.

There is only one study dealing with attitudes of teachers toward visually handicapped children. Murphy [145] administered rating scales to 309 teachers, special educators, principals, and other teaching personnel. They were asked to rank eight groups of exceptional children according to their preference for teaching them, and according to how much they knew about them. The groups were: visually handicapped, mentally retarded, emotionally disturbed, physically handicapped (crippled), hearing handicapped, gifted and talented, speech-disordered, and delinquents (overt-aggressive type). The visually handicapped were ranked as least preferred for teaching (except for the delinquents), and as those about whom the participants considered themselves least informed. However, special educators tended to rank the visually handicapped in a more favorable position. Murphy interprets the results as a moderate indication that favorable attitudes toward teaching a group are associated with knowledge about the group. Rusalem,[146] who conducts a valuable section, "Research in Review," in *The New Outlook for the Blind*, points out that the results of this study need to be considered with caution, since its participants were confronted with a forced-choice situation in which ranking distance was constant and, therefore, degree of differentiation could not be indicated. Also, attitudes toward a specific group are not necessarily expressed by this ranking—in which the teacher may indicate what he presumes to be the difficulties in working with this group. For instance, braille may be regarded as extremely difficult, and this may induce the teacher to assign a low-preference rank to the visually handi-capped. In any case, the area of teachers' attitudes toward the visually handicapped is in need of further exploration.

One final point should be made concerning public attitudes toward the blind—they are not something static but they are changing. Himes [147] points this out and discusses some indications of this change, such as the growth of a new social consciousness, the change in agency programs, the emphasis on rehabilitation, and the impact of the actively oriented war blind. He states: "Viewed in broad perspective, change appears as a tendency to melt down and remould the traditional stereotypes of the blind." The effects of continued and improved research also help in promoting this change.

Effects on Personality

A contribution unique in its kind and in its influence was made by Thomas D. Cutsforth with his book, *The Blind in School and Society*,[148] which was published in 1933. Cutsforth's own insight into the problems of blindness, his training as a clinical psychologist, his knowledge of the literature concerning the blind, his interviews with blind children, and his case studies make the book a most valuable source of information about the psychological effects of blindness. Many research studies were written later which only confirmed what Cutsforth stated, although he was often unable to provide adequate scientific proof of his assumptions. Some of them did not or will not stand up under scientific scrutiny, due, to a certain degree, to the fact that under the influence of his own writ-ings, conditions have changed so that they no longer support his supposi-tions. Cutsforth discusses the importance of the home environment for the pre-school blind child, the problems which blindness creates in his acquisition of language, his confinement to stimulation through touch and sound, his egocentric trends, his verbal unreality, and the develop-mental retardation which may be a result of all these factors. He considers the reasons for verbalism in blind and deaf-blind children and holds teachers who imposed visual experiences upon children without sight responsible for it. He wants to have the blind child educated "into his own world of experience so that he may live in harmony with himself and his world, whether it be among the blind or the seeing." [149] Cutsforth classifies fantasies of the blind into three categories:

> (1) Phantasies in which the individual eradicates the source of social annoyance; (2) phantasies in which the individual attains marked superiority or security; (3) phantasies in which the indi-vidual withdraws from the active situation in a surrender to a sim-ple, regressive preoccupation, largely emotional in nature.[150]

In considering voice and speech and its value for the blind, he emphasizes the psychogenic character of many of their speech defects. In a chapter on emotional problems, he discusses false attitudes toward the blind and false attitudes adopted by the blind and denies that there is anything like a "world of darkness" for the blind. "The dark experiential world of the totally blind from birth consists of visual nothingness so far as its nature can be discovered." [151] He also denies that the blind suffer because they cannot see or have a yearning for sight unless they adopt these attitudes under social pressure. He considers the fear of being watched an important factor in creating an emotional strain, particularly for pupils in schools for the blind, and believes that this phobia of being watched may persist long after the pupil has left the institution.

Cutsforth's book includes the only extensive treatment of sex behavior of the blind, on which information was and is quite meager and but partially understood. His basic assumption is that the blind child does not have as normal a sexual development as the seeing child. Since sexual growth takes place to the very limit which the environment provides, the environmental conditions and attitudes determine to a large extent the blind child's sexual growth. He does not have the same expanding social or the same stimulating objective environment and is confined in a much greater degree to stimulations which the self provides. The problems of masturbation and of homosexuality are discussed, and the need for a larger heterosexual environment is stressed. Cutsforth is very critical of the practice of segregation of boys and girls in schools for the blind and wants it replaced by a social environment in which the opposite sex is included so that pupils of residential schools can achieve normal growth under normal conditions. In a separate chapter, personality problems in institutions for the blind are considered, and some of Cutsforth's observations in this area are still valid. In general it is Cutsforth's conviction that "blindness changes and utterly reorganizes the entire mental life of the individual," [152] and that this reorganization, and its support or frustration, determines the influence blindness has on the development of the individual.

There are a few studies which deal with the influence of blindness on certain personality traits. Brown [153,154] reported two studies in which he used 359 seeing high-school seniors and 218 blind adolescents between the ages of 16 and 22. The Neymann-Kohlstedt Diagnostic Test for Introversion-Extroversion showed a higher incidence of introversion among blind girls than among blind boys—which did not seem to be true among the seeing. The comparison of responses to individual items revealed significant differences between the blind and the seeing, but a qualitative consideration of items did not show any typically differentiating syndrome. A comparison between blind and seeing boys gave the blind boys "a somewhat more 'extroverted' appearance." This was not indicated when the girls of both groups were compared. Brown believes that the differences revealed in the study are predominantly due to the effects of blindness, sex, and institutionalization. In the other study, Brown used the Clark Revision of the Thurstone Personality Schedule in which he changed item 15, "Do you cross the street to avoid meeting someone?" to "Do you try to avoid meeting certain people?" and eliminated for the blind group item 23, "If you see an accident does something keep you from giving help?" He found a higher incidence of "neurotic tendency" among the blind than among the seeing, and it was also higher among the girls than among the boys. There was a greater difference between the sexes in the blind group than in the seeing group. According to the results, the groups seemed to arrange themselves in order of decreasingly desirable adjustment as follows: seeing boys, blind boys, seeing girls, blind girls.

McAndrew [155,156] investigated the problem of rigidity in the deaf and the blind. She explains that she is using "a broad Lewinian-type concept of rigidity" and defines it as a lack of variability and adaptability which results in persistent repetition or continuation of an activity and interferes with the ability to adjust to small changes in a situation. Her groups of 25 deaf, 25 blind, and 25 normal individuals were equated for both chronological and mental age, but not for institutionalization. She arranged three experiments in which the blind participated. The Satiation experiment revealed that the deaf and the blind are more rigid than the normal, but that there were such large individual variations that the results may not represent real group differences. In the Level of Aspiration experiments, the records of the blind and normal were similar with reference to success, but the blind appeared slightly more sensitive to failure than the normal. The deaf appeared to be more rigid than the blind and normal groups. In the Restructuring by Classification experiment, in which she sought to determine the degree of social force needed to encourage a child to change his method of classification, all blind and normal subjects succeeded, but the blind required more trials than the normal. Of the deaf, only four of the 25 subjects solved the problem. She concludes:

> All of the data suggest that the deaf and the blind have smaller life spaces than the normal, being partially isolated from the objective environments in which they live by the barrier qualities of their handicaps; and that they, therefore, develop less-differentiated and more rigid personalities.[157]

According to the results, the blind are more rigid than the normal; the deaf, more rigid than the blind and the normal. McAndrew used in her experiments children from two southern states. It would be interesting to find out whether repetition of these experiments with a more representative sample of blind and deaf children would show different results. The reasoning behind these experiments and their execution make them very interesting and valuable contributions to the study of personality.

Jervis and Haslerud [158] placed twenty blind adolescents, twenty blindfolded sighted adolescents, and twenty sighted adolescents in a masked experimental situation which induced frustration. The three groups met the same age, sex, mental, and emotional criteria. Since blindness frustrates the individual directly as well as indirectly, they wanted to determine whether there are different patterns of response to frustration in any of the three groups and to find out if the reactions of the blind are due to inability to solve the problem or to the cumulative effects of blindness. In the frustrating situation of the experiment, the blind group reacted in a significantly different manner from the sighted group. The physiological reactions and verbal responses were recorded; quantitatively the blind exceeded the sighted in both significantly. In particular, they showed significantly more sighing and rapid and uneven respiration and significantly less flushing and biting tongue and lips than the sighted. In these reaction patterns, auditory and visual cues are of importance. The verbal responses of the blind were characterized by high intropunitiveness, while the sighted groups were highest in impunitive response. The blindfold did not change the reaction pattern of the sighted persons. The authors conclude:

> The apparent volubility and large amount of overt emotional expression in the blind do not reduce tension because in an unhealthy and immature way they generally have intropunitive reference. The desirability of promoting more direct outlets for tensions would seem indicated in the education of the blind.[159]

Morgan administered orally the *Personal Index* to 128 visually handicapped boys and girls of 12 years of age or older in a residential school for the blind (of whom only 30 per cent were blind).[160] The results of the blind group were compared with those of boys in a reform school and with the test norms. The scores of the blind subjects as a group ranked between those of the normal and the reform school boys. Morgan believed that his sample of visually handicapped children was not representative because it included a large percentage of partially seeing children who probably attended the residential school because they could not adjust to work in the regular public school where the well-adjusted ones were retained.

Brieland, in his *Comparative Study of the Speech of Blind and Sighted Children* gave the *Bell Adjustment Inventory* to the 84 matched pairs of blind and seeing pupils, 12 to 18 years old.[161] The test items were recorded and played back. The blind students were significantly inferior in health, social, and emotional adjustment, while the home adjustment did not show any significant difference.

A scale specifically designed to evaluate adjustment to blindness was developed by Fitting.[162] He interprets adjustment to blindness as including six areas: (1) Morale, dealing with the individual's confidence in himself, his hopes and his aspirations; (2) Outlook toward Sighted People, dealing with the individual's concept of others; (3) Outlook on Blindness, dealing with the individual and his concept of himself as a blind person; (4) Family Relationships, dealing with the attitudes toward members of the family in the home situation; (5) Attitudes toward Training, including the anticipated degree of success in adjustment training and outlook toward education in general; (6) Occupational Outlook, dealing with the individual's concept of himself as an employee, his expectations in an employment situation, and his feelings about expected concessions because of his disability. The scale includes 42 items which were standardized on a sample of 144 trainees in nine adjustment centers. Among other results, "the study indicated that there was a direct relationship between the amount of education, such as at a school for the blind, and the level of adjustment." [163]

Barker and his associates [164] reviewed fifteen studies in which various personality inventories were used, some of them unpublished theses. Of these studies, six indicated that the blind show greater maladjustment than seeing groups, while nine did not demonstrate any consistent and significant difference between blind and seeing groups. They agree with Sommers in questioning the general validity of personality inventories in research with the blind. The life situations of the blind differ greatly from those of the groups used in standardizing the inventories, and also many items in such inventories are of "different interpretive significance" for persons with normal sight and for those who are blind. They suggested detailed item analysis of personality inventories which may lead to hypotheses for further investigation.

Raskin and Weller [165] noticed in their survey of research current in 1953 that among studies in the area of adjustment, "there is not a single one which relies solely on the inventory-type of test in this field, but instead there is a noticeable development in the widespread use of projective tests of personality which aim at a deeper understanding of adjustment patterns." Lebo and Bruce [166] published in 1960 a current evaluative review of projective tests.

Projective tests for use with the blind obviously cannot offer visual stimuli such as inkblots or drawings, but must make use of stimulus situations which are either auditory, tactile-kinesthetic, or ideational-verbal.

For example, Wilmer and Husni [167] have used an auditory projective test with blind children which presented a recorded variety of sound sequences. The Twitchell-Allen Three-Dimensional Apperception Test is a tactile-kinesthetic projection test which makes use of 28 plastic pieces with ambiguous shapes. McAndrew [168] used this test with blind, deaf, and normal children and concludes that it is "applicable to the blind but must be interpreted cautiously." The Rotter Incomplete Sentences Blank is an example of an ideational-verbal projective test. In this test parts of sentences are presented, and the person is asked to complete them in a way which expresses his own feelings. Dean [169] used this test among others with blind persons and found that its value with the blind is more likely in the qualitative rather than in the quantitative evaluations.

The use of projective tests with the blind is still in an experimental stage. Frequently, new ones are devised rather than established ones applied and investigated. Lebo and Bruce [170] consider this a "dangerous manner."

Cholden [171] mentions three special preoccupations of the adolescent which make acceptance of blindness particularly difficult: "(1) The importance of bodily attractiveness in the female, and masculine strength and independence in the male. These preoccupations are of course related to sexual fears which are accentuated in the blind adolescent; (2) The problems of developing independence in an adolescent who must accept certain dependencies which are characteristic for blindness; (3) The exhibitionism accompanied with the desire for anonymity of the adolescent." [172]

Cole and Taboroff [173] report the successful therapy of a disturbed congenitally blind adolescent girl. They distinguish three categories of special problems of congenitally blind children: the cultural pressures which create a charged atmosphere in which the blind person must make his adjustment; the effects which blindness may have on personality and emotional development; and the problem of semantics of those blind from birth, since "their means of conceptualizing, their orientation, their perception of reality, may be different but also is poorly transmitted in a language manufactured by the seeing." [174]

Special needs of the blind adolescent are discussed by Abel.[175] He needs to be understood and respected as an adolescent who is blind; since he cannot observe visually, he needs to have his questions answered honestly and specifically by people around him and by professional persons; he needs to be a participating member of his family and of his peer group; he needs to acquire an optimistic outlook toward his future; he needs expert instruction in independent modes of travel; and he needs educational facilities and special equipment based on good practice and sound research.

Lowenfeld [176] examined some difficulties which blindness creates for the adolescent in the areas of sex curiosity, dating, mobility, and concern for the future. These difficulties may influence the blind adolescent's self-concept and his attitudes toward interpersonal relations, but "may be simply different but no more severe or serious manifestations of the process of maturation which goes on in all adolescents."

A growing interest in dynamically oriented research in the field of adjustment to blindness on the adult level is evidenced by such studies as those by Bauman,[177] by Gowman,[178] by Lukoff and Whiteman,[179] and by Cowen, Underberg, and Verrillo.[180] The main contribution in the general field of physical disability is B. A. Wright's [181] thought-provoking work, *Physical Disability—A Psychological Approach,* which integrates findings from all areas of disability, including blindness.

A major publication on the adjustment to blindness in adolescence reports on the three-year research program which has been carried on under Emory L. Cowen at the University of Rochester, New York.[182,183] Since the available research studies on attitudes toward the blind and adjustment to blindness have resulted in ambiguous and contradictory findings, the University of Rochester research group set out to examine afresh the essentially unresolved question of the comparative adjustment of visually disabled and sighted adolescents. They also wanted to test the proposition that characteristics of parent behavior (attitudes and understanding) are related to the adjustment of the visually disabled adolescent. They hoped that, in addition, their studies would clarify some other problems, such as the difference in adjustment between adolescents attending a residential school for the blind and those attending public school programs for the blind while living at home.

In their efforts to develop suitable measuring instruments for their research, the research team considered three factors as essential besides those which are required for all studies (reliability and validity): direct applicability to the visually disabled, objectivity of the indices of adjustment, and representation of a variety of situations. They developed, adapted, and adopted instruments to be used for the measurement of child adjustment, parental attitudes, and parental understanding. The child adjustment indices which yielded seven global measures of adjustment were: A Self-Concept and Ideal-Concept Sort, a Teachers' Behavior Rating Scale, and a newly developed, objectively scorable projective type device, the Situations Projective Test B (SPT-B). Measures of Parental Attitude consisted of the Master Scale of 150 items, testing generalized attitudes toward child rearing, sociopsychological attitudes toward minority groups and toward authority, and specific attitudes to blindness; and the Situation Projective Test A (SPT-A). Measures of Parental Understanding were in part the same as those used in measuring the adjustment of the children: the Predicted Self-Concept Sort and the Predicted SPT-B, so that the child's responses and the responses his parents predicted for him could be compared; and a "Dummy" Sort control in which the parent was asked to rank certain statements as she thought an "average teen-ager" would rank them.

The population of the study consisted of 167 adolescents aged 13 to 18 years, in the 7th through 12th grades. Of these, 71 were visually disabled adolescents attending public day-school facilities, and 56 were visually disabled adolescents from residential schools for the blind. The control group consisted of 40 sighted adolescents matched as closely as possible to the experimental group in age, grade placement, intelligence, and socio-economic status. The mothers of all 167 adolescents and the fathers of 66 were tested independently. The experimental groups were also broken down according to their degree of visual disability, and the sex distribution of all three groups was equated. The children were tested in their schools in two sessions of at least 45 minutes duration; parental tests were administered during individual home visits, in one session of about two hours.

So far as the problem of adjustment is concerned, the outstanding result of this study is that no systematic or consistent differences in personality attributes or adjustment were found among the three major groups tested. The authors state that their findings "cast an important shadow of doubt on beliefs about inherent associations between visual disability and maladjustment." [184] Although there were no significant differences, partially sighted adolescents ranked slightly lower in adjustment than the legally or totally blind. There were no sex differences found, except that within the residential-school sample, male adolescents were significantly better adjusted than their female fellow students. The study revealed no differences in adjustment between those living in residential schools for the blind and those living at home and attending public school facilities.

In their study of the relationship between attitudes of parents and child adjustment, the authors compared the mothers of the three major groups. They found mothers of adolescents in the residential-school group to have more favorable attitudes toward their children than did the other mothers. This they interpret as "a powerful contraindicant" for the belief that children are placed in residential schools because of unfavorable parental attitudes. To their concern the authors found that their data failed to show any relationship between maternal attitudes and child adjustment, a finding contrary to past research as well as to clinical observation and psychological theory. They call attention to the fact that their research used the questionnaire method, which depends heavily on what a parent is willing to verbalize publicly, and conclude that continued exploration of this problem is needed.

The third problem area, that of the relationship between parental understanding and adjustment of the visually handicapped child, has not previously been explored. The mothers of the three experimental groups showed no significant intergroup differences in the indices of understanding. However, a high degree of parental understanding, that is, accuracy in predicting the child's test behavior, correlated significantly and consistently with good adjustment of the child for all three experimental groups. This ability to predict apparently indicates an empathy and reality perception which is an essential condition for good child adjustment. The same pattern of relationship, though less clear-cut, was found for fathers.

The study also includes a preliminary attempt toward the construction of a prediction formula for adjustment. The adolescent who perceives a high degree of parental acceptance, who is seen by his mother as well adjusted and similar to other adolescents, and who has a relatively high socioeconomic status, is likely to be a well-adjusted individual.

The authors display a high degree of self-criticism in the appraisal of their research methods and results. This makes the reading of their study a stimulating intellectual exercise and the study itself a good one from which to learn scientific objectivity.

Jervis [185] used the self-concept for a comparison of blind and sighted adolescents. His subjects were twenty students, 17 to 19 years of age, from two residential schools. All were totally blind since their third birthday or before, of normal intelligence, and free from additional physical or severe emotional problems. As a control group he selected twenty sighted students, matched in all essential characteristics except blindness. Each subject had two open-ended interviews to yield a qualitative measure and was given a modification of the Chicago Card-sort to yield a quantitative measure. The interviews were used to explain the purpose of the study, to establish a good relationship, and to encourage the subject to talk freely about himself and his feelings in response to a set of twelve stimulus questions, such as "How would you describe yourself to a stranger? What do you consider some of your strengths? What do you see yourself doing in five or ten years?" In the Q-sorts the subjects were asked to sort twice statements concerning their feelings or attitudes toward themselves—once as they would best describe themselves, and once as they would describe their ideal selves. The interviews were independently judged by two psychologists, and no significant differences were found between the self-concepts of the two groups. A breakdown of the data revealed that blind subjects tended to be more apprehensive about their future, more aware of the need to get along with others, and felt less able to control outbursts of temper or aggression. Also, more of them felt that people in general did not expect enough of them. The Q-sort data also showed no significant differences between the two groups in their actual self-concept or in their idealized concept. However, more blind subjects had either high positive or high negative attitudes toward themselves, and the blind as a group exhibited a greater amount of variation. Jervis observes that "blindness may be considered more than sight-deprivation but not a completely crippling factor. The fact that the blind subjects pushed either to an extreme negative or an extreme positive attitude toward themselves would indicate that they have difficulty in normal adjustment." [186] He believes in the value of the self-concept for further research, which should be of a more specific nature.

In general the studies of the University of Rochester group and of Jervis agree that there are no essential and consistent differences between blind and sighted adolescents as a group, but there appear to be individual differences—and these should be further explored.

Blank [187] observed that "Psychoanalytic literature abounds in references to the symbolism of the eye, scoptophilia and exhibitionism, hysterical visual disturbances, and Oedipus and his blindness. . . . Yet contributions on the psychic problems of the blind are scant."

Burlingham [188] reports two case histories of blind children and concludes that the lack of sight disturbs and diminishes the testing of reality, one of the most important functions of the ego. Instead of compensating for this, the blind child turns to fantasy—which leads to denial of reality and to wishful thinking. She states that there was little new material concerning the early sexual development of the two children and concludes that "the instinctual processes and the attempts to repress them which cause anxiety, act independently of sight." [189] Her observations agree with those of Felix Deutsch,[190] who also noticed a striking readiness to give up reality and escape into fantasy.

Blank [191] believes that congenital blindness does not always cause ego defect, but blindness which occurs when ego functions are already developed is inevitably traumatic. He distinguishes three factors which underlie personality disturbances of the visually handicapped: "(1) The unconscious significance of the eye as a sexual organ, including the equation of eye with mouth and with genital. (2) The unconscious significance of the eye as a hostile, destructive organ, including the equation of eye with piercing phallus and with devouring mouth. (3) The unconscious significance of blindness as castration, as punishment for sin." [192] In two case presentations he demonstrates the problems of congenitally blind disturbed children and stresses that their ego development "depends primarily upon the physical contacts, consistent communication, and other components of mother love." [193] Therefore, psychotherapy with the mother and assistance to the whole family are important prerequisites for helping the child.

In his discussion of acquired blindness, Blank comes to the same conclusions as Cholden,[194] who distinguishes two stages in the reaction of healthy personalities to the loss of sight. The shock stage is a state of "psychological immobility," which can be thought of "as a period of protective emotional anesthesia which is available to the human organism under such stress." [195] The degree of ego strength and maturity will determine the individual's capacity to recover from this initial shock and to enter the next stage of depression. This stage is interpreted as a mourning for the loss of a loved object, and "the patient must die as a sighted person in order to be reborn as a blind man." [196] This stage must be lived through before blindness can be accepted, and attempts to prevent or prematurely shorten this depression may impede the rehabilitation process. Also, the raising of false hopes for the return of sight or, on the other hand, the premature offer of braille can prevent the acceptance of blindness as a reality.

Facial Expressions

The problem of facial expression and of its development in the blind is of practical as well as theoretical importance. The questions of the innateness of certain expressions and of the cultural determination of expressive mimicry have received considerable attention. The social value of "normal" facial expression for blind children and adults has been stressed by many educators. Thompson studied this problem in 26 blind children from six weeks to 13 years of age who had been blind from birth or shortly thereafter.[197] She compared them with a matched group of 29 seeing children. The children were observed and photographed in naturally occurring situations of an emotional nature. The purpose of the study was to determine the effects of maturation and of social mimicry upon the innate neuromuscular mechanisms of emotional expression. Expressions of laughing, smiling, and crying occurred in both groups of children, although there were certain differences between them. The effect of maturation showed itself in certain changes of facial expressions in blind children. These changes were considered to be maturational, since they could not have been brought about in any other way. The development of facial expressions in seeing children seems largely to be determined by mimicry. She concludes, "Since it is believed that the facial musculature is under a dual neural control, it seems that maturation effects the 'emotional' expressions whereas mimicry effects 'voluntary' expression." [198]

Fulcher asked 118 seeing subjects from 4 to 16 years of age and 50 blind subjects from 6 to 21 years of age to form facial expressions of emotions.[199] These were photographed by motion picture camera. The analysis of the requested expressions revealed: (1) The blind show less facial activity than the seeing in expressing every emotion. (2) The relative amount of facial activity in expressing emotions is about the same for the blind as for the seeing. (3) Facial activity increases with age in the seeing but decreases with age in the blind. (4) The blind show slighter, though similar, differences of facial movement in expressing different emotions. (5) The expressions of the seeing are more adequate than those of the blind. He concluded, therefore, that vision is an important means of acquiring the ability to form appropriate facial expressions, but that there are other ways of acquiring them besides visual imitation.

Dreams

How blind individuals dream is a topic of frequent discussions and numerous observations, but there are few studies available which investigate the dreams of blind children. Elinor Deutsch presents descriptions of dreams of various children and also her own dreams without discussing the symbolism contained in any of the dreams.[200] She found that children often said that they "saw" an object when they actually meant that they only heard or felt it or just knew that it was present. Therefore, she based her conclusions only on her own dreams and found that the imagery in them is "entirely auditory, kinesthetic, static, and tactile. The sense of hearing usually plays the most important part, while the other three sense modalities seem to be of about equal moment." [201] Taste and smell imagery did not play any part in her dreams. She often carried on long conversations and actually heard what was being said to her by voices which had all their usual inflections. An Italian study by Costa, in which he analyzed 80 dreams of 15 blind children, also showed that the dreams of totally blind children are predominantly of a tactual and auditory nature.[202] A French study by Bolli agrees with this observation and also stresses that the dreams of those born blind are not lacking in variety or richness.[203] In persons blinded later in life, visual imagery deteriorates in proportion to the age of the subject and the duration of his blindness.

That the congenitally blind and those who became blind before the age of about five do not have visual dreams is confirmed by the reports of Blank.[204] He also concurs with Deutsch and others that hearing ranks first in importance, tactile and kinesthetic next—but also found that sometimes blind people's dreams include taste, smell, and temperature perceptions. He describes five cases (three of whom were congenitally blind) and their dreams and concludes that the "typical dream of the blind is a dream 'from above,' one that is determined primarily by serious reality problems and it usually contains some prominent spoken statement, or other superego elements more closely related to the day's residue than to deeply repressed conflicts." He concludes: "The phenomenological differences between the dreams of the blind and the seeing are not fundamental. They require no revision of the psychoanalytical theory of dreams." [205]

Developmental Aspects

There is a large and growing literature which deals with descriptions, observations, and generalizations concerning the development of blind children. In most cases it also includes advice to parents on their functions in rearing a blind child. The number of scientific studies in this area, however, is rather small, although many of the research studies which were reported here have direct or indirect implications of a developmental nature.

Gesell, Ilg, and Bullis followed the development of a child, born with clinically complete bilateral anophthalmia (congenital absence of both eyes), up to the age of four years.[206] They took periodic moving-picture records of this child in order to answer such questions as: Is retardation of behavior caused by blindness or by complicating factors? Can blindness by itself produce retardation? How are patterns of behavior affected by blindness? Their observational data demonstrated that in general the sequences of development in this blind child were comparable to those of seeing children. The blind child progressed in the basic patterns of posture, manipulation, locomotion, exploration, language, and social behavior, thus confirming the basic role of maturation in the blind infant's growth. Due to the lack of visual control, the child showed atypical orientational behavior, established no eye-hand coordination, and his head remained in a consistently maintained mid-position. The authors concluded that blindness "profoundly alters the structure of the mental life, but not the integrity of a total growth complex." [207]

While Gesell and his associates found that blindness by itself does not produce a serious degree of retardation (at least up to four years of age), another study by Wilson and Halverson [208] reached a different conclusion. In this study, a totally blind child was observed and tested with a battery of tests including the Gesell Schedules, the Cattell Infant Scale, and the

Vineland Social Maturity Scale. Examinations were conducted at 15, 18, and 24 months, and the age at which the child passed various test items was recorded during regular weekly observations. The data indicated a general developmental retardation which was greatest in his motor and adaptive behavior—particularly in all activities involving prehension and locomotion, and least in language. In contrast to the aggressive attitude of seeing children, the child also showed a lack of initiative and spontaneity in his movements. The authors believe that much of the value of touch as an informative sense in early childhood is due to its association with vision and conclude that the blind child's retardation was for the most part caused by inadequate perception of space.

The difference in the findings of these two studies concerning the retarding influence of blindness may be due to a difference in innate potentialities of the two children, although the authors of the latter study do not consider this as a possible cause. It must, however, be recognized that even a single case of a blind child with essentially normal development is sufficient proof that blindness does not necessarily retard a child. As a matter of fact, there are innumerable blind children who have demonstrated normal growth in spite of total blindness, although data about them have not been scientifically recorded.

Two studies which used the Vineland Social Maturity Scale with blind children are available. Bradway asked in her study, "To what extent are total deafness, total blindness, and severe physical crippling social handicaps, and which of these is the greatest handicap?" [209] She tested 92 deaf pupils from 5 to 21 years of age, 73 blind pupils from 5 to 20 years, and also a group of crippled children. Her results gave the deaf a mean Social Quotient of 80 and the blind, one of 62. The Social Quotients of the blind showed a tendency to decrease with age, but she stated that neither deafness nor blindness constituted a permanent bar to successful performance but only resulted in a delay of it. The item comparison revealed that the deaf were superior to the blind in all categories except that of communication. Her finding that blindness is a greater social handicap than deafness is in contradiction to other studies comparing the deaf and the blind, particularly that of McAndrew mentioned before.

Nor are the findings of Bradway borne out by the research of Maxfield and Fjeld.[210] They used the Vineland Social Maturity Scale with 101 visually handicapped children ranging in age from nine months to six years and ten months. The Social Quotient for this group was 83.54 with a standard deviation of 29.28. The wide variability of this group is due to the fact that it included children whose mental ability varied from an extremely low level to very superior, and also to the inclusion of partially seeing as well as of blind children. Of great importance in this study are the qualitative results which led to a tentative revision of the

Vineland Social Maturity Scale for use with visually handicapped pre-school children. Maxfield and Fjeld used the first 77 items of the whole scale and found that 14 items were relatively more difficult for visually handicapped children than for the seeing. Among them were eating with spoon and fork, buttoning coat or dress, marking with pencil, fetching or carrying familiar objects, cutting with scissors, reaching for familiar person, and playing simple table games. Of the 14 items, at least four, such as marking with pencil and cutting with scissors, were obviously more difficult for visually handicapped children. Among fifteen items found to be relatively easier for visually handicapped children were sitting unsupported, discriminating foods, washing hands unaided, initiating own play activities, using names of familiar objects, and playing with other children. Thus the blind children revealed a tendency to succeed better on items requiring less initiative, less activity, and less aggressiveness. Maxfield and Fjeld, in their adaptation of the scale, adhered to the categories and age levels of the original scale but included new items and revised some others. They concluded that visually handicapped children as a group appeared to be more docile, less active, and to have less initiative than seeing children of corresponding ages. This trend was more striking in the blind than in the partially seeing. Hayes [211] used the Maxfield-Fjeld Adaptation of the Vineland Social Maturity Scale with three hundred blind babies and reported results closely corresponding to the findings of Maxfield and Fjeld.

In 1953 Maxfield and Kenyon [212] prepared a guide for the use of the Maxfield-Fjeld scale. Fnally, in 1957, Maxfield and Buchholz [213] presented their Social Maturity Scale for Blind Preschool Children. The use of the previous adaptation revealed that some items needed relocation or re-formulation, others should be eliminated, and new ones should be added. The new scale consists of 95 items and is based on data and observations of 484 children. The authors aim at providing "as objective a means as possible for comparing the present status, or the progress, of a given blind child, in his acquisition of personal and social independence and competence, with that of other blind children of corresponding chronological age." [24]

Sands stresses the importance of qualitative observation in connection with any use of pre-school tests with blind children; these observations should include:

> . . . the child's spontaneous play activities, his awareness and alertness; his methods of discrimination, exploration, and localization; his means of communication and use of language; his attention span and learning ability; his reactions to routine, and to people he knows as well as to new people.[215]

Lowenfeld [216] distinguishes three objective effects of blindness: (1) the limitation in the range and variety of experiences; (2) the limitation in the ability to get about, and (3) the limitation in the control of the environment and the self in relation to it. From these limitations he derives the following basic principles in methods of teaching blind children: Individualization, Concreteness, Unified Instruction, Additional Stimulation, and Self-Activity. The first two limitations have already been discussed here, but the third one, in the control of the environment and the self in relation to it, needs further elaboration.

Sight is the human sense which overcomes distance and, at the same time, gives details and relationships of form, size, and position. This "object quality" of vision permits more effective contact with and control of the environment than are achieved by the other senses. Therefore, lack of sight causes a detachment from the physical and, to a lesser degree, from the social, world. As a result, the blind individual is affected in different ways during his development. It has been noted, for instance, that the blind infant does not reach out for objects or crawl toward them because he is not attracted by them unless they emit sounds. Some blind children omit the crawling stage although they follow in general the same sequence of development as seeing children do. Also, the blind child cannot acquire certain behavior patterns on the basis of visual imitation. This factor plays an important role in his learning to walk, to talk, to play, to acquire expressive movements, and to perform the many other actions in which learning by imitation is important. Dressing, eating, and many daily activities are considerably more complicated when they must be learned and performed without sight. For this reason it is generally agreed that some retardation in the blind child's rate of development as compared with that of seeing children can be expected.

The blind child's inability to control his environment by sight also is responsible for his fear of being observed, which has been reported by many observers. He cannot determine whether he is being observed or when the observation begins or ends unless the observer makes himself known by some non-visual means. This fear by itself is liable to produce tension and self-consciousness. The question of how blind children learn to understand what it means to be watched has not yet received scientific attention. Reported observations have shown that the blind child realizes at an early age that people can tell what he is doing without having bodily contact with him. Thus he learns that others can do something to him which he cannot do to them. Also, he finds out at an early age that he must grope around for something he has lost, while his seeing brother or sister or friend can locate it immediately. Thus he learns by experience that he is in some way different from the others, although he may not know or may not be able to verbalize until much later that this is due to his blindness.

Cutsforth discusses "blindisms," which are acts of automatic self-stimulation such as rolling or tilting the head, thrusting the fingers into the eyes, and swaying the body.[217] He explains that, in contrast to the seeing child, the blind child must find his stimulation within bodily reach and turns to his own body as the source and the object of stimulation. Thus lack of stimulation from the external world furthers the blind child's concentration on the self and encourages the exercise of self-stimulation. Totman believes, on the basis of experience, that like any undesirable activity, blindisms must be replaced by more socially acceptable activities that give pleasure and satisfaction to the child.[218] Blindisms in their children are often quite disturbing to the parents because of the unfavorable reactions of other people to them. In most cases they disappear as the child grows up, although observers agree that emotionally disturbed children or those of low mentality may continue to practice them for a long time. This, however, is characteristic not only of blind but also of seeing children who are thus affected.

Retrolental Fibroplasia

Since RLF is a cause of blindness sui generis, the literature and research findings of this period will be treated separately, though they have important implications for and often direct pertinence to children blind from other causes.

The RLF wave released a veritable flood of articles, pamphlets, and conference reports dealing with psycho-educational problems of blind children of pre-school age. They all stress the importance of environmental influences, of emotional acceptance of the child by his parents, of providing the right opportunities for learning at the right time—principles which are accepted for children in general but which needed to be specially stressed with blind children.

Two books, widely acclaimed by parents and professional workers, have been found helpful. Lowenfeld's *Our Blind Children—Growing and Learning with Them* [219] is a psychologically oriented book dealing with the education of blind children. Spencer's *Blind Children in Family and Community* [220] is a more sociologically oriented picture story of preschool blind children.

A research volume, *Blindness in Children* by Norris, Spaulding, and Brodie,[221] reports a five-year longitudinal study conducted under the University of Chicago clinics by an ophthalmologist-psychologist-social worker team that cooperated with available community resources. Sixty-six of the 259 blind children in the study were studied intensively. Fifty-six of the former and 209 of the latter were blind as a result of retrolental fibroplasia. The first part of the study describes its research methods and findings; the second part presents case histories of six RLF children illustrating adjustment "ranging from very favorable to very unfavorable." The Cattell Infant Intelligence Scale, supplemented by certain items from the Kuhlmann Scale of Intelligence, and the Maxfield-Fjeld Tentative adaptation of the Vineland Social Maturity Scale were used with children up to three years. The Interim Hayes-Binet Intelligence Tests for the Blind were used with children above the three-year level. Detailed item analyses are reported for the Cattell and for the Maxfield-Fjeld scales. In interpreting the test results, it is stated that "In the experience of the project staff, any expectation that a psychological test result in itself could be regarded as a valid measure either of a child's capacity or of his functioning level proved unfounded." [222] The importance of readiness is recognized, and the results of the study suggest "that the more time that elapses between the time of optimum readiness and the time when the opportunity for learning is provided, the greater the difficulties in learning become." [223] Therefore, favorable opportunities for learning "are more important in determining the child's functioning level than such factors as his degree of blindness, his intelligence as measured by psychological tests, or the social, economic, or educational background of his parents." [224]

The study revealed no evidence that retrolental fibroplasia is associated with brain defects and concluded that, in the absence of any specific neurological findings, the functional retardation found in some retrolental fibroplasia children "must be presumed to be directly related to complex social and environmental factors."

The general conclusions of the study can be summed up by stating that under favorable conditions "the blind child can develop into an independent, responsible, freely functioning child whose use of his potential compares favorably with that of most sighted children of his age." [225] This result confirms for retrolental fibroplasia children what Gesell and his associates have found in their study of a child with congenital absence of both eyes.[226] But while Gesell states that blindness "profoundly alters the structure of the mental life, but not the integrity of a total growth complex," the University of Chicago study asserts: "There are no special problems or 'handicaps' which can be attributed directly to the blindness" [227]—a statement with which many would take issue.

The work reported by Norris and her associates is continued under Jerome Cohen at the Northwestern University Medical School.

Further support for the possibility of normal development in RLF children is found in Parmelee's studies on the mental development of children with blindness due to RLF. In a 1955 study [228] he used the Gesell norms to evaluate ten RLF infants less than one year of age, ten prematurely born infants with normal vision, and a control group of eighty full-term infants with normal vision. The developmental quotients (with age corrected for prematurity) of the RLF infants were "well within the normal range." In a 1958 study [229] of school-age children Parmelee compared 38 RLF children with 22 children blind from other causes. There was no significant difference between the groups in the incidence of mental retardation, but both groups had a higher incidence of it than is generally reported. In a third study Parmelee *et al.*[230] followed up, after a four-year interval, the ten RLF children reported in 1955 (when all were considered developmentally normal). In 1959, three of the children were "functioning at a mentally retarded level . . . have withdrawn considerably from social contact and have other behavioral difficulties suggestive of severe emotional problems. It was concluded that they probably have normal mental potential that is not manifest because of severe emotional problems." Parmelee believes "that developmental examination in the first year of life is a valuable adjunct in the evaluation of prematurely born blind children." [231] Revealing biographies of the ten RLF children are presented.

On the other hand, Keeler [232] reports that he observed a group of 35 RLF children of pre-school age in whom he found abnormal behavior similar to but much milder than that of five other RLF children who were under treatment for severe psychiatric disorders. He also studied two other groups of blind children: 18 who were congenitally blind and 17 who lost their sight in early childhood. In all of them he found developmental histories quite different from those in the RLF group. The congenitally blind showed normal development and far fewer abnormalities in behavior and motility than the RLF group. In the group of children with postnatal blindness, abnormalities in development and in behavior were least conspicuous, though some of them showed more anxiety and were more disturbed by changes in their environment. The latter two groups also did much better in school than the children with RLF.

The studies of Norris and her co-workers and of Parmelee used selected subjects and excluded some who did not meet certain standards. Therefore, they are not representative in the sense of giving a true picture of the condition of the group of children who became blind as a result of RLF. No wonder, therefore, that the practitioners in the field found themselves confronted with many RLF children who did not show the normal development expected according to the results of these studies. Their problems and therapy have been presented and discussed mostly by psychiatrists.

The behavior of a considerable number of RLF children has been observed as similar to or identical with that Kanner described under the term "early infantile autism." [233] Their behavior is characterized by self-isolation, developmental and mental retardation, lack of use of language for purposes of interpersonal communication, echolalia and inability to identify as "I," indifference to people and lack of affectivity, autistic patterns of activity and motility, tenseness to the point of appearing spastic, and primitive patterns of perception (exploring by tongue, smelling, and so forth). On the other hand, they often show an unusual rote and musical memory and are able to repeat songs or commercials—which their parents may interpret as a hopeful sign.

The cases of three blind children and their psychiatric therapy were presented by Green and Schecter.[234] Two were RLF cases showing severe disorders; the third, blind from early infancy, was not as autistic or retarded as the other two. Four phases of the therapeutic program are described: "(1) The individual work of the psychiatrist with the child. (2) Consultations with parents by the psychiatrist and the psychiatric social worker. (3) Placement of the child in daytime school programs, with regular consultations with the teachers. (4) Placement in institutions for disturbed blind children for those who could not be treated on a once-a-week clinic basis." Attention is called to the need for early detection of such emotional disturbances and the authors warn of "the danger of explaining, all too easily, the psychological deviations on the basis of a child's handicap, rather than exploring the severe child-parent disturbances which have become organized around the handicap."[235]

The most elaborate narrative of the psychoanalytic treatment and the recovery of a girl blind as a result of RLF, is presented by Omwake and Solnit.[236] Their contact with this severely disturbed child began when she was three and a half years old. Treatment continued through her seventh year. They selected for discussion in this presentation four of the child's difficulties: an arrest of libidinal and ego development; the development of an inhibition of touching; the disorganizing effect of memories of painful experiences from the first three years of life; and the gradually developing comprehension of her sensory defect.

The Educational Unit of the Hampstead Child Therapy Course and Clinic in London, England, works with blind children and their mothers. Burlingham's [237] chapter in The Psychoanalytic Study of the Child (1961) makes observations on the development of these children. Although the causes of blindness of the children are not given, their ages and other circumstances mentioned suggest that most, if not all of them, are RLF children. Burlingham observes that "retardation and restriction of muscular achievement are the order of the day. . . . The blind baby although not intentionally restricted yet behaves in many respects like a restricted sighted child."[238]

Burlingham considers blindness responsible for this because it prevents stimulation to reach out and causes lack of some incentive, such as the observed approval of the mother, to repeat achievements. The dependency stage of the blind child is enlarged and prolonged; frequent persistence of mouth pleasure is characteristic. Blind children are observed as showing much less aggressive expression and more fear of external aggression. They feel the need for controlling their aggression because they realize how dependent they are on the seeing. Burlingham also observed that blind children often ask strangers immediately for their names, where they live, and so forth. She believes that people are far more attractive to them than objects and imputes frequently occurring faulty methods of verbalization to such factors as speech, which is less firmly connected with sensory experiences, and lack in ego achievement. She raises the question whether this will affect later superego formation and produce "certain ego characteristics such as superficiality, hypocrisy, overcompliance, which are often considered to be connected with blindness." [239]

Many of Burlingham's other observations are similar to those made in the United States on disturbed RLF children, but the research on blind adolescents fails to confirm the presence of any of the expected ego characteristics mentioned above.

Keeler,[240] who contributed perhaps the best description of autistic patterns and defective communication in RLF children, also asks questions regarding the possible cause of the psychopathological syndrome observed in these children: (1) Does this condition result "from brain damage and mental retardation due to an insult to the brain brought about by the prematurity factor or perhaps through vascular involvement of the brain similar to that which occurs in the retina"? (2) Is this condition due to the blindness itself? (3) Are psychogenic factors, such as early emotional deprivation, responsible for the production of this disorder? (4) Do other factors not yet determined play a role? and (5) Is it a combination of any or all of these factors? Keeler leans toward the psychogenic factors theory. In this he is supported by such studies as those of Bender,[241] Spitz,[242] Mahler,[243] and others in the general field of child psychiatry; by Barry and Marshall,[244] Blank,[245] Hallenbeck,[246] Moor,[247] and others who have studied children blind as a result of RLF. Also, current research in sensory deprivation [248] appears to support the importance of psychogenic factors.

All studies agree that the prematurely born infant's relationship with his mother is severely disrupted because of his prolonged hospitalization, because of his mother's reaction to this separation and to his blindness, and because of other factors which are caused by the combination of prematurity and blindness. This emotional deprivation during the first year and the early years of life, and its results, have been found to cause serious problems in other children as well. Psychotherapy and social casework assistance [249] to the parents, and restoration of an accepting and warm emotional climate with psychotherapy or play therapy [250,251] provided for the child, offer the best hope for improvement of the child's condition.

There is, on the other hand, good evidence that the condition of at least some of the prematurely born children with RLF is due to neurological damage. In a carefully controlled longitudinal study by Knobloch et al.,[252] undertaken by the Maternal and Child Health Division of the Johns Hopkins University School of Hygiene and Public Health, 992 infants, about half of whom were prematurely born, were given a Gesell developmental examination at 40 weeks of age. "The smallest premature infants with birth weights under 1,501 gm., showed abnormalities in 50.9% of the cases. . . . Of the full-term controls, 12.8% had abnormalities." [253] A further breakdown showed that in the same group of lowest birth weight premature infants, "26.3% had neurological signs of sufficient severity (possible cerebral palsy plus overt neurological defect) to warrant close developmental supervision in order to be certain about future development. The comparable incidence for the remainder of premature infants was 7.2% and for full-term infants 1.6%." [254] A follow-up study [255] of 91 per cent of the children of the same group at ages 3-5 years confirmed the unfavorable position of the child with a birth weight below 1,500 gm. It appears "that the smaller the baby at birth, the less likely is he to maintain the status of 'normal' or to improve if not 'normal' between 40 weeks of age and 3 to 5 years." [256] Since RLF occurred most frequently in prematures with a birth weight of less than 1,500 gm., it stands to reason that they would show a similarly higher incidence of neurological damage.

Cruickshank and Trippe [257] have given some indication of the extent to which additional handicapping conditions are present in the blind population under 21 years of age. (This is the age group in which a considerable percentage must be blind as a result of RLF.) A total of 2,773 children are included in their extensive survey of services to blind children in New York State. Of these, 31 per cent had multihandicapping conditions, with cerebral palsy, epilepsy and brain injury ranking highest. This percentage does not include impairments of hearing, speech, or mental retardation. If these impairments are added, the authors state, "the problem of the multihandicapped blind child can be seen to be of major proportions."

Effects of Physical Factors

A number of physical factors related to the eyes doubtless affect the individual, although no research has clarified the extent and kind of this influence. Facial disfigurement is a frequent result of eye defects. The eyeball may be enlarged (as in congenital glaucoma) or abnormally small (microphthalmia), or there may be no eyeball at all (anophthalmia); the muscles controlling the movements of the eyeball or of the eyelids may not function normally and thus cause strabismus, nystagmus, or ptosis (dropping of the upper lid); X-ray treatment of the eyes to control malignant growths may have resulted in disfiguring X-ray burns; pathological changes in the eyeball or parts of it may be quite apparent. All these and other disfigurements are liable to make the individual quite self-conscious and ill at ease. The eye condition responsible for the visual defect may not be static but progressive, and this may cause anxiety and feelings of insecurity. There may be actual pain as a result of the eye defect (as, for instance, in glaucoma), or discomfort and irritation may sometimes serve to make the child acutely conscious of his eye trouble. Also, frequent and prolonged hospitalization because of eye pathology exerts its influence on the child, particularly if it necessitates separation from the mother during the earlier years of life. It may result in developmental retardation as well as in emotional reactions characteristic of deprivation of maternal care. Prolonged treatment of eye diseases by medication also has emotional effects on the child and his environment. Finally, any blindness which occurs late in life results in an emotional trauma which may manifest itself in various reaction forms.

Conclusion

BLINDNESS IS a defect of one sense, but it affects the individual in various ways. Efforts to connect behavior with specific effects of blindness have been sporadic. Studies on the psychological implications of blindness are either of a primarily descriptive nature with no or poor statistical support, or of a primarily statistical nature with little or no reference to actual behavior. Personality inventories, tests, scales, and interviews record only reported behavior, judgments (often about oneself), and opinions. Therefore, any analysis of these must be accepted with caution, no matter how refined and objective the statistical treatment may be. On the other hand, observed behavior cannot be related to blindness unless objective validation supports this connection.

In many studies the distinction between those who are totally and congenitally blind, and those who are only partially blind or partially seeing has not received due attention. The lack of this distinction is responsible for ambiguity in the results of many studies and for contradictions between the results of some of them. Barker and his colleagues [258] are justified in their conclusions that research in this area must overcome methodological problems and must be designed in terms of theory if it is to yield better results.

THE PARTIALLY SEEING CHILD

WHEN PINTNER in 1941 reviewed the literature on the partially seeing, he concluded his chapter by saying:

> This chapter shows our ignorance rather than our knowledge. The special education of the partially seeing child is so recent that practically all of the effort and interest in this work has been concentrated on the organization, administration, and equipment of these classes. About the children themselves from a psychological point of view we know practically nothing.[259]

Since then, conditions have not changed to any considerable extent, but we may be able to explain at least in part the reasons for the lack of research concerning the partially seeing child. He is, for all practical purposes, a seeing child, and his handicap, if it is one, does not affect him in any different way from other children who slightly deviate from "the normal." This is the conclusion of the few research studies that have been made, and it has undoubtedly discouraged others from further research. It would, however, be quite valuable to know more about the ways in which children react to visual handicaps which put them into the category of partially seeing children.

According to Hathaway's [260] revised book, the following children should be considered possible candidates for special education as partially seeing children: "(1) Children having a visual acuity of 20/70 or less in the better eye after all necessary medical or surgical treatment has been given and compensating lenses provided when the need for them is indicated. Such children must, however, have a residue of sight that makes it possible to use this as the chief avenue of approach to the brain. (2) Children with a visual deviation from the normal who, in the opinion of the eye specialist, can benefit from the special educational facilities provided for the partially seeing." Special educational opportunities should also be provided for children after eye operations, if readaptation in eye use and psychological readjustment is required, and for those with muscle anomalies, such as strabismus, which demand re-education of an eye and psychological readjustment.

Kerby reports on causes and degrees of defective vision in 4,179 boys and 3,131 girls in 600 classes for partially seeing children.[261] Of them, 20.8 per cent had vision of 20/200 or less, 29.5 per cent had vision from 20/70 to 20/200, 16 per cent from 20/50 to 20/70, 24 per cent better than

20/50, and for 9.7 per cent, vision was not reported. These figures show that only less than one third of these children really come within the visual acuity range of partially seeing pupils. One fifth of the pupils receiving education as partially seeing children fall under the definition of blindness. They are apparently able to take part in the instruction offered, and this may be taken as another proof of the already noted fact, that visual acuity by itself is not a true indication of "visual efficiency." Forty per cent of all pupils classified as partially seeing have vision better than 20/70 which, so far as visual acuity is concerned, would place them beyond the category of the partially seeing. It must be assumed that they either have progressive eye difficulties or suffer from other diseases that seriously affect vision. Also, they may have been placed in these classes for other than visual reasons. The wide visual acuity range of partially seeing children shows that they are a heterogeneous group so far as vision is concerned and may explain why the few research studies available do not reveal any differentiation between partially seeing and seeing children.

The group of partially seeing children reported on by Kerby [262] showed the following percentage distribution of causes of visual defects:

Developmental Anomalies of Structure		21.5%
Cataract and/or dislocated lens	11.3	
Albinism	3.7	
Other	4.3	
Multiple anomalies	2.2	
Diseases or Defects of Eyes		10.2%
Infectious diseases	3.4	
Injury	1.5	
Other	.4	
Cause unknown	4.9	
Refractive Errors		48.7%
Myopia (incl. myopic and mixed astigmatism)	35.5	
Hyperopia (incl. hyperopic astigmatism)	12.8	
Type not known	.4	
Defects of Muscle Function		18.2%
Squint (incl. strabismus and amblyopia ex- anopsia)	8.8	
Nystagmus	9.4	
Cause Undetermined		1.4%

There are no data available on the results of intelligence tests given to a representative group of partially seeing children, nor do adequate reports exist on their educational achievement.

Pintner and Forlano administered in large-type print the Aspects of Personality Test and the Pupil Portraits Test to more than four hundred children in classes for the partially seeing.[263] The scores did not reveal any consistent difference from the norms established for seeing children.

In a study limited to an unselected group of sixty partially seeing children in a large city school system, Livingston [264] collected data in order "to discover clues to the intelligence strengths and weaknesses of partially seeing children and whether enlarging the revised Stanford-Binet Intelligence Test would increase their score." [265] Photographic enlargements of the tests did not produce any significant I.Q. gains as compared with the standard forms. In comparing the partially seeing with 407 normally seeing children, the normally seeing did better in visual-motor coordination, and the partially seeing were superior in two abstract word tests. The author concludes that there was little evidence that the partially seeing child performs less adequately than the normally seeing in broad areas of mental functioning. Nevertheless, he refers repeatedly to the weaknesses of partially seeing children in certain areas such as social judgment involving interaction, conceiving and executing a planning operation, and emotional security. There are no data given on any of these and other observations which, as presented in this abridged version of a doctor's thesis, must be considered unconfirmed.

Since reading plays such an important role in our culture, particularly in acquiring an education, much attention has been given to the kind of print and the size of type which would be most adequate for partially seeing children. Past studies have not demonstrated how 24-point compares with 18-point type, the two types most widely used in books especially printed for partially seeing children. Nolan [266] studied this problem in a carefully designed experiment and found that both types were read with equal reading speed, the readability criterion selected for his study. Also, a common textbook letter type was read more rapidly than an experimental type thought to be more legible. These findings are an experimentally founded sanction for the enlarged presentation of regularly printed textbooks.

Eames [267] studied a population of 3,500 school children, half of them reading failures and half unselected. He found a much greater incidence of hypermetropia and exophoria at the reading distance (a type of strabismus) in the reading failure group, while myopia occurred with similar frequency in both groups. Also, "Pathological eye conditions as distinguished from eye defects and deficiencies have appeared to the extent of nearly five percent among reading failures which is slightly less than twice the frequency found among the non-failures." Eames offers a valuable discussion of the physiology of seeing to read and of the educational indications and implications of various eye conditions. It must be concluded that learning to read is affected by vision problems, and that partially seeing children need special attention in order to avoid reading difficulties, or remedial services if such have developed.

There are two studies available which investigated the relationship between visual defects and juvenile delinquency. Wallace found that refractive errors are more frequent in juvenile delinquents than in the normal population.[268] He concluded that the visual defect may cause discomfort which can lead to maladjustment in school, followed by truancy and ultimately by delinquency. Blumenthal described a case in which, after an eye was lost as a result of injury, such symptoms as disobedience, quarrelsomeness, cruelty, temper tantrums, and truancy were observed.[269] He believes that this adolescent wanted to regain status by being "tough" and thus compensated for the feelings of insecurity by developing aggressive behavior patterns.

Benton underlined the importance of parental responsibility and of the child's feelings of security. He emphasized that in the case of handicapped children, "their emotional difficulties bear a closer relationship to their early home experiences and to their general background than to their visual defect." [270] He also called attention to the possibility that emotional conflicts may be channeled through conversion to the visual apparatus, thus causing complaints of visual disturbance ranging from blinking to actual complete blindness.

Young discussed the results which some of the more common eye defects may have in causing fears and anxieties, self-centeredness or extroverted behavior, and worry about the cause and final outcome of the eye disorder.[271] She called attention to the effect of disfigurements due to certain visual handicaps, which may cause feelings of embarrassment or inferiority and make the individual avoid social experiences. Strabismus may lead to shyness and introverted behavior unless the eyes are straightened before school age when the social effects of the condition may become active. Myopia, in which distance vision is poor, may cause self-centeredness and a desire to confine oneself to solitary activities, but hyperopia, in which near vision is poor, may lead to neglect of school activities requiring close eye work and encourage interest in athletics. A panel presentation describes a multi-discipline approach in working with a partially seeing boy and his psycho-educational problems.[272]

Hackbush [273] recommended the use of various tests with the partially seeing, such as the Stanford-Binet, the Wechsler-Bellevue Intelligence Scale, the Jastak Wide Range Achievement Test, and the Vineland Social Maturity Scale. Some of these can be copied on yellow paper in as large size print as is necessary and comfortable for the child. She found the Human Figure Drawings Test and the Rorschach Test the most useful personality tests for this group, but does not give any results of their application. She called attention to "problem parents" whose anxiety, sadness, or ambitiousness affects the child. Some parents have "paranoid attitudes" and refuse to accept or face the child's handicap. Various instances of social and educational maladjustment are given in which visual defects were the causative factors but were not recognized until discovered in specific situations. Lowenfeld [274] called attention to the need for medical and psychological research in this area and discussed some basic needs of visually handicapped pre-school children. He found them to be identical with those of all children but stressed that they must be satisfied according to the child's sensory capacities.

Even if research on the effects of eye difficulties on the personality of children is practically nonexistent, there are enough observations available to prove that they may cause more or less severe forms of maladjustment. There are largely three ways in which an eye defect may show its psychological effects:

1. It may limit the child in his visual activities and in those others which are governed by vision. The kind and severity of the defect determines the nature of the limitations; its degree depends on personality and environmental factors.

2. The eye condition may be a changing one or cause actual discomfort or pain, thus creating or increasing feelings of insecurity and anxiety about imminent attacks as well as about the future progress of the pathological process.

3. There are various forms of mild or more severe facial disfigurements, for instance in strabismus or nystagmus, which may create a particular social reaction in the child's environment. The wearing of glasses, particularly heavy ones, is a cause of physical discomfort but also frequently evokes among children social reactions which are quite negative in their effects. Also the one-eyed child, even with good visual acuity in the remaining eye, may feel self-conscious, particularly if he must wear an artificial eye.

How an individual child reacts to any of these three basic factors will depend on his personality, his past experiences (which of course have become a part of his personality), and on his environment, which includes his family, his school, and his friends. We have no evidence of particular reaction patterns, but it is safe to assume that children react to eye difficulties essentially in the same way in which they react to other similar conditions affecting them.

H. R. Stolz and L. M. Stolz confirm this in discussing the emotional effects of wearing glasses:

> . . . for every example we may give of a girl disturbed because she has to wear glasses or a boy disturbed by his large, prominent nose, the reader can probably match a case with similar characteristics who gave no evidence of any disturbance. Of four girls in the California study who wore glasses, three were concerned about their appearance, while one showed no evidence of

disturbance, nor did the fact seem in any way to interfere with her satisfactory social relations.[275]

If a child is unable to succeed in his school work because of a visual defect, it may make him feel inadequate and inferior to his peers. Therefore, an effective screening program for eye difficulties is of great importance, since it is instrumental in finding those children who need special educational assistance in order to cope with their eye problems.

A few studies dealing with the blind have furnished some indication that the partially seeing tend to be less well adjusted than either the blind or the seeing.[276, 277, 278] Apparently the marginal position of the partially seeing child often intensifies his personality and adjustment problems. For example, teachers in schools for the blind have frequently voiced complaints that children with considerable sight in these schools are "problem cases." This may be explained as a reaction of children who are placed in an environment which does not permit them to make full use of their vision, which they consider their greatest sensory asset. Being frustrated in their visual functioning, they may develop resentment and asocial or even hostile behavior. For this and other reasons it is recognized by many that partially seeing children should attend regular classes in public schools and receive supplementary instruction in a special room with a resource teacher or from a special itinerant teacher, as described by Bertram.[279]

This survey shows how fragmentary and speculative the status of psychological literature on the partially seeing child at present is. The lack of positive results in a few research studies has undoubtedly discouraged further efforts, and so has the increasing trend to integrate partially seeing children educationally and socially with other "normal" children. A functional differentiation within the heterogeneous group of children with visual impairments appears to be a prerequisite for any more successful research efforts.

Notes

[1] M. D. Graham, *Social Research on Blindness: Present Status and Future Potentials* (New York: American Foundation for the Blind, 1960).

[2] R. G. Hurlin, "Estimated Prevalence of Blindness in the U.S., 1960," *The Sight-Saving Review*, XXXII (Spring 1962), 8.

[3] J. W. Jones, *Blind Children: Degree of Vision, Mode of Reading* (Washington, D.C.: U. S. Department of Health, Education and Welfare, Section on Exceptional Children and Youth, 1961).

[4] G. L. Abel, "The Education of Blind Children," in *Education of Exceptional Children and Youth*, eds. W. M. Cruickshank and G. O. Johnson (Englewood Cliffs, N.J.: Prentice-Hall, Inc., 1958), pp. 295-338.

5 C. E. Kerby, "Causes of Blindness in Children of School Age," *The Sight-Saving Review*, XXVIII (Spring 1958), 10-21.

6 Z. Toth, *Die Vorstellungswelt Der Blinden* (Leipzig: Johann Ambrosius Barth, 1930).

7 T. F. Schlaegel, Jr., "The Dominant Method of Imagery in Blind as Compared to Sighted Adolescents," *Journal of Genetic Psychology*, 83 (1953), 265-277.

8 H. R. Blank, "Dreams of the Blind," *The Psychoanalytic Quarterly*, XXVII (1958), 158-161.

9 J. W. Jones, "The Blind Child in School," *School Life*, January-March 1961, p. 9.

10 V. Lowenfeld, *Creative and Mental Growth*, 3rd ed. (New York: The Macmillan Company, 1957), p. 462.

11 R. G. Barker, et al., *Adjustment to Physical Handicap and Illness: A Survey of the Social Psychology of Physique and Disability*, rev. ed. (New York: Social Science Research Council, 1953), p. 271.

12 B. Lowenfeld, "Psychological Foundation of Special Methods in Teaching Blind Children," in *Blindness*, ed. P. A. Zahl (Princeton, N. J.: Princeton University Press, 1950), p. 91.

13 T. Heller, *Studien zur Blinden-Psychologie* (Leipzig: Wilhelm Engelmann, 1895).

14 W. Steinberg, *Die Raumwahrnehmung der Blinden* (Munich, 1920).

15 *Ibid.*, p. 139.

16 Heller, *op. cit.*, p. 68.

17 M. von Senden, *Space and Sight* (Glencoe, Ill.: The Free Press of Glencoe, Inc., 1960), pp. 289-290.

18 S. P. Hayes, *Contributions to a Psychology of Blindness* (New York: American Foundation for the Blind, 1941), pp. 16-48.

19 R. H. Wheeler and T. D. Cutsforth, "The Role of Synaesthesia in Learning," *Journal of Experimental Psychology*, IV (1921), 448-468.

20 R. H. Wheeler and T. D. Cutsforth, "Synaesthesia and Meaning," *American Journal of Psychology*, XXXIII (1922), 361-384.

21 R. H. Wheeler and T. D. Cutsforth, "Synaesthesia in the Development of the Concept," *Journal of Experimental Psychology*, VIII (1925), 149-159.

22 W. Voss, *Das Farbenhören bei Erblindeten* (Hamburg: Psychologisch-Aesthetische Forschungsgesellschaft, 1930).

23 Hayes, *op. cit.*, pp. 16-48.

24 *Ibid.*, pp. 63-80.

25 S. Axelrod, *Effects of Early Blindness: Performance of Blind and Sighted Children on Tactile and Auditory Tasks* (New York: American Foundation for the Blind, 1959).

26 *Ibid.*, p. 73.

27 R. V. Merry, "Adapting the Seashore Musical Talent Tests for Use with Blind Pupils," *The Teachers Forum*, III (March 1931), 15-19.

28 H. Cantril and G. W. Allport, *The Psychology of Radio* (New York: Harper & Row, Publishers, 1935).

29 Hayes, *op. cit.*, p. 291.

30 S. P. Hayes, "Measuring the Intelligence of the Blind," in *Blindness*, ed. P. A. Zahl (Princeton, N. J.: Princeton University Press, 1950), pp. 141-173.

31 S. P. Hayes, *First Regional Conference on Mental Measurements of the Blind* (Watertown, Mass.: Perkins Institution for the Blind, 1952), pp. 3-11.

32 Hayes, *Contributions, op. cit.*, pp. 90-98.

33 *Ibid.*, pp. 133-145.

34 *Ibid.*, p. 144.

35 S. P. Hayes, "Alternative Scales for the Mental Measurement of the Visually Handicapped," *Outlook for the Blind and the Teachers Forum*, XXXVI (October 1942), 225-230.

36 D. Komisar and M. MacDonnell, "Gains in I.Q. for Students Attending a School for the Blind," *Exceptional Children*, 21 (1955), 127-129.

[37] Hayes, "Alternative Scales," *op. cit.*, pp. 225-226.

[38] Hayes, "Measuring the Intelligence of the Blind," *op. cit.*

[39] L. L. Lewis, "The Relation of Measured Mental Ability to School Marks and Academic Survival in the Texas School for the Blind," *The International Journal for the Education of the Blind*, VI (1957), 56-60.

[40] J. B. Wattron, "A Suggested Performance Test of Intelligence," *The New Outlook for the Blind*, 50 (1956), 115-121.

[41] J. W. Jones, *"Blind Children, Degree of Vision, Mode of Reading,"* op. cit., p. 2.

[42] K. E. Maxfield, *Adaptation of Educational Tests for Use with Blind Pupils* (New York: American Foundation for the Blind, 1927).

[43] Hayes, *Contributions, op. cit.*, p. 155.

[44] F. F. Caldwell, *A Comparison of Blind and Seeing Children in Certain Educational Abilities* (New York: American Foundation for the Blind, 1932).

[45] B. Lowenfeld, "New Reading Practices," *The Teachers Forum*, XIII (November 1940), 31-40.

[46] Hayes, *Contributions, op. cit.*, p. 216.

[47] B. Lowenfeld, *Braille and Talking Book Reading: A Comparative Study* (New York: American Foundation for the Blind, 1945), p. 11.

[48] M. K. Bauman and S. P. Hayes, *A Manual for the Psychological Examination of the Adult Blind* (New York: The Psychological Corporation, 1951).

[49] V. Lowenfeld, *op. cit.*, p. 110.

[50] M. K. Bauman, "Studies in the Application of Motor Skills Techniques to the Vocational Adjustment of the Blind," *Journal of Applied Psychology*, XXX (1946), 144-154.

[51] Felix Deutsch, "The Sense of Reality in Persons Born Blind," *Journal of Psychology*, X (1940), 121-140.

[52] R. V. Merry and F. K. Merry, "The Tactual Recognition of Embossed Pictures by Blind Children," *Journal of Applied Psychology*, XVII (1933), 163.

[53] V. Lowenfeld, *op. cit.*, pp. 430-503.

[54] V. Lowenfeld, *The Nature of Creative Activity* (New York: Harcourt, Brace & World, Inc., 1939).

[55] V. Lowenfeld, *Creative and Mental Growth, op. cit.*, p. 446.

[56] T. D. Cutsforth, "The Unreality of Words to the Blind," *The Teachers Forum*, IV (May 1932), 86-89.

[57] C. Y. Nolan, "On the Unreality of Words to the Blind," *The New Outlook for the Blind*, 54 (1960), 100-102.

[58] K. E. Maxfield, *The Spoken Language of the Blind Preschool Child* (New York: Archives of Psychology, No. 201, 1936).

[59] S. M. Stinchfield, *Speech Disorders* (New York: Harcourt, Brace & World, Inc., 1933), pp. 62-76.

[60] D. M. Brieland, "A Comparative Study of the Speech of Blind and Sighted Children," *Speech Monographs*, XVII, No. 1 (1950), 99-103.

[61] M. F. Berry and J. Eisenson, *The Defective in Speech* (New York: Appleton-Century-Crofts, 1942), pp. 340-353.

[62] T. D. Cutsforth, *The Blind in School and Society*, rev. ed. (New York: American Foundation for the Blind, 1951), pp. 103-120.

[63] Brieland, *op. cit.*

[64] *Ibid.*, pp. 102-103.

[65] E. D. Rowe, *Speech Problems of Blind Children: A Survey of the North California Area* (New York: American Foundation for the Blind, 1958).

[66] K. Bürklen, *Touch Reading of the Blind*, trans. F. K. Merry (New York: American Foundation for the Blind, 1932).

[67] Heller, *op. cit.*, p. 93.

[68] K. E. Maxfield, *The Blind Child and His Reading* (New York: American Foundation for the Blind, 1928).

[69] B. F. Holland and P. F. Eatman, "The Silent Reading Habits of Blind Children," *The Teachers Forum*, VI (September 1933), 4-19.

[70] B. F. Holland, "Speed and Pressure Factors in Braille Reading," *The Teachers Forum*, VII (September 1934), 13-17.

[71] P. Fertsch, "Hand Dominance in Reading Braille," *American Journal of Psychology*, LX (1947), 335-349.

[72] P. Fertsch, "An Analysis of Braille Reading," *Outlook for the Blind*, XL (May 1946), 128-131.

[73] H. Horbach, *Taktiles Lesen* (Hannover: Verein zur Förderung der Blindenbildung, 1951).

[74] B. Lowenfeld, *Braille and Talking Book Reading, op. cit.*

[75] M. E. Enc and L. M. Stolurow, "A Comparison of the Effects of Two Recording Speeds on Learning and Retention," *The New Outlook for the Blind*, 54 (1960), 39-48.

[76] G. Fairbanks, N. Gutman, and M. Miron, "Effects of Time Compression on Auditory Comprehension of Spoken Messages," *Journal of Speech and Hearing Disorders*, 22 (1957), 10-19.

[77] L. Iverson, "Time Compression," *The International Journal for the Education of the Blind*, V (1956), 78-79.

[78] C. Y. Nolan, "An Overview of the Educational Research Program of the American Printing House for the Blind," *Proceedings of the 45th Meeting of the American Association of Instructors of the Blind* (1960), pp. 25-26.

[79] H. Chevigny and S. Braverman, *The Adjustment of the Blind* (New Haven: Yale University Press, 1950), p. 3.

[80] K. Bürklen, *Blinden-Psychologie* (Leipzig: Johann Ambrosius Barth, 1924).

[81] S. P. Hayes, *Facial Vision or the Sense of Obstacles* (Watertown, Mass.: Perkins Institution for the Blind, 1935).

[82] V. Dolanski, "Do the Blind 'See' Obstacles?" . . . *And There Was Light*, I (December 1931), 8-12.

[83] L. Truschel, "Der Sechste Sinn der Blinden," *Zeitschrift für Experimentelle Pädagogik*, III (1906), 109-142; IV (1907), 129-155; V (1907), 66-77.

[84] M. Kunz, "Das Orientierungsvermögen und das sog. Ferngefühl der Blinden und Taubblinden," *Internationales Archiv für Schulhygiene*, IV (1907), 80-179 and 181-185.

[85] A. Krogius, "Zur Frage vom Sechsten Sinn der Blinden," *Zeitschrift für Experimentelle Pädagogik*, V (1917), 77-89.

[86] W. James, *The Principles of Psychology* (New York: Holt, Rinehart & Winston, Inc., 1918), II, 202-211.

[87] P. Villey, *The World of the Blind*, trans. A. Hallard (New York: The Macmillan Company, 1930), pp. 101-117.

[88] V. Dolanski, "Les Aveugles Possèdent-Ils le 'Sense des Obstacles'?", *L'Année Psychologique*, XXXI (1930), 1-50.

[89] E. A. Jerome and H. Proshansky, "Factors in the Assay and Use of Guidance Devices," in *Blindness*, ed. P. A. Zahl (Princeton, N. J.: Princeton University Press, 1950), p. 466.

[90] M. Supa, M. Cotzin, and K. M. Dallenbach, " 'Facial Vision': the Perception of Obstacles by the Blind," *American Journal of Psychology*, LVII (1944), 133-183.

[91] Jerome and Proshansky, *op. cit.*, p. 467.

[92] Supa *et al.*, *op. cit.*, pp. 182-183.

[93] P. Worchel and K. M. Dallenbach, " 'Facial Vision': Perception of Obstacles by the Deaf-Blind," *American Journal of Psychology*, LX (1947), 502-553.

[94] M. Cotzin and K. M. Dallenbach, " 'Facial Vision': the Role of Pitch and Loudness in the Perception of Obstacles by the Blind," *American Journal of Psychology*, LXIII (1950), 485-515.

[95] B. M. McCarty and P. Worchel, "Rate of Motion and Object Perception in the Blind," *The New Outlook for the Blind*, 48 (1954), 316-322.

[96] C. H. Ammons, P. Worchel, and K. M. Dallenbach, " 'Facial Vision': the Perception of Obstacles Out of Doors by Blindfolded and Blindfolded Deafened Subjects," *American Journal of Psychology*, 66 (October 1953), 519-553.

97 P. Worchel, J. Mauney, and J. G. Andrew, "The Perception of Obstacles by the Blind," *Journal of Experimental Psychology*, XL (1950), 746-751.

98 P. Worchel and J. Mauney, "The Effect of Practice on the Perception of Obstacles by the Blind," *Journal of Experimental Psychology*, XLI (1951), 170-176.

99 *Ibid.*, p. 176.

100 D. L. Rouse and P. Worchel, "Veering Tendency in the Blind," *The New Outlook for the Blind*, 49 (1955), 115-119.

101 F. M. Norton, *Training Hearing to Greater Usefulness, A Manual* (Cleveland: Cleveland Society for the Blind, 1960).

102 Jerome and Proshansky, *op. cit.*, pp. 462-494.

103 *Ibid.*, p. 473.

104 D. R. Griffin, *Listening in the Dark* (New Haven: Yale University Press, 1958), pp. 297-322.

105 *Ibid.*, p. 320.

106 B. Lowenfeld, "Psychological Foundation," *op. cit.*, pp. 94-96.

107 Cutsforth, *The Blind in School and Society*, *op. cit.*, p. 73.

108 B. Lowenfeld, "Psychological Foundation," *op. cit.*, pp. 94-96.

109 *Dictionary of Psychology*, ed. Howard C. Warren (Boston: Houghton Mifflin Company, 1934), p. 189.

110 *Ibid.*, p. 154.

111 Villey, *op. cit.*, p. 126.

112 S. Finestone, I. F. Lukoff, and M. Whiteman, *Aspects of the Travel Adjustment of Blind Persons* (New York: American Foundation for the Blind, 1960).

113 P. Worchel, *Space Perception and Orientation in the Blind*, Psychological Monographs: General and Applied (Washington: American Psychological Association, 1951), LXV.

114 J. Drever, "Early Learning and the Perception of Space," *American Journal of Psychology*, 68 (December 1955), 605-614.

115 J. McReynolds and P. Worchel, "Geographic Orientation in the Blind," *Journal of General Psychology*, 51 (1951), 221-236.

116 R. J. Garry and A. Ascarelli, "Teaching Topographical Orientation and Spatial Organization to Congenitally Blind Children," *Journal of Education*, 143 (1960), 1-48.

117 H. L. Koch and J. Ufkess, "A Comparative Study of Stylus Maze Learning by Blind and Seeing Subjects," *Journal of Experimental Psychology*, IX (1926), 118-131.

118 J. R. Knotts and W. R. Miles, "The Maze-Learning Ability of Blind Compared with Sighted Children," *Journal of Genetic Psychology*, XXXVI (1929), 21-50.

119 R. V. Merry and F. K. Merry, "The Finger Maze as a Supplementary Test of Intelligence for Blind Children," *Journal of Genetic Psychology*, XLIV (1934), 227-230.

120 B. K. Duncan, "A Comparative Study of Finger-Maze Learning by Blind and Sighted Subjects," *Journal of Genetic Psychology*, XLIV (1934), 69-94.

121 D. C. MacFarland, "An Exploratory Study Comparing the Maze Learning Ability of Blind and Sighted Subjects," *The New Outlook for the Blind*, XLVI (1952), 259-263.

122 V. Lowenfeld, *Nature of Creative Activity*, *op. cit.*, pp. 115-124.

123 J. Berg and P. Worchel, "Sensory Contributions to Human Maze Learning: A Comparison of Matched Blind, Deaf, and Normals," *Journal of General Psychology*, 54 (1956), 81-93.

124 Barker, *et al.*, *op. cit.*, p. 276.

125 H. Rusalem, "The Environmental Supports of Public Attitudes toward the Blind," *Outlook for the Blind*, 44 (1950), 277-288.

126 *Ibid.*, p. 287.

127 Chevigny and Braverman, *op. cit.*

128 G. Schauer, "Motivation of Attitudes Toward Blindness," in *Attitudes Toward Blindness* (New York: American Foundation for the Blind, 1951), pp. 5-10.

129 Joseph S. Himes, Jr., "Some Concepts of Blindness in American Culture," in

Attitudes Toward Blindness (New York: American Foundation for the Blind, 1951), pp. 10-22.

[130] S. Braverman, "The Psychological Roots of Attitudes Toward the Blind," in *Attitudes Toward Blindness* (New York: American Foundation for the Blind, 1951), pp. 22-32.

[131] A. G. Gowman, *The War Blind In American Social Structure* (New York: American Foundation for the Blind, 1957).

[132] I. F. Lukoff and M. Whiteman, "Attitudes Toward Blindness—Some Preliminary Findings," *The New Outlook for the Blind*, 55 (1961), 39-44.

[133] Gowman, *op. cit.*, pp. 64-96.

[134] Lukoff and Whiteman, *op. cit.*

[135] V. S. Sommers, *The Influence of Parental Attitudes and Social Environment on the Personality Development of the Adolescent Blind* (New York: American Foundation for the Blind, 1944).

[136] *Ibid.*, p. 1.

[137] *Ibid.*, p. 102.

[138] *Ibid.*, p. 103.

[139] L. Kanner, *Child Psychiatry*, 2nd ed. (Springfield, Ill.: Charles C. Thomas, Publisher, 1948), pp. 117-132.

[140] Sommers, *op. cit.*, p. 105.

[141] L. Meyerson, "The Visually Handicapped," *Review of Educational Research*, XXIII (1953), 476-491.

[142] C. E. Buell, *Motor Performance of Visually Handicapped Children* (Berkeley: Charles Edwin Buell, 1950).

[143] *Ibid.*, p. 59.

[144] H. R. Blank, "Countertransference Problems in the Professional Worker," *The New Outlook for the Blind*, 52 (May 1958), 185-188.

[145] A. T. Murphy, "Attitudes of Educators toward the Visually Handicapped," *The Sight-Saving Review*, XXX (Fall 1960), 157-161.

[146] H. Rusalem, "Research in Review," *The New Outlook for the Blind*, 56 (1962), 66-68.

[147] J. S. Himes, "Changing Attitudes of the Public toward the Blind," *The New Outlook for the Blind*, 52 (1958), 330-335.

[148] Cutsforth, *The Blind in School and Society, op. cit.*

[149] *Ibid.*, p. 70.

[150] *Ibid.*, p. 75.

[151] *Ibid.*, p. 130.

[152] *Ibid.*, p. 2.

[153] P. A. Brown, "Responses of Blind and Seeing Adolescents to an Introversion-Extroversion Questionnaire," *Journal of Psychology*, VI (1938), 137-147.

[154] P. A. Brown, "Responses of Blind and Seeing Adolescents to a Neurotic Inventory," *Journal of Psychology*, VII (1939), 211-221.

[155] H. McAndrew, "Rigidity and Isolation: A Study of the Deaf and the Blind," *Journal of Abnormal and Social Psychology*, XLIII (1948), 476-494.

[156] H. McAndrew, "Rigidity in the Deaf and the Blind," *Journal of Social Issues*, IV (Fall 1948), 72-77.

[157] *Ibid.*, p. 77.

[158] F. M. Jervis and G. M. Haslerud, "Quantitative and Qualitative Difference in Frustration between Blind and Sighted Adolescents," *Journal of Psychology*, XXIX (1950), 67-76.

[159] *Ibid.*, p. 75.

[160] D. H. Morgan, "Emotional Adjustment of Visually Handicapped Adolescents," *Journal of Educational Psychology*, XXXV (1944), 65-81.

[161] Brieland, *op. cit.*, p. 102.

[162] E. A. Fitting, *Evaluation of Adjustment to Blindness* (New York: American Foundation for the Blind, 1954).

[163] *Ibid.*, p. 73.

164 Barker, *et al., op. cit.*, p. 282.

165 N. Raskin and M. F. Weller, *Current Research in Work for the Blind; A Survey* (New York: American Foundation for the Blind, 1953).

166 D. Lebo and R. S. Bruce, "Projective Methods Recommended for Use with the Blind," *Journal of Psychology*, 50 (1960), 15-38.

167 H. A. Wilmer and M. A. Husni, "The Use of Sounds in a Projective Test," *Journal of Consulting Psychology*, 17 (1953), 377-383.

168 H. McAndrew, "The Use of Projective Techniques in the Personality Evaluation of the Blind" (Abstract), *American Psychologist*, 5 (July 1950), 340.

169 S. I. Dean, "Adjustment Testing and Personality Factors of the Blind," *Journal of Consulting Psychology*, 21 (1957), 171-177.

170 Lebo and Bruce, *op. cit.*, p. 35.

171 L. S. Cholden, *A Psychiatrist Works with Blindness* (New York: American Foundation for the Blind, 1958), pp. 49-57.

172 *Ibid.*, p. 56.

173 N. J. Cole and L. H. Taboroff, "The Psychiatric Problems of the Congenitally Blind Child," *The American Journal of Orthopsychiatry*, XXV (1955), 627-639.

174 *Ibid.*, p. 630.

175 G. L. Abel, "The Blind Adolescent and His Needs," *Exceptional Children*, 27 (February 1961), 309-310, 331-334.

176 B. Lowenfeld, "The Blind Adolescent in a Seeing World," *Exceptional Children*, 25 (March 1958), 310-315.

177 M. K. Bauman, *Adjustment to Blindness* (Commonwealth of Pennsylvania: State Council for the Blind, 1954).

178 A. G. Gowman, *op. cit.*

179 I. F. Lukoff and M. Whiteman, *op. cit.*

180 E. L. Cowen, R. P. Underberg, and R. T. Verillo, "The Development of an Attitude to Blindness Scale," *Journal of Social Psychology*, 48 (1958), 297-304.

181 B. A. Wright, *Physical Disability—A Psychological Approach* (New York: Harper & Row, Publishers, 1960).

182 E. L. Cowen, R. P. Underberg, R. T. Verillo, and F. G. Benham, *Adjustment to Visual Disability in Adolescence* (New York: American Foundation for the Blind, 1961).

183 R. P. Underberg, R. T. Verillo, F. G. Benham, E. L. Cowen, "Factors Relating to Adjustment to Visual Disability in Adolescence," *The New Outlook for the Blind*, 55 (1961), 253-259.

184 *Ibid.*, p. 257.

185 F. Jervis, "A Comparison of Self-Concepts of Blind and Sighted Children," in *Guidance Programs for Blind Children*, A Report of a Conference, ed. C. J. Davis (Watertown, Mass.: Perkins Institution for the Blind, 1959), pp. 19-25.

186 *Ibid.*, p. 23.

187 H. R. Blank, "Psychoanalysis and Blindness," *The Psychoanalytic Quarterly*, XXVI (1957), 1.

188 D. Burlington, "Psychic Problems of the Blind," *American Imago*, II (1941), 43-85.

189 *Ibid.*, p. 81.

190 F. Deutsch, *op. cit.*, p. 140.

191 H. R. Blank, "Psychoanalysis and Blindness," *op. cit.*, pp. 1-24.

192 *Ibid.*, p. 1.

193 *Ibid.*, p. 6.

194 Cholden, *op. cit.*, pp. 73-83.

195 *Ibid.*, p. 74.

196 *Ibid.*, p. 76.

197 J. Thompson, *Development of Facial Expression of Emotion in Blind and Seeing Children* (New York: Archives of Psychology, No. 264, 1941).

198 *Ibid.*, p. 41.

199 J. S. Fulcher, *"Voluntary" Facial Expression in Blind and Seeing Children* (New York: Archives of Psychology, No. 272, 1942).

200 F. Deutsch, "The Dream Imagery of the Blind," *Psychoanalytic Review*, V (1928), 288-293.

201 *Ibid.*, p. 293.

202 A. Costa, "Sogni Difanciulli Ciechi e Semiveggenti," *Rivista de Psicologia*, XXXIII (1937), 44-52.

203 L. Bolli, "Le Rêve et les Aveugles," *Journal de Psychologie*, XXIX (1932), 20-73 and 258-309.

204 H. R. Blank, "Dreams of the Blind," *The Psychoanalytic Quarterly*, XXVII (1958), 158-174.

205 *Ibid.*, p. 173.

206 A. Gesell, F. L. Ilg, and G. E. Bullis, *Vision: Its Development in Infant and Child*, 3rd printing (New York: Paul B. Hoeber, Inc., 1950).

207 *Ibid.*, p. 273.

208 J. Wilson and H. M. Halverson, "Development of a Young Blind Child," *Journal of Genetic Psychology*, LXXI (1947), 155-175.

209 K. P. Bradway, "Social Competence of Exceptional Children: III. The Deaf, the Blind, and the Crippled," *Journal of Exceptional Children*, IV (1937), 64-69.

210 K. E. Maxfield and H. A. Fjeld, "The Social Maturity of the Visually Handicapped Preschool Child," *Child Development*, XIII (1942), 1-27.

211 Hayes, *First Regional Conference, op. cit.*, pp. 26-30.

212 K. E. Maxfield and E. L. Kenyon, *A Guide to the Use of the Maxfield-Fjeld Tentative Adaptation of the Vineland Social Maturity Scale for Use with Visually Handicapped Preschool Children* (New York: American Foundation for the Blind, 1953).

213 K. E. Maxfield and S. Buchholz, *A Social Maturity Scale for Blind Preschool Children: A Guide to Its Use* (American Foundation for the Blind, 1957).

214 *Ibid.*, p. 8.

215 H. H. Sands, "The Psychological Appraisal of Young Blind Children," in Hayes, *First Regional Conference, op. cit.*, p. 26.

216 B. Lowenfeld, "Psychological Foundation," *op. cit.*, pp. 90-99.

217 Cutsforth, *The Blind in School and Society, op. cit.*, p. 6.

218 H. E. Totman, "Training Problems and Techniques," in *The Blind Preschool Child*, ed. B. Lowenfeld (New York: American Foundation for the Blind, 1947), pp. 57-72.

219 B. Lowenfeld, *Our Blind Children—Growing and Learning with Them* (Springfield, Illinois: Charles C. Thomas, Publishers, 1956).

220 M. B. Spencer, *Blind Children in Family and Community* (Minneapolis: University of Minnesota Press, 1960).

221 M. Norris, P. J. Spaulding, and F. H. Brodie, *Blindness in Children* (Chicago: University of Chicago Press, 1957).

222 *Ibid.*, p. 15.

223 *Ibid.*, p. 23.

224 *Ibid.*, p. 65.

225 *Ibid.*, p. 65.

226 Gesell, Ilg, and Bullis, *op. cit.*, p. 273.

227 Norris, Spaulding, and Brodie, *op. cit.*, p. 65.

228 A. H. Parmelee, Jr., M.D., "The Developmental Evaluation of the Blind Premature Infant," *A. M. A. Journal of Diseases of Children*, 90 (1955), 135-140.

229 A. H. Parmelee, Jr., M.D., M. G. Cutsforth, and C. L. Jackson, "Mental Development of Children with Blindness Due to Retrolental Fibroplasia," *A. M. A. Journal of Diseases of Children*, 96 (1958), 641-654.

230 A. H. Parmelee, Jr., C. E. Fiske, and R. H. Wright, "The Development of Ten Children with Blindness as a Result of Retrolental Fibroplasia," *A. M. A. Journal of Diseases of Children*, 98 (1959), 198-220.

231 *Ibid.*, p. 219.

232 W. R. Keeler, "Autistic Patterns and Defective Communication in Blind Children with Retrolental Fibroplasia," in *Psychopathology of Communication,* eds. P. H. Hock and J. Zubin (New York: Grune & Stratton, Inc., 1958), pp. 64-83. By permission of the publisher.

233 L. Kanner, *Child Psychiatry,* 3rd ed. (Springfield, Illinois: Charles C. Thomas, Publishers, 1957), pp. 739-742.

234 M. R. Green, M.D. and D. E. Schecter, M.D., "Autistic and Symbiotic Disorders in Three Blind Children," *The Psychiatric Quarterly,* 31 (1957), 628-646.

235 *Ibid.,* pp. 645-646.

236 E. G. Omwake and A. J. Solnit, "'It Isn't Fair': The Treatment of a Blind Child," in *The Psychoanalytic Study of the Child* (New York: International Universities Press, Inc., 1961), XVI, 352-404.

237 D. Burlingham, "Some Notes on the Development of the Blind," in *The Psychoanalytic Study of the Child* (New York: International Universities Press, Inc., 1961), XVI, 121-145.

238 *Ibid.,* p. 123.

239 *Ibid.,* p. 137.

240 Keeler, *op. cit.,* pp. 75-76.

241 L. Bender, "Schizophrenia in Children," *American Journal of Orthopsychiatry,* 26 (1956), 499-506.

242 R. A. Spitz, "Anaclitic Depression," in *The Psychoanalytic Study of the Child* (New York: International Universities Press, Inc., 1946), II, 313-342.

243 M. S. Mahler, "On Child Psychosis and Schizophrenia, Autistic and Symbiotic Infantile Psychoses," in *The Psychoanalytic Study of the Child* (New York: International Universities Press, Inc., 1952), VII, 286-305.

244 H. Barry, Jr., and F. E. Marshall, "Maladjustment and Maternal Rejection in Retrolental Fibroplasia," *Mental Hygiene,* XXXVII (1953), 570-580.

245 H. R. Blank, "Psychiatric Problems Associated with Congenital Blindness Due to Retrolental Fibroplasia," *The New Outlook for the Blind,* 53 (1958), 237-244.

246 J. Hallenbeck, "Pseudo-Retardation in Retrolental Fibroplasia," *The New Outlook for the Blind,* 48 (1954), 301-307.

247 P. M. Moor, "Blind Children with Developmental Problems," *Children,* 8 (1961), 9-13.

248 L. A. Bachelis, "Some Characteristics of Sensory Deprivation," *The New Outlook for the Blind,* 55 (1961), 288-291.

249 F. Clay, "Social Work and the Blind Child," *The New Outlook for the Blind,* 55 (1961), 321-325.

250 N. J. Raskin, "Play Therapy with Blind Children," *The New Outlook for the Blind,* 48 (1954), 290-292.

251 J. Rothschild, "Play Therapy with Blind Children," *The New Outlook for the Blind,* 54 (1960), 329-333.

252 H. Knobloch, R. Rider, P. Harper, and B. Pasamanick, "Neuropsychiatric Sequelae of Prematurity: A Longitudinal Study," reprinted with additions, from *The Journal of the American Medical Association,* 161 (1956), 581-585.

253 *Ibid.,* p. 10.

254 *Ibid.,* p. 7.

255 R. A. Harper, L. K. Fischer, and R. V. Rider, "Neurological and Intellectual Status of Prematures at Three to Five Years of Age," *The Journal of Pediatrics,* 55 (1959), 679-690.

256 *Ibid.,* p. 683.

257 W. M. Cruickshank and M. J. Trippe, *Services to Blind Children in New York State* (Syracuse: Syracuse University Press, 1959), pp. 80-82.

258 Barker, *et al., op. cit.,* pp. 288-290.

259 R. Pintner, J. Eisenson, and M. Stanton, *The Psychology of the Physically Handicapped,* pp. 259-260. New York, Copyright, 1941. Used by permission of Appleton-Century-Crofts, Inc.

260 W. Hathaway, *Education and Health of the Partially Seeing Child,* rev. by

F. M. Foote, D. Bryan, H. Gibbons (New York: Columbia University Press, 1959), p. 16.

261 C. E. Kerby, "A Report on Visual Handicaps of Partially Seeing Children," *Exceptional Children*, XVIII (February 1952), 137-142.

262 *Ibid.*, p. 138.

263 R. Pintner and G. Forlano, "Personality Tests of Partially Sighted Children," *Journal of Applied Psychology*, XXVII (1943), 283-287.

264 J. S. Livingston, "Evaluation of Enlarged Test Form Used with the Partially Seeing," *The Sight-Saving Review*, 32 (Spring 1958), 37-39.

265 *Ibid.*, p. 37.

266 C. Y. Nolan, "Readability of Large Types: A Study of Type Sizes and Type Styles," *The International Journal for the Education of the Blind*, IX (1959), 41-44.

267 T. H. Eames, "Visual Handicaps to Reading," *Journal of Education*, 141 (1959), 1-34.

268 E. Wallace, "Physical Defects and Juvenile Delinquency," *New York State Journal of Medicine*, XL (1940).

269 F. Blumenthal, "Physical Defects in the Genesis of Juvenile Delinquency," *New York State Journal of Medicine*, XLI (1941).

270 P. C. Benton, "The Emotional Aspects of Visual Handicaps," *Sight-Saving Review*, XXI (Spring 1951), 25.

271 M. A. C. Young, "The Partially Seeing," in *Psychological Aspects of Physical Disability*, ed. J. F. Garrett (Washington: Office of Vocational Rehabilitation Service Series, Number 210, n. d.), pp. 162-178.

272 "Social and Emotional Adjustment of School Children with Eye Handicaps," *The Sight-Saving Review*, XXVI (Fall 1956), 156-162.

273 F. Hackbusch, "Psychological Study of Partially Seeing and Children with Other Visual Problems," *Sight-Saving Review*, XX (Fall 1950), 157-162.

274 B. Lowenfeld, "Meeting the Needs of Visually Handicapped Preschool Children," *Sight-Saving Review*, XX (Fall 1950), 145-150.

275 H. R. Stolz and L. M. Stolz, "Adolescent Problems Related to Somatic Variations," in *Adolescence*, National Society for the Study of Education, Year-book XLIII (Chicago: University of Chicago Press, 1950), I, 95.

276 Cowen, Underberg, Verillo, and Benham, *op. cit.*, p. 122.

277 D. Brieland, "Personality Problems of the Blind and Visually Handicapped as Revealed by a Projective Technique," (Abstract) *The American Psychologist*, 5 (July 1950), 340.

278 H. Greenberg and S. Jordan, "Differential Effects of Total Blindness and Partial Sight," *Exceptional Children*, 24 (1957), 123-124.

279 F. M. Bertram, "The Education of Partially Sighted Children," in *Education of Exceptional Children and Youth*, eds. W. M. Cruickshank and G. O. Johnson (Englewood Cliffs, N. J.: Prentice-Hall, Inc., 1958), pp. 265-294.

WILLIAM M. CRUICKSHANK

Professor of Education and Psychology
School of Education, Syracuse University

6 Psychological Considerations with Crippled Children

CHILDREN AND YOUTHS who are disabled by an orthopedic impairment will be considered in this chapter. Thus a child who has a deformity that causes interference with the normal use of bones, muscles, or joints would come within the province of this discussion. Included are children with poliomyelitis, osteomyelitis, tuberculosis of the bones or joints, and those with congenital deformities such as a clubfoot or spina bifida; also children and youths who are handicapped by cerebral palsy, with the recognition that although this condition is neurological rather than orthopedic, the cerebral palsied child is frequently considered with groups of orthopedic children and many times is grouped with crippled children in educational and therapeutic centers. Except for certain comparative purposes, cardiac children, who sometimes are included in legal classifications of crippled children, will be excluded from the discussion, but are considered elsewhere in this book.[1]

Theories of the Impact of Disability on Adjustment

NUMEROUS AUTHORS have developed theoretical statements regarding the impact of physical disability upon social and emotional adjustment. Although considerable thought has been given to this problem, little concrete research in support of any of the theoretical positions has been undertaken or completed. Since there is little experimental verification and since no attempt has been made to interpret theory in terms of degree of disability, length of period of disability in the development of the individual, congenital disability versus adventitious disabilities, and other pertinent factors, little can conclusively be stated.

The author feels that the basic adjustment problems of the crippled child are the same as those of physically normal children of comparable chronological and mental development. It has been stated that, if one approaches the problems from a phenomenological point of view,

> It is seen that the physically handicapped child in his social relationships is, as are all children, attempting to insure not his physical organic self, but his phenomenal self, the concept of himself of which he is cognizant. Two types of problems are to be observed in the handicapped child from this point of view: (1) adjustment problems which might occur in the normal developmental progress of any individual who is simultaneously striving for expansion of self and for the maintenance of the self-concept already developed, and (2) adjustment problems which are solely resultant from the fact that a physical handicap is inserted between the goal and the self-desire to achieve such a goal.[2]

It is recognized that such a dichotomy is artificial, and that no such clean-cut separation of adjustment problems ever exists. However, "the failure to recognize the duality of the problem accounts for much current misunderstanding with reference to the handicapped." [3] It also frequently accounts for the fact that the lay person and many professionals continue to conceive of all personality problems of crippled children as an inherent part of being crippled rather than to conceive of many of the adjustive attempts of crippled children as part of normative development and of others as efforts on the part of the child during normative developmental processes to integrate the crippling condition and his understanding of it into his life space.

Field Theory

The difference in adjustment potentials of crippled and non-crippled individuals has been interpreted in terms of Lewinian field theory.[4] Figure 1-1, as depicted earlier by Meyerson, illustrates the problem under consideration. It illustrates the life space of a person (P) in his attempt to effect an adequate adjustment in a new social situation ($N.S.$) different from an old situation ($O.S.$) that no longer holds value for him. In the course of his attempts to adjust, numerous avenues are open to him— direct movement into the new situation as the result of no barrier (B) or as a result of his ability to surmount the barrier or the development of substitute satisfactions (see Figure 1-1) if the barrier is temporarily or permanently insurmountable. Within the limits of his culture and his self-concept, great freedom of adjustment is permitted the individual. In rare instances, when both the new situation and substitute situations are unattainable, the individual may escape from his life space entirely into one of unreality or psychosis.

> These avenues are not equally open to the handicapped person. In the first place the barrier to achievement for the non-handicapped child rarely remains the same in the attempts of the personality to adjust to different situations. For the non-disabled person the barrier may change as the situation and the self-concept are subject to or have experienced modification.[5]

The barrier for the handicapped child may remain the same. If the child conceives his physical disability as a barrier, organically or psychologically, to satisfactory adjustment, the barrier always remains the same regardless of the type of adjustment being attempted. Note that, as will be discussed later, not all handicapped children conceive of their handicaps as being restrictive in nature. The theory thus holds only in those instances wherein the handicapped child conceives of himself as being handicapped. As will be shown, however, this comprises a relatively large proportion of disabled children.

The situation is basically different for a physically handicapped child attempting

> . . . to move from an old situation ($O.S.$) which at the moment holds no value to the self ($-$) into a new life space ($N.S.$) which does hold value ($+$). The barrier (B) to successful adjustment is the physical handicap . . . which is irremediable in actuality or which the child feels is irremediable. When the *normal* personality was confronted by the barrier . . . one of his avenues for successful adjustment was that of developing substitute satisfactions which contained nearly the same positive value as the originally desired new situation. Substitute satisfactions comparable to the original goal region are rarely possible to the handicapped child, because the same barrier to the original goal region is also a barrier to the development of substitute satisfactions of a value ($+$) equal in any respect to that contained in the originally desired new situation. Thus the handicapped individual's personality, in addition to the possibilities of escaping the life space into unreality or retreating to protect the self, has added *negative* pos-

sibility of developing substitute satisfactions within the old situation life space. All of these avenues have little value ($-$) to the personality as the behaver conceives his needs. Thus a condition of continued frustration frequently is to be observed in the handicapped person.[6]

This situation is well illustrated in a protocol of a counselling situation between the writer and a 16-year-old adolescent boy, a quadriplegic handicapped by athetoid cerebral palsy.

> *Subject:* I just don't know why the doctors let me live when I was born. I'm no use to anyone the way I am.
> *Counsellor:* You feel that you are of no value to society and that discourages you.
> *Subject:* Yes, I know what I want to do and I can talk O.K., but every time I try to do anything I'm stymied. I can't walk or even eat without some help.
> *Counsellor:* You feel, because of your physical condition, that you can't do many of the things you want to do and you feel frustrated when this happens.
> *Subject:* It's worse than that. When I can't succeed in something and when I know I could succeed if I weren't a C.P. (cerebral palsy), I get more than discouraged because I'm so helpless. You're stuck and you hate yourself for being stuck.[7]

This young man represents the situation demonstrated by numerous handicapped persons in their attempt to obtain satisfactions when the handicap represents a barrier organically or psychologically. The handicap sets into operation a circular situation: "the handicap is the barrier to success; frustration results; attempts are made to substitute satisfactions for the original activity; the handicap is again a barrier; greater frustration results; more activity; more blocking *ad infinitum.* . . ."[8] While no experimentation has been undertaken to test the adequacy of this hypothesis, Lewinian field theory may explain the problem of adjustment which is faced by some disabled children and young people. The recent publication by Wright goes far to establish definitively the somatopsychological relationship (suggested in the preceding discussion) of physical disability to general adjustment and personality development.[9]

Organic Inferiority

The theory of organic inferiority as developed by Adler has close relationship to the problem under consideration. However, as one evaluates the research and later theoretical considerations in comparison to Adler's earlier writings, the implications for real understanding of the handicapped become somewhat vague. Alfred Adler originally hypothesized and assumed an undetermined, but specific, neurological basis between organ inferiority and behavior mechanisms of a compensatory nature.[10] In later writings, the psychic need for control of inferiority of whatsoever kind was added, although Adler continued to refer to the organic basis of feelings of inferiority as the central theme around which his concepts were developed.[11] The hypotheses thus become more indefinite and less subject to careful experiment or control, so that today his concepts, while important in stimulating further thought, have largely been supplanted by other ideas. To completely discount Adler's contribution, however, would be to do him a real injustice, for without question his contribution was an important one, and the impact of his writings has weighed heavily on the later thinking of his students and his associates. Crookshank [12] and Dreikurs,[13] among others, have individually contributed detailed reviews of Adlerian concepts. Crookshank [14] feels that an individual may recognize his inferiority on a "somatic level," a "sympathetic level," or on a "psychic level." He feels, thus, that in a child with a clubfoot, for example, the "other leg may . . . try to grow longer to compensate." From the point of view of either a functional or sympathetic level, he feels that the body may "assume" an attitude or posture as a compensatory mechanism. On the psychic level, the individual is more conscious of the disability or physical inferiority, and he will attempt to deal with it with whatever techniques he can. Dreikurs, following the careful evaluation of three cases in which he applies Adlerian theory, states, ". . . the life style of each individual is not only influenced by the disability, but in turn determines the final effect of any physical disability." [15]

He further states:

> Each handicapped individual formulates his own response to his disability in accordance with his life style, which can only be determined through dynamic psychological investigation. Alfred Adler developed a specific technique to determine the life style of each individual. This life style is developed in early childhood through the interpretation which the child makes of all the experiences and difficulties with which he is confronted. The disability is only one, although often an important factor. Not what he has— in heredity endowment and environment—but what he does with it, is important. Courage and social interest, or the lack of them, determine whether a disability permits a good social adjustment or leads to permanent failure.[16]

Dreikurs' last statement, while leaning heavily on and in defense of Adler's views, is in effect more closely related to concepts of mental hygiene and compares to the thinking of Allen and Pearson, who feel that behavior problems of crippled children are directly related to inadequate parental attitudes rather than to the child's inability to encompass psychologically the physical disability per se.[17]

Freudian Theories and Body-Image

Numerous writers have looked to the writings of Freud as a basis for their concepts regarding physically handicapped persons. Chief among these are Meng and Schilder. Schilder sees a direct relationship between the perception of the body-image and action. He states:

> Our study is primarily a study of the body-image which lies on the impressive side of our psychic life. But there are no impressions which are not directional and do not find at the same time an expression. There are no perceptions without actions. Every impression carries with it efferent impulses. Even this formulation does not emphasize sufficiently that impression and expression form a definite unit which we can separate in its parts only by artificial analysis.[18]

From this he concludes:

> Experiences in pathology show clearly that when our orientation concerning left and right is lost in regard to our own body, there is also a loss of orientation in regard to the bodies of other persons. The postural model of our own body is connected with the postural models of the bodies of others. There are connections between the postural models of fellow human beings. We experience the body-images of others. Experience of our body-image and experience of the bodies of others are closely interwoven with each other. Just as our emotions and actions are inseparable from the body-image, the emotions and actions of others are inseparable from their body-images. The postural image of the body must be studied, if we desire to gain a deeper insight into social psychology.[19]

Bender,[20] and Bender and Silver [21] have further contributed to Schilder's concept of the body-image. The latter, in particular, have related the theory to an understanding of the brain-damaged child. They point out that a disturbance in the body-image may occur at any period in the development of the individual or at any level in the perceptual or integrative growth of the person. "In its early development, emphasis upon one particular part of the body by disease or by the attention of others, creates an increased psychological value to that part which disturbs the body-image." [22]

While not wholly related to the physically disabled child or youth, the important work of Machover is in large measure based upon the projection in drawings of unconscious determinants related to the body-image.[23] Although little research has been done with drawings of crippled children or youth, Machover reports on the drawings of twenty orthopedically handicapped persons. She states that the preliminary findings were notable, and that the individual's projections of the disability into the drawings varied "according to the basic personality of the individual afflicted, the degree of disability, and the duration of disease, but important features of the subject's reaction to the disease were made graphically explicit in most of the cases." [24] Studies utilizing large groups of physically disabled persons are needed to supplement Machover's findings, but the clinical evidence drawn from single cases wherein body-image manifestations are apparent in drawings of the human figure are common experiences of clinical psychologists.

Examples of the relationship between unconscious motivation for body-image projections are to be observed in Figures 6-1 and 6-2.[25] The drawing in Figure 6-1 was made by an 18-year-old boy with a congenital amputation of the left arm coupled with a mild paraplegic ataxic cerebral palsy. Without fully elaborating the personality dynamics depicted in

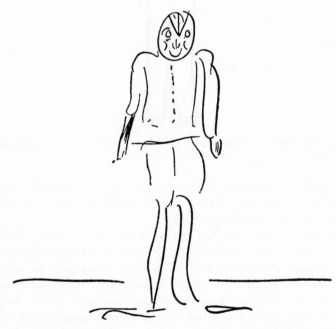

FIGURE 6-1. *Drawing of a man by an 18-year-old boy with congenital amputation of left arm and mild paraplegic ataxic cerebral palsy.*

the drawings, it is interesting to observe the treatment which is given the legs and the right arm in the drawing. The legs in the drawing are indefinite and generally appear useless. So too in reality, the subject's lower extremities were a source of worry to him insofar as gait and steadiness of locomotion were concerned. In a counselling session this boy commented, "If my pins would only go where I really want them to go,

I'd be a lot more satisfied." Although the boy's *left hand* is actually completely impaired, the drawing shows an incomplete right hand. Evidence of concern is depicted in interchange. It may be that in drawing the incomplete right hand, the boy is even more than in real life punishing himself for being handicapped, since the right hand symbolically relates to power and force. In the second drawing, Figure 6-2, the hands are again hidden from view. This drawing was made by an adolescent boy

FIGURE 6-2.   *Drawing of a man by an adolescent male with congenital deformities involving both hands.*

who also has a congenital deformity—one involving both hands. The usable fingers on the right hand include only the index finger and the thumb; on the left, the thumb alone.

Recently the author has had occasion to observe in another setting the impact of distortion of body-image concepts of learning and adjustment. Although insufficient data is available currently to substantiate the following statement, it is hypothesized that, until the child has a coordinated and coherent understanding of the body-image, learning in the form of reading and number concepts, for example, will either not take place or will be severely retarded. In working with a small group of hyperactive children, some with and some without the diagnosis of central nervous system impairment, it was observed that there was a close relationship in several children between the developing body-image concept as depicted in the children's drawings of a person and their initial development of reading and number concepts. In a group of forty such children, those who achieved most had well-developed body-image concepts and were able to depict these with accuracy. Those who did not achieve in reading and related learning areas, on the contrary, were those whose body-image concepts were immature or almost non-existent. It is the feeling of this author that there is a very close relationship between the two types of learnings. Until the child realizes that his total body functions in a coordinated way, that there is meaning and reason to the relationship of the several parts, and that each part has its separate and appropriate functions in relation to the total, learning of a socially acceptable nature apparently cannot take place. As these concepts enter the conscious understanding of the child, achievement may be observed to take place in the abstract areas of reading and arithmetic. Careful study of this situation should be undertaken, for if such is found to be generally true, there are major implications for pre-school and early elementary school and home activities, the goal of which would be the earlier development of positive and accurate notions of the body-image and self-concept. The unique relationship between self-concept and adjustment of many types has been emphasized also by Wright in her recent outstanding discussion.[26]

Any summarization of the Freudian formulations of Meng do him injustice, for without question much further consideration needs to be given to his understanding of the problem.[27] Both qualitative and quantitative research is needed for verification of his theory. Meng stresses the importance of the fact that with physically handicapped children a normal transition from the pleasure principle to the reality principle is frequently impossible because of the child's inability to participate in normal play activities. Little contact with reality through play brings the crippled child to an adult state of maturity too soon and without basic reality understanding. Meng also stresses the commonness of narcissistic pleasures among the handicapped group. As a result of his disability the individual lays claim to importance and distinction. He is different by reason of his disability, and as such, through such experiences as the necessity for undue physical exertion, pain, misfortune, fears, and other factors associated with the disability itself, the handicapped person considers himself in a position of uniqueness and narcissism.

Of considerable importance also in Meng's formulation is the factor of overcompensation, which, he points out, frequently occurs in handicapped individuals. Meng, however, draws a sharp distinction between overcompensation as he is considering it and overcompensation as a result of organic inferiority described by Adler. Meng is considering unfavorable parent-child relationships and unfavorable cultural-child relationships basic to compensatory behavior. As a result of too much parental attention or as a result of condescending attitudes on the part of society, for example, the handicapped child comes to feel inferior and unconsciously overcompensates so as to achieve psychic stability.

Closely related to this point is a second which Meng stresses. In keeping with Freudian concepts, stress is placed upon the close and intimate relationships between the child and his parents. The child comes to look upon the parent as the source of all his satisfactions and believes the parent to be the person who must supply all of the basic needs which he as a child feels. At the same time the child looks upon the parent (1) as the source of his handicap, which causes hate, and (2) also as the source of the solution to this handicapping situation, which results in ambivalence, since the emotions related to both roles in the same situation are distinctly different. Conflict and maladjustment ensue when the child is unable to rationalize the two opposing points of view confronting him. Often, when a satisfactory solution is not reached, the handicapped person is noted to resort to hypochondriacal solutions as a compensatory mechanism. The close relationship between the defect and the body structure increases the ego libido. As the individual feels rejected by the parent, by his peers, by the culture, the importance of this relationship becomes greater. As the need to protect the defect, the body, and, in fact, the ego itself becomes more apparent, hypochondriacal solutions are often used.

Other Theoretical Positions

The importance that Allen and Pearson place upon the parental attitudes as being basic in the development of healthy adjustment among handicapped children has been mentioned. Similarly, numerous other authors have made contributions to psychological theory relating to crippled individuals. Among these should be recorded the writings of Phelps,[28] Dembo,[29] Winkler,[30] Landis and Bolles,[31] Menninger,[32] Meyerson,[33] and Barker.[34] Clark,[35] also in psychoanalytic terms, has pointed out that the ego loss due to a somatic defect resolves itself in emotional compensatory behavior, while Kubie, in the same frame of reference, points out that the impact of the handicap will be the result of the interaction of three factors—reality, conscious fantasy, and unconscious fantasy and feeling.[36] Several studies based upon small samples of twins have in large measure supported the conclusion of Allen and Pearson, namely, that the impact of the disability is closely related to the adequacy or inadequacy of the parental attitudes which surround the child.[37, 38, 39, 40] Barker and his associates have summarized the theoretical assumptions which are proposed as etiological problems in individuals with physical disability: [41]

1. Compensation for inferiorities (Adler).
2. Easy narcissistic satisfactions deriving from pain and uniqueness (Meng, Clark).
3. Lack of normal plan and expressive actions (Meng, Wurtz [42]).
4. Easy cathexis to disabled part (Meng).

5. Unrelated anxieties transferred to bodily handicap (Meng, Stafford [43]).
6. Blame of parents (Meng, Allen, and Pearson).
7. Feeling of guilt for hostility toward parents (Meng, Winkler).
8. Body-image at variance with reality (Schilder, Bender).
9. Efforts to achieve social acceptance (Meng, Lowman,[44] Allen, and Pearson).
10. Dependent, demanding apathetic behavior deriving from over-solicitous protective situation (Meng, Allen, and Pearson).
11. Variable, conflicting behavior in response to variable, inconsistent attitudes of others (Allen and Pearson).
12. Goals beyond achievement possibilities due to pressure from parents, and to physical, social, and economic restrictions (Lord, Landis, and Bolles).
13. Conflict between withdrawal and compensatory tendencies (von Baeyer [45]).
14. Acceptance of disability as a punishment for sin (Winkler).
15. Retaliatory behavior for "unjust" treatment by nature (Meng).
16. Self-concept (Fishman [46]).
17. Degree of acceptance of disability by disabled person (Fielding [47]).
18. Value systems of disabled person and his associates (Dembo).
19. Cultural role of disabled person (Schneider,[48] Fitzgerald [49]).
20. Intergroup dynamics (Schneider).

Emotional and Social Adjustment

Studies of Adjustment

Information regarding the adjustment of crippled children in comparison to that of non-disabled children is, in general, unsatisfactory. Numerous studies in the literature point up differences in the adjustments of the two groups of children.[50, 51, 52] In most instances, however, such studies can be offset by others which generally show the converse of the situation—that the adjustments of crippled and non-crippled children can be favorably compared.[53] The situation is worthy of some detailed consideration. Cruickshank and Dolphin report the results of a study of the emotional needs of crippled and non-crippled children.[54, 55] These authors administered the Raths Self-Portrait N Test to two groups of children: one, a group of 87 crippled children; the other, a group of 193 non-crippled children. The group of crippled children consisted of 42 boys and 45 girls; the group of non-crippled children, 97 boys and 96 girls. The former included children handicapped by cardiac conditions, cerebral palsy, poliomyelitis, Perthe's disease, progressive muscular dystrophy, spina bifida, and other orthopedic or neurological impairments. Table 6-1 shows the mean scores achieved by both groups of children in eight areas of emotional need as included in the test. Of particular note in this

Table 6-1

*Significance of the Differences in Means Obtained by
Crippled and Non-Crippled Children* [a]

Need	Crippled Group n 87	Non-Crippled Group n 193	t-scores	Per cent level of significance of t
	Means			
Part A: Presence of Needs				
Belonging	3.46	2.88	1.4367	10–20
Achievement	4.45	3.81	1.4286	10–20
Economic security	3.90	3.97	.0147	90
Freedom from fear	6.37	6.07	.4517	60–70
Love and affection	2.56	2.28	.8505	30–40
Freedom from guilt	5.63	7.12	1.9487	5–10
Decision making	4.57	3.77	1.7010	5–10
Understanding world	4.99	5.99	1.5242	10–20
Part B: Fulfillment of Needs				
Belonging	5.92	5.82	.1558	80–90
Achievement	5.05	5.02	.0532	90
Economic security	4.24	3.83	.8888	30–40
Freedom from fear	4.09	4.43	.6730	50–60
Love and affection	5.34	6.19	1.2513	20–30
Freedom from guilt	3.49	3.47	.0488	90
Decision making	4.24	4.35	.2171	80–90
Understanding world	3.41	3.02	.9934	30–40

[a] By permission from W. M. Cruickshank and J. E. Dolphin, "The Emotional Needs of Crippled and Non-Crippled Children," *Journal of Exceptional Children,* XVI (1949), 33-40.

table is the fact that there are no statistically significant differences to be observed between the two groups of children.

The authors had earlier felt that the presence of a need to be free from feelings of fear and guilt would be predominantly characteristic of the crippled children,[56] but when the adjustment of the crippled children was compared later with normal children's emotional needs in these two areas, similar findings were obtained. It is the conclusion of this writer, in view of the findings of certain studies to be noted below, that objective tests such as the Raths Self-Portrait N Test and others used in earlier studies of the adjustment of crippled and non-crippled children are simply not sensitive enough to point up differences if they do exist. The objective tests certainly do not depict the possible differences in dynamics inherent in the quantitative results, and these quite probably differ between the groups. The objective test may contain too much of a threat to the child to permit honest responses; it may not anticipate wide enough scope of situations to produce answers that are typical of the child at the time he is completing the test; it may simply not be an adequate measure of emotional adjustment per se.

The Use of Projective Test Materials

Since practical experience with crippled children and the theoretical positions of previously discussed writers seemed to emphasize differences in the adjustment of certain crippled children, further study was given to this problem. Utilizing children from the same population as included in the Cruickshank and Dolphin groups, Broida and his associates made a more detailed study of the need to be free from intense feelings of fear, which was typical of both groups of children to a degree not noted in other areas of emotional need.[57] Broida administered a selected group of cards taken from the Symonds Picture Story Test, a thematic-apperception-type test, to three groups of crippled children: (A) a group where the need to be free from feelings of fear was over-met, (B) a group normal with respect to this need, and (C) a group where the need was not being met. The authors state:

> It is interesting that the children in Group C . . . produce the greatest number of social themas. Frequently these children expressed the desire in their stories for social acceptance and social participation. On the other hand the children in Group A, whose need to be free from fears was grossly over-met, also produce a large number of social themas. The significance of this is undoubtedly the same for Group A as for Group C. The earlier study of these children (Cruickshank and Dolphin) showed that the children of Group A were also those whose need for love and protection was, as was the fear factor, over-met. These crippled children who are overprotected to an extreme show in their themas hesitancy and insecurity about entering into social activities. The wish for social participation is nevertheless present. Conversely, children in Group C, whose fears were not alleviated, also expressed caution concerning social situations. The children of Group C produced almost four times as many social themas as did the children of Group B.[58]

A second area in which significant differences were observed between the three groups of children pertained to themas containing guilt. "Children of Group B, whose need to be free from feelings of fear is within normal limits, produce five times as many guilt themas as Group A and more than twice as many as the children of Group C."[59] The authors speculate that "morality is developed, at least in part, through social interaction both in and out of the family." Since the children of Group B (who were not impeded either through the presence of intense feelings of fear or through oversolicitation) were apparently emotionally free to move into social situations, the greater social participation and the lack of maturity to cope with the problems encountered in the social situations may have resulted in the production of guilt feelings. Since the children of Groups A and C were restrained from participation in social situations because of the factor of fear, no guilt was experienced and little, if any, was apparent in their themas.

Since Broida's study indicated that, with proper testing materials, differences are observable within a group of crippled children, Smock and Cruickshank, utilizing another projective-type test, studied differences between handicapped and normal populations of children.[60] The Rosenzweig Picture Frustration Study (Children's Form) was administered to matched groups of 30 handicapped children and 30 non-handicapped children. The groups were matched on the basis of age, sex, and intelligence. The handicapped children had a mean chronological age of 157.8 months (S.D.12.12) and a mean intelligence quotient of 93.73 (S.D.11.02); the normal children, a mean chronological age of 157.3 (S.D.11.39), a mean intelligence quotient of 95.57 (S.D.11.49). No statistically significant differences were obtained between the two groups on the matching criteria. Fourteen boys and 16 girls were included in each group. The handicapped group consisted of 15 orthopedically handicapped children, ten cardiac children, two partially-sighted children, and two hard-of-hearing children.

> One consistent difference between the groups is that the handicapped group responds to frustration in terms of its ego-threat value, whereas the normal children's responses were more in terms of reaction to frustration of a specific need or interference with immediate goal activity. The level of frustration tolerance of the handicapped child is apparently much lower than that of the normal child. Consequently, frustrating situations are likely to be perceived by the handicapped children as a threat to the total personality structure. This is not only true where the frustrating circumstances elicit a characteristic ego-defensive response from both groups, but is also the only area wherein a differential reaction is noted in the over-all comparison of two groups. Thus the handicapped child is likely to ignore the barrier to need-satisfaction and/or project blame and hostility upon the agent of frustration. The normal child is able to concentrate more of his attention upon the resolution of the problem with which he is immediately confronted.[61]

It will be recalled that Broida and his co-workers suggested that a desire for and a fear of social participation constituted one source of anxiety and fear reactions in the handicapped child. In keeping with this suggestion, one of the objectives of Smock and Cruickshank was to observe whether social relations did constitute an area of frustration in greater degree for the handicapped child than for the non-handicapped child.

Data from the present study confirm the findings of Broida *et al.*, and, furthermore, indicate that the handicapped child simply cannot tolerate any situation wherein personal inadequacy is . . . implied in the relationship. The lack of any difference between the groups' reactions to ego-blocking situations indicated that interference with goal activity is not significant enough to elicit characteristic group reactions. It is when an individual is accused of some offense by another person that the greatest differences between the groups are noted. In such situations the handicapped child manifests significantly more ego-defensive-extrapunitive responses. There seems to be no question but that the handicapped child is basically insecure in his relationship with others and that he feels quite inadequate in dealing realistically with external appraisal or criticism by others. The result seems to be that in these situations the handicapped child uses a characteristic defense mechanism, i.e., the projection of blame and hostility upon the interpersonal environment.[62]

Herein one sees partial verification of the retaliatory behavior which Meng says grows out of a feeling on the part of the handicapped that nature has been "unjust."

It should be stressed that, in the use of non-threatening projective techniques, basic differences in the adjustive mechanisms, in the emotional development, and in personality problems between crippled and non-crippled children become more apparent. The usefulness of the projective test is not a new observation, but its use in ascertaining differences in the dynamics of adjustment between handicapped and non-handicapped populations of children has not been too great.

Greenbaum and his colleagues have completed a study which indicates that care must be given in the selection of the stimulus materials in thematic apperception tests with crippled children.[63] Ray earlier had noted that the insertion into thematic materials of symbols of crippling, produced a variation in response patterns among a group of physically normal high school boys.[64] Greenbaum and his associates evaluated the Bachrach and Thompson modification of the Murray Thematic Apperception Test, which was intended for use with crippled children. The modification includes within the series of cards a number depicting symbols of physical disability—children with braces, wheel chairs, or other prosthetic devices. Utilizing carefully matched groups, the authors found that the introduction of the handicap per se into the stimulus pictures did not stimulate greater productivity on the part of handicapped children but, in effect, reduced the productivity significantly. Thus, although projective tests certainly have much greater clinical value than the objective materials used in early investigations with crippled and non-crippled groups, care must be taken in the selection of the content of the projective devices.

In keeping with the studies just reported, an investigation by Vivian

Harway is important.[65] The purpose of her study was to compare the behavior of orthopedically handicapped and physically normal children to determine the extent to which the children were able to evaluate their capacities in a situation and were able to set goals for themselves that were consistent with their capacities. She used two groups—eighty orthopedically handicapped children and forty physically normal children—matched for age, sex, and mental age. She employed two experimental situations: one, an intellectual task involving letter-symbol substitutions; the other, the Rotter Aspiration Board.

> The hypothesis that handicapped children would manifest behavior that was vacillating and inconsistent due to uncertainty in goal-setting situations was supported by the data. The low degree of association between the aspirations in the intellectual and motor tasks suggested, however, that both this variability and the tendency toward overestimation observed in the handicapped group were specific to particular situations or constellations of related situations and were not generalized behavioral approaches to the problem of self-evaluation. . . . The second hypothesis, that the handicapped child would be more likely to manifest unrealistic patterns of approach to the problem of self-evaluation, was supported in part by the experimental results. There was a tendency for more handicapped than normal children to utilize an unrealistically overambitious approach on both tasks. In addition, a greater proportion of handicapped than normal children used a confused and inconsistent approach on the intellectual tasks. However, the degree of similarity between the two groups in approach is so great that it cannot be said that this hypothesis was fully borne out by the data.

Here again one observes that in the careful selection of projective clinical test situations, differences in behavior and performance trends of crippled and physically normal children may be observed.

There is little question in the mind of the present writer that characteristic differences obtain in the adjustments of physically handicapped and normal children when considered as groups. This does not refute an earlier statement in this chapter to the effect that the adjustive problems of the two groups of children are basically the same. The problems to which both groups of children must adjust are in large measure identical. The techniques of adjustment and learning are comparable to both groups. The developmental processes of crippled children are considered to be no different than for normal children. The fact, however, that a physical and visible defect is inserted into the life space of the handicapped child constitutes a factor of adjustment that is not in any degree present in the physically normal individual. The manner in which the crippled child integrates the disability into his life space will, of course, vary widely, just as people demonstrate individual differences and uniqueness in most other human characteristics. This will become clearer in the following discussion of research related to the attitudes of the handicapped child toward his culture, and the attitudes of the culture toward handicapped individuals.

Attitudes of the Handicapped Child Toward the Culture

AMONG OTHERS, McKibben,[66] Franke,[67] Kammerer,[68] and Sohn [69] have reported studies which in whole or part deal with the attitudes of crippled individuals towards varying social situations. Stimulated by these earlier investigations, Cruickshank has reported on several aspects of this problem.[70] The value of the projective device has been commented upon, and therefore the projective sentence-completion test was utilized in the study now under consideration. An attempt was made to gain insight into the self-concepts of crippled children, into an understanding of the attitudes of handicapped children toward society and toward social situations, and into an understanding of the impact of the handicap upon the adjustment of the disabled child as the child evaluates the situation. To accomplish this, a projective sentence-completion test consisting of 45 incomplete sentences was developed. The test, together with a set of simple instructions, was furnished to personnel in six cities in the United States for administration to crippled children. A total of 264 handicapped children in junior and senior high schools cooperated in completing the test. The test was likewise administered to more than 400 junior and senior high school children who were physically normal. From the latter group, children were selected who could be matched with handicapped children on the basis of sex and chronological age. Known mentally retarded or borderline children had been excluded prior to test administration. A comparison of the results of the two groups of children was then made after the rough matching was completed. The composition of the group of handicapped children according to type of disability is shown in Table 6-2.

The quantitative results are important, but the qualitative aspects of the test results are also interesting and illuminating. For various reasons a number of the original 45 sentences were dropped from consideration in the final analysis. The remaining incomplete sentences and two children's responses to them are quoted as follows: [71]

Protocol of a 17-Year-Old Girl, Grade 10B
Handicap: poliomyelitis, left leg, and diabetes.

1. Most of all, I want to *get strong and regain my health.*
2. I'm afraid of *being in a dark room by myself.*
3. I would do anything to forget the time I *had the accident which most likely caused my diabetes.*

Table 6-2

Physical Disabilities Which Characterize the Children of the Experimental Group [a]

Disability	Number
Cardiac	75
Poliomyelitis	63
Cerebral palsy	40
Congenital deformity	13
Accident	13
Tuberculosis of joint, spine	10
Epiphysitis	10
Scoliosis	6
Muscular dystrophy	6
Osteomyelitis	5
Spina bifida	4
Perthe's disease	3
Arthritis	3
Hemophilia	2
Epilepsy	2
Pott's disease	1
Clubfoot	1
Dorsal kyphosis	1
Hyperthyroidism	1
Hypothyroidism	1
Diabetes	1
Frederick's ataxia	1
Hypercalcium	1
Hypocalcium	1

[a] With permission from W. M. Cruickshank, "A Study of the Relation of Physical Disability to Social Adjustment," *American Journal of Occupational Therapy*, VI (1952).

4. My father hardly ever *was sick in his whole life.*
5. Boys think I *can't run because I wear a brace.*
6. If people would only *stop looking at me, I wouldn't be so embarrassed.*
7. I know I could succeed if *I try hard enough.*
8. Girls think I *am very homely.*
9. My mother and I *get along very well.*
10. When there is a quarrel in my family, I *stay out of it.*
11. I could be happy if *I am not happy.*
12. I wish I could stop being afraid of *the hypodermic needle.*
13. People who watch me *are very nosey.*
14. Most girls like *boys.*
15. My mother hardly ever *misses work.*
16. When I am home with my family *I have lots of fun.*
17. I can *drive a car.*
18. My fears sometimes make me *worry.*
19. At times I have felt ashamed of *my bad temper.*
20. If my father would only *have lived longer.*
21. Other school children *walk to school while I ride a bus.*

22. When I am with boys *I don't know what to talk about.*
23. People who use crutches *are to be pitied.*
24. People who do things for others *are very nice and are the kind of people I like.*
25. When I am with girls I *find it easy to talk about anything.*
26. If I weren't blocked by *my poor leg I would ice skate and roller skate.*
27. My mother *tries her best to get me everything I want.*
28. Compared with others I *think I get around very good.*
29. I am worried about *my doctor.*
30. Try as I do, I *can't seem to find a way of avoiding things I don't like.*
31. I like to be treated *as a normal person should be treated.*
32. I think girls *of my age are less active.*

In the preceding responses one can see the impact of the girl's physical disability largely pervading her life adjustment. There are, of course, some responses which do not reflect the handicap. The general tone, however, of the protocol is one of personal concern and introspection. This is brought out strikingly when one compares the responses of the handicapped girl to those of a physically normal girl in the following protocol:

Protocol of a 17-Year-Old Girl, Grade 10
Physically normal.

1. Most of all, I want to *be a person who is fun to be with.*
2. I'm afraid of *being disliked or snobbish.*
3. I would do anything to forget the time I *had to come to school with a black eye.*
4. My father hardly ever *gets very angry.*
5. Boys think I *laugh too much.*
6. If people would only *judge people in and of themselves.*
7. I know I could succeed if *I became a social worker.*
8. Girls think I *am funny. (I hope.)*
9. My mother and I *are very close.*
10. When there is a quarrel in my family I *stay out of it.*
11. I could be happy if—*I am happy.*
12. I wish I could stop being afraid of *feeling self-conscious.*
13. People who watch me *make me feel self-conscious.*
14. Most girls like *boys.*
15. My mother hardly ever *gets real mad at me.*
16. When I am at home with my family I *do the dishes.*
17. I can *play the piano.*
18. My fears sometimes make me *think about them too much.*
19. At times, I have felt ashamed of *my previous actions.*
20. If my father would only *teach me how to drive a car.*
21. Other school children *go to school too.*
22. When I am with boys *I have a good time. I like to dance.*
23. People who use crutches *are just as good as anyone else.*
24. People who do things for others *are very considerate.*
25. When I am with girls *I have a good time.*

26. If I weren't blocked by *a guard I could make a basket in basketball.*
27. My mother *does the washing and I do the ironing.*
28. Compared with others, I *hope I'm not too bad.*
29. I am worried about *my Latin.*
30. Try as I do, I *am not always successful.*
31. I like to be treated *fairly.*
32. I think girls *gossip.*

It is not difficult to see the allocentric, extratensive characteristics of the latter protocol. Phrases which stimulated the handicapped girl to produce personalized, introspective sentences were often treated in an offhand, superficial manner by the physically normal girl, since the initial phrase contained no personal threat or implication.

General Considerations

Throughout the entire series of sentences, several factors merit comment. Almost universally, the physically normal children expressed either a positive or a negative feeling in completing the sentences, that is, they actually completed the sentence in some fashion meaningful to them. On the other hand, the physically handicapped children produced a larger statistically significant number of neutral, ambivalent, or nonsensical responses—or they entirely omitted responses. The latter almost never occurred in the responses of the normal children. This is interpreted as indicating the generally unsatisfactory situation in which physically handicapped children find themselves. The physically normal children, having had a continuous and varied series of contacts with many different aspects of society and involving numerous persons and situations, are able to evaluate and are able to react to social situations. Their reaction may be either positive or negative depending upon their feelings, self-concepts, and other psychosocial factors, but *the important fact is that they are aggressive and they do make a reaction of some kind.* The physically handicapped children, on the other hand, because of their markedly limited or curtailed opportunities for broad socializing experiences, are frequently unable to make appropriate responses or are unable to verbalize personalized self-expressions and self-concepts. Thus their responses take the form of neutral statements or statements which are ambivalent in nature; in many cases answers are completely omitted. This is an important and almost universal observation in the data under discussion.

Adjustment to Society

A number of sentences were developed to evaluate the adjustments of the children to broad social situations in which adults play an important role. A discussion, more detailed than with the remainder of the data, will be given to this phase of the study in order that the reader may gain an understanding of the type of data received from the two groups of children. Four stimulus phrases in the test were intended to produce evaluations of the child's social adjustment to people and society in general: (a) *If people would only . . .* (b) *People who watch me . . .* (c) *People who do things for others . . .* (d) *I like to be treated . . .* Table 6-3 shows the percentage of responses given by the children by category to these sentences.

Table 6-3

*Percentage of Responses Given By Subjects to Sentences
Dealing with Adjustment to Society* [a]

Sentence and Response Category	% Response Handicapped Group	% Response Normal Group	Critical Ratio	P Value
If people would only . . .				
handicap noted as an adjustment factor	7.5	00.0	4.69	.00001
miscellaneous	25.3	24.7	0.16	.88
no answer	2.8	1.5	0.97	.33
like me	38.3	52.3	3.30	.001
not pity me	1.7	00.0	2.13	.03
be more careful	3.9	8.5	2.13	.03
treat me equally	1.4	00.3	1.31	.19
mind their own business	18.6	12.5	1.96	.05
People who watch me . . .				
handicap noted as an adjustment factor	7.4	00.0	4.63	.00001
are nice	6.0	0.7	3.29	.001
are not nice	17.5	14.6	0.91	.36
make me feel bad	26.1	32.9	1.72	.08
pity me	2.6	0.3	1.98	.05
think I'm nice	11.9	13.8	0.66	.50
ambivalent in attitude toward me	0.4	0.3	0.12	.90
don't think I'm nice	5.5	10.8	2.19	.03
no answer	6.0	3.3	1.50	.13
ambivalence	0.7	00.0	1.17	.24
miscellaneous	16.4	18.7	0.71	.48
judge me	00.0	4.1	3.42	.001
People who do things for others . . .				
are nice	74.8	78.0	0.81	.42
aren't nice	1.9	1.1	0.74	.46
ambivalence	1.1	00.0	1.83	.07
no answer	4.6	2.2	1.45	.15
miscellaneous	6.1	8.3	0.97	.33
expect reward	11.1	8.3	1.10	.27
feel good	00.0	1.8	2.00	.05

I like to be treated . . .
handicap noted as an adjustment

factor	1.9	00.0	2.11	.04
nice	32.5	37.6	1.22	.22
no answer	4.9	1.1	2.66	.008
miscellaneous	7.6	5.2	1.12	.26
normal	2.6	1.1	1.20	.23
like others	34.9	26.1	2.18	.03
my age	5.7	1.9	2.18	.03
human	2.6	4.1	0.93	.35
fairly	1.1	7.0	3.47	.0004
equal	4.2	3.7	0.30	.76
like a boy	1.5	0.7	0.74	.46
as an adult	00.0	6.3	4.20	.00001
as a friend	00.0	2.6	2.60	.01
bossily	00.0	0.7	1.17	.24
badly	00.0	1.4	2.33	.02

[a] With permission from W. M. Cruickshank, "A Study of the Relation of Physical Disability to Social Adjustment," *American Journal of Occupational Therapy, VI* (1952).

In examining the responses to the first of these phrases,

. . . it is found that 7.5 per cent of the handicapped children's responses contain some reference to the child's handicap. As no such responses were given by the normal group, the *P* value associated with such a difference is less than .00001. As this sentence represents a wish and a wish with particular reference to adult society in contradistinction to society as represented by peers, the results point conclusively to the fact that adults are impressing upon the child an increased awareness of his physical disability. One may speculate by saying that perhaps a reason for the poor social adjustment of the handicapped child is the fact that members of adult society define the child in terms of his handicap. Another response to this sentence, "If people would only be nice," is given by 38.3 per cent of the handicapped children; by 52.3 per cent of the non-handicapped children (*P*, less than .001). Here both groups express rather strong dissatisfaction with adult society and a wish for improvement in relations with adults. One would probably expect, as a result of the relationship described in terms of the handicap above, that the handicapped group's responses would yield a larger percentage of such responses. However, there is apparently here a recurrence of the pattern observed so often in this study wherein the handicapped children, although showing currently poorer relationships with adults than do the non-handicapped children, seem to be satisfied with the status quo. The non-handicapped group, on the other hand, although seemingly better off in terms of adjustment with adults, is constantly striving for even better relationships.

The responses which indicate a wish for people to be nicer should, in reality, be added to other responses given to this uncompleted sentence which is similarly representative of a wish for better treatment on the part of adults and society. One such response, "If people would only treat me equally," is given by more of the handicapped children than non-handicapped children and is associated with a probability of .19. Here again there is evidence for the fact that adults are treating the handicapped child differently than the non-handicapped, and that such treatment can be attributed to the fact that a handicap exists. "If people would only not pity me" is found in 1.7 per cent of the responses of the disabled children and in none of the responses of the normal subjects (P, .03). The response, "If people would only mind their own business," is observed in 18.6 per cent of the handicapped children's responses; in 12.5 per cent, non-handicapped (P, .05). Thus, it would seem in terms of this last response that a good proportion of the children of both groups, and especially the children in the handicapped group, feel that there is too much adult interference in their lives. [This same finding obtained in the previously mentioned study by Dolphin and the present writer wherein it was noted that the need for love and affection was over-met in both the crippled and non-crippled groups of children.] Perhaps this is a further reason for the many negative feelings expressed by the children of both groups toward their individual parents and toward their families as a whole. In terms of this, the motivation can be understood for the last quoted responses on the part of the handicapped child, most of whose needs are taken care of by the parent. It will later be seen that these children have a strong need for independence and that this response, which is indicative of negative feelings toward adult interference, may well be a result of the fact that many handicapped children are not allowed to do things for themselves and may be over-protected by the parent.

Although both groups of children indicate a great deal of disfavor with adult society, in large measure a normal adolescent characteristic, the types of responses given by both groups seem to be basically different. Thus the responses indicating a wish for better relationships on the part of the handicapped group are responses directly connected with the handicap. In other words, the handicapped child is seeking better relations in terms of a hope that adult society will forget his handicap, ignore it.

In general, the remaining material in Table 6-3 serves to expand the concept discussed in the above paragraphs. One further aspect concerning social relationships warrants discussion, however. One of the sentences in this section began *I like to be treated.* . . . "I like to be treated nicely," is found in 32.5 per cent of the responses of the handicapped subjects; in 37.6 per cent, normal subjects (P, .22). Thus, one sees from this response and from the others below a strong wish to be treated somehow better and differently than they now are being treated. However, the reader shall see in the types of responses given by each group that the handicapped child wants to be treated *like others,* whereas the non-handicapped child wants to be treated *more than like others* and also in a positive manner. The non-handicapped children, having already attained the position of equality, are striving for something better. Evidence of these facts is seen immediately below.

The response, "I like to be treated not as a handicapped person," is seen in 1.0 per cent of the responses of the handicapped group and, as might be expected, in none of the responses of the normal group (*P*, .04). The handicapped group gives responses, such as, "I like to be treated normally" (*P*, .23); ". . . like others" (*P*, .03); ". . . equally" (*P*, .76); ". . . my age" (*P*, .03); and ". . . like a boy" or ". . . like a girl" (*P*, .46). The handicapped child is here observed asking to be treated as he is, namely, as a boy or a girl, and equally, as an individual of a certain age. He wants to be treated as others are treated. The non-handicapped children, however, give a different type of response, i.e., "I like to be treated as a human" (*P*, .35); ". . . treated fairly" (*P*, .0004); ". . . as an adult" (*P*, .00001); ". . . as a friend" (*P*, .01); and ". . . as the boss" (*P*, .24).

Examination of these latter responses given by the normal group subjects is evidence of the fact that these children are not seeking treatment in terms of the way others are treated as is seen in th case of handicapped subjects. Rather, they are seeking treatment in terms of specialized self-concepts, e.g., "adult," "friend," "boss," or "human." What the reader sees then is an expressed desire to be treated as special individuals rather than to be treated as others are treated. In addition, the non-handicapped children reveal their preoccupation with interpersonal relations in their desire to be treated as a friend or in other of the above categories. This latter is further emphasized by the fact that the disabled children once more produce more responses of omissions (*P*, .008) and more neutral responses (*P*, .26).[72]

Adjustment to Father and Mother

Four stimulus phrases were prepared to elicit feelings toward the father or father person; four others for the mother or mother person. In general both groups of children show a good relationship with the father or father person, although the physically normal children show a better relationship with the father figure than do the handicapped children.[73] On three of the four sentences relating to the father, the handicapped children give a statistically significant larger number of neutral responses indicating the difficulty which they are having in evaluating the relationship with their father. This may be due to the fact that the father is somewhat disrelated to the handicapped child, that is, he is away much of the time during the day and is interested in physical activities which are often impossible for the handicapped individual. It is also possible, although the study presents no evidence of this nature, that in the inability of the handicapped children to evaluate their father relationship satisfactorily, one gets a hint of possible rejection by the father or father person of the *handicapped per se* and thus of the *child* who presents the handicap.

In general both groups show a better relationship with the mother or mother person than they show for the father. The children of the handicapped group, however, demonstrate a more superior adjustment to the mother figure than do the physically normal children.[74] The handicapped are herein better able to define their relationship, and the children seem secure enough in their feelings to be able more adequately to make a critical evaluation of the relationship. Undoubtedly this is due to the fact that the handicapped children are of necessity placed in a closer relationship to the mother or mother person (nurse, teacher, physical therapist, occupational therapist, speech therapist) than are physically normal children. Dependency on the mother or mother figure brings the child into a unique and continuous feminine relationship which makes it possible for him to evaluate the relationship more realistically.

Peers

To the sentence, *Boys think I,* both groups show a strong positive feeling toward themselves. The percentage of responses in the "am nice" category for the physically handicapped children is 46.6; for the normal children, 40.1 (critical ratio, 1.53; P value, .12). However, in response to the same phrase, the handicapped children say "am not nice" in 28.4 per cent of their completions; the normal children, 45.4 per cent similar responses (critical ratio, 4.14; P, .0001). Here we see the handicapped children being less willing to be the recipients of negative feelings than are the normal children. In lieu of negative feelings the handicapped children give 4.0 per cent ambivalent responses, 3.3 per cent responses indicating the handicap itself as a barrier to peer relationships, and no answer in 7.0 per cent of their responses. Again one is impressed by the insecurity of the handicapped group of children in the face of possible recognition of feelings toward themselves. In general, however, the relationship of both handicapped and non-handicapped children toward boy peers is favorable, and, with a few minor exceptions, similar findings were obtained on sentences pertaining to girl peers.

Summary

With respect to adjustment of handicapped and non-handicapped children to general social situations, their parents, and peers, the following conclusions seem appropriate:

1. The adolescent children who have physical impairments dem-

onstrate better relations with the mother person than with the father person.

2. The handicapped children show a real interest in comparing themselves with others in an effort to determine their standings with others. This is considered a somewhat positive characteristic since it indicates that the children are maintaining a relatively aggressive attitude in social situations, but at the same time it indicates insecurity and anxiety in social situations.

3. The handicapped children indicate greater dissatisfaction with adults and adult society than do non-handicapped children.

4. The handicapped children frequently indicate a desire to be treated like other children rather than as children with handicaps.

A number of conclusions point to the fact that the handicapped adolescent group has difficulty in effecting happy social and emotional adjustments.

1. The handicapped children seem less able to evaluate interpersonal relations, and thus they produce many ambivalent and neutral responses and also omit many responses.

2. The responses of the handicapped group indicate a definite tendency to withdraw from social contacts and relations. The group is apparently satisfied with current adjustments despite the fact that the status quo is unsatisfactory in the area of social relations.

3. The handicapped children show fewer normal adolescent interests than the non-handicapped children, and they indicate that they are seeking substitute gratifications in fantasy.

4. The adjustment of handicapped children appears to be on a more immature level than that observed among normal children of the same age and sex.

5. The impact of the physical handicap is impressed on the disabled adolescents more by adults than by their peer group.

The normal group is almost universally characterized by factors which are essentially positive in nature.

1. The normal children show better relationships and greater identification with the father than do the handicapped children. The group of normal children, while showing less positive relationships with the mother than with the father, nevertheless shows greater and more positive relationships with the mother than does the handicapped group of children. More children of both groups show good relationships both with parents and with peers than show poor relationships. The normal group, however, shows a greater positive adjustment to parents and peers than do the handicapped subjects.

2. The normal group subjects seem better able to evaluate relationships with other people, both with adults and peers. There seems to be a better status quo arrangement for the normal subjects, but in spite of this they are continuing to strive for even better relationships. Their adjustment is characterized by allocentricity rather than self-interest as is seen with the disabled children. A critical evaluation of relationships is seen on the part of the non-disabled children as a part of a continuing drive for

self-improvement and a change in the status quo. Such a critical evaluation of social relations is observed to be absent with handicapped children.[75]

Fear and Guilt Feelings

A second aspect of the study dealt with an analysis of the sentences which related to fears and guilt feelings.[76] Nine stimulus phrases were developed in this connection. The writer was interested in this aspect of the total adjustment problem, since the degree to which fear and anxiety serve as motivating and inhibiting factors to all forms of learning is significant. Henri found that a statistically significant difference existed in the anxieties shown by crippled and non-crippled children on projective test material.[77] She utilized a relatively small sample in her study, but nevertheless the results are interesting and important. Further, in the earlier-quoted study by Broida, themas involving anxieties account for the third largest number of stories produced by the crippled children. Of particular interest with respect to fears are two stimulus phrases in the present study—*I am afraid of,* and *I wish I could stop being afraid of.*

> The first striking fact to be observed from this data is the strong fear of the handicapped group of their handicap. This is seen in the responses ". . . handicap," ". . . hospital," and ". . . disease." Other responses which are probably relevant to these in terms of fear of getting hurt are: "recreation," "vehicle," "aggression." The response of "being looked at" or "talked about" is likewise directly related to the handicap. The strong need for conformity and accord with the demand of society is seen in the responses of the non-handicapped children, i.e., *I am afraid of* "family," "people," "being alone in the dark," "war," "speaking before others," and "misbehaving." Although many of these responses appear in the handicapped children's completions, a greater percentage is found in those of the non-handicapped group.
>
> Further evidence of the immature and withdrawing type of adjustment which is made by the handicapped group is afforded by the responses, "dreams," the "unknown." The regressive type of adjustment characterizing the handicapped children is substantiated by the fact that the handicapped group gives larger percentages of those responses which we would expect from younger children. These include "animals," "water," "high places," and "fire." On the other hand, there is a restatement of the concern of the non-handicapped children which was seen in other aspects of this study with "education," the "future," and "success."
>
> It is most interesting to examine the possible dynamic differences produced by the different wording and interpretation of the two sentences. In one sentence there exists a plain statement of fact; in the other, a wish is involved, a wish to stop a definite threat. We would expect that responses threatening to the self would be suppressed when the individual was confronted with the state-

ment item. However, when the individual is given the task of completing the wish sentence, it is less threatening to him to state that of which he is afraid because partial relief is afforded him by the wish which, in a sense, reduced the threat.

If we accept this theoretical formulation, then, it is interesting to note that in 15 out of 23 categories of responses which are common to both of the items, percentages given per response by the handicapped group to the wish item are less than those given to the fear statement item. In two categories the percentages remain the same; in six, the percentages increase in response to the wish item. We can explain the decrease in percentage in the fifteen responses as due to the increase in the six responses which necessitated a reduction in other responses. Of the six items, one refers to recreation, and the decrease is only .3 per cent. Others are "omission" and "vehicles." However, the remaining three show greater increases and refer to interpersonal relationships. These are "being looked at" or "talked about," "people," and "family." What we may conclude, therefore, is that the handicapped group has a great fear of their position in interpersonal relationships, perhaps as a result of their lack of social techniques.[78]

The close relationship between guilt and fear has been recognized for a long time. Of the four sentences structured to sample feelings of guilt in the two groups of children, two will be discussed.

The first of these reads: *At times I have felt ashamed of . . .* "At times I have felt ashamed of my handicap" is found in 7.7 per cent of the responses of the handicapped; in 0.3 per cent of the non-handicapped (P, .00006). It is interesting to note that in addition to other responses which can be traced to the handicap, there also results the feeling of guilt at having a handicap.

The self seems to be that to which the most guilt is attached with both groups of children. "At times I have felt ashamed of myself" appears in 23.9 per cent of the completions of the handicapped, in 36.6 per cent of the non-handicapped (P, .001); ". . . ashamed of my behavior" is found stated by 22.8 per cent of the handicapped, 26.7 per cent of the non-handicapped (P, .30); ". . . ashamed of my personality" in 5.6 per cent of the handicapped, and in 1.0 per cent of the non-handicapped (P, .004); and "ashamed of my appearance" is found in 7.5 per cent of the handicapped and in 10.2 per cent of the non-handicapped (P, .08). It should be noted that the responses referring to being ashamed of the handicap are essentially similar to these responses indicating shame of the self.

Again, interpersonal relations seem to be an important area for both groups. For the handicapped group, the feeling concerning behavior toward members of the family, and especially the parents, is very strong. "At times I have felt ashamed of my ill-treatment of my family" is found in 6.3 per cent of the completions of the handicapped and 1.8 per cent of the non-handicapped (P, .008); ". . . ashamed of my family" appears in 4.5 per cent of the handicapped and 5.8 per cent of the non-handicapped (P, .50); and ". . . ashamed of people" occurs in 3.6 per cent of the handicapped and 7.6 per cent of the non-handicapped (P, .04). In the sentence, *I would do anything to forget the time I . . .* , the author is trying to ascertain what events in the children's lives they considered to be real traumas. The responses of the handicapped group are predominantly concerned with handicaps and the general state of health. Their handicap has produced tunnel vision in their perceptions.

Direct references to the handicap appear in 7.5 per cent of the responses of the handicapped and in none of the non-handicapped (P, .00001); references to injury constitute 13.2 per cent of the handicapped responses and 9.3 per cent of the non-handicapped (P, .15); allusions to being sick are found in 8.7 per cent of the handicapped and 3.7 per cent of the non-handicapped (P, .02); responses referring to time spent in the hospital are found in 7.1 per cent of the handicapped and 1.5 per cent of the non-handicapped (P, .002); references to accidents constitute 6.8 per cent of the handicapped and 20.4 per cent of the non-handicapped (P, less than .00001).[79]

Personal Aspiration

The effect of the physical disabilities on the aspirations of children was the final aspect considered in the evaluation of responses to the projective sentence-completion test.[80] In Table 6-4 are noted all the sentences to which the handicapped children gave a response directly related to the handicap. It will be observed that the sentences having the highest percentages of responses dealing with the handicap per se are those relating to personal aspiration. "*If I weren't blocked by* my handicap" is a response attributed to this stimulus phrase in more than a quarter of the children's responses. Similarly, 17.9 per cent of the handicapped children say, "*I could be happy if* I weren't handicapped." The impact of the handicap is clearly indicated in analyzing the responses of the group to sentences dealing with goals, wishes, and ambitions. The chief conclusions of this section of the study point to the following:

(a) The handicapped children express a wish to compensate for the limited scope of behavior imposed upon them by reason of a physical disability. (b) The handicapped children show a marked drive for acceptance. This factor has been observed in the self concepts of the handicapped children which referred to their adjustment to social situations involving peers, family, society generally and again in those situations which examined their feelings concerning fears and guilt. The handicapped children are striving for acceptance of a minimal nature. The normal children also desire to be accepted, but they are striving for something better than minimal acceptance. The normal child is not satisfied with the status which he now has which is already one of acceptance in

Table 6-4

*Percentages of Response to Sentences Which Relate Directly
to the Handicap*

Stimulus Phrase	Per Cent of Responses
If my father would only	.4
My father and I	.4
Boys think I	3.3
Most boys like	.4
When I am with boys	.4
If people would only	7.5
People who watch me	7.4
I like to be treated	1.9
I am afraid of	7.3
I feel most concerned about	5.5
I wish I could stop being afraid of	5.1
I am worried about	8.7
I am ashamed of	7.7
I would do anything to forget the time I	13.2
At times I have felt ashamed of	7.5
Most of all I want to	10.5
I could be happy if	17.9
I can	5.4
Compared with others I	8.3
I try	1.5
If I weren't blocked by	27.3

many areas. He strives for something better. The handicapped child on the other hand, not feeling that he has gained acceptance, strives for a feeling of minimal acceptance by society.

(c) Happiness, or a lack of personal happiness, is seen to depend directly upon the presence or absence of a handicap in a large number of instances. (d) The handicapped children evidence a need to engage in normal recreational activities. (e) Forty-seven per cent of the responses to one sentence by the handicapped children dealt with the handicap per se, recreational needs, and family adjustment, as opposed to 23 per cent of the responses of the normal children which were concerned with these categories.

(f) It is observed that the basis for comparison with others is a physical one, although there is a continuous insistence by the handicapped children that they are equal to others. Herein may be a vicious circle causing maladjustment in some handicapped children. There is a basic need to conceive of themselves as equal to their normal peers. The basis of comparison is physical. Upon being realistic, the handicapped child realizes his physical inadequacies. The reality of the situation coupled with his concept of comparison on a physical basis serves in combination to create an unsolvable situation. This fact is stressed moreover by the (g) finding that the handicap is recognized by the disabled children as a significant barrier, per se, to their success on whatsoever basis of evaluation.[81]

Hidden Versus Visible Disabilities

It will be recalled from Table 6-2 that among the children included in the group studied by the writer there were 75 children with cardiac disabilities. This group was large enough to warrant individual study. Of the original 75 children, four were excluded from this phase of the study because of illegibility of their responses; the remaining 71 cardiac children, with a like number of non-handicapped children, were matched in terms of age and sex as previously discussed. Two of the several areas discussed in the preceding pages with respect to the total group of handicapped children were re-evaluated with the cardiac group,[82, 83] namely, adjustment to parents and family, and fears. In general, it can be stated that the cardiac children responded in a manner much more closely related to the pattern of response of the normal children than of the handicapped children. Some findings are particularly interesting. Whereas the total group of physically handicapped children indicated a better relationship with the mother than with the father, the cardiac children, as did the normal children, indicated the opposite. It was stated earlier that the handicapped child's better relationship with the mother was probably due to the fact that the mother or mother person was the source of greatest assistance and comfort to the child. The cardiac children, however, because of the greater amount of time spent with the mother or mother person, may find her the source of numerous limitations. It is the mother who is constantly reminding the cardiac child to hold back, to stop running, to be quiet, or to rest. As such, the mother becomes a symbol of restraint, and thus the finding that the cardiac children function in this instance differently as a group from the larger group of physically handicapped children who have visible defects. Similarly, the finding noted earlier regarding ambivalence, neutral responses, and omissions did not pertain to the cardiac children. They, like the normal children, were much more able to evaluate their relationships than were the other crippled children. The authors point out that essential similarities rather than differences characterized the specific fears of the cardiac and physically normal groups. The cardiac children, like the crippled children, were differentiated from the normal children insofar as a fear of their handicap was concerned. In contradistinction to this, a greater fear of interpersonal relations characterized the non-handicapped group of children. The data did not indicate the regressive or immature behavior of cardiac children, as it had of the total group of crippled children when compared to their normal peers. In general, it was observed that the cardiac children did not show the degree of difficulty in evaluating their adjustment as did the total group of crippled children. It is hypothesized that this is due to the fact that the cardiac children are characterized by a handicap which socially is a hidden handicap. From an external point of view nothing in the visible picture serves to set this child apart from others. Insofar as society is concerned, the child is seen as normal in every sense of the word. Society accepts him as a normal member. The child does not have to feel different due to any barrier which his culture establishes. Thus he operates as a normal individual. It is only when the defect becomes a visible one that the handicap per se begins to have a serious impact on the adjustment process.[84] Earlier in this chapter statistically significant differences between the adjustments of handicapped and non-handicapped groups of children were noted. *Included within the former group were 75 cardiac children.* With the knowledge that cardiac children see themselves differently from other crippled children, the discussed differences undoubtedly have even greater statistical significance than reported earlier in the studies cited.

Attitudes Toward the Handicapped Child

SEVERAL INVESTIGATORS have reported studies dealing with the impact of the handicap on cultural attitudes toward disabled individuals.[85] However, the investigations on these problems which have dealt with children or youth are limited in number. Coughlin selected a group of 51 children from the files of the Detroit Orthopaedic Clinic.[86] In all cases the parents of the children were living and the attitudes of the parents were known to the worker. Coughlin finds four broad categories of parental attitudes. "The attitude considered most constructive was that of the relatively small number of parents who had sufficient intellectual insight and were so well adjusted personally that they were able, while fully realizing the implications of the orthopedic problem, to accept it and turn their attention and energies toward finding means of compensating for it." A second generally positive attitude was expressed by some parents who apparently had a "complete acceptance of a handicapped child on an emotional level with very little or no intellectual insight." A number of parents had an adequate intellectual understanding of the child's problem but emotionally were unable to provide him with complete acceptance. Thus these parents demonstrated such feelings as overanxiety, overprotection, and "overstimulation of the patient to accomplish more than he was capable." Finally, a group of parents were observed who neither intellectually nor emotionally were able to accept the child. These parents possessed both a lack of understanding of the physical condition of the child and "destructive attitudes" toward the child. Included among these latter were such factors as fear of surgery, fear that the child might get worse, fear of what society would think, and fear of inability to be economically independent.

Mussen and Barker also have reported a study on the attitudes toward cripples. While the study does not relate specifically to children or youth, the attitudes expressed toward crippled people in general undoubtedly apply to cripples regardless of age. The authors report on the results of ratings of 117 college students to a rating scale developed for the purpose of determining beliefs held toward the behavior characteristics of cripples.[87] On 24 personality characteristics the ratings varied from favorable to unfavorable. In general, the ratings concerning cripples were less favorable than "ideal ratings," although there were a few exceptions to this statement. Greatest variation was seen on such characteristics as "vitality," "self-confidence," "submissiveness," "realism," "aggressiveness," "social adaptability," and "sensitiveness." On each of these characteristics the ratings of attitudes toward cripples was in the unfavorable range.[88]

In an unpublished study with the present writer, Albert Wiberley and Linden Summers investigated the social acceptance of crippled children by their physically normal peers. Twenty-eight classrooms were located within a series of public school systems wherein no special programs differing from those planned for all of the children of a particular class were prepared for the crippled child. Twenty-nine crippled children and 807 physically normal children were included on the total class registers. Two crippled children were registered in one of the classes and the remaining 27 classes each contained one crippled child among the total group of children. To all of the children in the several grade groups the investigators administered a sociometric test to determine the degree of social acceptance or rejection of each child. The crippled children included those with poliomyelitis, cerebral palsy, congenital amputations, Perthe's disease, and other categories of disability. One finding of the study is pertinent at this point. Three classifications were made for the positions achieved by the children on the sociometric test through the responses given, that is, stars, neutral groups, and isolates. Among the physically handicapped children there were seven stars, seven neutrals, and fifteen isolates; among the physically normal children, 205 stars, 227 neutrals, and 375 isolates. When these two sets of figures are compared statistically there results a chi square of .342, which is, of course, not significant. There thus appears to be no difference in the rate of acceptance or rejection between the crippled and non-crippled children of these classrooms as demonstrated by the children's own choices. The factor of visible physical disability alone, in other words, is apparently not the basis on which acceptance or rejection of a crippled child is made.

Lord,[89] Kammerer,[90] Oettinger,[91] and Rosenbaum,[92] among others, have reported studies or have made comments regarding the intimate relationship between unfavorable parental attitudes toward crippled children and the development of emotional attitudes in such children. The closeness of the relationship is of such importance as to demand that in the study of the growth and development of crippled children, the parental attitude, the cultural attitude, and the attitudes of peers and siblings must be carefully evaluated. The impact of these attitudes on the maturation of the child must be noted and ascertained as one undertakes to provide the crippled child with experiences and activities which purport to enrich the child's life and to further his adjustment.

Intelligence

Studies of Children with Cerebral Palsy

Few studies of the intelligence of crippled children have appeared in the literature since the summary of Pintner and his associates in 1941.[93] An exception to this statement pertains to recent exceedingly important research in the area of cerebral palsy.

In 1946 McIntire reported the results of a study to which reference has been made by Phelps and by others.[94] Phelps suggests that approximately 30 per cent of the cerebral palsied group is mentally retarded as a result of brain damage; the remaining 70 per cent is normal "in the sense that these individuals show the normal spread of the population seen at large." [95] This statement has been widely accepted until recently when, simultaneously and independently, several studies have appeared—each of which is markedly similar to the others in methodology, treatment of data, and results.[96] Ann Heilman has compared the results of these studies in Table 6-5. It is interesting to observe the close similarity

Table 6-5

Comparison of Intelligence Test Ratings of Cerebral Palsied Children for Whom Ratings Were Determined in Five Recent Studies [a]

	Miller & Rosenfeld	Strong Memorial Hospital Staff	Asher & Schonell	Holoran	Heilman	Combined Data
	% of	% of	% of	% of	% of	% of
Estimated intellectual level.	261	90	340	133	178	1002
Mentally defective	49	43	47	36	47	45
Borderline dull	25	30	28	38	30	30
Average and above	26	26	25	26	23	25

[a] From A. Heilman, "Intelligence in Cerebral Palsy," *The Crippled Child*, XXX (1952), 12. By permission.

of the results of the five investigations and to note the results of the combined data. Among the 1,002 children included in the studies, 25 per cent have average or above average intelligence; 30 per cent, borderline-dull intelligence; and 45 per cent are in the mentally defective range. Fouracre reports similar findings in still another study, although his population was considerably smaller than those previously mentioned.[97] Likewise, Bice, in a study involving 992 cerebral palsied children, reports 487 children or 49.0 per cent with intelligence quotients between 0 and 69; 224 children or 22.5 per cent, between 70 and 89; 212 children or 21.9 per cent, between 90 and 109; and 69 children or 6.6 per cent, with I.Q.'s above 109.[98] All these studies have employed the 1937 Stanford revision of the Binet Intelligence Scale as a basis of their evaluations. It is recognized that the Binet-type tests are not the most satisfactory measures of intellectual evaluation for severely disabled children. However, the independent nature of the studies which have been cited, the knowledge that the psychologists involved in the studies were exceedingly well prepared for their responsibilities, and the increased understanding which clinical psychologists now have regarding the problems of mental meas-

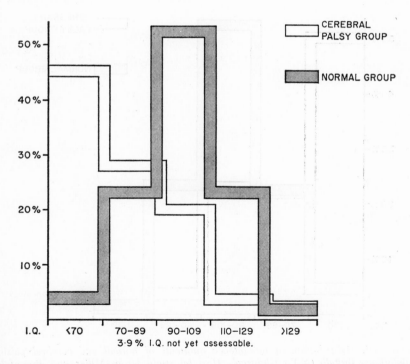

FIGURE 6-3. *Distribution of intelligence quotients of normal and cerebral palsied populations, British study [from Asher and Schonnel,* Archives of Diseases of Children, XXV (1950). *Reproduced with permission.]*

urement with handicapped children lend stature to these studies and credence to their collective findings.

The large population of cerebral palsied children reported by Bice, Hopkins, and Colton, and later analyzed in greater statistical detail by Bice and Cruickshank, supports the other studies with respect to the percentages of cerebral palsied children in the several classifications of intelligence. More important, perhaps, is the discussion of the latter authors which indicates no statistically significant differences between the major cerebral palsy classifications or between sexes with respect to intelligence. Some minor differences were noted particularly relating to the triplegia spastic group, but the meaning of these differences is not clear and is certainly not basic to psychological or educational planning. (It is recommended that the reader refer himself to an excellent discussion of intelligence and cerebral palsy which appears in Chapter 14 of *Cerebral Palsy: Advances in Understanding and Care* by Viola E. Cardwell. New York: Association for the Aid of Crippled Children, 1956.)

Taibl, utilizing the Raven's Progressive Matrices Test, examined 115 cerebral palsied children who ranged in age from six years to adult-

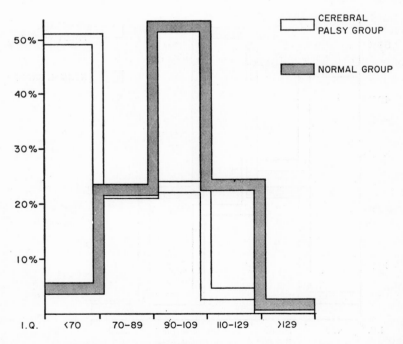

FIGURE 6-4. *Distribution of intelligence quotients of normal and cerebral palsied populations, Buffalo (N.Y.) Children's Hospital study [from Miller and Rosenfeld,* Journal of Pediatrics, XLI *(November 1952). Reproduced with permission.]*

hood.[99] The grade placement of the subjects was from Grade 1 through Grade 8 with the exception of Grade 5. No high-school students were represented in his study, although two university students were included. The group included 69 spastics, 6 ataxics, 1 rigidity, and 4 mixed types. Seventy-two of the children were educationally classified as either "special class" or "ungraded group." The findings indicated that the cerebral palsied children of Taibl's group ranged from intellectually superior to mentally defective, the distribution not being a "normal" one. The performance of the spastic group was in keeping with the distribution of intelligence scores in earlier studies cited. The athetoid group, however, showed a close relationship to normal comparative groups. In general, the author concludes that the cerebral palsied children perform on the Raven's Progressive Matrices in a manner closely similar to that of other North American children. This points to the need for further examination of the problem since this is in contrast to the findings of Bice, Holoran, Heilman, Asher, Miller, and others. Taibl also states that he is encouraged in the use of the Raven's Progressive Matrices as a test for cerebral palsied children. A later statement by Banks and Sinha, however, indicates that the average reliability (0.88) of the Matrices is considerably smaller than that given by Raven and "appreciably below the minimum needed for a satisfactory test of intelligence." [100] With respect to validity, the findings showed that some of Raven's items have undoubtedly been badly selected and poorly constructed. Banks and Sinha point out that several items have little discriminative value and others are comparatively worthless. "The average validity, whether judged by internal or external criteria, was decidedly poor (0.54)." Other statements from this study require that opinions regarding Taibl's data be held in abeyance until further basic work has been done on the test itself, and then corroborative studies must be completed. Further, Taibl's study can hardly have been considered conclusive, nor was it intended as such by the author, since it deals with a relatively small heterogeneous population. The small number of children per type of cerebral palsy, the wide chronological age span, the limited number of children at any one chronological age level, and the complete omission of children at certain age and grade levels necessitate that this study be considered as one pointing to new directions for investigation, but one which lacks definitive value. Thus, pending the publication of additional data, one must accept a rephrasing of earlier widely used figures regarding the incidence of mental retardation in cerebral palsy. Such data as that just cited require much serious thought with respect to their implications for education, therapy, and other social, psychological, and therapeutic programs for cerebral palsied children.

Studies of Intelligence of Crippled Children

As stated earlier, few recent investigations have been conducted regarding the intelligence of crippled children as a group. Lee reports the results of a study of intelligence of 148 crippled children in the Children's Orthopedic Hospital in Seattle, Washington. She utilized the Binet Test.[101] The age range of her group was between three and sixteen years; the intelligence quotient range, 35 to 138, with a mean of 86.8. Lee found that the children with poliomyelitis had the highest mean intelligence quotient score, 92. Children with "spastic paralysis" had a mean intelligence quotient of 69; tuberculosis of bone and joint, 88; congenital deformities, 61; and central nervous system involvements, 74. Witty and Smith have reported a study which included 1,480 crippled children.[102] They obtained a mean intelligence quotient of 84.5 with a range of from 50 to 130. Stanton,[103] and Gordon, Roberts, and Griffiths [104] present differing results with two populations of crippled children. The former, utilizing a group of 300 crippled children (which excluded cerebral palsied children), obtained a mean intelligence quotient of 88; the latter, a mean quotient of 103.9 from a group of 98 children with poliomyelitis. Fernald and Arlitt,[105] in one of the earliest studies reported, find a mean intelligence quotient of 82.35 and a range of 30 to 138 in a group of 194 crippled children, representing many different types of physical conditions, including cerebral palsy.

Practically all of the studies mentioned appeared prior to the publication of even the 1937 revision by Terman and Merrill of the Stanford-Binet Intelligence Scale. The 1960 revision of the Scale has a much more adequate standardization and, in general, is a great improvement in terms of items and administrative procedures over earlier forms of the same test. New studies need to be completed to provide information regarding the intelligence of crippled children on this scale. It has previously been pointed out that the intelligence range of children with cerebral palsy is apparently considerably different from that of the normal population and may, as well, be different from that of other types of crippled children. Hence, those studies which included cerebral palsied children within their populations need to be tentatively considered and need to be re-evaluated with populations which exclude this group of children. More and more information is being received from clinical observation and group study to the effect that crippled children cannot be considered as a homogeneous group insofar as psychological characteristics are concerned. Cardiac children, often included in group studies of crippled children, for example, appear to be characterized in many instances differently from other crippled children. Cerebral palsied children have already been discussed in this respect. It is very likely that other groups of crippled children will likewise have characteristics which distinguish one from the other. The impact of congenital defects on intelligence and personality versus adventitious disabilities needs to be seriously investigated. It can undoubtedly be expected that the intelligence level of some groups of crippled children will be below national norms or will have a different curve from that of the general population. Children who have been markedly restricted in their experiences and activities will, with the present instruments of evaluation, achieve lower-than-average scores. Children who have been restricted in their experiences through long periods of hospitalization and convalescence may be expected to show differences in intelligence scores and personality factors. Children who have suffered any sort of a cerebro-spinal involvement may be expected to achieve lower scores on tests due to the interaction in function of the cerebral cortex. However, studies which continue to group all types of handicapped children together, regardless of etiological factors or type of involvement, will add little to our present meager fund of knowledge of this problem.

The Binet-type tests and the revisions of them do have limitations in their application to disabled children. The preponderance of verbal material serves as a disadvantage to children with speech disorders or auditory impairments, while the heavy emphasis on motor activities in the remaining items often makes the test inappropriate for children with severe motor involvements. Such factors as these are basic to the criticism heard of the studies of the intelligence of cerebral palsied children noted earlier. Several authors have made serious attempts to circumscribe the criticisms of the Binet materials. Chief among these are Ammons and Ammons,[106] and Burgemeister, Blum, and Lorge.[107] Both of these groups of investigators have attempted to develop scales which require little or no verbalization and which can be completed through the utilization of gross motor activities rather than through the fine muscle movements required on previously mentioned intelligence scales. The attempt in each instance is to produce a scale which permits a more accurate evaluation of the innate ability of the crippled child and which reduces to a minimum the impact of the disability on test performance. Neither instrument has received sufficient use as yet to be able to ascertain accurately whether or not the goals of the authors have been achieved. The Leiter International Intelligence Scale was developed with the assessment of intelligence of physically handicapped children as one of its major goals. The test is ingenious in several of its parts; however, inherent in it is a major fault. The scale consists of dozens of items, many of which are composed of many tiny pieces to be placed together in a variety of ways. These pieces are so small, some measuring not more than one-half inch in width, that subjects with almost any degree of motor incoordination involving the hands are seriously restricted in their ability to participate in the test. As a test of motor performance the Leiter not only has all of the restrictions of performance tests generally but has intensified some of them to a point which renders useless an interesting and potentially useful instrument. These tests, however, together with careful modifications required on the Raven's Progressive Matrices may provide resources for clinical psychologists which in the future will permit more accurate research and greater understanding of the intellectual potential of individual crippled children.

Perception in Children with Cerebral Palsy

FOR MANY years psychologists have been interested in the effect of brain lesion upon learning, intelligence level, personality, and perception. Doll and his associates early pointed the relationship between birth injury, brain lesion, and mental retardation.[108] The universal effect of brain lesion is seen in Doll's statement that such may produce "(1) motor impairment, (2) retardation of intelligence, (3) disturbance of personality and conduct, and (4) consequent handicaps in learning." While Doll was not the first psychologist to be concerned with this problem, his organization of the problem stimulated many others to further consideration of it. Neurologists and psychiatrists likewise have contributed much to psychological understanding of this type of impairment.[109] Goldstein,[110] and Halstead,[111] who have worked primarily with adults, have also contributed much to the understanding of similar conditions in adulthood. Piotrowski,[112] and Harrower-Erickson,[113] also working with adults, have stimulated numerous later psychological investigations of central nervous system disorders through the use of Rorschach Test.

With children, Meyer,[114] Cotton,[115] Lord,[116] and Sarason,[117] among other research workers, have contributed important studies to the further understanding of the implications of brain injury for psychology. Werner and Strauss have made a remarkable contribution to an understanding of the impact of brain injury on the perception of exogenous mentally retarded children.[118] Since their work has received a penetrating critique from Sarason,[119] no further elaboration will be made here. Suffice it to say that while some limitations are inherent in the studies of Werner and Strauss, as Sarason points out so well, the importance of their contribution to psychology and education is exceedingly great. Further, it has a pertinent relationship to the cerebral palsied child.

Many of the contributions of the previously mentioned writers have directly or indirectly related to perception, and specifically to perception in individuals with brain pathology. Since cerebral palsy, in its numerous forms, is a cerebro-spinal condition, it has been the opinion of many that much of what has been written by these authors would normally also hold in a study of the psychopathology of children with cerebral palsy. It is recognized at the outset that the problem of individual differences is perhaps seen at its greatest among cerebral palsied children. Thus, there may be those who show marked degrees of impairment, psychologically, from brain injury, while others may show little or no effects of the lesion insofar as psychological growth, learning, and adjustment are concerned. This discussion will be amplified when the multiple-handicapped cerebral palsied child is discussed. Bender has stated, for example, that "cerebellar disorders often exist in relatively pure form and are not complicated with other perceptual or impulse disorders." [120] Later she states that "in some organic brain disorders, the ability to draw a man is not impaired due undoubtedly to different localizations of pathology." [121] The extreme variability of performance of brain-injured children and adults in psychological tests presents both interesting and sometimes baffling situations to psychologists and illuminates the paucity of accurate knowledge about these problems. Location of the lesion, extent of the lesion, innate intellectual capacity, and many other variables add to the complexity of the problem and make controlled research with large groups still to be desired.

Stimulated by the publications of Werner and Strauss relating to exogenous mentally retarded children, this writer has been concerned with their findings as they may relate to cerebral palsied children. In 1950 Dolphin [122] undertook a study of the psychopathology of cerebral palsied children which became the basis for later further investigation. As a preliminary study to ascertain the worth of further investigation, Dolphin obtained two carefully matched groups of thirty children each: one a group of cerebral palsied children; the other, physically normal children. The former group included children with a chronological age range of between eight and thirteen years, a mental age range from six to fifteen years, and an intelligence quotient range from 78 to 129. The mean C.A. was 10.02 years, the mean M.A., 9.55 years, the mean I.Q. (regressed), 93.46. The range for the physically normal children on the matching variables was quite similar to the cerebral palsied children, the mean C.A. being 10.17 years, the mean M.A., 9.57 years, and the mean I.Q., 93.66. Children were paired on the above bases and, as well, were matched by sex.

An experimental test battery consisting of six parts was administered to the two groups of children. In general, the results of these tests showed that the cerebral palsied children as a group differ significantly from physically normal children in several phases of perception.

The Figure-Background Relationship

The pathology of the figure-background relationship in individuals of all ages is an important differential diagnostic sign pertinent to cerebrospinal conditions and it has been recognized as such by clinical psychologists for some time. Rorschach himself commented upon the reversal-of-field phenomenon in individuals with organic pathology.[123] Since his first investigations with the cards later to bear his name, numerous others have commented upon this now common finding. Werner, in a study utilizing the Rorschach cards, noted the increased number of white-space responses perceived by brain-injured mentally retarded children and notes that this category of responses "was more than twice as high with the brain-injured in comparison to the non brain-injured group." [124] The Werner and Strauss study of the figure-background relationship stimulated a re-evaluation of their test with the cerebral palsied children in the present experiment.[125,126] Table 6-6 shows the results of the tachistoscopic presentation of nine stimulus pictures to the cerebral palsied and normal children of the Dolphin study.[127] It will be noted that the preponderance of responses of the normal children are those of the figure (either the correct figure or the incorrect figure, but nevertheless response to figure); those of the cerebral palsied children, the background (background with

Table 6-6

Comparison of Frequency Scores of Cerebral Palsied and Normal Groups for the Picture Test [a]

Type of Response	Cerebral Palsy Group Frequency Scores	Normal Group Frequency Scores	Chi Squares	Level of Significance
Correct figure	16	74	44.86	.001
Incorrect figure	8	56	40.84	.001
Background with correct figure	55	53	.0378	.90
Background with incorrect figure	97	60	12.36	.001
Background	94	27	47.8126	.001

a From J. E. Dolphin and W. M. Cruickshank, "The Figure-Background Relationship in Children with Cerebral Palsy," *Journal of Clinical Psychology,* VII (1951), 228-231. By permission.

incorrect figure and background only). A second test involved the children's matching an initial stimulus card with one of three other cards: (a) a card containing the background only, similar to that appearing on the stimulus card; (b) a card containing the original background with a different figure; and (c) a card with a different background and the original figure. While the difference was not statistically significant, a trend was observed in this test for the cerebral palsied children to select the card with the background only, whereas the normal children were differentiated statistically in their selection of the card which had the original figure but a different background.[128] The results of this portion of the study are in agreement with earlier studies of other types of brain-injured individuals to the effect that many of the cerebral palsied children have difficulty in distinguishing figure from background in a field which simultaneously contains both. The degree to which cerebral palsied individuals differ among themselves in this respect is not known from the reported data. However, the results indicated that not all of the responses of these children were psychopathological in nature and that individual differences were certainly present. Numerous cerebral palsied children responded in a manner similar to the normal children. For many cerebral palsied children, the figure-background differentiation is difficult or impossible, however and must be considered an important psychological characteristic of the group. Bender, in this connection, has stated that "perceptual or intellectual problems are due to difficulties in organizing or interpreting and appreciating the totality of perception, which leads to frustration due to poor relationship with reality." [129] Findings, almost identical to those described by Dolphin, are also reported by Klapper and Werner in the clinical reports of behavior of three cerebral palsied members of pairs of identical twins.[130] Also similar to the Dolphin study is the report of these latter authors with respect to the fact that the three physically normal members of the sets of twins responded to figure-background tests with predominantly figure responses.

An extensive study of figure-background relationships in the child with cerebral palsy is that reported by Cruickshank, Bice, and Wallen.[131] This study, sequential to the initial exploratory study of Dolphin, utilized large and relatively homogeneous groups of athetoid and spastic types of cerebral palsy children. One hundred fourteen athetoid and 211 spastic cerebral palsy children were examined and compared with 110 physically normal children. Chronological age, mental age, degree of stability, intelligence quotient, basis of physical diagnosis, and other variables were controlled.

In contradistinction to the earlier studies of Werner, Strauss, Dolphin, and others, the study of Cruickshank and his associates utilized a three-dimensional tachistoscopic method of presentation, the Syracuse Visual Figure-Background Test. The following findings, as reported by the authors, are significant in relationship to the present discussion:

   a. No sex differential was indicated in terms of the number of
      errors made by either sex within each age level within each
      diagnostic group.

b. Analysis of the number of slides correctly identified . . . revealed significant differences between the group means based on "number correct" scores for the three diagnostic groups; a mean of 7.04 for the spastic group, of 8.22 for the athetoid group, of 10.05 for the non-handicapped group.

c. Examination of the mean "number correct" scores at the various age levels for the three diagnostic groups revealed a fairly constant superiority of the non-handicapped group over the spastic group. The relative performance of the athetoid group, however, varied with age level approximating that of the spastic group at the younger ages and then approaching the performance of the non-handicapped at the older ages.

d. The spastic group made a significantly greater mean number of responses including reference to background (the number background score) than did either the athetoid or non-handicapped group. The difference between these latter two groups was not significant.[132]

It is the feeling of these authors that insofar as figure-ground relationship is concerned, the spastic group of cerebral palsy children presents the most significant problem, pathologically speaking, for the psychologist or educator. In general it can be stated that, if a learning problem is to be found in the cerebral palsy group, the problem will usually be most pronounced in the spastic subtype of cerebral palsy.

Visual-Motor Perception

A disturbance in the visual-motor relationship of brain-injured children has also been reported by Werner.[133] Marble boards similar to those used by Werner and described elsewhere [134] were administered to cerebral palsied and normal children by Dolphin. In this test one is able to ascertain to a large degree through the child's performance his method of visual perception. Although both groups of children utilized similar methods of visuo-motor performance, the trend established by the cerebral palsied children was toward a *constructive* and *incoherent* approach; the normal children tended to use a *constructive* and *global* approach in their responses. It is hypothesized that, as in the test of figure-background relationship, the cerebral palsied children were disturbed in their perception of the marble pattern (the figure) by reason of the large number of holes in the marble board and the marbles themselves, all of which constitute extraneous stimuli to which the cerebral palsied children find it difficult to refrain from reacting. Compulsivity to react, as described in numerous cited works, undoubtedly plays an important role in the performance of some of the cerebral palsied children of this study. A further evidence of the insecurity felt by the cerebral palsied children on the marble board test is gained when one observes that they moved marbles from place to place on the boards almost twice as many times as the normal children did. Further, it was observed that some of the cerebral palsied children, in an attempt to gain security in space on the marble board, compressed their figures close to the edge of the board itself and in numerous instances actually utilized the holes along the edge of the board as the point of departure for the remaining portion of the design on which they were working. So long as these children had the security and stability of an edge or fixed point, they could operate satisfactorily; when they attempted to operate in space in the center of the boards they were confused and were ineffectual in their efforts. It must be pointed out that these findings again pertained to an undetermined number of the cerebral palsied children. Nevertheless, this clinical observation involved a considerable proportion of the children. Similar behavior is also to be observed in the drawings of the Bender-Gestalt designs by two of the cerebral palsied members of pairs of identical twins reported by Klapper and Werner.[135]

The Cruickshank, Bice, Wallen study, to which earlier reference has been made, revealed a statistically significant difference between spastic, athetoid, and non-handicapped groups of children on the Marbleboard test. The median total error score for the spastic group was 23; for the athetoid group, 12.5; and for the non-handicapped group, 3. No consistent sex superiority was evidenced in this study. Examination of combined sex-age groups in terms of medians and proportions of perfect scores for "total error" and "total changes" scores respectively, supported previous findings of improved performance with increasing chronological age. These data further indicated that performance stabilized at an earlier age for the non-handicapped children than for the spastic or athetoid groups of children.[136]

It is felt from the work described above, and from similar observations which have been made with many adults having cerebral involvements, that the disturbance of visual perception and the inability of many patients to interpret visual stimuli into motor activity is another important psychological characteristic.

Tactual-Motor Perception

One set of form boards, consisting of raised wooden geometrical figures on wooden blocks, was presented to cerebral palsied and physically normal children.[137] A second set of forms consisted of the same geometrical figures—this time made up of large rubber-headed tacks surrounded by smooth metal thumbtacks pushed flat against the surface of the wooden blocks. The children, blindfolded, felt the surface of the blocks with their hands and fingers and then drew what they felt. In the first test situation there was marked similarity in the performance of the two groups of children. Even in this situation, however, where the background was purposely minimized, trends were observed for the cerebral palsied children toward *background responses;* for physically normal children, toward *figure responses.* However, in the second presentation, the results from the tactual-motor experiment were comparable to those obtained from the figure-background experiment noted before, that is, cerebral palsied children produce a significantly larger number of background drawings but physically normal children produce a significantly larger number of figure drawings. These findings from Dolphin's study are quite similar to the trends noted by Werner and Strauss in a comparable experiment with exogenous mentally retarded children.[138] In the Cruickshank, Bice, Wallen study of figure-background relationships, the non-handicapped children again performed significantly better than either the spastic or athetoid groups of cerebral palsy subjects on a tactual-motor performance test. This test involved a modification of the Bender-Gestalt test wherein Bender abstracts were converted into a tactual-motor test and administered to blindfolded subjects.[139] This study, which utilized large numbers of children, corroborated the findings of the earlier Dolphin pilot investigation.

Concept Formation

In their studies of concept formation with exogenous mentally retarded children, Strauss and Werner [140] had relied extensively on earlier work in grouping behavior reported by Cotton,[141] and Halstead.[142] Likewise, Dolphin modeled an experiment with cerebral palsied children, following these earlier investigators.[143] The Cruickshank-Bice-Wallen study did not extend itself to the problem of concept formation. Hence, no corroborative data to the Dolphin investigation is available from this source. The close relationship between the findings of Strauss, Werner, Halstead, Cotton, and Dolphin should be noted. Dolphin requested children to place before one of two pictures objects which they felt were appropriate to the picture. A miscellaneous collection of 102 objects was available for the children to choose from. All of the objects were either to be placed before one of the pictures or discarded. At that point the test was considered completed. The cerebral palsied children placed a mean of 8.26 objects before the first of the two pictures; the normal children, a mean of 4.03 objects. To the second picture the cerebral palsied children attributed a mean of 27.63 objects; the normal children, a mean of 17.36 objects. Statistically significant differences were obtained in each instance. The much larger number of objects and the more frequent usage of uncommon objects by the cerebral palsied children corroborates the similar findings of Strauss and Werner with exogenous mentally retarded children. It is also in keeping with the observation of Cotton that cerebral palsied children differed from normal children in three ways; namely, through a wider range of individual differences of the type of response within a given test situation, a greater tendency toward concrete types of responses with less ability to shift to more abstract forms of behavior, and a greater tendency toward stereotyped responses. The second characteristic is one which Goldstein feels is typical of individuals with organic brain pathology [144] and which clinical psychologists have come to feel is an almost classic sign in psychological evaluations.

Dolphin, as did others in similar experiments, observed the cerebral palsied children reacting to the objects on the basis of secondary characteristics—soap was placed before one of the pictures because soapsuds could be waves. A burned match "is a toothpick because it has a sharp end on it." The selection of objects because of their secondary characteristics was also noted by Strauss and Werner with their group of brain-injured mentally retarded children; in the Dolphin study this tendency was rarely demonstrated by the physically normal children. The selection of larger numbers of objects, the utilization of uncommon objects, and the projection of the static situations into three-dimensional realities are all in large measure due to the forced responsiveness of the cerebral palsied children to stimuli and to compulsivity characteristic of so many brain-injured individuals. The latter caused the child to feel forced to utilize all of the objects in his grouping activities. Strauss and Werner had observed a marked degree of meticulosity among their brain-injured subjects. To a lesser degree this was also observed by Dolphin in the performance of the cerebral palsied children during the grouping test. It was, however, a reported clinical observation made of the cerebral palsied children when drawings were done in connection with the previously discussed tactual-motor test.

Summary

Dolphin's study has reported differences between the two groups of children, cerebral palsied and normal, in discrimination of figure from background, in visual-motor and tactual-motor perception, and in generalized concept formation. It was not known from her study to what extent all of these aspects of psychopathology were present simultaneously in a single child or whether or not certain characteristics appeared in some children while others were absent. However, the Cruickshank, Bice, and Wallen study minimizes the notion of a general perceptional impairment. In general this study reported low relationships between the four tests which were employed within the three diagnostic groups studied. "Though the diagnostic groups differ considerably with respect to level of performance, there is not much evidence of individuals with over-all perceptual 'problems.'" [145] This fact would certainly emphasize the group importance of careful assessment and evaluation by competent clinicians of each cerebral palsied child and the necessity of adequate assessment information before educators can adequately prepare optimal learning situations for these children.

In addition to the differences already noted and discussed, certain other psychopathological characteristics were observed in the behavior of some of the cerebral palsied children. *Perseveration* was quite common among the cerebral palsied children. The impact of certain perceptions was observed to influence subsequent performance and activities of numerous occasions. *Dissociation,* the inability to relate objects in a unified Gestalt, has been observed by many investigators in the drawings by cerebral palsied children and during their performance on the marble boards. This does not appear to be a function of motor dysfunction due to gross motor impairment per se. Klapper and Werner likewise have reported this as a characteristic of varying degrees of severity in the cerebral palsied members of the pairs of identical twins whom they studied.[146]

The studies of Werner and Strauss, of Dolphin, and of Cruickshank, Bice and Wallen, and others tend to corroborate one another extensively. Further psychological studies reported in an educational demonstration lend further credence to the data reported herein.[147] In general it can be stated that statistically significant differences do obtain between groups of children with some type of central nervous system disorder and comparable groups of children without such disabilities. The implication of these findings, however, for learning and learning situations is still subject to much more needed research. The early reports of Strauss and Lehtinen, based on studies by Strauss and Werner, point out the necessity of significant modifications in the learning situation itself and in the educational methodology employed. The studies of Cruickshank and his associates referred to previously and the study of Gallagher [148] corroborate statistically much of what was suggested as important by Strauss, Werner, and Lehtinen. Certain other studies, however, demonstrate no difference or exceedingly minimal differences between populations of children with central nervous system disorders and those of normal physique. Studies by Capobianco and Funk [149] and Capobianco and Miller [150] are examples in this instance. These two studies, like the early studies of Strauss and Werner, were concerned essentially with the learning characteristics of exogenous and endogenous groups of mentally retarded children. In general no statistically significant differences were noted between the groups of children studied.

On the surface it would appear that the studies of Capobianco, Funk, and Miller were in opposition to the previous studies which have been discussed in this section of the chapter. Essentially, this author feels that there are inherent criticisms in the latter studies. On the other hand, to a degree they substantiate earlier findings.

From the point of view of critique, two factors which stand out in the studies by Capobianco and his associates must be considered, for they minimize the importance of the findings and impose serious limitations if comparisons are made with earlier studies. The studies of Dolphin utilized children up to a maximum chronological age of 16 years. The studies of Strauss and Werner were essentially limited to children between the chronological ages of 12 and 18 years. The studies by Cruickshank, Bice, and Wallen employed children between 6 years and 15 years 11 months. The later study by Cruickshank, Bentzen, Ratzeberg, and Tannhauser utilized children between the chronological ages of 7 and 11 years. The studies by Capobianco and his associates were, in effect, made on older populations, utilizing groups of subjects with chronological ages of 11 years seven months to 22 years of age (means in the range of 14 to 15 years). The heavy reliance on older subjects puts the findings of these authors in a position where comparisons cannot easily be made. The studies of Cruickshank, Bice, and Wallen, utilizing the Syracuse Visual Figure Background Test, indicate that at least two groups of cerebral palsy children show a marked loss in amount of psychopathology as age increases. It would not be expected, on the basis of the latter data, that statistically significant differences would obtain beyond the chronological age of fourteen (Capobianco's mean) if comparisons were made with endogenous type children. Thus the findings of Capobianco *et al.* are to be expected and are in line with previous studies.

The more significant criticism of the Capobianco studies, however, pertains to the rough methods employed in grouping. Two items were used. The Riggs and Rain classification system was employed in considering institutional records to differentiate the subjects into the two groups, that is, exogenous or endogenous. No neurological appraisal was employed. When one considers the generally unsatisfactory state of clinical records, the variability which may exist between medical and psychological diagnosticians, and the lack of reliability in a pencil-and-paper classification instrument, one has to reserve judgment as to the degree to which the two groups of subjects represented clear-cut differences and were indeed exogenous or endogenous. Furthermore, a second basis of grouping subjects involved the Syracuse Visual Figure-Background Test. A decision was made to define children as exogenous if they demonstrated four or more background responses on this test. While it might be assumed that all exogenous subjects produced four or more background responses, one has to raise the fact that numerous endogenous subjects may also produce four or more background responses. This fact, coupled with the crude appraisal through the Riggs and Rain system of the presence or absence of central nervous system disorder, makes it impossible to feel that two completely different groups of subjects were obtained; the results, therefore, must be questioned. One of the great needs in both psychology and education is for a carefully controlled study, longitudinal in nature, that seeks to study differences in psychopathology and achievement at various age levels from early childhood well into early adulthood. One of the values of the educational studies of Cruickshank and his associates was the availability of a unique medical-psychological-educational diagnostic team. The results obtained in this study can be compared to known quantified data. The children included in the study can be described with a unique degree of accuracy. Until similar careful diagnostic studies are made to precede psychological and educational investigations, the results of such studies will of necessity have to be considered tentative. In no way can the studies of Capobianco and his associates be considered comparable to earlier or later studies reported in this chapter. The data which are presented by the Capobianco studies are interesting and of value in the degree to which they corroborate the findings of earlier investigations regarding age changes.

The Multiply Handicapped Cerebral Palsied Child

The writer has commented previously in this chapter and elsewhere upon the problem of the multiply handicapped cerebral palsied child.[151] It is, however, such an important consideration for psychologists and educators that, at the expense of being redundant, further mention of the problem will be made here. Only three variables have been isolated for consideration in this connection, with the full realization that many others may be present in a given child and thus will have to be considered by the psychologist. The three which have been chosen for discussion are (a) the presence in the cerebral palsied child of other physical defects of whatever kind or degree, for example, impaired hearing, impaired vision, epilepsy; (b) the presence in the cerebral palsied child of retarded mental development; and (c) the presence in the cerebral palsied child of psychopathological characteristics of perception which are independent of mental retardation. Both of these last factors have been independently discussed earlier in this chapter. Table 6-7 illustrates the complexity of this problem and demonstrates the combinations of disabilities which may be observed in a consideration of the three variables which we have mentioned.

Table 6-7

Major Varieties of Multiply Handicapped Cerebral Palsied Children [a]

Type	Presence of Cerebral Palsy	Presence of Other Physical Defect	Presence of Retarded Mental Development	Presence of Perceptive Pathology
1	yes	no	no	no
2	yes	no	no	yes
3	yes	no	yes	no
4	yes	yes	no	no
5	yes	no	yes	yes
6	yes	yes	yes	no
7	yes	yes	no	yes
8	yes	yes	yes	yes

[a] From W. M. Cruickshank, "The Multiply Handicapped Cerebral Palsied Child," *Exceptional Children*, XX (1953), 16-22. By permission.

Type 1. This type simply involves the basic form of the disability, i.e., cerebral palsy of whatever variety and with no other physical or psychological deviations.

Type 2. This group of children includes those with cerebral palsy who also show defects of perception, but in whom there is no evidence of mental retardation or other type of physical disability. Type 2 in our classification of multiply handicapped cerebral palsied children constitutes a group about which we admittedly know relatively little at the present time. The validity of this clinical type is assured, however, in the opinion of this writer. Strauss and Werner briefly report findings which are subjective, but which were nevertheless gathered from the responses of a small group of children of normal intelligence and who demonstrated perceptive defects.[152] In the group of children studied by Dolphin and Cruickshank there were 14 children whose intelligence quotients were above 95. Within this group numerous children showed defects of perception which significantly differentiated them from their control subjects who were physically normal. . . . The prognosis for this type of multiply handicapped child is good educationally and psychologically provided the child receives his educational experiences in an environment which recognizes his basic learning problems,[153] and in the degree to which he can profit from a total program of physical reconstruction.

Type 3. This group includes those cerebral palsied children who show no physical handicap other than the basic one and who are free of perceptive disabilities but whose intelligence is retarded significantly. Psychologically these children appear like the endogenous mentally retarded children as defined by Strauss.[154] Many of these children show the classical symptoms of primary mental retardation, indicating that mental retardation might have existed even had cerebral palsy not been present. Such children, in addition to the physical characteristics of cerebral palsy (which are assumed throughout the remaining discussion of each type), exhibit lack of ability to form insight, poor comprehension, restricted memory functions, poor judgment, faulty reasoning, and limited problem-solving ability. These factors are those, among others, which characterize all primary forms of mental retardation. In general, each of the above factors will, of course, be accentuated in direct proportion to the degree of mental impairment. Both the rate of mental growth and the ultimate level of achievement, physical as well as mental, will be governed primarily by the innate mental ability of the child. While no adjustments are required in the learning environment, such as are suggested in connection with Type 2, the same sort of adjustments in curriculum and teaching materials are necessary as for endogenous mentally retarded children. Prognosis—educationally, psychologically, and to a somewhat lesser degree, physically—depends directly upon the intelligence level and the adequacy of the educational program. At best, the level of achievement is significantly limited.

Type 4. This group of cerebral palsied children included numerous problems of great seriousness. These are children who possess secondary physical disabilities other than cerebral palsy but whose intelligence is determined to be within normal limits and who do not show characteristics of perceptive difficulties. The frequency with which visual and auditory impairments accompany cerebral palsy is well known. Epilepsy . . . is common among children with cerebral palsy. As a matter of fact, there is no physical disability which might not also occur in conjunction with cerebral palsy. The degree of visual or auditory defect may, of course, vary from mild impairments to those of a profound nature. Epilepsy may take the form of petit mal or grand mal seizures.

Children who present this variety of multiple disorder constitute one of the most difficult educational and psychological problems of any to be mentioned. Teachers, psychologists, and medical personnel may well be confused with respect to the appropriate methods of education and physical training for these children. Secondary physical defects of mild degree may not constitute a serious block to the learning or to the adjustment of cerebral palsied patients. More involved physical defects, however, may seriously retard learning. Prognosis with Type 4 children is undetermined. Outcome is based primarily on the degree of severity of the secondary handicap and on the adequacy of the educational and therapeutic programs to cope with both primary and secondary disabilities. Educational methodology and therapy requisite to the secondary defect must, of course, be available to the child in order to insure even the most moderate psychological growth and educational achievement.

Type 5. With Types 5, 6, 7, and 8 the problem of multiple handicaps become more complicated. Cerebral palsied children in Type 5 category are those who have no secondary physical defects, but who demonstrate both retarded mental development and psychopathological perceptive functions. This group insofar as psychological development is concerned corresponds to the mixed category in the classification of mental deficiency as described by Strauss.[155] These children will demonstrate the psychological characteristics of both the exogenous and endogenous types of retarded children. Insofar as educational and therapeutic programs are concerned, this writer feels that the perceptive problems of exogeny will demand major consideration in program planning, in learning or therapy situations, and in teaching materials. On the other hand, the professional worker will also have to keep in mind those psychological characteristics briefly mentioned in connection with Type 3 which are typical of endogeny. Prognosis—educationally and psychologically—will depend directly on the level of innate intellectual ability and the extent of the cranial damage which has caused both the manifestations of cerebral palsy and those of exogeny.

Type 6. These cerebral palsied children are those who are characterized by secondary physical defects of a nature described in Type 4 who also show retarded mental development, but who do not have perceptive malfunction. It must be pointed out that to measure the intelligence of such children with accuracy is a most difficult operation since satisfactory instruments for the assessment of multiply handicapped children, and in particular, those with cerebral palsy, are not yet available. . . . When cerebral palsy, secondary physical disturbances, and mental retardation are found in combination, extreme caution must be exercised and careful periodic reassessments be made before a final decision is made regarding the mental level of the child. Even then accuracy in establishing a mental age may be impossible. If mental retardation is a bona fide diagnosis, then the prognosis for the child will depend upon the level of mental ability. At best, the outcomes, educationally and psychologically, may be significantly restricted.

Type 7. Type 7 includes those cerebral palsied children who have secondary physical disabilities and who also demonstrate the peculiarities of perception which have been commented upon above, but who are of normal intelligence. Prognosis here is better than in Type 6 because of the better intellectual ability of the child, although it, of course, depends upon the severity of the secondary physical disabilities. Experience has shown that some cerebral palsied children will superficially demonstrate auditory and visual impairments, but that in reality these may be manifestations of the perceptive difficulties and not actual sensory disorders. Such findings and observations would warrant careful and cautious psychological, audiological, and/or ophthalmological evaluations of cerebral palsied children to ascertain the exact etiology of the secondary physical manifestations.

Type 8. This final group of cerebral palsied children is one in whom are observed secondary physical disabilities, accurately diagnosed mental retardation, and the psychopathological perceptive characteristics. This group will constitute the most serious educational, social, and therapeutic problem. Prognosis will be exceedingly poor, and the possibility of any independent adult experiences will be significantly limited. Comments which have been made in connection with other appropriate groups of children will, in combination, all apply in this instance.

A classification of eight distinct types of multiply handicapped cerebral palsied children has been made. This classification is based upon the type of physical and psychological problem which the child demonstrates. It is a functional classification. Research of an educational and psychological nature is necessary with each type to determine the most adequate procedures which can be used to facilitate learning, social adjustment, and physical growth and development.[156]

Notes

[1] See Chapter 8.

[2] W. M. Cruickshank, "The Impact of Physical Disability on Social Adjustment," *Journal of Social Issues*, IV (Fall 1948), 78-83.

[3] *Ibid.*, p. 78.

[4] *Ibid.*, pp. 78-79.

[5] *Ibid.*, p. 79.

[6] *Ibid.*, pp. 79-80.

[7] *Ibid.*, pp. 81-82.

[8] *Ibid.*, p. 82.

[9] B. A. Wright, *Physical Disability—A Psychological Approach* (New York: Harper & Row, Publishers, 1960), pp. xx-408.

[10] A. Adler, *Study of Organ Inferiority and Its Psychical Compensation: A Contribution to Clinical Medicine* (New York: Nervous and Mental Disease Publishing Co., 1917).

[11] A. Adler, *The Neurotic Constitution* (New York: Dodd, Mead & Co., 1926).

[12] F. G. Crookshank, *Organ Inferiorities* (London: The C. W. Daniel Company, Ltd., 1936).

[13] R. Dreikurs, "The Social Psychological Dynamics of Physical Disability," *Journal of Social Issues*, IV (Fall 1948), 39-54.

[14] Crookshank, *op. cit.*, p. 49.

[15] Dreikurs, *op. cit.*, p. 50.

[16] *Ibid.*, pp. 52-53.

[17] F. H. Allen and G. H. J. Pearson, "The Emotional Problems of the Physically Handicapped Child," *British Journal of Medical Psychology*, VIII (1938), 212-235.

[18] P. Schilder, *The Image and Appearance of the Human Body* (New York: International Universities Press, Inc., 1950), pp. 14-15.

[19] *Ibid.*, p. 16.

[20] L. Bender, "Psychoses Associated with Somatic Diseases that Distort the Body Structure," *Archives of Neurology and Psychiatry*, XXXII (1934), 1000-1024.

[21] L. Bender and A. Silver, "Body Image Problems of the Brain Injured Child," *The Journal of Social Issues*, IV (Fall 1948), 84-89.

[22] *Ibid.*, p. 84.

[23] K. Mackover, *Personality Projection in the Drawing of the Human Figure* (Springfield, Ill.: Charles C. Thomas, Publisher, 1949).

[24] *Ibid.*, p. 26.

[25] See also drawings included in Z. S. Klapper and H. Werner, "Developmental Deviations in Brain-Injured (Cerebral-Palsied) Members of Pairs of Identical Twins," *The Quarterly Journal of Child Behavior*, II (July 1950), 288-313.

[26] Wright, *op. cit.*, chaps. vi and vii.

[27] H. Meng, "Zur Sozialpsychologie der Körperbeschädigten: Ein Beitrag zum Problem der praktischen Psychohygiene," *Schweizer Archiv für Neurologie und Psychiatrie*, XL (1938), 328-344.

[28] W. M. Phelps, "Description and Differentiation of Types of Cerebral Palsy," *Nervous Child*, VIII (1948), 107-127.

[29] T. Dembo, G. Ladieu, and B. A. Wright, *Adjustment to Misfortune: A Study in Social-Emotional Relationships Between Injured and Non-Injured People* (Washington, D.C.: War Department, Office of the Surgeon General, 1948), typescript.

[30] H. Winkler, *Psychische Entwicklung und Krüppeltum* (Leipzig: Leopold Voss, 1931).

[31] C. Landis and M. M. Bolles, *Personality and Sexuality in the Physically Handicapped Woman* (New York: Paul B. Hoeber, Inc., 1942).

[32] W. C. Menninger, "Emotional Adjustments for the Handicapped," *Crippled Child*, XXVII (1949), 4-7, 26-28.

[33] L. Meyerson, "Physical Disability as a Social Psychological Problem," *Journal of Social Issues*, IV (Fall 1948), 2-10.

[34] R. G. Barker, "The Social Psychology of Physical Disability," *Journal of Social Issues*, IV (Fall 1948), 28-38.

[35] L. P. Clark, "What is the Psychology of Little's Disease?" *Psychoanalytic Review*, XXI (1934), 131-145.

[36] L. S. Kubie, "Motivation and Rehabilitation," *Psychiatry*, VIII (1945), 69-78.

[37] R. L. Jenkins, "Dissimilar Identical Twins: Results of Brain Injury at Birth," *American Journal of Orthopsychiatry*, V (1935), 39-42.

[38] Klapper and Werner, *op. cit.*

[39] K. Bradway, "Birth Lesions in Identical Twins," *American Journal of Orthopsychiatry*, VII (1937), 194-203.

[40] H. W. Newell, "Differences in Personalities in the Surviving Pair of Identical Triplets," *American Journal of Orthopsychiatry*, I (1930), 61-80.

[41] R. G. Barker, *et al.*, *Adjustment to Physical Handicap and Illness: A Survey of the Social Psychology of Physique and Disability*, Social Science Research Council, Bulletin 55 (New York, 1953).

[42] H. Würtz, *Zerbrecht die Krucken* (Leipzig: Leopold Voss, 1932).

[43] G. T. Stafford, *Sports for the Handicapped* (Englewood Cliffs, N.J.: Prentice-Hall, Inc., 1939).

[44] C. L. Lowman, *Survey of the Vocational, Educational and Social Status of Poliomyelitis Patients* (New York: National Foundation for Infantile Paralysis, 1942), typescript.

[45] W. von Baeyer, "Zur Psychologie verkrüppelter Kinder und Jugendlicher," *Zeitschrift für Kinderforschung*, XXXIV (1928), 229-292.

[46] S. Fishman, "Self-concept and Adjustment to Leg Prothesis" (Doctoral dissertation, Columbia University, 1949).

[47] B. B. Fielding, "Attitudes and Aspects of Adjustment of the Orthopedically Handicapped Woman" (Doctoral dissertation, Columbia University, 1950).

[48] D. M. Schneider, "The Social Dynamics of Physical Disability in Army Basic Training," *Psychiatry*, X (1947), 323-333.

[49] D. C. Fitzgerald, "Success-Failure and TAT Reactions of Orthopedically Handicapped and Physically Normal Adolescents," *Personality*, I (1951), 67-83.

[50] F. Strauss, "The Initiative of the Crippled Child," *The Crippled Child*, XIII (1936), 164.

[51] A. Brockway, "The Problems of the Spastic Child," *Journal of the American Medical Association*, CVI (1936), 1635-1638.

[52] B. B. Rosenbaum, "Neurotic Tendencies in Crippled Girls," *Journal of Abnormal and Social Psychology*, XXXI (1937), 423-429.

[53] For example, see M. F. Gates, "A Comparative Study of Some Problems of Social Emotional Adjustment of Crippled and Non-Crippled Girls and Boys," *Journal of Genetic Psychology*, LXVIII (1946), 219-244.

[54] W. M. Cruickshank and J. E. Dolphin, "A Study of the Emotional Needs of Crippled Children," *Journal of Educational Psychology*, XL (1949), 295-305.

[55] W. M. Cruickshank and J. E. Dolphin, "The Emotional Needs of Crippled and Non-Crippled Children," *Journal of Exceptional Children*, XVI (1949), 33-40.

[56] Cruickshank and Dolphin, "A Study of the Emotional Needs of Crippled Children," *op. cit.*

[57] D. C. Broida, C. E. Izard, and W. M. Cruickshank, "Thematic Apperception Reactions of Crippled Children," *Journal of Clinical Psychology*, VI (1950), 243-248.

[58] *Ibid.*, pp. 244-245.

[59] *Ibid.*, p. 245.

[60] C. Smock and W. M. Cruickshank, "Responses of Handicapped and Normal Children to the Rosenzweig P-F Study," *The Quarterly Journal of Child Behavior*, IV (1952), 156-164.

[61] *Ibid.*, p. 162.

[62] *Ibid.*, pp. 162-163.

[63] M. Greenbaum, T. Qualtere, B. Carruth, and W. M. Cruickshank, "Evaluation of a Modification of the Thematic Apperception Test for Use with Physically Handicapped Children," *Journal of Clinical Psychology*, IX (1953), 40-44.

[64] M. H. Ray, "The Effect of Crippled Appearance on Personality Judgments" (Master's thesis, Stanford University, 1946).

[65] V. T. Harway, "Self-Evaluation and Reactions to Success and Failure Experiences in Orthopedically Handicapped Children" (Doctoral dissertation, University of Rochester, 1952).

[66] S. McKibben, "The Spastic Situation," *Journal of Speech Disorders*, VIII (1943), 147-153.

[67] K. Franke, "Erforschung der Krüppelpyche durch Selbstdarstellungen gebrechlicher Jungendlichen," *Zeitschrift fur Kruppelfursorge*, XXV (1932), 251-271.

[68] R. C. Kammerer, "An Exploratory Psychological Study of Crippled Children," *Psychological Record*, IV (1940), 47-100.

[69] D. L. Sohn, "The Psychic Complex in Congenital Deformity," *New York Medical Journal*, C (November 14, 1914), 959-961.

[70] W. M. Cruickshank, "A Study of the Relation of Physical Disability to Social Adjustment," *American Journal of Occupational Therapy*, VI (1952), 100-109.

[71] Words printed in roman type were the stimulus phrases included on the test; those in italics, the child's response.

[72] Cruickshank, "A Study of the Relation . . .," *op. cit.*, pp. 107-109.

[73] *Ibid.*, pp. 101-102.

[74] *Ibid.*, pp. 102-103.

[75] *Ibid.*, p. 109.

[76] W. M. Cruickshank, "The Relation of Physical Disability to Fear and Guilt Feelings," *Child Development*, XX (1951), 291-298.

[77] E. A. Henri, "The Emotional Reactions of Crippled Children Toward Their Physical Defects" (Master's thesis, Catholic University of America, 1949).

[78] Cruickshank, "The Relation of Physical Disability . . .," *op. cit.*, pp. 294-295.

[79] *Ibid.*, pp. 296-297.

[80] W. M. Cruickshank, "The Effect of Physical Disability on Personal Aspiration," *The Quarterly Journal of Child Behavior*, III (1951), 323-333.

[81] *Ibid.*, pp. 332-333.

[82] E. X. Freed, and W. M. Cruickshank, "The Effect of Cardiac Disability on Ad-

justment to Parents and Family," *The Quarterly Journal of Child Behavior*, IV (1952), 299-309.

[83] E. X. Freed and W. M. Cruickshank, "The Relation of Cardiac Disease to Feelings of Fear," *The Journal of Pediatrics*, XLIII (1953), 483-488.

[84] See also G. Ladieu, D. L. Adler, and T. Dembo, "Social Acceptance of the Injured," *Journal of Social Issues*, IV (Fall 1948), 55-61.

[85] See such studies as Landis and Bolles, *op. cit.*; Schneider, *op. cit.*; Gates, *op. cit.*; P. H. Mussen and R. G. Barker, "Attitudes Towards Cripples," *Journal of Abnormal and Social Psychology*, XXXIX (1944), 351-355; E. K. Strong, *Change of Interests with Age* (Stanford University: Stanford University Press, 1931); M. H. Means, "Fears of One Thousand College Women," *Journal of Abnormal and Social Psychology*, XXXI (1936), 291-311; and C. G. Randall, J. R. Ewalt, and H. Blair, "Psychiatric Reaction to Amputation," *Journal of the American Medical Association*, CXXVIII (1945), 645-652.

[86] E. W. Coughlin, "Some Parental Attitudes Toward Handicapped Children," *The Child*, VI (1941), 41-45.

[87] Mussen and Barker, *op. cit.*

[88] *Ibid.*, p. 353.

[89] E. E. Lord, *Children Handicapped by Cerebral Palsy* (New York: Commonwealth Fund, 1930).

[90] Kammerer, *op. cit.*

[91] K. B. Oettinger, "An Experiment in Teaching Physically Handicapped Children at Home," *Mental Hygiene*, XXII (1938), 245-264.

[92] S. Z. Rosenbaum, "Infantile Paralysis as the Source of Emotional Problems in Children," *Welfare Bulletin*, XXXIV (1943), 11-13.

[93] R. Pintner, J. Eisenson, and M. Stanton, *The Psychology of the Physically Handicapped* (New York: Appleton-Century-Crofts, Inc., 1941).

[94] J. T. McIntire, "The Incidence of Feeble-Mindedness in the Cerebral Palsied," *American Journal of Mental Deficiency*, L (1946), 491-494.

[95] W. M. Phelps, "Characteristic Psychological Variations in Cerebral Palsy," *Nervous Child*, VII (1948), 10-13.

[96] P. Asher and F. E. Schonnel, "A Survey of 400 Cases of Cerebral Palsy in Childhood," *Archives of Disease in Childhood*, XXV (1950), 360-379; I. M. Holoran, "The Incidence and Prognosis of Cerebral Palsy," *British Medical Journal*, 4751 (January 26, 1952), 214-217; E. Miller and G. Rosenfield, "The Psychological Evaluation of Children with Cerebral Palsy and Its Implications in Treatment," *Journal of Pediatrics*, XLI (1952), 613-621; A. Heilman, "Intelligence in Cerebral Palsy," *The Crippled Child*, XXX (1952), 11-13; and New York State Departments of Education and Health, *The Need for Special Cerebral Palsy School Classes in New York* (Albany: State Education Department, 1952). See also T. Hopkins, H. Bice, and K. Colton, *Evaluation and Education of Children with Cerebral Palsy* (Washington, D.C.: International Council for Exceptional Children, 1954); and H. Bice and W. Cruickshank, "Evaluation of Intelligence," in *Cerebral Palsy, Its Individual and Community Problems*, eds. W. M. Cruickshank and G. M. Raus (Syracuse: Syracuse University Press, 1955), chap. iii.

[97] In M. H. Fouracre and E. A. Theill, "Education of Children with Mental Retardation Accompanying Cerebral Palsy," *American Journal of Mental Deficiency*, LVII (1953), 402.

[98] Hopkins, Bice, Coulton, *op. cit.*

[99] R. M. Taibl, "An Investigation of Raven's 'Progressive Matrices' as a Tool for the Psychological Evaluation of Cerebral Palsied Children" (Doctoral dissertation, University of Nebraska, 1951).

[100] C. Banks and U. Sinha, "An Item Analysis of the Progressive Matrices Test," *The British Journal of Psychology, Statistical Section*, IV, Part II (1951), 91-94.

[101] M. V. Lee, "The Children's Hospital; A Survey of the Intelligence of Crippled Children," *Journal of Educational Research*, XXIII (1931), 164-167.

[102] P. A. Witty and M. B. Smith, "The Mental Status of 1,480 Crippled Children," *Educational Trends,* I (1932), 22-24.

[103] Pintner, Eisenson, and Stanton, *op. cit.,* p. 270.

[104] R. G. Gordon, J. A. F. Roberts, and R. Griffiths, "Does Poliomyelitis Affect Intellectual Capacity?" *British Medical Journal,* II (1939), 803-805.

[105] M. R. Fernald and A. H. Arlitt, "Psychological Findings Regarding Crippled Children," *School and Society,* XXI (1925), 449-452.

[106] See, for example, R. B. Ammons and H. S. Ammons, "The Full-Range Picture Vocabulary Test: I, Preliminary Scale," *Journal of Psychology,* XXVIII (1949), 51-64.

[107] L. H. Blum, B. Burgmeister, I. Lorge, "Trends in Estimating the Mental Maturity of the Cerebral Palsied Child," *Journal of Exceptional Children,* XVII (1951), 174-177. Also, the same authors in "The Mental Maturity Scale for the Motor Handicapped," *School and Society,* 73 (1951), 232.

[108] E. A. Doll, "Psychological Significance of Cerebral Birth Lesions," *American Journal of Psychology,* XLV (1933), 444-452; also E. A. Doll, W. M. Phelps, and R. T. Melcher, *Mental Deficiency Due to Birth Injury* (New York: The Macmillan Company, 1932).

[109] W. Penfield and T. Rasmusses, *The Cerebral Cortex of Man* (New York: The Macmillan Company, 1950).

[110] K. Goldstein, *Brain Injuries Due to War* (New York: Grune & Stratton, Inc., 1942).

[111] W. C. Halstead, *Brain and Intelligence* (Chicago: University of Chicago Press, 1947); and "Preliminary Analysis of Grouping Behavior in Patients with Cerebral Injury by the Method of Equivalent and Non-Equivalent Stimuli," *American Journal of Psychiatry,* XCVI (1940), 1263-1294.

[112] Z. Piotrowski, "The Rorschach Inkblot Method in Organic Disturbances of the Central Nervous System," *Journal of Nervous and Mental Diseases,* LXXXVI (1937), 525-537.

[113] M. R. Harrower-Erickson, "Personality Changes Accompanying Cerebral Lesions," *Archives of Neurology and Psychiatry,* XLIII (1940), 859-890.

[114] E. Meyer and M. Simmel, "The Psychological Appraisal of Children with Neurological Defects," *Journal of Abnormal and Social Psychology,* XLII (1947), 193-205.

[115] C. B. Cotton, "A Study of the Reactions of Spastic Children to Certain Test Situations," *Journal of Genetic Psychology,* LVIII (1941), 27-44.

[116] Lord, *op. cit.*

[117] S. B. Sarason and E. K. Sarason, "The Discriminatory Value of Test Pattern with Cerebral Palsied, Defective Children," *Journal of Clinical Psychology,* II (1949), 141-147.

[118] The reports of their research which have appeared in numerous professional journals are to be found in summary form in A. A. Strauss and L. Lehtinen, *Psychopathology and Education of the Brain Injured Child* (New York: Grune & Stratton, Inc., 1947).

[119] S. B. Sarason, *Psychological Problems in Mental Deficiency,* 2nd ed. (New York: Harper & Row, Publishers, 1952).

[120] L. Bender, "Psychological Problems in Children with Organic Brain Disease," *American Journal of Orthopsychiatry,* XXIX (1949), 407.

[121] *Ibid.,* p. 409.

[122] J. E. Dolphin, "A Study of Certain Aspects of the Psychopathology of Cerebral Palsy Children" (Doctoral dissertation, Syracuse University, 1950).

[123] H. Rorschach, *Psychodiagnostics,* trans. P. Lemkau and B. Kronenberg (Berne, Switzerland: Verlag Hans Huber, 1942).

[124] H. Werner, "Perceptual Behavior of Brain-Injured, Mentally Defective Children: An Experimental Study by Means of the Rorschach Technique," *Genetic Psychology Monographs,* XXXI (1945), 51-110.

[125] H. Werner and A. A. Strauss, "Pathology of Figure-Background Relation in the Child," *Journal of Abnormal and Social Psychology,* XXXVI (1941), 236.

126 Strauss and Lehtinen, *op. cit.*, p. 45.
127 J. E. Dolphin and W. M. Cruickshank, "The Figure-Background Relationship in Children with Cerebral Palsy," *Journal of Clinical Psychology,* VII (1951), 228-231.
128 Dolphin and Cruickshank, *ibid.,* p. 230.
129 Bender, "Psychological Problems of Children . . .," *op. cit.,* p. 414.
130 Klapper and Werner, *op. cit.,* pp. 294, 301, 306.
131 W. M. Cruickshank, H. V. Bice, and N. E. Wallen, *Perception and Cerebral Palsy: A Study in Figure Background Relationship* (Syracuse: Syracuse University Press, 1957), pp. xvi-123.
132 *Ibid.,* p. 109.
133 H. Werner, "Development of Visuo-Motor Performance on the Marble Board Test in Mentally Retarded Children," *Journal of Genetic Psychology,* LXIX (1944), 269.
134 J. E. Dolphin and W. M. Cruickshank, "Visuo-Motor Perception in Children with Cerebral Palsy," *Quarterly Journal of Child Behavior,* III (1951), 198-209.
135 Klapper and Werner, *op. cit.,* pp. 294 and 300.
136 Cruickshank, *et al., op. cit.,* p. 108.
137 J. E. Dolphin and W. M. Cruickshank, "Tactual Motor Perception of Children with Cerebral Palsy," *Journal of Personality,* XX (1952), 466-471.
138 Werner and Strauss, "Pathology of Figure-Background Relation . . .," *op. cit.*
139 Cruickshank, *et al., op. cit.,* p. 106.
140 A. A. Strauss and H. Werner, "Disorders of Conceptual Thinking in the Brain Injured Child," *Journal of Nervous and Mental Diseases,* XCVI (1942), 213.
141 Cotton, *op. cit.*
142 Halstead, "Preliminary Analysis of Grouping Behavior . . .," *op. cit.*
143 J. E. Dolphin and W. M. Cruickshank, "Pathology of Concept Formation in Children with Cerebral Palsy," *American Journal of Mental Deficiency,* LVI (1951), 392-396.
144 K. Goldstein and M. Scheerer, "Abstract and Concrete Behavior: An Experimental Study with Special Tests," *Psychological Monographs,* LIII (1941), 1-151.
145 Cruickshank, *et al., op. cit.,* p. 110.
146 Klapper and Werner, *op. cit.*
147 W. M. Cruickshank, *et al., A Teaching Method for Brain Injured and Hyperactive Children* (Syracuse: Syracuse University Press, 1961), pp. xxi-576.
148 J. J. Gallagher, *The Tutoring of Brain Injured Mentally Retarded Children: An Experimental Study* (Springfield: Charles C. Thomas, Publishers, 1960).
149 R. J. Capobianco and R. A. Funk, *A Comparative Study of Intellectual, Neurological, and Perceptual Processes as Related to Reading Achievement of Exogenous and Endogenous Retarded Children* (Syracuse: Syracuse University Research Institute, 1958).
150 R. J. Capobianco and D. Y. Miller, *Quantitative and Qualitative Analysis of Exogenous and Endogenous Children in Some Reading Processes* (Syracuse: Syracuse University Research Institute, 1958).
151 W. M. Cruickshank, "The Multiply Handicapped Cerebral Palsied Child," *Exceptional Children,* XX (1953), 16-22.
152 Strauss and Werner, "Disorders of Conceptual Thinking . . .," *op. cit.*
153 W. M. Cruickshank and J. E. Dolphin, "The Educational Implications of Psychological Studies of Cerebral Palsied Children," *Exceptional Children,* XVIII (1951), 1-18.
154 A. A. Strauss, "Typology in Mental Deficiency," *Proceedings of American Association on Mental Deficiency,* XLVI (1939), 85-90.
155 *Ibid.*
156 Cruickshank, "The Multiply Handicapped Cerebral Palsied Child," *op. cit.*

CHARLES KRAM

The Epilepsy Foundation
Washington, D.C.

7 Epilepsy in Children and Youth

Introduction

YOU PROBABLY have among your friends someone with epilepsy or who has a relative with epilepsy. You may not know this, however. Practical considerations of social and economic pressures motivate the person with epilepsy towards secrecy. Discovery may mean loss of employment for the adult, removal from the classroom for the child, as well as subjection to certain legal sanctions and painful ostracism. Later, you will see how these measures were inaccurately adopted and the extent to which some of them are still unjustifiably maintained. Unfortunately, the concealment practiced by many people with epilepsy enhances the mystery with which the illness is regarded. The uninformed person is thus encouraged to generalize erroneously on the basis of a few intractable cases he may have heard about.

Epilepsy is an ancient Greek term meaning "to be seized." It has been used since the Fifth Century B.C. to designate those conditions manifesting themselves by episodic and recurrent convulsive states. These conditions are also called attacks or seizures.

A seizure is a sympton. When it occurs we know that somewhere in the brain there is a functional disturbance experienced by a group of nerve cells and that these neurones are discharging their electrical energy at an accelerated rate. Changes in the usual pattern of electrical current discharged by brain cells can be measured by a machine called the electroencephalogram, more conveniently referred to as the EEG. A typical seizure consists of a sudden, involuntary, and temporary loss of consciousness accompanied by a varying amount of convulsive movements. Contributory factors are many and include head injuries, prolonged high fever, infections, interference with the normal supply of blood or oxygen to the brain—to name a few. A precise description of the specific way in which any one of these conditions precipitates a seizure is still lacking.

Epileptic seizures are symptoms of any one of a large number of illnesses brought about through any one of a great many causes. The person with epilepsy tends to have recurrent seizures. The exact form assumed by these seizures will vary from the imperceptible at the one extreme to the highly dramatic at the other. Diagnostic and therapeutic advances, especially since the mid-Thirties, have optimistically revised the prognosis for this illness. About 80 per cent of people with epilepsy can at the present time be largely or completely free of seizures as a result of current medical discoveries.

Historical Development *

EPILEPSY IS one of the oldest diseases known to man. Tower [58] reports that epileptic seizures were probably known long before the existence of written records. The early writings of various cultures and of a number of religions mention this illness in one form or another.

Prior to and including the Fifth Century B.C., people with epilepsy were variously regarded as being possessed either by good spirits or by demons. The adjective "sacred" was used to describe the disease by early man because of his belief that this was visited upon the patient by a deity; so that we find primitive man considering the epileptic as a holy being and one to be treated with reverence. Later, Neolithic medicine men [57] used trepanation procedures on the epileptic in order to release the demons considered to have entered the patient. For this purpose a shark's tooth was employed to perforate the skull so that the demon residing deep within the brain might escape. Sinful acts were also held responsible for

---

* Footnotes are arranged alphabetically-numerically at the end of this chapter and of Chapter 9.

producing this illness by way of divine retribution,[53] as for example, an act committed against the goddess of the moon, Selene.

Hippocrates (*ca.* 460-377 B.C.) is credited with the first known systematic attempt to introduce objectively determined evaluations in reporting on observations of seizures. His book, *On the Sacred Disease,* rebukes previous attitudes and replaces them with the suggestion that epilepsy is no more sacred than is any other disease. All illnesses spring from natural causes, and seizures are probably produced by some dysfunction in the cortical areas of the brain. The exactness of his observations may be attested to by the reliability of his description of a grand mal seizure which has retained its accuracy to the present time.

The writings of Hippocrates on this topic were to constitute medical dogma for a period of about 2,300 years following his death. However, it was not until the Fourth Century A.D. that the healers of that day began to interest themselves in these writings. Illustrating this gap of several hundred years is the writing of Pliny in the First Century A.D. He describes the Roman custom of spitting back over one's shoulder in the direction of the person with epilepsy who is displaying a seizure. The purpose of this is to throw back the evil or the contagion which was thought to emanate from the epileptic. Society still viewed the epileptic as unclean, endowed with evil, possessed by the devil, and as being insane. It was common practice to appeal to the church to exorcise the devil contained within the epileptic.

Medical literature from the Fourth Century up into the Nineteenth Century generally concurred with the opinions of Hippocrates as concerned the natural causes of epilepsy. Society as a whole seemed little influenced by this, however. Approximately for that identical period of time the same misconceptions, superstitions, and fears about epilepsy prevailed.

During the Nineteenth Century there was an awakening of interest in physiological studies of the nervous system. Certain of the ancient taboos relative to epilepsy were fading. Beliefs in possession by demon spirits, and related methods of releasing these evils, were being discarded. Replacing these were a number of remedial techniques based on inferential reasoning. Patients were advised not to eat meat, for example, because leopards display violent bursts of muscular activity and are meat eaters. Other therapeutic measures included stimulating the nervous activity of the patient, pouring cold water on the patient's face, providing him with a permanent tracheotomy, extracting all of his teeth, and amputating those extremities where seizures were noted to have started. Opposing views were also to be found. For example, since the obstruction of the blood flow to the brain produced convulsions, avoidance of bloodletting was advocated. A contrary remedy, however, was recommended by those who observed that the brain of the epileptic was congested and therefore concluded that too much blood overstimulates the brain. In 1857 Charles Locock [32] found that bromides were helpful in lessening the severity of seizures. Despite the dulling side effects, bromides would continue to be used as an anticonvulsant for the next 55 years.

Of particular importance to epilepsy was the work of John Hughlings Jackson, whose writings appeared in 1870. Jackson [52] stressed the importance of studying the entire course of each seizure in more detail and with greater precision than had been customary. He was interested as well in all factors preceding the seizures and, in addition, in closely observing the events immediately following. Convulsive movements formed patterns which enabled him to identify various types of seizures and to distinguish one from another. Recording these established convulsive patterns, he believed, would help to locate that portion of the brain from which the disturbance originated. Thus, additional information which would reveal the causes of seizures might be obtained.

It was Jackson who redefined epilepsy as only a name for occasional, sudden, excessive, rapid, and local discharges of brain cells. This disorderly discharge of nerve tissue, he explained, exhibited itself as a convulsion. He considered a convulsion to be nothing more than a symptom. In his writings he describes these nerve discharges as varying in degree and adds that he found them in a large variety of illnesses, at all ages, and under a wide number of circumstances.

In 1912 the bromides were replaced by phenobarbital as a more effective anti-epileptic medication. With the exception of this drug, there was little ostensible progress in the field of epilepsy for a period of more than sixty years following the publications of Jackson in 1870. The absence of significant and new information about epilepsy during this period may suggest a similar lack of interest on the part of society. This is not true, however. Interest had not waned and was energized in several new developments. It was simply that the major objectives had to do with the protection of society from the epileptic rather than the assistance of the epileptic with his illness. Special state institutions were set up in several parts of the country to remove the epileptic from society and to keep him in an isolated manner probably for a major portion of his life. In those states where special facilities were lacking, the person with epilepsy might be institutionalized along with other chronic and custodial cases. With the same purpose, legislation was enacted in a number of states preventing all people with epilepsy from marrying, bearing children, and obtaining an education.

You are correct in surmising from all of this that the person with epilepsy was viewed at that time as having an illness which is incurable, hereditary, and completely hopeless.

The impressions, social attitudes, and customs which developed and were strengthened throughout this period were accorded sufficient initial support and impetus to maintain them to an appreciable extent right up to the present.

The following may illustrate the effective retention of these negative views and also indicates how widespread they became. During the late 1920's a faculty member of a large eastern medical school presented a paper at a professional meeting. He reported a survey made of directors of state institutions for epilepsy located around the country, in which the observations and impressions of these directors and of their patients were evaluated. Describing what were claimed to be noteworthy characteristics of these people with epilepsy the author stated, "The group is composed of individuals who are on the whole not only incurable but who are steadily deteriorating. It is like a dying forest growing in a fertile soil. In this respect the group differs from that of the insane, and of the feeble-minded; the former has hope of cure, the latter of steadily improving."

Seizures

EVERY NERVE cell in the brain may be thought of as an electrochemical generator.[15] Each cell converts sugar and oxygen into electricity. The electricity may then be stored or discharged.[13] A neurone in its resting phase produces 8/100 of a volt ten times per second. This discharge frequency increases when the same neurone is activated. During a seizure the discharges increase in frequency to an excessive extent. The location of the neurones which start discharging excessively, the extent to which this discharge spreads to surrounding neurones, the speed with which the discharges spread (or march), as well as the locations into which the spread occurs, all help to determine the classification of that particular seizure.

Each group of neurones is capable of discharging excessively and producing a seizure.[36] You can therefore understand why it is not at all uncommon to experience an isolated seizure. Indeed, it is estimated that at least six per cent of the population has had just such a seizure at one time or another.[42] Pediatric neurologists believe that this percentage may be more than doubled with young children. A brief interruption in the normal supply of blood and oxygen to the brain may, for example, bring this about in many healthy individuals.

Gibbs [56] affirms that a seizure constitutes the body's normal reaction to injury of one or more nerve cells in the brain. When neurones are killed, they do not produce epileptic seizures. The injury, therefore, cannot be so severe as to make the neurones stop functioning but is just severe enough to make them function abnormally. Seizures cannot be attributed to a no longer functioning, destroyed area of the brain. Seizure activity often may develop in the surrounding zone which has sustained less severe injury. It is for this reason that epilepsy may be considered a hopeful and treatable disorder, in contrast to the classical neurological disorders which are largely irreversible and hopeless.

A seizure, as a defense mechanism, reflects the normal reaction of a group of neurones to excessive irritation. This explains why any person can have a seizure when the physiological condition of a portion of the brain is upset. A seizure which occurs once and is not repeated within a reasonable period, does not constitute epilepsy.[49] Just how ordinary and mild a seizure may be is illustrated by the occurrence of a benign nocturnal myoclonus. You may have noticed while falling asleep at night, and immediately before dozing off, a momentary muscular jerk of one of your limbs which may even have startled you and brought you back to wakefulness. The descriptive term is the only awesome factor about this. It is harmless, insignificant, and of unknown cause; with good reason, it usually merits no attention.

Seizures associated with epilepsy display the following characteristics: They come on so precipitously that in certain types of epilepsy the patient may suddenly fall to the floor as though he had been sandbagged; with a few exceptions they will be accompanied by either total unconsciousness or a modified loss of consciousness; the patient is unable to exercise any control in either starting or stopping the seizure; the seizure appears to terminate of itself; and the seizures will be recurrent.

If you were to observe a large number of people with epilepsy over a long period of time, you would notice that seizures appear in numerous and diverse forms. This is caused by the fact that the electrical disturbance responsible for the seizure may be located within any one of many portions of the brain.[48] This makes it possible for seizures to comprise combinations of all sensations and all movements available to the patient.[51] In part this accounts for diagnostic and classification difficulties.

Electroencephalograph (EEG)

THE EEG continues to be the most widely used laboratory procedure in the diagnosis of epilepsy. It was first described in 1929 by Hans Berger, who devised this instrument and had been working with it since 1907. This machine made possible the graphical recording of electrical activity in brain tissue. Berger reported the recordings he had made with a number of living organisms, including the first such tracing obtained from a person on July 6, 1924. Tracings made under various conditions appeared in his experimental work. He found, for example, that the tracings assumed different patterns when a number of varied stimuli were applied to the patient externally, that they were affected by a number of drugs and the relationship of these drugs to levels of consciousness, and that a substantial number of illnesses including epilepsy resulted in still other tracing differences.

Supporting this, Livingston [33] reports abnormal EEG tracings with brain tumors, migraine, behavior disturbances, endocrine disturbances, encephalitis, narcolepsy, sickle cell anemia, acute nephritis, allergy, and ophthalmological disorders.

The EEG, however, continued to be used for research purposes exclusively until Adrian published confirmatory reports of Berger's work in 1934.

Shortly thereafter two significant events occurred in fairly rapid succession. In 1935 Gibbs, Davis, and Lennox [50] described patterns of electrical tracings consistent with grand mal and petit mal seizures. They also demonstrated that abnormal EEG tracings could be found during intervals between seizures as well. This was followed in 1937 by the discovery of dilantin by Houston Merritt and Tracy Putnam.[46] This drug used alone, or in combination with phenobarbital, continues to provide effective control of seizures to the present time.

These two discoveries combined to motivate interest and to energize activity relative to epilepsy to an extent without parallel in the previous 2,000 years. Continued developments have proceeded from that period at an accelerated pace.

Today we know the EEG as a machine which measures the electrical discharges of brain tissue. A patient receiving what is popularly termed a "brain wave test" will be placed in a room screened off from outside electrical interferences as well as from all distracting stimuli. Electrodes in the form of small metal disks are placed around the patient's head in certain strategic locations. The brain's electrical activity is in this manner received by the machine, amplified, and converted into a series of written lines recorded continuously on a rotating drum. This record, the electroencephalogram, resembles a musical scale without the notes, with the exception that the lines are wiggly and contain numerous hills and valleys. The entire procedure may last about an hour, and during this time the patient usually assumes a reclining position of rest. Introducing certain stimuli, or altering the basic situation, is sometimes done for diagnostic purposes. Therefore, the patient may be encouraged to sleep during a portion of the examination or he may go through certain activities during this time or he may even experience an induced seizure in order to record as wide a range of electrical abnormalities as may be possible.

The resulting EEG tracings assist the physician in arriving at a diagnosis and in formulating a treatment plan individually designed for that patient.

Each major type of epileptic seizure possesses characteristic abnormal EEG tracings. In the diagnostic procedure it is common to employ the EEG to support clinical observations of the seizure. The rhythmical differences apparent when comparing normal EEG records with abnormal ones has led to the sometimes expressed opinion that the term "paroxysmal cerebral dysrhythmia" would more appropriately describe the illness than does the term epilepsy. However, between 10 and 20 per cent of clinically diagnosed epileptics produce normal EEG tracings.[18] Conversely, abnormal EEG patterns have been observed in from 10 to 15 per cent of individuals clinically free of any seizures. This has resulted in the common acceptance of the admonition, as expressed by Davis,[9] that the EEG not be considered *sine qua non* in medical management.

Classification

You will find disagreement in prevailing efforts to develop universally acceptable diagnostic categories suitable to the many kinds of seizures. The proper descriptive prefix before the term epilepsy, according to various systems, will be determined by the age when seizures began, the presumed cause, that area of the brain where the seizures originate, response to medications, or emotional factors attendant to the epilepsy. From a broader aspect the decision about which classification system to follow will also depend upon the particular bias of the diagnostician, the immediate circumstances of the study, and the short- or long-range purposes for that specific evaluation. In view of the abundant material describing epilepsy, it is surprising that within the legislation found in many states relevant to the person with epilepsy, in no instance is there an accompanying definition.

An accurate classification is important nonetheless to the physician, who must rely on precise methods in order to establish maximum seizure control with a given patient and to be able to plan effectively for the continued care and management of that same patient.

For purposes of medical management one or more of the following classification methods is used:

A dichotomous separation based on suspected etiology. In keeping with this method all cases which have a known and demonstrable cause are called organic or acquired or symptomatic.[23] About 25 per cent of all cases of epilepsy are considered to be organic.[21] Interestingly enough, a greater number of terms are applied synonymously to the 75 per cent of cases for which no known cause exists and of which the etiology is rather tenuous. The adjectives commonly used in this context are idiopathic, cryptogenic, genetic, essential, genuine, and metabolic.

Another procedure consists of EEG tracings occasionally supported by additional laboratory tests. High-voltage discharges in the form of rapid waves will appear on the EEG taken during a grand mal seizure. Slow waves with spike and dome discharges will appear on the EEG of petit mal seizures. Sharp waves, spikes, or still other aberrations generally referable to one or the other side of the brain will appear with psycho-motor seizures. In a number of instances of psychomotor epilepsy, additional laboratory study will reveal the location and cause of the seizures as a physiological defect in one of the temporal lobes.

A third method is based on making a division of seizures into either major motor or minor motor groupings. This method is supported by those who believe that this broad distinction is consistent with the amount of knowledge currently available about epilepsy, that using this method makes for fewer diagnostic inaccuracies, and that the method allows for optimum medical management. Minor motor seizures are more commonly seen and are estimated to constitute 75 per cent of all epilepsy.

Less discord exists in the application of a classification system that combines a detailed clinical description of the seizure pattern with the characteristic EEG tracings. Commensurate with this system, all cases of epilepsy are grouped into one of the following categories: grand mal, petit mal, focal, and psychomotor.

Grand Mal

Grand mal seizures are preceded by auras [44] in about half of the cases. The aura acts as a warning signal to the patient and may consist of any one of a number of sensations or feelings. Headache, abdominal pain, a visual experience of many bright lights, or a similarly self-produced auditory experience of a loud and persistent whistle are only a few of the many reported auras. The duration of the aura varies, so that in some instances the patient has sufficient time to prepare himself for the impending convulsion. The aura marks the beginning of the seizure, and the patient is unable to prevent the remainder of the seizure from following its usual course. Following the aura the patient will emit a cry caused by the lungs expelling air, there will be an abrupt loss of consciousness and falling, and then a rigid stiffening of the body (tonic spasm) which may last for about two minutes. This is rapidly changed to a period of rhythmical twitching (clonic) phase of the body which may last slightly longer than did the period of rigidity. While all of this is happening, the patient may also exhibit bladder or bowel incontinence, noisy and irregular breathing, as well as changes in skin color. If the patient has bitten his tongue or his cheek during the seizure, blood-stained saliva may appear at his lips. Termination of the seizure is indicated by the progressive relaxation of his body and the return of normal breathing and normal skin color. At this point the patient may drift into a state of sleep without awakening, or he may awaken and appear confused before going to sleep. (Most patients prefer to sleep from a few minutes to an hour or more after this seizure.) Even after he awakens, the patient may complain of muscular aches and of generally not feeling well. Ordinarily a period of rest is required before the patient can resume normal activities.

Status epilepticus describes a condition where the patient experiences repeated grand mal seizures without intervening periods of consciousness. The attention of a physician is imperative in this instance.

Petit Mal

Petit mal seizures consist of brief and transitory lapses of consciousness. They begin and terminate abruptly; their frequency may range from an occasional seizure to as many as two hundred a day. These may be so fleeting that they can go unnoticed and even be mistaken for daydreaming or for inattentiveness. The possibility for this illness to continue unrecognized is enhanced by the fact that this is almost always a children's disorder. A period of about three minutes of deep and rapid breathing (hyperventilation) will produce a seizure in someone with petit mal epilepsy and is therefore used as a diagnostic aid. These seizures may last from a couple of seconds up to about half a minute, they are not preceded by an aura, and they may be accompanied by small muscular movements of one or another part of the face. Termination of the petit mal seizure is free of any unusual symptoms or sensations. A milder petit mal seizure is sometimes called an "absence" for it does appear as though the patient simply flicked off the light of consciousness momentarily and then, just as abruptly, rejoined the stream of activities at the precise point where he had stopped a moment before. Usually there will be an amnesia for the duration of the seizure.

Focal

Focal seizures are thought to originate in the cerebral cortex. The beginning of a focal seizure will assume different forms, thus determining whether the seizure will be a Jacksonian seizure or a focal sensory seizure or a psychomotor seizure. In any of these forms it is possible for the excessive discharges of the nerve cells in that area of the brain originating the seizure to spread to the entire brain, producing a generalized grand mal seizure.

Jacksonian seizures start in the form of muscular twitchings within the tip of one of the extremities or on one side of the face. These movements then progress the length of the extremity or across the face, limiting their spread to that same side of the body where they began. Consciousness is retained, although the patient is unable to control these muscular movements. When these movements continue over to the other side of the body, they ultimately lead to a generalized convulsion similar to that observed in grand mal epilepsy and will then be accompanied by a loss of consciousness. These patients sometimes find that they can prevent the continued spread of the muscular twitchings by rapidly engaging in tasks demanding large expenditures of mental and physical energy.

Focal sensory attacks begin in a manner similar to the Jacksonian or focal motor seizures, the difference being that instead of a muscular twitching the patient experiences sensations of a tactile nature, of a sudden and marked temperature change within the extremity involved; or he may have experiences affecting the visual or auditory or olfactory senses.

Psychomotor

Psychomotor seizures may start with the patient experiencing unfamiliar and strange perceptions of his immediate environment. For example, it may appear to him that he is dreaming, that things are not real, that objects around him are smaller than they should be, or perhaps that everything is larger than usual. These sensations may be followed by some amount of abdominal discomfort concomitant with automatic motions—the most common of which are sucking and chewing movements. Automatic behavior may also be present so that the patient may get up, walk around, and perform one or more tasks. This automatic activity has a purposeful appearance but is usually unrelated to the situation. The psychomotor seizure may last from a few minutes to a period of several hours or even longer. Throughout this time the patient does not appear to lose consciousness, but neither does he seem to be aware of his actions. He will report amnesia for the duration of the seizure.

You will want to know that each of the above descriptions subsumes that we are discussing a patient with a single and pure form of epilepsy and with no additional complications. In actual practice patients will display mixtures of varying amounts of two or more types of epilepsy, fragments of any one of the seizures described, or symptoms which have not been described here or which even contradict some of the explanations given thus far.

Diagnosis

A COMPLETE and accurate evaluation has importance for the person with epilepsy. It has added significance for the epileptic child. It serves as a foundation underlying the structure of a long-range, comprehensive, and effective treatment plan. In the ideal situation the final product will reflect the diagnostic services of a number of people from the medical and paramedical professions.

The goals of a complete diagnostic study include: detection of the presence and type of epilepsy; determination of the existence and extent of problems in the emotional, social, familial, and educational areas; and formulation of a therapeutic program aimed at the resolution of any of the foregoing problems.

Continual medical supervision and periodic re-examinations are advocated for children, especially during the formative years. This is necessitated by the relatively rapid changes found in children—involving not only their epilepsy but other general adjustment factors as well. Reformulations of therapeutic programs are indicated with children from time to time in order for them to achieve a continuity of maximum gains and to exhibit uninterrupted progress.

The medical examination usually consists of neurological studies along with laboratory tests, a physical examination inquiring into the general health of the child, and a detailed medical history that thoroughly explores the family backgrounds of both parents.

Lennox [32] believed the unit of treatment in epilepsy to consist of the entire family. This recommendation should perhaps be expanded to include the community as well. Essential to a thorough work-up would be a careful social history of the child, inclusive of his attitudes about himself and his interpersonal relationships with peers as well as with adults in his environment. An account tracing the course of his home life should be provided, defining his position within the family, his attitudes and relationships with the other members of his family, and their attitudes towards him. Ways in which his family can participate in the treatment program set up for him must be assessed. Finally, resources and attitudes existing within his community need to be evaluated.

To complete the diagnostic procedure it is necessary to add the results of emotional and intellectual appraisals. Exploration of this area may include: one or more psychiatric interviews with the child as well as with the parents; psychological examinations to reveal the functioning level of his intelligence as compared with his potential endowment; a description of his personality make-up—including assets and liabilities, needs and levels of readiness for special educational or psychotherapeutic services, and the relationship between his epilepsy and any psychological problems which may be present; and aptitude, achievement, and interest tests whose results would be helpful in making educational and vocational recommendations consistent with the rehabilitation aspects of a therapeutic program.

Many children with epilepsy have no personality problems, nor do they display adjustment difficulties. Children who have attained good control of their seizures, who enjoy a wholesome family relationship, and who reside in an accepting and understanding community usually display a healthy emotional adjustment.

Participants in the evaluation should have an opportunity to share their findings at a case conference. One outcome of this meeting would be the preparation of a report containing a logical integration of all the available information. Another result might be the formulation of a treatment and follow-up plan devised by the same workers. To implement these plans, appropriate interpretations of the evaluation results must be meaningfully conveyed to parents, the family physician, school authorities, and others in the child's community who maintain roles important to that child's everyday activities.

Causes

You MAY recall that earlier in the chapter you were asked to survey a large population of epileptic patients. If you were to return to study this same group further—this time for the purpose of listing all factors apparently contributory to each patient's form of epilepsy, the severity of his seizures, and the circumstances surrounding the beginning of his epilepsy—you would probably find that each of the items on your list could be placed into one, or a combination of, the following categories: physiological disturbances, physical injuries, heredity, and psychological factors. Individually or collectively these factors assume both antecedent and precipitating roles in the onset as well as the entire course of epilepsy in a patient.

Physical and physiological causes may take the form of a head injury, a birth injury, an infection of the central nervous system, brain atrophy caused by lack of blood supply, brain tumor, certain childhood diseases associated with high fever and toxicity, as well as metabolic imbalances. Generally, the younger a child is at the time seizures begin, the more likelihood is there to be a known organic cause. It is not until after age ten that other causes assume prominence in the development of epilepsy. A second observation of related importance has to do with the greater incidence of epilepsy occurring in the early years and tapering off as maturity is reached. Tenny [54] studied 765 pupils in the Detroit school system who had epilepsy and reported that 44 per cent developed epilepsy during the first four years of life, 12 per cent experienced the onset of seizures between the fourth and sixth year, while 7 per cent started having seizures after the age of twelve. Mackay and Wortis [37] examined 352 patients in Norway and found that 40 per cent began having seizures before age five. In analyzing probable causative agents they found that 20 per cent of the patients had sustained a birth injury, 18 per cent suffered a head injury, 8 per cent had a history of an infection of the central nervous system, 4 per cent were found to have vascular abnormalities, and 2 per cent had brain tumors.

In still another survery [1] general practitioners in 67 areas in England were questioned about the epileptic patients they had been treating for a period of one year. They reported that the onset of seizures within their patients occurred most often during the first two years of life.

Lennox [32] offers three possibilities to explain the predominance of epilepsy in childhood. These are: a tendency for inherited predispositions to develop epilepsy to manifest themselves early in life, hair-trigger susceptibility along with the inadequate protection of the immature and undeveloped nervous system, and the greater likelihood for young children to sustain brain damage.

The hereditary factor does not apply to epilepsy itself but rather to a predisposition to attacks which usually requires the added stimulus of a precipitating agent in order to develop seizures. The matter of heredity will be discussed in more detail in the next section.

The causative role of psychological factors relative to epilepsy has led to considerable discussion and even personal disagreements. It is held by some that a seizure brought on by emotional factors is not epilepsy but hysteria. Gibbs [15] maintains that the patient's emotional reactions are less important determinants even of those psychiatric disorders associated with epilepsy than is the location in the brain of the epileptic discharge. He is severely critical of those who, in his opinion, would place major emphasis on psychotherapy and pay little attention to prescribing antiepileptic medication. Livingston,[34] on the other hand, vigorously describes the most common mistake in medical management as treatment which emphasizes medications while giving insufficient attention to the emotional factors involving the patient. Davis [60] demonstrated in a two-year study with children that seizures may result from emotional conflicts. She further found that it was not uncommon for a child to experience a lull in epileptic symptoms when disturbing aspects of that child's life were also quiescent. Livingston [33] supports this latter finding with his observations of many patients in whom seizures disappeared spontaneously upon admission to a hospital for study purposes. These patients, he adds, continued to be free of seizures for the duration of their hospital stay. Rose [16] found that early emotionally traumatic experiences can make for difficulty in later efforts to control seizures as well as to rehabilitate the patient. Emotional stress and conflict, he believes, may intensify and even bring on a seizure. In his opinion an effective treatment plan in certain cases may include placement in a non-threatening and socially accepting environment.

In this as in other areas where authorities take opposing stands, a careful examination of the literature suggests that the differences are more in degree than in kind; that the seemingly divergent views are more apparent than real; that certain of the disagreements are caused by insufficient communication rather than varying philosophies; and finally, that workers who confine their experience to settings and patient groups which differ markedly from one another will not always arrive at compatible conclusions about their observations. Of importance to the student is the observation that these very areas where agreement is lacking are those most in need of research and further study.

Heredity

THE MOST controversial topic in the field of epilepsy is the factor of heredity. Major differences revolve around the importance of heredity in causing epilepsy as well as the specific manner in which this happens. Available evidence does support the view that an inherited tendency or predisposition to develop epilepsy exists in certain people. Speculation attaches to the exact process of transmissal, whether males or females predominate in passing or receiving this tendency, and whether or not it exists in the form of a recessive gene. There is no evidence to indicate that epilepsy itself is inherited; there is rather a greater tendency to develop epilepsy from subsequent precipitating causes than is true for the general population.

Holowach [22] reports that, in a study of 120 cases of epilepsy, evidence of inheritance was found when seizures began early in life following trauma, whereas adults who developed epilepsy as the result of brain tumors had no greater incidence of close relatives with epilepsy than is found within a normal distribution of the population. Forster [12] found the incidence of seizures in close relatives of patients with idiopathic epilepsy amounted to 3 per cent in contrast to a comparable 1 per cent figure for those patients with a symptomatic (acquired) form of epilepsy.

These two studies were selected as typical of many reports confirming several commonly held theories. They are as follows: Heredity is considered to be a factor in cases of idiopathic epilepsy; what is inherited is only a predisposition to epilepsy so that the introduction of a precipitating cause is necessary before seizures can develop; idiopathic epilepsy is more prevalent in youth, especially between the ages of ten and eighteen; epilepsy which begins after age thirty is usually symptomatic, brought on by a demonstrable physical or physiological agent, and contains no hereditary components.

Additional confirmation is reported by Lennox,[32] who surveyed a total of 2,500 office and clinic patients and reported that the older the patient at the time epilepsy began, the fewer the number of close relatives who also developed epilepsy. Relatives of patients whose seizures began during the first five years of life showed an incidence of epilepsy four times higher as compared with relatives of patients who started their seizures after the age of thirty.

Current estimates suggest that approximately 1 per cent of the population has epilepsy. In actual numbers this amounts to a little under two million people with epilepsy in this country. Contrasting this figure with other illnesses,[42] epilepsy is as common as diabetes and active tuberculosis, and four times more prevalent than poliomyelitis. Because of the profound involvement of the immediate family when a member has epilepsy, the total number of people affected by epilepsy is more accurately reflected in the product obtained by multiplying the estimated prevalence by the three or four members constituting the average family.

For those people with epilepsy the probabilities dictated by the laws of heredity assume vast importance. Decisions about marriage and raising a family may be determined for them by the available information about heredity. Adults with epilepsy are thus forced to give serious consideration to the fact that, whereas when both parents have no epilepsy the chances of any of their offspring developing epilepsy are about one out of a hundred, this probability increases to one out of forty when one parent has epilepsy, with a still greater probability operating where both parents have epilepsy.

These probabilities when viewed alone may appear ominous and even alarming. It is therefore advisable that additional background information be provided so as to enable us to form a more realistic appraisal of this situation. It should first be noted that the inherited predisposition to epilepsy is equal to that found for diabetes, is one-half as great as with obesity, and only one-fourth as great as the inherited factor which accounts for migraine. Second, since about 1940, there has been rapid and continued progress in developing more accurate diagnostic procedures along with more effective medications. There is every reason to believe that these advances will continue. Third, it is heartening to realize that those patients in whom epilepsy develops at an early age and who are most influenced by the inheritance factor are the same group of patients who display the greatest favorable responsiveness to medications and who also demonstrate the best chances for reaching a point when they will be completely free of seizures without the assistance of medications. There is a tendency for all seizures to decrease in frequency as the patient grows older, but of all patients developing seizures in childhood, 50 per cent of them will be relieved of seizures by the time they reach age twenty, while 75 per cent of them may look forward to this freedom from seizures by the time they reach age thirty.

In addition to the foregoing information it is also pointed out by a number of studies that idiopathic epilepsy is least affected by deterioration resulting from associated disorders.

Intelligence

THE MORE commonly used intelligence tests are the two forms of the Stanford-Binet and the Wechsler Intelligence Scale for Children. With epileptic children, administering as well as interpreting these or other tests of intelligence requires arduous application of professional skill and experienced judgment. Several factors make it difficult to obtain the full measure of intelligence; they tend to cause a spuriously lower score than may be valid. These operational factors are as follows: The presence of organic damage in an appreciable number of children with seizures; frequently found gaps in their background of formal education; uneven and inadequate exposure to those daily living experiences which go to form social intelligence; the inability of the child to respond with his optimum performance because of long and continued use of certain medications; and his lack of experience in meeting a testing situation with the practice found in others of his age whose background has not been as limited.

A more accurate estimate of intelligence with these children must sometimes be made through means other than an intelligence test. In these instances the intelligence test assumes more importance as part of a periodic re-examination procedure in determining progress and the nature of that progress, rather than in yielding an I.Q. score.

Numerous studies reporting I. Q. scores for large populations of children with epilepsy concur that the distribution of their scores tends to be similar to the normal distribution of intelligence in the general population.[42,54,22,27,13,31,43,29] Deterioration is more apt to make itself evident in cases of organic etiology, of children who have developed epilepsy in infancy or early childhood, and of children having psychomotor and grand mal epilepsy. In the absence of brain damage along with seizures starting at a very early age, the intensity and the frequency of seizures have not been shown to have significance in affecting intelligence.

Efforts to establish subtest patterns consistent with epilepsy conclude that there is no typical epileptic patient. It would seem advisable that intratest variations be approached as an individual matter with any such children who are examined.

One final point of interest—in 1941 Penfield and Erickson [43] surveyed the psychological studies up to that date and concluded that the lack of uniformity in the results of careful workers was striking; they considered the matter sufficiently important to call attention to it. In 1962 Geist [14] summarized the psychological test literature up to about that date and concluded that the literature is replete with conflicting evidence.

Personality and Adjustment

EPILEPSY TENDS to create problems of emotional adjustment as does any other chronic illness.[26] The child is faced with the difficulties of his own acceptance and understanding of his seizures and of himself, his family's attitude towards his seizures as well as towards himself, the impressions and reactions he encounters in school and with his friends, repeated trips for medical attention, constant medications, limited participation in activity which other children may enjoy freely, and progressive realization of being different and of being treated differently than other children. The demand for continual readjustments imposed by these interminable problems would excessively strain the emotional health of any child. With the passage of time this child may develop painful self-consciousness and social awkwardness, and either retreat into a state of withdrawal or retaliate with bitterness and anger. Concomitant parental feelings of helplessness, guilt, perplexity, and shame may be conveyed to the child in the form of hostility, open rejection, segregation from the siblings, and restrictions from family and community activities. It is interesting to note that similar restrictions may be imposed by those parents who assume a position of the opposite extreme and become overconcerned, overprotective, oversolicitous, and overpermissive.

Parental attitudes and interactions with the child have central importance in shaping his immediate and future attitudes towards his epilepsy, towards himself, as well as towards his environment.

The frightened uncertainty experienced by parents may sometimes cause them to act in ways detrimental to the child's welfare. Concerned about community disapproval or about an injury sustained during a seizure, they may keep the child closeted at home; embarrassed by the social stigma, they may keep the child uninformed of his illness and instead provide him with some fuzzy explanation for his "fainting spells."

Such embarrassment may even motivate some parents to avoid all sources of care and treatment for the illness; their fear of the child being expelled from class and ostracized by his playmates may lead to the illness being treated as a closely guarded family secret. Refusal of some parents to accept the diagnosis or the absence of a cure may result in their being victimized by fraudulent remedies and practitioners, exhausting the family's financial resources through endless doctor-shopping tours, or engaging in repeated disagreements with the physician or clinic treating the child.

Lack of the full cooperation and understanding of the parents detracts from the effectiveness of even the best therapeutic program and interferes with the opportunity a youngster may have for making a wholesome adjustment to the classroom. It is generally agreed that the coordinated efforts of the teacher, the school nurse, the counsellor, and the school physician are essential ingredients to the treatment plan for that child. Yet without a frank approach by the parents, there is little chance of a teacher even knowing that she has a child with epilepsy in her class. A survey of 92,000 public school children in Boston [32] disclosed only 143 children with epilepsy, or one out of every 643 students. This gives a percentage of 0.15 in contrast to the 0.5 per cent of rejects for military service because of epilepsy in World War I and World War II, or the 1 per cent estimate of the people with epilepsy in the entire population. Since epilepsy is predominantly a children's disorder, we may assume that in the total children's population the percentage of epilepsy would possibly be in excess of either of the last two figures. There are three obvious reasons for this discrepancy. One has already been stated as the parental fear of exposing their children. Another becomes apparent when by computing the number of hours a child spends in school we find that about 85 per cent of his time is spent outside of the classroom and out of sight of his teacher. Finally, seizures are less prone to occur in class when the body and the mind are usually most active.

That the physician's role is difficult even with maximum parental cooperation may be more clearly seen by noting some of the ways in which epilepsy in children differs from epilepsy in adults.[9,32] Diagnosis is more complicated because of the high incidence of related disturbances. Brain lesions, other neurological defects, and deterioration processes are more common. EEG patterns change and display a greater variety of abnormalities. Even the seizure pattern is less static and tends to change with increased maturity. Locations within the brain from which the seizures presumably originate also shift and thereby become less meaningful. Response to medications are less predictable. Frequently establishment of good seizure control may only be temporary, and the seizures may suddenly recur. Treatment is broader in scope in that the whole family is involved. Physicians often find that they spend more time relieving the feelings of the parents than stopping the seizures of the child.

Emotional reactions aroused by epilepsy do not confine themselves to the patient. In subtle ways they are communicated to family, friends, and others—frequently in exaggerated forms. Insecurity and frustration in the patient, uncertainties and anxiety in family members, are central issues in these entanglements.

A sympathetic understanding is a necessary preliminary measure toward establishing a working relationship. The patient and his family may be exposed to an assortment of information about epilepsy which is occasionally conflicting and sometimes confusing. Apathy and ignorance continue to confront these people when they seek professional care and treatment in several parts of the country. Still encountered are attitudes and practices which tend to sweep all people with epilepsy into one category and then proceed to season this hash with generous sprinklings of obsolete beliefs. The basic insecurity experienced by these people is further compounded by the uneven and unpredictable course of the illness itself and by the absence of absolute qualities traditional with many other illnesses. For example, when a patient reports no seizures after a reasonable period of time, it is still general practice to advise that patient to continue taking his medications for a period of from two to four years following his last seizure. The person with epilepsy who is in good health and who has achieved complete or almost complete relief from his seizures feels unjustly harassed when he is deprived of those opportunities commensurate with his abilities, interests, and personal ambitions.

Investigation has shown that there is no typical personality pattern characteristic of epilepsy.[54] Behavior patterns as well as emotional reactions vary and, whatever their level of adjustment may be, appear to be the result of individual personality make-ups rather than being directly related to epilepsy. This contention is supported by the fact that recurrent seizures are only a symptom of a large number of conditions which in turn may affect any one of a large number of areas in the brain. Nevertheless, since the introduction of projective tests numerous attempts have been made to establish classification patterns in a number of personality tests characteristic of the epileptic. Studies have usually been made of small samples of patients (from ten to about twenty-five), and they often consist of cases with associated mental deterioration, severe emotional difficulties, or mental deficiencies. A comparison of many such studies, therefore, reveals inconclusive and inconsistent findings. Personality patterns suggested by these studies have not proven to be reliable, or else would tend to be characteristic of one or another of the attendant disorders within the sample population used. It is therefore advisable that psychological examinations confine themselves to an individualized assessment of the patient.

Treatment

PRIMARY TO a therapeutic program is the need to establish and maintain optimum reduction of the seizures. Only then can a broad range rehabilitative program be introduced with any assurance of success. Unhealthy attitudes along with the insecurity which may have existed up to this point will also need to be reduced. A typical treatment plan, therefore, includes work not only with the patient but also with his family, with his school, and with other people important to his everyday life.

Essential to the effectiveness of this plan is a mutually harmonious and cooperative relationship between the child's family and his physician, for the child will continue under medical supervision not only during the time he continues having seizures but for a period of several years following the cessation of his clinical symptoms. During this period parents may also have developed opinions and methods in need of modification. Sometimes family counselling is indicated for this purpose. Occasionally it may be advisable for the child to receive some psychiatric care as well.

As a rule, the child who has achieved good seizure control is encouraged to participate in all activities, as does the youngster without epilepsy. In a few instances the type of seizure the child has or the degree of control which has not as yet been attained, may suggest certain limitation of his activities unless they are under close supervision. Such matters are generally arranged individually with the youngster's physician.

Next to his parents, the classroom teacher may be the most important person to the child's daily experiences. Most children with epilepsy can attend regular schools in their own communities. Where medical management has successfully brought seizures under control, there is little needed in the way of special arrangements which the school or the teacher must make for that youngster. It is nevertheless not uncommon for a teacher to feel concern and anxiety about having a child with epilepsy in her class, and particularly so if she first learns of this through witnessing a seizure. Satisfactory arrangements can be made in almost all situations by providing the teacher and other school authorities with information to help them understand the youngster as well as his condition. The support and cooperation of the teacher will provide immeasurable help for the child in gaining acceptance with his peers.

Public Attitudes

THERE IS agreement that the general outlook for people with epilepsy is a bright one. Perhaps this is because they have already touched bottom. Knowledge and interest have increased exponentially since the 1940's. Diagnostic and therapeutic techniques have made dramatic advances in this relatively short period. It is currently estimated that about 50 per cent of all people with epilepsy can be helped, with the use of existing medications, to have their seizures completely removed. About another 30 per cent or more are able to have their seizures sufficiently reduced so that they can function as normally as any other person. The major problem for the person with epilepsy is no longer in the area of medical knowledge, but rather in the realm of public understanding and acceptance. The social image of the epileptic is lagging far behind the present availability of scientific fact, with the result that these people still face frustratingly unjust written and tacit restrictions devised in an era when all people with epilepsy were considered to be hopeless, untreatable, and unsafe.

Olender [41] completed a survey of state laws early in 1962. He found that in many states, by law or by administrative policy, people with epilepsy are not permitted to drive, to marry, and to have children. Davidson and Thomas [7] report the resistance adults with epilepsy face in finding employment. Although a concern for safety is usually given as a reason, their opinion was that emotional bias was the real cause for this. Further, surveys indicate that there are no significant differences for accident rates with properly placed epileptics than with others.[40] Nevertheless, Workmen's Compensation Laws often fail to give relief for injuries suffered by employees who have epilepsy. Similar difficulty is experienced in the epileptic's efforts to obtain life insurance.[2]

Caveness [5,6] reports on a public attitude study conducted over a ten-year period. Sampling technique included representative members of all groups of adults throughout the country. Some of his findings indicate that 90 per cent of the population have an awareness of epilepsy; that 18 per cent would object to their child playing with a child who has epilepsy; 4 per cent believe that epilepsy is another form of insanity; and 11 per cent firmly believe that people with epilepsy should not be employed. On the positive side, his last survey, completed at the end of the ten-year period, detected a distinct improvement in social attitudes in contrast with the findings of ten years before.

At the risk of oversimplifying a highly complex matter, it may be suggested that two basic needs still exist and will require much work towards their resolution. These are to bring the public up to date with current knowledge about epilepsy and to continue to increase the amount of knowledge and treatment methods available.

Notes

[1] "A Survey of the Epilepsies in General Practice, Research Committee of the College of General Practitioners," *British Med. J.*, August 6, 1960, pp. 416-422.

[2] Arieff, Alex J., "Epilepsy and Life Insurance," *Neurology*, VII, No. 1 (1957), 1071-1075.

[3] Bailey, Percival, "Lobectomy for Psychomotor Epilepsy," *Modern Medicine*, July 10, 1961.

[4] Baldwin, Maitland and Pearce Bailey, eds., *Temporal Lobe Epilepsy*. Springfield, Ill.: Charles C. Thomas, Publishers, 1958.

[5] Caveness, William F., "A Survey of Public Attitudes Toward Epilepsy," *Epilepsia*, IV (1949), 19-26.

[6] Caveness, William F., "Trend in Public Attitudes toward Epilepsy over the Past Decade," *Epilepsia*, I (1960), 385-393.

[7] Davidson, Elabel McL. and Joan C. Thomas, "A Sociological Study of Epileptic Patients," *Journal of Social Casework*, No. 30 (November 1949), 380-384.

[8] Davis, Ellen L., "Emotional Stress Can Trigger Seizures in Epileptic Children," *Pediatrics*, April 1962, pp. 63-66.

[9] Davis, Jean, "Management of Epilepsy in Children," *Tenth Western Institute on Epilepsy*, Denver, Colorado (1958), pp. 54-62.

[10] Eisner, Victor, Lydia L. Pauli, and Samuel Livingston; "Epilepsy in the Families of Epileptics," *The Journal of Pediatrics*, LVI, No. 13 (1960), 347-354.

[11] "Epileptic Pupils," *Colorado School Journal*, February 1962, pp. 1-11.

[12] Forster, Francis M., "Diagnosis and Treatment of Convulsive Disorders," *Modern Medicine*, July 15, 1957, pp. 69-79.

[13] Friedlander, Walter J., "Epilepsy," *The American Journal of Psychiatry*, CXVIII, No. 7 (1962), 623-627.

[14] Geist, Harold, *The Etiology of Idiopathic Epilepsy*. New York: Exposition Press, 1962.

[15] Gibbs, Frederic A. and Frederick W. Stamps, *Epilepsy Handbook*. Springfield, Ill.: Charles C. Thomas, Publishers, 1958.

[16] Green, John R. and H. F. Steelman, eds., *Epileptic Seizures*. Baltimore: The Williams & Wilkins Co., 1956.

[17] Green, John R. and Harry F. Steelman, eds., *Epileptic Seizures*. Baltimore: The Williams & Wilkins Co., 1956.

[18] Hefner, Ray, "Some Unusual Varieties of Visceral Epilepsy," *Missouri Medicine*, LVII, No. 3 (1960), 289-292.

[19] *Highlights of Progress in Research on Neurological & Sensory Disorders*. Washington, D.C.: U. S. Department of Health, Education and Welfare, Public Health Service, National Institutes of Health, 1958.

[20] Himler, Leonard E. and Theophile Raphael, "Epilepsy among College Students," *Mental Hygiene*, XXIV (July 1940), 459-468.

[21] Hinsie, Leland E. and Robert Jean Campbell, *Psychiatric Dictionary*. New York: Oxford University Press, Inc., 1960.

[22] Holowach, Jean, Yavuz A. Renda, and Irwin Wafner, "Psychomotor Seizures in Childhood," *The Journal of Pediatrics*, LIX, No. 3 (1961), 339-346.

[23] *Interviewing Guides*, rev. ed., "Epilepsy." Washington, D.C.: U. S. Dept. of Labor, Bureau of Employer Security, U. S. Employment Service, 1961, pp. 1-9.

[24] Juul-Jensen, Palle, "Vocational Training of Epileptics," *Epilepsia*, II, No. 3 (1961), 291-296.

[25] Kammerdiener, Jr., "Fundamental Facts Relating to the Counseling and Higher Education of Epileptic Persons," *Mental Hygiene* (October 1961), pp. 552-562.

[26] Kanner, Leo, *Child Psychiatry*. Springfield, Ill.: Charles C. Thomas, Publishers, 1960.

[27] Khan, Rafi Z., "An Etiological Reclassification of Epilepsy," *Journal of Mental Deficiency Research*, IV, Part II (1960), 108-114.

[28] "Laterality of Verbal Intelligence in the Brain," *Science*, March, 1962.

[29] Lennox, William G., H. Houston Merritt, and Thomas E. Bamford, eds., *Epilepsy*, XXVI. Baltimore: The Williams & Wilkins Co., 1947.

[30] Lennox, William G. and C. H. Markham, "The Sociopsychological Treatment of Epilepsy," *Journal of American Medical Association*, CLII (August 29, 1953), 1690-1694.

[31] Lennox, William G., "The Social and Emotional Problems of the Epileptic Child and His Family," *The Journal of Pediatrics*, XLIV, No. 5 (1954), 591-601.

[32] Lennox, William Gordon, *Epilepsy and Related Disorders*, I and II. Boston: Little, Brown & Co., 1960.

[33] Livingston, Samuel, *The Diagnosis and Treatment of Convulsive Disorders in Children*. Springfield, Ill.: Charles C. Thomas, Publishers, 1954.

[34] Livingston, Samuel, "Treatment of Epilepsy in Children," *Feelings*, IV, No. 2 (1960).

[35] Livingston, Samuel, Lydia L. Pauli, Irving Kramer, and Amir Najmabadi, "Clinical Evaluation of 1-Methyl-5, 5-Phenyl-Ethyl-Hydantoin in the Treatment of Epilepsy," *New England Journal of Medicine*, CCLXV, No. 9 (1961), 417-421.

[36] Mackay, Roland P., "All Epilepsy Is One," *American Medical Association Archives of Neurology*, II (March 1960), 237-246.

[37] Mackay, Roland P., S. Bernard Wortis, and Oscar Sugar, eds., *The Year Book of Neurology, Psychiatry and Neurosurgery*, 1959-1960 Year Book Series. Chicago: The Year Book Medical Publishers, Inc., 1960.

[38] Masland, Richard L., S. B. Sarason, and T. Gladwin, *Mental Subnormality*. New York: Basic Books, Inc., 1958.

[39] Meyer, V., "Cognitive Changes Following Temporal Lobectomy for Relief of Temporal Lobe Epilepsy," *American Medical Association Archives of Neurology and Psychiatry*, LXXXI (1959), 299-309.

[40] *Occupations of Epileptic Veterans of World War II and Korean Conflict*. Washington, D.C.: Department of Veterans Benefits, Veterans Administration, 1960.

[41] Olender, Jack H., *The Legal Rights of Persons with Epilepsy*. Washington, D.C.: The Epilepsy Foundation, 1962.

[42] *Patterns of Disease*, "Special Report: Epilepsy." Detroit: Parke, Davis & Co., 1958.

[43] Penfield, Wilder and Theodore C. Erickson, *Epilepsy and Cerebral Localization*. Springfield, Ill.: Charles C. Thomas, Publishers, 1941.

[44] Penfield, Wilder and Kristian Kristiansen, *Epileptic Seizure Patterns*. Springfield, Ill.: Charles C. Thomas, Publishers, 1951.

[45] Phemister, J. C., "Epilepsy and Car-Driving," *Lancet*, 7189 (June 10, 1961), 1276-1277.

[46] Putnam, Tracy J., *Epilepsy*. Philadelphia: J. B. Lippincott Co., 1958.

[47] Rasmussen, Theodore and Charles Branch, "Temporal Lobe Epilepsy: Indications for and Results of Surgical Therapy," *Postgraduate Medicine*, 31 (January 1962), 9-14.

[48] Richardson, William P., ed., *Convulsive Seizures*. North Carolina Health Council, 1961.

[49] Sakel, Manfred, *Epilepsy*. New York: Philosophical Library, Inc., 1958.

[50] Strauss, Hans, Mortimer Ostow, and Louis Greenstein, *Diagnostic Electroencephalography*. New York: Grune & Stratton, Inc., 1952.

[51] "Symposium on the Clinical Significance of Epileptic Seizures," *Proceedings of the Staff Meetings of the Mayo Clinic*. Rochester, Minn.: XXXIII, No. 20 (1958).

[52] Taylor, James, Gordon Holmes, and F. M. R. Walshe, eds., *Selected Writings of John Hughlings Jackson*, I. New York: Basic Books, Inc., 1958.

[53] Temkin, Owsei, *The Falling Sickness*. Baltimore: The Johns Hopkins Press, 1945.

[54] Tenny, John W., "Epileptic Children in Detroit's Special School Program," *Exceptional Children*, XXI, No. 5 (1955), 162-167.

[55] *The Child with Epilepsy*. Washington, D.C.: U. S. Department of Health, Education and Welfare, Childrens Bureau Bulletin No. 35, 1961.

[56] "The Patient with Epilepsy," *What's New*, No. 225 (1961), 4-9.

[57] Tilney, Frederick, Sanger Brown 2nd, and Henry Alsop Riley, eds., *Epilepsy and the Convulsive State*, Vol. VII of a Series of Research Publications by the Association for Research in Nervous and Mental Disease. Baltimore: The Williams & Wilkins Co., 1931.

[58] Tower, Donald B., *Neurochemistry of Epilepsy*. Springfield, Ill.: Charles C. Thomas, Publishers, 1960.

[59] Walker, A. Earl, *Posttraumatic Epilepsy*. Springfield, Ill.: Charles C. Thomas, Publishers, 1949.

[60] Wright, Beatrice A., *Physical Disability—A Psychological Approach*. New York: Harper & Row, Publishers, 1960.

JOSEPH NEWMAN

Chief, Psychology Service
Veterans Administration Hospital
Pittsburgh, Pennsylvania

8 *Psychological Problems of Children and Youth with Chronic Medical Disorders*

Psychological Implications of Chronic Disease

In Retrospect

A decade ago, the literature reporting research with chronically ill children was limited. For the most part, the guiding concepts for the study of illness among the younger age groups were derived from adult populations. The hazards in this procedure were widely recognized. In the ensuing ten years, a broad interest developed in the treatment and care of children and youth with medical disorders, whether acute or chronic. This interest was reflected in a burgeoning literature on the psychological aspects of disease and its ramifications among these early age groups. Basically, there has been a reemphasis of the principle of developmental psychology that the child is not an adult in miniature.

The current literature on chronic disease among children has affirmed a fundamental postulate of Chapter 1, that there are more similarities in the effects of different chronic diseases than dissimilarities. In the present chapter, we advance the postulate further, that these similarities make for a meaningful and coherent approach to chronic disease in general among children.

Psychosomatic Considerations

It was inevitable that psychosomatic variables would be sought in childhood disease. Nevertheless, extensive attention to these factors is relatively recent. Although the theoretical concepts pursued were formulated in studies of adults, there were early lines of investigation which observed somatic consequences to the infant of a disturbed mother-child relationship. Here psychoanalytic studies were prominent.[1]

While there is agreement that psychological factors play a role in many common ailments, there is little agreement about the basic mechanisms through which psychological and somatic factors interact to influence disease processes. There is even less agreement about the etiological role of psychological variables. Kaplan and Kaplan [2] insist that no one theory, construct, or set of variables is adequate to explain the observed and assumed relationship between psychological difficulty and physical malady.

The specificity theories, which assumed that specific psychological events caused specific psychosomatic diseases, and that specific personality features underlie specific psychosomatic conditions, have not been generally supported in research studies.[3,4]

More prevalent currently are the non-specific theories which attribute psychosomatic disease to general psychological stress reactions. Some writers emphasize the common origins of many diverse psychosomatic symptoms.[5] Thus, psychosomatic disturbances are multiply expressed in various systems of the body and not just in one organ system. They are the end-result of a series of events. This series of events may appear to have been initiated by some easily visible life stress such as school failure, injury, or death. However, the way in which a person reacts to stress is a highly individual matter which can be understood only by appreciation of the many factors operating in that person's situation.[6,7]

Hence, the psychological component in any one illness is variable, it may range from incidental to central importance. Starr [8] has conceptualized a scheme, a psychosomatic spectrum, in which he describes a continuum of psychological complications as they may occur in all types of clinical illness. The range is from illnesses in which the psychological factor is regarded as causative to those illnesses in which it is incidental. The categories of illness along this continuum are fourfold.[9]

The first group includes what Starr calls *psychological pseudosomatic reactions* in which the psychological factor is causative, such as in conversion hysteria, somatic delusions, and hypochondriasis. These are psychological states in which there is no demonstrable physiological dysfunction or organic change. Usually, emotional conflicts that explain the basis for the somatic complaints may be uncovered. Psychological pseudosomatic reactions can be essentially regarded as specific superficial manifestations of a disturbed emotional state which may otherwise not be in evidence.

The second category consists of *psychophysiological reactions* in which the psychological factor may vary from being precipitating to exacerbating, such as in anxiety states, tachycardia, hyperventilation, dyspnea, diarrhea, and diaphoresis. These reactions refer to the commonly observed close correlation between emotional states and concomitant physiological changes, which were demonstrated in the pioneering experiments of Cannon. In a host of affective disturbances (for example, fright, guilt, panic, depression) there are simultaneous and interrelated fluctuations in body physiology involving endocrine, metabolic, and neurophysiological mechanisms. These phenomena have been investigated more recently by Selye [10] who conducted a number of studies to the effects on organisms of extreme and long-continued strain or stress. The body will respond to stress in a stereotyped manner which Selye called the *general adaptation syndrome*. Emotional disturbances will act as "stress agents" and create neurophysiological, metabolic, and endocrine changes that are strikingly similar to those stress reactions created by physical or biological agents. Anxiety states point up psychophysiological reactions most conclusively. Grinker has conceptualized anxiety not only as a consequence of stress but also as a stress factor itself.[11]

The third category embraces *psychopathophysiological reactions* in which the psychological factor may range from an exacerbating role to a perpetuating one, such as in peptic ulcer, bronchial asthma, hypertension, thyrotoxicosis, diabetes mellitus, epilepsy, and neurodermatitis. Psychophysiological changes are essentially functional and reversible disturbances. However, when they become long-acting and frequent in their occurrence, tissue changes may result. These structural changes are what Starr describes as *psychopathophysiological reactions*. The psychophysiological reactions need not necessarily be the central determining factor in the origin of the structural change. Any other stress factor, perhaps nutritional, allergic, or infectious, may have been of primary significance in determining the onset of a disease condition, such as duodenal ulcer, ulcerative colitis, diabetes, and bronchial asthma.

The last group encompasses *somatopsychological reactions* in which the psychological factor is mainly incidental, such as in rheumatic fever, tuberculosis, encephalitis, and cerebral palsy. The existence of somatopsychological reactions is quite generally recognized. These disorders refer to the fact that the somatic disease creates and triggers emotional reactions that are secondary and incidental to the physical disorder.

In these four major sets of complexly related somatic and psychological states, it should be emphasized that, in any one individual with a clinical disorder, one or more of those reactions may be operating simultaneously or in sequence. This discussion is limited to two categories, psychopathophysiological reactions and somatopsychological reactions. Within the first category, we shall consider asthma and diabetes mellitus, and within the second category, heart disease and tuberculosis.

These four disease groups constitute severe and common diseases among children. Discussion of their psychological components will illustrate the experiences encountered with a whole host of diseases in childhood and youth. Indeed, it is the thesis of this discussion that the general or non-specific aspects of illness far outweigh the more specific effects of particular illnesses.

Developmental Factors in the Psychology of Illness

Recent reviews of developmental psychology note vigorous research activities in the effects of parental behavior and attitudes on child personality and behavior.[12] The research findings are generally consistent in demonstrating that the child's familial experiences are prime determiners of his personality. Within this context, there is mounting evidence on the pervasive and dramatic effects of early experience on later development. Thompson points out that "the living organism is a dynamic and developing system, variable in its functioning according to inherent genetic characteristics which interact with selected environmental antecedents. We now know that alteration in one part of this system can have widespread and enduring consequences."[13] This generalization finds wide support in the study of disease and its sequelae among children.

One avenue of investigation has been to relate psychosomatic disorders, psychopathophysiological reactions, to psychological traumas having their origin in the very early life of the individual. Mohr and others [14] studied a group of psychosomatically ill children. They found that these children were consistently exposed to inadequate mothering care during the first year of life. In view of the fact that early adaptation is mainly that of adjustment of the various body organs to extra-uterine function, later maladaptation may develop when emotional difficulties are experienced as physical and physiological traumas, as in the first few months of life when patterns of response are being initiated. In this period, any noxious stimulus, physical or psychological, tends to produce a generalized response.

In a later report, Garner and Wenar [15] more systematically explored the hypothesis that susceptibility to psychosomatic illness in children develops in the first year of life when somatic response patterns are soon laid down in an atmosphere of close but mutually frustrating mother-child interaction. Mothers of physically ill children had positive attitudes to pregnancy and early child care; mothers of neurotic children had negative attitudes toward both; and mothers of psychosomatically ill children had positive attitudes toward pregnancy, but not toward child care. Mothers in this last group were seen as ambitious, controlling, driving women, who victimized their children. They expect conformity, but lack tenderness and the spontaneous enjoyment of children. They are "quotation mark" mothers who "love" their children and do all the "right" things. While this study did not have a control group and the number of subjects was relatively small, it is regarded as a contribution to the growing literature about psychosomatically ill children.

In a study [16] of factors influencing the adjustment of organically handicapped children, the most prominent single factor in determining whether anxiety would become an important element seemed to be parental attitude. It was found that the amount of anxiety and the manner in which it found expression bore no predictable relationship to the handicap per se. There was no predictable relationship between the severity of the handicap and parental attitudes, such as over-protection or under-protection. The amount of parental anxiety and the manner in which it found expression seemed related more to the parents' own particular emotional needs and basic attitudes toward the child than to realistic elements of the handicap.

Again, Tuttman,[17] in an investigation of the influence of the severity of disability and parental authoritarianism in the child's acceptance of disability, found that children of authoritarian parents have more difficulty in accepting disability than do children of less authoritarian parents.

Parsons [18] has emphasized that the concept of illness as applied to the sick adult cannot be applied to the sick child. The immature child cannot be expected to assume the same roles and levels of responsibility as the adult. For example, the child cannot be held responsible for getting out of his condition by an act of will. He is not held responsible in usual dealings with others, and therefore, not responsible for recognition of his own condition, its disabilities, and his need for help. This means that third parties, parents, must play an especially important role in the child's illness.

General Psychological Effects of Illness

The literature on the psychological effects of acute illness among children is not large. Some of the psychological effects are not specific to illness. Illness, like any stress, may accentuate a pre-existing problem or awaken a previously dormant problem. Prugh,[19] for example, found that a child's reaction to illness was appropriate for age level rather than stemming from illness itself in a specific sense. Thus, anxiety was exaggerated by fantasies and fear of overwhelming attack on the part of the pre-school child, but not on the part of the older child.

Many authors have observed that physical illness in a child, no matter how trivial, has its own unique meaning to the child and to his parents.[20] When a child becomes ill, many things happen to him which are strange, new, and poorly understood. He does not feel well, understands little of why he has become sick, is irritable, and perhaps wants to be left alone. His own anxiety is often intensified by that of his parents, who may become guilty and anxious about their own part in the production of the illness or their failure to have prevented it. Indeed, many observers feel that parents form the most significant source of anxiety in children.[21,22,23]

Although the meaning of a specific illness to a particular child depends upon a large number of factors in his past experience and on the attitudes of his parents, there are certain common reactions in most children who become sick. Prominent among these is guilt and fear and the belief that illness is a punishment. In one study, 90 per cent of a group of hospitalized children stated that they became sick because they were "bad." Eighteen out of a group of 21 diabetic children said they "ate too much sugar." In a group of cardiac children, 90 per cent believed they were ill because they "ran too much." In another group of children with rheumatic heart disease, almost all thought that their illness was in some way caused by disobedience of parental commands. When these same children were placed for treatment outside their homes, some felt that they were being sent away because they were bad.[24]

To be sure, parental admonitions will intensify any latent fear that the child may have that his illness comes as a punishment. Thus, colds come because the child disobeys and does not wear his rubbers. A leg is broken because the child does not heed his mother's caution not to roller skate in the street. Upset stomachs could be avoided if the child would eat properly, and so on. When something does happen to the child, warnings are supplemented with "I told you so." These practices are very common and contribute to the child's belief that when he is sick, he is being punished. The use of the doctor as a "bogey" man will also reinforce the belief that illness is punishment. If the medical treatment is painful, it is looked upon as deserved punishment. Anna Freud[25] has discussed this aspect of illness in an enlightening way. She points out that the child is unable to distinguish between feelings of suffering caused by the disease and suffering imposed in order to cure the disease. The child is forced to submit uncomprehendingly. She identifies several factors as being sig-

nificant in illness. First is a change in emotional climate of the home—
increased attention and indulgence along with overconcern where formerly coercion may have been the rule. Then the experience of being
nursed may have negative psychological implications. In this, there is
infringement on developing processes of self-determination, independence, and privacy which may be difficult for the child to tolerate since
they are relatively recent acquisitions and hence more difficult to relinquish. A third factor is the restriction of bodily movement which inhibits the child's usual motoric activity and leads to irritability and rest-
lessness. Lastly, the threat of operations stimulates fears for bodily integrity and fantasies of mutilation.

The second group of common reactions are regressive phenomena.[26, 27]
It has been observed frequently that with almost any illness there occurs
some degree of regression to an earlier level of emotional and social functioning. In the child, regression takes place as an adaptive device to
mobilize defenses against anxiety. The degree of regression is dependent
upon the severity of emotional disturbance and length of illness. With
more prolonged and traumatic illnesses, there are more severe regres-
sions to infantile preoccupations with need for affection and purely physical functions such as food intake and excretion. The younger the child at
the time of illness, the more quickly the regression occurs. In general,
the most recently acquired behavior habits and social techniques are
first to go.

Persistent dependency reactions form the third group. Some children
try to perpetuate infantile relationships to their environment which have
given them an enjoyable security and satisfaction during illness. These
secondary gains of illness are reluctantly given up even though there
were no particular symptoms of maladjustment prior to illness. The most
persistent of these dependency states are those in which there is intense
anxiety on the part of parents because of illness in the child.

Fourth of the common reactions is rebelliousness. Some children react
by developing resentment and rebellion. They blame others for their
illness and incapacitation. This reaction is probably related to anxiety
over illness as a punishment and, as a compensatory mechanism, serves
to deny the presence of fears.

Chronic invalid reactions form the fifth group. These are the result of
parental overconcern, and they continue long after there is any need for
realistic concern about the effects of illness. There is continued preoccupation with bodily functioning on the part of the child.

Finally, there are the constructive reactions to illness. Some children
respond to difficult situations in a constructive manner, and illness may
cause a minimum of emotional disturbance. If illness is well handled

and the child stable and healthy emotionally, then illness may be a constructive growth experience.

Psychological reactions to illness also extend to the sequelae of illness, that is, to the reduced or limited function and disability. In addition to the awareness concerning his limitations gained in the family constellation, the child may become aware of his physical inadequacies as a result of limitations in his ability to compete and (consequently) because of the attitudes of his peers. This situation has a profound effect on his social adjustment, sense of personal adequacy, and very probably on the development of drives and motivation. Sontag has described such environmental settings into which the child may be thrust as being unyielding and disregarding of any differences and limitations.[28] Children may be unconsciously cruel in their uninhibited and unthinking treatment of physical defects and deficiencies of their fellows. "Fatty," "Skinny," "Shorty," nicknames implying physical differences, are indicative of the readiness with which children call attention to the physical differences and deformities of their fellows. This emphasis on lack of physical attractiveness or physical deformity comes at a time when it can be most important for personality delineation and emotional adjustment.

The child's physical state helps to shape his environment, which in turn affects his emotional life. His energy level is an important determining factor in the nature of his responses to environmental pressures, whether of resistive or passive sort. The adaptive process of a child to his handicap is quite different from that of an adult. The adult makes use of many past experiences in which problems were solved; the child's experience is limited. He must learn through experimentation.

These psychological phenomena continue to exert their influences when disease becomes long-term and/or chronic. The continued stress necessitates adaptive actions on the part of the family and the individual. In general, these adaptive maneuvers are not new but derive from the existing patterns established previously in the earlier phases of the illness.

One particularly useful and unifying frame of reference in understanding the effects of chronic illness is in terms of the body-image, body-concept, and self-concept.[29] Body-image and body-concept refer to the subjective impressions of one's own body and to the way in which it is perceived in relation to the outside world during growth and development. The self-concept is a broader construct; [30] it is also formed over time out of the rewarding and punishing experiences with the world and reflects how the individual sees himself. It is an organizing factor in behavior, a mediator between the individual and experience.

Wylie, in her review of the self-concept,[31] remarks on the theoretical importance of a person's body characteristics as he perceives them to the development of his self-concept. Self-concept theorists would agree on the general idea that body characteristics that have low value may be expected to undermine self-regard, while highly valued body characteristics should enhance self-regard.[32] However, no controlled study has explored this proposition directly. The total pattern of findings from different investigations is congruent with the assumption that deviations of body characteristics from the individual's ideal may lead to lowered self-regard. However, no firm cause-effect inferences can be drawn.[33]

It would seem reasonable and significant to relate the self-concept to physical health and specifically to illness. Some have theorized that low self-regard will lead to or involve anxiety and tension and that anxiety may lead to various psychophysiological expressions.[34] Wylie is of the opinion that there seems to be no strong support for the rationale that low self-regard will be connected with poor physical health.[35]

On the other hand, there is a persistent opinion that ill health will undermine self-esteem and distort the self-concept, that is, produce effects of a somatopsychological kind.[36] Wright feels that, while group data do not show consistent relationships between the self-concept and physical disability and, although there is wide variability in these data, there is a relationship in the attitudes of the disabled to personality characteristics existing prior to disability.[37] She feels that physical disability has a profound effect upon the individual. From this frame of reference, some recent studies may be considered.

Barker and Wright report that the attitudes of a disabled person toward self are frequently devaluating.[38] In a similar way, Shelsky[39] found that disabled and chronically ill patients are more self-rejecting and less self-accepting. This process is affected by the nature of the disability; persons with tuberculosis are more negatively affected than amputees. In a study by Kimmel,[40] the kind of personality problems created by orthopedic disability was related to the time of life the handicap occurred. Children with acquired orthopedic handicaps have greater confidence in and more esteem for their bodies. They can cope more adequately with anxiety than can children with congenital handicaps. Kimmel felt that the results supported theories of personality development which emphasized the importance of motor maturation in the development of body confidence and ability to cope with anxiety.

Hospitalization

As illness continues and especially as it becomes a chronic disorder, the prospect of hospitalization for the child becomes increasingly probable. Within the past twenty years, interest in the effects of hospitalization on the child has grown very rapidly, and an extensive literature has accumulated. Numerous studies have been reported, and one consequence has been significant change in hospital practices.[41]

Interest in the effects of hospitalization received stimulation from the work of Spitz [42] and Goldfarb,[43] among others, with institutionalized children. Their studies showed that the most favorable conditions of shelter, food, medical care, schooling, and supervised social life are not in themselves sufficient to assure adequate physical growth and emotional development. Critical in the institutional situation is the absence of stimulation derived from love and attention. The earlier the age at which such deprivation experiences occur, the longer the duration and greater the extent of maladjustment. While the results of the research in this area have not been fully accepted,[44] it seems fairly credible that restrictions and deprivations in infancy can have drastic effect on the development of behavior.[45, 46] Furthermore, these studies have only general applicability and suggestiveness for hospitalized children. The hospitalized child has a different psychological situation; he has a family, an illness, and continued contact with parents.

Investigation of hospitalization was spurred on also by the report of war experiences with children separated from their families. It was found that children separated from their mothers had adjustment difficulties even though placed in quiet surroundings far away from danger. Children who remained with their mothers did not have such difficulties even though they were in the midst of danger and privation.

The work of Bowlby [47, 48] followed these observations. His hypothesis was that separation experiences were pathogenic. Robertson,[49] an associate of Bowlby, states that when hospital admission deprives a child of warm, intimate, and continuing relationship with his mother, particularly before four years of age, he reacts emotionally in a characteristic manner. This reaction has three phases. The first phase is protest, in which the child strongly and consciously acts and demonstrates his grief. Next is despair in which the child is less active in showing a conscious need of mother but couples it with an increasing hopelessness. He may become withdrawn, apathetic and may make no demands. Sometimes this stage is presumed to indicate that distress has lessened. A common remark is "He was quite settled until his mother came." With short hospitalization, some children just reach this stage or may go home in the stage of protest. In the third phase, denial, the child shows more interest in his surroundings. He may appear stable and sociable. However, this is a superficial impression; actually it is a manifestation of a defensive or adaptive maneuver. When the previously lamented mother comes, the child hardly knows her and no longer cries when she leaves. He is reluctant to leave the hospital. Robertson believes that the aftermath of long hospitalization in the early years is an extended period of serious emotional maladaptation. The two main dangers of hospitalization are the traumatic (shock of losing the mother and the pain and fright of treatment) and the deprivational—a function of lengthy separation.

In this country, studies were also stimulated, and the most notable were those by Prugh and his associates.[50, 51, 52] The purpose of the studies was to investigate the nature of the effects of brief hospitalization upon both children and parents. Two groups of 100 children, matched for age, sex, and diagnosis and hospitalized for relatively acute illnesses and for relatively short periods of time, formed the basis of one investigation. The results supported the impression of other investigators that children under three years of age are the most susceptible to the negative aspects surrounding hospital care. Separation from the mother is often interpreted as a punishment or desertion. This reaction, separation anxiety, was most frequent among the younger children. It was also common in older age groups but in less severe form and not as frequently. Among the older children, anxiety was related more to experience than to separation. Separation anxiety was the most common persisting post-hospital reaction. Depression and various disturbances, such as in feeding, sleeping, and toilet behavior were noted. Regressive phenomena constituted the most common defense. Among older children, withdrawing behavior became common. Frequent among all children was the reaction to treatment and diagnostic procedures as punishment. In the main, children who showed the most successful adjustment to hospitalization were those who seemed to have the most satisfying relationship with their parents, especially the mother. The highest positive correlation was reported between apparent adaptive capacity and adjustment to hospitalization. Children with limited adaptive capacity showed the most severe reaction to the total experience of hospitalization. The reactions of the parents to hospitalization were found to be dependent upon the adjustment of the parents and the nature of their relationships with the child.

Other studies revealed essentially similar findings. Gofman, Buckman, and Schade [53] undertook to assess the preparation for hospitalization among 100 children, ages 3 to 15 years, as well as their understanding of illness and their reaction to hospital care. They found that 75 per cent of their group were not prepared for hospitalization. It was felt by these investigators that children as young as three or four years of age could understand something of their illness and the necessary treatment if the explanations were made in terms suited to their levels. Marlens [54] compared emotional attitudes toward self and the environment for a group of children hospitalized and a group with similar complaints but not hospitalized. The hospitalized children were significantly higher in feelings of rejection and punishment, somatic preoccupation, and in anxiety and depression. There was no difference between the groups in feelings of hostility.

At the University of Maryland Hospital, Glaser,[55] by means of group discussions with mothers, elicited descriptions of the reactions of their children to hospitalization. These reactions included: increased dependency needs and physiological regression in behavior; withdrawal from mother; need for continued contact with outside world. This last reaction made mothers fearful that mention of friends, pets, and other familiar aspects of home life would make the child homesick. Actually, it was evolved that talking about these matters was helpful. The technique of group discussions for mothers was found to be useful in dealing with the mother's anxieties, fears, and misconceptions about the illness and the hospitalization.

In another study, Vaughan[56] undertook to investigate the attitudes toward hospitalization and an impending operation for correction of strabismus in a group of twenty children and a group of twenty controls. He found that all the children had varied, bizarre, and sometimes frightening ideas about the hospital. The children reflected the parents' anxieties. However, he gave (to his experimental group) simple and brief explanations and reassurances of what to expect. He found that this was enough to result in a significant benefit.

These and similar experiences led to actions to minimize, if not eliminate, the hazards of hospitalization for children. This subject was the concern of a study group of the World Health Organization in meetings held in Stockholm in September 1954. It was pointed out that the best place to care for the ill child is at home. The child under five is unable to understand the meaning of illness. Even for an adult, going to a hospital is a major event. For the small child, the break in relationships occasioned by hospitalization seems final and irrevocable. The meeting suggested remedial measures.[57]

The remedial efforts proceeded along three lines: elimination of force or actual pain in contact between staff and child; preparation for hospitalization; continuing close contact between the mother and child. This last is most controversial and has met with the most resistance. Nevertheless, there have been efforts to modify the separation of mother and hospitalized child that is customary in this country.

On the other hand, some students of the problem, recognizing the potential deleterious effects of hospitalization, insisted that these effects were not inevitable. They were agreed that, with prophylactic measures, hospitalization could be a constructive experience.[58]

Illingworth,[59] in a balanced and comprehensive discussion of the problem, believes that the case has been overstated, particularly the danger that children who experience institutionalization and similar forms of severe deprivation, especially in early life, commonly develop psychopathic or affectionless characters. The exaggeration of the risk can cause much unnecessary anxiety in parents and might possibly delay necessary hospital treatment. It can also lead to the minimizing of this risk or denial of its existence. On the basis of his experience in the follow-up of all children discharged from a medical ward in an English hospital, Illingworth found that it was exceptional for the child to show behavior problems which could be ascribed directly to hospital stay and experiences. Certainly the majority of children cry in hospitals, especially young children, when parents leave at the end of visiting time. Some may show other types of emotional behavior, but this is quite different from suggesting that the hospital experience leads to behavior problems which persist for weeks or months after discharge. Indeed, it would be surprising if young children below four years of age were not upset by hospital admission. Nevertheless, Illingworth believes the problem of psychological trauma is great and the fact that "only a small majority" show any lasting ill effects must not be a basis for minimizing it.

Systematic study identifies the several factors as causative in behavior problems associated with hospital stay. First would be disturbance in parent-child relationship before admission or after; the better this relationship, the less likely the development of disturbance. Lack of or inadequate preparation for admission is another factor. A third is unwise or excessive preparation as a result of anxiety about hospitals on the part of the parents. Frequently encountered are threats to the child—to do as they are told or lose love. Also implicated is a lack of daily visiting. Parental anxiety during visits, along with unkept promises, are potent in creating problems. Finally, parental attitudes on discharge, overindulgence and the like, especially after serious illness, are important.

Unquestionably, there is broad recognition of the problem of psychological trauma for hospitalized children and the realization that many areas of hospital procedure can be modified for the welfare of the child. The measures recommended are implicit in the discussion of factors believed to be causative of disturbance. It is felt that many illnesses can be treated at home and hence unnecessary admissions should be avoided. When admission to a hospital becomes necessary then there should be appropriate preparation for such admission. Where possible, admission should be to a children's hospital rather than to a general hospital and certainly never to an adult ward. Upon admission, the child should not be separated from the mother; the mother should go up to the ward with him. Daily visiting should occur. Routines should be explained to the child. Unpleasant sights and sounds should be avoided, and painful procedures should be carried out in treament rooms away from the observations of children. Ward rounds should be conducted with some consideration of the child as an understanding individual with feelings. Educational and recreational facilities should be available. Contacts with the family, especially the mother, should be maintained either through individual or group meetings.[60, 61]

These measures, pediatric authorities are convinced, would contribute to positive experiences as a result of the hospital stay—in that solution of mother-child problems would be furthered and healthy maturational forces encouraged. There are many constructive forces within the hospital, and with the aid of these forces (for example, parent substitutes and family substitutes) the child may grow emotionally.[62]

Tuberculosis

Nature of the Disease

Tuberculosis is an infection to which apparently all humans are susceptible. It is caused by the *Bacillus mycobacterium tuberculosis,* which can and does infect almost any tissue or organ in the body. In addition to the pulmonary form, which accounts for the vast majority of cases of tuberculosis, the two most serious complications are hematogenous spread (miliary tuberculosis) and spread to the central nervous system (tuberculous meningitis).

The initial infection is called "primary" tuberculosis. This usually occurs in childhood but now appears increasingly in adulthood. A new infection after the primary lesion has been brought under control is referred to as "reinfection" tuberculosis. This usually happens in adulthood but may strike in childhood. Primary tuberculosis has a great tendency to heal and consequently is regarded as "benign." In contrast, reinfection tuberculosis has a tendency to progress. However, primary infection is not always benign and reinfection not always devastating. Because some authorities are of the opinion that arrested primary infection exerts an immunizing effect against reinfection, it is a controversial issue.[63]

In this country, the tuberculosis situation has undergone a remarkable change during the past three decades. In the early 1930's large numbers of children had primary tuberculosis. Many died in infancy and early childhood from acute reinfection forms of tuberculosis such as meningitis, pneumonia, and miliary disease. Large numbers were suffering from tuberculosis of the bones and joints. Over these years, a marked decline was observed in primary tuberculosis among children in nearly every region of this country. In the age groups under 21 years, 5 per cent have been infected with tuberculosis bacilli as determined by skin tests, compared with a rate of 90 per cent infected in former years.[64]

There has been a continued and marked decline in the mortality rate of tuberculosis since 1900, and a precipitous drop since 1947, corresponding with the introduction of antibiotic and chemical therapy. In 1900, the tuberculosis death rate in the United States was about 200 per 100,000; in 1945, the death rate was less than 50 per 100,000; and in 1958, 7 per 100,000. Tuberculosis workers feel this heralds the beginning of the complete eradication of tuberculosis; indeed, the Arden House Conference in November 1959 agreed that the elimination of tuberculosis as a public health problem was a realizable goal by 1970.[65]

While some observers felt that this decline in mortality rate did not reflect a corresponding decline in the incidence of the disease, the prevailing opinion is that there is a corresponding reduction in active case rate; the active case rate in 1950 was estimated at 80 per 100,000. The goal of 10 per 100,000 by 1970 has been set by tuberculosis workers.[66] Newer therapeutic and surgical techniques have provided many years of survival to persons who would have rapidly died of tuberculosis in the past. It is believed that more success was achieved in retarding death from tuberculosis than in protecting from infection or in curing the disease.[67, 68] The exact incidence of tuberculosis is not known.

During recent years there has also been a noticeable shift in the age period at which the height of tuberculosis mortality is reached. The active case rates are highest for those 65 years of age and older. Tuberculosis is now beginning to be spoken of as a disease of older people, particularly men. These older groups remain the largest source of infection.[69]

The implications of this situation are important for a work such as this text which covers the age groups up to about 21 years. The shifting of the greater incidence of tuberculosis to older age groups within the last twenty odd years has coincided with the rise in greater interest in the psychological factors in tuberculosis. Consequently, the groups to which psychological study has been applied have mainly been adults. Hence the number of psychological studies specifically dealing with tuberculous children have been very few—and have been even fewer in recent years.

Psychological Vulnerability in the Tuberculous

Before we consider specific studies, it will be of value to review some of the aspects of tuberculosis that have implications for psychological reverberations. First is the chronic nature of tuberculosis. The disease process, once brought under control, lies dormant. This dormancy is termed "inactive" or "arrested" but not "cured." Thus there is always the potentiality of reactivation, although with passage of time the probability of reactivation is reduced. Nevertheless, the danger is ever present.

This fact leads to the second aspect of tuberculosis which is important psychologically. Reactivation of dormant lesions can be caused by a variety of factors as apparently unrelated as puberty, fatigue, malnutrition, uncontrolled diabetes, and emotional disturbances.

Third is the contagious nature of the disease. This leads to isolation, most frequently carried out in a hospital. Isolation, entailing separation from family and friends, is continued until non-contagiousness is established and maintained, and the disease process is rendered inactive. A period of treatment extending over months and years may be required. During this time, the threat of possible lung surgery is constantly present. Paradoxically, the patient usually feels fine from the outset of treatment.

Fourth, tuberculosis as a leading cause of death carries with it the threat of death. To this statistical fact must be added the folklore about "consumption" as a wasting disease leading to certain fatality.

Fifth, in considering the folklore of tuberculosis, the sense of ostracism must be recorded. Further, tuberculosis is a disease, in the main, of the least-favored social classes. As one writer put it, "Tuberculosis is not a disease which spells retirement with honor." It is often felt by patients, and to a certain degree by society, to be evidence of failure.

Sixth, the susceptibility to tuberculosis becomes high shortly after puberty and during early adulthood, following the previous age period which is called the "golden age" of resistance to tuberculosis. Thus, for many young people, tuberculosis comes at a period of life in which important adjustments are being made, and the long illness serves to complicate these processes. This is not to say the tuberculosis contracted in childhood is of little consequence but that in numbers it will not be met frequently.

Finally, for those with reinfection tuberculosis, changes in the mode of life are necessary—the extent and length of time being dependent upon the extent of disease.

The literature on the psychological aspects of tuberculosis is extensive, and has been reviewed by several authors.[70, 71, 72, 73, 74, 75, 76] It has been concerned almost exclusively with adult groups. As a matter of fact, although there are references to add since our previous review, we have not been able to find any new studies involving age groups below adults and only one or two additional general discussions.[77, 78]

Until 25 years ago, the literature was the result of subjective observation and clinical experience. Observations were usually made on small numbers of cases; contradictory conclusions were frequent; systematic work with adequate experimental designs was virtually non-existent. In sum, this work served as a source of hypotheses for study, but it did not provide useful knowledge.

Within recent years, studies of a systematic and experimental nature have appeared, and a more consistent body of knowledge was evolved. Despite its hoary tradition, the notion of a "tuberculosis personality" has been discarded. Differences in scores on psychological tests of tuberculosis patients and non-ill people do occur, but these are seen in the context of the patients' experience of hospitalization; in other words, the effects seen in the tuberculosis patient may be reactive to the illness and its treatment. A number of studies report specific emotional characteristics such as depression and anxiety and enable us to conclude that these are frequently found in tuberculosis patients. Some relationship between psychological factors and response to treatment has been suggested.[79]

Attempts have been made to relate the onset of tuberculosis or its relapses to emotional stress.[80] This association has been noted by non-psychiatric observers as Rene Dubos.[81] The exact relationship of emotional factors to the onset of active disease has not been established. The various efforts to formulate tuberculosis as a psychosomatic disease have served to offer some explanation as to why a person falls ill and why he falls ill when he does but have failed to explain why he falls ill with pulmonary tuberculosis.[82]

Probably the most thoroughgoing psychological study has been reported by Vernier and her associates.[83] For some 814 patients in 18 hospitals, several psychological variables were related to hospital adjustment, response to medical treatment, and post-hospital adjustment. One psychological variable, anxiety, was found to be related to all three criteria. "Anxiety appears to play an important role in poor adjustment as seen both in the hospital and in the post-hospital situations. Further, among those hospitalized patients with far advanced disease, the presence of anxiety was significantly related to less satisfactory response to the medical treatment of the disease process itself. These results lend some confirmation to the concept that anxiety is a central psychological variable in determining a wide variety of behaviors." These investigators feel that in this disease, "the need to maintain anxiety at a minimal state makes sense both logically and psychologically."

This last study deals essentially with the somatopsychological effects of tuberculosis. From a practical point of view, these are especially significant. In addition, there is much agreement among the various studies on such psychological effects of the disease.

Somatopsychological Aspects

The effect of the diagnosis of tuberculosis is a traumatic one, a reaction of shock. This is followed by anxiety and depression. The specific reaction for each individual, Derner found, was related to the individual's perception of the meaning of the disease.[84] The defenses against anxiety and depression are frequently seen in defiance, cheerfulness, resentment, and apathy. The feelings of anxiety and depression are normal and adequate so long as they are in keeping with the nature and degree of the tuberculosis process and with the repercussions which the illness has for the individual's life situation. However, the situation may be complicated by existing conflicts and disturbances. In this fashion, neurotic anxiety may be superimposed on justifiable fear.

Tuberculous patients have to subject themselves to complete inactivity or enforced idleness for a prolonged period. Some surrender to this, finding in the disease a welcome refuge from the vicissitudes of life; others prematurely and unwisely try to escape this mode of existence. Derner has emphasized that the basic psychological problem in tuberculosis is the sharp conflict between dependence needs and independence needs.

Hospital and sanatorium life is highly artificial.[85] Tuberculosis is the center of all interest and the chief preoccupation of all patients. Surgery is an ever-present threat and a source of anxiety about mutilation. Hospitalization also keeps to the fore the fact that the patients are "social menaces." The most frequent thought of one group of patients studied was to go home. Often this thought is implemented by action, so that premature interruptions of treatment in hospitals and sanitoria have become a major problem in the treatment of tuberculosis. Interestingly enough, most patients feel anxious or insecure upon discharge.

Psychological Effects in Children

The psychological effects of tuberculosis upon children have been the concern of several investigators. Kramer [86] has not found any specific personality type among children suffering from tuberculosis, a finding consistent with other tuberculosis workers among both children and adults.[87,88] He also is of the opinion that the psychopathology of tuberculous children does not differ essentially from the psychopathology of those who are non-tuberculous. In addition, infection with tuberculosis does not necessarily lead to psychopathology; it is dependent on the reactions to the disease, not on the disease itself. Kramer found no specific reaction pattern among the tuberculous children. The last finding is at variance with the results of Dubo's study.[89]

Since Dubo's study is the most extensive investigation of tuberculous children available, it might be well to present its findings in some detail. Twenty-five children, ages six to thirteen years, were studied in Bellevue Hospital, New York City. These children came from deprived homes of low economic status in congested neighborhoods where the tuberculosis incidence is high. Data were gathered through individual interviews and group sessions. The Rorschach technique was also utilized.

It was found that, despite wide diversity of pre-morbid personalities, there was a remarkable similarity of specific reactions. These reactions appeared to be closely linked with the difficulties in medical management encountered with these children. Ward behavior was characterized by diffuse motor activity, aggressive outbursts, and inability to cooperate in bed rest. The necessary limitation of activity was intolerable. These reactions were believed to stem from the intense anxiety that characterized the children's reaction to tuberculosis. Their thinking was preoccupied with death and other morbid content. Tuberculosis was equated with death. Dreams, fantasies, and drawings were filled with morbid and threatening symbols.

To these children, tuberculosis was a highly abstract phenomenon. It was symptomless and yet terrible since they had seen relatives and other patients die of it. In face of this terrifying threat, the children could not react with the usual psychological response—fight or flight. They were constrained to remain inactive and passive. It is not surprising, therefore, that Dubo found that the fantasies of these children were filled with constant motion—running, dancing, roller-skating.

Regressive phenomena were observed but were expected in a prolonged, confining, and anxiety-producing illness. Yet strong resistance was found to these regressive trends. Another source of disturbance was the necessity for isolation. The children could not comprehend the abstract concept of contagion, much less the measures utilized to reduce contagion. They felt different and stigmatized; the most forceful term of opprobrium was to be called "TB patient." They believed tuberculosis to be contracted through lack of cleanliness and, therefore, shameful. In addition, the children tended to assume personal responsibility for being ill and looked upon the illness as punishment. The reactions to these feelings of guilt and shame were in resentment and a feeling of being wronged. Aggression and defiance of authority were frequent problems.

These results fit in with some of the findings of research with the adult tuberculous, particularly the reaction of anxiety. To be sure, this appears to be the basic generalized reaction to great threat. Important to note is the failure of the children to comprehend the meanings of tuberculosis and contagion, which remained abstract concepts. We may wonder, indeed, if adults do not have the same difficulty.[90] These results appear to have wide usefulness despite the fact that the study probably is of limited general applicability because of the nature of the group studied. It is quite possible that many of the attitudes and reactions expressed by these children reflect their sociocultural backgrounds.

Bellak, in a study of 46 patients, emphasizes the problems of the tuberculous adolescent.[91] These patients face many problems upon their return home after long absence. In the hospital sanatorium, they have lived under altogether different conditions in a sexually mixed group of all ages and have been exposed to many ideas. Thus, with the usual problems of adolescent growth, they encounter special difficulties at home and in their social relationships. Instead of "growing up" with their problems, absorbing changes in small doses, there are sudden changes and clashes. Bellak calls attention to these difficulties as one of the most clear-cut results of his study.

A Field Theory Contribution

A particularly clarifying approach to the understanding of the tuberculous individual has been formulated by Barker, Wright, Meyerson, and Gonick.[92] These authors have undertaken to state, in terms of Kurt Lewin's topological psychology, the nature of the problems encountered in the adjustment to tuberculosis. This approach considers the psychological position of the tuberculous as influenced by overlapping "healthy" and tuberculous situations which give rise to a great amount of interfering and antagonistic behavior. There are, to be sure, other elements developed in this analysis, and the interested reader would do well to consult the work of Barker and his associates.

Tuberculous Children in School

A practical issue in the care of tuberculous children, of particular interest to school authorities, is the provision of special facilities for education. In the past thirty years, attitudes have undergone considerable change. At one time there was much enthusiasm about the treatment of children with primary tuberculous infections by removal from the home to preventoriums and camps. For those at home, attendance in special buildings, special schools, and "fresh-air" classes was recommended. In addition, as measures to prevent tuberculosis, malnourished and anemic children were sent to institutions set up for that purpose.

Experience, however, has shown that these facilities make no difference in treatment, and the results are the same whether the children are treated at home or in any of these special facilities. Consequently, most of these facilities have been closed. The prognosis in primary tuberculosis is excellent. For those with active reinfection tuberculosis, the proper place is in the hospital. Many tuberculosis hospitals with patients of school age provide bedside instruction. Once the tuberculosis has been rendered inactive and the child discharged to his home, a period of progressive increases in activity is to be followed, during which the child may attend regular classes, beginning at first on a part-time basis. Segregation in special classes is not warranted medically or psychologically.[93] This is not to say that there will not be problems arising from the integration of children with inactive tuberculosis in class activities. However, to the interested teacher, these problems are no greater than for any child who requires some adjustment in classroom routine. In the last analysis, the problem of tuberculosis among children seems, happily, a vanishing one.

Heart Disease

Nature of Heart Disease Among Children

Fifty years ago, the focus of attention in diseases of the heart among children and youth was rheumatic heart disease. Today, in the light of a broadened interest in heart disease and with a more detailed examination of all the facts about heart disorders, it has become clear that there are many more children suffering from congenital heart disease than from rheumatic heart disease. However, until the advent of cardiac surgery, interest in congenital heart disease was academic. With remarkable advances in diagnosis and techniques achieved in the last decade, the prognosis in most forms of congenital heart disease was converted from "hopeless" to "surgically curable." [94]

There are many types of congenital heart defects; each may occur alone or in combination with other defects. The various anatomical subdivisions of the heart or of the great vessels leaving the heart may be affected. Some are more lethal or disabling than others; some produce little obvious handicap in childhood but may cause difficulty at a later age. The symptom which is most usually associated with congenital heart defects is cyanosis, hence the term "blue baby." However, not all heart defects present this symptom, and it may be associated with conditions other than congenital heart defect.

The causes of congenital heart defects are not known. Some implicate occurrence of German measles (*Rubella*) during the first three months of pregnancy. Other virus diseases are also believed to be involved. One author states that approximately six babies in a thousand live births are born with congenital heart disease; another author estimates this to amount to 30,000 to 45,000 children each year. Many die in the first few weeks of life, and a further number succumb before the end of the first year.[95] Congenital heart defects at present account for approximately half of the organic heart conditions found in school-age children.[96]

It is believed that 75 to 80 per cent of the children with congenital heart disease can be helped by surgery. Not all congenital heart defects can be successfully corrected. With some, children may be restored to a normal life; other defects may still require that the child be restricted in activity.[97]

The costs of diagnosis and surgical treatment of congenital heart defects are high. These procedures require large teams of many kinds of specialists and comparatively long periods of medical and hospital care. Hence, cardiac surgery is out of the reach of many families who can ordinarily meet medical expenses. Fortunately there are two major sources of help—the state crippled children's program and the state vocational rehabilitation program.

Rheumatic fever is a clinical syndrome whose chief manifestations are heart disease, arthritis, chorea, skin rashes, and subcutaneous nodules. The importance of the disease centers around the fact that it produces heart damage. Until the 30's, it was one of the chief causes of illness and death in childhood and early adult life. It is now less common and has dropped from being the second cause of death among school children to the third. One authority states that there is the clinical impression that rheumatic fever is milder in its virulence.[98]

The most important causative factor is accepted to be Group A hemolytic streptococcus. The disease rarely begins in the first four years of life. As adolescence is approached, the incidence rises from 40 cases per 100,000 at age 6 to 340 cases per 100,000 at age 14. The prevalence among school populations has been estimated from .2 per cent to 4.5 per cent. There is in the last 25 years a trend toward lowered incidence.[99]

Rheumatic heart disease is found in only one or two school children per thousand. Approximately an equal number have rheumatic fever but no residual heart involvement. Ninety-five per cent of children who have recovered from an attack of rheumatic fever are able to lead an average existence. Perhaps 5 per cent are semi-invalids and lead restricted lives. The vast majority is able to go to school and take part in ordinary activities that do not involve strenuous effort. In a study of 699 surviving patients out of 1000 rheumatic fever patients who twenty years before had acute attacks, it was found that three out of four had little or no limitation in their activities.[100]

Climate appears to be an important factor in incidence. The colder, wetter parts of the temperate zone as well as the colder, wetter seasons of the year favor rheumatic disease. It is far more common, also, among the poor than among the well-to-do in almost every community. It is infrequently seen in private schools but is relatively frequent in large public schools. Crowding, exposure to cold and wet without sufficient protection, malnutrition, and fatigue appear to be factors in susceptibility.[101]

The periods of illness in rheumatic fever are often prolonged despite the fact that the earliest infection is often mild. In addition, the child with rheumatic fever is subject to repeated attacks of acute infection, and if the heart escapes damage during earlier attacks, it rarely escapes as the result of the repeated attacks. The greater the number of recurrences, the greater the heart damage. After the acute infection phase is over, necessary convalescent care also lasts for long periods of time, sometimes extending even into years. There has been no specific therapy for rheumatic fever. Steroid therapy (ACTH and cortisone) has been found to be of value. Antibiotics are used to eradicate infection. Bed rest and good nursing care remain the basic essentials in treatment. Prevention of streptococcal infection is recommended by the prophylactic use of penicillin.

Many children with rheumatic fever may be regarded as being "cardiac," even though they do not have heart disease, because of the necessity for close health supervision and prophylactic medication.

Psychological Sensitivity of the Cardiovascular System

Psychological factors have been associated with the functioning of the heart since time immemorial. There are numerous allusions in literature to the particular vulnerability of the heart to emotional influence, if not to its being the actual seat of emotion. In view of the critical importance of the heart for life or death, it is not at all surprising that it has been probably the most heavily emotionally invested organ of the body. Any threat to the heart is a threat to life itself. Thus, the accumulated folklore concerning the heart would be expected to cause immediate psychological repercussions whenever there is the slightest implication of heart disease.

However, before discussing these somatopsychological aspects of heart disease, the psychosomatic elements of heart disease (which are here perhaps more clearly evident) should be considered. Interest in psychosomatic aspects of heart disease has been expressed along with the general development of psychosomatic medicine.[102] Dunbar, in particular, has formulated psychosomatic hypotheses in many forms of heart disease, including one for a psychosomatic predisposition to rheumatic heart disease.[103] Except for rheumatic heart disease, the diseases implicated are those of adulthood and so do not directly concern the age groups under study. Moreover, the evidence presented is based almost entirely on adult groups. Nevertheless, her hypotheses have not been supported—no distinct personality has been found for children with heart disease.[104,105,106]

In patients with structural heart disease, there is a basic physiological problem that can be stated in terms of supply and demand. As long as it is possible for the heart to maintain circulation at an adequate level, the patient is compensated, that is, an adequate blood supply is maintained to tissues in response to varying functional demands. Whenever the balance between circulatory demands and the capacity of the heart to meet these demands cannot be maintained, heart failure develops. That balance may be disrupted by factors which increase the demand to a level greater than can be met, or by factors that lead to reduction of the capacity of the heart of meet demands. In both these situations, psychological stress may operate to increase demand and/or decrease available supply.[107]

Many studies have been conducted that demonstrate this. Wolff and Wolff and the various studies of the Cornell group [108] have shown that variations in pulse rate, cardiac output, and blood pressure, as well as other cardiovascular changes, may be induced under conditions of psychological stress having specific meaning for the individual. These stress conditions included the persistent low-grade strains of "every-day" living. Insofar as the patient with heart disease is concerned, there is little doubt as to the influence of psychological stress on the course of his disease.[109] However, the etiological role of psychological stress is not firmly established.

Anxiety is an inevitable consequence of heart disease, as of disease in general. Koenig studied this phenomenon in children with rheumatic fever.[110] She investigated the relationship between recurrences of rheumatic fever and Rorschach indices of anxiety. She found that children with recurrences of rheumatic fever exceeded normal children in degree of anxiety. Children who had experienced several attacks exhibited more marked anxiety than those who had suffered a single attack. She also found that the younger the child during the first and ensuing attacks, the greater the anxiety in extent of indicators and intensity.

Reed [111] studied a group of children with congenital heart defects. He found that these children had greater social anxiety and were more eager to please than the control group. Josselyn, Simon, and Eells [112] describe the rheumatic children who came to a convalescent home after hospitalization as having "unwarranted anxiety in regard to their heart." They point out that anxiety may persist where damage to the heart is severe. Among their children, anxiety was also provoked by other factors than the actual cardiac condition—factors they classify under neurotic anxiety. Neurotic anxiety would include such sources of disturbances as the nature of the parent-child relationships, utilization of the illness for secondary gain—for attention, avoiding responsibility, controlling and tyrannizing the family, and the like.

In a group of 262 cardiac adolescents who responded to a questionnaire, about a half reported worries about their heart condition. About two thirds of the rheumatic heart cases reported a higher incidence of worries. In every group of this study, the adolescent felt that his parents were much more concerned about the cardiac limitation than he was.[113]

Neuhaus compared the personalities of asthmatic, cardiac, and normal children. The cardiac children exceeded the normals in degree of neuroticism and in dependency feelings but were not significantly different from asthmatic children. The younger sick children in the study groups showed more intense maladjustment.[114]

It seems clear that anxiety among cardiac children is invariably aroused. Once aroused, it cannot fail to reverberate to the cardiovascular system as a stress factor. Inevitably, the physiological reserve and heart function will be taxed—and possibly contribute to further disability. Finally, symptoms that are psychogenic in origin, the results of anxiety, may be misinterpreted as being based on heart disease.[115]

Psychological Factors in the Home

The outcome of these psychological forces is to place the heart in a central position in the phenomenological scheme of patients. With children, the intensity and content of anxiety about the heart seem to be derived from parental influences rather than from self-awareness except, of course, as children grow older. Holder found that parent-child relationships, particularly before illness, greatly influenced the way in which the child subsequently handled his disease.[116] This fact is emphasized by most investigators. It must be remembered, too, that anxiety in cardiac disease is realistic to a certain extent. The potential dangers of heart damage and death are constantly in the awareness of the parents who, in turn, impress them upon the child. As a result, Holder believes that rheumatic fever is a real trauma which, because of these threats, lowers the capacity of the child to withstand daily stresses.

Intensifying these effects is confusion about the nature of heart disease.[117] Children found it especially difficult to comprehend the concept of heart disease; their concepts are as vague as their mothers'.

Psychologically, another complication is that treatment programs, as for rheumatic fever, have been guided by the demands of the pathologic process. This means adherence to the need for strict bed rest with gradual resumption of activity. Emphasis is placed on lessened participation. Furthermore, most children with rheumatic heart disease are hospitalized because of the need for nursing care and close medical supervision. This experience of hospitalization is a very significant one, as we have seen.

In contrast, for his group of children, Bauer found that the anxiety coming out of separation was usually of short duration.[118] The adjustment to hospitalization seems to be dependent upon the nature of developmental relationships with parents. Those who adjust best have had opportunities for emotional security and growth with their parents. Other factors in hospital adjustment were found in the nature of the specific practices of the hospital to provide for emotional needs of the children, such as frequency of visits, and opportunities and encouragement to form attachments to parental substitutes. As we have noted, the aseptic and impersonal atmospheres in hospitals serve to enhance anxiety feelings.

The recognition among cardiologists of the importance of psychological factors in the care of children with long-term illness has led to increased attention to the extra-medical aspects of treatment. One study, for example, undertook to investigate the suitability of home care for children with active rheumatic fever.[119] It was found that children could be cared for as well as in the hospital, provided certain initial criteria were met. The most important criterion was the willingness and ability of the parents to undertake a long, exacting regimen of unpredictable duration and outcome. Both the children and parents preferred the home treatment to that in a hospital. There seems little doubt that the homes engaged in this study were in many ways superior to those ordinarily found among cardiac children. As such, this study is limited in its usefulness.

Restriction of Physical Activity

The single element running through every phase of the care of children with heart disease is the necessity for restriction of physical activity. This necessity dictates the need for long convalescence and continued efforts to teach the child to live within his limitations. It dictated the policy of many school systems to make arrangements for the education of children with heart disease in other than regular classes. It is important, therefore, that the psychological implications of restriction be considered.

Holder found that the restrictions placed upon children because of heart disease impressed upon them that they were sick and were constant reminders of their illness.[120] The child finds it difficult to understand the necessity for limited activity beyond the acute phases of illness when he readily accepts restrictions. As he begins to feel better, the restrictions become onerous. Hence, it is necessary to use pressure to maintain restricted activity and this is a constant source of conflict. The parents' anxiety may lead them to overcontrol. Bauer felt that much overemphasis on restrictions was an unconscious expression of the parents' hostility engendered by the hardships the illness caused the family.

It is not surprising to find that cardiac children dislike the restrictions placed on their activity.[121] They resent the segregation at school; they feel singled out and "different." They regard themselves as adequate and not different from other children. They miss the identifications with their peers and the competitive outlets afforded in their relationships

both at school and in their neighborhoods. The net effect of these restrictions is to engender hostility, anxiety, and feelings of low self-esteem
and insecurity. Passive children accept the restrictions, and the others
become resigned despite initial resistiveness.

On the other hand, a group of adolescent cardiac students on a self-
report questionnaire tended to underestimate the restrictions imposed by
the physicians. In distinction to the findings reported among elementary-
school cardiacs, very few of the adolescents felt that their limitation
had affected their ability to make friends. Virtually none of the students
reported having no friends. Two factors should be kept in mind in
interpreting these findings. One is that the data are based on self-reports
and two, adolescents would be loath to admit they have few or no
friends. This is a reflection of the cultural stereotype of popularity.[122]

The advisability for a regimen of limited activity and graded steps in
increasing activity usually means that the cardiac child goes to a convalescent home where he may stay up to a year after discharge from the
hospital. Here again, lack of understanding on the part of the child of
the need for a convalescent period was found. The reactions noted among
the children were accentuated guilt feelings and anxiety. During the
period of convalescent care, the concepts of controlling and limiting his
activity are emphasized as are the precautions necessary to avoid infection. Summer camps for cardiac children are also utilized to help these
children adapt to the regimen imposed by their illness.[123]

The Return Home

Eventually the child returns home and all observers agree that this
situation is fraught with difficulties. After so long an absence, the child
may have developed feelings of rejection and, hence, hostility toward
his parents and siblings.[124] In a sense, the child has grown away from
the family. Bauer found that while the home could have done much to
help the child in this difficult period, more often than not the child's
problems were enhanced.[125] The parents' anxieties tended to increase the
child's separation from his age group; overprotectiveness and overcontrol are common. Without the experience in relationships with healthy
peers, the child hesitates in or withdraws from competition with his
playmates. Holder saw the use of the uncertainties of outlook and the
possibility of recurrence of rheumatic fever to curb and cripple the
expression of positive aggressive trends.

Another contributing element to the cardiac child's negative psychological development is the ambivalent attitude of parents, exemplified in
a New York City Board of Education study. There was a limited acceptance of the child. The attitude of the parents was related to the degree

of marital harmony existing between them. When the marriage was harmonious, the attitudes toward the child were positive, and when disharmony prevailed, negative attitudes were the rule.[126]

Personality of the Cardiac Child

The net result of these forces seems to be to encourage passive, dependent reactions.[127] A recent study found that cardiacs exceed normal children in degree of neuroticism and dependency.[128]

The picture of the cardiac child, as drawn by the study of the New York City Board of Education, portrays him as one who has come to accept his disability with persistent withdrawal behavior. The data, based in part on the use of projective techniques, show definite personality trends. As a group, the cardiac children tended to be unresponsive. They were unable to cope with many situations in which they found themselves. They were passive and were lacking in initiative and drive for achievement. They did not make adequate use of their intellectual capacity and tended to be apathetic mentally. They required stimulation in order to be productive. Emotionally, the children were immature, constricted, and regressed. They were given to daydreaming and brooding.[129] As in other studies, a high percentage of children were judged to be maladjusted. They had few friends and did not engage in organized play activities outside of the home. Withdrawal behavior was characteristic.

On the other hand, a later study of adolescents reported that the cardiac group was representative of the general adolescent population. There was no distinct personality pattern for the adolescent "cardiac." Dependency was not a significant factor. The greatest amount of deviation from average was in sex anxiety. This finding was adjudged to be not unusual since one of the outstanding changes in adolescence is sexual maturity. The investigators in this study of adolescents felt that the evidence did not indicate that cardiac illness per se was related to any of the personality traits investigated. Where disturbances were found, it was not believed they were the results of cardiac illness. It is difficult to evaluate these results, whether they are the outcomes of the techniques and criteria of investigation or whether they represent developmental change. They stand in contrast to the findings of other investigations.[130]

In the New York City study, teachers of children in special cardiac classes evaluated their adjustment by means of a rating scale.[131] It was observed that the teachers were biased in favor of the children, tending to assign more favorable ratings in practically all categories of the scale. In contrast to the ratings by specialists, the children showed the best adjustment in (1) relationship to parents; (2) relationship to other children; (3) attitude to group control; (4) adjustment to handicap. Their poorest adjustment was reported in (1) leadership; (2) work habits; (3) nervous habits; (4) self-confidence; (5) responsibility. Furthermore, according to the teachers, the children tended to adopt aggressive, rather than withdrawing, mechanisms of adjustment.

In the study of adolescents, the teachers reported the majority of students as socially adjusted. With this group, the psychologists were in agreement.[132]

It is not easy to reconcile these contradictory findings within the same study and between studies. The reports do not attempt to do so. In addition to the probably different frames of reference for the teachers and specialists in rating the cardiac children, it seems that the biases of the teachers in favor of the children were potent factors in contributing to much of the difference.

In the high-school grades, the situation is altered. The student is less well known to any single teacher. The teacher usually felt competent to provide information on academic achievement but less able to provide information on other aspects of the student. The majority of students were reported as socially adjusted. Academic adjustment was rated as wholly positive for 48 per cent of the students and wholly negative for 20 per cent in the tenth grade. The majority of teachers felt that the cardiac students showed interest in the classroom and possessed other positive attributes about school.[133]

On both group and individual tests of intelligence, the cardiac children in elementary schools were found to fall into the low-average category. The distribution of scores showed a wide range of variability. There were no data available to evaluate this finding but it seemed to be due mainly to sociocultural phenomena. Most of the children came from below-average socioeconomic homes, and the deficit may be a function of cultural deprivation. It may be speculated, also, that the restriction of activities due to illness, with limited opportunities for social, cultural, and intellectual stimulation, were contributory.[134] Certainly the data presented previously on personality evaluation, indicating mental apathy and lack of drive, would tend to support these speculations.

Eighth-grade cardiacs attained an average I.Q. of 95.3 on a group intelligence test; the city-wide average for eighth graders was 101.8. Here again the cardiacs as a group fall into the low-average category.[135]

As part of the New York City study, a group of 108 cardiac students in the eleventh grade were examined with individual intelligence examinations. The average I.Q. for this group was 105.7. This places them in the slightly above-average group and compares favorably to the level achieved by the non-cardiac New York City eleventh-grade population.

The latter had achieved an average I.Q. of 103.7 on a group intelligence test when they were in the eighth grade.[136]

The discrepancy between the mean I.Q.'s of the eleventh-graders and eighth-graders is believed due to selective factors. Most of the school drop-outs occur in the tenth and eleventh grades and generally are for poor scholarship. Hence the eleventh graders are superior students. The proportion of drop-outs by school year is much the same in the "cardiac" and in the total school population.[137]

Cardiac Child in School

The New York City study found that in other areas as well cardiac children showed retardation. On tests of achievement, wide variability was seen. The children performed below the level of non-handicapped children in the same grade level. Analysis indicated that the cardiac children, as compared to the total school population of New York City in the grades studied, were in far larger proportion over-age for their grade. This high percentage of over-ageness was believed to be due, mainly, to irregular attendance and consequent non-promotion.[138]

In the eighth grade, cardiac adolescents obtained a mean grade reading score six months lower than that of the city-wide population (7.1 versus 7.7). In arithmetic, the corresponding grade scores were 7.3 for the cardiac group and 8.1 for the city-wide population.[139]

In the eleventh grade, about 2 per cent of the cardiac students were failing, that is, showed a high-school average below 65. For the entire group the average grade was 78.2. Again, the better achievement of the eleventh graders was undoubtedly due to selective factors.[140]

It is significant to note that those students who had received some type of special instruction—special classes, at home, or in the hospital—achieved scores below the intellectual and achievement scores of those who had attended regular classes for their entire school career.

It is appropriate at this point to discuss the advisability of special educational arrangements for cardiopathic children. In the past, there have been three types of school provisions for these children: (1) in day schools—special provisions in regular classes, special classes in regular schools, special centers for the handicapped in schools for normal children, and special schools; (2) residential provisions in institutions, sanatoria, convalescent homes, and hospitals; (3) homebound provisions for those children who are too handicapped to go to school, who cannot be transported, or who are excluded for whatever reason.

In the past, these educational provisions were dictated by purely medical considerations so as to provide for limited activity. Usually the anxieties of the school administrator and the teacher caused the child to be set apart. Furthermore, it had been customary to stress cardiac damage and resulting cardiac disability as the starting points in the education of the cardiopathic child. In other words, once the child was sick, he was to be trained for a life of cardiac disability. From this frame of reference, segregation in special classes and training in the realization of limitations were logical developments.

However, current medical thinking does not accept this point of view. The child is either completely handicapped because of rheumatic activity and cannot attend classes, or, as in the vast majority of cases, he can participate in all childhood activities when his illness is quiescent.[141] White shares this view and believes that most children with heart disease at any age, once the disease is not active, can safely attend school and need not or should not be separated in special categories or classes.[133] The exceptions would be those children with such congenital or organic defects as to make them actual cardiac cripples. Thus, with the medical necessity for special facilities for the education of cardiac children placed in doubt, it is not surprising that many educational authorities are taking another look at their special education facilities. This, of course, does not take into consideration the many compelling psychological arguments and findings against such segregation. These have been indicated throughout the present discussion.

In New York City, the Board of Education undertook to determine whether its program was meeting adequately the needs of children with physical limitations. This study was extremely broad and comprehensive and delved into every aspect of education of cardiopathic children. One part of the study was an evaluation of a sampling of special classes for physically handicapped children, not only for cardiac children. The physical and recreational facilities of these classes seemed to be adequate. The classroom climates in less than one third of the rooms observed were regarded as attractive; the others were "neat, staid, static." The large majority of the classes were friendly in atmosphere. About one third of the classes were conducive to the development of pupil initiative. Few were stimulating for the children; in most, interest was either forced or passive and indifferent. Formal control by the teacher was the role assumed in the great majority of classes. However, in most classes, the pupil-teacher attitudes were friendly and sharing. From these data, it does not seem that these classes reflect the best practices for providing the stimulation and opportunities for emotional growth. They tend to reinforce the trends towards passivity and lack of initiative.[143]

Studies such as these are difficult to evaluate because their results provide no frame of reference against which they may be evaluated. For example, for the special classes, it is necessary to know something of the regular classroom facilities and practices to learn whether the results are typical of the schools themselves or are specific for the special classes. This situation serves to point out again the need for controlled study.

Our discussion of heart disease among children and youth seems to have been concerned mainly with rheumatic heart disease. This is a reflection of the psychological literature which deals almost exclusively with children suffering from rheumatic heart disease. Until the advent of heart surgery, those were the children with heart disease who survived and came to the attention of other than medical disciplines. It is likely that this picture will change as the experiences with heart surgery among children develops and greater numbers of such children are encountered and studied. Nevertheless, the discussion presented should still be appropriate to all children with heart disorders.

Diabetes

Nature of Diabetes

The history of diabetes has been described to illustrate the progressive refinement of medical concern and care from a focus on the reduction of mortality and upon physical aspects of the disease to that of a lessening of morbidity and awareness of the psychological aspects of the disease. In the pre-insulin era, the central objective of the physician was quite simply that of the patient's survival. The early 1920's ushered in the insulin era, and there ensued an increasingly successful effort to reduce the physical aspects of diabetic morbidity. The 1940's heralded a third era in which increased attention was devoted to the psychological management of the diabetic, an interest epitomized by the ironic paraphrase "the diabetes was successfully regulated, but the patient decompensated emotionally." [144]

The progressive mastery of the disease permitted attention to casefinding and prevention. Contributing to the growing number of known diabetics is the rising number of aging individuals, among whom the incidence of diabetes is the highest, in our population.

Diabetes mellitus is a disorder of metabolism; the basic defect is an inefficient metabolism of carbohydrates. It is characterized by abnormal concentrations of sugar in the blood (hyperglycemia) and in the urine (glycosuria) and by abnormal metabolism of fat and protein. In untreated cases, there is marked loss of weight and the development of acidosis. The inadequately treated child under five years of age may be retarded in height and weight.[145] Eventually, if the diabetes remains uncontrolled, serious complications such as sepsis, nerve tissue damage, or vascular disease may develop.

There is no agreement on statistics regarding the prevalence of diabetes; no single figure would be acceptable to all authorities. Current estimates of the prevalence of diabetes in the United States is 2.9 million—roughly 1.5 million known cases and 1.4 million unknown cases—a rate of 16.9 for 1000 population.[146] It is estimated that about 150,000 children under the age of fifteen have diabetes.[147] There is an almost equal group of patients in whom the onset of diabetes is judged to have occurred after fifteen years of age.

The life expectancy of the diabetic is below that of the general population; 17 fewer years for the 10-year old diabetic to almost four years less for the 70-year old. However, the life expectancy is increasing. Nevertheless, diabetes is the eighth leading cause of death and the third leading cause of blindness. The mortality for diabetics under the age of 15 has been falling.[148]

A differentiation is made between diabetes in the younger age group (juvenile diabetes) and the disease in the older age group (adult diabetes); there is some opinion that the disease mechanism is different in each. Among the differences between the two types is the fact that diabetes tends to be more severe in the child. The disease runs a notoriously stormy course; it stabilizes as the child gets older but frequently becomes stormy again during adolescence. There is a greater frequency of symptoms among juvenile diabetics,[149] and greater fluctuations prevail in day-to-day control. Psychologically there are important differences. As a growing, maturing, and developing organism, the child is affected in a much more comprehensive and complex fashion. In addition, the child has the problem of rationalizing a regimen of living—an infinitely more difficult task for the younger age groups.[150]

There is not complete evidence to establish any specific cause for the disease. Many elements seem to be associated: hereditary factors, infection, over-eating, dysfunction of the endocrine glands, and psychological factors.

Treatment in Diabetes

Treatment of the diabetic child has as its criterion the ability of that child to compete with his peers physically, mentally, and socially. Insofar as he is not able to do so, to that degree is he considered inadequately treated; [151] the total welfare of the patient is the only acceptable medical goal.[152] In the treatment program, diet has to be watched and insulin taken. Exercise has to be watched in relation to the need for insulin, because exercise tends to lower blood sugar. Diabetic shock and coma are ever-present dangers, and the child has to learn to recognize the first symptoms of shock and to carry sugar to take for its avoidance. Infection is also a danger.

There is not complete agreement among physicians as to the degree of control necessary in the management of diabetic patients—whether there should be chemical control or clinical control.[153] Those who favor chemical control have rigid rules and procedures to be followed very strictly and carefully, such as frequent urine examinations, keeping of daily records, and others. Those physicians who favor clinical control usually recommend liberal handling of diabetic patients. Their patients have few rules to follow, one of which is never to omit insulin. These physicians emphasize psychological elements in the treatment of diabetes.[154,155] The development of oral preparations instead of insulin is very significant, but their use is presently restricted to adults.

Psychological Ramifications

The importance of psychological factors in diabetes has been recognized for a long time. However, in the pre-insulin era, it was quite impractical to be concerned with the emotional health of diabetics when the physician was struggling to stem the death-dealing effects of unregulated diabetes. With the discovery of the physiological mechanism, particularly insulin, there slowly evolved systematic attention to psychological variables.

The work of Menninger in 1935, pointing out striking temporal correlations between changes in diabetes and changes in the mental states of a number of psychotic patients,[156] helped to stimulate interest in the importance of psychological experiences. Other investigators noted that the severity of the metabolic disturbances in diabetes can be aggravated by emotional disturbances. Hinkle and his associates have demonstrated that emotional stress factors can produce undesirable changes in diabetic regulation which clear up upon the removal of stress.[157] They look upon diabetes as a disorder of adaptation. Others have also demonstrated these phenomena.[158]

To move to the position that diabetes can be caused by emotional factors is another matter. To be sure, the work pointing to emotional effects on regulation of diabetes is highly suggestive, but Danowski states "there is no extensive support for the suggestion that diabetes actually originates as a result of such stress." [159] As with tuberculosis, the data tell why an individual becomes ill at the time he develops symptoms, but they do not tell why he becomes ill with diabetes. Hinkle and his co-workers attempt to do so, but the stresses they describe are no different from the types of stresses which many individuals encounter without developing diabetes.[160] On the other hand, Danowski believes it is wise to keep in mind that emotional conflicts have very specific meaning for individuals, implying the possibility of a causative relationship under certain circumstances.[161]

Dunbar has been especially positive in asserting that the diabetic has a distinctive behavioral pattern.[162] However, her hypothesis has not been supported in subsequent research.[163] It seems well accepted that diabetics, adult or juvenile, do not have distinctive personality patterns that are different than those in other disease entities, rheumatic fever, for example.[164]

Starr places diabetes among the psychopathophysiological reactions in his psychosomatic spectrum. This would place the somatic component in the dominant relationship and psychological factors would be exacerbating and/or perpetuating of the somatic manifestations. This point of view is the one to which most writers in the field would subscribe. As a matter of fact, Hinkle's extensive investigation precisely demonstrates influence of emotional stress on the diabetic's course. It should be noted that the subjects involved in these studies were almost exclusively adults.

In some previous studies, a marked incidence of mental retardation among diabetic children was reported. However, the recent work of Kubany and his associates found that the intelligence of diabetic children is like that of the non-diabetic population.[165] They are of the opinion that the differences found in the past were mainly due to sampling biases.

Developmentally, the diabetic is not different from non-diabetic children except in height and weight. Hormonal secretions also are not strikingly variant from normals.[166]

Psychological Elements in Treatment

In addition to the effects of illness in general, diabetes has its specific implications. First of all, diabetes in childhood is a severe, life-long, life-threatening disease.[167] Diabetic children, as a rule, are healthy until they are struck by the disease. Within a short time, they become desperately ill, even comatose. With insulin, their outlook has changed in terms of life expectancy and normal functioning. Despite this more favorable outlook, diabetes in a child means constant awareness of danger. Ever present is the fear of hypoglycemic shock and possible coma. Avoidance of infections because they affect the physiology of the body calls for special vigilance. Blood vessel complications are always a danger. Consequently, a feeling of apprehension surrounds the life of the diabetic child. Complicating these fears are the usual bewilderment and lack of understanding of the illness on the part of both the family and the child.

The responses of the family to chronic illness, previously discussed,[168] have special pertinence here because of the critical responsibility of the mother in the daily management of the diabetes. The mother has the realization that the health and the life of her child depends upon her ability to get the child to follow the prescribed regimen. To be sure, the entire constellation of psychological elements in the family is involved, and, as Bruch and Hewlett have shown, the extent of success or failure in the daily management of the diabetic child is dependent upon these psychological elements in the home.[169]

In the prescribed regimen for the diabetic are fertile sources of psychological disturbance.[170] Fischer studied these various factors among a group of diabetic children followed for ten years.[171] The necessity for dietary restriction, although made more liberal with the advent of insulin, is still an important part of the daily routine. Parents develop many anxieties about food, fearing carbohydrates in particular. They hesitate to give sugar; they tend to repeat the same foods day after day, and lack of variety often provokes resistance. The children commonly become hungry after meals, and extra between-meal snacks are permitted. Not infrequently, diabetic children do their own supplementing, and this provokes violent reaction from the parents because of "cheating" or "stealing." The parents become overzealous in enforcing the diet and begin to use "detective" methods. The work of Hinkle and his associates suggests that the attempts to regulate the diets of many of the diabetic children is fruitless because such attempts are opposed by strong psychological drives. Food becomes an arena of struggle. The accusations of the parents bring guilt feelings and induce more concealment. Thus another vicious circle is set up—more guilt, more anxiety, and more conflict. Food comes to be regarded as a poison which not only intensifies the child's anxieties but also may be used as a weapon in his relationship to the environment.

Probably the most important aspect of daily routine is the necessity for insulin injections. This necessity more than any other aspect of diabetic care affects the emotions of the diabetic child. The use of the hypodermic syringe cannot be avoided even though the frequency of its use is reduced with slower-acting insulin preparations. The emotional effects of the injections are often traumatic. Some children regard them as punishment. Physiological reactions from insulin are very disturbing, and after a child has experienced several, he becomes very fearful and may seek to avoid or in some way weaken the insulin injection. This latter may occur when the child administers his own injection. Dread of insulin reactions may upset parents even more, particularly if the reactions come at night. Insulin reactions are indicated by pallor, sweating, and faintness. The effects of hypoglycemia are in irritability, sleepiness, crying, temper tantrums, and mischievousness. The child may fall asleep in the classroom or become unconscious after heavy exercise. Not infrequently, these symptoms of diabetic children are misunderstood and they are punished for "bad" behavior.[172]

A third aspect of the regimen of the diabetic child is the necessity to test the urine. Although testing of every voided specimen is unnecessary, urination takes on much emotional color. Aside from any diabetic disorder, this eliminative function seems to have an especially high potential for involvement in emotional disturbances. Added to this sensitivity is the anxiety of the diabetic surrounding the urine specimen and analysis. There is, not infrequently, bed-wetting among diabetic children because of a greater necessity for frequent voidings (polyuria) as a result of increased thirst and water intake (polydipsia). This bed-wetting is an aspect of the diabetes, but, of course, it may become involved with bed-wetting that is symptomatic of emotional disturbance. In any event, the parents and the child are upset and embarrassed by bed-wetting when it occurs. Here again, the relationships and the attitudes that exist in the family are important.

Anna Freud illuminates an inherent conflict in the management of the diabetic. The goal, as seen, is to teach the child the various requirements of self-care, among which is self-administration of insulin. The young child who is slowly and uncertainly moving away from dependence on the mother suffers a blow to this developmental progress when he falls ill with diabetes. The regimen of treatment requires that he begin to learn how to take care of himself. Anna Freud believes this burdens the child with excessively grave responsibilities and takes away the feeling that his parents will see to it that he is well and safe.[173,174]

Limitation of activity occupies a prominent place in the daily routine of the diabetic child.[175] The first limitation is in physical activity because of the fear of shock due to rapid depletion of blood sugar as the result of heavy exercise. While restriction is observed especially when the child is young and not fully capable of self-regulation, it seems all too frequently carried over into later years. The social life of the child is also limited. For example, a child is not permitted to attend parties because it is feared he may indulge in the excessive eating of sweets. In addition, parents may be fearful of letting the child out of sight for any length of time for fear of insulin reactions. Excursions and visits away from home are difficult because of insulin and meals. These difficulties serve to impress on the child the fact that he is "different."

The many and complex problems of the diabetic's life led Bennett and Johannsen to conclude that the disease makes a real and tangible impact on the personality of the child.[176] They are of the opinion the child never "gets used to" diabetes and its restrictions. They feel that the older child just gets more capable of controlling negative reactions. They go on to state that the results of the restricted life of the diabetic cannot but help to have effects on personality which, in their group, produced a constricted, passive-dependency.

Starr's comprehensive discussion of the psychosomatics of juvenile diabetes points up that the child's adjustment to the sudden illness depends upon the pre-morbid emotional state of affairs for the child and his family.[177] Given the same degree of life stress, that is, the appearance of diabetes, afflicted children and their families will react varyingly to such an emotional trauma. Where the intrafamilial adjustment has been adequately successful, the diabetic illness, after a short period of reactive disturbance, will be taken "in stride." On the other hand, where faulty interpersonal relationships and extensive conflicts were quite prevalent, diabetes will result in emotional upheavals.

The most interesting and crucially significant phenomenon observed in such poorly adjusted family situations is the fact that the diabetic management per se becomes the arena and battleground for the expression of irrational pre-existing attitudes in the mother-child relationship. The different problems of that situation contaminate the various details of diabetic regulation. The family's individualized reactions toward the child and his diabetes are of central importance in determining the type and specific nature of the adverse adjustment the child will make in connection with his illness. That adjustment may range from an excessively anxious and endangered personality to a compulsive, overly regulated, and regimented personality, a depressive and self-destructive personality, a delinquent and rebellious personality, and a submissive, passive, and excessively dependent personality.[178]

The Adolescent Diabetic

The social stigma of being diabetic becomes more apparent as the child moves into adolescence. In the earlier years, management is a problem mainly of the interplay between parents, particularly the mother, and child in order to achieve adherence to the diabetic regimen. Awareness that the diabetic routine does not make for social success begins to make its appearance as adolescence approaches. There seems to be general agreement among the workers in the field that adherence to the prescribed regimen becomes a real problem during adolescence.[179] It is interesting that this rebellion seems to coincide with the need in those years to achieve independence and emancipation from the home.

This rebellion is short-lived since there is no escape from diabetes.

We do not have information as to the consequences of the "defeat." There are suggestive data, as reported by Fischer, that many diabetic children begin to fail in studies after elementary school. Whether this is due to physical or psychological factors is not known. Still fewer go on to college, fewer of these complete college and go on to professional life. In general, there seems to be better adjustment after adolescence and college years have passed.

During adolescence, problems involving future aspirations arise—problems of marriage, parenthood, and career.[180] As for marriage and parenthood, there are many risks to be faced by the future mother with diabetes. There is a high rate of abortions, stillbirths, and neonatal deaths as well as hazards for the diabetic who is pregnant.[181] This is a matter for skilled and wise counseling; one which has to be faced candidly and honestly.

The employment of diabetics is a problem that is beginning to be given systematic attention. Surveys of the employment practices of industry pertaining to diabetics have been carried out.[182] In a sense, employability depends upon the diabetic. If control is achieved by diet alone, then the problem is relatively simple. If insulin is required, then questions arise. The problem of insulin is mitigated by the development and growing use of oral preparations.

The five most frequent reasons for rejecting diabetics for employment are: (1) Insulin shock (sudden unconsciousness); (2) Prolonged absenteeism; (3) Increased compensation costs (prolonged disability following industrial accident); (4) Complications of diabetes (prolonged or permanent disability which may be expensive to management); (5) Increased insurance costs (while frequently given is reported to be unfounded).[183]

The American Diabetes Association takes the position that although the poorly controlled, uncooperative diabetic should be refused employment, the well-controlled, cooperative diabetic is a good employment risk. The results of studies in industry show that the diabetic may be compared to the non-diabetic in his ability to work, caliber of work, and absentee record.[184]

Diabetic Children in School

In contrast to children with tuberculosis and heart disease, there is no mention in the literature of special educational facilities for the diabetic child. Certainly there do not seem to be compelling medical or psychological reasons for such. His educational needs apparently can be met most adequately in the regular class.

As with tuberculosis and heart disease but more obviously so, diabetes seem to require a style of life that would serve to set the diabetic apart, at least in his own eyes. Because of the necessity for training in this style of life and yet to make him feel as part of a group, summer camps for diabetics have been developed in many parts of the country. The stated values of these camps are to train the diabetic child in the prescribed diabetic regimen but to do so in an atmosphere of recreation, companionship, and emotional support. At present, there are more than thirty such camps.[185,186,187,188,189]

Finally, psychological attention is recommended consistently for the diabetic child. Throughout the literature, there is the theme that preventive measures should be observed and, when needed, psychotherapeutic programs should be set up for both child and parents. Group programs are also reported.[190]

Asthma

Nature of Allergic Disorders

Allergic disorders constitute a variety of reactions which may affect practically every organ and tissue of the body. These reactions result from antigen-antibody union, antigen being the substance (food, dust, drugs, bacteria) which, when introduced into the body, creates antibodies. These antibodies create tissue sensitivity, so that when there is additional antigen exposure in the future, the antigen-antibody union causes the allergic reaction. Histamine, or some similarly acting substance, is produced which, in turn, reacts on the neuromuscular apparatus of the affected organ. It is not known what determines for an individual the tissue or area to be involved, called the shock organ. This may be the skin, lungs, or another part of the body. The allergic reactions are well known, and may cause wheals, coughing, gasping, sneezing, among others. These reactions do not take place unless there is tissue sensitivity. Sensitivities may disappear spontaneously, or spread to new allergens, or antigens, or manifest themselves in new forms or in new shock organs.[191]

Allergies are long-lasting and may extend throughout life. Most children do not outgrow their allergies; rather they develop complications. Thus eczema, the most common allergic reaction in infants, is not outgrown, as is a prevalent misconception. More usually, the child will go through a sequence, referred to as the eczema-hay fever-asthma complex, and emerge with a respiratory allergy, asthma.[192]

In allergy, the inciting factors, once an antigen-antibody reaction is established, are extremely varied as are the manifestations elicited by them. There is no common agent, such as in tuberculosis, through which many quite different manifestations may be related; there is, instead, a number of non-specific factors in addition to allergens. The non-specific factors include infection and psychological stress. Actually the approach favored is the seeking of interactions among three forces—allergy, infection, and psychological stress—which ultimately produce the symptoms. Each of the forces may affect the other; each may be able to initiate vicious cycles or chain-type reactions. For any individual, the symptoms may be due to allergy, infection, or psychological stress, since they can arise from each of these.[193] This theoretical formulation follows Selye and Wolff in looking upon allergy as a maladaptive response to stress in which the protective mechanism an individual employs in his constant need for adaptation may produce disease, either because it is called into play when not needed, or because in "its magnitude and direction the adaptive protective reaction may be more damaging to the individual than the effects of the noxious agent per se." [194] In this situation, Prigal raises the intriguing possibility of the establishment of Pavlovian conditioned response. There is little known of this possibility in allergic disorders, except for a Soviet monograph describing the relationship of conditioned reflex and asthma.[195]

There seems to be general acceptance of the role of psychological force in allergic disorder but not as a specific mechanism of causation. Although psychological factors play a role in the modification of symptoms, and perhaps trigger symptoms, there is little or no evidence to demonstrate their ability to modify the actual antigen-antibody reaction.[196]

Some Statistics

There are no statistics on the incidence of allergic disorders on which there is agreement. Part of the difficulty lies in the matter of definition. If a liberal definition is followed, the incidence would be about 50 per cent of the population. This is indicative of the wide prevalence of allergic reactions. However, if only recognized allergic disorders are included, the general opinion is that the rate would be 10 per cent.[197] Asthma is taken to occur in about five per cent of the general population.[198] Figures for the incidence of asthma in groups of individuals in the United States are not readily available. In a study of 2,169 children under the age of 15 years, it was found that 20 per cent had major allergic disorders but only one third of this group was receiving treatment. The investigators felt that this situation pointed to a public health problem. If two thirds of the allergic children are untreated, how many learning problems and how much school difficulty and absenteeism may have roots in allergy? [199]

Psychological Determinants in Asthma

The psychological literature in asthma is a growing one. There has been extensive study but mainly from a psychoanalytic frame of reference. Impetus to this approach came from the work of French and Alexander who pointed out the particular significance of the interrelationships between the mother and the asthmatic child.[200] They found that the child is more or less rejected by the mother or both parents. The mother is much too preoccupied with her own problems to give adequate love to the child, although she often overcompensates for this unconscious rejection by an overprotective attitude. They also noted the overambition of the mother for the child and the overdependence of the child upon the mother, with the result that the child was immature and lacking self-confidence in most situations. Thus French and Alexander formulated their hypothesis that the psychological conflict in asthma is a repressed longing, basically for the mother. When this desire is frustrated or threatened with frustration, an asthmatic attack is precipitated. The asthmatic attack becomes symbolically the protest of a crying spell.

This hypothesis formed the basis for further investigations.[201] They followed psychoanalytic formulations and supported French and Alexander's observations. The most systematic and extensive series of studies were by Miller and Baruch.[202] They have observed and treated some 201 clinically allergic children since 1946. Psychological tests were used, and the parents were interviewed. Similarly treated was a group of 110 children with no allergic disorder but with behavior problems. They found that 97 per cent of the allergic children had mothers who verbally expressed rejecting attitudes, whereas 37 per cent of the mothers of nonallergic children did so—the difference being highly significant. This theme of maternal rejection has become the dominant one in the literature on asthma.

Miller and Baruch believe that maternal rejection preceded the development of symptoms. They studied hostility in allergic children as a reaction to the experience of rejection. As compared to non-allergic children, the allergic child did not dare to express his hostile feelings to the same extent or as freely as did the non-allergic child. He apparently developed guilt and anxiety in relation to his hostility and was more frequently in conflict about bringing out his hostile feelings. The allergic child is likened to a cornered animal. He feels and hates the impact of his mother's rejection, as all children do. But he is not able to express this hostility in either direct or indirect fashion. Consequently, he cannot get release from the tension of his hostile feeling. He turns his resentment on himself and uses his allergic condition as satisfaction for his conflicting needs.

An elaboration of Miller and Baruch's thesis is the concept of mutual engulfment advanced by Abrahamson.[203] The rejecting mother is found to be ambitious, willful, and oversolicitous of her child. She wants to mold the child along the lines she wishes. When the child rebels, as frequently happens, she rejects him. This raises anxiety for the child. Thus the basic conflict is dependence-independence, and the anxiety emerging from this conflict is expressed through a somatic response— asthma.

These concepts have found support in a number of studies which sought to verify the frequent observation that asthmatic children invariably showed an abatement of their symptoms when they were away from their homes and families—for example, in a hospital or a camp. Equally invariably, the symptoms would recur when they returned home.[204]

Long and his co-workers [205] undertook to investigate this phenomenon in a study of 18 children hospitalized for asthma. After their symptoms had been relieved while in the hospital, the children were exposed to heavy concentrations of house dust from their homes but showed no demonstrable reaction. This finding is interpreted to indicate that the allergen is not the only necessary factor to produce asthma and points to a complex etiology of asthmatic episodes.

An extension of these approaches is found in the development of therapeutic methods for the severely asthmatic child. One such method is the so-called "parentectomy" school of thought which recommends the separation of the asthmatic child from his family for effective treatment. The reported results of a residential treatment center in Denver which follows this method indicate that of five hundred children admitted over a period of years, only 10 per cent did not achieve any improvement or amelioration of symptoms.[206,207]

The results of the various studies delineating the different facets of the maternal rejection hypothesis are generally accepted. However, what is challenged is the concept itself—that the psychological conflict and trauma lead to the asthmatic reaction. Harris and Shure,[208] Leigh,[209] and others [210] insist that the psychological reactions observed are the results of the asthma, not the causes. For example, Fitzelle [211] in a controlled study involving a hundred mothers of asthmatic children and a hundred mothers of children with other ailments found no differences in personality tests and child-rearing attitude surveys between the two groups. Both groups deviated from the normal.

Coolidge has observed that the conflictual mother-child relationship is not specific for asthma but that the ambivalence conflict is a basic characteristic of development.[212]

Implicit in the challenge of the concept of maternal rejection as a causative factor is the questioning of the existence of a unique or specific personality pattern in the child as a significant etiological element. Harris and Shure in a survey of the incidence of asthma among school children ages six to twelve, found 25 cases of asthma. Among these 25 asthmatic children, they did not find any specific personality pattern.[213] Similarly, Knapp and others found no single personality type in their adult group.[214,215] Rees, reporting on his studies in England, did not find a specific personality type among his patients. Moreover, he did not find a significant psychological factor in 64 per cent of a group of fifty patients.[216,217]

Friend and Pollock have criticized the predominant focus on intrapsychic elements in the study of the asthmatic child. They believe there has been a neglect of situational and social factors.[218] Certainly the existing literature would support this criticism. The probable explanation is that the almost exclusive source of the hypotheses pursued in the study of asthma has been in psychoanalytic theory and remains so.

Psychological Effects of Asthma

The alternate approach to the psychological variables discussed above is that they are somatopsychological and result from the disorder. In this sense many of the psychological effects have already been considered. There is, as we have seen, virtually complete acceptance of the fact that psychological variables influence the frequency and severity of asthmatic episodes in children.[219] Bakwin [220] is of the opinion that when attacks occur frequently and are difficult to control, emotional factors should be suspected.

In general, he believes that any circumstance which makes the child anxious and unhappy may intensify the allergic symptoms. The asthmatic child, becoming aware of the agitation produced by his attacks and the concern displayed by his parents, finds in his illness a ready means of getting his own way and of evading responsibilities. Guilt feelings are common in both the child and parents. The child fears that he may have caused his illness or attacks by not carrying out his mother's directions, as by not wearing his rubbers or by eating something forbidden. When he becomes ill, he hurts himself and his guilt is relieved. He is conflicted over the restrictions which surround him—he wants greater freedom but also wants to obey his mother. On the other hand, the parents may also feel guilty that they are the cause of illness, through heredity or poor care. Then, the asthmatic attacks are in themselves very frightening, and the dread of future attacks may haunt the child and the parents. Finally, the characteristics of chronically ill children, discussed earlier, will be present.[221]

From backgrounds of experiences as these, it should not be surprising that there occur many of the personality characteristics ascribed to asthmatics. One writer has remarked on the "exclusiveness" in the relationship between the mother and asthmatic child. Another refers to the "mother's need" to be close to the child, that in this, their needs are complementary. Despite overt complaints, the mother actually rewards the dependence of the child. ". . . she can give love and care only to the sick child. . . . The illness provides the mother with the setting for acting-out more deeply repressed unconscious impulses. . . . Consequently the mother unconsciously fosters the illness." Little has been written of the father. He is described as "a passive individual who plays a subordinate role in the family." [223]

The closeness of the identification between mother and asthmatic child has led to observation that the mothers are overcontrolling and overambitious for the child, and that the child is overly dependent and overconforming.[224] Little and Cohen [225] and Morris [226] undertook studies in area of achievement, utilizing goal-setting tasks. In these studies, hypotheses were confirmed as to higher goals set by both asthmatic children and their mothers, and to the effect that the asthmatic child's level of aspiration rises when the mother is present and participating in goal-setting. Also, Morris found that asthmatic child-mother pairs were more alike in goal-setting than non-asthmatic child-mother pairs. Both studies used control groups.

Another personality characteristic noted in the asthmatic child was the presence of a significantly greater degree of neurotic behavior than normal; this behavior contained such traits as anxiety, insecurity, and dependency. However, the asthmatic children did not differ from cardiac children. Interestingly, Neuhaus did not find any significant differences between asthmatic children and their non-asthmatic siblings on these variables.[227] On the other hand, Fine found such differences in his study.[228]

The asthmatic child has also been described as being very sensitive emotionally and as being typically negativistic and emotionally inhibited.[229] Furthermore, he lacks self-confidence and has feelings of inferiority.[230]

There is little data on the school adjustment of asthmatic children. One report states that they are often retarded in their school achievement, mainly because of frequent absences.[231] Their school adjustment is described as poor; they tend to be fidgety, demanding, and immature. The experience of the Jewish National Home for Asthmatic Children in Denver, a residential treatment center, is very much the same. Many of the children admitted to the center have had difficulties in school because of frequent and extended school absences. In addition, the center found many of the children to have negative attitudes toward school. The children admitted to the center are the more severely asthmatic.[232]

Psychotherapeutic Procedures

More than the other illnesses we have considered, with the possible exception of diabetes, are psychotherapeutic procedures recognized as an integral part of the care of the asthmatic child.

Miller and Baruch have reported most extensively on psychotherapeutic efforts with asthmatics.[233,234] They see treatment as long and involved. The focus of therapy is the parents, and Miller and Baruch generalize that parents of severely ill allergic children are severely ill emotionally.

The asthmatic children who attend the residential home in Denver are also severely ill, and in this and similar facilities, psychological help is provided for the children. In addition, the parents of the children attend regular group therapy sessions on a continuing basis in their home communities. Here, too, the reported experience is that the parents need help.[235,236]

Conclusions and Implications

THE STUDY of these four chronic disorders serves to emphasize that the psychology of the ill and the disabled is to be understood in terms of the psychology of other groups, the normal and the deviant. The reactions of any child or youth to the stress of illness and disability depend upon a complex interplay of many forces, both internal and external. There is no simple predictable relationship between any single factor and the reaction displayed by the individual, whether this relationship is between a psychological variable and a physical response or between a physical event and a psychological response. Rather, the evidence is in the direction of interactional effects which, in turn, are influenced by situational, developmental, and psychosocial factors.

There are, to be sure, psychological reactions that occur with sufficient frequency to be regarded as being common, but those are by no means inevitable or invariant. Prominent among the common reactions to illness are anxiety and guilt feelings. Children often feel that their illness is a punishment. For them, illness is a poorly understood phenomenon and is clouded by subjective and irrational forces.

Inextricably implicated and strongly influential in these reactions are family forces which have their origin in parent-child relationships. There is a continuing interplay between these familial and subsequent experiences. Consequently, even though we are concerned with children and youth, it is appropriate to consider the reactions of adults to illness because the content of those reactions are communicated and provide the core of the children's reactions.

In our discussion, we began to discern developmental trends in reactions to illness and disability. There are suggestions that adolescence does not play an invariant role in chronic illness; the cardiac adolescent seems to be different from the diabetic adolescent.

Hospitalization is not inevitably a negative experience; certainly not with the changes in hospital practices being initiated to insure positive reactions.

Finally, in educational settings, chronically ill children are likely to appear in any classroom. As adults, teachers show the lack of knowledge, limited understanding, and distorted attitudes about chronic illness that adults as parents demonstrate.[237]

While there is much we still have to learn about the psychological aspects of chronic medical disorders among children, there is much we do know and can make available. Considerable research interest and activity are apparent; we also need a corresponding attack on the lag between knowledge about chronic disorders among children and the application of the knowledge.

Notes

[1] M. Sperling, "Psychosomatic Medicine and Pediatrics," in *Recent Developments in Psychosomatic Medicine*, eds. E. D. Wittkower and R. A. Cleghorn (Philadelphia: J. B. Lippincott Co., 1954), p. 381.

[2] H. I. Kaplan and H. S. Kaplan, "Current Theoretical Concepts in Psychosomatic Medicine," *American Journal of Psychiatry*, CXV (1959), 1091 ff.

[3] R. W. White, "Abnormalities of Behavior," in *Annual Review of Psychology* (Palo Alto: Annual Reviews, Inc., 1959), pp. 269 f.

[4] C. Buck and G. E. Hobbs, "The Problem of Specificity in Psychosomatic Illness," *Journal of Psychosomatic Research*, III (1959), 227 ff.

[5] L. S. Kubie, "The Problem of Specificity in the Psychosomatic Process," in Wittkower and Cleghorn, *op. cit.*, pp. 29 ff.

[6] O. F. Ehrentheil, "Some Remarks About Somatopsychic Compared to Psychosomatic Relationships," *Psychosomatic Medicine*, XXI (1959), 1 ff.

[7] I. Stevenson and R. A. Matthews, "Fact and Theory in Psychosomatic Medicine," *Journal of Nervous and Mental Disease*, CXVIII (1953), 289 ff.

[8] P. H. Starr, "Psychosomatic Considerations of Diabetes in Childhood," *Journal of Nervous and Mental Disease*, CXXI (1955), 494.

[9] *Ibid.*, pp. 494 ff.

[10] H. Selye, "Recent Progress in Stress Research, with Reference to Tuberculosis," in *Personality, Stress and Tuberculosis*, ed. P. J. Sparer (New York: International Universities Press, Inc., 1956), pp. 45 ff.

[11] R. R. Grinker, "Psychosomatic Approach to Anxiety," *American Journal of Psychiatry*, CXIII (1956), 443 ff.

¹² P. Mussen, "Developmental Psychology," in *Annual Review of Psychology* (Palo Alto: Annual Reviews, Inc., 1960), pp. 443 f.

¹³ G. G. Thompson, "Developmental Psychology," in *Annual Review* (1959), *op. cit.*, p. 1.

¹⁴ G. J. Mohr, *et al.*, "A Program for the Study of Children with Psychosomatic Disorders," in *Emotional Problems of Early Childhood*, ed. G. Caplan (New York: Basic Books, Inc., 1955), pp. 252 ff.

¹⁵ A. M. Garner and C. Wenar, *The Mother-Child Interaction in Psychosomatic Disorders* (Urbana: University of Illinois Press, 1959), pp. 160 ff.

¹⁶ V. E. Carter and S. Chess, "Factors Influencing the Adaptations of Organically Handicapped Children," *American Journal of Orthopsychiatry*, XXI (1951), 828.

¹⁷ S. Tuttman, "Children's Reactions to their Physical Disabilities in Relation to Parents' Personalities," *Dissertation Abstracts*, XV (1955), 1909-1910.

¹⁸ T. Parsons, "Illness and the Role of the Physician: A Sociological Perspective," *American Journal of Orthopsychiatry*, XXI (1952), 457.

¹⁹ D. G. Prugh, *et al.*, "A Study of the Emotional Reactions of Children and Families to Hospitalization and Illness," *American Journal of Orthopsychiatry*, XXIII (1953), 70.

²⁰ W. S. Langford, "Physical Illness and Convalescence: Their Meaning to the Child," *Journal of Pediatrics*, XXXIII (1948), 242.

²¹ S. A. Szurek, "Comments on the Psychopathology of Children with Somatic Illness," *American Journal of Psychiatry*, CVII (1951), 844.

²² L. W. Sontag, "Some Psychosomatic Aspects of Childhood," *The Nervous Child*, V (1946), 246 ff.

²³ L. W. Sontag, "The Genetics of Differences in Psychosomatic Patterns in Childhood," *American Journal of Orthopsychiatry*, XX (1950), 479.

²⁴ Langford, *op. cit.*, pp. 243 f.

²⁵ A. Freud, "The Role of Bodily Illness in the Mental Life of Children," in *The Psychoanalytic Study of the Child* (New York: International Universities Press, Inc., 1952), VII, 70 ff.

²⁶ I. M. Josselyn, "Treatment of the Emotionally Immature Child in an Institution Framework," *American Journal of Orthopsychiatry*, XX (1950), 397 ff.

²⁷ B. M. Korsch, "Psychologic Principles in Pediatric Practice: The Pediatrician and the Sick Child," in *Advances in Pediatrics*, ed. S. L. Levine (Chicago: The Year Book Medical Publishers, 1958), X, 11 ff.

²⁸ Sontag (1946), *op. cit.*, p. 300.

²⁹ B. Wright, *Physical Disability—A Psychological Approach* (New York: Harper & Row, Publishers, 1960), pp. 138 ff.

³⁰ C. M. Lowe, "The Self-Concept: Fact or Artifact," *Psychological Bulletin*, LVIII (1961), 325 ff.

³¹ R. C. Wylie, *The Self Concept* (Lincoln: University of Nebraska Press, 1961), p. 160.

³² *Ibid.*, p. 161 f.

³³ *Ibid.*, p. 221.

³⁴ *Ibid.*, p. 222.

³⁵ *Ibid.*, pp. 223 f.

³⁶ Wright, *op. cit.*, p. 376.

³⁷ *Ibid.*, pp. 377 ff.

³⁸ R. G. Barker and B. A. Wright, "Disablement: The Somatopsychological Problem," in Wittkower and Cleghorn, *op. cit.*, pp. 431 ff.

³⁹ I. Shelsky, "The Effect of Disability on Self Concept," *Dissertation Abstracts*, XVII (1957), 1598-1599.

⁴⁰ J. Kimmel, "A Comparison of Children with Congenital and Acquired Orthopedic Handicaps on Certain Personality Characteristics," *Dissertation Abstracts*, XIX (1959), 3023-3024.

⁴¹ H. H. Work, "Making Hospitalization Easier for Children," *Children*, III (1956), 83 ff.

42 R. Spitz, "Reply to Dr. Pinneau," *Psychological Bulletin*, LII (1955), 453 ff.

43 W. Goldfarb, "Variations in Adolescent Adjustment of Institutionally Reared Children," *American Journal of Orthopsychiatry*, XVII (1947), 449 ff.

44 S. A. Pinneau, "The Infantile Disorders of Hospitalism and Anaclitic Depression," *Psychological Bulletin*, LII (1955), 429 ff.

45 B. Pasamanick and H. Knobloch, "Brain Damage and Reproductive Casualty," *American Journal of Orthopsychiatry*, XXX (1960), 298 ff.

46 W. R. Thompson, "Early Environment—Its Importance for Later Development," in *Psychopathology of Childhood*, eds. P. A. Hoch and J. Zubin (New York: Grune & Stratton, Inc., 1955), pp. 133 ff.

47 J. Bowlby, *Maternal Care and Mental Health*, Monograph No. 2 (Geneva: World Health Organization, 1951), pp. 1 ff.

48 J. Bowlby, J. Robertson, and D. Rosenbluth, "A Two Year Old Goes to the Hospital," in *The Psychoanalytic Study of the Child, op. cit.*, VII, 82 ff.

49 J. Robertson, *Young Children in Hospitals* (New York: Basic Books, Inc., 1959), pp. 11 ff.

50 Prugh, *op. cit.*, pp. 71 ff.

51 D. G. Prugh and S. Cath, "Psychosocial Stress: Children's Reactions to Hospitalization and the Use of the Respirator," *Journal of Nervous and Mental Disease*, CXX (1954), 399 f.

52 D. G. Prugh, "Investigations Dealing with Reactions of Children and Families to Hospitalization and Illness: Problems and Potentialities," Caplan, *op. cit.*, pp. 307 ff.

53 H. Gofman, W. Buckman, and G. H. Schade, "The Child's Emotional Response to Hospitalization," *A.M.A. Journal of Diseases of Children*, IXCIII (1957), 157 ff.

54 H. S. Marlens, "A Study of the Effect of Hospitalization on Children in a Metropolitan Municipal Institution," *Dissertation Abstracts*, XX (1960), 3385-3386.

55 K. Glaser, "Group Discussion with Mothers of Hospitalized Children," *Pediatrics*, XXVI (1960), 132 ff.

56 G. F. Vaughan, "Children in Hospital," *Lancet*, CCLXXII (1957), 1117 ff.

57 M. Capes, "The Child in the Hospital," *Mental Hygiene*, XL (1956), 107 ff.

58 A. J. Sonit, "Hospitalization: An Aid to Physical and Psychological Health in Childhood," *A.M.A. Journal of Diseases of Children*, IXCIX (1960), 155 ff.

59 R. S. Illingworth, "Children in Hospital," *Lancet* (1958), 165 ff.

60 "The Welfare of Children in Hospital," *British Medical Journal*, I, Part I (1959), 166 ff.

61 R. A. Jensen *et al.*, "The Hospitalized Child," *American Journal of Orthopsychiatry*, XXV (1955), 293 ff.

62 G. E. Blom, "The Reactions of Hospitalized Children to Illness," *Pediatrics*, XXII (1958), 590 ff.

63 A. R. Rich, *The Pathogenesis of Tuberculosis* (Springfield, Ill.: Charles C. Thomas, Publishers, 1951), p. 808.

64 J. A. Myers, *Tuberculosis Among Children and Adults* (Springfield, Ill.: Charles C. Thomas, Publishers, 1951), p. 248.

65 E. M. Lincoln, "Eradication of Tuberculosis in Children," *Archives of Environmental Health*, III (1961), 444 f.

66 *Ibid.*, p. 447.

67 D. T. Smith, "Tuberculosis Today and Tomorrow," *American Review of Tuberculosis*, LXVII (1953), 719.

68 E. M. Lincoln and P. G. Vera Cruz, "Progress in Treatment of Tuberculosis," *Pediatrics*, XXV (1960), 1040 f.

69 R. J. Dubos, "Biologic and Epidemiologic Aspects of Tuberculosis," *American Review of Tuberculosis*, LXVII (1953), 4.

70 B. B. Berle, "Emotional Factors and Tuberculosis," *Psychosomatic Medicine*, X (1948), 366 ff.

71 E. Wittkower, "Psychology of the Tuberculosis Patient," in *Modern Practice in Tuberculosis*, eds. T. H. Sellors and J. L. Livingstone (London: Butterworth & Co., Ltd., 1952), p. 343.

72 R. G. Barker, *et al.*, *Adjustment to Physical Handicap and Illness: A Survey of the Social Psychology of Physique and Disability*, Social Science Research Council Bulletin 55 (New York, 1953), pp. 144 ff.

73 G. F. Derner, *Aspects of the Psychology of the Tuberculous* (New York: Paul B. Hoeber, Inc., 1953), p. 107.

74 B. R. Merrill, "Some Psychosomatic Aspects of Pulmonary Tuberculosis," *Journal of Nervous and Mental Disease*, CXVII (1953), 9 ff.

75 D. H. Harris, "Psychological Aspects of Tuberculosis," in *Psychological Aspects of Physical Disability*, ed. J. F. Garrett (Washington, D.C.: United States Government Printing Office, 1952), pp. 1 ff.

76 L. Korkes and N. D. C. Lewis, "An Analysis of the Relationship Between Psychological Patterns and Outcome in Pulmonary Tuberculosis," *Journal of Nervous and Mental Disease*, CXXII (1955), 524 ff.

77 C. B. Marker, "Psychological Care of Tuberculosis in Children," *Journal of the Maine Medical Association*, May 1956.

78 D. Rosenbluth and J. Bowlby, "The Social and Psychological Backgrounds of Tuberculous Children," *British Medical Journal*, I (1955), 946 ff.

79 C. M. Vernier, *et al.*, "Psychosocial Study of the Patient with Pulmonary Tuberculosis," *Psychological Monographs*, No. 510 (1961), 3.

80 J. Hartz, "Tuberculosis and Personality Conflicts," *Psychosomatic Medicine*, VI (1944), 17 ff.

81 Dubos, *op. cit.*, p. 2.

82 E. Wittkower, *A Psychiatrist Looks at Tuberculosis* (London: National Association for the Prevention of Tuberculosis, 1959), pp. 1 ff.

83 Vernier, *et al.*, *op. cit.*, pp. 3 ff.

84 Derner, *op. cit.*, p. 153.

85 A. O. Ludwig, "Emotional Factors in Tuberculosis," *Public Health Reports*, LXIII (1948), 883 ff.

86 H. D. Kramer, "Psychopathology of Childhood Tuberculosis," *The Nervous Child*, VII (1948), 102 ff.

87 E. L. Demuth, "Is There a Specific Personality in Tuberculous Patients," *Archives of Neurology and Psychiatry*, LXVI (1951), 30 ff.

88 Derner, *op. cit.*, pp. 1 ff.

89 S. Dubo, "Psychiatric Study of Children with Pulmonary Tuberculosis," *American Journal of Orthopsychiatry*, XX (1950), 520 ff.

90 J. Hartz, "Human Relationship in Tuberculosis," *Public Health Reports*, LXV (1950), 1293.

91 L. Bellak, "Psychiatric Aspects of Tuberculosis," *Social Casework*, XXXI (1950), 183 ff.

92 Barker, *et al.*, *op. cit.*, pp. 143 ff.

93 W. M. Cruickshank and W. G. Peacher, "Special Education for the Epileptic, the Tubercular, and Children with Glandular Disorders," *49th Yearbook of the N.S.S.E.*, ed. N. B. Henry (Chicago: University of Chicago Press, 1950), Part II, 218 ff.

94 J. D. Keith, R. D. Rowe, and P. Vlad, *Heart Disease in Infancy and Childhood* (New York: The Macmillan Company, 1958), p. x.

95 R. Gluck, *Diagnosis of Congenital Cardiac Defects in General Practice* (New York: American Heart Association, 1961), pp. 1 ff.

96 J. W. Wrightstone, *et al.*, eds., *Studies of Children With Physical Handicaps, No. 6, Adolescents With Cardiac Limitations* (New York: Board of Education, 1961), p. 15.

97 *If Your Child Has a Congenital Heart Defect* (New York: American Heart Association, 1960), pp. 8 ff.

98 Keith, Rowe, and Vlad, *op. cit.*, p. 640.

99 *Ibid.*, p. 5.

100 *Ibid.*, pp. 640 f.

[101] P. D. White, *Heart Disease* (New York: The Macmillan Company, 1951), p. 289.

[102] H. H. Garner, "A Psychosomatic View of Cardiovascular Disease," *Chicago Medical School Quarterly*, XIV (1952), 8 ff.

[103] F. Dunbar, *Psychosomatic Diagnosis* (New York: Paul B. Hoeber, Inc., 1948), pp. 433 ff.

[104] D. H. Crowell, "Personality and Physical Disease: A Test of the Dunbar Hypothesis Applied to Diabetes Mellitus and Rheumatic Fever," *Genetic Psychology Monographs*, XLVIII (1953), 117 ff.

[105] E. C. Neuhaus, "A Personality Study of Asthmatic and Cardiac Children," *Psychosomatic Medicine*, XX (1958), 181 ff.

[106] Wrightstone, *et al.* (1961), *op. cit.*, p. 114.

[107] W. F. Reiser, E. B. Ferris, Jr., and M. Levine, "Cardiovascular Disorders, Heart Disease, and Hypertension," in Wittkower and Cleghorn, *op. cit.*, pp. 300 ff.

[108] G. A. Wolff and H. G. Wolff, "Studies on the Nature of Certain Symptoms Associated with Cardiovascular Disorders," *Psychosomatic Medicine*, VII (1946), 293 ff.

[109] B. Boshes, "Emotions, Hypothalamus, and the Cardiovascular System," *American Journal of Cardiology*, I (1958), 212 ff.

[110] F. G. Koenig, "A Study of Anxiety in Children with Rheumatic Fever," *Dissertation Abstracts*, XX (1959), 1438-1439.

[111] M. K. Reed, "The Intelligence, Social Maturity, Personal Adjustment, Physical Development, and Parent-child Relationships of Children with Congenital Heart Disease," *Dissertation Abstracts*, XX (1959), 385.

[112] I. M. Josselyn, A. J. Simon, and E. Eells, "Anxiety in Children Convalescing from Rheumatic Fever," *American Journal of Orthopsychiatry*, XXV (1955), 109 ff.

[113] Wrightstone, *et al.* (1961), *op. cit.*, pp. 58 ff.

[114] Neuhaus, *op. cit.*, pp. 183 ff.

[115] L. Bellak and F. Haselkorn, "Psychological Aspects of Cardiac Illness and Rehabilitation," *Social Casework*, XXXVII (1956), 482 ff.

[116] T. B. Brazelton, R. Holder, and B. Talbot, "Emotional Aspects of Rheumatic Fever in Children," *Journal of Pediatrics*, XLIII (1953), 339 ff.

[117] I. L. Bauer, "Attitudes of Children with Rheumatic Fever," *Journal of Pediatrics*, XL (1952), 801.

[118] *Ibid.*, p. 4.

[119] D. Young and M. Rodstein, "Home Care of Rheumatic Fever Patients," *Journal of the American Medical Association*, CLII (1953), 987 ff.

[120] R. Holder, *Rheumatic Fever Project* (Boston: Massachusetts General Hospital, 1953), pp. 1 ff. (Typescript).

[121] J. W. Wrightstone, J. Justman, and S. Moskowitz, *Studies of Children with Physical Handicaps, No. 1, The Child with Cardiac Limitations* (New York: Board of Education, 1953), p. 67.

[122] Wrightstone, *et al.*, *op. cit.*, p. 63.

[123] M. A. Lammers, "Where Children Take Heart," *American Journal of Nursing,* LVI (1956), 854 ff.

[124] L. M. Taran and A. F. Hodsdon, "Social and Psychologic Problems Associated with Prolonged Institutional Care for Rheumatic Children," *Journal of Pediatrics,* XXXV (1949), 648 ff.

[125] Bauer, *op. cit.*, pp. 4 ff.

[126] Wrightstone, Justman, and Moskowitz, *op. cit.*, pp. 83 ff.

[127] *Ibid.*, p. 83.

[128] Neuhaus, *op. cit.*, pp. 183 ff.

[129] Wrightstone, Justman, and Moskowitz, *op. cit.*, p. 65.

[130] Wrightstone, *et al.*, *op. cit.*, pp. 114-115.

[131] Wrightstone, Justman, and Moskowitz, *op. cit.*, pp. 91 ff.

[132] Wrightstone, *et al.*, *op. cit.*, p. 82.

[133] *Ibid.*, pp. 78 ff.

134 Wrightstone, Justman, and Moskowitz, *op. cit.*, pp. 44-45.

135 Wrightstone, *et al., op. cit.*, p. 24.

136 *Ibid.*, pp. 104 ff.

137 *Ibid.*, p. 41.

138 Wrightstone, Justman, and Moskowitz, *op. cit.*, pp. 29 ff.

139 Wrightstone, *et al., op. cit.*, pp. 31 ff.

140 *Ibid.*, pp. 105 f.

141 J. Levitt and L. M. Taran, "Some of the Problems in the Education of Rheumatic Children," *Journal of Pediatrics*, XXXII (1948), 553 ff.

142 White, *op. cit.*, p. 261.

143 Wrightstone, Justman, and Moskowitz, *op. cit.*, pp. 113 ff.

144 Starr, *op. cit.*, p. 493.

145 T. D. Danowski, *Diabetes Mellitus* (Baltimore: The Williams and Wilkins Co., 1957), p. 407.

146 P. H. Forsham, ed., "Current Trends in Research and Clinical Management of Diabetes," *Annals of the New York Academy of Sciences*, LXXXII (1959), 231.

147 Danowski, *op. cit.*, p. 121.

148 Forsham, *op. cit.*, pp. 229 ff.

149 G. B. Forbes, "The Juvenile Diabetic," *G.P.*, XIII (1956), 99 ff.

150 J. P. Peters, "Management of Diabetes," *Yale Journal of Biology and Medicine*, XXVII (1954), 75 ff.

151 P. White, "Diabetes in Childhood," in *Diseases of Metabolism*, ed. G. G. Duncan (Philadelphia: W. B. Saunders Co., 1952), p. 1162.

152 Starr, *op. cit.*, p. 494.

153 White, in *Diseases of Metabolism, op. cit.*, pp. 947 ff.

154 C. C. Forsyth and W. W. Payne, "Free Diets in Treatment of Diabetic Children," *Archives of Diseases of Childhood*, XXXXI (1956), 245 ff.

155 E. Tolstoi, "The Objectives of Modern Diabetic Care," *Psychosomatic Medicine*, X (1948), 291 ff.

156 W. C. Menninger, "Psychological Factors in the Etiology of Diabetes Mellitus," *Journal of Nervous and Mental Disease*, LXXXI (1935), 1 ff.

157 L. E. Hinkle, F. M. Evans, and J. Wolf, "Studies in Diabetes Mellitus," *Psychosomatic Medicine*, XIII (1951), 184 ff.

158 H. Rosen and T. Lidz, "Emotional Factors in Precipitation of Recurrent Diabetic Acidosis," *Psychosomatic Medicine*, XI (1949), 211 ff.

159 Danowski, *op. cit.*, p. 417.

160 L. E. Hinkle and S. Wolf, "A Summary of Experimental Evidence Relating Life Stress to Diabetes Mellitus," *Journal of the Mount Sinai Hospital*, XIX (1952), 532 ff.

161 Danowski, *op. cit.*, p. 418.

162 Dunbar, *op. cit.*, pp. 481 ff.

163 E. I. Falstein and I. Judas, "Juvenile Diabetes and its Psychiatric Implications," *American Journal of Orthopsychiatry*, XXV (1955), 330 ff.

164 Crowell, *op. cit.*, pp. 117 ff.

165 A. J. Kubany, T. S. Danowski, and C. Moses, "The Personality and Intelligence of Diabetics," *Diabetes*, V (1956), 462 ff.

166 Danowski, *op. cit.*, p. 407.

167 H. Bruch, "Physiologic and Psychologic Interrelationships in Diabetes in Children," *Psychosomatic Medicine*, XI (1949), 200 ff.

168 See pp. 397-402.

169 H. Bruch and I. Hewlett, "Psychologic Aspects of the Medical Management of Diabetes in Children," *Psychosomatic Medicine*, IX (1947), 205 ff.

170 E. Podolsky, "Physical Ailments and the Frightened Child," *Mental Hygiene*, XXXIX (1955), 489 ff.

171 A. E. Fischer, "Factors Responsible for Emotional Disturbances in Diabetic Children," *Nervous Child*, VII (1948), 78.

172 *Ibid.*, pp. 79 ff.

173 A. Freud, *op. cit.*, pp. 70 ff.

174 Korsch, *op. cit.*, pp. 38 ff.

175 D. E. Johannsen and E. M. Bennett, "The Personality of Diabetic Children," *Journal of Genetic Psychology,* LXXXVII (1955), 175 ff.

176 E. M. Bennett and D. E. Johannsen, "Psychodynamics of the Diabetic Child," *Psychological Monographs,* LXVIII (1954), 1 ff.

177 Starr, *op. cit.*, p. 499.

178 *Ibid.*, p. 502.

179 P. White in *Diseases of Metabolism, op. cit.*, p. 946.

180 W. B. Kennedy, "Psychologic Problems of the Young Diabetic," *Diabetes,* IV (1955), 207 ff.

181 Forsham, *op. cit.*, pp. 229 ff.

182 *Ibid.*, pp. 258 ff.

183 *Ibid.*, pp. 263 ff.

184 "Analysis of a Survey Concerning Employment of Diabetics in Some Major Industries," *Diabetes,* VI (1957), 550 ff.

185 J. B. Hurd, "Report of the Committee on Camps," *Diabetes,* VI (1957), 97 ff.

186 A. Marble, "The Future of the Child with Diabetes," *Journal of the American Dietetic Association,* XXXIII (1957), 569 ff.

187 L. S. Smelo and S. Eichold, "Conduct of Camp for Diabetic Children," *Diabetes,* IV (1955), 219 ff.

188 H. G. Jacobi, "Nutritional Studies of Juvenile Diabetics Attending Summer Camp," *Journal of Clinical Nutrition,* II (1954), 22 ff.

189 W. B. Weil and M. B. Sussman, "Behavior and Diet and Glycosuria of Diabetic Children in a Summer Camp," *Pediatrics,* XXVII (1961), 118 ff.

190 L. Luzzati and B. Dittman, "Group Discussion with Parents of Ill Children," *Pediatrics,* XIII (1954), 269 ff.

191 S. J. Prigal, ed., *Fundamentals of Allergy* (New York: McGraw-Hill Book Co., Inc., 1960), p. 2.

192 F. S. Nelson and A. V. Stoesser, "Allergic Diseases of Infancy and Childhood," *International Record of Medicine and General Practice Clinics,* CLXVI (1953), 95 ff.

193 Prigal, *op. cit.*, p. 83.

194 *Ibid.*, p. 82.

195 *Ibid.*, p. 94.

196 J. Bostock, "Asthma: A Synthesis Involving Primitive Speech, Organism, and Insecurity," *Journal of Mental Science,* CII (1956), 559 ff.

197 H. G. Rapaport, S. J. Appel, and V. L. Szanton, "Incidence of Allergy in a Pediatric Population," *Annals of Allergy,* XVIII (1960), 45.

198 Prigal, *op. cit.*, p. 236.

199 Rapaport, Appel, and Szanton, *op. cit.*, pp. 46 ff.

200 T. M. French, *et al.*, "Psychogenic Factors in Bronchial Asthma," *Psychosomatic Medicine Monographs* (Washington, D.C.: National Research Council, 1941), Parts I and II, 1 ff.

201 C. H. Rogerson, D. H. Hardcastle, and K. Duguid, "A Psychological Approach to the Problem of Asthma and the Asthma-Eczema-Prurigo Syndrome," *Guy's Hospital Reports,* LXXXV (1935), 289 ff.

202 H. Miller and D. W. Baruch, "The Emotional Problems of Childhood and their Relation to Asthma," *A.M.A. Journal of Diseases of Children,* IXCIII (1957), 242 ff.

203 H. A. Abrahamson, "Evaluation of Maternal Rejection Theory in Allergy," *Annals of Allergy,* XII (1954), 129 ff.

204 L. Jessner, *et al.*, "Emotional Impact of Nearness and Separation for the Asthmatic Child and His Mother," in *The Psychoanalytic Study of the Child* (New York: International Universities Press, Inc., 1955), X, 353 ff.

205 R. T. Long, *et al.*, "A Psychosomatic Study of Allergic and Emotional Factors in Children with Asthma," *American Journal of Psychiatry,* CXIV (1958), 890 ff.

206 H. S. Tuft, "The Development and Management of Intractable Asthma of Childhood," *A.M.A. Journal of Diseases of Children,* IXCIII (1957), 251 ff.

207 M. M. Peshkin, "Management of the Institutionalized Child with Intractable Asthma," *Annals of Allergy,* XVIII (1960), 75 ff.

208 M. C. Harris and N. Shure, "A Study of Behavior Patterns in Asthmatic Children," *Journal of Allergy*, XXVII (1956), 312 f.

209 D. Leigh, "Asthma and the Psychiatrist: A Critical Review," *International Archives of Allergy*, IV (1953), 227 ff.

210 M. C. Harris, "Is There a Specific Emotional Pattern in Allergic Disease," *Annals of Allergy*, XIII (1955), 654 ff.

211 G. T. Fitzelle, "Personality Factors and Certain Attitudes Toward Child Rearing Among Parents of Asthmatic Children," *Psychosomatic Medicine*, XXI (1959), 208 ff.

212 J. C. Coolidge, "Asthma in Mother and Child as a Special Type of Intercommunication," *American Journal of Orthopsychiatry*, XXVI (1956), 165 ff.

213 Harris and Shure, *op. cit.*, p. 312.

214 P. H. Knapp, *et al.*, "Personality Variations in Bronchial Asthma," *Psychosomatic Medicine*, XIX (1957), 443 ff.

215 P. H. Knapp and S. J. Nemetz, "Acute Bronchial Asthma," *Psychosomatic Medicine*, XXII (1960), 42 ff.

216 L. Rees, "Physical and Emotional Factors in Bronchial Asthma," *Journal of Psychosomatic Research*, I (1956), 98 ff.

217 L. Rees, "The Role of Emotional and Allergic Factors in Hay Fever," *Journal of Psychosomatic Research*, III (1959), 234 ff.

218 M. R. Friend and O. Pollock, "Psychosocial Aspects in the Preparation for Treatment of an Allergic Child," *American Journal of Orthopsychiatry*, XXIV (1954), 63 ff.

219 E. Schneider, "Psychodynamics of Chronic Allergic Eczema and Chronic Urticaria," *Journal of Nervous and Mental Disease*, CXX (1954), 17 ff.

220 R. M. Bakwin, "Essentials of Psychosomatics in Allergic Children," *Pediatric Clinics of North America*, I (1954), 921 ff.

211 See pp. 402-407.

222 Coolidge, *op. cit.*, p. 176.

223 S. S. Kripke, "Psychologic Aspects of Bronchial Asthma," *American Journal of Diseases of Children*, C (1960), 935 ff.

224 P. A. Knapp and S. J. Nemetz, "Sources of Tension in Bronchial Asthma," *Psychosomatic Medicine*, XIX (1957), 466 ff.

225 S. W. Little and L. D. Cohen, "Goal Setting Behavior of Asthmatic Children and of Their Mothers for Them," *Journal of Personality*, XIX (1951), 376 ff.

226 R. P. Morris, "Effect of Mother on Goal Setting Behavior of the Asthmatic Child," *Dissertation Abstracts*, XX (1959), 1440.

227 Neuhaus, *op. cit.*, p. 183.

228 R. Fine, "The Personality of the Asthmatic Child," in *Abstracts of Dissertations*. New York (University Publishers, Inc.): University of Southern California Press (1948), 165 ff.

229 M. Creak and J. M. Stephens, "The Psychological Aspects of Asthma in Children," *Pediatric Clinics of North America*, V (1958), 733 ff.

230 Kripke, *op. cit.*, pp. 935 ff.

231 R. M. Bakwin and H. Bakwin, "The Child with Asthma," *Journal of Pediatrics*, XXXII (1948), 323.

232 S. C. Bukantz and M. M. Peshkin, "Institutional Treatment of Asthmatic Children," *Pediatric Clinics of North America*, VI (1949), 755 ff.

233 H. Miller and D. W. Baruch, "Psychotherapy of Parents of Allergic Children," *Annals of Allergy*, XVIII (1960), 990 ff.

234 H. Miller, "Evaluation of the Emotional Factors in Eczema and Urticaria," *Annals of Allergy*, XVIII (1960), 161 ff.

235 D. Hallowitz, "Residential Treatment of Chronic Asthmatic Children," *American Journal of Orthopsychiatry*, XXIV (1954), 576 ff.

236 H. A. Abrahamson and M. M. Peshkin, "Psychosomatic Group Therapy with Parents of Children with Intractable Asthma," *Annals of Allergy*, XVIII (1960), 87 ff.

237 F. P. Connor, "The Education of Children with Chronic Medical Problems," in *Education of Exceptional Children and Youth*, eds. W. M. Cruickshank and G. O. Johnson (Englewood Cliffs, N.J.: Prentice-Hall, Inc., 1958), pp. 498 ff.

G. ORVILLE JOHNSON
Professor of Special Education
Syracuse University

9 Psychological Characteristics of the Mentally Retarded

No FIELD of human behavior has been studied as extensively by persons in such a number of varied disciplines as mental retardation and the problems associated with it. No other field has been of as great concern to the state legislatures and national governing bodies. Each of these groups has selected terms to define the specific groups of children or aspects of the total problems in which they have an interest. As a result, there has been built up a large group of terms by physicians, social workers, rehabilitation counsellors, psychologists, educators and others. In some instances common terms have been employed by two or more disciplines—but not always to denote the same problem. In other instances, specific vocabularies have been developed to refer to narrow, clinical groups. The latter is true particularly of the medical profession.

One additional factor has entered the picture during the past two decades to further becloud or confuse clear communication. This has been the advent and expansion of organized groups of parents of retarded children. They have tended to use broad, descriptive terms when referring to their children, apparently feeling these terms make the children seem more nearly normal or less deviate in the eyes of the general public. The more specific and technical terms sound more "harsh" and leave little room for doubt. Newspapers and popular periodicals have tended to adopt these all-inclusive, non-specific terms. To add to the general confusion, they have also used the technical terms, such as moron, incorrectly and inappropriately.

The whole issue of terminology has been so acute that the *American Association on Mental Deficiency* has considered it a problem of major importance. Five manuals have been published in an attempt to propose solutions that will receive popular acceptance. The last [41] appeared in 1959 following two years of extensive work. The stated purpose of this manual is to increase uniformity in classification. If this is accomplished, it will prove to be a very real boon to research and communication.

Classifications can generally be divided into two major categories—medical and behavioral. The medical classifications are fairly well defined and accepted, although some disagreement sometimes exists concerning etiology or cause. When this occurs there may also be consequent lack of agreement in regard to the category in which an individual should be placed. The degree of agreement has been much less in the acceptance and use of behavioral classifications. This has been due to a number of factors. Two of the primary ones are scientists' inability to definitively describe categories and characteristics and the numbers of disciplines (sociology, education, and psychology—to name only a few) involved, each observing the behavior from its frame of reference and for its purposes. It is also in the descriptive, behavioral area that lay and legislative usage have been an added confusing factor.

It is, consequently, essential that any serious discussion concerned with a description of the mentally retarded, particularly in the behavioral area, must first be directed to the clarification of the terminology to be subsequently used. Only then can it become involved in the more fundamental aspects of the problem. This is true whether the discussion is centered around characteristics (physical, motor, psychological, social, educational and so forth) or programs (day-school, residential, workshops and so forth). Without a clear definition of terms effective communication between the discussant and the reader and/or listener is impossible.

The two basic classifications, medical and behavioral, are not mutually exclusive. A mentally retarded individual, in order to be adequately described and classified, must be included under each one. The medical classification is primarily concerned with etiology, physical characteristics, and consequent treatment and prevention. The behavioral classification is primarily concerned with the degree of mental retardation, the resulting performance level of the individuals in various situations, and programs. Persons interested in the behavioral aspects of the problems of and related to mental retardation have little need to know the medical classification. The exception to this statement is where unique patterns of behavior are existent in individuals belonging to a specific medical or etiological category.

The following discussion will, therefore, be largely descriptive in nature, directed to the behavioral characteristics and problems of the mentally retarded. The various medical categories will only be referred to as they are important within this context. Thus, the broad, generic term "mentally retarded" or "mental retardation" will be used as an all-encompassing concept to refer to all degrees of mental deficit. Where available information indicates psychological characteristics are restricted to an etiological group or to a group performing at a certain adaptive behavioral level, more specific terms with appropriate definitions will be introduced at that time.

Concepts of Mental Retardation

WHEN ONE discusses the field of mental retardation with persons from the various disciplines, he is often faced with more than the requirement of coping with a number of terminologies. He is likely to be faced with the problem of these persons having different conceptualizations of mental retardation. Mental retardation is literally many things to many people. To some it is a symptom. Some physicians may consider it a symptom indicating a chemical imbalance or the inability of the body to assimilate and digest certain foods. This would be in the case of such entities as phenolketonuria, galactosemia, and cretinism. Some psychiatrists and clinical psychologists consider mental retardation a symptom of a severe emotional disturbance. The individual is retarded intellectually only because of his inability to relate adequately with other persons and to his environment. In other instances, these same persons may consider that mental retardation is a symptom of a sensory handicap or that the sensory disability has been the indirect cause of the emotional disturbance. This attitude is also held by some educators and many parents. Thus, a deaf, blind, or cerebral palsied child cannot be mentally retarded. The apparent retardation in these children is merely a reflection or symptom of their inability to benefit from the normal environmental stimuli that encourages intellectual development in most children. The literature is replete with articles and statements purporting to prove or attempting to justify the assumption of normal intellectual development for the children and youth who compose these handicapped groups.

The sociologists and developmental psychologists often apparently feel that mental retardation is a reflection of a lack of psychosocial stimulation. It is a symptom of inadequate social concern and an inadequacy of social structure. The fact that most mentally retarded persons (particularly where there is no apparent etiological factor such as disease, trauma, or chemical imbalance present) tend to be born to parents residing in subcultural, low socioeconomic environments indicates to them the validity of their contention. Numerous educators feel mental retardation is a sympton of poor or inadequate instruction. It may also be a symptom of disinterest and inattention on the part of the child or youth. Consequently, the individual does not derive adequate or sufficient benefit from the instruction provided him.

Where mental retardation is considered as purely a symptom, the solution is either a simple one or hopeless as far as present knowledge is concerned. Cure by attacking the cause is the only correction possible. If the cause cannot be corrected with presently known methods, techniques, or treatment, there is nothing that can be done at least at the immediate time. Selective feeding, changing bodily chemical balance, and providing psychotherapy are all purported cures. When the cure does not produce results it is because it is not specific for the disease under treatment or because there is inadequacy of available information and treatment. Similarly, children having severe sensory disabilities cannot be helped unless substitute stimuli can be provided to compensate for the lack of experiences in certain areas. The latter solution, of course, is far more acceptable and commonly practiced. Following this train of reasoning, there can be no truly retarded blind, deaf, or cerebral palsied children.

The sociologist would feel that mental retardation along with many social ills are strictly the product of slum area living. They can all be eliminated by the razing of substandard dwellings and the erection of community housing projects; addition of parks, playgrounds, and recreational facilities; and the provision of various "cultural" experiences for the residents. More homework, higher academic standards, different methods, and insistence on attention and satisfactory performance in the schools will solve the problem of the mentally retarded child in the school, according to the educator.

These theories sound fine and attract many disciples. They make it possible to conceive of a society where nothing so unpleasant as the mentally retarded exist. They are not proven by pointing at a case where apparently dramatic changes occurred following a prescribed treatment. No one has ever held that some of these factors do not cause mental retardation or that some persons having problems in the previously mentioned areas may not also have a number of behavioral characteristics usually attributed to mental retardation. Mental retardation, however, must be accepted as an entity in itself. It may also be associated with one or more of these symptoms, but it exists as a valid, unique characteristic. In the case of phenolketonuria, if treatment is initiated at an early enough date, the individual *may* never become mentally retarded. In other words, the inability of the body to assimilate certain foods may be a cause of mental retardation, but mental retardation is not necessarily a symptom. Severe emotional disturbance may cause an individual to be inadequate insofar as his abilities to relate to other persons and his environment are concerned. Mentally retarded persons, like the normal and superior, may become emotionally disturbed. But because a mentally retarded person is emotionally disturbed does not mean that the retardation is a symptom.

The mentally retarded, particularly those who are capable of independently maintaining themselves, tend to reside in the subcultural, low socioeconomic areas of the community. They hold jobs that are rated toward the bottom of the vocational ladder. In childhood and youth they do poorly in school. Does this mean that the environment is the sole cause of their retardation, or does this environment reflect their behavioral level? Where else in the community could they maintain themselves without outside help? What kinds of better jobs could they hold? What else could they do in school? Studies [7,17,44,72] have not indicated that the educable mentally retarded perform any higher in special classes, theoretically designed in consideration of their characteristics and needs, than they do in the regular grades. Others beside the mentally retarded also live in these areas, are employed on similar low-level positions in industry, and do poorly in school—but for numerous other reasons. Again, mental retardation cannot be considered a symptom.

Mental retardation, by definition, is exactly what the term itself describes. The mentally retarded are individuals who are retarded and inadequate in their intellectual development and ability. The term states unequivocally that this is their characteristic now. It indicates nothing in regard to either the past, the future, or the cause. The definition thus used is one concerned with the intellectual operational level of individuals. Measures of the more finite variety (pound, ounce, gram, inch, centimeter, and so forth) used in the physical sciences have not been developed. Yet, intelligence can be measured by comparing the behavior of one individual to that of the population. These comparisons have been made in many ways. Gross or severe retardation has been recognized down through the centuries much as it is today, by merely observing the behavior of an individual and making a gross comparison to the way persons of his age behave. This kind of evaluation fails at the higher levels where the deviation from the norm is relatively small. It was not until the advent of the standard intelligence test that an instrument that could make these finer differentiations was available. Binet's original instrument was designed for the purpose of measuring those aspects of intelligence that are important to school success. This is still its primary application, although the Terman and Merrill Revision [91] has been found to be one of the best predictors of vocational success for the retarded as well.[63] Since Binet completed his original work, numerous revisions of his scale, as well as additional intelligence tests, have been developed. A number of these have attempted to measure other, or additional, facets of intelligence. Thurstone, for example, attempted to determine all of the factors that contribute to a concept of total intelligence. After defining and describing these factors, he selected and devised items designed to measure them. These items were combined into the *Tests of Primary Mental Abilities*.

Intelligence is measurable on a comparative basis today. The intelligence tests have been designed and standardized to perform this function. Since mental retardation is some degree of deficit in intelligence, the intelligence tests are the instruments that have been developed to determine the intellectual level at which an individual is functioning. Through use of the intelligence tests, it can be determined whether or not a person is mentally retarded. Clinical judgment, use of projective material, and psychiatric and psychological interviews can help only in determining if the individual performed at or near his ability level on the intelligence test, and/or other kinds of psychological problems he may have in addition to mental retardation.

Once an instrument had been developed that was capable of making finer measurements of intellectual development than had been possible using observation alone, placement of persons (particularly children) in categories began. It was, of course, recognized immediately that those categorized as mentally retarded were incapable of learning the same things as normal children of the same age. They could, however, often learn these things at a later date. Thus the concept of their being "slow to learn" or "slow learners" developed.

Diagnostic instruments have also provided the means whereby fairly accurate estimates of the incidence of mental retardation can be made. Unfortunately, no extensive and reliable epidemiological studies have been made to either verify or refute estimates, based upon school surveys and the assumed distribution of intelligence, that are available. School surveys are poor because numbers of the lowest pupils have been excluded. In addition, they are subject to errors engendered by the nature of the population being served. As a result, other methods must be relied upon. If intellectual abilities follow the same normal distribution as other physical characteristics (and there is no reason to think they do not), the incidence of mental retardation should be between 3 and 4 per cent. About one half of 1 per cent will be of such a low level that they will require custodial care, supervision, and direction for their entire lives. The majority of the remainder are educable as children and able to care for themselves socially and economically as adults. Of the low-grade retarded, more than half of them can be considered trainable. They can learn to take care of their personal needs. There are approximately 2.7 trainable children per 1,000 school children. Of these, one has been institutionalized and 1.7 are still residing in the community.[55,75]

As psychology gradually came of age and more and more information concerning human behavior and individual differences became available, theories or hypotheses began to be developed regarding the psychological characteristics of persons included in the several intellectual categories. Psychologists began to look for ways in which the mentally retarded differed from the normal and a whole psychology of the retarded began to develop. Work has been done in the areas of learning, adjustment, social maturity, psychomotor skills, and even differentiation of characteristics for special etiological groups. The basic assumption seems to have been that here was a unique organism [3,26,95] (or possibly a number of unique organisms) [90] that needed to be described psychologically in order that educators, social workers, and other persons who might be responsible for them would, in having this information, become more knowledgeable and able to plan more effective programs.

Influence of Psychosocial Stimulation

THERE ARE several ways in which cultural factors may be related to and have an influence on mental retardation. One is in the impact that cultural factors have upon the individual who is, for any reason, retarded. Another is in the effect the retarded person has on his society. The third concerns the part which cultural factors play in the etiology of mental retardation.

There is little question that cultural factors play some part in the development of an intelligence that is appropriate to the society in which an individual exists. It has been shown that different attitudes and values in different cultures are associated with different child-rearing practices. Further, sociologists contend that more than one culture exists in the United States. The predominant one is the "middle class"; thus poor performance of "lower-class" children on mental tests can be explained, at least partially, in terms of their lack of environmental stimulation. The fact that there is a markedly higher percentage of mentally retarded persons among the lower socioeconomic groups is commonly accepted. In fact, the statement is circular because any test item which did not indirectly measure socioeconomic status would probably be discarded as not assessing intelligence. Depending upon one's philosophical persuasion, it may be argued that people belong to the lower classes because they are unintelligent or that they may be unintelligent because they get insufficient stimulation from their lower-class environment.

There have been many different approaches used to study the extent to which cultural factors are responsible for the incidence of mental retardation. Or, to put it in another context, many studies have attempted to determine how the rate of intellectual growth can be controlled by changes in environment. One of these methods is to study children who have been reared in an environment other than the home of their natural parents. They may then be compared to their earlier development or with siblings who remained in the original home.

Freeman, Holzinger, and Mitchell [36] studied 130 pairs of siblings who had been separated for at least four years in various foster homes. They found that the correlation between siblings was only .25, whereas the correlation between the intelligence of children and the socioeconomic conditions of the foster homes was .48. In order of ascending economic levels of their foster homes, mean I.Q.'s of the children were 91, 103, and 111. The twin studies reported by Newman, Freeman, and Holzinger [69] showed that I.Q.'s of fraternal twins correlated .63; those of identical twins reared together correlated .88; and those of identical twins reared apart correlated .77. In a few cases where identical twins were reared in very different environments, I.Q.'s showed differences as great as 24 points. A number of additional studies have been conducted using siblings raised in different environments. In most of these studies, while correlations continued to remain positive, they dropped significantly lower as the environments changed. This was especially true for children under five or six years of age.

In studying children with parents of subnormal intelligence and/or coming from lower socioeconomic group homes which provided them with little stimulation, a number of interesting results were reported. Skeels and Fillmore [84] found that, although the intelligence of young children showed fluctuation by age, it remained higher than the intelligence of the older children. A successive drop in intelligence was noted for each successive age group of children who remained in these homes over seven years. In another study, Skeels [82] followed a group of children who had been taken out of the poor environment into which they were born and placed in foster homes at an early age. He found that their average intelligence was higher than one would expect in terms of their parentage. Whereas a correlation of .50 is consistently found between the intelligence of parents and children, the correlation between the intelligence of these children and their true mothers was zero. The average I.Q. of the mothers was at the borderline level, while the average for the children was 115.5. When comparing the intelligence of the children with the occupational level of the foster father, no correlation was found for children under two years of age. After this age, the correlations tended to become positive.

Skeels and Dye [83] report what is probably the most dramatic study in the literature relating to the effects of environmental change on I.Q. Thirteen children under three years of age having an average I.Q. of 64 were taken from an orphanage where they had received a minimum of attention and placed in an institution for the feeble-minded. They were assigned to various wards where they received a great deal of attention from older patients and attendants. After a year and one half, their I.Q.'s showed an average increase of 27.5 points. A contrast group of twelve infants remained in the orphanage. The initial average I.Q. of this group was 87.6. After thirty months, with adequate physical care but a minimum of stimulation, they had dropped an average of 26.2 points in I.Q.

In relation to the findings concerning increases in I.Q. or tested mental ability, a number of persons have discussed the age at which a child must be taken from a poor environment and placed in a stimulating one, if the change is to prove of value. The general consensus of opinion among investigators holding that environment is an extremely important factor in mental development is that the change must be made very early in life. Wells [96] felt that if children were taken from poor homes and placed in good foster homes before five years of age, sufficient change upward in intellectual development would occur to render invalid earlier predictions concerning intellectual attainment at adulthood. If, however, the change in environment were made after the age of five, neither significant gains nor losses would occur. Reymert [76] felt that the change must be made before the age of six. He found, by examining children at the time they entered school and annually throughout the ensuing five years, that no changes in I.Q. occurred for those whose home environments were changed during this period of time.

One of the most recent and extensive studies in this area was done by Kirk.[54] He identified 81 mentally retarded children from three to six years of age. They were divided into four groups: Community Experimental, Community Contrast, Institutional Experimental, and Institutional Contrast. The Experimental groups attended pre-school programs, the Contrast Groups did not. It was found that the rate of mental growth of 70 per cent of the children who received the pre-school education was accelerated during the pre-school period; the rate was maintained after they entered a regular school program. When the social and intellectual growth increases of the experimental groups were compared to similar evaluations of the contrast groups, the differences were significant at the 5 per cent level of confidence. Additional analyses were made on such factors as organicity and home environment. The study strongly indicates that a stimulating pre-school program can do much to materially increase the rate of intellectual growth of many mentally retarded children, but if optimum results are expected, the program must extend beyond the school and into the community where the children reside in undesirable homes that provide little in the way of psychosocial stimulation.

The foregoing statements are applicable to the high-grade retardate (those with I.Q.'s of approximately 50 and above). It is with this group that the studies have been concerned. There is little or no evidence to indicate that similar findings will obtain for the low-grade, custodial groups.

Learning Characteristics

STUDIES CONCERNED with the learning characteristics of mentally retarded persons are by far the most numerous among all the reported research projects conducted for the purpose of obtaining information related to their psychological behavior. The investigator who begins to examine the literature is faced by one problem that at first glance appears to be almost insurmountable. How is it possible to bring the many results together into some kind of a meaningful relationship when they have been obtained by study of quite diverse groups or populations? At times, it is difficult, because of differences in terminology, to even determine the exact nature of the group from which the subjects were selected. When the types of groups are clearly defined, one finds that some comparative studies have used institutional mentally retarded and non-institutional normal subjects. Other studies have included subjects selected in a variety of ways—from public school, special class, and so forth. The various studies have also used mentally retarded subjects of differing degrees or levels of retardation. One soon begins to speculate upon the influences the matter of selection of subjects may have on the reported results. Yet, with all these apparently contaminating influences there is remarkable agreement in the results, regardless of the environment or degree of intellectual deficit.

A number of kinds of learning, and use of a variety of appropriate tasks, have engaged the attention of many investigators. The verbal learning ability of two groups of retarded subjects and one group of normal subjects, all of equivalent mental ages, was reported by Cassell.[16] He was primarily interested in the problem of retroactive inhibition although he studied serial learning as well. The subjects were first required to learn an experimental list of six words. Next, an interpolated list of words was presented to half of each group. While the results indicated that retroactive inhibition did obtain, there was no evidence of any significant difference between the groups (the two retarded and one normal) either on this factor or on the serial learning. Johnson [46,48] also studied serial learning and pro-active and retroactive inhibition. Both the subjects and tasks selected were different from Cassell's. The normal and retarded subjects were selected from the public schools. The serial learning task consisted of memorizing a list of nonsense syllables by using the anticipation method. A cancellation task was used in the other study. He found no significant differences in serial learning between the normal and retarded groups. Like Cassell, he also found that the learning of normal children and mentally retarded children was affected by a previously learned task of the same nature. However, on the particular tasks used, which were somewhat psychomotor in nature, the mentally retarded were affected to a significantly smaller degree than the normal children. Berkson and Cantor [9] concerned themselves with a problem of verbal mediation. Following an A-B, B-C, A-C paradigm with the experimental subjects and an X-B, B-C, A-C paradigm with the controls, they compared the performances of a normal group and a mentally retarded group. The results indicated that the facilitation effects were of a comparable magnitude for the two groups. There was no significant difference between their performances.

Cruickshank and Blake [24] and Blake [48] reported the results of comparative studies with normal and retarded institutionalized boys on tasks requiring associative learning, transfer, sensory-motor learning, and discovery and application of a principle. The only differences they found caused them to conclude that the normal subjects were "probably superior" on the paired associates task. McCullock, Reswick, and Roy [66] studied the abilities of institutionalized mentally retarded subjects on tasks involving repetitive learning. Their results indicated that there was a positive relationship between mental age and initial scores, final scores, and the amount learned. Sloan and Berg,[88] using a similar task—also with institution inmates—reported the same results.

The problem of transfer has also been investigated, and is the subject of a number of published reports. Among the earliest is a study by Woodrow,[97] in which he compared the abilities of normal and mentally retarded children of the same mental age. He concluded that there was no significant difference between the performances of the two groups. Johnson,[46,48] using a psychomotor task, found that his retarded group showed significantly superior performance on a task requiring the transfer of a principle than did his normal group. Tizard and Loos [93] reported considerable transfer of training took place and that, among a group of residential retarded subjects, practice brought improvement in performance of a complex laboratory task.

Several studies on "set" have been conducted with the mentally retarded. Unlike the majority of the previously cited investigations, these are not comparative in nature. Rather, the investigators were interested in determining whether the same theories that had been postulated for learning in general held true for the mentally retarded. Barnett and Cantor [5] took a group of adult mentally retarded subjects and provided them with stimuli and instructions that were designed to facilitate learning. Their performance was then compared to that of another group which had not had the training. It was reported that discrimination set facilitated performance. When the experimental group was divided into groups of "high" and "low" mental-age subjects, it was further found that the degree to which performance was facilitated was comparable for these two groups. Bensberg [8] concluded from his work that by developing in the mentally retarded sets to attend to appropriate or inappropriate aspects of presented stimuli, the rate of learning can be controlled.

The search for qualitative learning differences between normal and mentally retarded children has resulted in very little data to support the thesis that the differences exist. The concept that the mentally retarded require more time to learn a task they are capable of learning than do normal children certainly has not been verified by most of the reported research. The same is true for the often expressed necessity for the inclusion of more repetition or practice in their learning activities. Most of the evidence, instead, indicates that the mentally retarded learn in the same way as normal children, youth, and adults. The laws of learning that hold true for the normal also hold true for the mentally retarded. They are not "slow learners" in the sense that they comprehend slowly or grasp new concepts slowly or learn a skill slowly. The slowness is related to their rate of intellectual development. That is one of the prime determiners of when they will be able to comprehend, grasp a concept, or learn a skill.

Studies using mentally retarded persons as subjects have carefully employed tasks that are within their ability to master. When they can learn to perform the required task, they follow the same laws of learning and show little or no difference from normal persons of the same intellectual developmental level—mental age. If more difficult tasks were posed, the normal subjects of the same *chronological* age would be able to learn them; the mentally retarded would not. Then a difference would be demonstrated between the two groups. The difference, however, would not be one of learning but rather one of development.

Many statements concerning the learning rate of retarded children are undoubtedly made by persons who (a) are unfamiliar with the basic concepts involved in an understanding of the learning process, (b) have failed to differentiate immediate and sequential learning, or (c) lack an understanding of child development. Often they have not differentiated in their own thinking between learning and development, using the terms interchangeably. As a result, articles concerned with development rate have appeared where the author has used the term "learning," and in other writing, the author has used a reverse of the terms and concepts involved. This has resulted in a great deal of confusion on the part of readers. The confusion on the part of authors has thus been compounded to the extent that numerous dogmatic statements appear in print concerning the learning abilities (or disabilities) and characteristics of retarded children that are erroneous in light of interpretations that can be made concerning the findings reported in the learning studies.

When concerned with child development and rate of development in general, one may be referring to the growth rate of an individual or group in one or more of a number of somewhat discrete and only distantly related areas—physical, mental, academic, social, and so forth. The mentally handicapped group for education purposes is defined (as the name implies) upon the basis of retarded or slow intellectual development. This is reflected in the theoretical meaning of the I.Q. which, on most standardized intelligence tests, is a ratio showing the relationship between intellectual growth and number of years lived. The individual's present intellectual behavior upon a selected sample of tasks is compared to the average responses of a large sample of the population of the same life age.

Thus, a child with an I.Q. of 75 has an intellectual developmental rate three fourths that of the average or normal. A child with an I.Q. of 66 or 67 is developing intellectually at two thirds the rate of the average or general population. It will, consequently, take this individual from one-fourth to one-third times longer to "pass through" a specified developmental growth period than is required for the "average" or normal child. Assuming each of three children has an intellectual developmental level (mental age) of 6-0 years, the normal child will achieve one year of intellectual growth in one chronological year, and after a one-year interval will have an intellectual developmental level of 7-0 years. During this same period of time, the child with an I.Q. of 75 will have grown intellectually 9 months, and the child with an I.Q. of 66 or 67 only 8 months. The child with an I.Q. of 75 will require one year and 4 months and the child with an I.Q. of 66 or 67 will require one year and 6 months to develop intellectually the one year that the normal child accomplished in a one-year period of time.

The I.Q., therefore, does not provide the observer with an evaluation of the present intellectual power or ability of the individual but is rather derived from this knowledge plus a knowledge of the individual's life age. On such standardized instruments as the *Stanford Binet*, the intellectual developmental level (mental age) may be derived from a knowledge of the developmental age (intelligence quotient) and life age (chronological age.)

Learning is dependent upon a number of variables of which intellectual developmental level is an important one. This factor will largely determine the maximum complexity and level of learning that can possibly take place at any specified time. Thus, in comparing the learning ability (level, rate, and so forth) of two groups of children at the same intellectual developmental level, and assuming the same degree of readiness to learn in terms of background experiences, attitudes, desires, quality of instruction, and so forth, one would expect that they would learn the skill or concept in the same period of time. Although the two groups (normal and mentally handicapped) may differ significantly on such developmental factors as life age, physical and motor development, or social development, as long as they are equated for intellectual developmental levels, experiences, and previous learnings to ensure equal readiness, they should have similar patterns of learning, require the same amounts of practice, and retain equal amounts of the material learned.

The preceding statement should hold true in terms of immediate learnings within the intellectual abilities of the subjects included within the respective group. In the case of learning studies, it should hold true for the younger, normal subjects and older, retarded subjects of the same mental age. This statement would not apply, however, to a sequence of learning activities (such as learning to read, which actually consists of many discrete learnings). Where sequential learning is properly placed in terms of an intellectual developmental scale and each successive learning activity requires: (1) greater intellectual maturity as well as, (2) previous learning, then the concept of intellectual rate of development as well as the concepts involved in learning must be incorporated into planning for the learning of the entire, total sequence.

The subject with normal or "average" intelligence will learn the sequence in a specified period of time. The subject developing more slowly requires that successive learning be spaced farther apart, thus extending the sequence of learnings over a longer period of time, but no more practice time in learning a specified skill or concept and consequently no more total instructional time to learn the entire sequence should be necessary. The only additional time devoted to skill instruction for the slower group should be in terms of additional review to overcome the factor of forgetting.[47]

The basic learning characteristics of the mentally retarded, summarized briefly, are in all probability the same as for normal children of approximately the same mental age. Differences that have been noted by teachers using rather subjective observational methods and by some research

workers probably are due to controllable factors. Cruickshank [23] found
that mentally retarded boys were retarded in their arithmetic vocabulary,
had less understanding of the correct process to use in solving problems,
and tended to guess or give some unsuitable response more often than
did normal boys. In the area of reading, Dunn [27] found, when comparing
two groups of boys (retarded and normal equivalent mental ages), that
the mentally retarded did not do as well in silent and oral reading. In
addition, the two groups differed markedly in regard to the patterns of
reading errors. Numerous other studies of somewhat less extensive nature
have amply supported these findings.

Since the learning of arithmetic and reading are important skills, usually
highly emphasized by the schools, it would appear that the results discussed above would be contradictory to the earlier statement concerning
no learning differences. The results reported by Cruickshank, Dunn,
and others may have been influenced by many factors unrelated to
"ability" to learn. An important factor may be one of instruction. Kirk,[56]
in surveying the reading progress of an institutional population, reported
good reading ability. The average reading achievement of a hundred
children (averaging 14 years-10 months of age, 69 I.Q., and mental
age slightly over 10 years) was grade 4.3. MacIntyre [65] also states that
mentally retarded children can perform at a level at least equal to their
mental age. Numerous comparative studies, such as those reported by
Bennett,[7] Pertsch,[72] and Johnson,[44] further indicate the probable influence of instruction. These studies compared the achievement of mentally retarded children in special classes with the achievement of like
children in regular classes. They showed that those mentally retarded
children who remained in the regular grades were achieving higher than
those who had been placed in special classes. Since in Johnson's study
the factor of selection for placement in the special class was controlled,
the differences had to be caused by instruction or emphasis of academic
instruction in the respective curricula.

Anyone desirous of knowing more about the mentally retarded and/or
working with them should also be aware of some of the other variables
that may affect learning. The various groups within the total "society"
place varying amounts of value upon different kinds of learning. The
middle- and upper-class groups as well as the upwardly mobile in American culture tend to stress academic accomplishment as a means of maintaining or improving their status. The lower-class groups tend to emphasize traditional academic learnings and the need for formal education
to a much lesser degree. Since the majority of the higher-grade retarded
who can benefit from education and eventually maintain themselves independently come from lower-class homes, their felt needs for high academic achievement are often much less than for children in general.

This statement should not be construed to mean that mentally retarded children do not want to learn. It means that anyone working with them must have an awareness of individual backgrounds and values. Only in this way can learning experiences be placed in contexts whereby each child will understand the value of learning and have the necessary desire to achieve.

Another important variable is the satisfaction the individual has derived from previous learning experiences. When the mentally retarded child or youth is constantly compared with normal or bright siblings and/or classmates, he may soon become so sufficiently frustrated that he will refuse to apply himself to school-centered activities. If the variables mentioned, as well as many more, are not understood, it is very easy to come to the conclusion that mentally retarded children learn differently from normal children. It should be remembered that these same factors also operate with the normal. Teachers, psychologists, and social workers who work with the retarded are usually most familiar personally with middle-class values and objectives. It is difficult to understand that other value systems exist. Since most of society is designed to meet the needs of this large, middle group, these variables that affect learning adversely have much less chance of achieving the same degree of importance with normal children than they do with most of the mentally retarded.

The continuity of the learning process across all I.Q. levels was commented on by Ellis [28] *et al.* in a discussion of their findings on serial verbal and finger-maze learnings with subjects at various intelligence levels. This concept, along with a recognition of variables effecting learning, has been accepted by numbers of psychologists and educators. Future research is undoubtedly going to include larger numbers of studies directed toward factors (psychological, physiological, and sociological) that influence learning. As information of this kind becomes available, more realistic and influential programs (educational and community) will be able to be planned for the mentally retarded. As a result, the mentally retarded will learn to operate more effectively in society and to improve their positions and conditions within the community.

Psychomotor Abilities

THE RELATIONSHIP of general physical growth and maturation of the mentally retarded was investigated fairly thoroughly during the first third of the twentieth century. From these studies it is generally accepted today that the high-grade mental retardate who is potentially capable of maintaining himself independently follows the same sequence of growth at approximately the same rate as the normal individual.

Some evidence indicates that the mentally retarded may be, on an average, slightly smaller and somewhat more prone to illness than the general population. This is supported in a series of recent reports by Klausmeier,[57] Klausmeier, Lehman, and Beeman,[59] and Klausmeier and Check.[58] They studied the relationship between chronological age, height, weight, grip, number of permanent teeth, carpal age, intelligence, reading, arithmetic, and language for three groups of children 8 years-5 months of age. The group classified as "low" in I.Q. was not significantly different from the "average" or "high" groups in any of the physical measurement areas. They were, however, fairly consistently lower on most of the measures.

As one considers the physical development of the low-grade retardate that requires perpetual supervision and direction, the similarity in physical growth no longer holds true. These persons develop significantly more slowly than the normal in all areas of physical growth. Many never achieve complete physiological maturity no matter how long they may live. A strong contributing factor here, of course, is that much of the severe retardation is either caused by or associated with gross physical deviations or malfunctionings.

The area of motor and psychomotor abilities is a much newer field of study. As a result, less information is available. Historically, Europe seems to have been more interested in the entire subject of physical and motor development at an earlier date than the Western Hemisphere. It is only in recent years that this, too, has changed. Three tests are European in origin, but not all have found equal favor in this country. A test of motor proficiency developed by a Russian named Oseretsky has proved to be the most popular of the three. Many investigators have made use of it or adapted it to their use. The Vineland [15] adaptation was one of the first to be used. Later, Sloan [87] developed and standardized the *Lincoln-Oseretsky Motor Development Scale.*

In 1960 Francis and Rarick [35] reported a study concerned with the motor characteristics of the mentally retarded. Their subjects included 284 children (boys and girls) from special classes in Milwaukee and Madison, Wisconsin. They found that the mentally retarded children were from two to four years retarded as compared to published norms. They also found that the discrepancy tended to increase with age. They felt that their evidence indicated that the motor abilities of the mentally retarded were organized in much the same way as in children with normal intelligence but that the ability level is lower than has often been suspected.

Beaber [6] compared mentally retarded and normal children in four tests of simple motor performance. The subjects were divided into three groups—two normal and one retarded. One normal group and the retarded group were matched on mental age. The other normal group and the retarded group were matched on chronological age. The results showed that the performance of the mentally retarded was below that of normal children of the same chronological age but was very similar to the performance of intellectually normal children of the same mental age.

Howe [43] also compared the motor skills used on eleven tests of mentally retarded and normal children. He used 86 subjects ranging from $6\frac{1}{2}$ to 12 years of age. The groups were matched with respect to chronological age, socioeconomic background, and sex. He found that the normal children were consistently superior to the mentally retarded.

A number of studies concerned with motor skills have been conducted using institutional populations. Sloan,[86] using the Oseretsky, determined that normal children were significantly better than the mentally retarded on all subtests. Malpass,[64] using institutionalized and non-institutionalized mentally retarded subjects, reported that when he compared the motor performance of the combined group to the performance of a group of normal children of the same chronological age the normals were significantly better. Rubin,[78] using the *Lincoln-Oseretsky*, studied the relationship of age, intelligence, and sex to motor proficiency in a group of institutionalized retarded children. He found motor proficiency to have a significant positive relationship to age, to be insignificantly related to intelligence, and to bear no relationship to sex at these ages (10 to 14 years). He comments, however, that the lack of significant relationship to intelligence may well have been due to the method of statistical analysis used.

The preceding studies, while few in number, are consistent in the information provided. The psychomotor (defined as pertaining to activities requiring coordination or direction from the brain) development of the mentally retarded is significantly below that found in the normal population. All the evidence strongly indicates a high, positive relationship between level of intelligence and level of psychomotor development.

Personal and Social Adjustment

ATTITUDES CONCERNING personal adjustment, mental illness, social behavior (including delinquency and crime), and their causes have undergone long and interesting development. Notwithstanding the information that has been provided through research, many of the ancient attitudes continue to persist. When efforts were first made to understand deviate and asocial behavior, the assumption was that abnormality was basically physical and that deviates could be typed. Further, it was felt that criminals, for example, were born. Measurements of hundreds of prison inmates were eventually required to help dispel this idea. The next assumption was that criminals and delinquents were mentally retarded.

Today it is generally argued that there is no direct cause-and-effect relationship between discernible mental defect and delinquency. Mental retardation is usually considered to be associated with from 15 to 20 per cent of the cases of delinquent behavior, although studies such as that reported by Levy [62] indicate that the relationship may be as low as 1 per cent. Sociologists feel that delinquent behavior is actually produced by a multiplicity of causes. The focus on unitary causes, such as physical type, race, nationality, or mental retardation, is gradually being replaced by theories of frustration and multiple factors and their effects upon one another. Haggerty [40] suggests that low intelligence may be of importance but indicates that the cause is basically extreme deviation from the normal. Thus the same factor may, on occasion, also operate for the very bright as well.

Kvaraceus [60] emphasizes that the nature of the curriculum in school is an important element to consider. The delinquent is typically a non-bookish, non-intellectual, non-academic, non-verbal student who does poorly in the traditional school subjects. For instance, in a group of 761 delinquents, 44 per cent had repeated at least one term of school, as compared with only 17 per cent of all other children in the same school. He also found that 60 per cent of these delinquent children expressed a definite dislike for school, and 34 per cent had been truants as compared with 7 per cent among the non-delinquents. It is obvious that the majority, if not all, of these young delinquents had experienced a considerable degree of frustration in connection with their school life.

Following the thinking connected with the multi-factor theory, a delinquency-producing environment consists of several of the listed items or elements: a home in which parents are unsuccessful economically, are of average or below-average intellectual ability, are of undesirable personal habits, are of questionable morality, are ineffective in discipline, are unable to furnish the children with a feeling of emotional security, and are inclined to reject their delinquent child both before and after his misdeeds; a neighborhood that is devised for adults, without safeguards for children, largely without safe outlets for emotional and social life, and full of unsatisfactory models and conflicting standards; and a school that attempts to make academic scholars out of non-academic children and sometimes furnishes them with teachers who are too rejecting in their attitudes. When these elements are affecting the same, unstable child, retarded or normal, a delinquent is likely to be produced.

That this is the environment of many of the mentally retarded is well recognized. The majority of the mentally retarded children and youth are raised (or allowed to grow up) in the delinquency-producing areas of the community. It is little wonder that most studies show a higher delinquency rate for them than is true for the total population. The question that has not been answered is, "How does their delinquency rate compare with others raised in the same environment, in the same culture?" Understanding that these are the contributory factors that result in delinquent behavior, it is now possible to understand such behavior when it is observed in the mentally retarded. It is also possible to establish school and community programs designed to eliminate these conditions.

The past quarter of a century has seen many of the earlier attitudes and feelings regarding the relationship of mental retardation and behavior vanish among professional workers as greater understanding has developed. Unfortunately, this is not as true of the public in general. In the late 1930's another movement relating behavior, adjustment, and intelligence came to the forefront. During the decade between 1940 and 1950 there was a flurry of activity related to the testing of personality and the use of projective tests with the mentally retarded. Some of the reports (Jolles [51] and Sloan [85]) went so far as to intimate that certain types of mental retardation may be a symptom of personality disorder. In these cases the apparent limited mental ability is due to the problems related to personality and adjustment. These persons can, consequently, be better diagnosed or differentiated with projective than standard intelligence tests. Both Sarason [81] and Wallin [94] were extremely critical of these studies.

The general feeling among psychologists is that projective tests and psychological interviews have primary value in determining the existence and nature of problems related to personal adjustment that may be facing the mentally retarded person. From studies, such as those reported by Sarason,[80] Abel,[2] and Gothberg,[38] it is apparent that the mentally retarded have much the same psychological needs and face much the same kinds of personality stresses as normal persons. They have fears and feelings of inadequacy, anxiety, aggression, and guilt like anyone else. These stresses may or may not interfere with their intellectual functioning. The one point that was brought out in a number of studies was that the feelings usually thought of as being unhealthy in nature were exaggerated in the mentally retarded. Since most of these studies were performed with institutional populations, one cannot generalize from their findings to the total population. The high-grade mentally retarded persons who are ordinarily committed are either dependent or delinquent in their behavior. Furthermore, they represent a very small fraction of the total retarded population. Johnson,[44] using the *California*

Test of Personality, found that the mentally retarded children who remained in regular grades, as well as those who had been placed in special classes, scored significantly lower than normal children on both the Personal Adjustment and Social Adjustment parts of the test. These results can be explained on the basis of the added frustrations faced by mentally retarded children in school situations.

During the years of high activity with personality assessment and recommendations advocating greater use of projective instruments, their use with the mentally retarded was frequently discussed in professional literature. The general thesis contained in the writing of Cassel,[14] Guertin,[39] Kanner,[52] and others was essentially that often unrecognized personality disorders may be misinterpreted as mental retardation, since their learning and responses to items on standard intelligence tests were in many ways similar. At a slightly later date this movement also provided another explanation than that used earlier for apparent retardation in children with physical or sensory disabilities. Not only could the reduced level of intellectual operation now be blamed upon lack of learning due to deprivation of sensory stimulation; it could also be explained by the presence of an assumed severe personality disorder. For a time it almost appeared as if it were impossible for blind, deaf, or cerebral palsied children to be mentally retarded, although it was known that a number of the causes of these disabilities were also causes of mental retardation.

The hypothesis upon which these assumptions are founded is that a person will be unable to perform adequately in either a learning or testing situation if a severe personality disorder is present. Knowing that this is true in mental hospitals where one is dealing with cases of schizophrenia and autism, it seems reasonable that it would still hold for somewhat less acute problems in children who are still capable of relating to a certain extent with persons about them and of having an awareness of their environment. The hypothesis can also be very easily tested. Reduction or alleviation of the problem should increase learning and test performance. Although counselling and psychotherapy have been used with the mentally retarded (as well as with children who have physical or sensory disabilities and behave like retarded persons), no research reports using numbers of subjects and control groups have been published that show significant I.Q. changes. Undoubtedly success has been achieved in individual cases. But that the problem of pseudo-retardation is an extensive one or can be ordinarily solved in this manner has not been demonstrated.

There is no reason to suspect that the mentally retarded, because they are retarded, are consequently immune to personality disorders. They are, instead, probably somewhat more prone to having emotional problems because of their limited intellectual abilities. As a result they understand their problems less clearly, perceive the demands of their environment less accurately, and are more restricted in the number of available possible solutions to their problems. The discussions and reviews concerning psychotherapy with the mentally retarded by Abel,[1] Burton,[12] Neham,[68] and Sarason [81] indicate that the use of this treatment approach with the retarded was not generally received with enthusiasm by the majority of the therapists. The various reasons for this are as follows:

1. A feeling that, due to an unawareness of his problems, the retarded would not seek help.
2. A feeling that the mentally retarded lacked sufficient intelligence essential to developing understanding and insights required in modifying behavior.
3. A feeling that the mentally retarded were unable to delay or control expression of impulses or, due to lack of ego strength, to develop self-dependence.
4. A feeling that any small results obtained were not worth the necessary involvement of time, effort, facilities, and money.
5. A feeling that many therapists who attempted treatment of this type had insufficient understanding of mental retardation.
6. A conflict of values between those of the therapists and those that were appropriate for the mentally retarded.

Despite these initial rather negatively biased attitudes, a goodly amount of work has been done, particularly in institutions, with some apparent success. Only a few of the studies, in which groups of subjects were used, will be briefly cited. Heisner,[42] using individual psychotherapy with 14 subjects over about a one-year period, reported little increase in I.Q. The majority, however, showed an improvement in behavior and adjustment. Thorne,[92] working with 30 males and 38 females over a two-year period, reported that 66 per cent improved. Cotzin,[21] using group therapy with 9 boys, reported initial improvement of behavior for each one. After an interval of time a re-evaluation indicated continued behavioral changes—some positive and others negative. A methodological study using 54 chronically delinquent males is reported by Snyder and Sechrest.[89] Their results indicated a significantly greater increase in positive behavior on the part of those subjects with whom directive therapy was used as compared to those with whom other methods were employed. General success in psychotherapy with 12 female subjects was also reported by Fisher and Wolfson.[33]

These articles, as well as most other studies, indicate more successes than failures, which is also true for normals. Such factors as the generally subjective tone of the majority of the evaluations, the unreliability of many of the more objective attempts at rating therapy, the lack of control groups in many instances, the general lack of control for such variables as mental age, chronological age, length of stay in the institution, positive or negative influences of the institutional environment, types of behavior manifested, and personality and theoretical orientation of the therapists leave most of the results open to question. Considered as a group, however, the studies repeatedly indicate that the mentally retarded individual is capable of deriving some benefit from psychotherapy. There is no doubt that the processes and outcome are difficult to measure in a reliable and objective manner. One is eventually impressed by the quantity if not the individual quality of the evidence.

The greatest success appears to be achieved when the therapist is accepting, relatively permissive, but by no means passive. He allows and encourages expressions of feeling but, when necessary, places definite limits on overt behavior. In many of the studies reported the therapist continually found it necessary to take an active role in defining the purpose of therapy, in giving the patients direction and structure in recognizing and delineating their problems, and in some cases developing topics of discussion or activities to be developed. Practically no studies reported the use of a classical psychoanalytical approach. Where a completely non-directive approach was utilized in a group therapy situation,[67,77] complete failure was reported. There seems to be a feeling developing among therapists generally that a reality oriented approach (which may also apply to the mentally retarded) is most effective. The flexibility and sensitivity of the therapist himself to the needs of his patients, however, may be more crucial than any specific technique.

The fundamental problem then appears to eventually center around the effectiveness of the social adjustment of the mentally retarded—the effectiveness with which they can relate to others. While this problem has been investigated sporadically over an extended period of time, little in the way of direct, definitive information is available for a number of reasons. First, most comparisons have been made against a norm or average for the total population. Although the mentally retarded show up at a disadvantage on these comparisons, there is good reason to believe they are neither valid nor meaningful. These comparisons do not take into consideration the society with whom the retarded ordinarily associate and maintain themselves. The social maturity of those who are able to operate independently in society over an extended period of time must be satisfactory, at least in terms of the demands made on them. Second, instruments available for evaluating social maturity are poorly standardized and seldom based upon any theory of social behavior or adjustment. In this area, as in a number of others, instrumentation is badly needed.

According to Clarke [20] all mentally retarded above the very lowest levels have some degree of social adaptation although this level will vary widely. He lists the reasons for social maladjustment as lack of educational achievement, poor home and background conditions, prolonged stays in residential situations, poor emotional control, lack of experience, resentful attitudes toward authority, poor work habits, and lack of initiative. In order to effect proper social adjustment a program based upon the learning of good work habits should be emphasized. This idea is comparable to those expressed in curricula used for the mentally retarded in numbers of school systems.

One of the major reasons for the placement of mentally retarded children in special classes is that many educators feel that adequate social adjustment does not and cannot take place in the regular class. Johnson [45] and Johnson and Kirk [50] report that the mentally retarded are less accepted than normal children. They are also more actively rejected. The reasons given for the rejection are in relation to the retarded children's unacceptable behavior rather than low academic ability. Lapp [61] and a number of other investigators have supported these findings with respect to lack of acceptance. Blatt [10] compared mentally retarded children in special classes with those in regular classes. He found the special class children are socially more mature and emotionally stable.

Pero [71] conducted a study in which he used a social orientation method of social training with a group of mentally retarded persons within an institutional setting. His sample consisted of twenty students selected on the basis of the possibility that they might eventually be released. The objectives of the project were to prepare the students for a better-adjusted life while in and after leaving the school. The program was set up to be a guidance medium through which the personnel might delve deeper into the true nature of each student as an individual and as a member of a group.

Tests were used to measure the amount of responsibility that could be handled, how well each student undertook and completed tasks, leadership potential, awareness of daily needs and responsibilities, the ability to make and keep friends, self-confidence, dependability, and social adjustment in school. The results were discussed with the group. In addition, individual conferences were provided for those who desired them. Each student was thus given an opportunity to seek advice on anything that might be troubling him. The orientation lessons were so prepared as to give a complete social training related to occupational and social adjustment, human relations, improved daily living, personal growth and development, and total school adjustment. It was observed that the students formed a code of ethical values helpful to everyday living and that conduct and behavior improved within the institution. There was a general increase of competencies necessary for adequate social adjustment.

With young children, Capobianco and Cole [13] showed that play activities produce more acceptable behavior among mentally retarded children. It has long been recognized that the level of social behavior has a positive, although not perfect, relationship to the mental age of the individual. This was verified in this study. That is, the lower the mental age, the lower one can generally expect the social level of the individual to be. His rate of social growth will also follow the rate of intellectual growth more closely than his rate of chronological growth. This is of utmost importance when one plans programs taking into consideration the kinds of occupations and social relations the mentally retarded adult will be capable of maintaining for himself.

The final criterion of effective personal and social adjustment is the effectiveness with which the mentally retarded adjust to society. Two primary sources have commonly been used for purposes of obtaining populations of retarded adults for studies in these areas. One source is the institution; the other, special classes within the public schools. In interpreting results obtained using these populations, some cautions must be observed. It is estimated that only about 5 per cent of the mentally retarded population can be found in institutions and that only 20 to 40 per cent can be found in special classes, depending upon the state and community. Any conclusions are consequently based upon samples taken from approximately 30 per cent of the mentally retarded population. It is obvious that a certain amount of care need be applied in generalizing from these studies, since one is not completely aware of the factors that determine the composition of the population.

Once information has been collected, there still remains the task of determining a causal relationship for the behavior. If one group performs in a superior manner to another is this the result of special training? A study by Porter and Milazzo [74] would seem to indicate that special class training does result in better social and economic efficiency. This view receives some support from Bobroff.[11] Closer examination of the study indicates that one cannot make too broad generalizations based upon these results alone. First, the populations were small, only 24 subjects. Second, the amount of time spent in a special class was fairly short, ranging from 1.1 to 5.5 years with a mean attendance of only 3.2 years. Fortunately, a number of additional studies concerned with the social and vocational adjustment of the mentally retarded are available.

One of the earliest extensive studies is reported by Channing.[18] She studied the work success of 949 mentally retarded adults who had been enrolled while still children in special classes in a number of cities. Ninety-four per cent were found to have been employed, although first jobs tended to be of short duration. Baller [4] compared the status of a group of former special class pupils with a group of normal adults. He found that the mentally retarded were socially, economically, and vocationally inferior. Less than 50 per cent were maintaining themselves independently continuously. The rate of permanent employment was very low. On the more positive side, the mentally retarded only had a few more contacts with law enforcement agencies, and these were of a minor nature. Charles [19] followed the same group of mentally retarded about fifteen years later, when their mean age was in the early forties. He found the majority of them were now maintaining themselves and that their whole social and economic adjustment had improved considerably. Kennedy [53] studied 256 mentally retarded adults who were matched with 129 normal adults. She concluded that the mentally retarded had come from families that were less well adjusted, more disturbed, and economically less well off. Despite this and the mental retardation, the families were very similar in their economic, marital, and social adjustment. Again the mentally retarded had a few more contacts with the police—but of a minor nature such as traffic violations and disturbing the peace.

Peterson and Smith [73] also compared groups of mentally retarded and normal adults. The groups were matched on the basis of age. The retarded had attended special classes an average of four years. It was observed that the mentally retarded worked at low-level jobs and maintained their first jobs for varying periods of time. Ninety-three per cent of the retarded group lived in substandard housing. More than 50 per cent were unmarried. Among those who had married, the divorce rate was high. As in other studies, they showed a higher incidence of minor civil offenses. The area in which the two groups were most similar was in their avocational interests—reading and television.

The relationship between personal adjustment, social skills, and vocational success with the mentally retarded has received some attention. Although the answers to these problems are still problematical some indications are available from work done with vocational rehabilitation. Generally speaking, the results of these programs have been good. It should be remembered, however, that the state vocational rehabilitation agencies accept only those clients who show not only eligibility for service but also show high feasibility. The local office determines eligibility, often through the use of achievement and aptitude tests. Many of the most difficult cases are never accepted.

Cowan and Goldman [22] concluded that level of education and past work experience were not significant factors in vocational adjustment. The effort exerted to find employment, however, is significant. Peckham [70] studied eighty closed rehabilitation cases. The following job adjustment problems were noted: (1) a lack of acceptance by co-workers was felt, (2) a lack of social and vocational sophistication existed, (3) the retarded employees indicated a dissatisfaction with level of salary, (4) they quit their jobs for capricious reasons, (5) parents were unrealistic regarding the capacity of their children, (6) the family tended to over-protect the retarded person. Personnel from Departments of Vocational Rehabilitation attempted to solve these problems by counselling with employers, parents, and clients and providing an on-the-job training program. As a result of the study, recommendations concerning job practice supplemented by classroom instruction, guidance on the job, and an active follow-up program were made.

Engel [29] made an extensive survey of studies related to the employment of the mentally retarded adult. The following points and recommendations seemed to be important in their achieving success.

a. Social and vocational adjustment should be given specific attention.
b. School programs should be centered around personal adjustment, social skills, and good work habits.
c. The mental level is not as important as personal traits and characteristics of the worker. The most important traits in workers according to employers are dependability, ability to get along with co-workers, ability to accept criticism, and a desire to do one's best.
d. Hand work in school has no apparent relationship to success on the job.
e. Students should be encouraged to remain in school until they are ready for employment.
f. There is a need for good guidance of the mentally retarded.
g. Counselling, personal and vocational, should be provided before the termination of schooling.
h. A follow-up program is necessary to provide support for the initial job experience.

Follow-up studies with low-grade or severely retarded persons presents quite a different picture. Contribution to the general welfare of the home and community, or even demonstrated ability for self-direction, is the exception rather than the rule for these persons. Delp and Lorenz [25] did a follow-up study of 84 severely retarded persons who had been in special classes. By the age of twenty-two (average), 9 were deceased, 25 had been institutionalized, 9 had moved out of the state, and 41 were still at home in that community. A more extensive study of somewhat higher-grade retardates was reported by Saenger.[79] His findings are based upon a sample of 520 cases taken from a population of 2,640 persons who between the years 1929 and 1955 had attended special classes for children with low I.Q.'s. Sixty-six per cent of these retardates were still residing in the community, 26 per cent had been committed to an institution, and 8 per cent were deceased. Of those still living in the community, only 33 per cent were able to leave the home and neighborhood unattended. Thirty-six per cent were employed or had worked at some time. Less than half of them had found positions themselves, outside of jobs directly or indirectly controlled by parents, relatives, or family friends.

Parental and Family Adjustment

AMONG PSYCHOLOGISTS it is widely recognized that many of the problems presented by children are reflections of and/or caused at least in part by problems in their parents and family. It is almost axiomatic that the parents must be included in the treatment when therapy or counselling with children is done. It is, therefore, appropriate that a brief look be taken at the problems facing parents of mentally retarded children. As a better understanding of their problems and attitudes is developed, greater insights into the behavior and problems of retarded children and youth should result.

Most of the research that has been conducted to date in this area consists of studies involving parents of severely retarded children who come predominantly from the middle class. A much smaller amount of work has been concerned with the attitudes and problems of parents (again from the middle class) of higher-grade, educable retarded children. The problems faced by these parents are in many ways identical, therefore it should come as no surprise that the findings of the studies are very similar. Middle-class parents are faced with a problem that essentially has no satisfactory solution. The mentally retarded child, whether severely or mildly retarded, is a deviate of such a nature that it is impossible for him to achieve at or even near the hopes and aspirations his parents have for him. He poses a problem of perpetual care and supervision for them. They usually cannot accept institutional care because it represents rejection of the child.

In some ways the problems are less acute and better defined (consequently, easier to deal with) when the child is severely retarded. Then the deviation is so great from early childhood or even infancy that it is obvious some kind of custodial plans must be made. Even so, many parents never face it and die leaving the problems still unsolved. The higher-grade retardate has the potential of self-support and self-direction when the environmental demands are not too great. Too often the level at which he can maintain himself is unacceptable to the middle-class parent. As a result he is seldom given the opportunity. If he does find employment he continues to reside in his parents' home where many of his middle class-needs are still provided. Once the father has retired, or the parents have died and can no longer supplement his income, make many of his purchases, and so forth, his problem becomes acute. He has not learned how to provide for many of his needs nor has he been prepared for the lower standard of living he must assume. Relatives and agencies must take over the role of the parents at this point.

The presence of a severely retarded child within the middle-class home, as previously indicated, is a very traumatic occurrence. Farber [30,31] and Farber, Jenne, and Toigo [32] studied the problem of marital integration. Farber found that the degree of marital integration among middle-class, Caucasian families having a severely retarded child was dependent upon a combination of the severity of the problem and the methods used by the parents. That is, the type of family orientation was very important to marital integration. If institutionalization of the retardate were to be recommended, it should be recommended upon this basis. As far as the effect of the retardate upon the siblings was concerned, mothers saw their daughters as being affected to a greater degree than their sons. He also found the marital integration of families with severely retarded boys lower than those with retarded girls. The boys, in addition, became a more disruptive influence as they became older. This sex difference vanished where the children had been placed in an institution. Among the supportive factors reported were religion and close interaction with the mother of the child.

Parental aspiration and ability to evaluate their children in regard to their growth and potential has also been studied to some degree for the severely retarded. Goldstein [37] found that the aspirations of parents were quite unrealistic but tended to improve (become more realistic) following the enrollment and attendance of their children in a school program. Johnson and Capobianco [49] provided a parent education program in conjunction with a school program for the children. Only a few of the parents attended the sessions with any regularity. It appeared that parents who did participate could evaluate the present behavioral level of their children quite accurately. However, they had relatively little understanding of either what other children of the same chronological ages are usually capable of doing or what this level of behavior in their own children meant in terms of ultimate abilities in the future. About half of the parents felt that their children would become fairly normal, be able to learn academic skills, and eventually earn their living. It would only take them longer than the normal.

Fliegler and Hebeler reported a study of middle-class parents who had an educable retarded child. In regard to parental attitudes they stated:

Adjustment for the entire group . . . showed that greater relief was evident in a reconciliation to the handicap and parental
satisfaction with educational and organized activities-goals. Somewhat less familial adjustment was noted in the reaction of the
local community members toward the retardate, intrafamilial relationships which concern disciplinary measures, special considerations and the relationship between the retardate and his siblings,
and the impact upon the parents' social life as a consequence of
the retardation. Although the patterns for mothers and fathers was
similar to the combined group, mothers indicated a greater dissatisfaction with the neighborhood contacts. Since mothers are more
directly related to the neighborhood, this difference is plausible.

It seems that acceptance of retardation and the ways of coping
with it through education are viewed with comparatively less concern than the more personalized areas. Significantly, in each of the
cities from which the population emanated, special classes and
clinical medical facilities are available. However, neglect of the
more personally involved areas of behavior leads to greater discomfort. The interpretation of retardation for personal adjustment
to the familial and community relationships is obviously needed to
enhance over-all adjustment.[34]

The studies mentioned are related to the parental problems of approximately 25 per cent of retarded children. The remainder of the children
and their parents are of the lower class. Since no studies are available,
one can only hypothesize concerning parental attitudes, family adjustment, and the impact of these factors upon the children. With this group
the total problem of mental retardation is probably considerably different
and in many ways simplified for both the retardate and his parents. For
one thing, among parents of severely retarded children evidence indicates
that lower-class families institutionalize their children much more readily
than parents in the middle class. Thus, this problem is fairly readily
solved to a large extent. The retardate receives care and supervision in
an environment designed in terms of his needs and abilities. The demands
placed upon him are realistic. The parents, at the same time, are relieved
of the necessity for care, direction, and planning.

As far as the high-grade, educable retardate is concerned, the hopes
and aspirations of the parents are in harmony with the ability of the
child. He is living at a socioeconomic and cultural level that it is within
reason to expect him to at least maintain. The jobs he qualifies for and
can obtain as a youth and adult are equal to those held by his parents.
Here the primary problem should not be one of family integration due
to the presence of a retarded child or unrealistic aspirations on the
part of the parents. Often he is not recognized as being mentally retarded. The primary problem is that the retarded child is too often
growing up in an environment where the value system is inappropriate

for keeping out of trouble with the law and the community in general. Ways must be devised that will provide him with more appropriate values if he is to be able to use his abilities in maintaining himself.

Summary

MENTAL RETARDATION is based upon a concept of the distribution of intelligence in the total population. The mentally retarded ordinarily include those persons in the lowest 3 or 4 per cent of this distribution. If this concept is kept clearly in mind, a clearer and more accurate understanding of the mentally retarded and their psychological characteristics can be developed. The entire field has been plagued too long with misconceptions and misunderstandings unfortunately still fostered by groups because they are thus enabled to keep the truth from coming into the foreground of their own thinking. Too much time has been devoted to studying the characteristics of the mentally retarded from biases based upon an assumption of uniqueness or that they comprise a population apart from the rest of the human race.

Recent studies indicate quite conclusively that the mentally retarded learn in the same way as the normal. Their motor development follows the same sequence and pattern as the normal. Their level of achievement or performance, however, can be best estimated upon the basis of mental rather than chronological age. The modes or methods of adjustment are also like those of the normal. This is, they have desires, fears, hopes, frustrations, and so forth as does anyone else. The dynamics of their approach to solutions to problems is also the same, although the methods may vary somewhat due to the nature of the problem, their background of experience, and the depth of understanding they can bring to bear in seeking to reduce tension.

The majority of the mentally retarded come from lower-class homes that provide a minimum of psychosocial and cultural stimulation. Thus, it has been found that, for many, a dramatic change in their environment may cause significant changes to occur in their intellectual developmental rate. When and if a solution is found for this broad sociological problem it does not mean that mental retardation will vanish from the scene, although it may well be materially reduced at least insofar as it is recognized at the present time. There is no reason to suspect that intelligence does not follow the same characteristics in regard to its distribution that has been found to be true for other physical growth.

The mentally retarded who reside in the low socioeconomic areas of the community face many problems—problems that the retardation tends to make more acute. These areas of the community are also the high delinquency areas. Placing a child with limited intelligence in continuous contact with antisocial values and behavior over an extended period is providing him with learning experiences that will make his total community adjustment even more difficult. Often he may be unable to foresee all the implications and consequences of his behavior. As a result, much of the crime and delinquency attributed to the retarded is due not to the retardation directly but rather to the lack of appropriate learning experiences. Society is at fault.

The mentally retarded child, youth, or adult in a better home is, in many ways, no better off. While parents may intellectually understand his problems it is seldom that they can truly accept them emotionally. The program of training or the most appropriate disposition of his problems may not be acceptable to them. They may intellectually understand that he can only earn his living as an adult in an unskilled position but be unable to accept his employment in a position of this type. In some instances he, his siblings, and the parents might be better off if he were placed in an institution, but they feel they are rejecting him by placing him there—"Nice" people do not reject their children and furthermore, what would their neighbors and friends think?

Programs cannot be planned for the total population of mentally retarded. The mentally retarded represent a broad cross section of the human race in terms of their social, physical, motor, and cultural abilities and backgrounds. Experiences that may be correct for one child may be all wrong for another. By understanding the laws of learning in the individual's intellectual development, the level of learning experiences can be recommended. By understanding human behavior and adjustment, the individual's behavior can be understood and controlled. Each retardate is an individual with his characteristics, problems, abilities, and experiences. Individual rather than group or category understanding and appropriate planning must be provided.

Notes

[1] Abel, Theodora M., "Resistances and Difficulties in Psychotherapy of Mental Retardates," *Journal Clinical Psychology*, IX (1953), 107-09.

[2] Abel, Theodora M., "Responses of Negro and White Morons to the Thematic Apperception Test," *American Journal Mental Deficiency*, XLIX (1945), 463-68.

[3] Baker, Harry J., *Introduction to Exceptional Children*, rev. ed. New York: The Macmillan Company, 1953, pp. 258-59.

[4] Baller, Warren R., "A Study of the Present Social Status of a Group of Adults, Who, When They Were in Elementary Schools, Were Classified as Mentally Deficient," *Genetic Psychology Monographs*, XVIII, No. 3 (1936), 165-244.

[5] Barnett, Charles D. and G. N. Cantor, "Discrimination Set in Defectives," *American Journal Mental Deficiency*, LXII (1957), 334-37.

[6] Beaber, James D., "The Performance of Educable Mentally Handicapped and

480 G. ORVILLE JOHNSON

Intellectually Normal Children on Selected Tasks Involving Simple Motor Performance." Doctoral dissertation, Syracuse University, 1960. 146 pp.

[7] Bennett, Annette, *A Comparative Study of the Subnormal Children in the Elementary Grades*. Teachers College Contributions to Education. New York: Teachers
College, Columbia University, 1932. 81 pp.

[8] Bensberg, Gerard J., "Concept Learning in Mental Defectives as a Function of
Appropriate and Inappropriate 'Attention Sets'," *Journal Educational Psychology,*
XLIX (1958), 137-43.

[9] Berkson, Gershon and G. N. Cantor, "A Study of Mediation in Mentally Retarded
and Normal School Children," *Journal Educational Psychology,* LI (1960), 82-86.

[10] Blatt, Burton, "The Physical, Personality, and Academic Status of Children Who
Are Mentally Retarded Attending Special Classes as Compared With Children Who
Are Mentally Retarded Attending Regular Classes," *American Journal Mental De-
ficiency,* LXII (1958), 810-818.

[11] Bobroff, A., "Economic Adjustment of 121 Adults, Formerly Students in Classes
for Mental Retardates," *American Journal Mental Deficiency,* LX (1956), 525-35.

[12] Burton, Arthur, "Psychotherapy With The Mentally Retarded," *American Journal
Mental Deficiency,* LVIII (1954), 486-89.

[13] Capobianco, Rudolph J. and D. A. Cole, "Social Behavior of Mentally Retarded
Children," *American Journal Mental Deficiency,* LXIV (1960), 638-51.

[14] Cassel, Robert H., "Notes on Pseudo-Feeblemindedness," *Training School Bulletin,* XLVI (1949), 119-27.

[15] Cassel, Robert H., "The Vineland Adaptation of the Oseretsky Tests," *Training
School Bulletin,* Supplement to XLVI (1949), 1-32.

[16] Cassell, J. T., "Serial Verbal Learning and Retroactive Inhibition in Aments,"
Journal Clinical Psychology, XIII (1957), 369-72.

[17] Cassidy, Viola M. and J. E. Stanton, *An Investigation of Factors Involved in the
Educational Placement of Mentally Retarded Children.* Ohio State University, 1959.

[18] Channing, Alice, *Employment of Mentally Deficient Boys and Girls.* Washington,
D.C.: U.S. Government Printing Office, 1932. 107 pp.

[19] Charles, Don C., "Ability and Accomplishment of Persons Earlier Judged Mentally
Deficient," *Genetic Psychology Monographs,* XLVII (1953), 9-71.

[20] Clarke, A. D. B., "The Social Adjustment of the Mentally Deficient: A Symposium," *American Journal Mental Deficiency,* LXII (1957), 295-99.

[21] Cotzin, Milton, "Group Psychotherapy With Mentally Defective Problem Boys,"
American Journal Mental Deficiency, LIII (1948), 268-83.

[22] Cowan, L. and M. Goldman, "The Selection of the Mentally Deficient for Vocational Training and the Effect of this Training in Vocational Success," *Journal Consulting Psychology,* XXIII (1959), 78-84.

[23] Cruickshank, William M., "A Comparative Study of Psychological Factors Involved in the Responses of Mentally Retarded and Normal Boys to Problems in Arithmetic." Doctoral dissertation, University of Michigan, 1946.

[24] Cruickshank, William M. and K. A. Blake, *A Comparative Study of the Performance of Mentally Handicapped and Intellectually Normal Boys and Transfer.* Syracuse: Syracuse University Research Institute, 1957.

[25] Delp, H. A. and M. Lorenz, "Follow-up of 84 Public School Special Class Pupils
with I.Q.'s Below 50," *American Journal Mental Deficiency,* LVIII (1953), 175-82.

[26] Duncan, J., *"The Education of the Ordinary Child."* New York: The Ronald
Press Company, 1943, p. 55.

[27] Dunn, Lloyd M., "A Comparison of the Reading Processes of Mentally Retarded
and Normal Boys of the Same Mental Age," in *Studies of Reading and Arithmetic in
Mentally Retarded Boys.* Monographs of the Society for Research in Child Development. Serial No. 58, XIX, No. 1, 1954, 7-99.

[28] Ellis, Norman R., M. W. Pryer, M. K. Distefano, and R. S. Pryer, "Learning in
Mentally Defective, Normal and Superior Subjects," *American Journal Mental Deficiency,* LXIV (1960), 725-34.

29 Engel, Anna M., "Employment of the Mentally Retarded," *American Journal Mental Deficiency*, LVII (1952), 243-67.

30 Farber, Bernard, *Effects of a Severely Mentally Retarded Child on Family Integration*. Monographs of the Society for Research in Child Development, Serial No. 71, XXIV, No. 2, 1959. 112 pp.

31 Farber, Bernard, *Family Organization and Crisis: Maintenance of Integration in Families With a Severely Mentally Retarded Child*. Monographs of the Society for Research in Child Development, Serial No. 75, XXV, No. 1, 1960. 95 pp.

32 Farber, Bernard, W. C. Jenne, and R. Toigo, *Family Crisis and the Retarded Child*. C. E. C. Research Monograph, No. 1, 1960. 66 pp.

33 Fisher, L. A. and I. N. Wolfson, "Group Therapy of Mental Defectives," *American Journal Mental Deficiency*, LVII (1953), 463-76.

34 Fliegler, Louis A. and J. Hebeler, *A Study of the Structure of Attitudes of Parents of Educable Mentally Retarded Children and a Study of a Change in Attitude Structure*, I. Syracuse: Syracuse University Research Institute, 1960. 556 pp.

35 Francis, Robert J. and G. L. Rarick, *Motor Characteristics of The Mentally Retarded*, U. S. Office of Education, Cooperative Research Monograph No. 1. Washington, D.C.: Superintendent of Documents, 1960.

36 Freeman, Frank N., K. J. Holzinger, and B. C. Mitchell, "The Influence of Environment of the Intelligence, School Achievement and Conduct of Foster Children," *Twenty-seventh Yearbook National Society Study of Education*, I (1928), 103-217.

37 Goldstein, Herbert, *Report Number Two on Study Projects for Trainable Mentally Handicapped Children*. Springfield, Ill.: State Superintendent of Public Instruction, 1956. 42 pp.

38 Gothberg, Laura C., "A Comparison of the Personality of Runaway Girls with a Control Group as Expressed in the Themas of Murray's Thematic Apperception Test," *American Journal Mental Deficiency*, LI (1947), 627-31.

39 Guertin, Wilson H., "Differential Characteristics of the Pseudo-Feeble-minded," *American Journal Mental Deficiency*, LIV (1950), 394-98.

40 Haggerty, M. E., "The Incidence of Undesirable Behavior in Public School Children," *Journal Educational Research*, XII (1925), 113-14.

41 Heber, Rick, *A Manual on Terminology and Classification in Mental Retardation*. American Association on Mental Deficiency, 1959. 111 pp.

42 Heiser, Karl, "Psychotherapy in a Residential School for Mentally Retarded Children," *Training School Bulletin*, L (1954), 211-18.

43 Howe, Clifford E., "A Comparison of Motor Skills of the Mentally Retarded and Normal Children," *Exceptional Children*, XXV (1959), 352-54.

44 Johnson, G. Orville, *A Comparative Study of the Personal and Social Adjustment of Mentally Handicapped Children Placed in Special Classes with Mentally Handicapped Children Who Remain in Regular Classes*. Syracuse: Syracuse University Research Institute, 1961. 56 pp.

45 Johnson, G. Orville, "A Study of the Social Position of Mentally Handicapped Children in the Regular Grades," *American Journal Mental Deficiency*, LV (1950), 60-89.

46 Johnson, G. Orville, *Comparative Studies of Some Learning Characteristics in Mentally Retarded and Normal Children of the Same Mental Age*. Syracuse: Syracuse University Research Institute, 1958. 166 pp.

47 Johnson, G. Orville, "The Relationship of Learning Rate and Developmental Rate," *Exceptional Children*, XXVI (1959), 68-69.

48 Johnson, G. Orville, and K. A. Blake, *Learning Performance of Retarded and Normal Children*. Syracuse University Special Education and Rehabilitation Monograph Series 5. Syracuse: Syracuse University Press, 1960. 216 pp.

49 Johnson, G. Orville and R. J. Capabianco, *Research Project on Severely Retarded Children*. Special Report to New York State Interdepartmental Health Resources Board, Albany, 1957. 230 pp.

482   G. ORVILLE JOHNSON

[50] Johnson, G. Orville and S. A. Kirk, "Are Mentally Handicapped Children Segregated in the Regular Grades?" *Exceptional Children*, XVII (1950), 65-67, 87-88.

[51] Jolles, Isaac, "The Diagnostic Implications of Rorschach's Test in Case Studies of Mental Defectives," *Genetic Psychology Monographs*, XXXVI (1947), 89-197.

[52] Kanner, Leo, "Emotional Interference with Intellectual Functioning," *American Journal Mental Deficiency*, LVI (1952), 701-7.

[53] Kennedy, Ruby Jo R., *The Social Adjustment of Morons in a Connecticut City*. Hartford: Social Service Department, State Office Building, 1948. 120 pp.

[54] Kirk, Samuel A., *Early Education of the Mentally Retarded*. Urbana, Ill.: University of Illinois Press, 1958. 216 pp.

[55] Kirk, Samuel A., *Public School Provisions for Severely Retarded Children*. Special Report to New York State Interdepartmental Health Resources Board. Albany, 1957. 87 pp.

[56] Kirk, Samuel A., "The Effects of Remedial Reading on the Educational Progress and Personality Adjustment of High Grade Mentally Deficient Problem Children," *Journal Juvenile Research* (1934), pp. 140-162.

[57] Klausmeier, Herbert, "Physical Growth of Mental Retarded Children," *School and Society*, XXCVI (1958), 140.

[58] Klausmeier, Herbert and J. Check, "Relationships Among Physical, Mental, Achievement, and Personality Measures in Children of Low, Average, and High Intelligence at 113 Months of Age," *American Journal Mental Deficiency*, LXIII (1959), 1059-68.

[59] Klausmeier, Herbert, I. J. Lehman, and A. Beeman, "Relationships Among Physical, Mental, and Achievement Measures in Children of Low, Average, and High Intelligence," *American Journal Mental Deficiency*, LXIII (1959), 647-56.

[60] Kvargceus, William C., "Delinquency—A By-Product of the School?" *School and Society*, LIX (1944), 330-41.

[61] Lapp, Esther R., "A Study of the Social Adjustment of Slow-Learning Children Who Were Assigned Part-Time to Regular Classes," *American Journal Mental Deficiency*, LXII (1957), 254-66.

[62] Levy, Sol, "The Role of Mental Deficiency, the Causation of Criminal Behavior," *American Journal Mental Deficiency*, LVIII (1954), 455-64.

[63] Loomis, Chester M. (Coordinator), *A Study of Social Adequacy and of Social Failure of Mentally Retarded Youth in Wayne County, Michigan*. Wayne State University, 1959. 530 pp.

[64] Malpass, Leslie F., "Motor Proficiency in Institutionalized and Non-Institutionalized Retarded Children and Normal Children," *American Journal Mental Deficiency*, LXIV (1960), 1012-1015.

[65] MacIntyre, G. Mildred, "Teaching of Reading to Mentally Defective Children," *Proceedings American Association on Mental Deficiency*, XLI (1937), 59-67.

[66] McCulloch, T. L., J. Reswick, and I. Roy, "Studies of Word Learning in Mental Defectives. I. Effects of Mental Level and Age," *American Journal Mental Deficiency*, LX (1955), 133-39.

[67] Mehlman, B., "Group Play Therapy With Mentally Retarded Children," *Journal Abnormal and Social Psychology*, XLVII (1953), 53-60.

[68] Neham, Sara, "Psychotherapy in Relation to Mental Deficiency," *American Journal Mental Deficiency*, LV (1951), 557-72.

[69] Newman, H. H., F. H. Freeman, and K. J. Holzinger, *Twins: A Study of Heredity and Environment*. Chicago: University of Chicago Press, 1937.

[70] Peckham, R. A., "Problems in Job Adjustment of the Mentally Retarded," *American Journal Mental Deficiency*, LVI (1959), 448-53.

[71] Pero, John F., "Social Orientation Method of Social Training in an Institution," *American Journal Mental Deficiency*, LX (1955), 390-96.

[72] Pertsch, C. Frederick, "A Comparative Study of the Progress of Subnormal Pupils in the Grades and in Special Classes," Doctoral dissertation, Teachers College, Columbia University, 1936. 101 pp.

[73] Peterson, L. and L. L. Smith, "A Comparison of the Post School Adjustment of

Educable Mentally Retarded Adults With That of Adults of Normal Intelligence," *Exceptional Children,* XXVI (1960), 404-8.

[74] Porter, R. B. and T. C. Milazzo, "A Comparison of Mentally Retarded Adults Who Attended a Special Class with Those Who Attended Regular School Classes," *Exceptional Children* (1958), 410-12.

[75] *Report on Study Projects for Trainable Mentally Handicapped Children.* Springfield, Ill.: State Superintendent of Public Instruction, 1954. 43 pp.

[76] Reymert, M. L., "The Effect of a Change to a Relatively Superior Environment Upon the I.Q.'s of One Hundred Children," *Thirty-ninth Yearbook National Society Study of Education,* II. 1939.

[77] Ringelheim, Daniel and I. Polatsek, "Group Therapy With A Male Defective Group," *American Journal Mental Deficiency,* LX (1955), 157-62.

[78] Rubin, H. M., "The Relationship of Age, Intelligence, and Sex to Motor Proficiency in Mental Defectives," *American Journal Mental Deficiency,* LXII (1957), 507-16.

[79] Saenger, Gerhart, *The Adjustment of Severely Retarded Adults in the Community.* A Report to New York State Interdepartmental Health Resources Board, Albany, 1957. 176 pp.

[80] Sarason, Seymour B., "Dreams and Thematic Apperception Test Stories," *Journal Abnormal and Social Psychology,* XXXIX (1944), 486-92.

[81] Sarason, Seymour B., *Psychological Problems in Mental Deficiency,* 3rd ed. New York: Harper & Row, Publishers, 1959. 678 pp.

[82] Skeels, Harold M., "Mental Development of Children in Foster Homes," *Journal Genetic Psychology,* XL (1936), 91-106.

[83] Skeels, Harold M. and H. B. Dye, "A Study of the Effects of Differential Stimulation on Mentally Retarded Children," *Proceedings and Addresses of the Sixty-Third Annual Session of the American Association on Mental Deficiency,* 44(I) (1939), 114-36.

[84] Skeels, Harold M. and E. A. Fillmore, "Mental Development of Children from Under-privileged Homes," *Journal Genetic Psychology,* L (1937), 427-39.

[85] Sloan, William, "Mental Deficiency as a Symptom of Personality Disturbance," *American Journal Mental Deficiency,* LII (1947), 31-36.

[86] Sloan, William, "Motor Proficiency and Intelligence," *American Journal Mental Deficiency,* LV (1951), 394-406.

[87] Sloan, William, "The Lincoln-Oseretsky Motor Development Scale," *Genetic Psychology Monographs,* LV, 183-252.

[88] Sloan, William, and I. A. Berg, "A Comparison of Two Types of Learning in Mental Defectives," *American Journal Mental Deficiency,* LXI (1957), 556-66.

[89] Snyder, Robert and L. Sechrest, "An Experimental Study of Directive Group Therapy With Defective Delinquents," *American Journal Mental Deficiency,* LXIV (1959), 117-23.

[90] Strauss, Alfred A. and L. E. Lehtinen, *Psychopathology and Education of the Brain-Injured Child.* New York: Grune & Stratton, Inc., 1947. 270 pp.

[91] Terman, Lewis M. and M. A. Merrill, *Measuring Intelligence.* Boston: Houghton Mifflin Company, 1937. 461 pp.

[92] Thorne, Frederick C., "Counseling and Psychotherapy with Mental Defectives," *American Journal Mental Deficiency,* LII (1948), 263-71.

[93] Tizard, J. and F. M. Loos, "The Learning of a Spatial Relations Test by Adult Imbeciles," *American Journal Mental Deficiency,* LIX (1954), 85-90.

[94] Wallin, J. E. Wallace, *Children With Mental and Physical Handicaps.* Englewood Cliffs, N.J.: Prentice-Hall, Inc., 1949. 549 pp.

[95] Wallin, J. E. Wallace, *The Education of Handicapped Children.* Boston: Houghton Mifflin Company, 1924, pp. 58-9.

[96] Wells, J. and G. Arthur, "Effect of Foster-Home Placement on the Intelligence Ratings of Children of Feebleminded Parents," *Mental Hygiene,* XXIII (1939), 277-85.

[97] Woodrow, H., "Practice and Transference in Normal and Feebleminded Children," *Journal Educational Psychology,* VIII (1917), 85-96, 151-65.

RUTH STRANG

Emeritus Professor of Education
Teachers College, Columbia University and
Professor of Education, University of Arizona

10 Psychology of Gifted Children and Youth

PSYCHOLOGY, BROADLY defined, is the study of the way an individual's mind works, the reasons why he behaves as he does—the whole complex of interactions between mind and body, and between innate and environmental forces. The psychology of gifted children is a large subject, too large to treat here in its entirety. The comprehensive case study and the projective techniques offer the best means of studying the individual as a whole. What is usually done is to view one facet of the child's personality at a time and try to see its relation to the whole.

Much has been written about the characteristics of gifted children and about educational programs for them. Detailed information on these subjects is available in the monumental developmental study by Terman and his associates,[1,2,3,4,5] in the pioneer studies of gifted children by Leta A. Hollingworth,[6,7] in the explorations by Witty [8] into giftedness on different socioeconomic levels, in Sumption's follow-up of three hundred gifted children,[9] and in excellent summaries of research.[10,11]

Far less research has been done on the psychology of gifted

children. Of late, more attention has been given to such questions as how their hereditary "gifts" are developed, whether their motivations are different from those of other children, how the social, emotional, intellectual, and physical aspects of their development are interrelated, how they learn, and why they often fail to realize their potentialities. Nevertheless, the dynamic psychology of gifted children is still to be written.

Who Are the Gifted?

GIFTEDNESS HAS been defined in many ways. Some writers put the emphasis on superior endowment; others on exceptional performance. Some seek manifestations of giftedness in measurable intelligence; others in a variety of human abilities. Since endowment can only be judged by its products, and since modern psychology emphasizes the functioning of the organism as a whole, the most acceptable definition should include these two aspects. Witty's definition, adopted by the American Association for Gifted Children, characterizes as gifted "children whose performance is consistently remarkable in music, art, social leadership, and other forms of expression." [12] If this broad definition is accepted, not only is high performance on intelligence tests included, but also creative talent in an almost unlimited range of socially useful endeavor.[13]

Indeed, special talent is usually associated with above-average intellectual ability. In a school population of a quarter of a million, Terman found only twenty specially talented children who did not have superior mental ability. Exceptional scientific and literary achievement seems to require a high degree of general ability, whereas creativity as measured in accomplishments in music and art do not correlate so highly with intelligence.

The development of special talents seems to require special patterns of aptitudes, opportunities, and interests. For example, Subarsky proposed that the following combination be considered characteristic of science talent: curiosity, ability to recognize problems and to detect incongruities in facts, ability to think quantitatively, and manipulative ability.[14]

Certain qualities of character and temperament such as energy level, drive, determination, and perseverance also enter into this definition. A gifted person does not lead an effortless existence. Most people know individuals who fail to achieve outstanding success because of their inability to maintain a high level of performance.

This emphasis on performance or functioning highlights the individual's responsibility for making full use of his resources. Those who have

a great capacity for achievement have a correspondingly large obliga-
tion to contribute to the welfare of all.

Does Giftedness Occur Singly?

THERE IS no simon-pure kind of giftedness. Although researches have
shown substantial positive correlations among many kinds of ability,
one finds giftedness appearing in many different patterns of general
ability and specific aptitudes. A mathematical or a musical genius sometimes has a physical deformity. Any of the types of physical handicap
mentioned in previous chapters may be associated with high intelligence
or special talents. Among a group of gifted adolescents taking part in
a panel discussion, one was a spastic. His parents had to help him walk
to the platform, and his facial muscles were contorted when he spoke.
His physical appearance was in marked contrast to that of the other
members of the panel—who were well developed, good-looking youngsters. But when he spoke, his high intelligence and social sensitivity
shone through his physical limitations; he had the entire audience with
him after the first few sentences.

The reader is undoubtedly also familiar with the occasional gifted individual who is socially inadequate or emotionally disturbed. Any physical, social, or emotional handicap may occur in combination with high
intelligence or special talent, though this is not common. When it does
occur, it requires special treatment.

How Can Gifted Children Be Identified?

IN EVERY age there is need for gifted persons who will make a major
contribution to new developments in technology, social science, and art.
There is need to discover those who will demonstrate ways of living
peacefully and constructively with others, who possess social intelligence,
emotional maturity, and the perseverance to accomplish their social
purposes.[15] Exceptional creative talent is especially needed in the critical
situations of today—situations that will tax to the utmost the abilities of
the gifted.

The first step is early identification of these gifted individuals. Unless
they are identified, special provision for their needs cannot be made.
Worse still, they may be subjected to experiences that discourage the
natural use of their abilities. When they enter school, they may be given
primers to read, although they are able to understand books on the
second- or third-grade level. They may have to waste time while the rest
of the class catches up with them. They may be required to do unneces-

sary routine drill exercises. Their eagerness to ask and to answer questions may be suppressed.

The following incident which occurred in a language arts class shows how extremely insensitive one teacher was toward a gifted ten-year-old child:

Miss Jones was showing a colored picture to her language arts class. "What do you see?" she asked.

Some answered, "An Arab."

"Why do you think he is an Arab?"

"Because of his clothes."

"What about his skin and complexion?"

"It's dark," several children said.

"Yes, you can always recognize an Arab by his dark skin."

Paula's hand went up but she received no recognition. "But, Miss Jones, I saw an . . ."

Miss Jones, ignoring Paula's attempt to comment, went on. "You can also tell he's an Arab by his dirty clothes."

"But," Paula persisted, "all Arabs are not dirty. I saw. . . ."

"Paula, will you speak when you're spoken to. Now, class, another way you can recognize an Arab is by his straight black hair. He . . ."

"But, Miss Jones," Paula interrupted, "I saw blond Arabs when I was traveling in Syria and the Near East. They . . ."

"I told you to speak when you are spoken to. You have interrupted me three times. This time I am going to send you to the office."

Here was a child so eager to share her experience with the class that she interrupted when she was not recognized. She was punished instead of rewarded for her eagerness to make a valuable contribution to the class discussion. Experiences such as these tend to reduce superior children to mediocrity, or to make them passive or rebellious.

How should gifted children be identified? Parents may not be able to identify gifted children; they do not have sufficient basis for comparison. Their observations may be distorted by their ambitions. However, they may be able to furnish details about the child's early development that indicate to the discerning teacher or psychologist the presence of superior ability.

Teachers who are familiar with the characteristics of gifted children and who have a chance to observe children in an informal and challenging environment can give evidence that is valuable in identifying the gifted. Teachers have daily opportunity to observe how skillfully children use language, how quickly they see relations, how sensitive they are to things in their environment, how readily they learn, how easily they remember. Moreover, gifted children usually show outstanding resourcefulness and imagination, sustained attention, and wide interests.

Classroom and playground also offer opportunities to identify children who get along exceptionally well with others and handle frustrating situations with exceptional maturity. It is most rewarding to study children's interaction in groups. However, teachers have been given little help in using these daily opportunities to identify and educate the socially gifted.

Like parental observation, teacher observation also has its pitfalls. Some teachers have a tendency to overrate the abilities of docile, obedient, conscientious children. Others fail to recognize potential giftedness that is suppressed by emotional conflicts or by boredom with dull, routinized, teacher-dominated situations.

Identification of the gifted is best achieved by a combination of methods. To supplement accurate observation by parents and teachers, standardized tests are widely used. Tests of achievement or attainment identify scholastic aptitude; however, they may fail to identify, especially in elementary school, bright children whose economic and cultural backgrounds have been such as to lower their scholastic attainment. Group tests of intelligence, supplemented by individual examinations such as the Binet or the Wechsler Intelligence Scale for Children, have been used effectively in identifying the intellectually gifted. Profiles or patterns of abilities that are derived from a battery of tests are much more enlightening than a general estimate such as that provided by the I.Q.; a child who is gifted in one area does not necessarily score equally high in other tests and subtests.[16] If a discrepancy is apparent between teacher observation and test results, the child should be given opportunity, over a period of time, to function at his true level.[17]

Special tests of creativity have been devised to detect a kind of ability that is not measured by the available intelligence tests. Among other qualities these tests measure sensitivity to problems, associative and ideational fluency, flexibility of ideas, originality, and ability to improvise. Torrance[18] reported a low correlation between tests of intelligence and tests of creativity.

The cumulative record and the case study, both of which collect and synthesize information from various sources, are most likely to give clues to giftedness in the school population as a whole. An important function of the guidance staff is to make periodic surveys of the cumulative records of all the pupils, looking for individuals whose superior potentialities are shown by test results, school marks, and teacher observations.

Were They Born That Way?

CERTAIN HEREDITARY factors condition intellectual development. Two children who have the same physical environment will use that environment in different ways. One will learn to organize and to relate his experiences; the other will apparently learn very little. Histological studies and microscopic studies of the brain support the conclusion that "differences in intelligence are strongly inherited." [19] "Culture-free" tests given to eminent, as compared with average, persons and studies of identical twins further confirm the biological inheritance of intelligence.[20] It is well known that for identical twins, resemblance in physical and mental traits is high (correlations of .80 to .97); for children of the same parents it is substantial (.42 to .55); for unrelated children it is negligible (−.19 to .09). When identical twins are reared apart, the difference in environments shows a clearer influence on social behavior and school achievement than on personality structure or general mental ability.

At birth individuals differ in the degree to which they possess "a deductive and organizing activity of the mind . . . which leads to generalizations." [21] This inherited structure enables certain persons to select experiences from the environment, to relate, integrate, and organize them, and to achieve a favorable relationship between themselves and the environment. "From its beginnings . . . intelligence finds itself entangled in a network of relations between the organism and the environment." [22] Intelligence, thus conceived, contributes to the physical development of the child; his organs are modified by the experiences that his intelligence selects and makes possible. The intelligent child becomes increasingly able to handle his environment. His verbal ability is an important tool in helping him to assimilate new experiences.[23] At every stage of life, experience is necessary to the development of intelligence. Intelligence is not ready-made; it is not received at birth like the gift of the fairy godmother. "Intelligence elaborates itself." [24] It is constantly creating itself and developing its "house of clay" through the selection and use of life experiences. In this sense, intelligence is learned.

The relative influence of nature and nurture has long been a controversial topic. Barbara Burks' early estimate of "the total contribution of innate and inheritable factors" as "probably not far from 75 or 80 per cent" [25] has been supported by a study of London children.[26] The relative proportion would vary with different groups. But every individual has potentialities that he may develop; he also has hereditary limitations that he cannot transcend.

Although studies have shown that gifted children as a group have an unusually large number of accomplished relatives, persons of outstanding achievement have come from homes of low economic and apparently low intellectual status; they have overcome severe environmental handicaps. The Harvard "gamble" experiment [27] has demonstrated that boys who ranked high in certain character traits were able to meet high college academic standards despite relatively poor home backgrounds.

Studies of Negro children of superior intelligence indicate that race per se is not a limiting factor in intelligence.[28] Negro children who rated 160 I.Q. or higher on the Binet Test came from different sections of the country and from varied school and home environments.[29] The Negro children who were studied achieved best in "verbal subjects least dependent upon school instruction." [30]

Since one inherits genes, not characteristics, every observable trait is developed only with the aid of environmental conditions. Observation of gifted children supports the theory that an evolving intelligence influences physical development, achievement, and use of the environment. From birth, the child who has this initial organizing tendency is likely to be precocious in all aspects of his development. He uses his environment to good advantage. If he is in a family of high ability, he is fortunate in being exposed to books, stimulating conversation, and other experiences that are favorable to the further development of intelligence. The influence of environment is often seen still more clearly in the development of talent.[31]

In some instances, children who have a special mental facility for using their environment to fulfill their needs are deprived as they grow older of the experiences that would be necessary for the highest development of their intelligence. Gifted children who come from subcultural and low socioeconomic groups have special problems in realizing their potentialities. Their families and neighbors often are unsympathetic to their aspirations; they may have difficulty in financing the kind of education they should have, and in getting into the vocations for which they have prepared.

Pritchard reported the case of a highly gifted Negro boy who was unusually inventive and creative.[32] In both elementary and high school he made a good adjustment. One indication of his leadership ability was his election as president of the high-school student government association. He won a scholarship to a large metropolitan university. Here his gifts for leadership were not recognized by the college authorities. He became a leader in an off-campus group, one of the so-called youth movements, which sent him to a foreign country as a student representative. His increasing entanglement with subversive movements finally brought him into serious difficulty. Although he had been given a good free education, a combination of experiences in both his personal and his academic life gave rise to attitudes that closed the doors of opportunity to him. As an adult he expressed dissatisfaction with both his vocation and his personal life, and was "cynical and bitter." Had he received effective guidance during his college years, he might have fulfilled his potentialities for personal happiness and social usefulness.

Different situations evoke different types of talent and elicit talent differently in different people.[33] Social conditions in school may make it impossible for a gifted child to achieve the growth in mental ability that might be expected of him in childhood and adolescence. Gifted children often complain, "The other kids don't like me." Children of lower ability may feel jealous of or threatened by the high achievement of the gifted child; they may display resentment of him. The teacher who singles out the gifted child and holds him up as an example to others increases his unpopularity. Gifted children sometimes defy the teacher or deliberately get low marks in order to be accepted by their peers. Environmental conditions such as these may account in part for the fact that some gifted pupils, especially girls, score lower on the Stanford-Binet test when their intelligence is rechecked after a seven-year interval.

Investigations substantiate the conclusions drawn from Terman's study regarding the relation of socioeconomic level and high intelligence. Surveys both here and abroad have shown that a much larger proportion of the fathers of identified gifted children belonged to the professional or semi-professional occupational groups than was the case among fathers of the general school population; comparatively few gifted children sprang from skilled or unskilled laborers.[34] More recent evidence indicates that in the lower strata of society there are many gifted children who have not been identified. Faris' life histories showed clearly how favorable social background, family relations, and opportunities stimulated gifted children to develop their abilities.[35] Lewis likewise noted that gifted children are more frequently found in small families and homes of superior socioeconomic status.[36]

However, knowledge of the parents' occupation and socioeconomic condition is not an adequate basis for predicting a child's level of intelligence. The correlation between children's intelligence and their parents' socioeconomic status is positive, but not high.[37] Both superior and retarded children are found in homes of every socioeconomic level. In actual numbers, according to McGee and Lewis' study of 45,000 children in grades four through eight, the majority of gifted children come from average homes.[38] An investigation of the socioeconomic levels of 26,000 German boys resulted in a similar conclusion—that the broad middle class and the upper levels of the lower class constitute the most important seed-bed of gifted children. Perhaps the intelligence test that is used in most studies gives disproportionate weight to upper socioeconomic levels. With "culture-free" tests, a larger proportion of the gifted might be found in other occupational groups.

A more important factor than socioeconomic status may be the attitude of the parents toward the child and his education. Different cultural groups tend to have different orientations; Jews tend to reach high levels of achievement in relation to their ability; Negroes and Catholics, in general, do not.[39]

Freedom to use the environment to best advantage also should be considered. Experiments with rats in a comparative psychology laboratory showed that those in a free environment performed better in problem-solving than those in a restricted environment. Gifted children, too, need a free environment and especially what Olson has called a "lush environment." With their special capacity to organize and to use their environment, the gifted may be expected to make the optimum use of a free environment from the earliest years.

Beyond the home and the school extend the wider relationships of the local community, the nation, and the world. These wider relationships exert an increasing influence on the development of the gifted child as he grows older. A social matrix fraught with anxiety and intergroup tensions may depress creativity and restrict the use of individual talent. Moreover, society's expectations of the individual may either stimulate him or discourage him from developing his gifts and using them for social purposes. Group membership may be conducive to creativity, productivity, and the building of self-esteem or to the opposite qualities. The tenor of the times has a strong effect on adolescent development. We know this from observing the waste that occurs when young lives are governed by the spirit of irresponsibility and abandoned to the pleasure motive.

It seems clear that the majority of the children who are called gifted have indeed been blessed with exceptional heredity, a fortunate childhood, and favorable community conditions. This combination of factors has enabled them to maintain a continuous development of their intelligence and special talents through interaction with their environment. The processes by which potential talent is developed under various circumstances is a most important area for research.

Why Should Different Levels of Intelligence Be Recognized?

MEMBERS OF the group designated as gifted display individual differences. They do not constitute a homogeneous group. There are various levels of giftedness, as well as manifold patterns of intellectual development, social and economic conditions, family relations, educational experiences, and opportunities for success.

It has been estimated that the I.Q. range of 130-160 embraces about 3 per cent of the total population; that is, about thirty thousand in a million may be expected to show this level of mental ability. These people speak the same language as others but use words in a superior way.

This is "the most comfortable range of intelligence." Scores of from 165-180 I.Q. are rare; less than one person in a million will be found with an I.Q. over 180. These higher levels of ability have some distinctive characteristics. On the WISC test, children with I.Q.'s of 150-205 scored relatively high on subtests of verbal comprehension and ability to associate and synthesize.[40]

Children above 180 I.Q. are exceptionally precocious. One such child, described by Leta S. Hollingworth, wrote the following poem at the age of five:

> If I had Aladdin's lamp, you see,
> I'd give one wish to you and me.
> And then we'd wish for every toy,
> That every child should have some joy.[41]

Another exceptionally gifted boy with an I.Q. of 200 began to read at four years of age. His playmates were considerably older than he. When taking tests he generally gave more detail than was required for credit. If he did not know the answer, he did not hesitate to say, "I don't know." He showed excellent insight into his work and spontaneously criticized it. He often gave lectures to his classmates on such special topics as "history of timepieces, ancient theories of engine construction, mathematics, and history." [42]

A biographical study of twenty men of genius [43] showed a childhood pattern characterized by intense parental attention, intellectual stimulation, affection from parents and other adults, restricted contacts with other children of the same age, and a very rich fantasy life. Individuals designated as *geniuses* show very deep insights. Their superlative original, creative power is harnessed to a given task with unremitting effort supported by great physical stamina. Whether a certain degree of emotional instability and ill health is necessary to the highest achievement is still a moot question. Tsanoff has reviewed the relations between abnormality and genius and has discussed manifestations of creative genius in different fields.[44] He has illustrated the creative powers of the mind by means of incidents from the lives of artists, poets, musicians, and other geniuses. They collect and organize knowledge, then integrate and transform it in original ways. The genius sees things "in their harmonious and significant relation to others . . . in their beauty and their inner truth and reality." [45] The genius seems to possess greater intensity of mind than other persons.

With respect to insanity and genius, Tsanoff suggests four possibilities:

1. Neuropathic troubles are the cause of intellectual superiority.
2. Nervous troubles and genius are independent of each other.
3. Genius is the cause of neuropathic troubles.

4. Nervous troubles and intellectual superiority are different expressions of the same underlying conditions.[46]

The last two explanations seem to be the most plausible. By its very intensity a high kind of creativity may cause nervous strain and tension, and a supersensitivity of the nervous system may be conducive to both inner conflict and creative expression.

Still more positive conclusions were reached by Juda on the basis of a study, carried on over seventeen years, of the heredity, background, and physical and mental health of 294 highly gifted persons—113 artists and 181 scientists.[47] She concluded that there is "no evidence to support the assumption that the genesis of highest intellectual ability depends on psychic abnormalities." [48]

There is also some difference of opinion about the adjustment of children with I.Q.'s above 180. Terman found few reliable differences between those with I.Q.'s of 170 or above and his total group of gifted children. However, the exceptionally high I.Q.'s were rated somewhat less satisfactory in mental and social adjustment than the total group, especially during the middle teens. He concluded that "although children of this type are faced by difficult problems of adjustment, they have very superior intelligence with which to meet them." [49]

Hollingworth's more intensive study of a small number of children above 180 I.Q. indicates that there is some basis for the general impression that persons of such outstanding mentality have special problems of adjustment.[50] They suffer a certain amount of isolation and are likely to lose contact with other children of their own age. They are apt to play solitary games. They may live apart in their own world of intellect and may use a different vocabulary. They may become intolerant of less gifted people.

However, with respect to most characteristics, they are superior to the general population of children. They read at an early age, have exceptional vocabularies, a wide range of interests, and a desire to classify and sort information. Even in their play this organizing ability is evident.

Part of the problem of the highly intelligent stems from the responses that they evoke from other persons. Too few parents and teachers recognize the importance of helping these children integrate the intellectual, emotional, and physical aspects of their development. Adults sometimes encourage the very intelligent child to specialize in intellectual pursuits before he has achieved sufficient social and emotional development. Too often he receives little or no chance to experience the satisfaction of using his abilities in social service to the community.

Some of the failures that occur in this high intellectual group may be traced to early childhood experience. One child of 180 I.Q. who at six years of age already showed a retarded development was clearly rejected by the mother and involved in a sexual complex with the father. In other cases, failure to realize potentialities is difficult to understand.

Although persons at this level of I.Q. may have the intelligence for achieving outstanding success, they may lack other essentials such as strong drive, a purpose, a stimulating early environment, opportunity for advanced study, energy reserve, or capacity for sustained effort. Deficiencies in social adjustment and emotional stability also may affect their performance. Moreover, success in any work depends upon the individual's deriving sufficient emotional satisfaction to sustain continued effort.

What Are the Characteristics of Gifted Children?

DESPITE THE manifold individual differences among gifted children, certain characteristics are common to the majority of the gifted children studied by Leta S. Hollingworth, Terman and his associates, Witty, British psychologists,[51] and more recent investigators.[52] For the purposes of identifying gifted children, as well as for understanding them as a group and meeting their needs, teachers and parents should recognize these typical characteristics.

Physique and Health

It is well established that gifted children as a group are "slightly superior physically to the various groups used for comparison." [53] They are not the undersized, stoop-shouldered, clumsy, pathetic creatures often pictured. They maintain their good health as adults. These differences in favor of the gifted may be due either to biological superiority or to better health care and other conditions over which the individual has some control.

In the majority of cases the mother's health was good and the conditions of birth were normal; more than the average were breast-fed; and the child's health during the first year was rated by the mother as "excellent" or "good."

During their school years teachers reported a lower incidence of headaches, malnutrition, mouth-breathing, and defective hearing for the gifted group. They caught about as many colds and other contagious diseases as did the other children. Eye examinations showed about the same incidence of visual defects, although their history of early reading habits might lead one to predict more eye trouble. Medical examinations confirmed most of the teachers' impressions that the gifted children had better health and a lower incidence of defects of all kinds than were reported in the general population.

The health habits of this gifted group were also superior. They slept longer. They spent, on the average, two-and-a-half to three hours daily out-of-doors. Their dietary habits also were superior.

This physical superiority may be to some extent both a cause and an effect of their mental development. The healthy child, without auditory, visual, or orthopedic defects, is freer to explore his environment and to select and use the experiences he needs. His activity is not limited by general weakness or pain. On the other hand, a handicap that makes a child feel inferior and unfavorably affects his self-concept may depress his intelligence rating. According to Piaget's theory of the role of intelligence in child development, the gifted child and his parents would be likely to establish and maintain a healthful environment. They would recognize the value of sleep, outdoor play, and good food habits.

School Achievement

Many stories about geniuses who were dunces in school have been shown to be false, when all the facts were known. For example, Charles Darwin's failing marks might well be attributed to the disturbances he caused by carrying insects and small animals into the classroom. Sir Walter Scott never attended the school in which he was reported to have failed; on the other hand, he showed marked literary ability in early childhood.

Most gifted elementary school children, especially in the lower grades, like their school if it is a reasonably good one. Gifted high-school graduates are likely to be more critical of their schools; they mention poor teachers, low standards of achievement, and lack of special interest groups. While in school the gifted are often accelerated, almost never retarded, and are absent less than the general population. They often have a keen sense of humor and enjoy free discussion. They like science. They are not content with collecting facts and dislike rote memorization and "busy work." They want to have time to do things on their own; they do not like to be too closely scheduled. They show early the following indications of superior intelligence: "Quick understanding, insatiable curiosity, extensive information, retentive memory, large vocabulary, and unusual interest in such things as number relations, atlases, and encyclopedias." [54] It is significant that in the majority of the cases these abilities and interests are not artificially stimulated by the parents; 70 per cent said they "had allowed the child to go at his own pace."

Results of standardized tests show a superiority in achievement far beyond that recognized by most teachers and parents. Some children rated as average by teachers have scored as much as two to four years above their actual grade placement. There are varied reasons for this discrepancy, as Terman and Oden point out: A shy child may not make his ability known in class; a vociferous child may annoy the teacher by his insistence upon communicating his knowledge; another child may rebel at having to spend time on what he considers "busy work," which in fact is what much homework is; a bored child may withhold his attention from assigned tasks that are neither interesting nor challenging to him in favor of other activities that are not approved by the teacher; an undiplomatic child may correct the teacher's mistakes, and thus make him feel inferior and resentful of the child's superior ability.

Poor teaching and lack of proper guidance in the choice of a major field also may inhibit the gifted child's performance in school. When such conditions are corrected, gifted children often respond by showing improved achievement and interest.

Social reasons, too, may account for poor school performance or even failure in some subjects. Like other children and adolescents, the gifted seek status in their group. If the morale of the group is low and academic achievement is disparaged, then the gifted child sometimes does poor work just to be accepted by the group. He thus avoids being called "a brain" or "a square" by his peers. As one bright high-school girl said, "If you're taller than the boys, it's bad enough, but if you're brighter, it's fatal."

The gifted child's superiority on standardized achievement tests is not related to the duration of his school attendance: the number of months spent in school has almost no effect in raising the achievement quotient. Once started in the three R's, the gifted child increases his command of reading, language usage, number concept, arithmetical reasoning, and information.

Having acquired effective tools of learning, gifted children can take the initiative and go ahead on their own.[55] All they need is some teacher help when they are ready for it, parental encouragement, rich laboratory and library facilities, and opportunities for experiences in art, music, and social activities.

Like other individuals, the gifted show some unevenness of achievement in various fields. The two subjects in which they are likely to be either specially high or specially low are arithmetic and spelling. Usually they are better in arithmetic, history, and English than in writing, art, and handiwork—subjects requiring manual coordination or dexterity. Even in their poorest subjects, however, they tend to maintain a higher level of performance than the average pupil. Outstanding achievements in certain fields may be attributed to opportunity to progress in those fields rather than to the ease or inherent interest of the given subject.[56]

Some verbally gifted children overemphasize intellectual pursuits. Occasionally, this exclusive interest in books and academic subjects is unwittingly encouraged by parents and teachers who do not recognize its detrimental effect on other important tasks of adolescent development.

Underachievement

The dynamics of underachievement are complex. It may stem from such diverse motivations as fear of failure or desire for independence or security; it may be the expression of a hostility, anxiety, or inner conflict that withdraws the child's energy and effort from his studies. The current point of view is that underachievement is part of a total personality pattern—a feeling of personal inadequacy,[57] a low level of aspiration, unclear educational and vocational goals, narrow interests, and poor personal and/or social adjustment. Only a clinical study can give the true picture in an individual case.

The various elements that may be related to achievement and underachievement have been summarized by Burt,[58] Gowan,[59] and others.[60] The results of research are conflicting. Some studies failed to find that poor mental health and lack of sociability are clearly related to underachievement. There is more agreement that school failure tends to be associated with or arise from a value system that is characteristic of low rather than of high socioeconomic status. Home conditions, relationships, and attitudes toward learning tend to differentiate the high from the low achievers. The underachiever usually dislikes school, does not enjoy learning from books, and lacks effective study and reading habits.

The characteristics of gifted achievers and underachievers vary from grade to grade as well as from individual to individual. In the third grade, the high general achievers "were sensitive and responsive to socialization pressures, had largely accepted adult values, and were striving to live up to adult expectation." [61] They were more secure and confident at this point than they were in the seventh grade, when they had become somewhat antagonistic toward adults and more aggressive and competitive. In high school, the achievers tended to make a better adolescent adjustment than the underachievers.

Reading Development of Gifted Children

The development of reading ability is a prelude and a prerequisite to the child's personal development through reading. Without adequate reading proficiency, the child is handicapped in communicating, as well as in acquiring knowledge in any field. Reading contributes to children's personal-social development in many ways. It builds up self-esteem; it is

a satisfying way to use leisure time; it helps them to understand themselves and others.

Studies of gifted children have referred briefly to (1) the early age
at which they learn to read, (2) their exceptional interest in reading,
(3) their precocity in reading adult books, (4) their intensive reading
in particular fields. Reference has been made also to deviations from
these general tendencies. There are case studies of gifted children who
used reading as an escape from social situations to which they were
making a poor adjustment. Many gifted children are retarded in reading
development. They are often bored with the assigned books, memorize
beginning stories rather than read them, "talk around" a question instead
of finding the answer. With effective instruction they can improve in
speed and comprehension.[62]

To supply needed information on how gifted children read, the author
made a study of the reading autobiographies of 54 seventh, eighth, and
ninth grade pupils with I.Q.'s of 120 or higher. These autobiographies
yielded a wealth of introspective reports on the reading interests and
methods of these children.

Gifted children learn to read early; 43 per cent of the gifted children
in Terman's study learned to read before going to school. About the
same proportion has been found in other studies. One youngster with an
I.Q. of 160 wrote, "I looked at pictures when I was one and read simple
books at three."

How do gifted children learn to read? A few learn all by themselves
to associate printed words with meanings. As one boy said, "I got interested in books and read them; that was all there was to it." However,
most of these youngsters said they had been taught to read by various
methods and by various people. "Sounding out words" was most frequently mentioned. One youngster described a common combination of
methods:

> My mother and father were firm believers that books play a
> very important part in a child's life. When I was about one or two
> years old my mother or father read to me every night and after-
> noon. After a month or two of constant reading of my favorite
> stories over and over, or the reading of a poem, I learned them
> from memory. I was about four when I would sit down by my-
> self, and telling by the pictures which was the poem or story pre-
> sented, I would act as if I was reading. Soon I could distinguish
> words or sound them out.

Some profit by more systematic instruction in independent word recognition.[63] Once they have acquired a basic sight vocabulary and mastered
word recognition skills, they begin to read extensively.

What do gifted children read? In the lower grades their reading interests are not much different from those of other children. Their first-grade reader seems to make a strong impression on them, and their supplementary reading of children's series, animal stories, and humorous books includes the favorite books for these grades. Their reading interests are broad.

Their specialized interests begin to emerge earlier than those of other children. Gifted children report interest in travel, science, biography. In general the gifted children move more quickly into teen-age and adult reading. However, unless they receive guidance, many read books that are trivial, below their level of ability, and of poor quality.

How much do they read? It is well known that gifted children are usually great readers. In their reading autobiographies they make comments such as these: "I spend much of my free time reading." "I read more than anything else." "I spend half my time reading." As they go into their teens, the time they spend in reading decreases as they become occupied with clubs, social activities, special lessons, television, and radio. Still they find considerable time for reading. This is because they find reading an enjoyable and rewarding experience that challenges their active minds and satisfies their desire for knowledge.

What are their reading habits? Some of them describe reading methods that, on the whole, are sound and mature. One boy described his habits of selecting books as follows:

> Usually in selecting a book I am very choosey. If I feel that I want information, I will be found delving into the non-fiction type book. But occasionally, though not very often, I have some leisure at hand, so to arouse some interest I will read a fiction book. I happen to be *very* critical as to the fiction books I read, and I usually read very well-known novels. In a fiction book, once I start, I read continuously until either the book ends or until an interruption interferes.

Gifted children usually like media of communication that give exercise to their alert minds. Books demand more thought and give more stimulus to the imagination than do media in which ideas are pictured or interpreted by the producer.

Creativity

A special factor of creativity is gaining increasing recognition as a component of giftedness. Its characteristic features are what Guilford has called "divergent thinking," productive imagination, and fluency of original ideas.[64] A minimum I.Q. of around 120 seems to be essential for products of interest and value. Getzels and Jackson [65] were able to distinguish two groups of adolescents: (1) those in the top 20 per cent on creativity measures but below the top 20 per cent in I.Q.; and (2) those in the top 20 per cent on I.Q. measures but below the top 20 per cent on creativity. Both groups were superior in academic achievement but were quite different in other respects; those in the high I.Q. group were preferred by both teachers and classmates to those in the high creativity group.

The expressed values of the two groups were different: the high I.Q. put more emphasis on success, character, and goal-directedness; the high creativity, on sense of humor and on qualities that were the opposites of those they believed their teachers favored. The high I.Q.'s responses to pictures and theme topics were more conventional and stereotyped; the high creative group's responses were more humorous, unconventional, and original. As the highly creative children go through the elementary school, other children at first think their ideas are silly or naughty; later they are more often chosen as having good ideas.

Interests

Gifted children are characterized by enthusiasm. Contrary to the general impression, they enjoy playing games with other children, especially games that require thought and skill. Gifted girls engage in slightly more play activities than the average; gifted boys, slightly less. They have a tendency to play with older children. Because they are usually younger than the other children in their group, they have less chance for leadership experience and by contrast may seem socially immature. It is the atypical gifted child who withdraws markedly from social contacts. However, they also enjoy their individual hobbies and solitary activities, especially curling up in a comfortable position with a good book. They spend less time than the average boy or girl in going to movies and watching television. They usually persist in the face of difficulty, if the activity appeals to them as worth while.

Social and Emotional Development and Adjustment [66]

The organizing activity of the mind, which, as has been said, gifted children possess in a high degree, influences their emotional development; it makes them active participants in the process of growing up emotionally. They see that they have two choices: to yield to the demands that are made upon them, or to resist them. They learn at an early age that they cannot always have what they want. Since they understand or perceive a situation clearly, they tend to act on thinking rather than on the impulse of the moment. Since they see more clearly the consequences of certain behavior, they are more willing to forego an immediate satisfaction in favor of a more distant goal.

This does not mean that the gifted child is never aggressive or obstreperous. He may try to override controls at home or at school that seem to him unreasonable or detrimental to his development. If the demands are actually unreasonable or detrimental, his aggressive behavior is justified. For example, an adolescent girl was referred to a guidance clinic by an older sister who said that Ethel "went all to pieces in a difficult situation." The psychologist observed that the opposite was true in the testing situation. In an interview with the counsellor Ethel confided, "I know it's childish to have temper tantrums, but it's the only way I can get the things I need." She was referring to social and educational experiences that she needed for her adolescent development.

Many gifted adolescents work out these problems of growing up with a minimum of conflict with their parents. They recognize the parents' point of view, present their own side of the question clearly and reasonably, and often arrive at some satisfactory integration or compromise. For example, one boy, the oldest in the family, solved the problem of the family car one evening by suggesting that he first drive his little sister to her Scout meeting, his younger brother and sister to the party they were attending, and his mother to her friend's house. Then he would go on his own date and pick up the members of the family later in the evening. To prevent a recurrence of similar confusion he suggested that they all sign up for the car a week ahead.

On the Farfey test of developmental age for boys and the analogous form prepared by Sullivan for girls, 26 gifted boys and 24 gifted girls, as compared with an unselected group, showed a wide variation in maturity from item to item. The gifted group, however, tended to rate higher on certain esthetic and intellectual aspects of development.[67] Although they are similar to average groups in personality structure, as indicated by their responses on the group Rorschach, the gifted group, by virtue of their greater verbal facility, may be able to talk out their life problems instead of acting them out in destructive ways.[68]

Gifted adolescents frequently display more emotional maturity than some of their parents and teachers. Few adults have analyzed the problem of drinking as maturely as the 16-year-old boy who wrote:

> In my crowd the problem was drinking. They thought it was smart to have beer parties, or to have wienie roasts where a bottle was included. I think it is wrong for teen-agers to drink. It is bad for our health and it is not smart, but what is one to do or say when everyone else in the crowd likes to drink? A person feels different and left out when he isn't like the others in his group. This was my problem and it weighed heavily on my mind for a long time.
> Then I started observing the other people in my crowd. The

more I thought about it, the surer I was that they drank, not because they really liked to, but because it gave them a thrill to indulge in something which was thought wrong for teen-agers and because they didn't want to feel different from the group, as I had felt. I found that teen-agers who drank were not the ones who were respected. I talked it over with several of the other kids in our crowd and I was glad to hear that they shared my views on the subject.

This is a problem which confronts most of the teen-agers today. . . . I really believe that if every person who drinks would analyze his views on the subject and find out why he does and what he gets out of it, there would be fewer cases of teen-age drinking in America today.[69]

With younger children especially, a parent often has to hold fast to the controls which he knows are necessary. At the same time he can recognize the child's feeling, help him to express it, and help him to understand and accept inevitable frustration. By establishing adequate discipline, in the sense of control, the parent helps the child to attain a sound, healthy basis for maturity.

The social adjustment of accelerated pupils in high school and college has been studied extensively. Although individual cases of poor social adjustment have been reported, acceleration of one or two years, determined on the basis of individual study of the pupil, appears to be "beneficial and healthful." [70] This is because intellectually gifted children tend to be physically and socially, as well as intellectually, in advance of their chronological ages. The reason why some high-school and college students have a hard time making social adjustments may lie in physical immaturity or unfavorable earlier social experiences.

Jarecky [71] described the characteristics of the socially gifted adolescents whom he studied as follows: They are physically attractive in appearance; are accepted as equals by both peers and adults; engage in constructive social enterprises, are often arbiters and policy-makers; are non-defensive in their behavior; are fairly free from obvious emotional tensions; have enduring relationships—their friendships are not subject to rapid turnover; stimulate positive, productive behavior in others; handle difficult situations with intelligence, humor, and insight.

Studies of social acceptance made by means of the Ohio Classroom Social Acceptance Scale, other sociometric methods, and teacher and parent estimates have shown that gifted children are not social isolates. They are socially accepted and wanted as friends more than the average and far more than the least able children.[72,73,74] Their degree of social acceptance tends to be higher among younger elementary school children than among older children; it varies with the school and the community, and with the general level of intelligence. Social status with peers tends to decline more with decreasing I.Q. than it rises with increasing I.Q.

Although gifted children accept classmates who have lower ability, they may have stronger friendship ties in the neighborhood. One reason why they are accepted in the classroom is that they do not flaunt their abilities,[75] even though they may actually be achieving beyond expectancy. Children are able to assess quite accurately the learning ability of their classmates.

Attending a special class for fast learners did not seem to affect these children's social relations in the regular classroom. However, teachers may contribute to the isolation of the gifted child by singling him out and assigning him enriching experiences of a solitary kind. Gifted children sometimes feel lonely, even though they are apparently popular with their classmates.

Although the majority of gifted children make a good social adjustment, some need help in establishing satisfying social relations. A senior high-school girl with an I.Q. of 150 poignantly expressed her dissatisfaction with her school adjustment:

> When I entered high school (after a year spent with an invalid sister) I found that I no longer knew how to get along with my contemporaries. Trying to convince myself it didn't matter, I threw myself into my studies and outside reading. Unfortunately studies aren't a very good substitute for friends, and I was extremely unhappy and lonely during my first three years in high school. Whenever I was particularly hurt or miserable, I retired to my books—to forget. This, as anyone can see, was not wise as it made me even more out of place and self-conscious. If anyone was ever heading directly for a nervous breakdown, it was I.
>
> At the beginning of my senior year, I acquired a new teacher, who tried to give me confidence in myself. To a large extent, she succeeded, although there is a great deal more to do. I can at the moment carry on a conversation without wishing to be on the other side of the world. As yet I find it much easier to get along with older people than with my own age group.
>
> I think a great deal of suffering could have been avoided if someone had taken some interest in me earlier, if someone had tried to bring me out of myself. If someone *had*, I don't think I would have cried myself to sleep so many nights during my first three years of high school. If there had been someone to help at the beginning, I don't think it would have been as hard as it is now for me to get along with people.[76]

Gifted individuals generally rank superior in measures of adjustment and score high on personality and character tests, both in childhood and in later life. Terman reported that almost 80 per cent of his gifted group later rated their adjustment as "satisfactory." This is as one would expect; individuals who possess high powers of mental organization should be able to recognize and analyze their problems of adjustment, bring their broad background of experience to bear on them, and see clearly the consequences of certain courses of action.

These qualities perhaps account for the fact that the emotionally disturbed persons in Terman's gifted group showed a high proportion of recovery from their disorders. Only one case seemed hopeless. Terman and Oden made this comment:

> Superior intelligence does not appear to be a causal factor in mental disorder as found in this group, but seems, rather, to have helped those affected to overcome their difficulties. The insight and intelligent cooperation shown by those who become mental patients have almost certainly contributed to the improvement noted in several of the cases.[77]

Writers have emphasized the fact that children need a harmonious home life, good family relations, and consistent and reasonable treatment in the early years.[78] Neville [79] made a clinical study of 78 children with Binet I.Q.'s ranging from 140 to 180 who were referred to a psychological clinic. Of these, 35 were considered "difficult"; they showed such maladjustments as fits of depression, stammering, stealing, outbursts of temper, parental overprotection, and extreme jealousy. More than half were extremely nervous, and a considerable number were unhappy at school. Eight showed scholastic backwardness, while more than half were troubled by difficulties in social adjustment.

In almost all of the relatively few cases of mental breakdown, alcoholism, delinquency, and homosexuality in Terman's study, unsatisfactory home conditions were evident. Among these were overattachment of son to mother, overprotective, oversolicitous mother and reticent or passive father, overindulgent or overstrict parents, and homes broken by divorce. In most of these cases some difficulty in social adjustment was manifested during the school years.

Because of their greater competence, gifted children are less likely than other children to have the kind of personal problems that stem from concern with one's efficiency in mental tasks. But their level of aspiration is also likely to be high. They may compare themselves with eminent persons whose autobiographies they read. They are often held up to very high standards of achievement by ambitious relatives and friends. They live under considerable social pressure. It is significant that many Harvard freshmen expressed feelings of inferiority and inadequacy.[80]

The problems of gifted children vary with the community and with the general level of intelligence. In a midwestern city, the major problems of 35 children with Binet I.Q.'s of 150 or higher were lack of motivation and creativity, and presence of apparently minor conflicts which tended to interfere with the realization of their potential.

A number of individual cases have been reported in which mental functioning was restricted by unfavorable emotional development. Kanner described a child who, when four years old, could "read" magazines like *The National Geographic* and *The Atlantic Monthly* without in the least comprehending the meaning of the words he pronounced correctly.[81] On the Binet-Simon scale and on the Vineland Social Maturity Test his psychometric rating was extremely low, although he could read mechanically everything that was shown to him and handled formboards adroitly. The psychiatrist recognized that certain features of his home environment were having a detrimental effect—the pressures put upon the child by "a rigid, detached, machine-like father," "the instability of a neurotic grandmother," "the rivalry with a fully accepted younger sister," and "the ambivalent attitude of a filially and matrimonially unhappy mother." The child was put into a foster home where these unfavorable influences were replaced by fondness and permissiveness, tempered by a gentle firmness. At six he was admitted to a public school where he was handled with exceptional skill. Psychiatric work with the mother during the child's absence enabled her to help him when he returned from the foster home.

> At ten years of age he achieved a Binet I.Q. of 150 and at twelve was attending junior high school. He is still a peculiar child, preoccupied with mathematical puzzles and the collection of maps, but he has a reasonably good relationship with his mother, his sister, and his teachers and has made a few friends.[82]

In brief, there is a relationship between the emotional development and adjustment of gifted children and their mental ability. Their ability to understand and organize, and their insight into situations favor good emotional adjustment. But this intellectual ability is not always able to overcome the effects of unfavorable early home conditions or lack of guidance in the elementary and high-school years. Without the desire to learn, they will not show the expected mental development. One child asked a very pertinent question of the adult who told him he could accomplish anything he wanted to. He replied, "But how do you get to want to?" Emotional development, as part of the total development of the child, obviously affects his mental functioning.

Character and Personality

Through his own experiences, the gifted child develops a concept of himself as an individual in his own right. This basic self-concept emerges within the family group. During the first half of his first year of life he senses the world as friendly or hostile, depending upon the kind of physical care and affection he experiences. Soon he begins to think of himself as dependent or independent, competent or inadequate, depending upon his experiences. The gifted child's superior ability to organize and relate his experiences favors good personality development. As his personal contacts widen, he has the problem of integrating his early egocentric idea of himself with the idea of a social self. This integrating process results in a sound, stable self-concept, an important factor in emotional adjustment.

The great majority of intellectually gifted children show superiority in character and personality.[83,84] An extensive study of school children in 36 states appeared "to justify the conclusion that the child of superior intelligence has a much better chance of developing a desirable personality than does the child who is retarded in intelligence." [85] Some of the details that we are familiar with in the false picture of gifted children may have been drawn from observation of pseudo-gifted children— children whose parents have coached and pushed them to attempt tasks that are beyond their real mental ability, with the result that they have developed emotional strains and have become unable to maintain early levels of achievement.

Although Terman and his associates used a number of ingenious tests to appraise character and personality traits, the results are not conclusive. As Terman and Oden pointed out, the superiority of bright children on these tests may be attributed to their ability to figure out the purpose of the tests and answer in the approved way.[86] The superiority of the gifted group over the control group was highest in social attitudes and in preference for admirable characters. On the Raubenheimer-Cady series of character tests, the gifted children expressed far more social preferences and social attitudes than the average; they indulged in less boastful exaggeration and less cheating, and showed greater trustworthiness under stress. It is possible that some of these desirable traits—including sociability, friendliness, restraint, and cooperation—may stem as much from socioeconomic environment as from "giftedness" per se.

Ratings by teachers and parents were in substantial accord with other sources of information except in the appraisal of social development. Teachers and parents rated the gifted children from between 97 to 84 per cent above the mean of the control group in general intelligence, desire to know, originality, and common sense. Their next highest group of ratings were those on will power and perseverance, desire to excel, self-confidence, prudence and forethought (84 to 81 per cent). On emotional traits they rated the gifted, on the average, 67 per cent superior; on moral traits, 74 per cent; and on social traits, from 57 to 54 per cent. Gifted children were rated as 70 per cent superior to the control group in leadership. It would be interesting to know the nature of the observations on which these teachers' ratings were based. What behavior, for example, did they consider as indicative of superior emotional and moral traits and of leadership?

In Britain, where more rigid class differences made the conditions affecting social and moral behavior more complex, the percentage of serious maladjustment among the gifted was barely 1 per cent—much less than that found among the controls.[87]

Intellectual functioning should be viewed against the background of personality structure and dynamics. Personality should be interpreted with reference to environmental conditions and other non-intellectual factors, as well as with respect to intellectual ability. Studies are needed of talented children with average intelligence; of intellectually gifted children who are handicapped physically, socially, or emotionally; and of gifted children who have developed in an all-round way.

How Do Gifted Children Learn?

THERE ARE several sources of information on how gifted children learn: (1) statements by gifted children about conditions that they consider conducive to learning; (2) general learning theory, which probably applies to gifted as well as to average children; (3) experiments on the learning of gifted children; and (4) introspective reports in which gifted children describe their ways of learning. The information available from the third and fourth sources is very meager. It is not known whether gifted children employ learning procedures that are similar to those of the average pupil, or whether their methods of learning and reading are quite different. From his experience with and study of exceptional children, Baker [88] concluded that superior learners tend to (1) "learn by complex associative methods rather than by simple direct rote drill"; [89,90] (2) "look for abstract or generalized rules underlying all school subjects"; [91] (3) be able "to do independent work." [92] They will do excellent work in vocational and manipulative subjects, if they are interested and can use associative learning methods and apply general principles. Under favorable conditions they will also "develop and cultivate comparatively unselfish and social points of view." [93]

Conditions which Gifted Pupils Consider Conducive to Learning

In criticizing their schooling gifted children say, "Why didn't we have more experiences of the kind we needed?" "Why didn't teachers hold us up to standards of achievement appropriate for us?" "Why didn't high-school teachers teach us effective methods of reading and study, which we needed in college?" They complain bitterly about having to drill on skills they already possess. They complain about dull required books, meaningless topics, and lack of challenging assignments.

With respect to the kinds of teachers who have helped or hindered them, gifted children have definite ideas. Writing about the ideal teacher, one 16-year-old high-school pupil with a Binet I.Q. of 132 said:

> I think the ideal teacher is one who is very understanding. She must be able to talk individually with each student and help him to straighten out any difficulties he might have. I think this is very important because if a person starts out wrong in grammar school it might be hard for him to find himself in junior high school. The teacher must have a lot of patience—she shouldn't lose her temper too often. The teacher should be creative. She should be able to think of different things for the pupils to do.

Speaking of her recent experience with teachers, one junior high school girl with a Kuhlmann-Anderson I.Q. of 131 wrote:

> One of the best teachers I have had was Mr. Y. He made me feel at ease in his class so that I could work better. For compositions he had me write about things that I really knew and liked. He helped me study for tests by talking to me about it and showing me what points to cover.
>
> Another good teacher was Mr. X. He was very fair about marks and considered every angle. He seemed to get me to work hard. Without my really trying I could get things done. I think that these two teachers are good because they don't use force in teaching.

One youngster summed up his ideas of the ideal teacher by saying, "Give us bright, interesting teachers for bright, interesting students." The gifted appreciate teachers who arouse their curiosity, insist on reasonably high standards of excellence, and provide for activities that call for initiative and self-reliance.

In panel discussions, gifted pupils mentioned the following conditions which they consider to be conducive to learning:

> Don't let us drift into the habit of loafing through our classes. Instead, give us opportunities: (1) to take additional subjects in which we are interested; (2) to engage in creative work, such as marionette shows; (3) to learn to speak before an audience; (4) to take part in discussions that move forward toward their goal; (5) to apply principles and theories to life problems; (6) to match wits with other gifted persons, as in a special class, debating club, or discussion group; and (7) to learn the most efficient reading and study methods.
>
> Let bright pupils occasionally tutor pupils who are having difficulty in learning. This helps prevent unnecessary repetition of subject matter in class and gives the tutors the satisfaction of being of service.

Learning Theory Applied to Gifted Children

The gifted individual's performance is determined by (1) his drive or state of need, (2) the present stimulus situation, (3) his previous learning experiences, and (4) that organizing, creative quality of mind which seems to be the essential element in giftedness.

Incentives of various kinds improve performance of a goal-directed activity. Gifted children may be expected to understand the nature of an incentive. But this understanding may lead them to reject certain incentives. For example, public praise by a teacher is very likely to decrease the learning of a gifted child because he senses its detrimental effect on his relations with his classmates. Under such circumstances, praise does not motivate the gifted pupil to achieve recognition for his work. Certainly there are wide differences in the effects of praise and blame, and in the kinds of incentives that will motivate the learning of gifted children.

It is probable that satisfaction in the learning process itself—reading, solving problems, and other intellectual activities—is for the gifted child an important intrinsic incentive. He is curious and eager to learn and often does things because he sees that they are worthwhile in themselves. Or, looking ahead, he sees that the accomplishment of a given task will achieve some goal. Within the gifted group, various incentives exert varying appeals; individuals differ in the type and degree of their ego-involvement.

Gifted children from middle- or upper-class homes tend to be more highly motivated to succeed in academic work than do children from lower socioeconomic levels. Accordingly, they may take failure more seriously. If their ego-involvement is very great, the threat of failure may have a disorganizing effect on their performance. The extent of this effect depends somewhat on their previous experiences and on their ability to do the task. There is probably an optimum amount of motivation.

There is a little evidence that among children and adolescents, the effect of group rivalry as a stimulus to learning decreases with intelligence. With highly intelligent adults, the effectiveness of group rivalry almost disappears. Rivalry between individuals, under traditional school conditions, is also effective in increasing the performance of some school children—the gifted more than the mentally retarded. But the influence of this incentive will vary greatly with the culture.

Stimulus situations affect learning. Depending upon how they are perceived by the individual, they may arouse an inner response that serves as a drive toward problem-solving. They may also increase the strength of a response; this is called *reinforcement*. Stimuli that satisfy a need promote learning, providing the situation is constructively perceived. The individual is selective in responding to situations. Do certain kinds of stimuli have more potency for gifted children than for children of average or below-average mental ability? Are different things considered useful by gifted children? Does the amount of reinforcement that is necessary to increase the strength of a response vary with mental ability? These are still unanswered questions.

Retention is another factor to be considered in the learning process. Long ago Plato differentiated the gifted by their ability to "remember and not forget." Remembering is selective.[94] Since motivation, background of experience, and verbal ability are important factors in memory, we should expect the gifted child to be superior in his ability to remember. Gifted children feel a strong need to connect past and present events into a meaningful whole. This organizing ability is a well-known aid to remembering.

The degree of retention varies with a wide variety of conditions, in addition to the ability of the learner. These include his need for learning the material, the completeness with which he is learning it, the quality of the instruction given, the relationship between learner and teacher, cultural conditions, and other factors.

Certain practical suggestions for remembering would seem to apply to gifted as well as to other students:

1. The nature of the material affects the degree of one's retention; it is most important to sense the structure or principles underlying the content.

2. Thoroughness of learning is a factor; well-learned material is retained better than material that is not brought to the point of mastery.

3. There seems to be less forgetting when the material is learned just before going to sleep than when the learning is followed by daily activities.

4. Review and use of the material should accompany, or follow soon after, the initial learning. It pays to take time to recall and recite what you have learned.

5. Interest and satisfaction facilitate learning.

Similarly, certain methods of teaching would usually be effective with gifted children:

1. Students like to take initiative in learning. When they are allowed to do so, they put forth more effort than when they are under compulsion.

2. Guidance is most effective at the beginning of the learning process; it helps the student get off to a good start. Most students are restive

during lengthy verbal explanations. The effectiveness of any verbal guidance depends on whether the student is ready for it and considers it important to him.

3. It is more effective to give approval of each step in a carefully analyzed learning process than to reward only the end result.

4. Certain methods of studying and of teaching may be more effective for gifted pupils than for the class as a whole. Brownell and Mosher showed that one method of learning subtraction was more effective, when used with bright pupils and by able teachers, than another method that was generally considered to be superior.[95] Even a bright child who is taught by rote methods may have difficulty in applying what he has learned to the solution of general problems. In discussing the alleged superiority of any method of teaching, one should take into account the complex interaction between the method, the interest and ability of the student, and the skill of the teacher. Some individuals respond well to a method that others find baffling.

There is a great need for intensive studies of the ways in which gifted children learn. Such experiments should recognize emotional drives as well as the problem-solving process that these drives evoke. Two individuals of equal intelligence who show the same initial achievement may progress at quite different rates because there is greater motivation in one case. The learning process is complex. It is affected by many factors such as motivation, unconscious inhibitions, the nature and usefulness of the learning task, the methods of instruction, and the interpersonal relations in the classroom.

What Motivates Gifted Children?

ALTHOUGH REFERENCE has already been made to the motivation of gifted children, this topic is important enough to warrant further treatment. Follow-up studies of groups of children who were apparently equally gifted show that some succeeded and some failed in later life, as judged by vocational and economic achievement. These divergent outcomes point to the importance of motivation or drive.

In Terman's genetic study of genius, a comparison of the successful and unsuccessful groups who were quite evenly matched in intelligence, shows that the successful group excelled the unsuccessful in integration toward goals, perseverance, and self-confidence; undertook more extracurricular and leadership activity in elementary school; and did superior work in high school.[96] From this phase of their study Terman and Oden concluded:

. . . intellect and achievement are far from perfectly correlated.

Why this is so, what circumstances affect the fruition of human talent, are questions of such transcendent importance that they should be investigated by every method that promises the slightest reduction of our present ignorance. So little do we know about our available supply of potential genius, the environmental factors that favor or hinder its expression, the emotional compulsions that give it dynamic quality or the personality distortions that make it dangerous.[97]

A Hierarchy of Motivations

Psychologically, the motivation of gifted children is complex; it involves much more than a simple physiological need or some external social pressure. Motives may be arranged in a hierarchy from the most deep-seated and pervasive to the most superficial and transient. Most basic is the drive toward "self-actualization"—the desire to develop one's potentialities, to make oneself as "good" and complete as possible. Almost equally deep-seated is the gifted child's desire to know—his curiosity about himself and his world. His self-concept is influenced by his life experiences, especially by the responses and expectations of persons who are close to him. The kind of person he thinks he is, and the kind of person he would like to be—these ideas are persistent and pervasive; they motivate much of his behavior and shape many of his values.

These basic motives underlie the more evident motives, or lack of positive motivation, that we observe in gifted children and adolescents: their "will to work" or "habits of idleness," their eagerness to learn or apathy, their intellectual curiosity or nonchalance, their determination to do well or merely "get by," their willingness to sacrifice present satisfactions for future goals or absorption in immediate pleasures.

In a sense, motives reside in the situation as well as in the individual. There are attractions and repulsions, rewards and punishments. But the influence of the situation depends upon the way the individual perceives it. Thus, by changing his perception of the situation we may modify his response to it. For example, Ausubel[98] found that children's "responsiveness to an incentive of personal prestige or recognition" might be on two levels: (1) a general level of competitive aspiration determined by personality organization and development; and (2) a specific level largely determined by factors of ego-involvement in the particular situation but influenced also by early experiences.

Case studies of gifted school children raise baffling questions about the conditions that are preventing them from realizing their potentialities.

> Alice, 16-years-old, was brought to a reading clinic by her father because, he explained, "She feels the need of help in reading." She especially wants to learn to read plays aloud at sight, without embarrassment. In her family, going to college is taken for

granted. However, her scholastic record in high school has been below average, and she scored at only the 25 percentile for her grade in reading comprehension on the Nelson-Denny Silent Reading Test. Alice feels that she entered high school poorly prepared in reading; she hopes to increase her speed without loss in comprehension. She wants to present herself as a person with no difficulties; she is not willing to admit mistakes. Yet she is afraid of failure and seems to be reading under great tension. She wants to succeed but takes no positive steps to correct her mistakes. Poor performance on reading exercises in class, constant self-comparison with classmates she feels are better students than she, unsuitable instruction in school, the attitude of her family toward her recent rejection by one of the well-known women's colleges— all these factors increase the very feeling of inadequacy that seems to be preventing her from putting forth maximum effort.

On the other hand, Alice has much to reinforce her self-esteem. She talks courteously and fluently. Her conversational vocabulary is mature; she uses and pronounces correctly such words as *prejudice, distinctions, complimentary.* She approaches a practice exercise with the reasonable question, "What am I reading this for?" She frequently makes comments such as these: "I find Shakespeare more interesting than the 'little dog and the rat' of the Gates Diagnostic Test." "I can't spell long hard words, but I don't want to express myself in words like that anyway."

In this case the worker's goals were to help Alice (1) to handle positively her deep anxiety about her reading and her generally low scholastic achievement, and (2) to build a clearer, realistic concept of herself. How would a person with her many good qualities handle these difficulties in reading? Not by denying them, but by learning how to correct them. The worker is ready to suggest suitable instruction and practice, by means of which Alice can progress with as little failure and frustration as possible. Alice's superior mental ability should aid her in solving this problem that involves both emotional stress and reading difficulty.

Case studies emphasize the importance of non-intellectual factors and reveal many subtle aspects of motivation and personality organization.

What Is the Dynamics of Their Development?

Early Childhood Experiences

Home is where one starts from. As we grow older
The world becomes stranger, the pattern more complicated
Of dead and living. Not the intense moment
Isolated, with no before and after,
But a lifetime burning in every moment
And not the lifetime of one man only
But of old stones that cannot be deciphered.[99]

Most of the gifted children in Terman's study had the advantage of growing up in well-to-do, intellectually stimulating environments. Some, however, were brought up in families with barely enough money to keep going. A few came from extremely wealthy families. In most cases, the family income was more than adequate to provide educational and cultural opportunities, although only one family in twelve had an income above $10,000. The mean amount of schooling for both fathers and mothers was four or five grades more than the average person. The gifted children had access at home to many more books than does the average child. Their parents were verbally minded: "words are their way of life."

The parents of the gifted were in the prime of life when the children were born. Thus the children suffered none of the disadvantages of immature parents on the one hand or, on the other, of parents whose age makes them too remote from the younger generation. There were few broken homes among these families. In general, the home conditions of the gifted children seemed to be distinctly superior to those of other children in the same neighborhoods.

Since the early years have such an effect on child development, the psychological climate in the homes of gifted children is of great importance. Parents who are in good health, free from serious financial worries, able to keep abreast of new developments in nutrition and child development, successful in keeping their home intact, permissive to the extent of allowing the child to progress in his own best way, firm in helping the child to meet reasonable social demands, and ready to listen and to answer questions—such parents seem likely to provide the affection, understanding, and stimulation that infants and young children need. These conditions enable the gifted child to get off to a good start.

At any stage in a gifted child's development, parent-child relations may confirm or deflect his developmental trend. Available evidence shows that infants who are seriously deprived of maternal affection and the normal stimulation that is provided by things to look at, listen to, and manipulate become apathetic little creatures. Under extreme deprivation, even a child who is born with superior ability to select experiences from his environment and to relate and organize them may fail to develop his potentialities. Moreover, he may fail to acquire that basic sense of trust in his world and in himself which helps him cope with his problems later on in life.

Similarly, the gifted child who, between the ages of one and three, is deprived of affection and of opportunities to explore his expanding world may fail to realize his intellectual and social potentialities. During this period the attitudes and expectations of the people who mean most in the child's life shape his personality development. Mothers of high-achieving boys were democratic in their attitudes and encouraged verbalization.[100] Even a gifted child may acquire a sense of unworthiness if he is constantly belittled. If he is excessively coerced and controlled, he may become either hostile or oversubmissive and dependent. The personal relations which he experiences during these early pre-school years largely determine how he handles the dependency-independency problem and whether he emerges with a comfortable sense of autonomy.

These predispositions, which are acquired in the early years, persist, especially if they are reinforced by subsequent experiences. They often determine the way in which a child perceives new situations. If he has successfully handled his early developmental tasks of gaining a sense of trust and appropriate independence, he is ready to explore the wider world of social relations and to become established in his masculine or feminine role, with all that this development involves. Emotional conflicts and distorted attitudes that become crystallized during this preschool period may block the all-round development of gifted children.

Unlike the majority of the parents in Terman's study, some parents seem indifferent to the child's success. They are definitely opposed to higher education on the grounds that going to college will keep the child from contributing to the family income and may make him feel superior to his own parents.

School Experiences

During the elementary school years, gifted children aged six to twelve have experiences that may either promote or impede their best development. Some unfavorable school conditions that foster habits of idleness and suppress enthusiasm for learning have already been mentioned. One gifted child, I.Q. 132, described the ideal educational program for the upper elementary grades as follows:

> I think the program should be quite varied, with recreational as well as educational things to do. . . . Pupils should have a chance to do projects for others, such as making things for hospitals, and so forth. Also, they should have a lot of creative work; this would be helpful later in showing the pupils what they like to do and what they don't. I think a sound program of arithmetic, grammar, and spelling should be taught. This always comes up later in life, and I think that if the pupils got a good knowledge of the fundamentals their work later would come a little easier.

Like other children, the gifted need the following experiences during the elementary school years: opportunities to relate themselves congenially to their classmates, to make their own rules and establish socially accepted standards of conduct, to be of service, to take responsibility for group enterprises, to learn fundamental skills, to do work suited to their ability, to match wits with their intellectual peers. They need ample time, appropriate materials of instruction, and freedom to learn and create and live happily with one another. When these experiences are not forthcoming, the gifted child at first feels frustrated; later he may become either antagonistic or indifferent.

Adolescent Problems of Adjustment

Adolescence is a time for sorting out childish ways of behaving and for cultivating more mature responses. The instability of this period is to be viewed as an opportunity, not a calamity. It is an opportunity for the child to develop a concept of his more acceptable self and to see clearly the knowledge and skills he needs to attain it. Many gifted adolescents view this in-between period with insight and optimism. In anonymous introspective compositions, they give us more insight into the dynamics of growing up than is found in most books on adolescent psychology.[101]

Gifted adolescents usually are a little earlier than average teen-agers in facing the adolescent tasks originally described by Leta S. Hollingworth and subsequently confirmed by later investigations. This applies especially to the task of working out a religion and a philosophy of life. Friendships formed in late adolescence often last a lifetime, and heterosexual relations established then frequently lead to marriage.

Many gifted adolescents need help in making their educational and vocational plans. Since their interests are wide, they sometimes have difficulty in choosing a vocation. One boy described his varied vocational interests as follows:

> At about the age of five, medicine appealed to me as a career. As the years passed, I wasn't so sure, but I gave it little thought as the future seemed so far away. In high school I have discovered that I derive pleasure from writing. I can say, with no intention to brag or show conceit, that I have done fairly well in it. Then again I have always been interested in science, especially chemistry. In my daydreams, I have seen myself a world-famous novelist or a great chemist working unselfishly for humanity. Although I have made no defiinite plans, I now feel that I've had some experience on which to make a sound choice.

Conflict between the parent's ambition for the child and the child's own vocational interest sometimes has profound emotional reverberations, as in the following instance:

> I feel sick and miserable when I think of my future. My mother wants me to teach. She thinks teaching is a respectable and needed occupation, and she tries to drive me into it. I don't want a restricted life. I want to be a musician. But I'm scared to tell her.

She always seems to laugh when I'm serious. I hate the sound of
her laugh and almost hate her for trying to force her plans upon
me. I don't want to hate her because she's really good and I love
her, honestly. When I play my beloved piano, time passes un-
heeded. While I am playing, there is only one future for me:
music.[102]

Some people have the unfortunate attitude that the gifted child should
be able to look out for himself. Since he has been lucky in his heredity
and early childhood experiences, they are not ready to give him the
same break that they would willingly accord to the mentally or physically handicapped.

At every stage of development, the path to better adjustment is open.
The personality patterns formed during the early years may change if
environmental conditions improve early enough in the life course. Only
when multiple negative factors continue to conspire against him does
the gifted child succumb to circumstances.[103] Pritchard describes two
highly gifted individuals who came from homes that would be labelled
economically submarginal; one was a broken home, and the other a home
in which there was a great deal of parental disharmony. The elementary
school teachers recognized that both of these children had serious problems of adjustment and tried to help them. But by the time the child
from the broken home was fifteen he had come into conflict with the
law. One completed high school; the other did not. Both are married;
both express dissatisfaction with their vocations; both are looking for
a chance to "get rich quick." Their grudge against society, coupled with
their superior potential ability, makes them threats to the social order.

A brighter picture is reflected by the vast majority of the gifted
children in Terman's study; for more than thirty years they have maintained and used, in socially acceptable ways, their high level of intellectual ability. Intensive and valuable as this study is, we need additional clinical studies of gifted children, which may reveal more of the
subtle dynamics of their successful progress into maturity.

The psychiatric case study, non-directive interview, and projective
techniques constitute promising methods of studying the personality
dynamics of gifted children. Little work has been done with the Rorschach Test. Mensh reviewed about fifty studies in which the Rorschach
was used; [104] only one of these dealt exclusively with Rorschach characteristics of gifted children. Seven-year-olds in a class for gifted children (Stanford-Binet I.Q.'s of 135-174 with a mean of 146) gave a
larger number of responses, more whole responses, and fewer detail
responses; and showed greater emotional maturity and a wider range of
interests than average children. The pattern of their responses indicated
that they were well adjusted.[105] A later study showed no significant

differences between average and gifted groups in the categories of Rorschach responses; [106] might this mean that as they have grown older the gifted have learned more effective responses for coping with their conflicts?

What Happens to Gifted Children?

Do "MENTALLY precocious kids grow up to be dopes"? Do they become more and more peculiar? Are they failures in later life?

Terman's developmental studies show clearly that most gifted children become gifted adults, that they are happily married and are successful in business or the professions. For people like this, who have high levels of ability, there is an increasing demand.

On intelligence tests the gifted show marked gains in mental age up to and beyond their sixteenth year. As they grow older, there is a widening gap between their mental ages and those of borderline and very dull individuals.

A comparison between the 150 most successful and the 150 least successful men thirty-five years or older in Terman's original group revealed characteristics that had been identified eighteen years earlier. The least successful received lower ratings for traits such as emotional stability, perseverance, self-confidence, and social adjustment.

However, far too many gifted children continue to fall by the educational wayside. In 1960, 71 per cent of the students (85 per cent boys and 64 per cent girls) in the upper 10 per cent of the high-school graduating classes in Indiana continued their education beyond high school. But this leaves 1,011 able students who did not go on.[107] Absence of motivation and lack of money are reported as the major reasons why students do not continue their education. Of those who do enter college, a large percentage fail to meet the academic standards. Witty highlights this unfortunate situation by an individual example:

At eight years of age, Bill's I.Q. was 182. Teachers predicted a brilliant career in science. Two years later the record read: "Exceptional ability; brightest boy in his class; strong interest in science." Today, without college training, he heads the credit department of a store.

Such waste of human resources might be prevented if teachers and parents learned to recognize gifted children early and to give them the guidance they need. The gifted child is characterized by his

. . . precocity in using words and sentences, extreme rapidity in learning and remembering, great sensitivity to various things in the immediate environment, interest in books, ability to tell a story and reproduce accurately a number of incidents or events, unusual imagination and resourcefulness, power of sustained attention, and versatility of interests. Creative ability, too, will be revealed as the child is given opportunities for varied experiences in the arts.[108]

What Are Some Implications for Their Education?

IT HAS been estimated that there are 1,500,000 gifted children in the United States, and that we are doing something for only 10 per cent of that number. The two main problems are: how to identify those "with high potentialities, wherever they are, and whatever early gifts they may have"; and what to do about them.

Although this chapter is not concerned with the education of gifted children, certain implications for their education may be summarized briefly.

Full use of our human resources should be made. Although "the promise of youth" seems to have been fulfilled in many cases, it is probable that very few, if any, of the gifted children who have been studied have developed to the full limits of their capacities. If they had had more affectionate and understanding parents; more challenging home, school, and college experiences; more capable, interesting, and perceptive teachers who maintained high standards of excellence; and greater stimulation from associating with their intellectual peers for part of the school day, they would have reached even higher levels of achievement.[109] Gifted children need someone, preferably the father in the case of boys, who will expect and help them to attain suitable standards. They need instructional material that evokes inventiveness. By grouping the gifted with their intellectual peers part of the time, and in a heterogeneous group the rest of the time, we can effectively meet both their social and their intellectual needs.[110] A certain amount of acceleration, individually determined, enables gifted children to contribute to society for a longer period of years. The gifted child needs special education because he is "keen intellectually with unusual insight, and is a sensitive person." [111] Without released time for supervision by the teacher and by various experts, it is difficult to make adequate provision for gifted children in the regular classroom. However, it is not impossible.[112] A large proportion of the gifted do not get a suitable preparation for life.

Children who are becoming too narrowly intellectual should be helped to achieve a more rounded development without sacrificing high achievement in the field in which they are most competent. By guiding them in planning a balanced program inclusive of creative work and play, social and solitary pursuits, and the use of varied avenues of learning, parents and teachers can help them to acquire the over-all maturity that is the source of superb achievement.

Notes

[1] L. M. Terman *et al.*, *Mental and Physical Traits of a Thousand Gifted Children, Genetic Studies of Genius* (Stanford, California: Stanford University Press, 1925), I. The first volume of a monumental study of gifted children. Comprehensive measurements show the group to be, on the average, more or less superior in educational achievement, health and physical development, and desirable personality traits, and to have a high percentage of famous relatives.

[2] C. M. Cox, *The Early Mental Traits of Three Hundred Geniuses, Genetic Studies of Genius*, ed. L. M. Terman (Stanford, California: Stanford University Press, 1926), II. A more intensive study of part of the gifted group described by Terman in 1925.

[3] B. S. Burks, D. W. Jensen, L. M. Terman *et al.*, *The Promise of Youth, Follow-up Studies of One Thousand Gifted Children, Genetic Studies of Genius* (Stanford, California: Stanford University Press, 1930), III. A brilliant follow-up study of Terman's original gifted group after a period of ten years.

[4] L. M. Terman, M. H. Oden, *et al.*, *The Gifted Child Grows Up: Twenty-five Years' Follow-up of a Superior Group, Genetic Studies of Genius* (Stanford, California: Stanford University Press, 1947), IV. The follow-up of the gifted group after twenty-five years reinforces the conclusions drawn from the earlier studies in the series.

[5] L. M. Terman and M. Hoden, *The Gifted Group at Midlife: Thirty-five Years' Follow-up of the Superior Child, Genetic Studies of Genius* (Stanford, California: Stanford University Press, 1959), V.

[6] L. A. Hollingworth, *Children Above 180 I.Q.: Origin and Development*, ed. H. L. Hollingworth (New York: Harcourt, Brace & World, Inc., 1942). The records of twelve children are presented, together with the author's interpretation of her observations of highly intelligent individuals.

[7] L. A. Hollingworth, *Gifted Children: Their Nature and Nurture* (New York: The Macmillan Company, 1926). A pioneer, authoritative publication on gifted children and the education they need if they are to make their maximum contribution to society.

[8] P. Witty, *A Study of One Hundred Gifted Children*, University of Kansas Bulletin of Education, II, No. 7 (Lawrence, Kansas: Bureau of School Service and Research, University of Kansas, 1930). An initial study of the characteristics of gifted children in the Kansas City, Missouri, Public Schools, together with a follow-up made five years later; in general, it corroborates Terman's *Genetic Studies of Genius*.

[9] M. R. Sumption, *Three Hundred Gifted Children* (New York: Harcourt, Brace & World, Inc., 1941). A follow-up study of the development of gifted pupils who had been in the special classes of the Cleveland schools. The emphasis in this study is educational rather than psychological.

[10] Catharine Cox Miles, "Gifted Children," in *Manual of Child Psychology*, 2nd ed., ed. Leonard Carmichael (New York: John Wiley & Sons, Inc., 1954), pp. 984-1063.

[11] Kenneth E. Anderson, ed., *Research on the Academically Talented Student* (Washington 6, D.C.: National Education Association of the United States, 1961), pp. 11-92.

[12] P. Witty, "How to Identify the Gifted," *Childhood Education*, XXIX, 7 (1953), 313.

[13] P. Witty, "Who Are the Gifted?" in *Education for the Gifted, Fifty-seventh Yearbook National Society for the Study of Education* (Chicago: University of Chicago Press, 1958), pp. 41-63.

[14] Z. Zubarsky, "What is Science Talent?" *Scientific Monthly*, LXVI (May 1948), 377-382.

[15] H. A. Carroll, *Genius in the Making* (New York: McGraw-Hill Book Co., Inc., 1940). The emphasis in this book is on the mental, social, and physical development of the intellectually gifted child. Full use is made of the results of research.

16 Frederick B. Davis, "Identification of the Intellectually Gifted," *Science Teacher*, XXVIII, 3 (1961), 45.

17 Ruth A. Martinson and Leon M. Lessinger, "Problems in the Identification of Intellectually Gifted Pupils," *Exceptional Children*, XXVI, 5 (1960), 227-231.

18 Paul E. Torrance, "Explorations in Creative Thinking," *Education*, LXXXI, 4 (1960), 216-220.

19 P. B. Medawar, *The Future of Man* (London, England: Methuen & Co., Ltd., 1960), pp. 78 and 86.

20 C. Burt, "General Introduction: The Gifted Child," in *The Yearbook of Education* (New York: Harcourt, Brace & World, Inc., 1962), p. 12.

21 J. Piaget, *The Origins of Intelligence in Children*, trans. M. Cook (New York: International Universities Press, Inc., 1952), p. 2.

22 *Ibid.*, p. 19.

23 B. McCandless, "Environment and Intelligence," *American Journal of Mental Deficiency*, LVI, 4 (1952), 679.

24 J. Piaget, *op. cit.*, p. 359.

25 B. Burks, "The Relative Influence of Nature and Nurture upon Mental Development," *Twenty-seventh Yearbook National Society for the Study of Education* (Chicago: University of Chicago Press, 1928), p. 309.

26 C. Burt, "General Introduction: The Gifted Child," *op. cit.*, p. 12.

27 Robert P. Crossley, "The Secret of Getting into Harvard," *McCall's Magazine*, LXXXVIII, 10 (July 1961), 45, 134-136.

28 M. D. Jenkins, "The Upper Limit of Ability Among American Negroes," *Scientific Monthly*, LXVI (1948), 399-401.

29 M. D. Jenkins, "Case Studies of Negro Children of Binet I.Q. 160 and Above," *Journal of Negro Education*, XII, 2 (1943), 159-166.

30 P. Witty and M. D. Jenkins, "The Educational Achievement of a Group of Gifted Negro Children," *Journal of Educational Psychology*, XXV, 8 (1934), 585-597.

31 J. Bahle, *Hans Pfitzner und der geniale Mensch: eine psychologishe Kulturkritik* (Konstanz: Curt Weller, 1949).

32 M. Pritchard, "Total School Planning for the Gifted Child," *Exceptional Children*, XVIII, 5 (1952), 146. See also total reference to Pritchard in *Exceptional Children*, Nos. 4-6 (1952), 107-110, 143-147, and 174-180, respectively. Describes concretely the committees which might be formed in a school system to plan for the education of gifted children.

33 David C. McClelland, "Issues in the Identification of Talent" in *Talent and Society*, eds. Donald C. McClelland, Alfred L. Baldwin, Urie Bronfenbrenner, and Fred L. Strodtbeck (Princeton, N.J.: D. Van Nostrand Co., Inc., 1958), pp. 1-28.

34 C. Burt, "General Introduction: The Gifted Child," *op. cit.*, pp. 26-31.

35 R. E. L. Faris, "Sociological Factors in the Development of Talent and Genius," *Journal of Educational Sociology*, IX, 9 (1936), 538-544.

36 W. D. Lewis, *A Study of Superior Children in the Elementary School*, Contributions to Education No. 266 (Nashville, Tennessee: George Peabody College for Teachers, 1940).

37 W. McGehee and W. D. Lewis, "The Socio-Economic Status of the Homes of Mentally Superior and Retarded Children and the Occupational Rank of Their Parents," *Pedagogical Seminary and Journal of Genetic Psychology*, XL, 2nd half (1942), 375-384.

38 R. J. Havighurst, "Conditions Productive of Superior Children," *Teachers College Record*, LXII, 7 (1961), 524-531.

39 D. C. McClelland, "Issues in the Identification of Talent," *op. cit.*, pp. 19-21.

40 L. Lucito and J. Gallagher, "Intellectual Patterns of Highly Gifted Children on the WISC," *Peabody Journal of Education*, XXXVIII, 3 (1960), 131-136.

41 Hollingworth, *Children Above 180 I.Q. Stanford-Binet*, *op. cit.*, p. 191.

42 *Ibid.*, p. 217.

43 H. C. McCurdy, "The Childhood Pattern of Genius" from *The Smithsonian Re-*

port for 1958, Publication 4373 (Washington, D.C.: Smithsonian Institute, 1958), pp. 527-542.

44 R. A. Tsanoff, *The Ways of Genius* (New York: Harper & Row, Publishers, 1949).

45 *Ibid.*, p. 7.

46 *Ibid.*, p. 23.

47 A. Juda, "The Relationship Between Highest Mental Capacity and Psychic Abnormalities," *American Journal of Psychiatry*, CVI, 4 (1949), 296-307.

48 *Ibid.*, p. 306.

49 Terman and Oden, *The Gifted Child Grows Up, op. cit.*, p. 288.

50 Hollingworth, *Children Above 180 I.Q. Stanford-Binet, op. cit.*, pp. 274-275.

51 C. Burt, "General Introduction: The Gifted Child," *op. cit.*, pp. 24-25.

52 Miriam L. Goldberg, "Recent Research on the Talented," *Teachers College Record*, LX, 3 (1958), 150-163.

53 Terman and Oden, *The Gifted Child Grows Up, op. cit.*, p. 20.

54 *Ibid.*, p. 25.

55 *Ibid.*, p. 29.

56 H. C. Lehman, "Young Thinkers and Great Achievements," *Journal of Genetic Psychology*, LXXIV, 2nd half (1949), 245-271.

57 Ann Marie Walsh, *Self Concept of Bright Boys with Learning Difficulties* (New York: Bureau of Publications, Teachers College, Columbia University, 1956).

58 C. Burt, "General Introduction: The Gifted Child," *op. cit.*, pp. 46-51.

59 J. C. Gowan, "Dynamics of the Underachievement of Gifted Students," *Exceptional Children*, XXIV, 3 (1957), 98 ff.

60 R. J. Havighurst, "Conditions Productive of Superior Children," *op. cit.*

61 E. A. Haggard, "Socialization, Personality, and Academic Achievement in Gifted Children," *School Review*, LXV, 4 (1957), 388-414.

62 R. A. McCracken, "Accelerating the Reading Speed of 6th Grade Gifted Children," *Exceptional Children*, XXVII, 1 (1960), 27-28.

63 D. G. Schubert, "How Gifted Junior High Students Attack Unknown Words," *California Journal of Educational Research*, X, 2 (1959), 90 ff.

64 E. P. Torrance, "Measurement and Development of the Creative Thinking Abilities," in *The Yearbook of Education* (New York: Harcourt, Brace & World, Inc., 1962), chap. 6.

65 J. W. Getzels and P. W. Jackson, "The Highly Intelligent and the Highly Creative Adolescent," in *The Third University of Utah Research Conference on the Identification of Creative Scientific Talent* (Salt Lake City, University of Utah Press, 1959), pp. 46-57.

66 R. Strang, *Helping Your Gifted Child* (New York: E. P. Dutton & Co., Inc., 1960). A book designed to help parents develop the potentialities of their gifted children.

67 R. L. Thorndike, "Performance of Gifted Children on Tests of Developmental Age," *Journal of Psychology*, IX, 2nd half (1940), 337-343.

68 Janet E. Bleckner, "The Responses of Average and Gifted Students on the Group Rorschach Test," *California Journal of Educational Research*, X, 5 (1959), 200-206.

69 R. Strang, "Manifestations of Maturity in Adolescents," *Mental Hygiene*, XXXIII, 4 (1949), 566.

70 W. L. Wilkins, "The Social Adjustment of Accelerated Pupils," *School Review*, XLIV, 6 (1936), 445-455.

71 R. K. Jarecky, "The Identification of Socially Gifted Adolescents," (Doctoral dissertation, Teachers College, Columbia University, 1958).

72 J. J. Gallagher, "Social Status of Children Related to Intelligence, Propinquity and Social Perception," *Elementary School Journal*, LVIII, 4 (1958), 225-231.

73 R. V. Miller, "Social Status and Socioempathic Differences among Mentally Superior, Mentally Typical, and Mentally Retarded Children," *Exceptional Children*, XXIII, 3 (1956), 114-119.

74 Meta F. Williams, "Acceptance and Performance among Gifted Elementary-

School Children," *Ohio State University Educational Research Bulletin*, XXXVII, 8 (1958), 216 ff.

[75] H. A. Grace and Nancy Lou Booth, "Is the 'Gifted' Child a Social Isolate?" *Peabody Journal of Education*, XXXV, 4 (1958), 195-196.

[76] R. Strang, "Inner World of Gifted Adolescents," *Journal of Exceptional Children*, XVI, 1 (1950), 100.

[77] Terman and Oden, *The Gifted Child Grows Up, op. cit.*, p. 108.

[78] D. A. Thom and N. Newell, "Hazards of the High I.Q.," *Mental Hygiene*, XXIX, 1 (1945), 61-77.

[79] M. E. Neville, "Brilliant Children: with Special Reference to Their Particular Difficulties," *British Journal of Educational Psychology*, VII, Part 1 (1937), 247-257.

[80] H. A. Murray, *Explorations in Personality* (New York: Oxford University Press, Inc., 1938).

[81] L. Kanner, "Emotional Interference with Intellectual Functioning," *American Journal of Mental Deficiency*, LVI, 4 (1952), 701-707.

[82] *Ibid.*, p. 702.

[83] Gertrude Hildreth, "Characteristics of Young Gifted Children," *Pedagogical Seminary and Journal of Genetic Psychology*, LIII, 2nd half (1938), 287-311.

[84] H. H. Davidson, *Personality and Economic Background: A Study of Highly Intelligent Children* (New York: King's Crown Press, 1943).

[85] W. McGehee and W. D. Lewis, "A Comparison of Certain Personality Characteristics of Mentally Superior and Mentally Retarded Children," *Journal of Educational Research*, XXXV, 8 (1942), 609.

[86] Terman and Oden, *The Gifted Child Grows Up, op. cit.*, p. 47.

[87] C. Burt, "General Introduction: The Gifted Child," *op. cit.*, pp. 40-41.

[88] H. J. Baker, "Characteristics of Superior Learners and the Relative Merits of Programs of Enrichment and Acceleration for Them" in *Classroom Techniques in Improving Reading*, ed. W. S. Gray, Supplementary Educational Monographs, No. 69 (Chicago: University of Chicago Press, 1949), pp. 153-157.

[89] *Ibid.*, p. 153.

[90] *Ibid.*

[91] *Ibid.*, p. 154.

[92] *Ibid.*

[93] *Ibid.*

[94] T. G. Alper and S. J. Korchin, "Memory for Socially Relevant Material," *Journal of Abnormal and Social Psychology*, XLVII, 1 (1952), 25-37.

[95] W. A. Brownell and H. Mosher, *Meaningful vs. Mechanical Learning* (Durham, N. C.: Duke University Press, 1949).

[96] Terman and Oden, *The Gifted Child Grows Up, op. cit.*, p. 342.

[97] *Ibid.*, p. 352.

[98] D. P. Ausubel, "Prestige Motivation of Gifted Children," *Genetic Psychology Monographs*, XLIII, 1st half (1951), 57.

[99] T. S. Eliot, *Four Quartets* (New York: Harcourt, Brace & World, Inc., 1944), p. 17.

[100] J. V. Pierce and Paul H. Bowman, "Motivation Patterns of Superior High School Students," in *The Gifted Student*, OE-35016 Cooperative Research Monograph No. 2, U. S. Office of Education, Department of Health, Education, and Welfare (Washington 25, D.C.: U. S. Government Printing Office, 1960), pp. 33-66.

[101] R. Strang, *The Adolescent Views Himself* (New York: McGraw-Hill Book Co., Inc., 1957).

[102] R. Strang, "Mental Hygiene of Gifted Children" in *The Gifted Child*, ed. Paul Witty (Boston: D. C. Heath & Company, 1951), p. 146.

[103] Pritchard, *op. cit.*, pp. 143-147.

[104] I. N. Mensh, "Rorschach Study of the Gifted Child: A Survey of the Literature," *Journal of Exceptional Children*, XVII (1950), 8-15.

[105] M. Gair, "Rorschach Characteristics of a Group of Very Superior Seven-Year-Old Children," *Rorschach Research Exchange*, VIII, 1 (1944), 31-37.

106 Janet E. Bleckner, "The Responses of Average and Gifted Students on the Group Rorschach Test," *op. cit.*

107 W. W. Wright, "Why Capable Indiana High School Students Do Not Continue Their Schooling" in *Higher Education, Incentives and Obstacles,* Invitational Conference on Encouraging Personal Incentive for Higher Education Among Talented but Disadvantaged Youth (Washington, D.C.: American Council on Education, 1960), pp. 67-73.

108 *Ibid.,* p. 21.

109 M. Krugman, "Identification and Preservation of Talent," *Teachers College Record,* LXI (1960), 459-463.

110 Mary Goldworth, "The Effects of an Elementary School Fast-learner Program on Children's Social Relationships," *Exceptional Children,* XXVI, 2 (1959), 59-63.

111 N. B. Scharer, "How Can the School Meet the Needs of Gifted and Superior Students?" *Bulletin of the National Association of Secondary-School Principals,* XXXVI, 185 (1952), 99-109.

112 J. J. Gallagher and Thora Crowder, "The Adjustment of Gifted Children in the Regular Classroom," *Exceptional Children,* XXIII, 7 (1957), 306 ff.

EMORY L. COWEN

Department of Psychology
University of Rochester
    and

MATTHEW J. TRIPPE

Department of Special Education
George Peabody College for Teachers

11 *Psychotherapy and Play Techniques with the Exceptional Child and Youth*

CONCERTED INTEREST in the use of psychotherapeutic methods with the disabled is a relatively recent development. It is, in all probability, a logical consequence of events in the field of rehabilitation subsequent to World War II. With increased attempts in the direction of total rehabilitation for the disabled and an awareness that the psychological aspects of disability may be more of a problem than the physical aspects, considerable attention has been directed to study of the sociopsychological aspects of disability.[1] Following an extensive survey [2] of publications dealing with the effects of physical disability on personality and behavior, Barker stated ". . . physically disabled persons more frequently than physically normal ones exhibit behavior which is commonly termed maladjusted." [3] This conclusion is in keeping with the notion that impaired functioning and negative social evaluation represent additional problems with which disabled people must contend in their attempts to achieve maximally effective functioning. Reference to the increased prevalence of maladjustment among the disabled provides support for the plea to make psychotherapeutic services more readily available for this group. Although more recent research findings suggest that the relation between disability and disturbance is not simple or direct, the need for widespread utilization of effective psychiatric, psychological and social-work services with the disabled is indicated to the extent that further research supports the generalization made by Barker.

We shall attempt to survey critically the available studies in psychotherapy and play conducted with the exceptional child, in order to determine what has been accomplished and to achieve a better understanding of future service and research needs. Since psychotherapeutic methods used with the handicapped may be identical to or considerably overlap those developed with the non-handicapped, it seems appropriate to begin by considering the general nature of psychotherapy and the play techniques that have been developed for the latter group.

The Nature of Psychotherapy

Psychotherapy Defined

Very probably, universal agreement on a single definition of psychotherapy would be impossible. The types of activities that are labeled psychotherapy by workers vary considerably along many dimensions. For example, one well-accepted, broad distinction is made between the so-called intensive and supportive types of psychotherapy, each of which involves basically different objectives and techniques.[4] Several others propose that only the psychoanalytic and psychoanalytically oriented therapies may be truly classified as intensive psychotherapies.[5] When we add to this the many differences in philosophies and techniques among various schools of psychotherapy,[6] the difficulties involved in settling upon a completely satisfactory definition become more apparent. One inclusive definition, which might be expected to have fairly widespread acceptability, was proposed by Snyder, who defined "psychotherapeutic counseling" as:

> . . . a face to face relationship in which a psychologically trained individual is consciously attempting by verbal means to assist another person or persons to modify emotional attitudes that are socially maladjusted, and in which the subject is relatively aware of the personality reorganization through which he is going.[7]

Group therapy may be seen as falling within Snyder's definition, but certain other kindred procedures, though essentially therapeutic in nature, would not be classified primarily as *psycho*therapies; for instance, physical and chemical therapies, environmental therapies, art, music and occupational therapies, book and film therapies, all of which are essentially non-verbal in nature. Play therapy also falls somewhat outside this definition because it is largely non-verbal, and because the child is frequently quite unaware of the personality reorganization through which he is going. The limitation here, however, relates to the nature of the child rather than to the theory or purpose of the therapy and, as such, play therapy is an area of major interest in the present review. Educational procedures and guidance activities, however, are not considered primarily psychotherapeutic because of their frequent emphasis on information-giving, as opposed to modification of emotional attitudes.

Countless other definitions of psychotherapy have been proposed.[8] In citing a specific definition, we seek only a broad common understanding of the meaning of the concept and, roughly, to designate approaches which will be emphasized in our review of work with the handicapped.

Objectives of Psychotherapy

It is only at a very gross level that we may speak of common objectives in psychotherapy. Illustratively, Shaffer and Lazarus stated, ". . . the objective of psychotherapy . . . is to secure the soundest degree of mental or psychological health that is possible." [9] Stated otherwise, the single goal which all psychotherapies share is that of doing the most to promote optimal mental health in any patient. Beyond that common goal, objectives differ considerably from one type of psychotherapy to another. In the intensive, or uncovering types, we seek to effect basic personality changes. It is hoped that such changes will be the consequence of the insights deriving from the uncovering of the relatively deeply rooted bases of the patient's difficulties. By contrast, in the supportive psychotherapies we do not seek to produce a major personality change, nor do we ordinarily anticipate that the patient will be entirely able to deal satisfactorily with difficulties that may arise subsequent to therapy.

Fromm-Reichmann cogently summarized the different objectives in the two approaches:

> The goal of intensive psychotherapy . . . is . . . alleviation of patient's emotional difficulties in living and elimination of the symptomatology, this goal to be reached by gaining insight into and understanding of the unconscious roots of the patient's problems, the genetics and the dynamics . . . whereby such understanding may frequently promote changes in the dynamic structure of the patient's personality.
>
> The therapeutic goal of intensive psychotherapy is in contradistinction to the aim of other important psychotherapeutic methods

and techniques. . . . Their goal is to cure symptoms and effect social recoveries. They operate without promoting personality changes and without producing insight into the genetics and dynamics of a patient's problems, or they center upon only a limited focal amount of insight.[10]

The emphasis in supportive psychotherapy thus is on buttressing existing defenses. It is most widely used when time is extremely limited and with patients who, either by virtue of chronicity of illness and tenuous adjustment are considered poor risks for intensive psychotherapy, or where an otherwise psychologically sound individual is confronted with a largely situational maladjustment.[11]

By these criteria most of the reported work in psychotherapy with the handicapped has been essentially supportive in nature.

Common Denominators in the Process of Psychotherapy

It has frequently been observed that each of the schools of psychotherapy succeeds in helping some people.[12] This suggests the presence of certain common denominators which, if not absolutely universal, are at least usual in all forms of psychotherapy. What are these common factors?

Whether or not the client is willing to assume responsibility for such action, the common starting point for psychotherapy is an individual seeking help. Though clients vary considerably in terms of dissatisfaction with their pre-therapy adjustment as well as in their motivation for change, most experts would regard the seeking of help per se as the first important factor in psychotherapy.[13]

All forms of psychotherapy have at their core a relationship between therapist and client. It is in this relationship that we probably find the single most fundamental common denominator in psychotherapy.[14] Frequently we are inclined to differentiate psychotherapies on the basis of utilization of specific configurations of therapeutic techniques. In doing so we tend to overlook the fact that techniques take on meaning only from the context in which they emerge—the therapeutic relationship. The essence of therapy is not the response of the client to therapeutic techniques, whether interpretive, reflective, or persuasive; it is his response to another person. A crucial determining factor in client movement will therefore be the impact of the therapist's personality upon the client —his warmth, sensitivity, understanding, spontaneity, and empathy—in short, the ability of the therapist to create a maximally facilitating psychotherapeutic atmosphere. The emphasis on the therapeutic importance of the therapist's personality as contrasted to his technique was cogently stated by Rosenzweig:

> Given a therapist who has an effective personality and who con-
> sistently adheres in his treatment to a system of concepts which
> he has mastered and which is in one significant way or another
> adapted to the problems of the sick personality, it is of compara-
> tively little consequence which particular method the therapist
> uses.[15]

Since the personal attributes which contribute to the establishment of
an effective relationship do not belong exclusively to the adherents of
any one school of therapy, the fact that all methods of psychotherapy
report successful treatment becomes highly understandable.

Support for the notion that the relationship is a basic common aspect
of diverse approaches to psychotherapy is found in a series of studies
reported by Fiedler.[16] When therapists of various persuasions were asked
to describe an ideal therapeutic relationship, greater agreement was found
among expert therapists representing different schools, than among experienced and inexperienced therapists of any given school. The statement, "The therapist is able to participate in the patient's communication," was reported as most characteristic of an ideal therapeutic
relationship. Included among the group of statements classified as very
characteristic were the following: "The therapist's tone of voice conveys
the complete ability to share the patient's feeling," and "The therapist
is well able to understand the patient's feelings." [17]

A factor variously described as catharsis, expression of feeling, or
release of emotional tensions represents still another important general
feature of psychotherapy. Largely as a function of the therapeutic atmosphere, the patient is able to release pent-up emotional tension that
he has not been able to express elsewhere. Though the intensity of
release varies among individuals, expression of feeling, or catharsis,
probably occurs to some extent in almost all psychotherapeutic experiences.

Psychotherapy also involves the systematic utilization of a group of
therapeutic techniques by a therapist. Although specific techniques vary
as a function of objectives and philosophy of psychotherapy,[18] the existence of what Rosenzweig referred to as a "formal consistency of therapeutic responses and belief in a systematic position . . ." may constitute
an important general therapeutic factor.[19] Quite possibly the client reacts
at a rather subtle level to the security which a therapist feels about his
operating principles. Less direct than a formal set of operating techniques but nevertheless of considerable importance in psychotherapy are
the non-verbal aspects of the interaction between client and therapist—
facial expressions, postural change, inflections, gestures, and the like.[20]
These frequently understudied behaviors doubtless contribute profoundly to the basic relationship and give meaning to the verbal be-

havior of both client and therapist. As such, they constitute a basic common factor in all approaches.

At least several other common features are likely to be observed in instances of successful psychotherapy. To the extent that these factors are present, we are more likely to have successful psychotherapy, and to the extent they are missing, it would be difficult to conceive of significant psychotherapeutic gain. The first of these is the achievement of insight, a term used broadly to refer to some change in self-understanding or increase in self-awareness by the client. Watson's comments on this point are pertinent:

> In psychotherapy there should be an enlargement of the patient's understanding of himself, of the relation of his symptoms to his personality pattern and of his relation to other persons. . . . The insight achieved is directly relevant to the treatment goals. It may be an essentially modest one—the realization of one's limitations and abilities in relation to some particular problem—or it may be wider in scope, such as a veritable reconstruction of the personality of the patient.[21]

Behavior change in real life situations is another further common denominator in psychotherapy. This is generally seen as consequent to the achievement of insight. Rogers referred to this as the phase of positive action—first at a minute level and ultimately in terms of "integrated positive action on the part of the client." [22] On this point Shaffer and Lazarus said, "The success in the psychotherapeutic hour is in part a rehearsal which must be followed by actual performance. No insight or emotional discharge can be as rewarding as accomplishment in real life." [23] We may regard the implementation of positive action as one barometer of psychological growth that has taken place in psychotherapy.

Notwithstanding obvious divergencies in objectives and techniques, it seems possible to delineate a common core of factors which may be found in all approaches to psychotherapy. These common denominators constitute the essence of therapy—the factors which lie behind reports of successful treatment by all schools. They may be summarized as follows: (1) a person seeking psychological help; (2) a unique client-therapist relationship; (3) an opportunity for release (catharsis) of emotional tension; (4) a formally consistent body of therapeutic techniques; (5) the impact of non-verbal communications and the personality of the therapist. Two other factors, though not necessarily common to all instances of psychotherapy, are at least to be found in instances of successful psychotherapy: (1) a reorganization of self-understanding (insight), leading to (2) psychological growth and the initiation of positive changes in behavior.

Play Techniques and Psychotherapy with Children

IN SEVERAL important respects psychotherapeutic methods and techniques used with adults have not been found to be entirely translatable to work with children. Because of certain special problems that children present in therapy, it has been necessary to develop new and more appropriate techniques in working with them. One of the most important differences between adults and children is the relative lack of development of verbal expression in the child. As many authors have noted, play constitutes a natural and spontaneous medium of expression for the child.[24] Hence much therapeutic work with children, especially with young children, has been built around play activities, and has come to be known as play-therapy.

The term "play-therapy" has proven so popular that it has become a substitute for the more generic concept of psychotherapy with children. Some workers, however, continue to distinguish between the two, regarding play as but one of many techniques used in psychotherapy with children. Illustratively, Watson stated, "Play is merely one way of allowing the therapist to interact with a child patient." [25] It would be inaccurate then, to speak of play as the sole method of therapy with children, although practically speaking it is, at the very least, one extremely important and widely used approach with that group. Thus Jackson and Todd reported, "Whether play predominates or is only an adjunct to treatment, it is now accepted as the best method of access to the young child." [26]

Objectives in Psychotherapy with Children

Actually the objectives of psychotherapy with children, certainly at a gross level, are quite similar to those in adult psychotherapy, that is, to facilitate the maximal improvement in the child's adjustment within a given set of circumstances. As with adults, however, specific objectives in therapy with children vary considerably in different situations.[27] Jackson and Todd distinguished between two types of play-therapy, one designed to provide for abreaction or release in connection with a circumscribed situational problem or traumatic experience, and the other for "those in whom there is a slow-growing but subtle personality change extending over years." [28] In this distinction we may find a partial parallel to some differences between supportive and intensive psychotherapies with adults. Watson used the following terms to describe extreme points of a continuum of approaches to play-therapy: "active" or "passive," "controlled" or "free," and "standardized" or "spontaneous." [29] In contrast to the "passive," "free," and "spontaneous" situations, the "active," "controlled," and "standardized" situations are characterized in terms of greater intercession by the therapist, as well as by more specific focalized therapeutic objectives. Differential emphases in objectives among various schools of psychotherapy with children add to the difficulties involved in attempting a universally acceptable statement of specific objectives in child therapy.

Differences Between Children and Adults: The Need for Play Techniques

It seems appropriate to examine somewhat more carefully certain differences between children and adults so that we may better understand the bases for change in therapeutic methods and the widespread use of play techniques with children.[30] One important difference between children and adults occurs in the approach to the therapy situation. In most instances the adult enters into a psychotherapeutic relationship because he wishes, for any one of a number of reasons, to change himself. This is not usually the case with the child, who more typically is directed into therapy by an adult, with little or no information about why he is there. The adult is likely to be aware of certain common goals that he shares with the therapist and is relatively sensitive to the personality reorganization which is taking place. For the child, however, there may be little knowledge of the purpose of the periodic therapy contacts and a lack of feeling of common striving with the therapist.

A second difference of fundamental importance between children and adults is the relative lack of verbal development in the child. If we were to go no further than these differences, we would already have two powerful reasons for the development of play techniques in therapy with children. In the first instance, since the child is generally not motivated or even necessarily oriented towards personal change, much of the motivation, if he is to remain in therapy, must come from the intrinsic gratifications of the situation itself. Talking about himself to an adult may not be an especially enjoyable diversion for the young child. Play, on the other hand, is both natural and pleasant. It can, because of its inherent appeal to the child, motivate him to continue in the therapy situation. Second, if therapy is to take place, expression and communication are necessary, and in these regards the child's relative lack of verbal development is a limiting factor. Through his spontaneous play and nonverbal behaviors, however, it is possible for him to give expression to his problems and conflicts and to communicate with the therapist. These two fairly basic differences between children and adults have pointed to the development of play techniques as a preferred method of therapy with children.

Slavson cited several additional differences between children and adults which further underscore the potential value of play techniques for children. Illustratively, the child is considerably more impulsive than the adult; he is less subject to repressive forces and more willing to ". . . act out and speak about matters that are embarrassing to an older person"; [31] his fantasy life is closer to the surface; his attention span is shorter; he is more concerned with locomotion and expression, and physical activity is of greater importance to him.

In an attempt to determine some of the conditions attending the use of play as a therapeutic medium, Filmer-Bennett and Hillson [32] reported on the responses of 118 child clinics to a questionnaire designed for this purpose. Surprisingly, 68 per cent of the clinics reported the use of play with children 12-15 years of age. Concerning the purposes of play, 77 per cent reported that it is used to facilitate the patient-therapist interaction in preparation for "straight" psychotherapy.

Other differences between adults and children warrant consideration although, unlike the preceding differences, they are not necessarily factors that have led to the development of play techniques. The young child, because he is still in the process of developing, tends to be more plastic than the adult and probably has a greater potential for change. His resistance and defenses are likely to be less deeply rooted, and he may be more amenable to opportunities for modification and new learning inherent in the therapy situation.[33] Several authors have pointed out that, because the child's ego organization is weaker and his ego boundaries are more elastic, he tends to be more fluid than the adult. There is greater lability, inconsistency of behavior, and intermingling of reality and fantasy in the child.[34] Consequently there is likely to be less continuity in the over-all course of child therapy, or in any given session, during which frequent shifting from one activity to another, from fantasy to reality, and from deeper to more peripheral aspects of the problem, is to be expected.

A final important difference between children and adults concerns their respective levels of dependency. The adult is relatively independent in that his therapy experience does not typically involve collateral contact with other people. This is not true for the child, who is highly dependent on one or more adults—most frequently the parents. Therapy with the child usually starts because he has been referred by an adult. At several stages in the child's therapy experience, direct involvement of some adult on whom he is dependent may be required (as an informant in describing the nature of the problem situation or in matters of on-going evaluation of therapeutic progress, and possible conjunctive environmental change).[35]

A very important issue in this area is that of parallel therapeutic contacts with the parent. Most experts would agree that the problems of the child are usually closely interwoven with those of other family members, and that coordinate treatment of parents is essential. Illustratively, Slavson wrote, "There are psychotherapists, especially psychoanalysts, who are convinced that little can be done therapeutically for young children without basically altering the personality of the mother. There is ample foundation for this belief." [36] Similarly, Jackson and Todd stated that ". . . change is not likely to be permanent unless a considerable modification in the parents' outlook is also achieved, and their influence on the child is fundamentally altered." [37] Other therapists regard collateral parent treatment as perhaps helpful, but not necessary. Thus Axline stated, ". . . *It is not necessary for adults to be helped in order to insure successful play-therapy results.*" [38] More recently, Anna Freud stated that the necessity of providing therapy for parents is only one of a number of possible approaches making for beneficial change, prevention, and enlightenment.[39] She suggested that therapy for the mother is appropriate in those instances where the mother's and the child's pathology are interrelated and in cases where the child's pathology reflected deprivation of mothering even though the mother is with the child. In cases of the latter type, the mother's disturbance is so incapacitating that she is unable to provide adequate mothering for her child. For other types of cases, Freud recommended: (1) guidance for the parents to assist them in understanding the child's treatment, (2) therapeutic guidance for mothers of handicapped children, (3) helping a mother to guide her own child through treatment, and finally, (4) influencing the socially accepted and prevalent patterns of child rearing. Concerning this last point, she stated,

> For the child guidance clinic this opens up the possibility of playing a part in the setting up of new traditions . . . they have gained the confidence of the public already where the treatment of problem children is concerned. It should not be difficult for them to establish a similar position of trust with regard to the handling of normal children during the all-important first four or five years of life, very much in the manner in which the well-baby clinics have established their traditions with regard to the healthy infants' physical needs. This will be slow work, supplanting gradually what is left of religious, national, and class traditions, but it will be no less effective so far as influence on the mothers is concerned.[40]

Despite some disagreement, then, as to its necessity, it would seem desirable to determine for each case if some type of coordinate parent service is needed and, if it is needed, to provide that type which is most appropriate. Work with parents is probably of even greater importance when we are dealing with the exceptional child. This point will be amplified in a later section.

Essential Aspects of Play-Therapy

Overlooking special emphases and biases of any given persuasion, the basic constants of play-therapy include: the relationship, opportunities for expression, and a configuration of therapeutic techniques.

Probably the area of greatest agreement among child therapists representing different schools, would be in the fundamental importance of the therapist-child relationship. So significant is this factor that one approach to psychotherapy with children has been called "relationship therapy." [41] Other approaches, whether eclectic, non-directive, or psychoanalytic, while differing considerably in practice, have agreed on the crucial therapeutic role of the relationship. Strong emphasis is given to this point by Witmer, who in her volume on child therapy devoted a full chapter to its careful enunciation. Referring to the therapist-child relationship Witmer stated, "It . . . is the underlying dynamic, and upon its proper use most of therapy depends." [42] Similarly, Despert, in trying to account for the successful results obtained by various schools of child therapy, commented, ". . . In all approaches, a common element is found, which is the therapist-patient relationship." [43] Important as the patient-therapist relationship is in psychotherapy with adults, it is probably of even greater significance in work with children because of the relative reduction of verbal interchange in the latter situation.

Although there is little disagreement about the basic importance of the therapeutic relationship, it would probably be somewhat more difficult to obtain complete agreement on the nature of the ideal child-therapist relationship. Nevertheless there is considerable overlap in the writings of representatives of various schools on this point. Illustratively, Witmer, writing from a psychiatric frame of reference, summarized the important elements in the therapist's attempt to establish a relationship, as follows:

> They are friendly and kind and keenly sensitive to the child's moods, actions, and words. They may anticipate his fears and doubts, and explicitly or, more likely, by implication let him know that his ideas will receive serious attention. They are very careful to be non-judgmental, neither condemning nor praising, but receiving all information in an accepting manner and permitting free expression of feeling and opinion even if the accompanying behavior has to be forbidden. They define for the child, in one way or another, what therapy is to consist of and they are then careful to allow him freedom of choice, even if he chooses to be totally non-communicative or, after some experience with therapy, to withdraw from treatment. [44]

It is both surprising and encouraging that Axline's description of the essential elements of the non-directive play-therapy relationship is so similar to Witmer's statement. In her summary of the basic principles of non-directive play-therapy, Axline stressed the development of a warm, friendly relationship, the establishment of a feeling of permissiveness in the child so that he will be able to give complete expression to his feelings, total acceptance of the child as he is, a non-judgmental attitude, and a willingness to allow the child to lead the way.[45] Doubtless these two statements of the nature of the relationship in therapy with children are reasonably representative of current thinking.

Closely related to questions of relationship is the significance of non-verbal aspects of psychotherapy with children. Since play-therapy proceeds with considerably less verbalization than does psychotherapy with adults, its nonverbal aspects assume a more central position. This, as Watson has indicated, is a two-way proposition. The therapist must be particularly sensitive to the child's facial expression, postural adjustments and expressive movements, since these may be the child's major channels of expression. The child, in turn, reacts to similar non-verbal behaviors of the therapist.[46] Thus, Moustakas commented: "What the therapist says and does is important. How he feels is even more important." [47]

Although most workers would agree that the opportunity for free expression is another essential element in play-therapy, there is nonetheless an issue as to the need for limiting such expression. Ginott pointed out the divergent opinion on the use of limits and related the differences of opinion to the definition of permissiveness employed by different workers.[48] Permissiveness may mean the acceptance of any and all behaviors that the child may display or it may refer to the acceptance of symbolic behavior. Ginott argued that limits are necessary. He presented six reasons for the use of limits in play-therapy and a discussion of the technique of limit setting. Ginott and Lebo [49] studied the use of limits in play-therapy by therapists of differing theoretical orientation. The results of questionnaires sent to psychoanalytic, non-directive and "other" types of therapists indicated that therapists of varied orientations did not differ in the number of limits employed.

Axline spoke of play-therapy as ". . . an opportunity which is given to the child to 'play out' his difficulties." [50] The child's ability to give expression to his feelings derives in part from the relationship that has been established and in part from the construction of the playroom and the choice of play materials. They should be planned to facilitate expression. Many suggestions along these lines have been made.[51]

The playroom should be built to withstand plenty of wear and tear (washable walls and floors, protected glass, and so on). Privacy of location and sound-proofing may reduce the necessity of unduly restricting vocal expression. Running water, a sand box, and a platform stage for psychodramatic activities, have been found to encourage expressive play, as have certain play materials. Included in the latter group are various "expressive media"—plasticene and clay, water color and finger paints, crayons, scissors and cutting paper, and a blackboard with chalk; "outlets for aggressive activity"—punching bags, knives, balloons, military equipment, soldiers, vehicles, and planes; "doll play facilities"—a doll house fully furnished, dolls representing various family members, a wide variety of other types of dolls including amputation dolls, wetting dolls, and rag dolls, puppets, and masks; "household items"—pots, brooms, mops, rags, utensils, and baby carriage; "regressive toys"—nursing bottles, nipples, and rattles. While successful play-therapy can take place without some or many of these materials, their presence tends to encourage freer expression in diverse problem areas.

The final essential element in play-therapy is a specific pattern of therapeutic behaviors and techniques. It is primarily on the basis of these differences in techniques that we distinguish various approaches to play-therapy. Some child therapists rely heavily on interpretation, others prefer reflection of feeling, and so on. Despite these differences in techniques there remains a certain internal consistency in the verbal behaviors of each therapist, which may help to make the child feel more secure in the therapy situation.

A steady series of recent contributions continues to deal with a variety of aspects of play-therapy. Ginott [52] has provided us with an excellent review and critique of its current status. This investigator, after reviewing studies of process and outcome, cites the need for more critical research in demonstrating the effectiveness of play techniques. Gondor [53] has discussed the importance of understanding and the use of fantasy material for investigating crucial conflict areas and for evaluating the course therapy is taking. Solomon [54] has considered the dynamics of psychoanalytic play-therapy and in particular has stressed the importance of interpretations made to the child. Hambridge [55] has presented an excellent exposition of structured play-therapy, while Kaplan, Ryan, Nathan, and Bairos [56] have proposed that with delinquents a true therapeutic relationship can be established by controlling acting-out behavior, thereby building-up anxiety. Lebo and Lebo,[57] in an experimental study, have concluded that child's age and the level of aggression affect his responses to the non-directive play-therapy situation. Moustakas [58] found that more frequent and more intense negative attitudes were expressed in play-therapy by disturbed children than by their matched but well-adjusted peers.

Collectively, the foregoing contributions reflect a continuing and active interest in the process of play-therapy as well as in its outcome. Though we cannot yet be assured of the over-all level of its effectiveness or of particular favored areas for its applicability, current clinical investments in this type of activity remain substantial.

Group Psychotherapy

An important trend in the field of psychotherapy is the use of group procedures either exclusively or in combination with individual therapy. Much of the therapeutic work that has been done with adults and children, the disabled, and the physically normal has been conducted in a group setting. Activities in this direction are on the upswing. It is at once obvious that increased demands for service can be more realistically met through group therapy and, in addition, there is some suggestion that group procedures may possess specific advantages under certain sets of circumstances or in instances where individual therapy has been ineffective. Axline, for example, proposed that where the child's problems are centered primarily in the area of social adjustment, group therapy is likely to be more helpful than individual treatment.[59] Slavson, as a result of careful exploration of the potential uses of group approaches to psychotherapy, has developed four different types of group therapy situations for young children and adolescents, each suited to a particular age group and a particular type of problem. He has found these group situations to be quite effective in dealing with a wide variety of problems.[60]

In his presentation of a theoretical framework for group play-therapy, Ginott observed that the inner experience responsible for curative effects is the same in all therapies and proposed five questions which must be answered in evaluating a particular therapeutic approach.[61] In his analysis, group play-therapy has unique advantages over individual play-therapy in establishing a therapeutic relationship, promoting catharsis (expression of feeling), achieving insight, providing opportunities for reality testing, and facilitating the development of sublimations. Other child therapists have not been nearly so enthusiastic concerning the usefulness of group therapy, claiming that it is, at best, of limited usefulness. Illustratively, Jackson and Todd stated, "In our opinion, all deeper psychological treatment ought to be individual. Groups can be used to help children whose difficulties are mainly due to their environment rather than to deep-seated inner conflicts." [62]

The issue is not necessarily a popularity poll of the virtues of group versus individual procedures. Both may be used in combination in any particular instance. Brammer and Shostrom reported Buhler's suggestion of four basic alternatives which vary in the relative emphasis placed on group methods when used together with individual methods.[63]

In our review of psychotherapy and play techniques with the exceptional child we shall refer frequently to group therapeutic work with handicapped individuals. There is ample reason to believe that for the disabled such an approach may provide some unique and important benefits.

Applications to Exceptional Children

IT HAS been frequently observed that the exceptional child must adjust not only to those problems which he shares with all other children, but also to emotional difficulties that stem more directly from his disability.[64] All exceptional children are not equally successful in making these adjustments. Some, in spite of their additional problems, adapt quite satisfactorily and perhaps even better than many physically normal children. Others fare less well. Certainly there is no automatic relationship between either incidence or degree of disability and presence or extent of maladjustment. Other things being equal, however, the exceptional child is likely to be confronted with a greater number of adjustive difficulties because of the additional problems growing out of his disability. Hollingshead remarked, "Severe physical handicap places intrinsic limitations on the child in his attempts to reach the ordinary life goals of his age group." [65] One might expect, on this basis, that the relative prevalence of maladjustment should be higher in a randomly selected group of disabled individuals than in an otherwise similar but physically normal group. The results of research on this question are not nearly so clear and appear to be due to different investigators' employing different methods with different samples. When this is considered with the problem of specifying and measuring maladjustment, it is not surprising that these studies do not permit unequivocal generalization. More hopeful are those studies directed towards the delineation of characteristic personality problems of specified groups of disabled children and adults. Since it may be now concluded that the relationship between disability and personality is not a direct one,[66] more studies of the type reported by Mussen and Newman are needed.[67] After detailed study of previous research, two hypotheses related to dependency and achievement were investigated by studying two groups of 15 children, each selected from a total sample of 79 handicapped children. So far as the investigators could determine, the two groups differed only in the quality of personal adjustment and did not differ significantly from each other in other important factors. The disabling conditions present in both groups included poliomyelitis, cerebral palsy, and muscular dystrophy. The authors concluded that personal adjustment appeared to be enhanced by the acceptance of dependency needs and by aspirations to achieve realistic goals. They suggested that warm, permissive parent-child relationships, together with parental understanding of the disability, may foster the development of this desirable motivational pattern. Studies of this type appear to point the way to the kinds of procedures necessary to prevent the development of personal problems, as well as to the types of interventions that will be needed to deal with such problems.

Certainly there is no reason to believe that maladjustment is any less prevalent among the disabled than it is among the non-handicapped. This alone is sufficient reason for great concern over the technical development and the availability of psychotherapy and other promising provisions for reducing the almost intolerable tensions, anxieties and conflicts which are to be found in disturbed disabled children and youth.

Sensory Defect

Although research on the application of psychotherapy and play techniques in instances of sensory defect is extremely limited, there is increased awareness of the need for additional work in this area. Levine commented on the usefulness of psychotherapy with the deaf and pointed out some problems in its application.[68] On several occasions, Lowenfeld has called attention to the potential usefulness of psychotherapy for the blind.[69] Therapeutic techniques are viewed as promising not only for the treatment of severely disturbed children with sensory defects but also from the point of view of preventing the development of problems and promoting wholesome development.

Only a few published reports of work in psychotherapy or play-therapy with children having sensory defects are available. Omwake and Solnit presented an account of the treatment of a congenitally blind child.[70] Treatment was started at the age of three and one-half and had continued through the age of seven, when the report was made. The therapist was the nursery school director; her role initially had been conceived as that of a teacher. During the second year of treatment, conflicts emerged which required specialized assistance. Rather than transfer the child to another person, therapy was continued by the nursery school director under the supervision of a child analyst. An educational program was also provided by another person. This report included a detailed case presentation, an account of the therapeutic process, and a discussion of the child's major difficulties as they appeared in treatment, with implications for her development. There is a theoretical discussion of the effects of blindness on development and the value of therapeutic and educational measures.

Axline presented an account of the therapeutic treatment of a severely

disturbed nine-year-old boy who was almost totally blind.[71] This youngster was included on an experimental basis in a non-directive play group
with four other disturbed but physically normal boys. All were living in
the same foster home. The children were seen for eight sessions. Axline
felt that the boy's handicap was not a deterrent to therapy. At the end
of therapy, he was considered by the therapist to have gained in insight
and personal satisfaction. The foster mother felt that his behavior had
improved. Interesting as both accounts are, they are in no way conclusive.
They may, however, serve as a source of encouragement to those interested in studying the potential usefulness of psychotherapeutic methods
with visually handicapped children.

Rothschild reported on play-therapy with blind children conducted at
the Industrial Home for the Blind.[72] Most of the children treated were
of pre-school age, and all were congenitally and totally blind. A modified
approach is recommended since the children were observed to be limited
in their expression and participation in play situations. More beneficial
results were obtained when the mothers were also involved in therapy.

A remotely relevant report in the area, is that of Dickinson, who described how a combination of parent guidance and the therapeutic
orientation of a nursery school teacher helped a pre-school blind child
to make a more satisfactory adjustment.[73] Psychotherapy or play-therapy
as we have defined them, however, were not actually utilized with
this boy.

The research and service needs in this area have received considerable
attention at a number of conferences and workshops.

A group of workers interested in the general areas of diagnosis and
counselling with the blind met at the University of Michigan in 1947.
These workers first surveyed available information and then established
an organization known as the National Psychological Research Council
for the Blind.[74] Subsequently, this organization has published a compilation of research suggestions on psychological problems associated with
blindness. Several studies directly pertinent to the area of psychotherapy
with the blind are outlined. Illustrative of this group are the following:

> What is the role of group activities, such as sociodrama or group
> psychotherapy, in helping the newly blinded to develop more re-
> alistic social and vocational goals? . . . What is the relative effec-
> tiveness of role-playing in group situations involving only blind
> persons as compared with situations involving blind and seeing
> individuals? . . . Is the Rogerian form of non-directive counselling
> effective with the blind in dealing with personal adjustments?
> Under what conditions and with what kinds of problems should
> this method be employed? [75]

While much of this suggested work is geared primarily toward the adult blind, the proposed program illustrates the type of planning for coordinated research in therapy with the disabled that is sorely needed even today. Wright, in her report of the Princeton Conference, presented the results of a survey on needed research reported by members of the National Council on Psychological Aspects of Disability. More research studies were recommended in the area of psychodynamic and psychosocial aspects of adjustment to disability than in any other. Research in psychotherapy ranked fourth in the list of twenty.[76]

McQuie reported on a conference at Northwestern of professionals from many disciplines concerned with emotionally disturbed blind children. A major recommendation was that day schools and residential schools for the blind participate in the work with severely disturbed blind children. McQuie proposed a plan for such action, with major emphasis on the therapeutic teaching of children in small groups.[77] This suggestion to consider alternative provisions for children who urgently need services that are in short supply is an important one. It will be expanded in the final section of this chapter.

Speech Disorders

Although the field of speech pathology and speech therapy is an area of activity somewhat separate from traditional psychotherapy, it should be mentioned in passing that some speech problems are viewed as reflecting personality maladjustment. In such instances, psychotherapy either exclusively or in association with other specified interventions is recommended. The technical research in this area is outside the province of this chapter. The authors, therefore, will call the reader's attention only to the fact that speech therapists frequently employ psychotherapeutic procedures. Two recent publications give support to this statement. In a recently published volume Hejna presented transcripts from his own practice to illustrate non-directive psychotherapeutic techniques in actual use.[78] In his experience, psychotherapy can bring out underlying problems so that conventional speech therapy procedures may then be used. The subtitle of *Stuttering and Personality Dynamics* by Murphy and Fitzsimons is *Play Therapy, Projective Therapy and Counseling.*[79] Stuttering is viewed as a deep-seated personality problem and a psychodynamic, interpersonal approach is advocated. There are two main sections in this book: one on the psychodynamics of stuttering and the other on a detailed exposition of what is called psychodynamic speech therapy. Included in the second section are chapters on diagnosis, play-therapy, group play-therapy, projective therapy, client-centered counselling, and counselling with parents.

Cerebral Palsy and Orthopedic Defect

The potential contributions of psychotherapy in dealing with emotional concomitants of disabilities in this group have been cited frequently. Some preliminary work in this area has been reported.[80] Axline and Rogers described the therapeutic handling of a six-year-old child with a constricted throat.[81] He had an impressive array of personal problems and had been rejected and abandoned by his mother. Therapy consisted of non-directive individual and group play sessions during a seven-month period. The child was able to work through his need for affection, adapt more satisfactorily to his foster home, act out his infantile needs in an accepting environment, and consequently adopt more mature behavior.

A report of psychotherapy in the case of a 12-year-old boy with a markedly atypical physique was presented by Schiffer.[82] This youngster, who was both retarded in school and disturbed in interpersonal relationships, was seen for 18 months in case work and group therapy. Highly dependent at first, he was inept in manual skills, and was subjected to teasing by other members of the group. Eventually, as he gained acceptance by the group, he became less dependent, more confident and outgoing, and able to participate constructively in the group situation. Further, these improvements seemed to generalize in terms of a better community adjustment.

Bychowski and Despert summarized three instances (from the records of the Institute for Crippled and Disabled in New York) of psychotherapy with disabled youths.[83] The first of these was an 18-year-old male with congenital cerebral palsy accompanied by a rather severe speech defect. Psychotherapy by a social worker was essentially supportive and its consequences included: strengthening the ego, helping the patient to accept his limitations, and enabling him to hold a job successfully. The second, a 23-year-old cerebral palsied male, with a speech disturbance, considerable manifest anxiety, and a marked dependency conflict, was also described. Originally seen by a social worker, the patient later was transferred to a psychiatrist for depth treatment. Progress was reported. The third report dealt with a 22-year-old post-poliomyelitis female with a residual paralysis of the trunk and lower extremities. The patient seemed markedly anxious and insecure when treatment was undertaken. Following seven months of therapy with a social worker, and six months of additional psychiatric therapy, remarkable mental and physical improvements were observed, and the patient was able to hold down a job very successfully. In all of these cases, the authors stressed the necessity of a team approach in working with the disabled person.

Bernabeu reported on the analytic study of eight children hospitalized because of the severe consequences of poliomyelitis.[84] The report covers an eighteen-month period and describes the therapeutic problems and treatment. Another clinical study focusing on the role of body-image in psychotherapy with the physically handicapped was reported by Cath, Glud, and Blane.[85] A description of the therapeutic process was provided, and emphasis was placed on getting the patient to justify the discrepancy between his body-image and his body-structure. Elsa Miller reported on four groups of children seen in a child guidance clinic, two of which were mildly disabled children with cerebral palsy and a third group which consisted of cerebral palsy children with severe disabilities.[86] One group consisted of twelve mildly disabled children who, with their parents, received psychotherapy for periods of from eight months to two years. This clinical report emphasized the importance of parent-child relationships and described the problems in this area found in the children with mild cerebral palsy. She pointed out the confusion concerning what to expect of the child since he seemed so variable in his capabilities. Treatment was judged to be highly effective with positive changes in self-concept, parental relationships, anxiety and hostility. The cases were re-evaluated from one to four years after treatment, and the gains were found to be maintained. The problems were found to be basically unchanged in the majority of the cases of the untreated, mildly handicapped groups. The following conclusions were reached: (1) parent-child relationship problems represent a significant factor in the adjustment of mildly handicapped children with cerebral palsy, (2) the disability does not remain the basic problem, (3) adjustment problems appear to be more severe in the mild group than in the severe group, (4) the troubled child shows the same emotional responses whether or not he is disabled. Miller concluded her report with a plea for greater sensitivity to the emotional health of the mildly disabled child and his parents and argued that the presence of a physical disability should not be used to exclude emotionally disturbed children and their parents from obtaining needed mental health services.

Several studies in group therapy were also reported in this area. Rubenstein described a group therapy program for adolescents in an orthopedic hospital school.[87] In particular, he summarized the experiences of one adolescent group consisting of seven post-poliomyelitis boys between the ages of 15 and 19 years. This group was structured to provide opportunity for recreation, "gripe" sessions, and self-government. The permissive role of the therapist was designed to encourage free expression and discussion of problems. Though some members profited considerably more than others, the greatest values of the situation appeared to derive from the opportunities for expression and for working through fears and anxiety. Three of the four group members who were discharged from the hospital succeeded in adjusting satisfactorily to the home situation.

Cruickshank and Cowen described a non-directive group play-therapy experience with five physically handicapped children, ranging in age from seven to nine.[88] The group was heterogeneous with respect to disability, including two with severe cardiac conditions, and one each with diagnoses of post-poliomyelitis, cerebral palsy, and hemophilia. All, however, had given evidence of emotional disturbance in the school situation, as indicated by pre-therapy reports from their teachers. The therapy experience, which took place in the school setting, consisted of a total of 13 sessions during a two-month period. It was hoped that the permissive therapy environment, and acceptance by the group members would enable the children to work through their emotional problems, including those stemming from their physical limitations. On the basis of reports submitted both by parents and teachers at the end of therapy, it appeared that three of the five children improved considerably, one very slightly, and one not at all.[89]

Brain Injury and Epilepsy

There are several reports of psychotherapy designed to alleviate concomitant personality disturbances with brain-injured children. Schiffer described the treatment of a 14-year-old brain-injured boy with marked adjustive difficulties.[90] Treatment by means of activity group therapy lasted about 18 months. Considerable progress was reported within the framework of the boy's limitations.

In considerable detail, Slavson reported the treatment of a nine-year-old boy with diffuse organicity as indicated both by diagnostic psychological testing and electroencephalography.[91] The boy was markedly disturbed at the start of therapy, isolated in interpersonal relations, fearful, living at a fantasy level, and was functioning inadequately in school. Therapy lasted for three years, consisting first of individual treatment by a psychiatric case worker, then individual plus group contacts, and finally group contacts alone. Follow-up study 18 months after the termination of therapy, revealed marked improvements in adjustment, despite the irreversible nature of the organicity. The boy appeared to be more mature and realistic, he was less anxious and fearful, and he had become considerably more effective in social relationships.

Miller, in the previously mentioned article, commented in detail on the disorganized, hyperactive behavior associated with brain injury shown by one of the children treated.[92] The boy was a severe behavior and learning problem; his difficulties were attributed to organic factors. Remarkable improvement was observed within eight months of therapy.

Miller raised the question of the extent to which the extremely hyperactive behavior had been learned and was the result of the child's emotional difficulties superimposed upon the basic organic deficit. However, the perceptual and conceptual problems observed did not disappear and were still present at follow-up from one to four years later.

Although primarily concerned with non-organic epileptic children, Deutsch and Wiener emphasized the value of psychotherapy for brain-injured children in the following quotation:

> Psychotherapeutic treatment of organics should not be ruled out, except in cases showing considerable brain damage or progressive deterioration. It is well known that many organic conditions are accompanied by a reactive neurotic-like superstructure, which if removed makes possible effective functioning within the limits imposed by the organic condition. In some cases which presented an organic picture, the changes in behavior after treatment were remarkable.[93]

Relative to the paucity of work in areas thus far considered, the use of psychotherapy in treating emotional problems associated with epilepsy is somewhat more extensive. Here, however, the largest proportion of the work has been done with adults.[94] Nevertheless, there are some relevant reports dealing with the epileptic child and youth. Bridge devoted an entire chapter in his volume on epilepsy in children to a careful consideration of the possible applications of psychotherapy and play techniques in dealing with the emotional problems of the epileptic child.[95] Though Bridge does not report actual therapeutic work, his discussion is thoughtful and detailed and contains valuable suggestions regarding the potential usefulness of varied therapeutic approaches. Bridge suggested that the need for psychotherapy with epileptic children is often overlooked because of the outstanding nature of the physiological disturbances.[96] He pointed out that even in those instances were personality factors are not initially causative of seizures, they may later become ". . . an integral part of the causative mechanism," and that eventually ". . . emotional disturbance may be the dominant causative factor, and in psychotherapy lies the best possibility of cure." [97]

Bridge differentiated three levels at which psychotherapy may be applied with the epileptic child. In cases of mild emotional disturbance, *"preventive psychotherapy or mental hygiene"* is applicable. This consists primarily of a therapeutic orientation on the part of the physician and direct education of the patient and his family. At a second level, there are epileptic patients who have acute and unchecked emotional symptoms, coincident with seizures, that must be controlled. Here *"symptomatic or psychosomatic therapy"* is recommended. This is essentially supportive psychotherapy. Bridge proposed that both "preventive" and "symptomatic" psychotherapy can be carried out effectively by the medical practitioner dealing with the epileptic child.[98]

Still another group of epileptic children face much more serious emotional difficulties that may or may not coincide with their seizures. About these children Bridge said:

> There are the individuals who have been treated medically but neglected psychologically, who have faced insurmountable obstacles to normal living because of seizures, or who have failed to receive in the home the security necessary to compensate for the handicaps and disappointments that result from epilepsy. Still others have developed personality disturbances that antedated the appearance of epilepsy; the disease adds only a complication, although nevertheless a serious one.[99]

Bridge believed that an intensive form of psychotherapeutic treatment is essential for these children—such work of necessity falling outside the province of the medical practitioner.

Bradley proposed that group therapy may be particularly useful with epileptic children because they may be excluded (with subsequent feelings of isolation) from community activities.[100] In this connection Deutsch and Zimmerman described as one important objective in group therapy with epileptics the development of an "esprit de corps" to reduce the tendency of such patients to perceive themselves as social outcasts.[101]

Insofar as actual therapy reports go, Hart reported an instance in which a seven-year-old epileptic child was so seriously disturbed that formal psychotherapy was impossible.[102] A "relationship therapy" was set up, consisting primarily of a concerted effort by ward nurses and attendants to meet the child's tremendous affectional needs. In one year's time the child's behavior had improved considerably.[103]

In one of the few studies in the entire area of therapy with the disabled, involving a sizeable number of subjects, Deutsch and Wiener used analytically oriented play and interview techniques with 57 epileptic children and adolescents.[104] Conjunctive individual and group therapy was undertaken with parents wherever possible. Based on reports of behavioral changes obtained from the family and the school, 24 of the 42 patients for whom treatment had been completed were rated improved, and 18 unimproved. With some patients who had not responded to medication over a period of years, there was a reduction, following therapy, both in seizure frequency and in the required amount of medication. The authors proposed that psychotherapy permitted release of tensions and anxiety which presumably were contributing significantly to the onset of the seizures. To study the stability of positive change, nine subjects from the improved group were followed-up after one year. Seven showed notable improvement on both Rorschach and Binet, four of these showing increases of 19 to 26 I.Q. points on the latter measure.

Gottschalk described applications of psychoanalytic therapy with three emotionally disturbed epileptic children, studied at the Child Psychiatry Clinic of Michael Reese Hospital.[105] Reasoning that psychological factors may exacerbate seizures, he hypothesized that ". . . there should be a possibility through psychologic means of modifying the frequency and/or form of the seizures in certain epileptic patients . . . ," and ". . . the electroencephalogram may possibly also be modifiable through psychologic means . . ."[106]

The three subjects, all of whom showed serious personality disturbances, were selected in terms of two criteria: (a) an established diagnosis of idiopathic epilepsy following extensive neurological examination, and (b) assured cooperation of the parents in a long-range therapy program. The first subject, a five-year-old boy, was seen intensively in play-therapy for 140 sessions during a 14-month period, after which further therapy was considered unnecessary. The second subject, a ten-year-old boy, also was seen in a playroom setting for approximately 100 sessions during a 27-month period. The last subject was a 17-year-old adolescent. Here, interview therapy was used for about 100 sessions during a 36-month period. For the last two subjects, therapy was discontinued because the therapist had to leave town before its completion.

Evaluation of the outcome of therapy, which had a welcome objective flavor, was based on clinical indices (such as seizure frequency, modifications in form of seizures and behavior under stress, and change in dosage of anticonvulsants), electroencephalographic change, and psychological tests including the Rorschach and I.Q. measures. Marked over-all improvement was observed in the five-year-old boy and the 17-year-old adolescent. Perhaps the most striking aspect of change was the initial diminution and ultimate disappearance of seizures without recurrence in a two-year follow-up period, notwithstanding reduction or elimination of anticonvulsant medications. This was accompanied by a considerably less deviant EEG, which, in the case of the five-year-old, seemed entirely normal after therapy. Behaviorally, both subjects seemed to have adjusted much more adequately and many symptoms disappeared. Comparison of pre- and post-therapy Rorschachs for the 17-year-old boy corroborated other indices of improvement. With the ten-year-old boy, although there were indications of improvement behaviorally and in terms of seizure reduction, electroencephalographic and Rorschach findings were equivocal. Apparently some progress has been made, but further therapy seemed indicated. In all three cases an increase of three I.Q. points was observed in post-testing.

Gottschalk proposed that epileptic seizures may be activated psychologically, particularly when a conflictual drive is blocked from gratification or expression. He concluded that psychotherapy can reduce seizure frequency, though in the absence of control subjects it is impossible to be sure that some combination of time and medication could not have produced similar results. Gottschalk felt that the failure of anticonvulsants to have effected change before therapy was undertaken, suggests that the psychotherapy was the crucial factor underlying the observed changes. He proposed that a judicious combination of psychotherapy and medication would be far more effective than the medication alone.

Despite the fact that it is based on only three subjects, Gottschalk's study represents a significant contribution because of the intensive nature of the therapy experience and the extensive and objective aspects of his evaluation. By buttressing an approach of this type with a more substantial number of subjects, and more adequate controls, we would be approaching a model for more rigorous scientific study of the applicability of psychotherapy and play techniques to the exceptional child.

Mental Deficiency

Although the area of mental deficiency has been described in the past as a forgotten field of psychology,[107] there has been far more work in psychotherapy and play-therapy with mentally defective children than with any other single group of exceptional children. This is not to suggest that we have had nearly enough studies of psychotherapy with the defective, for we have not. The studies that have been reported are more varied and at least as good technically as those done with any other group of exceptional children, but it would be misleading to characterize this area as more than the least understudied of the various areas of disability. There has, however, been at least sufficient material on therapy with defectives for several reviews of the literature and a book of collected readings.[108]

The tradition and conceptions of both mental deficiency and psychotherapy are such that many reports, particularly the earlier ones, begin by raising the question of whether psychotherapy is useful with this group.[109]

By now, however, accumulated studies of individual, group, and play-therapy, with various expressive media, and with widely divergent therapeutic orientations lend strong support to the following appraisal: "Despite the earlier pessimism, there can be no doubt now as to the effectiveness of counselling and psychotherapy with the mentally deficient." [110]

One of the first to explore the possibilities of therapy with defectives was Clark, who has discussed applications and modifications of analytic techniques with this group.[111] A series of three papers emanating from the Menninger Clinic shortly thereafter described further applications of psychoanalytically oriented therapy with some defectives.[112] Apparently reports of therapy with defectives were so scarce at that time, that it was considered desirable by Chidester and Menninger to report in some detail the same case that Ackerman and Menninger had described earlier. In this instance, over-all behavioral improvements following therapy were accompanied by a marked increase in I.Q. score.[113]

Since these early papers there has been a reasonably steady trickle of case reports of individual psychotherapy with defectives in varied settings, some of which were summarized by Sarason.[114] Hartwell described the treatment of an introversive feeble-minded boy of 11, who was seen for two years in psychiatric therapy.[115] Therapy seemed to have helped him to become somewhat more outgoing, happier, and to make at least a minimal adaptation to the environment.

Feldman presented a summary of therapy with a 19-year-old, dejected, anxious soldier with an I.Q. of 41, hospitalized for headaches.[116]

Sarason summarized the course of individual psychotherapy with two young defectives in an institutional setting.[117] The first of these was a 23-year-old girl, described as an acute behavior problem. Psychotherapy, lasting 10 months with the staff psychologist, helped considerably to reduce sullenness and depression, increase spontaneity, and improve interpersonal relationships and work efficiency. The second report summarized a year of individual therapy with a 16-year-old defective boy described as destructive, moody, and unhappy. As a result of therapy, feelings of guilt and worthlessness were considerably reduced. Follow-up indicated that he had adjusted well after his discharge from the institution.

Sion described a series of 11 supportive therapy contacts with an immature adolescent defective in an institutional setting.[118] The boy's basic problem involved working out a relationship with a rejecting mother. Ultimately, through therapy, he was able to prepare himself for an adequate adjustment outside the institution. Follow-up after 18 months revealed that the boy was entirely self-sufficient.

A more extensive study on the effects of individual psychotherapy with the defective is that by Cooley. The results of therapy with "dull" and "bright" children ranging in age from three to fifteen were compared.[119] The "bright" subjects were above 115 I.Q., while the "dulls" consisted of nine children ranging in I.Q. from 61-74 and 16 children with I.Q.'s between 75 and 84. The two groups were matched for age, sex, and socioeconomic status. Cooley found no apparent differences in the results of therapy either between the dull and bright groups or between the two dull subgroups—nor did the dull children require more time in treatment. Eight of the nine children in the 61-74 I.Q. group were able to make at least partial progress in therapy, and three of these eight showed very definite improvement.

Of considerable interest is a report by Thorne summarizing the results of a systematic program in counselling and psychotherapy with defectives at the Brandon State School.[120] Sixty-eight defectives, 30 male and 38 female, each of whom had been referred for psychiatric study and treatment because of a serious conduct problem, were seen in therapy. Some non-directive but mostly directive techniques such as reassurance, persuasion, advice, and suggestion were used. Therapy was evaluated on the basis of conduct records of the children, breaches of discipline, school and work records, and clinical judgment. By these criteria 45 children (66 per cent) were rated improved, 16 (23 per cent) unchanged, and seven (10 per cent) worse. In evaluating this study, Thorne stated, "This . . . program of systematic counselling and psychotherapy has been an unqualified success, both in terms of general institutional morale and the adjustment of individual cases." [121] Unfortunately, since psychotherapy was but one aspect of an entirely revised, more progressive institutional program, it is difficult, in the absence of a non-therapy control group, to know what portion of the observed improvements in the therapy group derived specifically from the therapy experience rather than from the improved institutional program. This caution notwithstanding, Thorne's study is a worthwhile contribution, which supports his conclusion that ". . . counseling and psychotherapy with defectives is both possible and profitable. . . ." [122]

In a subsequent article, Thorne described his technique of tutorial counselling with mental defectives and stated that they are capable of learning high social skills, including psychological techniques, by being taught what a normal person would do in a number of specific situations.[123]

The use of play techniques with the defective has been described by Axline, who used non-directive play therapy with a five-year-old boy. On the basis of medical diagnosis and successive Binet I.Q.'s of 65 and 68, he was thought to be mentally defective.[124] Initially constricted, lethargic, and disinterested in the play situation, he became more alert and responsive. Later, group play contacts were also provided. Marked physical and psychological improvements were observed as a consequence of therapy. Follow-up after one year indicated that he had continued his good adjustment in the home and had adapted very well to the school situation. At that time his Binet I.Q. was 105.

Maisner described the use of play therapy with 15 children, between eight and thirteen, referred for bad behavior or indications of maladjustment noted in psychological testing, as part of a general personality re-educative program at the Wayne County Training School.[125] The personality difficulties presented were varied, including autistic-schizoid adaptations, negativism, destructiveness, hyperactivity, and aggression. The children had been in residence from one month to three years; I.Q.'s ranged from 41-86. Each child was seen for a minimum of six individual play-therapy contacts, and most were seen for additional individual or group play, or counselling.

An emphasis in therapy was placed on the establishment of rapport and acceptance of the child, followed in turn by clarification of feeling, desensitization, and interpretation. The play-therapy program was considered to have been quite successful on the basis of test results, school progress, and written reports by teachers and cottage workers evaluating the children's behavior. Maisner stated that ". . . every one of the fifteen children . . . has shown some major indication of improved adjustment." [126] Maisner was aware that the improvements noted cannot, in the absence of a non-therapy control group, be attributed solely to a play-therapy experience that was but one aspect of a total personality re-education program. One other complicating factor in evaluation is that Maisner did not specify whether the 15 children who improved after play therapy were randomly selected before their therapy experience from a population of similarly disturbed children or whether they form an *ad hoc* group selected to be subject of a written report partially because of successful therapeutic outcome.

Under the title "Mental Deficiency—Symptom or Disease," Axline reported on play therapy with 15 emotionally disturbed young children, aged six and seven.[127] Three subgroups, each containing five children, were identified on the basis of the therapy records. The children in the first two of these groups had I.Q. scores ranging between 66 and 74 when therapy began. In one group there was no change in post-therapy I.Q., while in the other there was a marked increase (averaging 21 points) in post-therapy I.Q. The third group, consisting of children with pre-therapy I.Q.'s between 105 and 114, showed no change in post-therapy scores. Each child was seen individually in non-directive play for eight to twenty contacts. The published report consists essentially of 15 discrete synopses of treatment. Most of the children appear to have been helped to a better adjustment by their play-therapy experiences, though all did not benefit to the same extent.

It is quite difficult to evaluate some aspects of Axline's study. It is not entirely clear why she uses the term mental deficiency in the title of the paper, or says that ". . . the material presented seemed to lend itself to this study of mental deficiency. . . ." [128] Apparently the children studied had not been diagnosed as defective, and the prime basis for describing them in those terms seems to have been the low pre-therapy I.Q. It would perhaps be more defensible to say that Axline has shown that some children with low I.Q.'s may show considerable I.Q. gain after a play-therapy experience. Axline's explanation of such change on the basis of the child's becoming more able to express his basic capacities is certainly a reasonable hypothesis. However, an essential prerequisite to any study of the basic or symptomatic nature of mental deficiency, whether it is by means of educational, chemical, environmental, or psychotherapeutic procedures, is the initial establishment of a competent diagnosis of mental deficiency.

In raising this specific criticism of Axline's study we do not wish to bypass an important underlying point. In our review, we have noted at least several instances of increase in I.Q. scores, accompanying other and more general behavior improvements following therapy with individuals competently diagnosed as defective. About such changes, Neham stated, ". . . when and if psychotherapy resulted in the restoration of normal intelligence . . . this was a case of mistaken diagnosis due to poor testing, emotional or social involvements, or a combination of these factors." [129] This explanation derives from Doll's inclusive criteria of mental deficiency, two features of which are mental subnormality and the presence of this (and other conditions) at maturity.[130] If one accepts this viewpoint it is of course impossible for a defective to change intellectually (or socially) for if such a change takes place, then, by definition, the affected individual was not defective. Unfortunately many practitioners tend to lose sight of the fact that it *is* a definition and endow all those who have been labeled as defective and/or institutionalized with the quality of essential incurability contained in it. To the extent that this is done, it will serve as a deterrent to research in psychotherapy or any remedial procedure with the defective.

Stating the matter otherwise, if one inclusive criterion of mental deficiency is, as Doll stated, that the condition obtains at maturity, then it is impossible to diagnose finally any child as defective, since there can be no certain foreknowledge of his status at maturity. Practically speaking, when a child is diagnosed as defective, it can only be on the basis of the most complete information available *at the time of diagnosis*. That there are some children, *competently diagnosed* as defective on the basis of all available social, behavioral, and test data, who are capable of making significant intrapersonal, social, and intellectual improvements following a psychotherapeutic (or other remedial) experience is entirely consistent with our best knowledge at this time.

Mundy reported on her work with children certified as imbeciles at the Fountain Hospital.[131] In one experiment, two matched groups were used; the experimental group consisted of 15 children who received nondirective therapy for from nine months to a year. The control group of 10 children received only the regular services of the hospital. After a one to one and one-half year period, the treated group increased in social behavior and showed a significant increase of 7 I.Q. points. In another experiment, eight physically disabled children were treated after an initial control period. A performance test was used to measure changes in I.Q. Following therapy, a significant increase of 22 I.Q. points was observed as compared with a change of 2 I.Q. points following the control period. The treatment was non-directive play-therapy and was provided over a period of from 9 to 12 months. Staff members judged the behavior of all subjects to be improved.

Institutionalized retardates between the ages of 8-12 with emotional problems were studied by Subotnick and Callahan.[132] The I.Q.'s of the eight boys were between 53 and 88. A variety of measures were used, and the subjects served as their own controls. The control period was followed by an eight-week therapy period during which the therapy was provided for two 45-minute sessions a week. No significant changes were found.

Several stimulating reports of group therapy with defectives are available. Some early applications of group techniques with institutionalized defectives were reported by Boyd.[133] Subsequent work has for the most part, also been done in institutional settings.

Cotzin described a therapy group of nine mentally defective boys between 11 and 15.[134] The I.Q. range was from 50-62, excepting one boy with 79. All the boys referred for group therapy were classroom problems and had shown various aggressive, defiant, and asocial behaviors. The group met for ten 75-minute sessions during a three-week period. The first session, in which the therapist was passive, was quite chaotic and characterized by uncontrollable physical and verbal aggression. The therapist therefore assumed a more active role, and in the next few meetings more structured activities, including boxing matches as an outlet for diffuse aggression, story telling, and work with expressive media, were introduced. During this phase of therapy, hostile, aggressive, and negativistic behaviors subsided somewhat. In order to encourage release and insight, a courtroom scene was set up with the therapist as judge, and each child as prosecutor, defendant, and jurist at different times. Though the study was carried out primarily at an exploratory level, improvements were observed in the behavior of all children during the two months following the termination of therapy. Six of the eight children who were followed-up for a year maintained these improvements, which were attributed to the opportunities for release and achievement of insight provided by the experience.

Abel used a group therapy approach with three institutionalized defective boys described as restless and destructive.[135] Therapy consisted of a series of weekly two-hour sessions for three months with an emphasis on the use of role-playing and various expressive media. Presumably because of acceptance gained in the therapy situation and satisfactions derived from constructive rather than destructive activities, important outside behavioral changes took place. The boys became leaders among their peers and functioned more adequately in school.

Fisher and Wolfson used Slavson's activity interview therapy, a combination of play and interview techniques, with two groups of institutionalized defective girls,[136] There were eight girls between the ages of 10-3 and 11-6 in one group, and four between 12-6 and 13-3 in the other. The groups were seen for 36 sessions constituting six identifiable therapeutic stages. In evaluating the contributions of the group therapy experience, beyond the improvements observed during the actual sessions, ratings of the children were obtained from staff members and attendants. On this basis, eight of the twelve children showed definite improvment.[137]

Mehlman reported an important study of non-directive group play therapy with institutionalized "familial" (endogenous) defectives.[138] The subjects were 32 boys and girls between the ages of seven and eleven. The average age was ten years. During the six-week period before therapy each child was given a diagnostic battery including two individual intelligence tests (the Binet and Grace Arthur II) and three personality measures by an examiner other than the therapist. All children were given the same test battery during the six-week period immediately after therapy ended. For the entire group, mean pre-therapy I.Q.'s were 65 on the Binet and 67 on the Arthur.

On the basis of an over-all adjustment rank obtained from judges' ratings of the Rorschach records, the children were assigned alternately to one of three groups. The first of these was the experimental or play-therapy group, while the other two were control groups. Of the latter, one was a simple non-therapy control group in which the children were given only the pre- and post-therapy test batteries. The other group was shown movies and was included to insure that any observed changes in the experimental group were a function of the therapy experience, rather than the ameliorative effects of a pleasant break in institutional routine, or the interest and attention of an adult. There were no significant differences among the groups with respect to chronological age, length of institutional residence, and, with a few minor exceptions, pre-therapy test performance. To reduce the effects of non-significant differences among groups on pre-test measures, analysis of covariance was used as a statistical control.

The 11 experimental (play-therapy) children were divided into two play groups of six and five, each of which was seen for 29 sessions during a 16-week period. With respect to the personality indices used, there were few reliable changes. Only on the Haggerty-Olson-Wickman Behavior Rating Scale did the play-therapy group show significant improvement in comparison to the non-therapy controls. In addition there were no significant changes on the two intelligence measures following therapy. In discussing these findings, Mehlman described some factors specific to his therapy situation, which may have been operating to reduce its effectiveness. He also pointed out that the essentially negative results refer only to a limited, and perhaps not representative or optimal, set of objective criteria of evaluation.

One critical comment about Mehlman's study may be pertinent. In his criteria for selection of children for therapy, no reference is made to the presence of an emotional disturbance in the child or the need for therapy. It is conceivable that before therapy some of the children were reasonably well adjusted within the framework of their limitations. To the extent that this factor may have been operating, the likelihood of finding change consequent to therapy was reduced. Nevertheless, insofar as sophistication of experimental design, objectification and comprehensiveness of evaluation, and extent and precision of control are concerned, Mehlman's study represents a significant methodological advance.

Positive changes in behavior were reported by Woodward, Siegel, and Eustis following two years of group play-therapy.[139] The subjects were eight pre-school retarded children. Their parents were also seen, and all were judged to have personality problems. The authors concluded that psychogenic factors were related to the retarded development shown by the children. It was found that the children with less marked psychotic features showed more favorable response to the total program. The children were referrals to a pediatric service and showed uneven maturational rates and delayed speech. All but one showed some schizoid characteristics. The general impression of this group is that it consisted of severely retarded children with complicating emotional factors. The children were all overconcerned about themselves, fears were quite common; their participation in group activities was limited. The report was prepared when the children had been under treatment for two years. Activity level and aggressiveness had increased. Participation in group play activities had developed to a level of about one year below chronological age. The children were more responsive, less guarded, less fearful; overcautiousness had decreased.

O'Connor and Yonge worked with older (16-20 years) defective delinquents in therapy for 32 one-hour meetings held twice a week.[140] A matched control group was selected, and both groups were assigned to a workshop under the same supervisor, who provided ratings on both experimental and control subjects. The results indicated that the experimental group showed positive changes in attitude, work, and I.Q. rating together with a decrease in negative comments in their ratings.

A well-planned and carefully controlled study of therapy with defective delinquents was reported by Snyder and Sechrest.[141] Subjects were assigned to three groups. One group received directive psychotherapy and consisted of 16 subjects. The second group was a placebo group of 16 subjects. The third group of 13 subjects received no special treatment. The therapy group met for one hour a week for a period of 13 weeks. Its members were told in the first session that therapy was being provided to help them to improve their behavior. The placebo group met on the same schedule and was told that it was participating in a study. During their meetings they were permitted to engage in free discussion of topics of their own choosing. Evaluation of therapy was made on the basis of routine evaluation reports and comments by staff members in regular reports on inmates. The therapy group received significantly more positive comments than did either the placebo or control group. This study could have been improved with the addition of more objective, behavioral measures of improvement and change.

With the defective child, even more frequently than with the intellectually normal one, verbalization may not be the best method of expression. Whether or not this is a result of the defective's inferior language development and concept formation is relatively unimportant. What is essential is that some medium be found whereby expression and communication by the defective can be optimally facilitated. Abel described this as a need for a transference between the defective child and the medium of therapy.[142] To this end there has been considerable exploratory work in the use of expressive media, creative arts, and play as avenues for therapy with this group.

Artistic activity is one approach which may have considerable therapeutic value with the defective.[143] Several reports of such work are available. Schaefer-Simmern and Sarason described the use of art as a therapeutic medium with a 30-year-old, institutionalized female defective who was uncooperative, phlegmatic, and inarticulate.[144] Parallel to the unfolding of artistic abilities in this girl, behavioral improvement was noted.

With a 16-year-old institutionalized defective boy, described as silent, morose, and verbally uncommunicative, Abel used drawing as an approach to therapy during a four-month period.[145] As the boy's drawings became freer and more spontaneous, his verbalization increased and he was able to discuss his problems with the therapist. Ultimately he was able to adjust well to farm life. Abel also reported work by Kadis, who had experimented with finger painting as a method of expression and communication in therapy with defectives.

Various forms of occupational therapy have been used with defectives. Menzel described the application of such techniques to an institutionalized adolescent Negro girl diagnosed as defective.[146] Referred because of stubbornness, destructiveness, and general unmanageability, the patient was able to gain expression and to achieve satisfaction through creative work. Menzel felt that the work in occupational therapy helped this girl to fulfill strong need for acceptance and recognition, to feel her own worth, and to find her niche in life. Follow-up during a seven-year period revealed that the patient had succeeded in making a good adjustment and a successful marriage. Abel also used occupational therapy techniques with an institutionalized, verbally unresponsive, adolescent girl with severe sexual problems.[147] Constructive work in weaving constituted a success experience for the girl, and after about a year she was able to talk through her problems with the therapist. Ultimately, the deviant sex behavior diminished, and the girl seemed to be more content. The creative accomplishments served also to increase acceptance of the girl by her mother. Other instances of the use of art, occupational therapy, and recreational therapy with the defective were summarized by Neham.[148]

This discussion of effective media through which to reach the defective child raises an interesting question. There is no denying the virtue of professional workers concerned with the mentally retarded searching for more effective interventions which will be of assistance in improving behavior. However, in examining the literature one is impressed by the tendency of workers to append the therapeutic label to activities which cover a wide range of provisions. Thus one can find reports on music therapy, art therapy, work therapy, recreational therapy, and so forth. Also, techniques that may be essentially conversational, tutorial, or discussion-centered often are variously referred to as case work, group work, remotivation, re-education, counselling, or psychotherapy. Unfortunately the pressures are in the direction of applying the more status-laden labels, with the result that many reports are classified as psychotherapy when some other label would better serve the purpose of more effective communication. There is an urgent need for greater detail and more complete specification of just what is done and to whom and for what purpose. This confusion of terms appears to result from a failure to distinguish between, on the one hand, psychotherapy as a set of procedures with a purpose and, on the other hand, certain environmental changes, opportunities or expressive media which may have beneficial or *therapeutic results*. In Abel's article, cited previously, expressive media were used by the therapist to facilitate communication and to effect a relationship. In other studies that reported the use of expressive media or other techniques, the purpose is not nearly so clear. In some reports, at least, a particular procedure was awarded the therapeutic label because it was found to have beneficial results.

There are, then, at least three purposes which may be identified in looking over the work that has been done in this area with the mentally defective. The first purpose relates to the reorganization of the social structure of institutions for the mentally retarded. For example, Heiser used the term psychotherapy to include the warm affectionate attitude of a cottage mother and the sympathetic understanding of a school teacher.[149] Certainly nothing should be spared in an attempt to make institutional living more wholesome and beneficial for the patient population, but little is gained by labeling these attempts as psychotherapy. There has been much discussion of milieu therapy as applied to the institutional treatment of emotionally disturbed children,[150] and certainly these conceptions are important in planning for the residential care of mental defectives or of any children, for that matter, who are removed from their families and communities and placed in residential homes or schools. Konopka's excellent discussion of institutional treatment for emotionally disturbed children is also applicable to other groups.[151] Leland and Smith pointed out that the retarded child who comes to an institution today does so after he has presented problems to his parents and community.[152] The child knows he is a problem and that the hospital or school is to some extent a treatment facility. Kaldeck observed that their emotional difficulties, more than their retardation, cause many children to be institutionalized for years.[153] Gunzburg noted the mounting realization that character and temperament are frequently more decisive in the rehabilitation of the feeble-minded than are the intellectual aspects.[154] Thus the improvement of sociopsychological factors through more wholesome environments and the provision of a variety of related services can result in improved behavior and expedite the return of many children to their homes and communities. The previously cited article by Thorne is in this tradition.[155] Psychotherapy is one intervention which holds promise for assisting persons to return to productive useful lives in the community, but everything which is done to achieve this goal is not psychotherapy.

In this connection, it is entirely possible that much of the encouragement springing from the applications of psychotherapy to institutional populations is a result of attempts to change behaviors which in part, at least, may have been induced by institutional living. Tizard's work with institutionalized trainable children lends some support to this observation.[156] He used staffing ratios and methods of child care usually employed in residential nurseries for normal pre-school children. By giving the children opportunities for expression and play, together with small grouping and more individual attention than is likely to be received in large institutions, impressive changes were observed in social and emotional development and in physical health.

A second purpose of the application of psychotherapy to the area of mental deficiency is in the direction of increasing intellectual functioning —some of the studies previously considered in this chapter have reported I.Q. changes. In all likelihood, those studies that show no attempt to select their subjects on the basis of disturbed behavior seem, of necessity, to have been conducted with this purpose in mind. A third purpose (and at once, the most obvious) is to treat maladjusted behavior present in a person who is also mentally defective. The studies that identified and selected defective children with personality or behavior problems for psychotherapy are in this direction.

Any attempt to summarize the results of psychotherapeutic work with the defective child in a concise or confident manner must be regarded as hazardous. Although there has undoubtedly been more work with defectives than with any other group of exceptional children, most authors have with good reason described their studies as exploratory. Firm generalizations would be difficult indeed to defend. It is, for example, not entirely clear why Neham, after a partial review of work in therapy with defectives concluded: "The experiments presented seem to indicate that the directive supportive method in which a warm friendly personal relationship is developed seems to be the best approach adapted to mental defectives." [157] Certainly the evidence at that time is not sufficiently clear-cut to indicate that any one approach to therapy is best for mental defectives in general and even less for any specific group of defectives. Leland and Smith described an approach consisting of unstructured materials and unstructured therapist's role (U.-U). This is but one of four different combinations of materials and therapist's role that they suggest.[158] They consider that the therapist's role and the materials may be structured or unstructured. It is to be hoped that presentations of this type will lead to more definitive research comparing the relative merits of various approaches to psychotherapy with specified groups of defectives with clearly formulated purposes or objectives. Similarly, one might question the basis of another of Neham's conclusions, namely that the ". . . weight of evidence indicates that high moron intelligence is necessary for therapeutic success." [159] One must be careful to distinguish between what may appear logical and what is an interpretation of sound research. A generation ago the notion that therapy with defectives could not be successful may have seemed both logical and acceptable to most practitioners. Subsequent research has demonstrated otherwise. In the absence of comparative research in therapy with defectives at different intellectual levels, what Neham stated as a conclusion should be regarded at best as a tentative hypothesis. Many clinics do, however, screen potential therapy cases on the basis of intelligence.[160]

In a more positive vein this much can be said: Instances of successful therapeutic outcomes with defectives have been reported from many settings by practitioners with diverse orientations. Sources include case reports, studies of interview therapy, reports of play-therapy and expressive media, studies in group therapy—provided by psychoanalysts, directivists, non-directivists and eclectics who have worked with institutionalized and non-institutionalized defectives. Though many of these reports are open to serious criticism if considered alone, together they underscore the conclusion that therapy with at least some defectives can be successful. Further, the few comparative studies of therapy with the defective and intellectually normal child offer no support for the notion that the former has a poorer therapeutic prognosis.

Although there are some instances of increases in I.Q. following therapy with competently diagnosed defectives, there is no basis for concluding that such increases are either general or typical. Most subjective evaluations of personality and behavioral changes after therapy with these children suggest that significant improvements have taken place. Regrettably, diagnostic test data before and after therapy are extremely rare and are not consistent enough either to support or to contradict generalizations derived from subjective reports.

A strong indication of a growing conviction that therapy with the defective is both feasible and potentially fruitful, may be found in the ever increasing number of studies reported in this area in recent years. Unfortunately there have been few systematic attempts to analyze research problems and formulate research needs. Notable exceptions to the preceding statement include Sarason's suggestions of some basic research problems in individual psychotherapy with defectives, Cotzin's proposals for a research program in group psychotherapy, and Mehlman's analysis of methodological problems in research on therapy with the defective.[161]

There can be little question of the effectiveness of psychotherapy with some defectives. Much needed information in this area, however, is still lacking. It is not yet clear which children in this heterogeneous group can be helped by therapy and which cannot, nor do we know about the relative effectiveness of various types of therapies or different therapeutic media, with either the defective group as a whole or any of its subgroups. These are some of the important future research problems that face us.

Their solution should extend the usefulness of psychotherapy to many defective children heretofore regarded as essentially unapproachable.

Illustrative Excerpts of Play-Therapy

SINCE THE literature contains many illustrations of non-disabled children working through emotional problems in therapy, two excerpts have been selected to show how the handicapped child may use the therapy situation in dealing with problems stemming more directly from his disability.

The first of these occurred during play-therapy with a six-year-old boy with a constricted throat. Every three weeks this boy had to go to the hospital to have his throat dilated, a source of considerable anxiety for him. The following is a partial transcript of a play session one day previous to such a hospitalization:

> E. (*Goes to paint table and starts to paint blobs of red on a large paper.*) I'm going to the hospital tomorrow. I'm going to have my throat dilated.
>
> T. You're going to the hospital tomorrow.
>
> E. I'll bet you'll miss me.
>
> T. You know I'll miss you.
>
> E. Yes. You will! (*Hits paint with paintbrush and splatters the paint.*) It'll hurt! It'll hurt! It'll hurt!
>
> T. You think it will hurt to have your throat dilated.
>
> E. Sometimes it bleeds! Look! (*Points to paper painted red.*) Look! Bloody! Like my throat.
>
> T. You think your throat will be bloody like that.
>
> E. Yes. (*Puts down brush. Tears up paper.*) I'll throw it away! I'll get rid of it!
>
> T. You'll get rid of the blood on the paper.
>
> E. Yes. (*He crams it in the wastebasket and gets it and tramps on it. Then he gets a baby doll and beats it with his fist.*) Bad, Bad, baby! I'll beat you up! (*Does so. Then gets hammer and pounds doll's head—it was a rag doll.*) I'll hurt the baby's head. I'll hammer it to pieces. I'll make *it* bleed (*defiantly*).
>
> T. You'll make the baby's head bleed.
>
> E. (*Getting gun*) I'll shoot it. Bang! Bang! There I fixed it. (*Aims gun at the teacher.*) Bang! Bang! There! I shot you, too.— Not really, though—just pretend. (*Comes over and pats teacher's hand.*)
>
> T. You just feel like shooting everyone.
>
> E. (*Screaming*) I don't want to go to the hospital!
>
> T. You don't want to go to the hospital, and because you have to go you feel like shooting everyone. That's all right to feel that way!
>
> E. (*Grinning*) Bang! Bang! Bang! (*Then he gets the hammer and pounds the workbench.*)

T. It makes you feel good to pound the old workbench.

E. (*Drops the hammer, kicks it across the room. He comes over and sits down beside the teacher and puts his head in her lap.*) I'm tired now. Let's go walking.[162]

One day after the dilation the following interchange took place during the therapy hour.

E. I'm tough, I am. The doctor was surprised when I told him I was eating everything and everything was staying down.

T. You're pretty pleased about that.

E. You bet. He said, "You're telling me tall tales." I said, "Oh no! Not me!" And it didn't hurt me a bit.

T. The doctor was pleased, too. And it didn't hurt a bit this time.

E. I told the doctor I eat and keep it down because I like it at school—I like the kids—I like my teacher. I like where I'm living now. (*Laughs. Picks up doll and dances around table top. Sings.*) I like! I like! I like! [163]

The authors believe that play-therapy helped the child to adjust more maturely and courageously to the emotional difficulties arising from his disability.

Another illustration of the handicapped child's use of the play session in trying to reduce anxiety resulting from his disability occurs in the ninth of a series of group play-therapy sessions with physically handicapped children, reported by Cruickshank and Cowen.[164] This sequence centers around the fantasy play of a seven-year-old hemophiliac boy and differs from the preceding one in that the child was apparently not aware of a relationship between his play activities and his disability.

P. (*To G and J*) Do you want to play cowboy and crook? (*No response*) (*To C*) Would you be the robber?

C. You'd like me to play the robber. I'll be anything you'd like for me to be.

P. Okay. You must sit here. (*C sat down on the piano chair and P tied him up flimsily.*) Now I must cut your finger off. (*P took a pair of scissors and went through the motion of cutting off a finger.*)

C. You're going to cut off a finger. (*P cut it off.*)

P. (*Very realistically*) Oooooooh—it's bleeding!

C. You cut off my finger and now it's bleeding.

P. I'll cut off all your fingers now. (*Went through the motions.*) They're all bleeding. You're losing all your blood. Maybe you'll bleed to death.

C. You think I may bleed to death?

P. We'll have to save the blood. (*Runs and gets two jars and puts C's right hand in one jar and left hand into the other.*) All your blood is dripping into the jars. (*He filled up the two jars which he had.*) It hasn't stopped; you're still bleeding to death. I must get some more jars. (*He got some more jars and filled them up with blood from C's fingers.*) Now look at all the blood we have. (*To the others*) Look we've got all these jars full of blood. We've got all this blood in case anyone gets hurt and needs blood. (*Suddenly he realized that C was bleeding to death.*) We must get some medicine to stop the bleeding. (*He poured some grains on C's hand.*) Leave them there; it hasn't stopped bleeding yet. (*After several minutes he shook the grains off into a box.*) It's better now. It looks like it's going to stop. I'll untie you now.[165]

Apparently, through his play behavior, the child was seeking to dissipate anxiety resulting from his precarious physical condition. The authors discuss the sequence as follows:

. . . P went out of his way to "cut off the bandit's fingers," an extremely purposeful and unique move. His actions during the entire scene were dramatic, painstaking, and realistic. He collected blood in the jars as if the cut were really dripping blood. He created a threat of death for the bleeding victim, indicating the possible seriousness of the problem in terms of his own meanings. . . . However at the end of the fantasy the victim was saved by means of medication. P, who evidenced sincere fright during the fantasy, appeared relieved and emotionally unburdened when it was over.[166]

Work with Parents

Since the child's problems are frequently either interwoven with or a reflection of parental difficulties and require unique parental understandings, many child therapists regard conjunctive parental contacts as essential. For parents of handicapped children this need has been felt even more strongly. Though actual work with parents of disabled children falls beyond the scope of this chapter, an attempt will be made briefly to indicate some considerations which suggest that the need for such work is compelling.

Actually there is no single uniform pattern of parental reactions to children's disabilities. Some may accept the situation completely; for others, it will be a source of constant concern. In general, however, the presence of a handicap in the child may serve to make the parent more vulnerable to certain attitudinal disturbances. For example, (particularly with parents of congenitally handicapped children) there may be fairly marked guilt feelings at a conscious or unconscious level. Frequent stigmatization of the disabled child may promote the development of embarrassment and shame for some parents. The parent in his identification with the child may be considerably disturbed by the ridicule and abuse which the child (and sometimes the parent) may continually have to absorb. Such attitudes toward the disabled child in the immediate community may force an unwanted social isolation upon the parents. In many instances the disability may result in excessive financial obligations, added child care responsibilities, and consequent restriction of activity that may be very difficult for the parents to accept. In addition, disability frequently places restrictions upon the child's potential for accomplishment in our culture. This may be a source of frustration for the parent who is depending on vicarious need-satisfaction through the child's accomplishments. Certainly, with parents who are disturbed individuals in the first place, it should be expected that disability in the child will tend to exacerbate their problems and anxieties.

Westlund and Palumbo stressed the importance of parental problems when, in describing an over-all approach to the treatment of the disabled child, they stated, "Frequently the best results with the patient may be obtained only through the parents." [167] It is probable that attitudinal difficulties such as those discussed, underlie the observation of a higher incidence of rejecting and overprotecting behaviors in the parents of disabled children.[168] Other writers, however, have suggested that emotional reactions on the part of professional personnel may result in an unfair appraisal of the attitudes of parents of exceptional children. Gallagher analyzed the term "rejection" with a view toward helping workers use the concept in context with appropriate limitations.[169] Wright re-examined the concepts of overprotection, dependency, and independence as applied to persons with disabilities.[170] She raised the question of whether in emphasizing independence, the importance of dependency needs was being overlooked and whether the effect of overprotection is as deleterious as it is reputed to be. It was further observed that overprotection frequently depends on who is making the judgment, and Wright expressed concern that warmth, love, and understanding in the relationship between parents and their disabled children may be lost in pursuing the vague and abstract goal of independence.

With children showing behavioral deviation, conjunctive work with parents is designed to help parents with their conflicts and to provide an opportunity for them to develop more favorable attitudes towards the child. This should make it less difficult for the child, already facing imposing pressures, to adjust more adequately to his environment. Since not all parents of disabled children, or even disturbed children, are necessarily disturbed themselves, coordinate work with them does not necessarily have to be psychotherapy. Such work can serve an important educative function. Many parental anxieties may be alleviated when sound information about the child's limitations and potential is made available. In the earlier mentioned article by Anna Freud, special reference was made to work with mothers of handicapped children:

. . . there is no reason to expect that mothers [of handicapped children] are equipped automatically for the specialized task of bringing up such a child in a manner calculated to minimize the handicap. On the contrary, the mother's natural hurt and despair concerning her child's defect, the injury to her pride and pleasure in the child will all work toward estranging her from the task of mothering, thereby increasing the initial damage. There is here a specially difficult therapeutic task with the mothers which has been tackled in few places. But there is, besides it, also the need for expert advice, based on knowledge of the abnormalities concerned, such as the following: how to insure with the blind infant that contact with the object world by sight is substituted for through other channels; how to provide motor outlet for the blind toddler, thereby preventing many of the abnormalities following on motor restriction; how to prevent necessary dietary restrictions from being understood by the child as punishments and experienced as intolerable deprivations; how to minimize the effect of inevitable separations from the mother; how to prepare for operations and meet their equally inevitable aftereffects, etc., etc. There are a whole host of emergency situations of this kind in which the normal mother will feel helpless without guidance.[171]

Much conjunctive work with parents has successfully combined educative and therapeutic goals. There has also been a strong tendency to utilize group approaches in this work. Since parents of disabled children often feel atypical, ashamed, and inferior, verbal interchange with others having similar feelings may be a source of considerable implicit reassurance and an important therapeutic catalyst. There have been a number of reports in the literature for, by, and about parents of disabled children and the important services these parents need. Many plans for providing these services have been discussed and include the need for parent education,[172] parent counselling,[173] parent associations,[174] group therapy,[175] case works,[176] and short-term group meetings.[177] This listing is by no means inclusive, and it does not exhaust the number of different plans that have been suggested. They are mentioned here only to give the reader an idea of the extent of the concern for parents to receive needed information, guidance, and therapy and to point out some of the provisions that have been attempted or proposed.

Overview, Discussion, and Research Suggestions

ALL EVIDENCE considered, sound knowledge about psychotherapy and play techniques with the exceptional child is very limited. Published reports focusing primarily on this area, whether of a theoretical or research nature, are few. That this is so should not be surprising. It is but one aspect of a broader lag in research on psychological aspects of disability,[178] and of a reluctance to provide equal opportunities for deviant persons. With a great shortage of trained personnel, adequate facilities, and equipment, those working with the handicapped have been hard-pressed to meet the demands for services. Faced with practical responsibilities that must be met on a day-to-day basis, it would be difficult for such people to undertake research even if they had the needed technical skills.

Despite the great need for such work, it would be unrealistic to expect that research in psychotherapy with the handicapped could be put on a very substantial footing without the development of more socially favorable attitudes toward the handicapped and a greater interest in the research needs. But such changes do appear to be developing, albeit painfully slowly at times. Contrasted with a generation ago, interest in the application of psychological theory to the understanding of disability and an emphasis on the sociopsychological aspects of disability have grown considerably.[179] Even in a basically understudied area such as psychotherapy with the disabled, a specific subarea of a broadly construed social psychology of disability, indications of activated interest in recent years can be discerned.[180]

Another reason why there has been so little work in therapy with the disabled is that the field of psychotherapy itself is undermanned relative to its present service and research needs. As Sarason stated, "The tremendous demand for psychotherapeutic help, the scarcity of trained personnel, and the amount of time which such efforts entail have forced clinicians to give what little time they have to those cases which promise the most results in the shortest period of time." [181] In the apportionment of the limited man-hours available for service and research in therapy, we have tended to overlook the exceptional child.

Research in psychotherapy, because of the variety and complexity of the variables involved, presents extremely difficult problems, for only in most recent years have we begun to develop specialists with the prerequisite clinical training and experience and the research skills needed to study this area adequately. Effective study of psychotherapy with the exceptional child calls for individuals who combine a sound background in therapy with a thorough grasp of research methods, and an interest in and knowledge of disability. There are altogether too few such people available at the present time.

In evaluating the relatively few available published reports of psychotherapy with exceptional children, several general critical comments seem indicated. A very high percentage of these reports are descriptions of the course of psychotherapy or play-therapy with one or, at the most, several handicapped individuals. Studies involving more than 12 or 15 subjects are few, and most are lacking in rigorous control and objective evaluation.

Generalization about psychotherapy with the exceptional child must, therefore, be tentative. The comparative absence of data, combined with the need for information, produces a situation in which speculation may be confused with fact. Certainly authoritative pronouncements in this area must be regarded with a jaundiced eye. Perhaps the strongest statement that can be made at this time is that there are reports of successful psychotherapy in almost all areas of disability. The relatively high percentage of successful cases among those reported, however, should not be taken as an indication of any general success of therapy with these groups. In many instances, successful outcome may have been one reason why a particular case was selected for publication. A given published report of successful psychotherapy with a disabled person may be based on one out of one, or one out of twenty attempts. Further, the criteria used to evaluate the outcome of therapy in a number of these case reports have been highly subjective and quite possibly unreliable.

While it is true that all groups of exceptional children have been grossly understudied insofar as applications of therapy are concerned, this lack seems most pronounced in the case of visual, auditory, and orthopedic defects, including cerebral palsy. In terms of sheer number of studies reported, variety of approaches used, and methodological contributions, the area of mental deficiency is in the forefront.

We can only speculate as to why this is so. Techniques for working in therapy with the handicapped have not been developed *de novo*. Workers have taken as a point of departure those techniques which have been effective with the non-handicapped individual. Therapy with the non-handicapped person depends heavily on communicative, locomotor, and manipulative functions, the latter two being particularly important in play-therapy. The frequently drastic impairment of one or more of these functions in sensory defect, orthopedic disability, and cerebral palsy may make direct application of therapeutic methods used with the non-disabled difficult and cause therapists and researchers to neglect the study of applications to these groups.

Considerable modification of the therapist's attitudes and customary pattern of responses and behaviors is required if applications are to be undertaken. That most of the studies with mental defectives have been conducted with institutionalized subjects is suggestive of another possible reason. Since communities have increased their efforts to provide locally for mental defectives, those that do migrate to the institutions frequently do so because they have violated community norms. They are problems to themselves and to others, and psychotherapeutic provisions are made in an effort to alter or modify the problem behavior. Also, the tendency has been to provide positions on institutional staffs for professionals who are interested and skilled in conducting research related to the formidable problems faced by these facilities.

Greater flexibility may be required in the application of therapeutic techniques to the disabled child in comparison to the physically normal child. We are not likely to discover any single approach to psychotherapy which is applicable to all disabled groups. In many cases the child's disability will make him less amenable to one medium of therapy than to another. With mental defectives, encouraging results have been obtained using a wide variety of therapeutic media. Because of the extreme heterogeneity of the many handicapped groups, continued study of numerous therapeutic media should be regarded as an essential prerequisite to the development of a sound over-all program in psychotherapy.

Several authors have proposed that play and group activity may be especially valuable for the handicapped child, even in instances where the disability does not preclude the use of individual interview methods. Both Barker and Shiffer pointed out that handicapped children often are deprived of play experience and the normal adjustive and exploratory values that derive from such activities.[182] To the extent that this is true, a sheltered play situation may constitute an ideal therapy setting. A frequent social consequence of disability is the stigmatization and ostracism of the handicapped child. Normal gratification of socialization needs and acceptance by a group may be severely restricted. Consequently the child may be deprived of opportunities to form peer-group identifications, and he may develop feelings of social rejection and isolation. In such instances the potential value of a group approach to therapy seems to be very great.[183]

While the presence of disability may necessitate modification in standard therapeutic practice with various handicapped groups, it would be misleading in planning a therapy program for the disabled to regard them as a breed apart from the non-disabled. For it is also true, as so many writers in this field have stressed, that the handicapped child is first of all a child: "The mentally retarded child, the child with visual impairment, the crippled child, and every other exceptional child has fundamental motives and drives common to all children in general. . . ."[184] Such a viewpoint should be reassuring to those who are discouraged by the relative dearth of information about psychotherapy with the disabled, since it follows that much of our general knowledge about therapy with the non-disabled may be applicable to the handicapped. It does not, therefore, seem either necessary or desirable that we build a new psychotherapy of disability, independent of what we already know about psychotherapy with non-handicapped individuals. We need to overcome the reluctance which limits full engagement in psychotherapy with the handicapped on the part of responsible professional personnel—without overemphasizing the similarities which exist between normal and disabled to the extent that needed modifications or the implications of unique aspects of specific disabilities are ignored.

The therapeutic value of certain core factors in the therapy process, such as the relationship, and the provision of opportunities for expression should apply to the handicapped as well as the non-handicapped. The goals of personal and social amelioration should be roughly constant for both groups. It is primarily in the discovery of techniques and media, which in the light of a particular disability will optimally facilitate the achievement of these goals, that significant differences may be anticipated. Secondarily, it is probable that some concrete modifications in normal therapeutic procedures may be a necessary consequence of certain disabilities. Several investigators who have worked in therapy with the handicapped have already suggested such modifications. Illustratively, Garrett commented, "In view of the effect of brain damage . . . interviews with cerebral palsied clients in crowded, noisy offices will also prove misleading." [185] Bradley emphasized the importance of the therapist's being able to recognize such behaviors as hyperactivity and agitation as prodromal symptoms of convulsions in epileptics, so that he may be able to provide opportunities for the constructive expenditure of the excess energy, thereby helping to forestall the seizure.[186] Cowen and Cruickshank pointed out that unrestricted physical activity with severe cardiacs might have dangerous physical consequences. They stated as a general point that therapy ". . . must operate within a matrix of limitations which protect the child from physical injury resulting from his handicap." [187]

Suggestions for research in psychotherapy with the exceptional child may be made at many levels. Because of the number of pertinent variables involved, if we were to take all possible permutations and combinations into account, research problems numbering into the thousands could be proposed. Many of these would, of course, be problems with implications beyond the area of disability.

In the light of certain general shortcomings of past research in psychotherapy with disabled children, it would be well to indicate several methodological considerations which should have general applicability to subsequent work in this area. The problem of evaluation of therapeutic outcome has frequently been handled unconvincingly.[188] Essentially, the question is: "Is psychotherapy effective?" Although there are many excellent articles on the methodological problems in conducting research in psychotherapy, it is appropriate to comment briefly here on methodology. To determine the effectiveness of what was done requires a determination of what the patient's behavior was prior to therapy and what it is after completion of therapy. The most outstanding methodological problems in this area of outcome research are in sampling and design, control and criteria. Before the development of formal research in psychotherapy, the case study report was frequently used. We have commented on the problem of not knowing whether a case report represents one successful case out of one attempt or one out of twenty. Associated with this are the biases and distortions which may result from the enthusiasm of the investigator. Clinical case studies can be quite useful in developing insights and generating hypotheses, but they are not adequate for testing hypotheses. Proper scientific method calls for controlled observation,[189] and case-study data do not fulfill this requirement.

In designing psychotherapy research, the problem of follow-up should be considered. Changes resulting from therapy and apparent at its termination should persist, and the individual should not return to his original status once therapy has been concluded. In order to determine if observable gains persist over time, evaluations must be made subsequent to the termination of therapy.

What constitutes successful therapy is another methodological problem which must be considered. Improved mental health is one goal we might all agree on but the problem of specifying what is meant by optimal health is yet to be resolved.[190] Agreement is complicated by philosophical and cultural considerations, and the positions taken are strongly influenced by values. Zax and Klein argued recently for more intense use of behavioral criteria, and attempts in this direction appear to be promising.[191]

Pre-therapy evaluation should include detailed information about presenting symptoms and problems, statements concerning the child's behaviors and adjustment from informants who have had frequent contacts with him, and extensive psychodiagnostic data. Thus, clinical and objective data relevant to the patient's pre-therapeutic personality structure and dynamics and outside behaviors in varied settings would be available. Post-therapy evaluation should provide for procurement of additional accounts of the child's behaviors and adjustment from the informants, and readministration of the original test battery. Since therapy cannot always be evaluated accurately at its conclusion, follow-up is essential. Some children who seemed to have progressed in therapy may not continue to show improvements at the time of follow-up, and conversely, some who, at the end of therapy, seem to have been helped little or not at all, may show considerable improvement in follow-up. Evaluation will be more meaningful to the extent that comparable data can be collected during the several appraisal periods. Not infrequently other objective data may also be available (school grades, attempted institutional elopements, number of discipline reports, and the like). Utilization of such data will further enhance an over-all evaluation program.

If we are to conclude that the changes following any intervention came about as a result of the intervention and not from any of a number of possible resources, then controls are needed. In many of the studies cited in this chapter, psychotherapy was only one of a number of program modifications introduced at the same time so that it is difficult to conclude that the observed changes came about as a result of the therapy. With epileptics, for example, there may be conjunctive drug therapy; in some settings psychotherapy may be one aspect of a general re-educative and rehabilitative program. If we hope to identify the particular contribution of the psychotherapy experience in such situations, it will be necessary to use as control subjects individuals who have been exposed to all aspects of the ameliorative program except the therapy experience. Still another type of control group may be necessary in the case of therapeutic work done in an institutional setting. Observed changes in such instances could be independent of the psychotherapeutic experience —perhaps attributed to the value deriving directly from an affectively positive interruption of a boring routine, and the attention of an interested outsider. The proper control here would require the establishment of a "pleasurable activity—non-psychotherapeutic" group, as in the studies by Mehlman and by Snyder and Sechrest.[192] Particularly in research with children, there is the problem of development and, without adequate controls, it is difficult to conclude that the child would not have improved anyway. For some people, and in some circumstances, just the special recognition and attention necessarily accompanying the provision of treatment may be sufficient to produce changes. Finally, as has been observed with patients in mental hospitals, some just seem to get better even though no specific treatment had been provided.

A shortcoming of work in therapy with the disabled child has been the neglect of the basic problem of controls. Lacking these, the degree of confidence that can be placed in research findings is seriously reduced. In this area, controls should enable the experimenter to attribute observed changes in certain dependent variables, such as personality and behavioral measures, to the effects of a specific independent variable— the therapeutic experience. To do this, other pertinent variables which could also account for change in the dependent measures must in some way be held constant.

Several other general approaches to control may be of particular value in research with handicapped groups because of frequent difficulties encountered in obtaining adequate control groups. In some instances there may be differences on pre-test measures between the therapy group and the best control group available. These differences may be taken into account in evaluating post-therapy and follow-up measures by analysis of covariance. Where a control group is not available at all, it may be possible to design the experiment so that each subject can serve as his own control as was done in a study reported by Dorfman.[193] This can be achieved by having a pre-therapy control period, measuring change during this period, and using this as a baseline against which change during a therapy period of similar duration can be compared.

With the exceptional child our confidence in the meaningfulness and stability of results obtained in psychotherapy will increase as studies involving considerably large numbers of subjects are reported. Further, it seems highly desirable that speculations and arbitrary judgments be replaced, or at least augmented, by appropriate tests of statistical significance as criteria in evaluating changes resulting from psychotherapy.

So much for determining the effectiveness of psychotherapy. If we are to improve effectiveness and if broader application to disabled persons is to be made, we need to better understand the process of therapy. The first step in studying the process is to develop useful instruments for description and measurement. Once this has been accomplished, it is possible to analyze a series of cases with respect to relevant aspects of the process. It is also possible at this point to utilize theory for the generation of hypotheses related to cause and effect or relationships between variables. Research of this type is very complex, costly, and time consuming.

With these general methodological considerations as a backdrop, some suggestions may be made regarding more specific research needs. In attempting to set up even the skeleton of a comprehensive research program in psychotherapy with the disabled, the problems involved and variables whose operations we must eventually comprehend are both numerous and complex. It seems clear that at the present stage of our knowledge, the approach to research in this area must be largely empirical, though not necessarily unsystematic in nature. The nature of the therapeutic process with the disabled needs to be studied. Another fundamental problem is: What therapeutic techniques are most effective with which handicapped persons or, given a disabled individual, what operations yield maximal "therapeutic mileage"? To answer this second question: Studies within all disability groups and major subgroups are needed, in which a wide variety of therapeutic approaches constitute the independent variables, and their effects on the dependent personality and behavior measures are compared. Specifically, this will require experimentation with: (a) individual and group therapy, alone and in combination; (b) varied therapeutic media, such as the interview, play techniques, psychodrama, expressive methods, and new approaches which must be developed to deal with special problems presented by some handicapped individuals in need of therapeutic assistance but not amenable to presently available approaches; and (c) differing therapeutic orientations.

A large number of other variables, including age, sex, intelligence, personality configurations, will further help to determine the best therapeutic approach for a given disabled individual. They present problems that are also important determinants of the optimal approach to therapy with the non-disabled. Other factors such as degree of disability, congenital versus acquired disorders, institutional versus non-institutional settings, and length of institutionalization are considerations more specific to handicapped children. The contribution of all of these variables must be taken into account individually and interactively in an experimental program designed to identify preferred approaches to therapy with various handicapped children.

Experimental analogue applications may be helpful in determining the implications of variables of this type for psychotherapy with the disabled. An experimental analogue of psychotherapy is a "controlled laboratory situation involving two or more people, in which the behavior of one person (E) is designed along some relevant dimension(s) to simulate that of a psychotherapist, while in one or more ways the other person (S) is experiencing a feeling of stress, discomfort, or a 'symptom' which in some way approximates that brought by the patient to an actual psychotherapeutic situation. Primarily through the medium of verbal interchange, E seeks to relieve S's present difficulty." [194] An approach of this type significantly reduces the number of variables with which one must contend in an actual therapeutic session with a client. The analogue approach restricts the operation of extraneous variables and permits a cleaner experimental design. While such research is potentially valuable, it should be used as a complement to more traditional approaches in an attempt to gain a more complete understanding of the process and to render it more effective. Work on experimental blindness [195] and experimental deafness [196] suggests possible applications for research on psychotherapy with the disabled.

With this already vast array of problems, we have scarcely skimmed the surface of the potential reservoir of needed research in therapy with the handicapped. In any single approach to therapy, additional problems of considerable import could be proposed. Illustratively, in group therapy, such questions as optimal size of group, frequency and length of

sessions, personality factors in group composition, use of groups containing individuals with different disabilities, or mixed groups of disabled
and non-disabled individuals are all pertinent.

A comprehensive research program taking into account the many variables that have been considered potentially relevant to therapy with the
disabled does not give promise of immediate execution when we attempt
to make a judgment on the basis of the amount or level of current work
in this field. There is a need to exercise considerable selectivity in choosing problems to be studied and to use experimental designs which yield
maximum information for a given time and energy expenditure. Even so,
to gather information carefully on just a few major problems will undoubtedly require several years of intensive study.

In trying to determine the relative immediacy of potential research
problems, it is necessary to draw heavily on our best present knowledge
of the psychology of disability and of psychotherapy with non-disabled
people. In these areas, we may find certain general principles, with at
least clinical if not always research soundness, that may be applied
logically to eliminate many of the potential research problems from the
category of the immediately pressing. Illustratively from our knowledge
of therapy with the non-disabled, the late adolescent and young adult
might be expected to be more responsive to verbal techniques than to
play methods. On this basis we might be willing to accept as a "best
hunch" that the most pressing research problems with the late adolescent
and young adult handicapped will center around systematic variations of
approaches to verbal therapy methods in the light of differences in intelligence and degree and type of emotional disturbance. Such a general
emphasis would, however, have to be appropriately modified by our
knowledge of disability. With the blind, for example, because of frequent
restriction of non-verbal aspects of expression, we might feel even greater
justification than with other handicapped groups in stressing variations in
verbal techniques as the most important variables for study. By contrast,
with the deaf, because of frequent underdevelopment or absence of verbal
communication, it will be imperative at any age level, to explore carefully many types of non-verbal therapeutic media.

The magnitude of the research problem can also be reduced through
judicious use of experimental design. In this regard, analysis of variance
and covariance are tools of great potential usefulness, not only because
they are well suited for use with relatively small numbers of subjects,
but also because they provide a framework within which it is possible
to gain information about the interactions of some of the many variables
operating in the therapy situation.

For those particularly concerned with problems of personality theory and theory of psychotherapy, there is much valuable information which an experimental program in psychotherapy with the disabled may be expected to yield. For example, students of psychotherapy have long been aware that growth through therapy is dependent upon factors over and beyond the actual content of the therapist's responses, such as his vocal intonation, postural adjustments, and facial expression. These variables operate very subtly and are difficult to isolate experimentally in non-disabled people. With deaf and blind individuals, however, we have a situation in which at least one of these more subtle modes of communication in therapy is not available. Through careful analysis of therapeutic sessions with such subjects, it may be possible to gain important general information about the role of these factors in therapeutic growth. Such information gained from work with the disabled would be extremely helpful in therapeutic practice with the non-handicapped.

In general, the detailed protocol of psychotherapy is one of the richest sources of information about personality functioning. Much can be learned about the personality development and defense mechanisms in the handicapped person, through systematic study of the protocols of therapy with such individuals. This, too, represents an area in which study of the handicapped person can be very useful to general personality theory. For example, one frequently mentioned attribute of the handicapped person is his psychological isolation. If, through analysis of therapy protocols with the handicapped, we can come to understand better the reasons for such isolation and the behaviors which it generates, we shall have gained information which should have general applicability to other psychologically isolated but non-handicapped individuals. The usefulness of this approach has already been demonstrated by Barker, who characterized the handicapped in terms of such properties as underprivileged minority status, and marginality. Knowledge gained from the handicapped person about the behavioral consequences of an underprivileged position should presumably have generalized applicability to underprivileged minority groups, while information about their marginal status should be equally meaningful for other marginal groups, such as adolescents and immigrants.[197] Study of these problems of general theoretical interest is highly dependent on the availability of accurate reports of what has taken place in therapy. To this end, the use of movies, sound recordings, and observer accounts of therapy with the disabled will be invaluable.

The scientific study of the use of psychotherapy with the disabled is at a very early age. We have reached a point where uncontrolled observation and armchair speculation are beginning to be augmented by controlled, objective experimentation. Ultimately, we may hope that the fruits of a comprehensive research program in psychotherapy and play techniques will be measured in the better adjustment of a considerable number of exceptional individuals.

Beyond Psychotherapy: An Epilogue

THE VERY title of this chapter and its orientation, thus far, toward the actual usage and estimated potential of psychotherapy and play techniques with the exceptional child and youth may carry with them hidden assumptions that are, at the very least, unwarranted and, at the extreme, dangerous. At least three of these assumptions should be brought out into the open in order to establish a matrix within which the potential contributions of psychotherapy can be effectively and realistically evaluated. These are: (1) That there is a one-to-one correspondence between the psychotherapy or the play experience and the subsequent occurrence of significant personality, intra-psychic, and/or behavioral change; (2) that services in the area of psychotherapy and play are available to the disabled person when needed and desired; (3) that psychotherapy and play techniques constitute the only, or even the primary, basis for the transition from a state of maladjustment, personal unhappiness, and/or maladaptive behavior to one of internal satisfaction and adequate external adjustment. The first two of these assumptions touch on practical, concrete, and empirical issues; the third, however, evokes considerations of a somewhat more conceptual nature.

Since its very beginnings there has been concern, more or less manifest, about how effective psychotherapy is. Although we do not here propose a detailed consideration of the now substantial body of relevant theorizing and research data in this area, several observations are in order. Few, even its most ardent advocates, would argue the 100 per cent effectiveness of psychotherapy. Professional opinions in the matter range from those who view it as virtually always a useful, helping procedure to those who see it as totally ineffectual either with adults [198] or with children.[199] Perhaps the truth will ultimately be found to lie between these positions and will point to more specific and circumscribed, rather than indiscriminate, bases for its applicability. Concerning our first hidden assumption, then, it is not justifiable to assume that the mere application of psychotherapy or play techniques guarantees a positive outcome. Psychotherapy, in its present state, is an approximate and quite fallible procedure—not a panacea or a cure-all. Though it may be the best approach for some problems it is not the best approach for all problems. And even where it is the best approach, there is no guarantee of its effectiveness. Sometimes these limitations are not known to the potential "consumer" who may be inclined to endow psychotherapy with magical and sure-fire properties that it does not possess. Anna Freud has spoken to the point, as follows:

> There is no lack of confidence in the clinic on the part of the public; again, if anything, there is too much. With many people, the concept of treatment in a clinic has acquired a magical connotation. Little difference is made between children who suffer from environmental neglect, unsuitable parents, tragic bereavements, and those cases where something has gone wrong in the development and personality structure for internal reasons. In both instances to know that a child is in treatment seems to spell safety to parents, welfare agencies or public authorities, as if every nonorganic disturbance were automatically suitable for psychological treatment, and as if treatment guaranteed a cure in all cases. Paradoxically enough, it will soon be necessary on the part of the clinics to disabuse the public, i.e., to induce people to lower their expectations of therapy to a level more justified by the conditions and limitations imposed by reality.[200]

With respect to matters of effectiveness, there is the very real danger that psychotherapy can be "oversold," relative to what we can realistically hope it to be able to achieve.

The question of effectiveness of psychotherapy aside, we are coming to appreciate more fully that there is an ever-increasing number of adults and children with mental health problems who require help. Whether this recognition reflects a growing sensitivity to psychological function and its perturbations by the public at large, keener diagnostic techniques, or whatever, the net result is a deeper skepticism concerning the extent to which psychotherapy will ever be able to meet these needs. Prior to the report by Albee on the manpower situation in the mental health field [201] it was thought that expanded training opportunities would turn out trained personnel in sufficient numbers to meet the need if we would but wait. Albee concluded, however, that adequate services would never become available if the present increase in population continues without an accompanying increase in the training of mental health personnel. Speaking generally, we cannot now adequately provide professional mental health services for those who require them. The demonstration of greater need for such services among the disabled will not necessarily alter this fact.

Certain other considerations, some relatively subtle, may mean that the disabled person will be in an "underprivileged" position regarding the availability of psychotherapeutic services. It has been proposed, for example, that consciously or otherwise therapists exercise biases about the type of patient who can best use psychotherapy. Strupp [202] has indicated that the "ideal" adult therapy prospect is young, attractive, and well educated. He belongs to the upper middle class, has good ego strength, and has no serious neurotic symptoms. He communicates well, is willing to talk about his problems, and shares the therapist's value system. Whether or not it is warranted, there may be a tendency to perceive the disabled individual as one who does not fully conform to the profile of the ideal patient. To the extent that this may happen, we should anticipate the possibilities either of outright denial of service or else of a downgrading of the individual's attractiveness as a candidate for services by private therapists or by clinic personnel based on the additional complicating fact of disability. Realistically then, it may make little sense to argue that disabled children should receive psychotherapy when in fact is not readily available.

Two directions for future action suggest themselves as logical consequents of the foregoing view. First, since much current effort with the disabled child is aimed toward keeping him at home, in school, and in the community, it is important that considerable energy be expended with professional workers, both in private and clinic settings, so that those youngsters who need and can effectively use mental health services will in fact receive such services. Regrettably, judgments about the disabled child's suitability for treatment may too often be based at this time upon the fact of disability and the therapist's lack of experience with such conditions, rather than upon objective evaluation of his mental health status and his ability to profit from therapy. And secondly, support and encouragement should be extended in the search for effective alternative approaches to large-scale containment and reduction of maladjustment.

Perhaps the least tangible of the three assumptions that we are reviewing is the last one—i.e., that the choice of psychotherapy and play as the primary foci of this chapter may subtly suggest that these are the only, or even the dominant, approaches to amelioration of mental health problems. Such a presumption would not be defensible. Broadly speaking, there are two types of approaches to problems of mental health: the *curative* or *therapeutic* ones, which seek to deal with identified instances of disturbance by the best available means, and the *preventive* or *prophylactic* ones, which orient themselves in a longer range sense toward the elimination of sources of maldevelopment.

The therapeutic orientation subsumes a wide variety of interventions. Included would be such treatment methods as physical and occupational therapies; surgical, medical, and chemical therapies; environmental-manipulative therapies; and psychotherapy. The latter, at best, cannot be regarded as more than a single, limited component of a comprehensive, multi-faceted orientation. Moreover, its intrinsic nature is such that it requires more or less concentrated attention with a given individual for substantial periods of time. Culturally speaking, psychotherapy as we now know it cannot be expected to reach great numbers of individuals. This problem is further complicated by the noticeable tendency for the most highly trained professional specialists to serve only a selected portion of the population in need of help.

Faced with the increasing realization of these "facts of life," it becomes important to encourage budding, but nevertheless evident, reappraisals of our traditional preferences for dealing with mental health problems, and to devise alternative techniques, methods, and facilities in a manner that will provide help for greater numbers of people who are emotionally disturbed.[203] Clearly, greater exploration must be directed to interventions that, in addition to being effective, can also be made broadly available. Illustratively, Schiffer has reported a training program for teachers and counselors to lead therapeutic play groups [204] and, going a considerable step further, Rioch is now involved in training housewives in a therapeutically oriented type of function.[205] This is not to establish the effectiveness or the validity of such approaches; it is merely to suggest that the area is very worthwhile and extremely important one for research. Growing efforts may also be observed toward increased involvement in and increased responsibility by the schools for the mental health needs of school children. Laycock has identified five reasons justifying greater involvement on the part of schools in relation to emotionally disturbed children.[206] There have been numerous other articles on the role of the teacher and education in work with emotionally disturbed children.[207] These efforts being made by schools are but part of the larger picture, which also includes the need for a wide range of community resources and facilities presently in short supply if adequate attention is to be given to the emotional problems of the disabled child.

The point to be emphasized is that research along these lines, coupled with rigorous studies to assess the effectiveness of these innovations, is sorely needed. A principal implication here is that the social reward will be much greater if techniques can be found with which relatively untrained workers can provide these necessary services. It should also be possible to find groups of professionals with natural ability and relevant prior training, capable of profitably applying specially designed mental health principles and programs. The mental health specialist could vastly increase his functional effectiveness by providing pertinent training for others and by serving as a consultant to those who are actually providing service.[208]

Also, psychology in general is becoming increasingly aware of the historic underdevelopment of its preventive as contrasted with its treatment potential. The original spirit underlying the development of the term "mental hygiene" was indeed preventive in nature. But preventive work, in addition to being expensive and time consuming, tends to give the illusion of being less concrete, less dramatic, and less pressing than therapy, which is directed to immediate, tangible, and already manifest disturbance. Hence it has been neglected. There is reason to find gratifying the recent resurgence of interest in preventive functions. We shall not review this work here, since it has been considered elsewhere.[209] It may, however, be appropriate to cite a point of view about such work.

> Preventive work . . . because it precedes the full-blown occur-
> rence of pathology carries with it the potential for reaching large
> segments of the population early in their careers and in a manner
> which vastly extends the effectiveness of resources of existing pro-
> fessional specialties. A strong case can therefore be made for the
> thesis that preventive approaches to mental health should be re-
> garded as the primary focus of any comprehensive program de-
> signed to bring about a "saner society" of tomorrow.[210]

Quite likely there are many prospective indirect benefits to the disabled inherent in any large-scale preventive mental health oriented program. There is, in addition, much to be gained from careful consideration of specific facets and details of prevention programs that might hopefully be of direct value to the disabled person.

Our analysis leads us to the view that psychotherapy cannot be regarded as an unqualifiedly effective procedure, that even if it were, necessary services for the exceptional individual are not now available and do not appear to be available in the foreseeable future. In fact it is to be expected that this situation will become increasingly, rather than decreasingly, acute. Fundamentally, however, it would be a mistake to view psychotherapy as the only weapon in the mental health armamentarium. It is not! We must be increasingly oriented in the future toward greater exploration of potential resources in the area of prevention and toward the broadening of our ameliorative approaches so that greater numbers of less highly specialized workers become involved in service contacts with substantially greater numbers of exceptional individuals.

Psychotherapy should not be oversold; nor should it be sold down the river. There is, indeed, an important place for it in a balanced and reasoned over-all approach to the mental health problems of the disabled. But progress in this area will be accelerated only if we do not constrict ourselves by thinking first of psychotherapy and grafting other approaches on to that corpus. Perhaps it is somewhat ironic that the authors of a chapter on psychotherapy and play techniques appear to be approaching the view that their contribution on this level must be sharply limited. Indeed, it may be more useful in future compendia to replace a chapter on psychotherapy and play techniques with a somewhat broader one on mental health approaches with the disabled. Certainly such a title would suffer less from implicit ills of prejudgment.

From one point of view we need to be clear about what psychotherapy is and what it clearly is not. However, this plea for conceptual clarity should not be misused to discourage the development of other "helping" techniques, particularly those that give promise of reaching greater numbers of disabled individuals. In the final analysis, it does not much matter what a technique is called so long as the method itself can be clearly specified and its effectiveness determined.

Notes

[1] B. A. Wright, *Physical Disability—A Psychological Approach* (New York: Harper & Row, Publishers, 1960), p. 53, and E. L. Cowen, R. P. Underberg, R. T. Verrillo, and F. G. Benham, *Adjustment to Visual Disability in Adolescence* (New York: American Foundation for the Blind, 1961).

[2] R. G. Barker, *et al.*, *Adjustment to Physical Handicap and Illness*, 2nd ed. (New York: Social Science Research Council, 1953).

[3] R. G. Barker, "The Social Psychology of Physical Disability," *Journal of Social Issues*, IV (1948), 28.

[4] G. W. Shaffer and R. S. Lazarus, *Fundamental Concepts in Clinical Psychology* (New York: McGraw-Hill Book Co., Inc., 1952), chap. ix.

[5] See F. Fromm-Reichman, *Principles of Intensive Psychotherapy* (Chicago: University of Chicago Press, 1950), p. x; and R. Waelder, "Areas of Agreement in Psychotherapy," *American Journal of Orthopsychiatry*, X (1940), 705.

[6] W. U. Snyder, "The Present Status of Psychotherapeutic Counseling," *Psychological Bulletin*, XLIV (1947), 297-386; and R. A. Harper, *Psychoanalysis and Psychotherapy, 36 Systems* (Englewood Cliffs, N.J.: Prentice-Hall, Inc., 1959).

[7] W. U. Snyder, *op. cit.*, p. 298.

[8] See E. J. Shoben, "Some Observations on Psychotherapy and the Learning Process," in *Psychotherapy: Theory and Research*, ed. O. H. Mowrer (New York: The Ronald Press Company, 1953), p. 125.

[9] By permission from *Fundamental Concepts in Clinical Psychology*, by G. W. Shaffer and R. S. Lazarus, p. 298. Copyright, 1952. McGraw-Hill Book Company, Inc.

[10] By permission from *Principles of Intensive Psychotherapy*, by F. Fromm-Reichman, p. x. Copyright, 1950. University of Chicago Press.

[11] G. W. Shaffer and R. S. Lazarus, *op. cit.*, pp. 298 ff.

[12] See S. Rosenzweig, "Some Implicit Common Factors in Diverse Methods of Psychotherapy," *American Journal of Orthopsychiatry*, VI (1936), 412; and C. R. Rogers, *Client-Centered Therapy* (Boston: Houghton-Mifflin Company, 1951), p. 31.

[13] See G. Watson, "Areas of Agreement in Psychotherapy," *American Journal of Orthopsychiatry*, X (1940), 706; and C. R. Rogers, *Counseling and Psychotherapy* (Boston: Houghton-Mifflin Company, 1942), p. 31.

[14] Fuller discussion of this very important point may be found in Shaffer and Lazarus, *op. cit.*, chap. ix; "Areas of Agreement in Psychotherapy," *op. cit.*, pp. 698-707; R. I. Watson, *The Clinical Method in Psychology* (New York: Harper & Row, Publishers, 1951), chap. xviii; and H. L. Witmer, ed., *Psychiatric Interviews with Children* (New York: The Commonwealth Fund, Harvard University Press, 1946), chap. iii.

[15] S. Rosenzweig, *op. cit.*, pp. 414 ff.

584   EMORY L. COWEN AND MATTHEW J. TRIPPE

16 F. E. Fiedler, "The Concept of an Ideal Therapeutic Relationship," *Journal of Consulting Psychology*, XIV (1950), 238-245; F. E. Fiedler, "A Comparison of Therapeutic Relationships in Psychoanalytic, Non-Directive and Adlerian Therapy," *Journal of Consulting Psychology*, XIV (1950), 346-445; and F. E. Fiedler, "Factor Analyses of Psychoanalytic, Non-Directive and Adlerian Therapeutic Relationships," *Journal of Consulting Psychology*, XV (1851), 32-38.

17 F. E. Fiedler, "The Concept of the Ideal Therapeutic Relationship," *Journal of Consulting Psychology*, XIV (1950), 239-245.

18 See K. M. Colby, *A Primer for Psychotherapists* (New York: The Ronald Press Company, 1951), pp. 8 ff., for a discussion of some differences in the use of techniques between classical analysis and his framework for psychotherapy.

19 S. Rosenzweig, *op. cit.*, p. 412.

20 Fromm-Reichmann, *op. cit.*, p. ix; S. Rosenzweig, *op. cit.*, p. 412; and R. E. Pittenger, C. F. Hockett, and J. J. Danehy, *The First Five Minutes, A Sample of Microscopic Interview Analysis* (Ithaca, N. Y.: Paul Martineau Publ., 1960).

21 By permission from *The Clinical Method in Psychology*, by R. I. Watson, pp. 563 ff. Copyright, 1951. Harper and Brothers. See also "Areas of Agreement in Psychotherapy," *op. cit.*, pp. 708 ff.; and Rogers (1942), *op. cit.*, p. 40.

22 C. R. Rogers (1951), *op. cit.*, pp. 43 ff.

23 By permission from *Fundamental Concepts in Clinical Psychology*, by G. W. Shaffer and R. S. Lazarus, p. 310. Copyright, 1952. McGraw-Hill Book Company, Inc.

24 V. M. Axline, *Play Therapy* (Boston: Houghton-Mifflin Company, 1947), p. 9; and L. Jackson and K. M. Todd, *Child Treatment and the Therapy of Play*, 2nd ed. (New York: The Ronald Press Company, 1950), p. xi.

25 R. I. Watson, *op. cit.*, p. 669.

26 L. Jackson and K. M. Todd, *op. cit.*, p. 51.

27 For a comprehensive summary of seventeen specific objectives in one form of child psychotherapy see S. R. Slavson, *Child Psychotherapy* (New York: Columbia University Press, 1952), pp. 158 ff.

28 L. Jackson and K. M. Todd, *op. cit.*, p. 129.

29 R. I. Watson, *op. cit.*, pp. 674 ff.

30 Cogent discussion of this question is available in R. I. Watson, *op. cit.*, pp. 622 ff.; Slavson, *op. cit.*, pp. 143 ff.; and E. Dorfman, "Play Therapy," in Rogers (1951), *op. cit.*, chap. vi.

31 Slavson, *op. cit.*, pp. 143 ff.

32 G. Filmer-Bennett and J. S. Hillson, "Some Child Therapy Practices," *Journal of Clinical Psychology*, XIV (1959), 105-106.

33 R. I. Watson, *op. cit.*, p. 662; Slavson, *op. cit.*, p. 114.

34 R. I. Watson, *op. cit.*, p. 664; Slavson, *op. cit.*, p. 143.

35 R. I. Watson, *op. cit.*, p. 665.

36 Slavson, *op. cit.*, p. 257.

37 L. Jackson and K. M. Todd, *op. cit.*, p. 75.

38 Axline, *op. cit.*, p. 68.

39 A. Freud, "The Child Guidance Clinic as a Center of Prophylaxis and Enlightenment," in *Recent Developments in Psychoanalytic Child Therapy*, ed. J. Weinreb (New York: International Universities Press, Inc., 1960), pp. 32 ff.

40 By permission from *Recent Developments in Psychoanalytic Child Therapy*, by J. Weinreb (ed.), from "The Child Guidance Clinic as a Center of Prophylaxis and Enlightenment," by A. Freud, pp. 37-38. Copyright, 1960. International Universities Press, Inc.

41 F. H. Allen, *Psychotherapy with Children* (New York: W. W. Norton & Company, Inc., 1942).

42 Witmer, *op. cit.*, p. 48.

43 J. L. Despert, "Play Therapy," *Nervous Child*, VII (1948), 288.

44 Witmer, *op. cit.*, pp. 40 ff.

45 Axline, *op. cit.*, pp. 75 ff.

[46] R. I. Watson, *op. cit.*, p. 663.

[47] C. E. Moustakas, *Children in Play Therapy* (New York: McGraw-Hill Book Co., Inc., 1953), p. 1.

[48] H. G. Ginott, *Group Psychotherapy with Children* (New York: McGraw-Hill Book Co., Inc., 1961), pp. 102 ff.

[49] H. G. Ginott and D. Lebo, "Play Therapy Limits and Theoretical Orientation," *Journal of Consulting Psychology*, XXV (1961), 337-341.

[50] Axline, *op. cit.*, p. 9.

[51] See R. I. Watson, *op. cit.*, p. 670; Slavson, *op. cit.*, p. 294; Axline, *op. cit.*, chap. iii; and H. G. Ginott, *op. cit.*, chaps. v and vi.

[52] H. G. Ginott, *op. cit.*, chap. x.

[53] L. H. Gondor, "Use of Fantasy Communications in Child Psychotherapy," *American Journal of Psychotherapy*, XI (1957), 323-335.

[54] J. C. Soloman, "Therapeutic Play Techniques, Symposium, 1954: Play Technique and The Integrative Process," *American Journal of Orthopsychiatry*, XXV (1955), 591-600.

[55] G. Hambridge, "Therapeutic Play Techniques, Symposium, 1954: Structured Play Therapy," *American Journal of Orthopsychiatry*, XXV (1955), 601-617.

[56] M. Kaplan, *et al.*, "The Control of Acting Out in the Psychotherapy of Delinquents," *American Journal of Psychiatry*, CXIII (1957), 1108-1114.

[57] D. Lebo and E. Lebo, "Aggression and Age in Relation to Verbal Expression in Non-Directive Psychotherapy," *Psychological Monographs*, LXXI, No. 449 (1957).

[58] C. Moustakas, "The Frequency of Negative Attitudes Expressed in Play Therapy: A Comparison of Well Adjusted and Disturbed Young Children," *Journal of Genetic Psychology*, LXXXIV (1955), 309-325.

[59] Axline, *op. cit.*, p. 26.

[60] Slavson, *op. cit.*, chap. xi.

[61] Ginott, *op. cit.*, pp. 2 ff.

[62] L. Jackson and K. M. Todd, *op. cit.*, p. 51.

[63] L. M. Brammer, and E. L. Shostrom, *Therapeutic Psychology: Fundamentals of Counseling and Psychotherapy* (Englewood Cliffs, N.J.: Prentice-Hall, Inc., 1960), pp. 290-291.

[64] See, for example, W. M. Cruickshank, "The Impact of Physical Disability on Adjustment," *Journal of Social Issues*, IV (1948), 78-83.

[65] M. T. Hollingshead, "The Role of Discipline in Psychotherapy with the Handicapped," *Nervous Child*, IX (1949), 157.

[66] B. A. Wright (1960), *op. cit.*, p. 53.

[67] P. H. Mussen and D. K. Newman, "Acceptance of Handicap, Motivation, and Adjustment in Physically Disabled Children," *Exceptional Children*, XXIV (1957), 255-260 and 277-278.

[68] E. S. Levine, "The Deaf," in *Psychological Aspects of Physical Disability*, ed. J. F. Garrett, Rehabilitation Services Series, No. 210 (Washington, D.C.: Office of Vocational Rehabilitation, 1952), p. 144.

[69] See B. Lowenfeld, "The Blind," in Garrett, *op. cit.*, p. 191, and B. Lowenfeld, "Mental Hygiene in Blindness," in *Psychological Diagnosis and Counseling of Adult Blind*, eds. W. Donahue and D. Dablestein (New York: American Foundation for the Blind, 1950), p. 42.

[70] E. G. Omwake and A. J. Solnit, " 'It Isn't Fair': The Treatment of the Blind Child," in *The Psychoanalytic Study of the Child*, eds. R. Eissler, A. Freud, H. Hartmann and M. Kris (New York: International Universities Press, Inc., 1961), pp. 352-404.

[71] Axline, *op. cit.*, chap. xxi.

[72] J. Rothschild, "Play Therapy with Blind Children," *New Outlook For The Blind*, LIV (1960), 329-333.

[73] R. M. Dickinson, "Counseling Services for Pre-School Blind Children," *Outlook for the Blind*, XLII (1948), 75-79.

74 The major portion of these proceedings are reproduced in Donahue and Dablestein, *op. cit.*

75 *Research Suggestions on Psychological Problems Associated with Blindness* (Washington, D.C.: Federal Security Agency, Office of Vocational Rehabilitation, 1956), p. 11.

76 B. A. Wright, ed., *Psychology and Rehabilitation* (Washington: American Psychological Association, 1959), p. 80.

77 B. McQuie, "Severely Disturbed Blind Children," *The International Journal for Education of the Blind*, IX (1960), 93-96.

78 R. F. Hejna, *Speech Disorders and Nondirective Therapy: Client-Centered Counseling and Play Therapy* (New York: The Ronald Press Company, 1960).

79 A. T. Murphy and R. M. Fitzsimons, *Stuttering and Personality Dynamics* (New York: The Ronald Press Company, 1960).

80 See, for example, T. M. Abel, "Facial Disfigurement" in Garrett, *op. cit.*, p. 122; and D. H. Harris, "Psychological Aspects of Tuberculosis," in *ibid.*, p. 108.

81 V. M. Axline and C. R. Rogers, "A Teacher Therapist Deals with a Handicapped Child," *Journal of Abnormal and Social Psychology*, XL (1945), 119-142.

82 M. Schiffer, "Activity Group Therapy with Exceptional Children," in S. R. Slavson (ed.), *The Practice of Group Therapy* (New York: International Universities Press, Inc., 1947), chap. iii.

83 G. Bychowski and J. L. Despert, "Psychotherapy with Crippled and Disabled" in *Specialized Techniques in Psychotherapy* edited by Bychowski and Despert (New York: Basic Books, Inc., 1952), pp. 185-206.

84 E. P. Bernabeu, "The Effects of Severe Crippling on the Development of a Group of Children," *Psychiatry*, XXI (1958), 169-194.

85 S. H. Cath, E. Glud, and H. T. Blane, "The Role of the Body Image in Psychotherapy with the Physically Handicapped," *Psychoanalytic Review*, XLIV (1958), 34-40.

86 E. A. Miller, "Cerebral Palsied Children and Their Parents," *Exceptional Children*, XXIV (1958), 298-302.

87 B. Rubenstein, "Therapeutic Use of Groups in an Orthopedic Hospital School," *American Journal of Orthopsychiatry*, XV (1945), 662-674.

88 W. M. Cruickshank and E. L. Cowen, "Group Therapy with Physically Handicapped Children I, Report of a Study," *Journal of Educational Psychology*, XXXIX (1948), 193-215.

89 E. L. Cowen and W. M. Cruickshank, "Group Therapy with Physically Handicapped Children II, Evaluation," *Journal of Educational Psychology*, XXXIX (1948), 281-397.

90 Schiffer, *op. cit.*, pp. 67 ff.

91 S. R. Slavson, "Treatment of a Neurotic Nine-Year-Old Boy with Organic Deficiency," in Slavson, *op. cit.*, chap. xi.

92 Miller, *op. cit.*

93 A. L. Deutsch and L. L. Wiener, "Children with Epilepsy: Emotional Problems and Treatment," *American Journal of Orthopsychiatry*, XVIII (1948), 71.

94 K. A. Menninger, "The Psychoanalytic Study of a Case of Organic Epilepsy," *Psychoanalytic Review*, XIII (1926), 187-199; O. Deithelm, "Brief Psychotherapeutic Interviews in the Treatment of Epilepsy," *American Journal of Psychiatry*, CIII (1947), 806-810; S. Cobb, "Psychiatric Approach to the Treatment of Epilepsy," *American Journal of Psychiatry*, XCVI (1940), 1002-1022; A. L. Deutsch and J. Zimmerman, "Group Therapy as Adjunct Treatment of Epileptic Patients," *American Journal of Psychiatry*, CIV (1948), 783-785; and G. C. Randall and W. C. Rogers, "Group Therapy for Epileptics," *American Journal of Psychiatry*, CVII (1950), 422-427; and N. Michael, "Epilepsy in College Students," *Ohio State Medical Journal*, XVIII (1952), 42.

95 E. M. Bridge, *Epilepsy and Convulsive Disorders in Children* (New York: McGraw-Hill Book Co., Inc., 1949), chap. xiii.

[96] *Ibid.*, p. 419; see also C. Bradley, "Treatment of the Convulsive Child in a Children's Psychiatric Hospital," *Nervous Child*, VI (1947), 81.

[97] By permission from *Epilepsy and Convulsive Disorders in Children*, by E. M. Bridge, p. 420. Copyright, 1949. McGraw-Hill Book Co., Inc.

[98] *Ibid.*, pp. 434 ff.

[99] *Ibid.*, p. 436.

[100] Bradley, *op. cit.*, p. 81.

[101] Deutsch and Zimmerman, *op. cit.*, p. 783.

[102] R. G. Hart, "Relationship Therapy in a Children's Psychiatric Ward," *American Journal of Psychiatry*, CIV (1947), 132-134.

[103] *Ibid.*, p. 132.

[104] Deutsch and Wiener, *op. cit.*, pp. 65-72.

[105] L. Gottschalk, "Effects of Intensive Psychotherapy on Epileptic Children," *A.M.A. Archives of Neurology and Psychiatry*, LXXX (1953), 361-384.

[106] *Ibid.*, p. 361.

[107] See K. F. Heiser, "Applications of Clinical Psychology to Mental Deficiency," in *Progress in Clinical Psychology*, eds. D. Brower and L. E. Abt (New York: Grune & Stratton, Inc., 1952), I, 450; and S. B. Sarason, "The Psychology of Exceptional Children," in *Helping Parents to Understand the Exceptional Child* (Langhorne, Pa.: The Woods Schools, 1952), p. 20.

[108] See S. B. Sarason, *Psychological Problems in Mental Deficiency* (New York: Harper & Row, Publishers, 1949), chap. x; S. Neham, "Psychotherapy in Relation to Mental Deficiency," *American Journal of Mental Deficiency*, LV (1952), 557-571; C. L. Stacey and M. F. DeMartino, eds., *Counseling and Psychotherapy with the Mentally Retarded* (Glencoe: Free Press of Glencoe, 1957); and H. C. Gunzburg, "Psychotherapy with the Feeble-Minded," in *Mental Deficiency, The Changing Outlook*, eds. A. Clarke and A. Clarke (Glencoe: Free Press of Glencoe, 1958).

[109] See, for example, Sarason (1948), *op. cit.*, p. 263; Neham, *op. cit.*, pp. 559 ff.; and T. M. Abel, "Resistances and Difficulties in Psychotherapy of Mental Retardates," *Journal of Clinical Psychology*, IX (1953), 107.

[110] Heiser, *op. cit.*, p. 456.

[111] L. P. Clark, *The Nature and Treatment of Amentia* (Baltimore: The William & Wilkins Co., 1933), pp. 218 ff.; and L. P. Clark, "The Present and Future Outlook in the Treatment of Amentia," *Psychiatric Quarterly*, VII (1933), 50-70.

[112] L. Chidester, "Therapeutic Results with Mentally Retarded Children," *American Journal of Orthopsychiatry*, IV (1934), 464-472; N. W. Ackerman and C. F. Menninger, "Treatment Techniques in a School for Personality Disorders in Children," *American Journal of Orthopsychiatry*, VI (1936), 294-312; and L. Chidester and K. Menninger, "The Application of Psychoanalytic Methods to the Study of Mental Retardation," *American Journal of Orthopsychiatry*, VI (1936), 616-624.

[113] Other studies dealing with the modifiability of intelligence following therapy have also grown out of this early work. Since they deal primarily with children of borderline intelligence or higher, they will not be treated here. See, for example, E. Miller, "Emotional Factors in Intellectual Retardation," *Journal of Mental Science*, LXXIX (1933), 614-626; S. G. Dulsky, "Affect and Intellect: An Experimental Study," *Journal of Genetic Psychology*, XXVII (1947), 199-220; and G. Kriegman and J. R. Hilgard, "Intelligence Level and Psychotherapy with Problem Children," *American Journal of Orthopsychiatry*, XIV (1944), 251-265.

[114] Sarason (1949), *op. cit.*, pp. 268 ff.

[115] S. W. Hartwell, *Fifty-Five "Bad" Boys* (New York: Alfred A. Knopf, Inc., 1946).

[116] F. Feldman, "Psychoneurosis in the Mentally Retarded," *American Journal of Mental Deficiency*, LI (1946), 247-253.

[117] Sarason (1949), *op. cit.*, pp. 282 ff.

[118] A. Sion, "Casework with an Adolescent Boy of Moron Intelligence," *American Journal of Mental Deficiency*, LVII (1953), 709-718.

[119] J. M. Cooley, "The Relative Amenability of Dull and Bright Children to Child Guidance," *Smith College Studies in Social Work*, XVI (1945), 26-43.

[120] F. C. Thorne, "Counseling and Psychotherapy with Mental Defectives," *American Journal of Mental Deficiency*, LII (1952), 263-271.

[121] *Ibid.*, p. 269.

[122] *Ibid.*, p. 271.

[123] F. Thorne, "Tutorial Counseling with Mental Defectives," *Journal of Clinical Psychology*, XVI (1960), 73-79.

[124] V. M. Axline, "Some Observations on Play Therapy," *Journal of Consulting Psychology*, XII (1948), 209-216.

[125] E. A. Maisner, "Contributions of Play Therapy Techniques to Total Rehabilitative Design in an Institution for High Grade Mentally Deficient and Borderline Children," *American Journal of Mental Deficiency*, LV (1950), 235-250.

[126] *Ibid.*, p. 246.

[127] V. M. Axline, "Mental Deficiency—Symptom or Disease?" *Journal of Consulting Psychology*, XIII (1949), 313-327. Axline notes, in presenting background information about these children, that four were visually handicapped, one deaf, two spastic, one post-poliomyelitis, and that all the others had speech problems. Little reference to these disabilities is made in the subsequent report, however.

[128] *Ibid.*, p. 314.

[129] Neham, *op. cit.*, p. 569.

[130] See E. A. Doll, "Essentials of an Inclusive Concept of Mental Deficiency," *American Journal of Mental Deficiency*, XLI (1946), 215.

[131] L. Mundy, "Therapy with Physically and Mentally Handicapped Children in a Mental Deficiency Hospital," *Journal of Clinical Psychology*, XIII (1957), 3-9.

[132] L. Subotnik and R. Callahan, "A Pilot Study in Short-term Play Therapy With Institutionalized Educable Mentally Retarded Boys," *American Journal of Mental Deficiency*, LXIII (1959), 730-735.

[133] N. L. Boyd, "Some Experiments in Group Work and Play as Related to Change in Social Behavior," *Welfare Bulletin, Illinois State Dept.*, XXXV (1944), 17-19.

[134] M. Cotzin, "Group Psychotherapy with Mentally Defective Problem Boys," *American Journal of Mental Deficiency*, LIII (1948), 268-283.

[135] Abel (1953), *op. cit.*, p. 109.

[136] L. A. Fisher and I. N. Wolfson, "Group Therapy of Mental Defectives," *American Journal of Mental Deficiency*, LVII (1953), 463-476. There are several other reports of applications of Slavson's activity group therapy with markedly retarded, though not defective, children, including that by M. Shiffer in S. R. Slavson (1947), *op. cit.*, chap. iii; and S. R. Slavson, H. Wiener, and S. Schedliger, "Activity Group Therapy with a Dull Delinquent Boy of Eleven," *Nervous Child*, IV (1945), 274-290.

[137] Fisher and Wolfson, *op. cit.*, p. 474.

[138] B. Mehlman, "Group Therapy with Mentally Retarded Children," *Journal of Abnormal and Social Psychology*, XLVIII (1953), 53-60.

[139] K. Woodward, M. Siegel, and M. Eustis, "Psychiatric Study of Mentally Retarded Children of Pre-School Age: Report on 1st and 2nd Years of a Three Year Project," *American Journal of Orthopsychiatry*, XXVIII (1958), 376-393.

[140] N. O'Conner and K. A. Yonge, "Methods of Evaluating the Group Psychotherapy of Unstable Defective Delinquents," *Journal of Genetic Psychology*, LXXXVII (1955), 89-101.

[141] R. Snyder and L. Sechrest, "An Experimental Study of Directive Group Therapy with Defective Delinquents," *American Journal of Mental Deficiency*, LXIV (1959), 117-123.

[142] T. M. Abel (1953), *op. cit.*, p. 108.

[143] H. Shaefer-Simmern, *The Unfolding of Artistic Activity* (Berkeley: University of California Press, 1948).

[144] H. Shaefer-Simmern and S. B. Sarason, "Therapeutic Implications of Artistic Activity in a Case Study," *American Journal of Mental Deficiency*, XLIX (1949), 185-196.

145 Abel (1953), *op. cit.*, pp. 108 ff.

146 M. Z. Menzel, "Psychotherapeutic Techniques Among the Mentally Deficient," *American Journal of Mental Deficiency*, LVI (1952), 796-802.

147 Abel (1953), *op. cit.*, p. 109.

148 Neham, *op. cit.*, pp. 557-571.

149 K. F. Heiser, "Psychotherapy for the Mentally Retarded Child," *Training School Bulletin*, XLVIII (1951), 111-119.

150 F. Redl, "The Concept of a Therapeutic Milieu," *American Journal of Orthopsychiatry*, XXIX (1959), 721-736.

151 G. Konopka, "Institutional Treatment of Emotionally Disturbed Children," *Crime and Delinquency*, VIII (1962), 52-57.

152 H. Leland and D. Smith, "Unstructured Material in Play Therapy for Emotionally Disturbed, Brain Damaged, and Mentally Retarded Children," *American Journal of Mental Deficiency*, LXVI (1962), 621-628.

153 R. Kaldeck, "Psychiatric Approach to Mental Deficiency," *American Journal of Mental Deficiency*, LXIV (1959), 50-56.

154 H. C. Gunzburg, *op. cit.*, p. 367.

155 F. Thorne (1952), *op. cit.*

156 J. Tizard, "Residential Care of Mentally Handicapped Children," *British Medical Journal*, 5178 (1960), 1041-1046.

157 Neham, *op. cit.*, p. 568.

158 Leland and Smith, *op. cit.*

159 Neham, *op. cit.*, p. 568.

160 G. Filmer-Bennett and J. S. Hillson, *op. cit.*

161 S. B. Sarason, "Individual Psychotherapy with Mentally Defective Individuals," *American Journal of Mental Deficiency*, LVI (1952), 803-805; Cotzin, *op. cit.*, p. 282; B. Mehlman, "Non-Directive Group Play Therapy with Institutionalized Endogenous Mental Defective Children" (Doctoral dissertation, Syracuse University, 1951), pp. 6 ff.

162 By permission from *Journal of Abnormal and Social Psychology*, for "A Teacher Therapist Deals with a Handicapped Child," by V. M. Axline and C. R. Rogers, p. 129. Volume XL. 1945.

163 *Ibid.*, p. 130.

164 By permission from *Journal of Educational Psychology*, for "Group Therapy with Physically Handicapped Children I, Report of a Study," by W. M. Cruickshank and E. L. Cowen, pp. 212 ff. Volume XXXIX. 1948.

165 *Ibid.*, p. 213.

166 *Ibid.*, p. 214.

167 Westlund and Palumbo, "Parental Rejection of Crippled Children," *American Journal of Orthopsychiatry*, XIV (1946), 272 ff.

168 Barker, *et al.*, *op. cit.*, p. 83.

169 J. Gallagher, "Rejecting Parents?" *Exceptional Children*, XXII (1956), 273-276.

170 B. A. Wright, "A New Look at Overprotection and Dependency," *Exceptional Children*, XXVI (1959), 115-122.

171 A. Freud, *op. cit.*, pp. 35-36.

172 A. Auerbach, "Group Education for Parents of the Handicapped," *Children*, VIII (1961), 135-140; M. E. Frampton and E. D. Gall, eds., *Education for the Parents of Exceptional Children* (Boston: Porter Sargent, Publishers, 1955); B. Lowenfeld, *Our Blind Children: Growing and Learning With Them* (Springfield, Ill.: Charles C. Thomas, Publishers, 1956); and E. Fleischer, M. Karl, M. Eversdan, "An Idea for a Guidance Program," *Crippled Child*, XXXIV (1956), 27.

173 H. L. Beck, "Counseling Parents of Retarded Children," *Children*, VI (1959), 225-230; Woods Schools, *Counseling Parents of Children with Mental Handicaps; Proceedings of the 33rd Spring Conference of the Woods Schools, May 2 and 3, 1958* (Langhorne, Pa.: The Woods Schools, 1958); A. E. Winder, "A Program of Group Counseling for the Parents of Cerebral Palsied Children," *Cerebral Palsy Review*, XIX (1958), 8-11; H. Ray Barsch, "Counseling the Parent of the Brain-Damaged

Child," *Journal of Rehabilitation*, XXVII, 40-42; and R. M. Nadal, "A Counseling Program for Parents of Severely Retarded Preschool Children," *Social Casework*, XLII (1961), 78-83.

174 A. Katz, "Therapeutic Aspects of Parent Association for the Handicapped," *Cerebral Palsy Review*, XXII (1961), 6-7, 13.

175 G. Boles, "Simultaneous Group Therapy With Cerebral Palsied Children and Their Parents," *International Journal of Group Psychotherapy*, IX (1959), 488-495; and I. A. Kraft, "An Experimental Group Approach Supplementing Rehabilitation," *Archives of Physical Medicine and Rehabilitation*, XXXIX (1958), 509-513.

176 A. Hersh, "Casework with Parents of Retarded Children," *Social Worker*, VI (1961), 61-66.

177 M. L. Yates and R. Lederer, "Small, Short-term Group Meetings with Parents of Children with Mongolism," *American Journal of Mental Deficiency*, LXV (1961), 467-472.

178 Wright (1959), *Psychology and Rehabilitation*, op. cit.

179 Wright (1960), op. cit.

180 Wright (1959), *Psychology and Rehabilitation*, op. cit.

181 Sarason (1949), op. cit., p. 264.

182 Barker, op. cit., p. 30; Shiffer, op. cit., p. 60.

183 Bradley, op. cit., p. 81; Shiffer, op. cit., pp. 60 ff.; and S. I. Gochman, "Developing a Comprehensive Guidance Program in a Hospital or Clinic School for the Handicapped," *Journal of Child Psychiatry*, II (1952), 278.

184 The Yearbook Committee, "Basic Facts and Principles Underlying Special Education," in *The Education of Exceptional Children*, National Society for the Study of Education, 49th yearbook, N. B. Henry, ed. (Chicago: University of Chicago Press, 1950), p. 10.

185 Garrett, op. cit., p. 66.

186 Bradley, op. cit., p. 81.

187 Cowen and Cruickshank, op. cit., p. 289.

188 M. Zax and A. Klein, "Measurement of Personality and Behavior Change Following Psychotherapy," *Psychological Bulletin*, LVII (1960), 435-448.

189 M. H. Marx, "Sources of Confusion in Attitudes Toward Clinical Theory," *Journal of Genetic Psychology*, LV (1956), 19-30.

190 M. Jahoda, *Current Concepts of Positive Mental Health* (New York: Basic Books, Inc., 1958); E. J. Shoben, "Toward a Concept of the Normal Personality," *American Psychologist*, XII (1957), 183-189; and M. B. Smith, "Research Strategies Toward a Conception of Positive Mental Health," *American Psychologist*, XIV (1959), 673-681.

191 M. Zax and A. Klein, op. cit., p. 446.

192 Mehlman, op. cit.; Snyder and Sechrest, op. cit.

193 E. Dorfman, "Personality Outcomes of Client-Centered Child Therapy," *Psychological Monographs*, CXXII, No. 456 (1958).

194 By permission from *Psychological Reports*, for "The Experimental Analogue: An Approach to Research in Psychotherapy," by E. L. Cowen, pp. 9-10. Volume VIII. 1961.

195 F. M. Jervis and G. M. Haselrud, "Quantitative and Qualitative Differences in Frustration Between Blind and Sighted Adolescents," *Journal of Psychology*, XXIX (1950), 67-76.

196 L. Meyerson, "Experimental Injury: An Approach to the Dynamics of Physical Disability," *Journal of Social Issues*, IV (1948), 68-71.

197 Barker, op. cit., pp. 31 ff.

198 H. J. Eysenck, "The Effects of Psychotherapy: An Evaluation," *Journal of Consulting Psychology*, XVI (1952), 319-324; H. J. Eysenck, "The Effects of Psychotherapy," in *Handbook of Abnormal Psychology*, ed. H. J. Eysenck (New York: Basic Books, Inc., 1960).

199 E. E. Levitt, "The Results of Psychotherapy with Children: An Evaluation," *Journal of Consulting Psychology*, XXI (1957), 189; E. E. Levitt, H. Beiser, and

R. Robertson, "A Followup Evaluation of Cases Treated at a Community Child Guidance Clinic," *American Journal of Orthopsychiatry,* XXIX (1959), 337-346.

[200] By permission from *Recent Developments in Psychoanalytic Child Therapy,* ed. J. Weinreb from "The Child Guidance Clinic as a Center of Prophylaxis and Enlightenment" by A. Freud, pp. 27-28. Copyright, 1960. International Universities Press, Inc.

[201] G. W. Albee, *Mental Health Manpower Trends* (New York: Basic Books, Inc., 1959).

[202] H. H. Strupp, "Psychotherapy," in *Annual Review of Psychology,* XIII, ed. P. Farnsworth (Palo Alto: Annual Reviews, Inc., 1962), pp. 470-471.

[203] Joint Commission on Mental Illness and Health, *Action For Mental Health* (New York: Basic Books, Inc., 1961).

[204] M. Schiffer, "The Use of the Seminar in Training Teachers and Counselors as Leaders of Therapeutic Play Groups for Maladjusted Children," *American Journal of Orthopsychiatry,* XXX (1960), 154-165.

[205] M. Pines, "Training Housewives as Psychotherapists," *Harper's Magazine,* CCXXIV (1962), 37-42.

[206] S. R. Laycock, "Helping the Emotionally Disturbed Child in the School Setting," *Canada's Mental Health,* Supplement, No. 26.

[207] R. G. Newman, "Conveying Essential Messages to the Emotionally Disturbed Child at School," *Exceptional Children,* XXVIII (1961), 199-204; I. Tallmann and S. Levine, "The Emotionally Disturbed Child in the Classroom Situation," *Exceptional Children,* XXVII (1960), 114-126; W. C. Rhodes, "Psychological Techniques and Theory Applied to Behavior Modification," *Exceptional Children,* XXVIII (1961), 333-338; S. Jacobson and C. Faegre, "Neutralization: A Tool For The Teacher of Disturbed Children," *Exceptional Children,* XXV (1959), 243-246; N. G. Haring and E. L. Phillips, *Educating Emotionally Disturbed Children* (New York: McGraw-Hill Book Co., Inc., 1962); E. Rubin and C. B. Simpson, "A Special Class Program for the Emotionally Disturbed Child in School: A Proposal," *American Journal of Orthopsychiatry,* XXX (1960), 144-153; E. L. Phillips and N. G. Haring, "Results From Special Techniques for Teaching Emotionally Disturbed Children," *Exceptional Children,* XXVI (1959), 64-67; K. B. Douglas, "The Teacher Role in a Children's Psychiatric Hospital Unit," *Exceptional Children,* XXVII (1961), 246-251; C. D. Price and B. Strongin, "The Emotionally Disturbed Children in a Residential Treatment Center," *Exceptional Children,* XXIV (1957), 160-164; and R. W. Colvin, "The Education of Emotionally Disturbed Children in a Residential Treatment Center," *American Journal of Orthopsychiatry,* XXXI (1961), 591-597.

[208] Project Re-ED, George Peabody College for Teachers, *Reeducation of Disturbed Children: A Demonstration Project,* Bulletin No. 1 (Nashville, 1961).

[209] E. L. Cowen, L. D. Izzo, H. Miles, E. F. Telschow, M. A. Trost, and M. Zax "A Mental Health Program in the School Setting" (monograph, in press).

[210] *Ibid.,* p. 2.

Name Index

A

Abel, G. L., 229, 278
Abel, T. U., 467, 469, 555, 558-59
Abernathy, E. A., 191
Abrahams, P., 191
Abrahamson, H. A., 436, 447
Abt, L. E., 116, 587
Ackerman, N. W., 551
Adams, G. M., 51-52
Adler, A., 314, 319
Adler, D. L., 366
Albee, G. W., 579
Albright, R. W., 203
Alexander, F., 435
Allen, F. H., 315, 320, 584
Allen, R. M., 113
Allport, G. W., 51, 240
Alper, T. G., 524
Altable, J. P., 187
Alves, G. J., 189
Amatruda, C. S., 73

American Association for Gifted Children, 485
American Association on Mental Deficiency, 449
American Diabetes Association, 432
American Foundation for the Blind, 227
American Printing House for the Blind, Louisville, Kentucky, 229, 252
American Schools for the Deaf, 122-23
American Speech and Hearing Associations Committee on Legislation, 194-95, 205-6
Ames, L. B., 116
Amin, D. L., 129
Ammons, C. H., 257
Ammons, H. S., 85, 349
Ammons, R. B., 85, 349
Amoss, H., 128
Anderson, Kenneth E., 521

Subject Index

A

Abnormality and genius, relation between, 493
Acceptance of disability situation, 49-51
Acculturation, commonality of, 100-101
Achievement testing of the blind, 242-43
Acidosis, 425
Acoustically handicapped, *see* Hearing impairment
Acquired blindness, 283, 295
ACTH, use in rheumatic fever, 416
Adaptation of Educational Tests for Use with Blind Pupils, 242
Adenoids and voice disturbance, 201-2
Adjustment:
  adolescent, 270-71, 336
    problems of gifted, 517-19

Adjustment (*Cont.*):
  anxiety, 51
  blindness, 277, 280-81
  children with high IQ's, 494
  crippled children, 321-23
  diabetic child, intrafamiliar, 431
  epilepsy, 386-89
  to father and mother, 334-35
  impaired hearing, 144-47
  to peers, 335
  pupils, accelerated, in high school and college, 503
  speech defects, 208-9
  to society, 330-34
Adjustment to Visual Disability in Adolescence, 271, 583
Adlerian concepts and the crippled child, 314-15
Adolescence:
  blindness, 270-71, 278-79
  cardiac impairment, 420-22
  diabetes, 431-32